T0392494

Israelite Religion

THE ANCHOR YALE BIBLE REFERENCE LIBRARY

Israelite Religion

From Tribal Beginnings to Scribal Legacy

KAREL VAN DER TOORN

 YALE AYBRL

Yale UNIVERSITY PRESS

NEW HAVEN AND LONDON

Published with assistance from the foundation established in memory of
James Wesley Cooper of the Class of 1865, Yale College.

Yale University Press books may be purchased in quantity for educational,
business, or promotional use. For information, please e-mail
sales.press@yale.edu (U.S. office) or sales@yaleup.co.uk (U.K. office).

Set in Adobe Caslon type by Newgen North America.
Printed in the United States of America.

Library of Congress Control Number: 2024943188
ISBN 978-0-300-24811-1 (hardcover : alk. paper)

A catalogue record for this book is available from the British Library.

This paper meets the requirements of ANSI/NISO Z39.48-1992
(Permanence of Paper).

10 9 8 7 6 5 4 3 2 1

To Bob Becking and Pieter van der Horst,
friends since the days of DDD

Contents

List of Abbreviations, ix

Introduction, 1
Prologue: Ancient Near Eastern Religion, 17
1. Tribal Religion, 47
2. Royal Religion, 78
3. Local Religion, 119
4. Diaspora Religion, 153
5. Ethnic Religion, 178
6. Scriptural Religion, 211
Epilogue, 242

Notes, 247
Acknowledgments, 357
Index of Subjects, 359
Index of Modern Authors, 371
Index of Ancient Sources, 384

Abbreviations

AAeg	Analecta Aegyptiaca
AASOR	Annual of the American Schools of Oriental Research
ÄAT	Ägypten und Altes Testament
AbB	Altbabylonische Briefe
ABS	Archaeology and Biblical Studies
ActAnt	*Acta Antiqua Academiae Scientiarum Hungaricae*
ADPV	Abhandlungen des Deutschen Palästina-Vereins
AfO	*Archiv für Orientforschung*
AfOB	Archiv für Orientforschung: Beiheft
AIL	Ancient Israel and Its Literature
AION	*Annali dell'Istituto Orientale di Napoli*
ANEM	Ancient Near East Monographs
ANET	*Ancient Near Eastern Texts Relating to the Old Testament.* Edited by James B. Pritchard. 3rd ed. Princeton: Princeton University Press, 1969
AOAT	Alter Orient und Altes Testament
AoF	*Altorientalische Forschungen*
AOS	American Oriental Series
ARM	Archives royales de Mari
ASOR	American Schools of Oriental Research
ATANT	Abhandlungen zur Theologie des Alten und Neuen Testaments
ATD	Das Alte Testament Deutsch
AuOrSup	Aula Orientalis Supplementa
AYB	Anchor Yale Bible

AYBD	*Anchor Bible Dictionary.* Edited by David Noel Freedman. 6 vols. New York: Doubleday, 1992; reprint, New Haven: Yale University Press.
AYBRL	Anchor Yale Bible Reference Library
BA	*Biblical Archaeologist*
BaghM	*Baghdader Mitteilungen*
BAIAS	*Bulletin of the Anglo-Israel Archaeological Society*
BAR	*Biblical Archaeology Review*
BARIS	BAR (British Archaeological Reports) International Series
BASOR	*Bulletin of the American Schools of Oriental Research*
BETL	Bibliotheca Ephemeridum Theologicarum Lovaniensum
BiOr	*Bibliotheca Orientalis*
BJS	Brown Judaic Studies
BKAT	Biblischer Kommentar, Altes Testament
BRL2	*Biblisches Reallexikon.* 2nd ed. Edited by Kurt Galling. HAT 1/1. Tübingen: Mohr Siebeck, 1977
BWANT	Beiträge zur Wissenschaft vom Alten und Neuen Testament
BZAW	Beihefte zur Zeitschrift für die alttestamentliche Wissenschaft
BZNW	Beihefte zur Zeitschrift für die neutestamentliche Wissenschaft
CAD	*The Assyrian Dictionary of the Oriental Institute of the University of Chicago.* Chicago: Oriental Institute of the University of Chicago, 1956–2006
CANE	*Civilizations of the Ancient Near East.* Edited by Jack M. Sasson. 4 vols. New York, 1995. Reprint in 2 vols. Peabody, MA: Hendrickson, 2006
CBET	Contributions to Biblical Exegesis and Theology
CBQ	*Catholic Biblical Quarterly*
CBQMS	Catholic Biblical Quarterly Monograph Series
CdE	*Chronique d'Égypte*
CHANE	Culture and History of the Ancient Near East

CHJ	*Cambridge History of Judaism.* Edited by William D. Davies and Louis Finkelstein. 4 vols. Cambridge: Cambridge University Press, 1984–2006
Cl.-G.	Ostraca from the Clermont-Ganneau collection, published by H. Lozachmeur, *La collection Clermont-Ganneau.* Paris: De Boccard, 2006
CM	Cuneiform Monographs
ConBOT	Coniectanea Biblica: Old Testament Series
COS	*The Context of Scripture.* Edited by William W. Hallo. 3 vols. Leiden: Brill, 1997–2002
CRINT	Compendia Rerum Iudaicarum ad Novum Testamentum
CUSAS	Cornell University Studies in Assyriology and Sumerology
DDD	*Dictionary of Deities and Demons in the Bible.* Edited by Karel van der Toorn, Bob Becking, and Pieter W. van der Horst. Leiden: Brill, 1995. 2nd rev. ed. Grand Rapids: Eerdmans, 1999
DNWSI	*Dictionary of the North-West Semitic Inscriptions.* Jacob Hoftijzer and Karel Jongeling. 2 vols. Leiden: Brill, 1995
DSD	*Dead Sea Discoveries*
DULAT	*A Dictionary of the Ugaritic Language in the Alphabetic Tradition.* Gregorio del Olmo Lete and Joaquín Sanmartín. 2 vols. 3rd rev. ed. Leiden: Brill, 2015
EANEC	Explorations in Ancient Near Eastern Civilizations
EBR	*Encyclopedia of the Bible and Its Reception.* Edited by Hans-Josef Klauck et al. Berlin: de Gruyter, 2009-
EBW	*Encyclopedia of Material Culture in the Biblical World.* Edited by Angelika Berlejung. Tübingen: Mohr Siebeck, 2022
EJL	Early Judaism and Its Literature
EPRO	Études préliminaires aux religions orientales dans l'empire romain
ErIsr	*Eretz-Israel*
ETL	*Ephemerides Theologicae Lovanienses*
ExpTim	*Expository Times*

FAOS	Freiburger altorientalische Studien
FAT	Forschungen zum Alten Testament
FOTL	Forms of the Old Testament Literature
FRLANT	Forschungen zur Religion und Literatur des Alten und Neuen Testaments
GAT	Grundrisse zum Alten Testament
Gesenius[18]	*Hebräisches und Aramäisches Handwörterbuch über das Alte Testament.* Wilhelm Gesenius. 18th ed. Edited by Herbert Donner and Johannes Renz. Heidelberg: Springer, 2013
HACL	History, Archaeology, and Culture of the Levant
HAL	*Hebräisches und aramäisches Lexikon zum Alten Testament.* Ludwig Koehler, Walter Baumgartner, and Johann J. Stamm. 5 vols. 3rd ed. Leiden: Brill, 1967–1995
HAT	Handbuch zum Alten Testament
HBAI	*Hebrew Bible and Ancient Israel*
HBM	Hebrew Bible Monographs
HCOT	Historical Commentary on the Old Testament
HdO	Handbuch der Orientalistik
HKAT	Handkommentar zum Alten Testament
HSM	Harvard Semitic Monographs
HSS	Harvard Semitic Studies
HTR	*Harvard Theological Review*
HTS	Harvard Theological Studies
HUCA	*Hebrew Union College Annual*
ICC	International Critical Commentary
IDB	*The Interpreter's Dictionary of the Bible.* Edited by George Arthur Buttrick. 4 vols. Nashville: Abingdon, 1962
IDBSup	*The Interpreter's Dictionary of the Bible: Supplementary Volume.* Edited by Keith Crim. Nashville: Abingdon, 1976
IEJ	*Israel Exploration Journal*
INJ	*Israel Numismatic Journal*
JAJ	*Journal of Ancient Judaism*
JANEH	*Journal of Ancient Near Eastern History*

JANER	*Journal of Ancient Near Eastern Religions*
JAOS	*Journal of the American Oriental Society*
JBL	*Journal of Biblical Literature*
JCS	*Journal of Cuneiform Studies*
JEA	*Journal of Egyptian Archaeology*
JHebS	*Journal of Hebrew Scriptures*
JHNES	The Johns Hopkins Near Eastern Studies
JNES	*Journal of Near Eastern Studies*
JNSL	*Journal of Northwest Semitic Languages*
JSJ	*Journal for the Study of Judaism in the Persian, Hellenistic, and Roman Periods*
JSOTSup	Journal for the Study of the Old Testament Supplement Series
JSQ	*Jewish Studies Quarterly*
JSS	*Journal of Semitic Studies*
KAI	*Kanaanäische und aramäische Inschriften.* Herbert Donner and Wolfgang Röllig. 2nd ed. Wiesbaden: Harrassowitz, 1966–1969
KAT	Kommentar zum Alten Testament
KTU	*The Cuneiform Alphabetic Texts from Ugarit, Ras Ibn Hani and Other Places.* Manfred Dietrich, Oswald Loretz, and Joaquín Sanmartín. 2nd ed. Münster: Ugarit-Verlag, 1995
LÄ	*Lexikon der Ägyptologie.* Edited by Wolfgang Helck, Eberhard Otto, and Wolfhart Westendorf. 6 vols. Wiesbaden: Harrassowitz, 1972–1992
LAI	Library of Ancient Israel
LAPO	Littératures anciennes du Proche-Orient
LCL	Loeb Classical Library
LHBOTS	The Library of Hebrew Bible/Old Testament Studies
LSS	Leipziger semitische Studien
LSTS	The Library of Second Temple Studies
LXX	Septuagint (LXX^A = Codex Alexandrinus)
MARI	*Mari: Annales de recherches interdisciplinaires*
MC	Mesopotamian Civilizations
MRS	Mission de Ras Shamra

NABU	*Nouvelles assyriologiques brèves et utilitaires*
NEAEHL	*The New Encyclopedia of Archaeological Excavations in the Holy Land.* Edited by Ephraim Stern. 5 vols. Jerusalem: Israel Exploration Society & Carta; New York: Simon & Schuster, 1993 (vols. 1–4). Jerusalem: Israel Exploration Society & Biblical Archaeology Society, 2008 (vol. 5)
NJPS	*Tanakh: The Holy Sciptures: The New JPS Translation According to the Traditional Hebrew Text*
NRSV	New Revised Standard Version of the Bible
NTOA	Novum Testamentum et Orbis Antiquus
NTS	*New Testament Studies*
OBO	Orbis Biblicus et Orientalis
OED	*Oxford English Dictionary*
OEANE	*The Oxford Encyclopedia of Archaeology in the Near East.* Edited by Eric M. Meyers. 5 vols. New York: Oxford University Press, 1997
OIMP	Oriental Institute Museum Publications
OLA	Orientalia Lovaniensia Analecta
OTL	Old Testament Library
OTS	Old Testament Studies
OtSt	Oudtestamentische Studiën
PIHANS	Publications de l'Institut historique-archéologique néerlandais de Stamboul
PTMS	Pittsburgh Theological Monograph Series
RA	*Revue d'assyriologie et d'archéologie orientale*
RAC	*Reallexikon für Antike und Christentum.* Edited by Theodor Klauser et al. Stuttgart: Hiersemann, 1950–
RAI	Rencontre assyriologique internationale
RB	*Revue biblique*
RevQ	*Revue de Qumran*
RGRW	Religions in the Graeco-Roman World
RHPR	*Revue d'histoire et de philosophie religieuses*
RIDA	*Revue internationale des droits de l'antiquité*
RIME	The Royal Inscriptions of Mesopotamia, Early Periods
RINAP	Royal Inscriptions of the Neo-Assyrian Period

RlA	*Reallexikon der Assyriologie.* Edited by Erich Ebeling et al. 15 vols. Berlin: de Gruyter, 1928–2018
SAA	State Archives of Assyria
SAAS	State Archives of Assyria Studies
SANE	Sources of the Ancient Near East
SBLDS	Society of Biblical Literature Dissertation Series
SBLMS	Society of Biblical Literature Monograph Series
SBLSS	Society of Biblical Literature Symposium Series
SBS	Stuttgarter Bibelstudien
SBT	Studies in Biblical Theology
SEL	*Studi epigrafici e linguistici sul Vicino Oriente antico*
SHCANE	Studies in the History and Culture of the Ancient Near East
SJ	Studia Judaica
SJLA	Studies in Judaism in Late Antiquity
SJOT	*Scandinavian Journal of the Old Testament*
SO	Symbolae Osloensis
SOTSMS	Society for Old Testament Studies Monograph Series
SSN	Studia Semitica Neerlandica
STDJ	Studies on the Texts of the Desert of Judah
StOr	Studia Orientalia
StPohl	Studia Pohl
SVTP	Studia in Veteris Testamenti Pseudepigraphica
TA	*Tel Aviv*
TAD	*Textbook of Aramaic Documents from Ancient Egypt.* Bezalel Porten and Ada Yardeni. 4 vols. Jerusalem: Hebrew University, Department of the History of the Jewish People, 1986–1999
TDOT	*Theological Dictionary of the Old Testament.* Edited by G. Johannes Botterweck, Helmer Ringgren, and Heinz-Josef Fabry. Translated by John T. Willis et al. 15 vols. Grand Rapids: Eerdmans, 1974–2006
THAT	*Theologisches Handwörterbuch zum Alten Testament.* Edited by Ernst Jenni, with assistance from Claus Westermann. 2 vols. Munich: Chr. Kaiser Verlag; Zürich: Theologischer Verlag, 1971–1976

ThWAT	*Theologisches Wörterbuch zum Alten Testament.* Edited by G. Johannes Botterweck, Helmer Ringgren, and Heinz-Josef Fabry. 8 vols. Stuttgart: Kohlhammer, 1970–1995
TLOT	*Theological Lexicon of the Old Testament.* Edited by Ernst Jenni, with assistance from Claus Westermann. Translated by Mark E. Biddle. 3 vols. Peabody, MA: Hendrickson, 1997
TLZ	*Theologische Literaturzeitung*
TSAJ	Texte und Studien zum antiken Judentum
TWNT	*Theologisches Wörterbuch zum Neuen Testament.* Edited by Gerhard Kittel and Gerhard Friedrich. Stuttgart: Kohlhammer, 1932–1979
UCOP	University of Cambridge Oriental Publications
VT	*Vetus Testamentum*
VTSup	Supplements to Vetus Testamentum
WAW	Writings from the Ancient World
WBC	World Biblical Commentary
WDSP	Wadi Daliyeh Samarian Papyri; Douglas M. Gropp, *Wadi Daliyeh II: The Samaria Papyri from Wadi Daliyeh.* Discoveries in the Judaean Desert 28. Oxford: Clarendon, 2001
WMANT	Wissenschaftliche Monographien zum Alten und Neuen Testament
WO	*Die Welt des Orients*
WUNT	Wissenschaftliche Untersuchungen zum Neuen Testament
WZKM	*Wiener Zeitschrift für die Kunde des Morgenlandes*
YNER	Yale Near Eastern Researches
ZA	*Zeitschrift für Assyriologie*
ZABR	*Zeitschrift für altorientalische und biblische Rechtsgeschichte*
ZAW	*Zeitschrift für die alttestamentliche Wissenschaft*
ZDPV	*Zeitschrift des deutschen Palästina-Vereins*

Israelite Religion

Introduction

If everything before the Middle Ages belongs to the realm of antiquity, Israelite religion is like a relic from a very distant past. The first evidence for its existence is from the Early Iron Age (ca. 1200–1000 BCE). During the millennium that followed, it went through several phases until, about two thousand years ago, it branched out into Judaism, Samaritanism, and what was then the sect of the Christians. Ancient history, as they say. Yet despite the distance in time, the religion of the ancient Israelites has rarely suffered from lack of interest. Owing to centuries of Christian culture, many Western historians look at the history of Israelite religion as a kind of prelude to their own history. So do Jewish historians and, at some remove, Muslim scholars. Echoes of the Bible in contemporary culture—names, phrases, narratives—reinforce a sense of familiarity with the ancient Israelites. Somehow they feel close—much closer than other peoples of those faraway times, such as the Assyrians, the Phoenicians, or the Egyptians.

The sense of familiarity is deceptive, however, and potentially misleading. It easily becomes an obstacle in the search for the historical reality. In the venture of investigating Israelite religion, we need to be prepared for an encounter with the unknown and unfamiliar. The Israelites lived in another world. They shared that world with the other peoples of the early Middle East. The area was one cultural zone. Even if the various peoples and polities of the period were each in their own way unique, the differences were embedded in a shared set of cultural patterns and assumptions. Religion was part of those cultural patterns. Gods would have different names and stories from one region to another, but they did have a family resemblance. Scholars of the time drew up catalogues in which they identified gods of different areas on the basis of similarities in profile.[1] Such translations point to a common understanding of the nature of superhuman beings. Seen against this background, Israelite religion was a particular variant of ancient Near Eastern religion. The claim that it stood out "against its environment" is tendentious inasmuch as the implied claim of uniqueness is a thinly disguised theological assertion.[2] To the historian, such exceptionalism is taboo. Would we be able to go back in time and meet the ancient Israelites, their religion might strike us as being just as foreign and distant as the religion of the Babylonians.

Sources: The Bible, Archaeology, and Ancient Near Eastern Religion

In a classic study of Mesopotamian civilization, A. Leo Oppenheim gave the section on religion the provocative title "Why a Mesopotamian Religion Should Not Be Written." The reasons he adduced were of two orders: first, "the nature of the available evidence," and second, "the problem of comprehension across the barriers of conceptual conditioning."[3] The same problems beset the study of Israelite religion. The nature of these difficulties is not such, however, as to render the entire venture impossible. On the contrary, the challenges of problematic and fragmentary evidence, on the one hand, and of the culture gap between them and us, on the other, are a stimulus to try to overcome them. The very effort to come to terms with the evidence and to bridge the cultural divide is a useful and rewarding exercise in its own right. When successfully performed, it yields a new appreciation of an important chapter of human history. But first, let us take a closer look at the issues of evidence and cultural difference.

The sources for the study of Israelite religion fall into three categories: the Bible, the archaeological record, and the evidence on other ancient Near Eastern religions. Each of these sources requires a few words of caution. Because the Bible is Israel's legacy to the world, it is tempting to think that Israelite religion was the religion of the Bible. Such was indeed the dominant view among Jewish and Christian scholars until early modern times. The nineteenth century brought about a paradigm change. Masterfully synthesized and presented in the work of Julius Wellhausen, the new insights of critical biblical scholarship showed there was considerable discrepancy between the biblical narrative and the historical reality.[4] The Hebrew Bible as we know it did not see the day before the second century BCE. Though it contains older texts, some perhaps as early as the eleventh century BCE, the collection as a whole was brought together and edited by Judean scribes from the Hellenistic period (third and second centuries

BCE). It was their selection, their edition, and often reflected their ideas about the past. According to some scholars, the editorial bias of the Hebrew Bible disqualifies it as a historical source.[5] Others acknowledge the bias but nevertheless use the Bible as the main narrative thread to tell the story of Israel's religion.[6] While the skepticism of the former chooses to ignore—at least in theory—an essential source of information, the approach of the latter is in danger of mixing religion (a historical phenomenon) with theology (an ideological stance).[7] In spite of such risks, the Bible still ranks as the main source on the religion of Israel. It would be impossible to write a history of Israelite religion without it. If we rigorously apply the tools of critical analysis, remain suspicious of its theological framing, and have a sharp eye for detail and unintentional snippets of information, the witness of the Bible is invaluable.

If it is impossible to reconstruct the religion of Israel without the Bible, it would be equally impossible if the Bible were all we had. The archaeological record is a crucial second source. It may be divided into three sets of data: architecture and utensils (remains of houses, city walls, sanctuaries, altars, cult stands), iconography (figurines, images on seals and other objects), and epigraphy (written texts). The order corresponds to one of increasing clarity. Ruins are silent and images are mute, but texts still speak their messages. Because of the inclemency of the Palestinian climate, in combination with the use of perishable writing materials, the epigraphical remains, especially for the preexilic period, are scant by comparison with those of Mesopotamia (where texts were inscribed on clay and the tablets were baked) and Egypt (where arid sands protected the papyri). The significance of the rare texts we do have is often tremendous. The Balaam inscription from Deir Alla (Jordan, ca. 800 BCE), for instance, has some literal correspondences with the Balaam stories in Numbers 22–24, illustrates the renown of the legendary figure, and gives precious information on a number of deities.[8] The texts from Kuntillet Ajrud (Sinai peninsula, ca. 800 BCE) provide another example. They show that YHWH, the god of Israel, had the goddess Asherah as his consort.[9] Such instances could be multiplied. They do not contradict the data from the Bible but reveal that much of what the biblical authors described as deviant religion was not marginal but mainstream. The presence of a temple at Elephantine in southern Egypt in the fifth century BCE, where local Jews venerated Yaho, his consort Anat (Anat-Bethel or Anat-Yaho), and a god named Eshem-Bethel, is another case in point.[10] The temptation is to assume that such data reflect exceptional situations, but there is no good reason to do so. It is preferable to take them as a means to counterbalance the ideological perspective of the Hebrew Bible.

The significance of archaeology for the reconstruction of Israelite religion is such that a number of scholars feel that the order of sources should be reversed. Instead of the Bible, the archaeological evidence should come first. Sometimes the advocates of this approach are archaeologists by profession, but text people too can be found to make a case for the priority of the archaeological evidence.[11] Others are less explicit about it but follow a similar route.[12] A special application of the archaeological approach is the systematic study of Palestinian iconography as a means of entry into the religious universe of early Israel.[13] In this instance, too, some have hailed the result as "the first true history of Israelite religion."[14] Over the years archaeology has revolutionized some of the traditional tenets about Israelite history and religion. Whether this is enough to merit priority as a historical source is debatable, however. Nearly all archaeological contributions on the history of Israelite religion presuppose knowledge of a paradigm that goes back to the Hebrew Bible. The counterevidence they marshal challenges several aspects of that paradigm but has not replaced it. It would be very difficult to do so. If the Bible is a *deforming* mirror of Israelite religion, the archaeological record consists of *shards* of a mirror. Instead of a distorted image, they reflect merely fragments. The particular value of those fragments is the fact that they are random and unedited. They must seamlessly fit in with our reconstruction of Israel's religious past. If they do not, the reconstruction stands in need of revision.

The third source on Israelite religion is perhaps the hardest to handle. It is also the most contested one. If Israelite religion is a variant of ancient Near Eastern religion, as argued above, the patterns of religious belief and practice in the surrounding cultures should be recognizable in Israelite religion as well.[15] Whether we refer to this shared heritage as the "common theology of the ancient Near East" or as its common cosmology or other terms to that effect, the basic assumption is that Israelite religion conforms to patterns of thought and practice that are characteristic of its cultural environment.[16] It is easy to see why this postulate has caused concern and critique. The concern, especially among some of the more conservative scholars, is that this angle of inquiry fails to do justice to the unique qualities of Israelite religion, such as its monotheism, aniconism, and morality—"unique" being code for "superior." The critique holds that this "patternism" is too facile as it ignores all the variety among the cultures of the time. From on high we may discern common patterns, but on the ground people experienced difference. Both objections are real. Even though we must lay aside all preconceived ideas about the superiority of Israelite religion, its distinct developments (such as its eventual monotheism and aniconism) must find their rightful place in our historical reconstruction. Whether those developments were as unique as is often claimed is a separate matter. The distinction between the perspective from on high and on the ground is perhaps less problematic from an ideological point of view. "Map is not territory," to quote an epigram that captures the predicament of the scholar who studies the religion of others.[17] The view from outside is not the view from inside. While it is impossible to really step inside the world of others, we must be mindful of our position as outsiders. A position for better or worse, perhaps. The one advantage we have is, precisely, the distance that allows us to see things that would be invisible from nearby. All this is not to imply, of course, that common patterns do not allow for differences. On the contrary, one might say. The postulated similarity is what makes the methodical comparison of difference truly interesting.[18]

The Historian as Anthropologist

The second reason why A. Leo Oppenheim believed it was not really possible to write a "Mesopotamian religion" consisted of "the barriers of conceptual conditioning." The world the Mesopotamians lived in was so different from ours—most of all in terms of apperception—that they are bound to remain a mystery to us. Oppenheim's conviction did not prevent him from using the next fifty pages to give an excellent introduction to Mesopotamian religion.[19] Apparently, the principle of transcultural incommunicability was more rhetorical than real. If the latter were the case, the entire field of cultural anthropology would be doomed. Cultural difference does not condemn us to incomprehension. Instead, it forces us to go beyond our own cultural horizons in an effort to make sense of what is going on in the world of others. Historians of ancient history must use the mindset of a cultural anthropologist, in addition to the traditional tools of their discipline.

Much of the cultural divide between them (the early Israelites) and us (inhabitants of the modern world) is already contained in the word "religion." The way in which we use this term to refer to a complex of beliefs, values, and practices makes it easy to forget that we are introducing a concept that was foreign to the Israelites. Their language did not have a word for religion. Instead they spoke of "fear of God" or "calling upon God's name." This is not merely a different way of saying the same thing, for the Hebrew expressions are referring to morality and worship. Religion as a separate province of human culture—distinct from law, ethics, arts, and sciences—did not exist for them. It was so much woven into the fabric of their lives that they would have been unable to recognize it as religion. That is no reason for us to abandon the term altogether, provided we realize we are using a modern category. Before the Enlightenment, people did not think of their religion as religion.[20] One of the presuppositions of the modern use of the term "religion" is that it is possible not to have religion.[21] For the ancient Israelites, this was not an option. They might be devout or less devout, live by the rules or ignore them, but a world without gods was inconceivable.

From an anthropological perspective, religion is to be approached as a cultural phenomenon. It did not come down from heaven but originated in human societies. Up to a point the ancients had a similar view. A Sumerian myth opposes nomads to civilized people by saying that the former are tent-dwellers who offer no prayer and do not visit the places of the gods.[22] Also the book of Genesis implies that cultic worship is a social institution and a hallmark of civilization. Next to a passage that describes the invention of music and metallurgy (Gen 4:21–22), the author notes, "At that time people began to invoke the name of the LORD" (Gen 4:26 NRSV; unless otherwise noted, as here, biblical translations are my own). In other words, at some point in the course of human history, people began to worship the gods. The social roots of religion have important consequences for its study because they imply that religion cannot be understood in isolation from its social environment. In Israel, societal changes profoundly affected the religious imagination. During the long millennium in which Israelite religion flourished, the metaphors for God went through several changes. When the Israelites were a coalition of tribes, their god was the divine warrior; in the time of the monarchy, he was their king; when they became part of the Persian Empire, God assumed traits of a world emperor with a host of intermediaries between himself and his subjects. A similar morphing of metaphors is evident in the way people thought about sin: first as a stain or burden, but when barter gave way to a money economy, as debt and guilt.[23] New metaphors did not displace earlier ones but added another layer that, for a time, dominated the landscape. Religion being a cultural construct, it mirrors the evolution of the society that produced it. This is true as much of Israelite as of any other religion.

Religion or Religions? Internal Diversity and Historical Development

In keeping with a general trend in religious studies, scholars of Israelite religion have become increasingly aware of its internal diversity.[24] Such diversity or pluralism has both a synchronic and a diachronic dimension. At a synchronic level it is possible to distinguish between state religion, on the one hand, and family religion, on the other.[25] Equivalents of "state religion" are "national religion," "royal religion," or, at some remove, "urban religion."[26] "Household religion" is the principal alternative for family religion.[27] Whatever the preferred terminology for the binary, the common point is to acknowledge the simultaneous existence of two levels of religious experience. Some scholars prefer to refine the distinction and posit a tripartition, consisting of "personal," "official," and "local" religion;[28] others would even identify four levels.[29] Much depends on the vantage point of the researcher. It is possible to define a series of other binaries. A very fundamental one compares the religious experience of women with that of the male population.[30] Since men and women lived in almost separate worlds, the gender approach is a must in order to obtain a balanced picture. Professional environment also affected the religious experience; a soldier's religion differed from the religion of a peasant. An exhaustive catalogue would be pointless. Suffice it to say that Israelite religion had room for great diversity.

Diversity of a different order is extant between the religions of Israel and Judah. So far, this introduction has spoken about "Israelite religion" as though it were a single stream of tradition. But this unitary vision of the past is a projection of later times. Historically we have to distinguish between Israel and Judah. During two centuries (ca. 920–720 BCE) these territories were separate kingdoms: "Israel" or "the house of Omri" in the north, and "Judah" or "the house of David" in the south (fig. 1).[31] According to the Judean editors of the historical books of the Bible, the division was secondary. It was allegedly the result of a schism. The northern tribes had separated themselves from the kingdom of David in a rebellious pursuit of independence. In the eyes of the postexilic community, Israelites and Judahites originally all belonged to one family. This family model itself is a construct. Various clans and regional populations, on occasion confederated for military purposes, were retrospectively presented as twelve tribes, each named after an ancestor descending from Jacob the son of Isaac the son of Abraham.[32] In reality, the populations of Israel and Judah—in the political sense of the terms—had a sense of kinship, not on account of blood ties but because of a common veneration for the god Yhwh. How the cult of Yhwh gained such a hold on the population, both in Israel and in Judah, is a question to be addressed in the discussion of the origins of Israelite religion—Israelite in the nonpolitical but ideological sense of the term. Though both Israelite and Judahite religion were Yahwistic—meaning Yhwh was the main god—they differed in forms of worship and religious tradition. After the demise of the Northern Kingdom in the late eighth century BCE, the characteristic elements of northern religion survived. In the wake of the migration of Israelite refugees to Judah, the religious traditions of the north found their way to the south. In the postexilic era, Israel ceased to exist as a political entity; under foreign rulership, it was known as Samaria. Judah incorporated the religious heritage of Israel and appropriated the name. From that time on, Judeans were Israelites too. Comparing themselves to David and Solomon, the rulers of the last independent Jewish kingdom before the Common Era, the Hasmoneans—in power between 152 and 63 BCE—promoted the use of the term "Israel" for their state, and "Israelites" for all of their subjects.[33]

The dual use of the term "Israel"—for all worshippers of Yhwh in the broader sense and for the Northern Kingdom in the narrow sense—is confusing but hard to avoid altogether. It is part of a wider set of terminological issues. The Hebrew Bible speaks of "Israelites" but also, on more than one occasion, of "Hebrews," as though the latter were an ethnic group more or less coterminous with the former. Modern scholarly use restricts the term "Hebrew" to the language spoken in Israel and Judah and used throughout the Hebrew Bible. In this book too, "Hebrew" refers solely to language. "Palestine" is another name that may cause some perplexity. In modern usage the term designates a specific territory west of the Jordan River (the West Bank and the Gaza Strip), but under the pen of historians of Israelite religion, the reference is to the geographical area extending from the sources of the Jordan in the north to the Dead Sea in the south, and from the Mediterranean in the west to Transjordan in the east. In fact, the scholarly use of the term perpetuates the Latin designation of the area. "Palestine" and "Palestinian" are best used as geographical designations only.

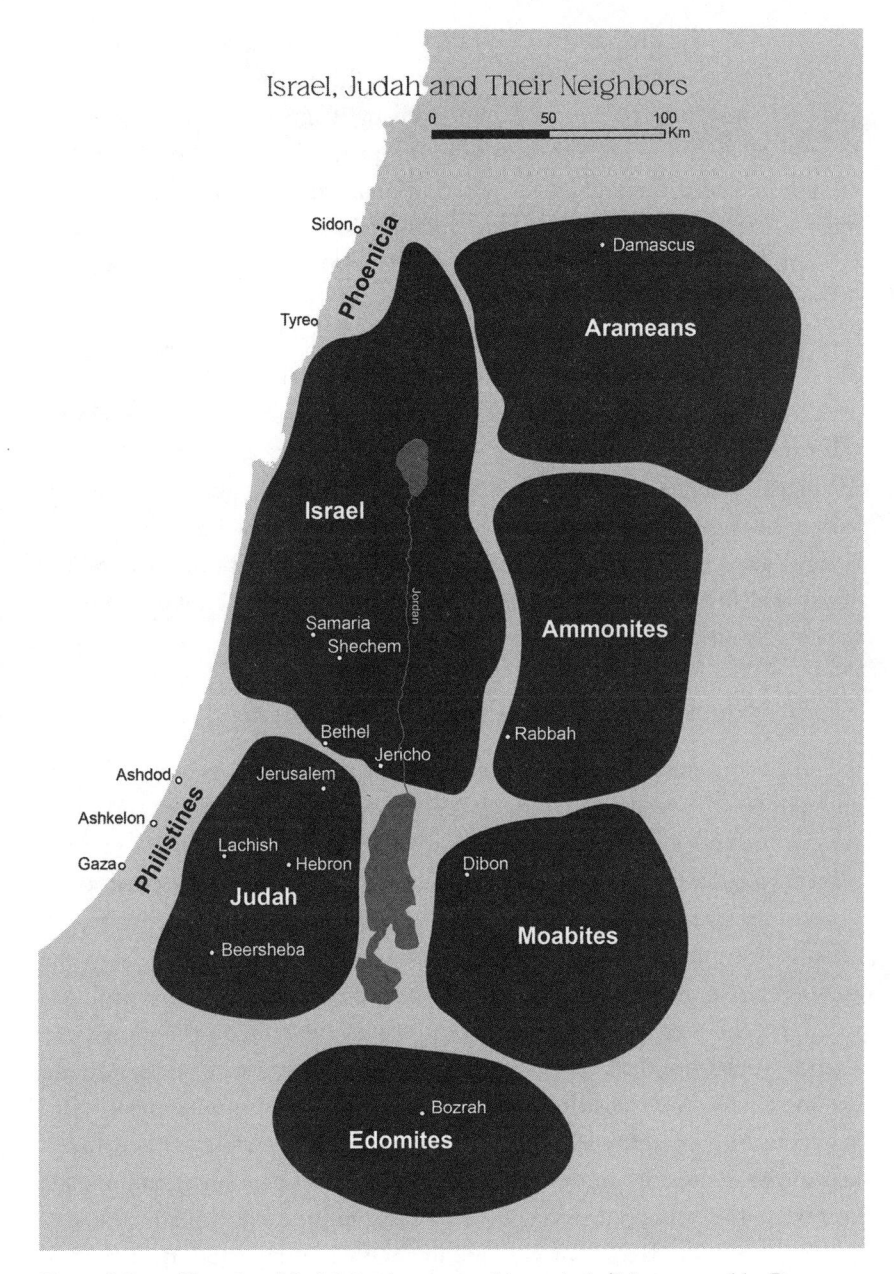

Fig. 1. Map of Israel and Judah in the monarchic period. (Map created by Jip Zinsmeister.)

All in all, the diversity within Israelite religion is significant. At a synchronic level it is both sociological and geopolitical. There is family religion and state religion, religion as experienced by women vis-à-vis that experienced by men, the religion of soldiers and the religion of farmers, urban versus rural religion, and a host of additional varieties. Geopolitically we must distinguish between Israelite and Judahite religion. The diachronic diversity of Israelite religion will become clear in the chapters discussing its historical development. The transformations are sometimes so significant that the various phases of Israelite religion might look like a succession of religions. Does all this mean that we should abandon the singular and speak of "Israelite religions" instead? Some scholars do.[34] Yet a majority stays with the singular "religion." They take diversity in religion the way linguists take dialectal variety. Just as a dialect is not a language, so religious variety does not imply a plurality of religions. As long as the common core is significant enough, the variants are part of one tradition. This book is about Israelite religion in the singular, though it does pay a lot of attention to the diversity within.

The Storyboard of This Book

The more than thousand years of history this book covers saw the rise and demise of Israelite religion, from its tribal beginnings to its scriptural turn in the end. Over the course of the long millennium, Israelite religion went through a series of stages. Each new stage brought about transformations of collective beliefs and practices, even as earlier phases deposited an active substratum. Religions tend to be conservative: the legacy from the past—often most tangible in certain phrases and metaphors—continues to inform the present. The development of Israelite religion was closely related to social-political developments and major historical events. Among the former are the transition from tribal chiefdoms to monarchical states and, centuries later, the loss of political independence as Israel and Judah became provinces of foreign imperial powers. Most prominent among the events are the fall of Samaria (722/720 BCE) and the Babylonian conquest of Jerusalem (587 BCE), in conjunction with the deportation of part of the population. The order of the following chapters roughly follows the successive stages of Israelite religion: as tribal religion, royal religion, local religion, diaspora religion, ethnic religion, and scriptural religion—of these, only the chapters on royal and local religion cover the same period. The adjectives highlight aspects of Israelite religion, most of them linked to the particular period in which they gained prominence. A prologue puts Israelite religion in the perspective of its ancient Near Eastern environment, while the epilogue looks at the nearly imperceptible transition between Israelite religion and the various religious communities that regard themselves as its legitimate heirs with a claim to its legacy.

The prologue is based on the premise that Israelite religion is a particular variant of ancient Near Eastern religion. Underneath the different forms of religious life of Moabites, Assyrians, Babylonians, Israelites, and Judahites there is a shared heritage of concepts about the cosmos, the gods, the purpose of worship, morality, and human destiny. This common ground made it possible for people from different religious communities to comment on the beliefs of others. Thus an Assyrian army commander to the population of Jerusalem, in 701 BCE: "Do not let Hezekiah mislead you by saying, The LORD will save us. Has any of the gods of the nations saved their land out of the hand of the king of Assyria? Where are the gods of Hamath and Arpad? Where are the gods of Sepharvaim? Have they delivered Samaria out of my hand? Who among all the gods of these countries have saved their countries out of my hand, that the LORD should save Jerusalem out of my hand?" (Isa 36:18–20 // 2 Kgs 18:32–35 NRSV; cf. Isa 37:10–13 // 2 Kgs 19:10–13). Israelites might make comparable observations. "So now the LORD, the God of Israel, has conquered the Amorites for the benefit of his people Israel. Do you intend to take their place? Should you not possess what your god Chemosh gives you to possess? And should we not be the ones to possess everything that the LORD our God has conquered for our benefit?" (Judg 11:23–24 NRSV). Different gods, similar beliefs. The latter were not limited to situations of conflict and warfare. On a wide range of subjects, from cosmology and the experience of time to notions about gods, ghosts, and demons, there was a common understanding. The prologue deals with all of the above in order to put the religion of Israel in its appropriate cultural context.

Six chapters follow the prologue. Each one of them focuses on an aspect of Israelite religion as it took shape in a particular period. The order, then, is chronological rather than thematic—only the chapters on royal and local religion study phenomena of the same period. This book gives a history of Israelite religion, not a thematic treatment. Instead of one section on sanctuaries and another one on ritual purity, topics such as those will come up in several chapters, as the context requires. If one wants to know all about temples, one will need to consult the index and browse through various chapters. Though perhaps inconvenient for quick consultation, this setup seeks to prevent the misguided impression that Israelite religion was static and almost timeless. Three thousand year ago things changed too—in our eyes perhaps at a very slow pace, but in the experience of those living, then maybe just as fast as history moves today.[35]

In order to follow the narrative thread of this book it is helpful to summarize here the main lines of each of the six chapters. Israelite religion began as tribal religion (Chapter 1). At the turn of the Early Iron Age (ca. 1200–1000 BCE), the population of the Palestinian highlands was ethnically mixed and politically fragmented. Alongside descendants of the original Canaanite population, there were, especially in Transjordan and northern Israel, groups with Aramean roots and, in both Judah and Israel, clans that had come from the south, sometimes from as far as southern Edom and the Sinai peninsula. Clan and tribe were the dominant forms of social organization. In religion, three gods could claim a special status: Baal as the traditional god of the Canaanites, El as the main Aramean deity, and YHWH (most likely pronounced as "Yaho" or "Yahu") as the tribal god of the southern migrants. YHWH came, as theophany texts tell us, "from Teman" or "from the fields of Edom" (Deut 33:2–3; Judg 5:4; Hab 3:3; cf. the reference to "YHWH of Teman" in texts from Kuntillet Ajrud).[36] To better defend themselves, clans and tribes would unite, first temporarily but later on more permanent terms. To that purpose, they entered into a covenant: the partners made a solemn promise of nonaggression and military aid in case of attack. Warfare, in antiquity, was the business of gods. The god who led the troops to victory was the greatest. In this capacity, YHWH would eventually gain ascendency over Baal and El as the ultimate divine warrior (Exod 15:3; Ps 24:8). He became the god of the covenant. For a time, Baal receded into the background, while El and YHWH would eventually merge, a development that the kings of Israel solemnized by hailing the icon of the bull (the animal of El—"Bull El" in texts from Ugarit) as icon of YHWH (1 Kgs 12:28–29). As a result of the identification, YHWH, originally a bachelor god, was coupled with Asherah, in Ugaritic texts the consort of El ("YHWH of Samaria and his Asherah").[37]

The beginning of the first millennium BCE saw an important change in political structures. Tribal coalitions under the leadership of local chiefs got caught up in a process that led to the emergence of territorial kingdoms. The early kings, such as Saul and David, may have begun their career as warlords, but they soon became the heads of real states, with a staff of government officials and a standing army. The religion these kings sponsored was royal religion (Chapter 2). Owing to the religious background of the first kings, YHWH rose to the position of national god. The veneration he received was hardly ever exclusive, however. For reasons of political expediency (respect for the religion of all the king's subjects, international diplomacy), other gods might receive cultic recognition too (Baal, for instance). In the new order, the human king claimed the status of God's lieutenant: he acted as lawgiver, supreme judge, and leader of the army. He was a "son of God" (2 Sam 7:14; Ps 2:7, 45:7–8), though such mythological language was normally used only in the context of special celebrations. Kings were also temple builders and generous patrons of major local sanctuaries. This was, up to a point, a matter of self-interest. Royal religion was national religion, and national religion was politics. Religion provided the monarchy with ideological legitimacy. The members of the priesthood of the royal sanctuaries were civil servants, and the chief administrator of the temple (the high priest) was a royal appointee. Part of their duties was to teach the population that fear of God and respect for the authorities were two sides of the same coin. Under the monarchy, the importance of the main state temples (Jerusalem, Bethel) increased considerably. In addition to their role as places of worship, both for daily offerings and as theater of annual festivals, they developed secondary functions as courthouse, bank of savings, bureau of weights and measures, armory, and tax collection center.

Whereas royal religion was designed to foster national unity, social stability, and civil obedience, the scope of local religion (Chapter 3) was the welfare and continuity of the family and its wider kinship group, the clan. Royal religion and local religion existed side by side in the same period; the two hardly intersected. The rites of local religion took place in a domestic context and at graves or at local sanctuaries. There was a double focus: the family ancestors and the family gods. Both of them received daily invocations and food offerings. Periodically, at the time of the new moon, the wider kinship group would gather for a larger ceremony for both the ancestors and the gods. In Babylonia and Syria, each family venerated its own local god. Judging by the personal names of the period, YHWH was the dominant family god in Israel and Judah. However, since it was YHWH in his capacity as god of a local shrine, the divine name functions almost as homonym of distinct local deities.[38] YHWH of Hebron was not exactly the same as YHWH of Samaria. In the performance of the daily rituals, women had a central role, even if on more solemn occasions the paterfamilias would lead the liturgy. Prophets also were mainly active at a local level—the biblical picture of national prophets notwithstanding. Historically, prophets had a wide range of activities, as soothsayers, intercessors, healers, and charismatic leaders of a band of disciples. Many of them were itinerant, making the rounds of various local sanctuaries. These local prophets were not in the king's pay. Their independent position allowed them a critical stance vis-à-vis royal religious politics, especially where they felt the latter conflicted with their own, more local, religious loyalties.

A transformative new period began after the fall of Samaria (722/720 BCE) and, some 130 years later, Jerusalem (587 BCE). The Assyrian invaders of Israel deported part of the population to Assyria and Media. Under the pressure of the times, many Israelite families sought refuge in Judah. More than a century later, the Babylonians defeated Judah and settled many of the captives in southern Mesopotamia. Their traditional religion became diaspora religion (Chapter 4). In most textbooks, the Israelite diaspora remains in the shadows of the Babylonian exile of Judah. Yet the forced migration of Israelites to Jerusalem and surroundings was hardly less momentous. The Israelite diaspora in Judah included priestly families, such as the priests of Anathoth from whose circles the prophet Jeremiah came (Jer 1:1). Some of these priests from the north were closely involved in the religious reforms of King Josiah (r. 640–609 BCE); they were likely the minds behind the cult centralization program of Deuteronomy. Owing to the migration, other Israelite traditions (the exodus, Elijah, Elisha) and oracle collections (Hosea, Amos) became part of a common religious heritage. The impact of the diaspora in Babylonia was quite different. More so than ever before, religion became a means to remain anchored in the past and preserve a collective identity. Ancestral customs, such as circumcision, turned into religious duties. Though the historical record attests to the existence of Yahwistic temples outside Palestine (as in Elephantine and, later, Leontopolis), there is no evidence that the Judahite community in Babylonia had such sanctuaries.[39] This circumstance triggered various developments. On the one hand it led to the cultivation of new religious practices, such as periodical fasts and community prayers at places appropriate for worship. On the other, it spurred a Zionist movement among the second generation of exiles. They knew about Jerusalem only from stories, but they fixed their hopes on a return to what they regarded as the Holy City (Isa 48:2, 52:1). Toward the end of the sixth century BCE, these men and women would be in the forefront of the religious nationalists who founded a new temple community in Judah.

Even though many Judahite families preferred to stay in Babylonia, several groups of exiles chose to move to Judah when the opportunity presented itself—not all at once, but in waves. That moment was near when Cyrus the Great invaded Babylon (539 BCE). As the new masters of the Middle East, the Persians implemented a policy that allowed groups of deportees to return to the land of their ancestors. Provided there should be law and order—which included the regular payment of taxes—Judah was granted some measure of self-regulation, particularly in the domains of religion and family law. During this period, religion became a hallmark of ethnic identity owing to which Israelite religion turned into ethnic religion (Chapter 5). With the consent and approval of the Persian authorities, various Babylonian Jews made the journey to the province of Yehud to restore some of the monumental infrastructure of Jerusalem (temple, city walls) and reorganize its religion. This was the time Ezra promulgated "the law of the God of heaven" as a kind of constitution for all Yahwists in the satrapy known as Beyond the River (Syria-Palestine). One major effect of Ezra's mission was the imposition of a common festival calendar for all Judeans in the empire. Also the Judeans at Elephantine Island, in the deep south of Egypt, had to conform to the written prescriptions about the religious feasts, as a document from their community archive indicates. The Judean diaspora throughout the empire was beginning to develop a Jewish identity—a characteristic mix of ethnicity and religion. The "Israelites," as the book of Ezra likes to call them, had lost political independence, also in Judah and Samaria, but they survived as a nation with a religion all of their own.

The final phase of Israelite religion falls in the Hellenistic and Roman periods, the time between the conquests of Alexander the Great (r. 336–323 BCE) and the destruction of the Second Temple (70 CE). The Hellenistic culture that swept over the Eastern Mediterranean changed the landscape. Amphitheaters, public baths, gymnasia, and schools became common features. Judean culture with its religious tradition now entered an era of full-blown literacy. Looking back at the period, we can see a flowering of what is now known as Jewish literature. The scribal workshop of the Jerusalem temple produced a final edition of the Law, the Prophets, and the other Writings. Diaspora novellas, wisdom collections, apocalyptic revelations, legends about biblical and parabiblical figures, and other edifying literature catered to the needs of an ever-increasing reading public. The Dead Sea discoveries also attest to the presence of written commentary on the ancestral literature. Israelite religion had become scriptural religion (Chapter 6). The increased prominence of the "holy books" gave birth to various reading communities, whose different views on the number of divinely inspired books as well as their interpretation led to the existence of several Jewish sects (Sadducees, Pharisees, Essenes). Some of them also embraced the apocalyptic literature that flourished during the period. The latter would at times spark an eschatological fever that made the coming of the prophet and the materialization of messianic expectations seem very near. But the final era turned out to be for another time. The one end that did come was the end of the Second Temple. History continued. In the aftermath of the temple's destruction, the Pharisee rabbis came to determine the profile of mainstream Judaism. As guardians and interpreters of the ancestral books—the books that *they* deemed ancestral—the sages and scholars would shape the future of Judaism.

Israelite religion has a prologue and an epilogue. The prologue is the tapestry of ancient Near Eastern religion that Israelite religion was linked to by a thousand threads. It is a prologue that did not end when the story of Israelite religion began, because religion continued alive and well throughout the Near East for the entire first millennium BCE. The epilogue is its aftermath, most tangible in Judaism, Samaritan religion, and early Christianity. Every ending is also a new beginning. There is no date for the demise of Israelite religion, nor an exact birthdate for Judaism, Samaritanism, and the Jewish sect that would become Christianity. To the naked eye there is no transition. Looking back, we see a strong historical connection between the one and the three others. What they inherited from Israelite religion was a text, a sacred scripture that they read as divine law for eternity (Judaism, Samaritanism) or as prophecy of Jesus the Messiah (Christianity). One need not share the belief in the sanctity of the text to recognize the latter as a lasting contribution of Israelite religion to the heritage of humankind. Israelite religion is now a dead language, but it left a scribal legacy that still resonates.

Prologue: Ancient Near Eastern Religion

There are many ways to define religion. One that has commanded wide assent says that religion is "an institution consisting of culturally patterned interaction with culturally postulated superhuman beings."[1] This definition captures some of the essential elements of what we nowadays call religion. Religion is not merely belief in God. In that respect, books on Israelite religion that focus on the origin and profile of Yhwh, some of them studies of outstanding merit, provide a historical theology rather than a history of religion.[2] Religion consists of *interaction* with beings from the superhuman sphere. Such interaction presupposes belief; however, that belief is not individual but a cultural postulate. In the ancient Near East, this postulate was common to all ethnic and linguistic groups that lived in the area. Nobody realized this involved an act of belief. The presence of gods seemed the most natural thing in the world. Within the general category of superhuman beings, there were gods and ancestors, both entitled to acts of worship and devotion, but also demons and ghosts, to be kept at bay by spells and incantations. All of them were superhuman rather than supernatural, for at the time people did not make the distinction between the natural and the supernatural. Gods and ancestors inhabited the same universe that humans lived in, albeit in separate places out of reach for ordinary men and women. In the perception of the early inhabitants of the Eastern Mediterranean, the cosmos was vertically divided into three zones: the earth as the human habitat, heaven above as the realm of the gods, and the netherworld below for the ancestors. Demons and ghosts were harder to locate: they roamed the places betwixt and between, the fringe areas that were neither here nor there. Before we discuss the nature of gods, ancestors, ghosts, and demons, we need to familiarize ourselves more intimately with this cosmology.

Cosmology and the Separation Principle

The world we live in is both a physical reality and a place of the imagination. As physical reality, the world of the ancients did not differ all that much from ours. In their minds, however, their picture of the world departed significantly from modern views of the universe. Pascal felt terrified by "the eternal silence of these infinite spaces."[3] With the progress of science, the universe has expanded into thousands of galaxies, and the infinite spaces have become only more infinite. By comparison, the ancient Near Eastern cosmology had the reassuring simplicity of domestic architecture. There was a ground floor (earth), a second floor (heaven), and a basement (underworld). None of those spaces was empty. Gods lived upstairs, the ancestors in the basement, and humans and animals occupied the ground floor. In some respects, however, this domestic metaphor is skewed, for it fails to convey the awe people felt when contemplating the sky or thinking about the underworld. In their imagination, heaven was incredibly "high" and "vast," just as the underworld was terribly "deep" and "wide." Those were domains to which humans had no access:

> Can you find out the deep things of God?
> Can you find out the limit of the Almighty?
> It is higher than heaven—what can you do?
> Deeper than Sheol [the underworld]—what can you know? (Job 11:7–8 NRSV; cf. Prov 30:3–4; Deut 30:11–14)[4]

In the imagination, the immensity of heaven and the profundity of the underworld gave rise to the idea that they consisted of multiple levels. In the learned literature of the Babylonians, heaven has three levels: the upper heavens as the abode of the high god, the middle heavens as residence of various other gods, and the lower heavens for the stars and constellations.[5] Though less explicit, the topography of the ancient Israelites was similar. The reference to "a pavement of sapphire stone, like the very heaven for clearness," under God's feet (Exod 24:10 NRSV; cf. Ezek 1:26–28, 10:1) compares to the blue stone floor of the middle heavens in cuneiform texts.[6] Also the poetic triad of "heavens," "highest heavens," and "waters above the heavens" conveys the idea of superimposed levels (Ps 148:1–6). The apostle Paul's mention of an ascent to "the third heaven" shows he was familiar with the tripartition (2 Cor 12:2). Along with the three-tiered heaven was the idea of seven heavens (see, e.g., 2 En. 20:1), which occurs already in Sumerian texts. The seven heavens have their cosmological counterpart in the seven levels of the underworld.[7] In the Mesopotamian myth about the descent of Ishtar to the underworld, the goddess has to pass through seven gates in order to get to the innermost part of the shadow society below.[8] Up to a point, these speculations about the topography of heaven and the underworld cater to human curiosity about the unknown. More significantly perhaps, they express a sense of the distance that separates the gods in the high heavens, on the one hand, and the world of the dead, on the other, from the humans who live on earth.

The division of the universe into three compartments is not merely a cosmological theory. It reflects a concern with separation. Just as there is a proper *time* for every matter under heaven (Eccl 3:1), so there is a proper *place* for gods, human beings, and the spirits of the dead. As long as all of them stay in their designated zone, there is no danger. Blurring of the boundaries, however, might bring disaster. In the story of Ishtar's descent, the goddess threatens the gatekeeper of the underworld: "If you do not open the gate for me to come in, I shall smash the door and shatter the bolt, I shall smash the doorpost and overturn the doors, I shall raise up the dead and they shall eat the living: the dead shall outnumber the living!"[9] Should the gate to the underworld be shattered, the dead would engulf the world of the living and "eat" them (the verb is *akālu*, related to *ukultu*, "epidemic").[10] In a similar manner the gods must stay in their realm. In the Bible, when the sons of God took wives for themselves from the daughters of humans, they fathered a breed of hybrid heroes. Their act set in motion a process that resulted in the flood—a disaster that nearly spelled the end of humankind (Gen 6:1–8). Underneath these mythological tales runs a deep-seated fear of disorder and destruction as possible consequences for transgressing boundaries. What is meant to be separate must remain separate.

Also in the realities of daily life, the separation principle plays a role—subtle sometimes, but not for that reason any less imperative. Under the form of disease and decay, the realm of the dead encroaches upon the world of the living. And in temples and sanctuaries, the gods dwell on earth as well. In these instances, the separation principle demands that humans observe a respectful distance. Contact with a corpse leads to a state of impurity (Num 5:1–4). The return to regular life requires ablutions and perhaps other purifying measures, as well as a period of social isolation (Num 19:14–22). Before the body of the deceased is buried, it has to be washed, anointed, and wrapped in cloth in preparation of its passage to the netherworld (Matt 27:59; John 19:40).[11] Temple visits cannot be made without due precaution either. Here, too, worshippers must separate from the secular realm by washing, changing their clothes, and taking off their footwear (Gen 35:2–3; Exod 19:10; 2 Kgs 10:22; Exod 3:5; Josh 5:15). Depending on local tradition, additional rules may apply, such as the avoidance of leeks, garlic, and onions.[12] It may seem paradoxical that contacts that are either inevitable (the burial of the dead) or desired (the encounter with gods) are fraught with danger. This follows from the dual nature of the gods and the dead. When rightly treated, gods and ancestors can be a source of blessing, yet the slightest error might prove fatal. The LORD blessed the house of Obed-edom when the ark of God stayed there, but when Uzzah touched the ark to keep it from falling, God struck him dead (2 Sam 6:6–11).

The separation principle also applies in certain social contacts. In some cases, the reasons that require separation are quite transparent. Illness, especially when obvious to the eyes of others, leads to social isolation. The motive is not hygienic precaution in the modern sense of the term, but fear of contamination by what was perceived as an incursion of the realm of death into the world of the living. Those disfigured by skin disease would spend their days outside the city walls (Lev 13:45–46; 2 Kgs 7:3–5). When healed, they had to submit to purification rites (aspersion, change of clothes, shaving, baths) before they could mix with the rest of the population (Lev 14:1–9).

A special area where separation rules prevail are intergender relationships. Up to a point, men and women moved in separate circles. There was the world of men, gathering at the city gate when the day is done, and the world of women, meeting one another in their private quarters or in the shadows of their homes. The royal palace would have a harem, and many private houses had separate living quarters for women.[13] Adult women covered their heads to preserve their privacy. When the husband entertained guests, his wife would not be in the room.[14] Gender roles came with distinct vestiary codes, emphasized by the Deuteronomic prohibition of code switching (Deut 22:5). Each gender, moreover, had its characteristic implements: for women the spindle and the mirror, for men the axe and the club (2 Sam 3:29).[15] But though men and women lived in parallel universes, they had to come together to produce offspring. Intercourse was not carefree, however. Especially the first time, it was fraught with peril—hence the popular tales about grooms who died on their wedding night (Tob 3:7–9, 6:14–15; cf. Exod 4:24–26). By crossing the boundary between the sexes, the partners became "unclean" and had to perform various rites of purification afterward—bathing being the most common one (Lev 15:18).[16]

As the discussion above suggests, there is a close connection between the separation principle and the binary of pure versus impure or the less solemn-sounding one of clean versus unclean. Cleanliness or purity stands for a state of safety and vitality; its opposite refers to a situation of impaired vitality and exposure to harm. For humans, neither purity nor impurity is ever absolute. It all depends on context. By crossing the boundaries that separate the sacred from the secular, the world of the dead from the world of the living, or the sphere of men from the sphere of women, humans become impure. The vision and call of Isaiah illustrate the mechanism. Isaiah was safe until he found himself in the presence of the deity, where he feared for his life because he was "a man of unclean lips" (Isa 6:5). It took a rite of purification to dispel the danger and make him fit to act as God's messenger (Isa 6:6–8). Purification, then, is a rite of passage. It allows one to make the transition from one realm to the other. Similar principles underlie the biblical laws about clean and unclean animals. Uncleanliness attaches to animals that cross the boundaries that separate earth from heaven (the sky) and the underworld (the waters underneath the earth). The priestly codification of dietary customs may be artificial in some respects, but the logic of the rules agrees with the concern for separation characteristic of much of the ancient Near East.[17]

Cosmology and the Experience of Time

While the three-tiered universe of ancient Near Eastern cosmology is primarily about spatial organization, it also frames the division and experience of time. Sun, moon, and stars make the rounds of the firmament, some of them slower than others, and thereby determine the rhythm of day and night, the month and its divisions, the fixed times for holy days and festivals, and the succession of the years (Gen 1:14–19). In the collective imagination of the Near East, the astral bodies were not merely luminaries but gods. Variants of the Hebrew word for sun (*šemeš*) occur as the proper name of the sun god in Mesopotamia (Shamash) and the sun goddess in Ugarit (Shapshu). The same is true with respect to the Hebrew word for moon (*yārēaḥ*), which at Ugarit served as the name of the moon god Yarikh. Sun-god worship was widespread in Egypt too (where the god was called Re). To the authors of the Hebrew Bible, sun and moon were not gods but just heavenly bodies. Polemical references to the worship of sun and moon, however, suggest that many Israelites saw them as divine beings (Deut 4:19, 17:3; 2 Kgs 23:5; Jer 8:2; Job 31:26–28; Wis 13:2). Such place-names as Beth-Shemesh ("temple of Shemesh") and Jericho ("place of Yarikh") preserve the memory of their worship in Palestine.[18]

Since the predominant notion of gods was anthropomorphic, Mesopotamian texts and images picture the daily course of the sun as the journey of a manlike figure, with rays emanating from his shoulders, emerging at dawn from the doors of heaven in the east, traveling across the skies, and eventually entering the interior of heaven again through another double door in the west (fig. 2).[19] At night, the god sleeps in his bedroom.[20] At times, the imagery is slightly more elaborate: "O Shamash, you have opened the locks of heaven; you went up a staircase of pure lapis lazuli."[21] Echoes of such imagery survive as poetry in some biblical passages. Thus the image of the sun coming out as a bridegroom from his wedding canopy to run its course like a strong man (Ps 19:6 [19:5]) may be compared to "the hero, young man Shamash, the husband whom you love," phrases used in a prayer to his consort Aya.[22] In keeping with the Mesopotamian imagery, the sun is said to "come out" at dawn and to "go (back) in" at dusk.[23] The Hebrew terminology for sunrise (*mizraḥ haššemeš*) and sunset (*mēbô' haššemeš;* literally, "entry of the sun") conforms to this usage and thereby retains a fossilized memory of the Near Eastern solar mythology.

In the Near East, people did not measure time by clocks and calendars. There is some evidence for water clocks and sun dials in Mesopotamia and Egypt, but their use was rare.[24] As for calendars, the ones that were in existence were prescriptive, listing lucky and unlucky days, the times of monthly and annual rituals, or the proper periods for various agricultural activities.[25] The three main units of time—day, month, and year— were commonly determined by the position of the sun, the phases of the moon, and the succession of the seasons. Time, to the ancients, was neither an abstraction nor an empty space. It had religious significance. Not only because the markers of time—sun, moon, and constellations—were conceived of as deities, but also by the fact that various religious occasions, from daily offerings to annual festivals, punctuated the passage of time and were, for most people, the main references when they needed to put events on a timeline. Thus, a narrator can say something happened "[t]he next day, about the time of the morning offering" (2 Kgs 3:20), or, "As midday passed, they raved on until the time of the offering of the oblation" (1 Kgs 18:29, cf. 18:36). These are the morning and evening offering (the *minḥâ*), the one brought at dawn and the other around three o'clock in the afternoon.[26] Religion was so much part of everyday experience that such references to the daily temple ritual as time indications felt quite natural.

Fig. 2. The sun god Shamash coming out to illuminate the world. Artist's impression after third-millennium BCE Mesopotamian seal engraving. (Drawing by Willem Zijlstra.)

In view of the religious significance that the main divisions of time were invested with, there is reason to make a few observations about the day, the month, and the year. In Israel, the *day* used to be reckoned from one sunrise to the next, a full day consisting of "day and night." In Babylonia, on the other hand, the day began when the sun disappeared and ended the next evening.[27] It is this Babylonian reckoning that the Judeans, during the time of their exile, eventually adopted and later introduced in Judah. In the postexilic era, then, the day ran from sunset to sunset (Neh 13:19), a custom surviving in Judaism where the Sabbath starts on "Sabbath evening." The working day was a Mediterranean day. It started early in the morning, when temperatures were still mild, and came to a halt around noon. That was the time for the first real meal, usually followed by a nap in the shade to avoid "the heat of the day."[28] Evening began after the siesta.[29] For those accustomed to more temperate climates it may take a mental adjustment, but in the Mediterranean, from about three in the afternoon onward, people wished one another "good evening." Most people would use the remainder of the day for activities that were not too strenuous. In the early evening the girls of the village would come out, usually in groups, to draw water at the well (Gen 24:11; 1 Sam 9:11). A little later it was time for the second meal of the day. The rhythm of two meals a day—breakfast did not amount to much—had a parallel in the sacrificial regime.[30] Throughout the Near East, the gods would receive two meals a day, in some cases supplemented by secondary offerings as a kind of snack in between.[31] The time of those sacrifices was widely regarded as the propitious moment to approach the deity with praise and petition (Ps 141:2; Dan 9:21; Jdt 9:1; Luke 1:9–10).

Days added up to *months* rather than weeks, the seven-day week being another postexilic innovation in Judah. The principal moments of the month were new moon and full moon. Leading up to the appearance of the new moon—a small sliver of silver in the sky—was the period during which the moon was invisible. It had been "taken away," as the Akkadian expression has it, or gone to "lie down," according to the Sumerian phrase. In Babylonia, the interlude between two moons counted as "the beginning of the month."[32] The Egyptians followed a similar reckoning.[33] In Israel, too, such seems to have been the case, as the "new moon" (*ḥōdeš*) lasted up to three days (1 Sam 20:5–29).[34] These were days off, often used by the extended family to gather around a meal that included offerings for the family ancestors.[35] The calendrical setting was related to the fact that the moon god had left heaven for the underworld. He was believed to be able, precisely during these days, to "release" the dead so that they might participate in the celebrations.[36] The second high point fell at midmonth. In Israel, new moon (*ḥōdeš*) and full moon (*šabbāt*) were apparently the appropriate times to visit a sanctuary (2 Kgs 4:23; cf. Hos 2:13 [2:11]; Amos 8:5; Isa 1:10–17). Though *šabbāt* normally means "Sabbath," a period of rest returning every seventh day, the Hebrew word is related to Akkadian *šapattu* (variant *šabattu*), "festival day," which fell on every fifteenth day of the month. In other words, Sabbath was, originally, full-moon day; the identification with the seventh day of the week is a later development.[37] Another Hebrew term for full moon is *kese'/keseh* (Job 26:9). The rare occurrences of the term confirm the cultic significance of the occasion, as it marked the time of festivals and sacrifices (Ps 81:4; Prov 7:19–20; cf. 1 Kgs 12:32–33).[38]

The *year* was identical with the agricultural year. When in Hellenistic times the correct calculation of festival dates became an issue, Jewish scholars had recourse to astronomical observations. For the average population of Palestine, however, the agricultural year offered sufficient orientation. They put a time frame to events by saying something had happened "at the beginning of the barley harvest" (2 Sam 21:9; Ruth 1:22), "in the days of the wheat harvest" (Judg 15:1; cf. 1 Sam 6:13, 12:16–17; Ruth 2:23), or "at the time the latter growth [*leqeš*] began to sprout" (Amos 7:1). Before the exile, month names were seldom used. The Gezer calendar (tenth century BCE), too, organizes the year by agricultural activity, starting with the "ingathering" in autumn, passing by the latter growth (*leqeš*), the harvest of barley and wheat, to end with the time of the summer fruit.[39] Apparently, the year began in the fall. In this respect, the epigraphical evidence from Gezer is consonant with the biblical passages that speak of the autumnal harvest festival "at the turn of the year" (Exod 34:22; 1 Sam 1:20). The latter phrase shows that the harvest festival was a New Year festival. Calendrically, it fell in either the seventh or the eighth month of the year (1 Kgs 12:32).

The fact that the Bible puts the New Year in the seventh month (e.g., Lev 23:39) is due to the postexilic introduction of the Babylonian calendar (including the Babylonian month names). Although the Babylonian year starts with the spring equinox (around March 20), the New Year celebrations oscillated between spring and autumn, as is demonstrated by the fact that the Akitu festival came around twice a year: the first time in the first month, and the second time in the seventh.[40] This was the general pattern throughout the Near East. Also on the Syrian coast, in the port town of Ugarit, there was a spring festival and an autumn festival—the one marking the beginning of the seafaring season, and the other inaugurating the new agricultural year.[41] In the myth that served as the libretto to the rituals, the first festival celebrated the triumph of Baal over Yamm (the unruly sea of the winter months; cf. Acts 27:12, 28:11), and the second Baal's victory over Mot (ruler of the underworld, personifying the scorching summer heat). In Israel, too, the New Year festival in autumn had a pendant in spring. Whereas the autumn New Year festival was Succoth (the Festival of Booths), the spring festival was Passover. Passover was in origin a pastoralist festival, marking the time of seasonal transfer of the herds, whereas Succoth was an agriculturalist festival celebrating the harvest. In the monarchic period, the spring new year was the beginning of the political year because spring was the season for warfare: "In the spring of the year [literally, "turn of the year"], the time when kings go out to battle" (2 Sam 11:1 NRSV; 1 Kgs 20:22, 26; 2 Kgs 13:20).

When the main parameters of time are sun, moon, and the seasons, the predominant experience of time is likely to be cyclical. The Hebrew expression for the beginning of the new year, "at the (re)turn (*těšûbâ* or *těqûpâ*) of the year," says as much. Still it would be a serious misrepresentation to say that the only form of historical awareness was cyclical. People then did not live in an eternal present any more than they do now. To them, too, history was a sequence of generations and events. Genealogical lists were a venerable literary genre, carefully kept and handed down, as the bare-bones of family, tribal, and even national history.[42] All over the Near East, royal chancelleries produced annals. These yearbooks put the acts of kings in a religious frame because failure and success were believed to be in the hands of the gods. Gods not only had been active in the mythical time of the beginning but continued to act in history.[43] The one thing absent from the ancient Near Eastern perception of time is the notion of progress. Progress should not be confused with historical development, however. There was development, but that development was one of decadence rather than progress. Babylonians, Egyptians, Israelites—they all had a sense that world history could be divided into three or four periods. Each new period marked a decline with respect to the previous one. The Golden Age was in the distant past, when humans lived to an inordinate old age (Gen 5:1–32), and gods still imparted revelations in person.[44] Against this background, innovation was by definition deterioration. When renovation was inevitable, those responsible took care to present it as a return to the pristine purity of the beginning.[45]

Gods of Nature and the Nature of Gods

In light of the discussion of ancient Near Eastern cosmology it is clear that nature was a powerful source for the religious imagination.[46] Whereas the modern metaphor of nature is that of a machine lacking free will, to the ancients nature was the stage on which gods acted and interacted.[47] Throughout the Near East, people personified the sun, moon, and stars as gods. So they did with rainstorms, mountains, rivers, and seas. It did not stop there. Animals might be gods or closely associated with them. Particular places could be deified. On the borderline between nature and culture, strong emotions, too, were gods or closely related to gods, such as love and desire and the frenzy of warfare. Similarly beer, wine, and strong drink counted as gods, since they could induce altered states of consciousness. In addition, there were the cult objects such as the drum, spear, and harp, closely linked with the sphere of the sacred and therefore deified.[48] The cuneiform script, widely used at the time, put the classifier *dingir*, "god," before all nouns that were regarded as divine names. The god lists the scribes compiled could be very long.[49]

Fig. 3. The storm god Baal standing on the waters of his slain enemy Yamm and brandishing a thunderbolt; stela from Ugarit. Louvre, Paris, AO 15775. (Wikimedia Commons.)

What makes a god? The common quality of ancient Near Eastern gods is their superhuman nature. They are more than human, foremost because they are far more powerful. This is true of the heavenly bodies that dictate the rhythm of the days and the seasons. But the sun, moon, and stars are predictable, even though they might on occasion depart from their course. More awe-inspiring are the gods whose behavior is unpredictable, such as the gods of winds, storms, rain, hail, and thunder (fig. 3). A classic phrase for the Mesopotamian god Enlil (literally, "Lord Wind") says that he "sleeps a deceptive sleep."[50] The meaning is clear. Even when the air has been hardly stirring, a storm may suddenly rise and leave a trail of devastation. Now storms can be terrible, but rainfall is a necessity, especially in areas that lack other supplies of water. This explains the dual nature of gods, and the ambivalent feelings they inspire. Agrarian societies of the type that prevailed in Palestine depended totally on seasonal rainfall. This dependence inspired sentiments of fear and trembling toward the gods, who could both give or withhold it. "Fear of God" was real fear. That is why people went to such lengths to stay on the good side of their gods.

Though all sorts of associations could be at the origin of Near Eastern deities, most of the major gods were related to natural phenomena. This is one of the reasons why ancient Near Eastern religion has often been categorized as "nature religion." The authors who came up with this classification held an evolutionary view of religion.[51] They believed in the survival of the fittest. The most primitive form of religion was supposed to have been the belief in and use of totems. Totemism had been succeeded by nature religion. But nature religion would in its turn be surpassed and made redundant by higher, more spiritual forms of religion, a process that was to culminate in Christianity—seen by some as the summit of religion, with one god only, no human-made idols, and a strong ethical code. The popular secularization theory is in fact an offshoot of such thinking, taking the secular worldview as the ultimate stage and natural end of religion. Few scholars of religion today would embrace this evolutionary perspective. Also, the qualification of ancient Near Eastern gods as gods of nature is questionable. Many of them do have their origins in natural phenomena, but all of them were endowed with agency and were commonly pictured, in the mind of their worshippers and in cultic representations, as having human emotions and human forms. Anthropomorphism was the rule.[52] The gods were superhuman, which meant they possessed all the human faculties without being subject to human limitations. The natural phenomena they were connected with functioned almost like etymologies. They were a reminder of where these gods came from, but it would be an error to equate them with the gods. People did distinguish between the sun as a celestial body (the natural object) and the heavenly power associated with the sun (the god).[53]

The profile of the Mesopotamian sun god Shamash provides some further insight into the correlation between the deity and the natural phenomenon he took his name from. The sun god is the god of justice. He is the supreme judge, punisher of the lawless and protector of those who, on account of their social position, were often victims of violence (such as orphans and widows). This is related to the fact that the sun's rays were believed to penetrate everywhere. Shamash could read a letter while it was still in its sealed envelope (cuneiform tablets of a confidential nature could be put in a casing made of clay).[54] Since the sun god is all-seeing, no human action is hidden from his sight. This made Shamash the patron god of judges, and the one invoked by all who had suffered or feared maltreatment. Owing to his role as divine judge, Shamash was also the god of oracular inquiries, since the oracle was believed to be a divine verdict.[55] Wayfarers too would turn to Shamash to protect them. It does not take an extraordinary leap of the imagination to see how these various facets of Shamash could spring from his association with the sun. At the same time, though, the various dimensions of the sun god's profile make it clear it would be a serious error to reduce Shamash to a deified natural phenomenon. The god was believed to have human form and to fulfill roles that were modeled on human roles, although he lived up to these roles with a grandeur possible only for gods. Much the same goes for the other "nature gods" of the Near East. Nature was the springboard of the imagination, but the imagination came up with gods who looked more like humans than like natural elements.

Speaking of gods, the inhabitants of the ancient Near East normally used the plural—their world was polytheistic. It seemed the most natural thing since the cosmos itself was operated by many forces, sometimes harmoniously, at other times in conflict. To reduce such diversity to a single factor felt like an amputated version of reality. Out of religious fervor for the god of his forebears, a king might neglect the regular cult of other gods, as Nabonidus did in his devotion to the moon god.[56] Such exclusive worship of one deity (monolatry) does not deny the existence others. Monotheistic "revolutions," such as the one promoted by Akhenaten in mid-fourteenth century BCE Egypt, were interludes rather than lasting reorientations.[57] Throughout the three millennia of its recorded history, ancient Near Eastern religion has tended to identify similar gods with one another, or to present various local gods as aspects of a major national one. At the same time, though, gods might multiply when divine titles (such as Baal, "Lord," for the storm god Hadad) came to serve as proper names. Such developments do not change the overall picture. There was a multitude of gods, and that very multiplicity belonged to the essence of the religious imagination.

The world of the gods was not one of equals. Also in the pantheon there existed rank and hierarchy. To define the position of the various gods with respect to one another, people would use two models: one is that of the heavenly council presided by a senior god; and the other, that of a divine tribe, in which gods were grouped in related families, the complete family tree being headed by a divine ancestor. The two models are not mutually exclusive and do occur side by side. In the Babylonian Story of Creation the text opens with a genealogical account of the gods (the model of

Fig. 4. Akkadian seal representing Ishtar, goddess of sex and warfare, holding her lion. Museum of the Institute for the Study of Ancient Cultures (ISAC), University of Chicago. (Wikimedia Commons, CC-BY-3.0, https://creativecommons.org/licenses/by/3.0/deed.en.)

the tribe), whereas later in the text, the divine hero Marduk "convened the great gods in assembly" (the council model).[58] To harmonize the two models, one might say that the council consisted of the tribal elders under the presidency of their leader. In Syria and Palestine, the council model was the more common one.[59] It is hierarchical as the members of the council must bow to the god that presides over them, but otherwise they are more or less equal. Also the Bible has preserved a few references to the divine council, as in Psalm 82: "God has taken his place in the divine council; / in the midst of the gods he holds judgment" (Ps 82:1 NRSV).

In keeping with the anthropomorphism of the ancient Near Eastern deities, the gods of the various pantheons formed a divine society that paralleled in many ways society as humans knew it. In addition to such phenomena as labor division and social hierarchy, gods had different roles and positions based on gender and age. There were gods and goddesses. Most of the major gods had an official female consort (Marduk and Zarpanitum, Shamash and Aya, Baal and Anat, and so on), and at times a lady lover on the side (Marduk and Nanay). Gods married and had sex. In Mesopotamian temples and elsewhere, there were periodical sacred marriage rites to celebrate the love of the gods, to promote the fertility of the land, and to present the human ruler as divine offspring.[60] Divine couples had children. Ugaritic texts speak about the "seventy children of Asherah" (a designation of the pantheon headed by El and Asherah), motherhood putting Asherah in a position where she could plead with her consort that he might grant the wish of the one or the other of her offspring.[61] Human worshippers, too, would ask goddesses to put in a good word.[62] Divine fatherhood is most prominently present in the classic father-son constellation of a senior god and his successor, such as Marduk and Nabu.[63] The one goddess with no respect for the social conventions is Ishtar, just like her Syrian counterpart Anat, both bearing some distant resemblance to Egyptian Isis (fig. 4). She is the wild one, the maiden who does not grow old, the goddess of sex and warfare whose presence is often intoxicating.[64]

City Gods and Tribal Gods

The ancient Near Eastern gods are closely connected with a variety of natural and seminatural phenomena—so much so that modern authors can paraphrase them as sun god, moon god, storm god, wine god, and the like. These connections are about the different profiles of the gods. Many of them also have another kind of connection, since they are related to a particular social group. The two principal varieties of such groups are the urban community and the tribe, the former living in a city, and the latter wandering about or settled in the country. There are, then, city gods and tribal gods. In the great civilizations of the time, such as Mesopotamia and Egypt, most gods were city gods. Almost every deity had its own city, where it lived in temples as rulers would in a palace. The city belonged to the deities; it was their estate. The citizens worked for the benefit of the city god and/or goddess, providing them with everything they might need. In return, the gods would extend their special protection over the city. It was, in many ways, a symbiotic relationship. The renown of the city would reinforce the reputation of its god, just as the acclaim of the god would enhance the position of the city. Hence the attempts of city scribes to come up with compositions that presented their god as the most eminent of all. The Babylonian Story of Creation is a good example. It seeks to raise Babylon's city god, Marduk, also known as Bel, to the highest rank of the pantheon on account of his epic exploits at the time of creation.[65] A similar purpose may have inspired the Memphite Theology, an Egyptian document that presents the city god of Memphis (Ptah) as the true creator.[66]

The association of tribal gods is not with cities but tribes, or perhaps more precisely, with tribal territories. A Babylonian creation myth describes how in primeval times each god "took" his own city: "Bel took Babylon, Nabu took Borsippa, Nergal took Cuthah, Zababa took Kish, Shamash took Sippar, Sin took Ur, Adad took Bit Karkara, Enlil took Nippur, Urash took Dilbat, Erimabinutuka took Isin. All the gods got territory."[67] It is instructive to compare this passage with a similar account preserved, in lightly garbled form, in the Bible:

> When the Most High apportioned the nations,
>   when he divided humankind,
> he fixed the boundaries of the peoples
>   according to the number of the gods;
> the LORD's own portion was his people,
>   Jacob his allotted share. (Deut 32:8–9 NRSV)

Whereas the Babylonian text focuses on cities, the biblical passage deals with nations. The principle is the same. At some point in the distant past, the gods have been allotted their portion. But while the Babylonian gods took cities, the gods of the Deuteronomy passage received nations. The difference is not theological. It has to do with a difference in social and political organization. In Iron Age Palestine there were no real city-states. The dominant forms of social organization were tribes and tribal confederacies, some of which might amount to what today we would call a nation. As a matter of consequence, the gods were tribal or national deities. YHWH was the god of the Israelites, just as Milcom was the god of the Ammonites, and Chemosh the god of the Moabites. Tribal gods were not unknown in Mesopotamia either. Amurru was the tribal god of the Amorites, without any privileged link to a city.[68] In a similar manner, many Aramean tribes had their tribal gods, such as El, Shamash, Sin, and Ashtar.

The origins of the particular veneration of a particular deity by a given city or tribe are mostly a matter of speculation. In the mythological explanation that the ancient texts offer, the initiative had come from the gods. They had "taken" their cities or, as the biblical texts say, "chosen" their people. The historical reality must have been different. Maruduk, for instance (biblical Merodach), is the pre-Sumerian name of Marduk the local god of Pabila (the later Babylon), a minor city in the third millennium BCE.[69] Nearly all such cities had a local god. Originally, most of these local deities had a general profile, the labor division among the gods being one of the consequences of their organization into a pantheon. Such theological constructions occurred in the wake of processes of state formation during which formerly independent cities were joined into larger polities. The spread of a common script over the Mesopotamian area favored these intellectual developments.

As for the tribal gods, we may note that many of them are related to astral or atmospheric phenomena. Sun, moon, morning star, storm clouds—they are all manifestations of gods who are not tied to one place but move along with the groups that worship them. This is not to say that all tribes were by definition itinerant, but at an early stage of their formation most of them had been. When settled, they would usually live in a territory rather than in one city. In some rare cases, the tribal god carries the same name as the social group he is connected with. Amurru the god of the Amorites is a classic example. A closer investigation of his profile shows he had traits of a storm god and may have been a doppelgänger of El, especially since his consort was Ashratu (biblical Asherah). In fact, many of the tribal gods differ by name rather than profile. This hardly comes as a surprise since tribal gods might have a small entourage (consort, son, some servants) but were usually not integrated into a larger pantheon. Here, again, Amurru might be cited as an example. His incorporation into the Mesopotamian pantheon was clearly a late development.[70] City links of tribal gods, such as that of YHWH with Jerusalem ("YHWH who dwells in Zion," Joel 4:21 [3:21]), are likewise secondary.

Ancestor Cult and the Deified Dead

Surveys of gods worshipped in Mesopotamia reveal the existence of a number of deities with names that look suspiciously like proper names of human beings. The most compelling cases are theophoric names, that is, names that include a reference to a deity (a good example of a simple theophoric name is Jonathan, "YHWH-has-given"). When such theophoric names occur as divine names, it is clear they refer to humans who, posthumously, have achieved the status of gods. Mesopotamian examples include the gods Ikrub-El (variant Yakrub-El, "El has blessed"), Itur-Mer ("Mer has returned"), and Aba-Enlil-gim (Sumerian name, "Who is like Enlil").[71] Does this mean that all the gods and goddesses of Mesopotamia were deified men and women, as the theory of euhemerism claimed of the Greek gods?[72] That would be most unlikely. But these names are evidence of a category of gods who are actually deified ancestors. As such they provide an oblique insight into an aspect of ancient Near Eastern religion that probably had greater significance than most textbooks suggest.

In the mind of the early inhabitants of the Near East, the dead were not really dead. They were, for quite some time after their departure, still very much alive, not merely in the memory of their descendants but as beings that could affect what happened in the real world. The dead had some uncanny powers. They possessed foresight and the gift of healing, as well as the ability to afflict the living with illnesses of the body and the mind. Like gods, they could move around invisible to the human eye. Like gods, they could bring blessing or cause great harm. On the strength of the analogy, the dead were classified as gods—not only in Mesopotamia, where some ancestors received worship like full-fledged deities, but throughout the Near East. In Judah and Israel, too, the population at times referred to the dead (*mētîm*) as "gods" (*'ĕlōhîm*; 1 Sam 28:13; Isa 8:19–20). It was not just a matter of semantics. The cult of the ancestors had such importance in the daily life of the ancients that they put it on a par with the veneration of the gods. On his wanderings, Gilgamesh is to sprinkle cool water every day for the sun god Shamash as well as for the spirit of his father, Lugalbanda.[73] According to a testament clause common at Emar (northern Syria), the main heir was to call upon and to venerate "the gods and the dead" of the—at times adoptive—father.[74] In like manner, a literary text from Ugarit mentions the funerary cult alongside participation in the sacrifices for El and Baal in a list of filial duties.[75]

At first sight, the divine status of the dead offers a strange contrast with the inferior conditions to which they had been reduced. Gods are not less but more than human. Human beings who have moved to the world of the dead, however, would seem to have descended to a lower form of existence. According to a classic description, found in several Mesopotamian texts, the underworld is "the house where those who enter are deprived of light, where dust is their food, clay their bread. They see no light, they dwell in darkness. They are clothed like birds, with feathers."[76] Conditions in the netherworld are unpleasant, to say the least. It is a place without hope, as the author of the book of Job intimates: "If I must look forward to Sheol as my home, and make my bed in the dark place, say to the Pit, 'You are my father,' to the maggots, 'Mother,' 'Sister'—where, then, is my hope? Who can see hope for me? Will it descend to Sheol? Shall we go down together in the dust?" (Job 17:13–16 NJPS). Those who have died ("descended to Sheol" or "the Pit," in Hebrew parlance) have gone to a place of perpetual sleep (Jer 51:39, 57; cf. Ps 13:4). Why, then, should the dead be regarded as gods?

The dead are gods on account of their powers, not because they live in bliss. In order to better understand why they were gods, we need to circumscribe more closely the power they were credited with. That power is, first and foremost, the power to "bless" their descendants. The literary genre of the patriarchal blessing, familiar from the Bible (e.g., Gen 49:1–28; Deut 33:1–29), has its background in the custom for the paterfamilias to determine what each of his children would inherit. His blessing determined rank among the children and thereby provided legitimacy to the son or daughter invested with the paternal authority (Gen 27:1–45; contrast Deut 21:15–17). If the father was a king, his "blessing" would decide which of his sons would be his successor (1 Kgs 1:1–2:12). Having passed to the realm of death, the paterfamilias still loomed large as a figure of authority for his children. So did the ancestors he was descended from. Rank, authority, and ownership among the living derived legitimacy from the blessing by the family ancestors. Should the dead withhold that blessing, the very foundations of power and possession would erode. Other abilities of the dead are related to the blessing. Blessing and curse are a form of prophecy since they predict what will happen (Gen 49:1; Numbers 22–24). Like the father on his deathbed, the ancestors were believed to foresee the future. Common throughout the Near East, this belief underlies the practice of necromancy.[77] The third blessing of the ancestors for their descendants was the gift of offspring. Such personal names as Abi-iddinam, "My father has given (a child)," and Abi-asaph, "My father has added (a child to the family)," are reflections, the one in Babylonian and the other in Hebrew, of the concern of the ancestors for the continuity of the family line.[78] It is in this capacity that Ugaritic texts address the ancestors as *rāpi'ūma*, "healers."[79] In Hebrew, the related verb *rāpā'*, "to heal," does occur with the connotation "to restore fertility" (Gen 20:17; 2 Kgs 2:19–22).

The divine powers of the dead, then, are more properly speaking the powers of the family ancestors. Accordingly, the cult of the dead is not performed indiscriminately but always in a family setting. It consisted of two elements: invocation and offering. Every day, normally at the time of the family meal, the ancestors were invited to come and receive some cool water and a few morsels of bread. In Mesopotamia, this rite was known as the "regular *kispu*," the latter term being derived from the verb *kasāpu*, "to break (bread) in small pieces."[80] With local variations, the custom was observed throughout the Near East. In some places it was usual to put the offerings near or on the grave; in other places it was a domestic rite performed before statuettes or other symbols of the ancestors. Periodically, the celebration took on a more solemn aspect. The extended family came together for a festive meal in communion with the ancestors. At some point of the ceremony, the paterfamilias would invoke the ancestors by name, inviting them to eat and drink and to bless their descendants. Records of such ceremonies normally mention up to three generations by name. Apparently, the dead whom no living family remembered having seen in person had joined the anonymous group of "family, kin, and relatives."[81] The one exception to this rule are the rituals for the royal ancestors. Those may contain a litany of more than twenty-five names, tracing back the dynastic line to the presumed founding fathers.[82]

The invocation of the royal shades of the dead shows how the ancestor cult could function as a ritual claim of legitimacy. Going back to the founders of the dynasty, the monarch implied he reigned with the full approval of his forebears. On a more modest scale, the leading male of the extended family made a similar claim. Participation of family members living at some distance was compulsory, precisely as a demonstration of solidarity with the family and its authority structure (1 Sam 20:6). Yet it would be an error to reduce the ancestor cult to this more formal aspect. The feelings toward the ancestors also had an element best captured by the Latin *pietas*, often translated as "devotion," but actually a mix of emotional attachment and respect, with a hint of compassion. The biblical story about Rachel and the teraphim provides an illustration. The teraphim are ancestor statuettes that served as the focus of the daily funerary offerings.[83] After her marriage to Jacob, Rachel had to leave her father's house to join the family of her husband. When she left, she secretly took the teraphim—much to the dismay of her father when he discovered their disappearance (Gen 31:19, 30–35). Rachel's motives have been the subject of much speculation. The most simple explanation is that she was attached to the statuettes, the way one can be attached to family pictures. The daily gifts to the ancestors were a concern to women; they prepared the food for the household, including its ancestors. Michal, married to the future king David, also exhibited a certain familiarity in the handling of the domestic teraphim (1 Sam 19:11–18). But pietas for the dead was not the prerogative of women. Take the Babylonian father whose son had disappeared eight years before. Since he did not know whether the son was still alive, the father had been making funerary offerings as if the boy were dead.[84] As it turned out, he had been kidnapped. The sad story shows that the cult of the dead could also be a disinterested demonstration of attachment to a lost child who had no grave and whose whereabouts were unknown.

Demons and Ghosts

In the collective imagination of the ancient Near East, there were gods in heaven, dead in the underworld, and demons and ghosts roaming about the earth where humans lived. Such demons were related both to the gods above and to the spirits of the dead below. Unlike the gods and the dead, however, demons had not stayed in their proper realm. They operated in disregard of the separation principle and thereby constituted a source of constant danger for humankind. A paradigmatic case is that of Lamashtu. She had been a goddess for she was a daughter of Anu, the Mesopotamian high god. Yet "[f]or her malicious ideas, her improper spirit, her father Anum threw her out of heaven, (threw her down) to earth." Lamashtu is "evil." Though of divine descent, she has turned into a demon.[85] Whereas Lamashtu had her origins in heaven, other demons have come from the underworld. Born of the queen of the netherworld, they have been "hurled from the earth as castoffs." They are "creatures of hell" that have not stayed in place.[86] In the general perception, demons were misfits, nowhere at ease and always dangerous. The evil demon has a dusky shadow, and "there is no light in his body, he slinks about in secret places."[87]

It was hard to tell what demons looked like because they entered houses unseen and they blew about as evil winds. But in the descriptions of spells and conjurations, demons are closely associated with animals. The demon Samana has the "mouth of a lion, teeth of a dragon, claws of an eagle, tail of a scorpion."[88] Lamashtu, for her part, had the head of a dog and the teeth of a donkey.[89] Amulets depict her with the head of a dog, a bird of prey, or a lion (fig. 5).[90] With the combination of human and animal features, these demons have the appearance of monsters. In what may have been an earlier stratum of popular belief, demons were thought to manifest themselves in the form of animals. Incantations of the third and early second millennia BCE address black dogs, snakes, and scorpions as demonic agents.[91] A biblical oracle mentions the demon Lilith, well-known from Mesopotamian texts, keeping the company of jackals, ostriches, wildcats, hyenas, and goat-demons (Isa 34:13–14 NRSV). The early translators of this passage found it difficult to decide whether these creatures were real animals or actually demons.[92] Demons, apparently, were hybrid creatures most likely to be encountered in the border zones of the civilized world. They made their lair among ruins, in deserts, in the steppe, or in forested areas that were hard to penetrate. The animal form some of them had underscores their mixed and impure nature.

Fig. 5. Stone amulet of the demon Lamashtu standing on a donkey and suckling a wild pig and a jackal. British Museum. (Wikimedia Commons, CC-BY-SA-4.0, https://creativecommons.org/licenses/by-sa/4.0/deed.en.)

A major difference between demons, on the one hand, and gods and ancestors, on the other, is that demons are inherently evil and evil only. They are almost impossible to deal with because they have very little in common with humans: "Neither males are they, nor females, they are winds ever sweeping along. They have not wives, engender no children, know not to show mercy, hear not prayer and supplication."[93] When gods do harm, they are normally responding to human misbehavior. The diseases they send are in retribution for transgressions. Even when the targets of the gods' anger don't know where they have gone wrong, they realize they must have done something to bring about punishment. Nor do the dead turn against the living for no reason. Perhaps they have been neglected or disturbed. Ultimately, gods act for motives not unlike the motives that inform human behavior. Demons are different. They can only harm, and they do so indiscriminately and regardless of circumstances. The evils they bring—anxiety attacks, insomnia, infant mortality, migraine, loss of appetite, sudden death—are blind to the identity of the victims. The only way to keep them at bay is by means of magic. A branch of religion rather than its opposite, magic seeks to ward off demons by the use of apotropaic figurines, amulets at the door, spells to frighten them, and a wide range of rites of elimination.[94]

Sanctuaries and Temples

The definition quoted at the beginning of this prologue identifies "interaction" as a core concept in religion. In so doing, it takes religion primarily as performative behavior. Religion presupposes belief, but it is in essence something that people act out. The central acts of ancient Near Eastern religion were sacrifice and worship, which followed, as the definition intimates, certain cultural patterns.

Though temples are the customary setting for interaction with the gods, the encounter can take place anywhere. The proper habitat of gods is heaven, but in order to receive the gifts that worshippers offer, the gods have to come down to earth. The Babylonian flood story has an almost comical passage in which the hero of the deluge prepares a sacrifice on the mountaintop where the ark has come to rest. When the gods smelled the incense, they "gathered like flies around the man making sacrifice."[95] The point is not the simile of the flies, but the fact that the gods gather to a place where they do not normally live. Mountains are closer to heaven than the plains, but in this case the gods simply come to where the sacrifice is. The wayfarer in the wilderness may offer cool water to Shamash at any point of his journey.[96] A similar idea informs an old rule about sacrifice in the Bible: "You need make for me only an altar of earth and sacrifice on it your burnt offerings . . . ; in every place where you call out my name I will come to you and bless you" (Exod 20:21 [20:24]). A later scribe took offense and corrected the text slightly to read "in every place where I cause my name to be remembered" (NRSV), but there can be no mistake. The original idea is that God will come to any place where worshippers invoke him and offer sacrifice (cf. Exod 23:13). The similarity with the words used in the liturgy for the funerary offerings is striking. There, too, the officiant invokes the ancestors, invites them to come and to partake of the offering, and prays for their blessing.[97]

Though sacrifice might be brought at any place, the more common practice in the Near East is to have sanctuaries devoted to the interaction with the gods. Sanctuaries could be very simple. The archaeological area known as the Bull Site in northern Palestine is an open-air cult place, located on a mountaintop, delimited by a low wall of boulders, and had a stone stela and an offering space (see fig. 26, below, Chapter 3).[98] It was certainly not the only place of its kind. In cities and towns with a sanctuary, however, the latter would usually be a roofed building with a courtyard. It was the local temple. The word "temple" sounds lofty, but the common term for temple, in Semitic languages and Egyptian, is "house." The temple is the house of God or, more accurately, the house of a particular god. The basic floor plan is rectangular and divided into two spaces: at the back the chamber where the god resides, and in the front a larger room, designed as a kind of audience hall. A wall surrounds the temple area. Its main gate leads to an open courtyard that had to be crossed to get to the entrance of the building. Temple builders with ambition could add all sorts of annexes, porticos, and decorations, but those would not change the basic design. The latter obeyed a domestic logic: there was a private room for the deity, an audience hall, and a yard for sacrifice and public ceremonies (fig. 6).

Since the temple was a house of God (whether Ishtar, Bel, Amon, Dagon, Yhwh, or any other god), the deity was presumed to live there. Such a belief seems difficult to reconcile with the notion of a dwelling in heaven or on a majestic mountain in the far distance. The objection that gods are everywhere fails to take into account that omnipresence was not a standard attribute of godhood (*ilūtu*, "divine nature," is the Akkadian term) in antiquity. Only some gods could be in more than one place at a time (such as the sun god). There is perhaps no solution that would satisfy all the demands of logic. But was it a problem of pure logic? This is about the coexistence of two parallel realities. In order to harmonize them, the mythology of the temple presented the house of God here below as the replica and counterpart of God's mansion in the inaccessible parts of the universe. The Babylonian Story of Creation contains the most explicit expression of this idea. To honor Marduk for his role in restoring order, the other gods built him a shrine in the city of Babylon. It is the Esagila temple, a "replica of the Apsu."[99] In the Babylonian story, Apsu is the name of the proper abode of Marduk and some of the other great gods. The Babylonian temple is its *mehertu*, "copy" or "equivalent," built not by human hands but by the gods themselves.[100] In the presentation of the book of Exodus, the Jerusalem temple is the exact copy of the "prototype" (*tabnît*) that God showed to Moses on Mount Sinai (Exod 25:9, 40). The upshot of these and other myths of origin is that the presence of the temple is due to the initiative of

Fig. 6. Temple of Baal-shamin at Palmyra. (Photograph copyright © 2008 by Erik Hermans, Ancient World Image Bank [New York: Institute for the Study of the Ancient World, 2009–], https://www.flickr.com/photos/isawnyu/5514623047, used under terms of a Creative Commons Attribution license.)

the gods. They have built it or given detailed instructions so that the earthly structure corresponds to a heavenly model.

In the ancient Near East, temples could have many secondary functions, including that of a savings bank and treasury, court of justice, dining hall, and arsenal. But the essence of a temple was the presence of the deity. There were different ways to conceptualize this presence, just as there were different means to make it real. The usual practice was to have a sculpted image of the god set up in the inner sanctum. The size of the image differed from place to place. Since gods looked like human beings (or humans were "in God's image," as the first chapter of Genesis has it), the images usually had human form, the deity's identity being indicated by the appropriate attributes. Most of the time the body of the image consisted of wood with a coating of precious metal. Gods were typically "beaming" and "brilliant" and shining like the heavens where they came from.[101] Icon production followed strict protocol. A special ritual activated the image and transformed the lifeless material into a living presence.[102] Anthropomorphic statuary was not the only option to materialize divine presence. The Egyptians often used animal forms, much like the "calves" in Bethel and Dan. In western Mesopotamia, Syria, and Palestine there was a tradition to set up a stone stela, at times roughly carved, to serve as an embodiment of the god.[103] The symbol is referred to as "stone" (Akkadian *abnu*, Hebrew *'eben*), "stela" (*sikkanu*, in Mari, Emar, and Ugarit), "erected stone" (*maṣṣēbâ*, the usual expression in Biblical Hebrew), and "bethel," that is, "sacred stone" (fig. 7).[104]

Modern scholars tend to stress that it would be a mistake to think the ancients actually identified their gods with the images.[105] They have a point. If for some reason the gods take fright, they might abandon their sanctuaries and go up to heaven, leaving their images behind.[106] On the other hand, the departure of the divine image—taken as spoil by an aggressor or temporarily away for purposes of repair—meant that the god had left.[107] In the absence of some material token, people found it hard to believe the deity was still present. The devotion of most worshippers focused on the image. They rarely saw it, because it normally stayed behind closed doors, but when it came out, as for the New Year procession, the sides of the street were thronged with people who tried to glimpse and touch the god. As an object of religious fervor, there was little difference between a sculpture or a standing stone. Both could kindle the enthusiasm of the crowd. In their eyes, the god was truly present in either symbol. In the minds of most

Fig. 7. Three standing stones (*maṣṣēbôt*) from the sanctuary at Dan; artist's impression. (Drawing by Willem Zijlstra.)

believers, the association between the gods and their local symbols was so strong that distinct images in different temples were taken for different deities, even though they carried the same name. Sacrificial rituals from Ugarit have separate offerings for Baal of Ugarit and Baal of Aleppo.[108] The phenomenon compares to the veneration of different local images of the Madonna in our time.

Guardians of the Code of Conduct: Worship and Morals

The term "interaction" in our definition of religion to characterize the kind of relations humans entertain with the superhuman agents of their culture might cause modern readers to raise an eyebrow. Interaction implies reciprocity, which in turn supposes that gods, ghosts, and demons—"culturally postulated superhuman beings"—somehow respond to human action. Doesn't that mean that the definition, for all its scientific-sounding phraseology, is actually a piece of crypto-theology? Instead of dismissing our definition as unscientific, however, it is preferable to focus on the cultural patterns the interaction is supposed to follow ("culturally patterned interaction"). We need not become believers in order to study the forms divine actions and reactions were expected to take according to the collective imagination of the time.

Narrowing the motley group of superhuman agents to the category of gods, the actions ascribed to them are basically of three kinds: positive, negative, or neutral. In the religious terminology of the time, the gods can bless, curse, or be silent. Each type of divine action covers a range of possibilities. Blessing can involve fertility, healing, prosperity, success, and a host of other things; a curse can consist of the absence of all that, or more seriously, its very reverse, such as illness, destitution, and defeat. Silence, in the case of gods, is usually ominous, divine inaction leaving humans to their fate. When ghosts or demons do nothing, on the other hand, it may be a relief—the only kind of action demons perform is harassment. In the ancient Near East there was relatively little concern about what the gods might do in the hereafter; the focus was almost entirely on the connection between human behavior now and its consequences in this life. Behavior did have consequences. The model that underlies the postulated interaction between humans and gods was based on the notion of retribution. There is a code of conduct, both written and unwritten, that determines what the gods will do. If humans live by the code, they shall be rewarded; if not, they shall be punished or, in the best case, meet with divine disapproval. The code has rules about things to do and things to avoid in the realms of religious worship—homage paid to the gods in public ritual and ceremony, acts of individual devotion—and social morals. It bears stressing that the ancient Near Eastern codes of conduct were both religious and social. Gods were supposed to care a great deal about the offerings they received but were nonetheless demanding when it came to social behavior, in terms of both ethics and etiquette. They were the guardians of correct behavior.

Offerings and sacrifice are major items in the religious code of conduct. Gods compare to humans, and temples are their houses; providing them with sustenance is a religious duty. To A. Leo Oppenheim, the "care and feeding of the gods" was the core of the Mesopotamian cult.[109] It is hard to disagree. According to the epic of Atrahasis, the gods created humankind in order to be relieved from toil and labor, and to enjoy their meals in a leisurely manner, without having to work for their food.[110] The myth is not without a hint of humor. As humans prove to be rather boisterous, the gods send the flood to reduce noise levels. The din disappears, but so do the offerings. Which is why, at the first sacrifice after the flood, the hungry gods gather around it "like flies." It sounds like a parody, but the underlying idea is serious enough. It is humankind's duty to feed the gods. When hunger strikes, the cult is in jeopardy—which ultimately harms the good relations with the gods. This peril to regular worship was acknowledged in Judah too. When a locust plague ravages the harvest, the priests, being "ministers of the altar," pass the night in sackcloth and lament because "[g]rain offering and drink offering / are withheld from the house of your God" (Joel 1:13 NRSV). In Israelite religion, sacrifice was understood, as it was throughout the Near East, to be "food" (*lehem*) for the deity (Lev 3:11).

Yet it would be misleading to reduce the sacrificial cult to donations of food and drink for domesticated deities. Especially in the western zone of the Near East (in some other places too), there is at times a more violent aspect to sacrifice—a response to what one might call the wild side of some gods that makes them prone to savagery. These are typically warrior gods and goddesses, such as Anat, Ishtar, Adad, and, at least in the eyes of some of his worshippers, YHWH (Ps 68:22–24; Isa 34:6). Violence is part of their profile, which makes them, when aroused, thirsty for blood. In some periods and parts of the Near East, the fear of aggression from the side of the gods led to the practice of human sacrifice.[111] To avert a complete onslaught in a lost battle against the united armies of Israel and Judah, King Mesha of Moab offered his firstborn son as burnt offering (2 Kgs 3:27). It was a human sacrifice to appease the anger of the god of Israel. Echoes of the practice are found elsewhere in the Bible (Mic 6:7).[112] In Israelite religion this has given rise to the custom of animal sacrifice as substitute: a lamb instead of the firstborn son (Exod 11–12; 24:20; Gen 22:1–14). Substitute sacrifice was not unknown among Mesopotamians and Hittites either, though there it was typically offered to demons or angry ghosts.[113] At any rate, occurrences of substitute sacrifice show that offering could have a dimension beyond "care and feeding." While most sacrifices were an invitation for the gods to come, some sacrifices were meant to make them go away.

If offerings of different sorts—food, frankincense, and precious gifts— were necessary to stay on the right side of the gods, the behavior adopted toward fellow human beings mattered just as much if not more. In nineteenth-century Europe it was customary, especially among Protestant theologians and liberal Jewish thinkers, to celebrate Israelite religion as the triumph of "ethical monotheism" over the ritualistic polytheism of the time.[114] This is a very tendentious contrast. In the polytheistic universe of Babylonians, Canaanites, and Egyptians, the gods cared very much about human honesty, compassion, and generosity. "As for you, unblenchingly anoint the parched, feed the hungry, give water to the thirsty to drink"— such is the command of the god to his worshipper in an Old Babylonian composition.[115] Similar admonitions echo in other texts.[116] Incantations to dispel the effects of a divine curse list as possible causes slander and false accusations, oppression of the weak woman, disruption of family ties, cruelty against prisoners, the use of false measures and weights, the changing of field boundaries, adultery, and much more of the like.[117] The fact that all of these actions provoke divine displeasure and put the offender under a curse demonstrates that the Babylonian gods acted as the custodians of the moral order. Things were the same in Egypt. The "negative confession" contained in the Book of the Dead (spell 125) lists sins very similar to the ones mentioned in the Babylonian incantations, such as defamation, the use of a false balance, and other such things.[118]

In Mesopotamia and Egypt, the precepts and prohibitions of the code of conduct were never proclaimed as divine law. Nobody needed a revelation to know what was the moral thing to do. The rules of human interaction were a matter of common sense and general wisdom. Where conflicting principles came into play, one could consult legal verdicts, such as the "laws" of Hammurabi—exemplary cases that illustrated the wisdom the gods had given to this enlightened monarch.[119] Disregard for the rules did not spring from ignorance; it indicated a moral flaw. Some people find it hard not to act selfishly. It took the supervision of the gods to curb the human tendency to pursue individual gain at the cost of the common good. The gods were believed to fulfill this role not because they stood on higher moral ground, but on account of their superior powers of perception and retribution. Their custodianship of morals was ultimately anchored in anthropomorphism, which made them endorse the very values human beings knew to be right. The model was the same throughout the Near East; so were the basic rules of social conduct.[120] This common Near Eastern doctrine of divine justice, even if it did not deter every possible offender, was a powerful source of social cohesion. In that sense, the cultural postulate of superhuman beings and their presumed interaction with humans contributed to the survival of the societies of yore.

1 Tribal Religion

During the period that archaeologists identify as the beginning of the Iron Age (ca. 1200 BCE), it would have been difficult to predict that the inhabitants of the Palestinian highlands would adopt, over the course of the next centuries, the worship of YHWH as their common religion. The clans and tribes that inhabited the area had very different backgrounds. Alongside the population that was native to the land, traditionally known as Canaanites, there were Arameans who had come from northern Syria and settled in Transjordan and in patches of the central hill country, as well as various groups that had migrated, either by way of Transjordan or southern Judah, from Edom, Midian, and the Negev. "Israelites" were living there too. An Egyptian stela from about 1200 BCE commemorating a campaign of Pharaoh Merenptah mentions an ethnic group, "Israel," located in central Palestine (fig. 8).[1] Aside from the fact that these Israelites would eventually lend their name to the Northern Kingdom as a whole, we know as good as nothing about them. The name Israel suggests they worshipped El, just as the Arameans did—not El the quiescent patriarch known from Ugaritic texts, but the Aramean El, divine warrior and head of the Shadday-gods.[2] The Canaanite element of the population worshipped the storm god Baal, most likely in conjunction with his consort Anat. Toponyms from the period preserve the memory of various local cult centers for Baal (e.g., Baal-hamon, Baal-shalisha) and Anat (e.g., Beth-anath, Anathoth).[3] The god YHWH was foreign to the area. He came, as the ancient theophany texts say, "from the fields of Edom," an area associated with such mountains as Paran, Seir, or Sinai (Judg 5:4–5; Deut 33:2; Hab 3:3,7). His cult reached Palestine when various groups from Edom, Midian, and the Negev made their way to the hill country. How this relatively obscure deity from the desert rose to the highest rank among his peers is one of the riddles this chapter seeks to resolve.

Fig. 8. Merenptah stela. Egyptian Museum, Cairo. (Wikimedia Commons, CC-BY-SA 3.0, https:// creativecommons.org/licenses/by-sa/3.0/deed.en.)

The Ancestors of the Israelites

In the area that would become the homeland of the Israelites, the transition period that ran from the Late Bronze Age deep into the Early Iron Age (ca. 1250–1050 BCE) was a time of dramatic change in demography and settlement patterns. While many cities in the agricultural regions of Palestine were destroyed or abandoned, the slopes of the hill country witnessed a sudden growth of small rural settlements. As the old Canaanite city-states collapsed, new population groups arrived, including Sea Peoples, Aramean tribes, and pastoralist nomads from Edom, Midian, and the Negev.

The changes of the time were part of a pattern that was in evidence throughout the Eastern Mediterranean. The principal cause of this "Late Bronze Age Collapse" was most likely climate change.[4] It affected the entire region and made the Early Iron Age more arid than previous periods. Agricultural production declined sharply.[5] Many urban centers were unable to sustain their populations. In the ensuing struggle for survival, the traditional inhabitants were forced to find means of subsistence elsewhere. The new settlements of Early Iron Age Palestine, found both on the coastal plain and in the hill country, were mostly modest in size, offering accommodation for small groups of related families. Fields of wheat and barley were replaced with olive orchards and vineyards, both better adapted to the arid conditions of the time. Small-scale cereal production did not disappear altogether, though. In due course, rainfall would return to its regular rhythm. Over the course of the following centuries, agriculture picked up again. During all of the last millennium BCE, Israel was essentially a peasant society.[6]

The migrations that brought new populations to Transjordan and Palestine had the same cause. Because of dramatic changes in the climate, peoples from different parts of the Mediterranean basin traveled to other places hoping to find better conditions for survival. The so-called Sea Peoples came from the west, over land by way of Anatolia and the Syrian coast and over sea via Crete (Caphtor) and Cyprus; they eventually settled the southern Palestinian coast, where they would come to be known as the Philistines (distant ancestors of the Palestinians). Two other migrant groups would end up as Israelites. In the search for sustenance, Arameans moved in from Upper Mesopotamia and Syria (Kir) and found shelter in Transjordan and the northern hill country. About the same time an assortment of nomadic tribes from Edom, Midian, and the Negev (Egypt) migrated in the direction of Palestine (Amos 9:7). These migrants were the main forebears, alongside part of the native Canaanite population, of the people who would come to be known as the Israelites (fig. 9).

The proto-Israelites, as we may call them, were ethnically diverse and had different subsistence strategies. Many of the groups that made their way into Palestine during the Early Iron Age were pastoralist nomads. They lived in tents and moved about in search of pasture grounds for their small cattle. The seasonal transfer of sheep and goats to different pastures often over long distances—transhumance is the technical term—was a traditional element of their lifestyle.[7] Pastoral nomadism was an element that would never totally disappear from Israelite society, though it came to be embedded in a basically agricultural mode of life. The Israelite cultic calendar has preserved remnants of pastoralist rites of transhumance in Passover (celebrated in spring) and the Day of Atonement (celebrated in autumn). The sacrifice of a Passover lamb and the application of some of its blood to doorposts and lintels on the eve of the departure to distant pastures (Exod 12:1–13) was a rite of protection against a demon known as the Destroyer (*mašḥit*). The offering of one goat and the dispatch of another to the wilderness for the demon Azazel originated as a rite of pacification on the return from transhumance.[8] These pastoralist rites have been reinterpreted and inserted into a calendar whose main festivals have an agrarian background (various seasonal harvests), in keeping with the way of life of the majority population.[9]

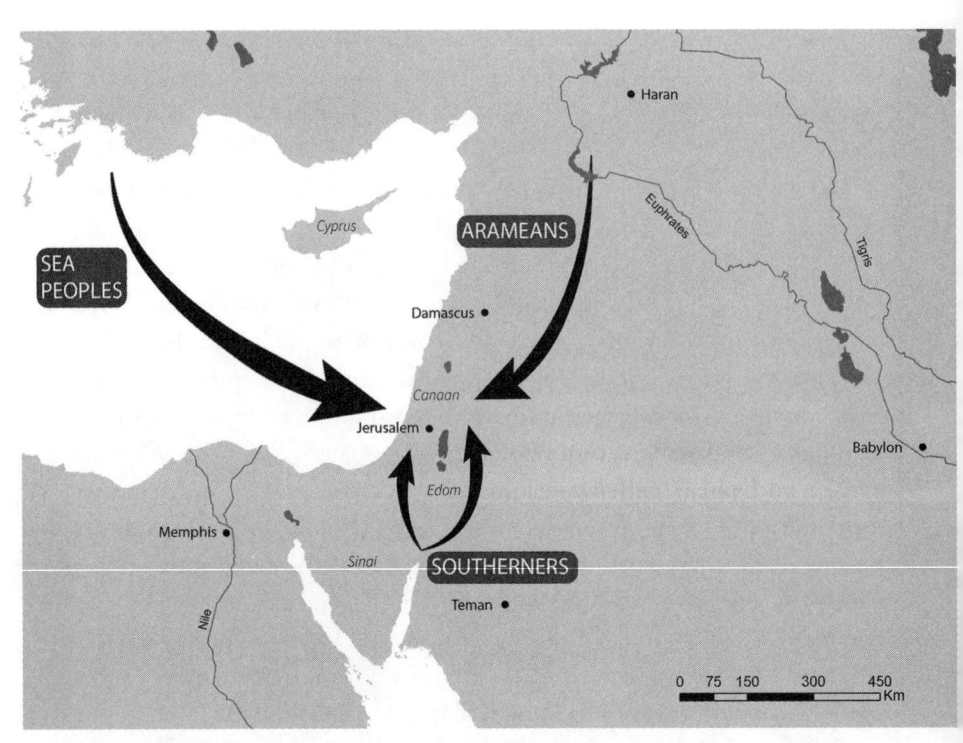

Fig. 9. Map indicating the infiltration of Palestine by Sea Peoples, Arameans, and southern nomads during the early Iron Age. (Map created by Jip Zinsmeister.)

Alongside agriculturalists and pastoralists, there was another demographic element in Late Bronze and Early Iron Age Palestine with less peaceful means of subsistence. These were the "Hebrews." Egyptian sources refer to them as *'apiru*, itself a loan from Akkadian *ḫabiru*. The term designates a social class, the variant Akkadian terms *ḫabbātu*, "robber, raider," and *munnabtu*, "fugitive, refugee," providing a sense of their status and background.[10] The fact that the term has survived in Biblical Hebrew as a marker of ethnicity applied to the early Israelites and their ancestors is an indication of the importance of the social phenomenon in the making of early Israel.[11] Up to a point it was a cultivated memory, as demonstrated by the liturgical phrase that describes Jacob, ancestor of the Israelites, as "a wandering Aramean" (Deut 26:5). The Hebrew verb translated as "wandering" (*'ābad*) is related to Akkadian *abātu*, "to run away, to flee," and its derivative *munnabtu*, "fugitive, refugee."[12] It would be preferable to render the expression, then, as "a fugitive Aramean" (as NJPS does). An example of a band of "Hebrews" in the sociological sense of the term is extant in the description of David, who broke away from his master (1 Sam 25:10) to become the leader of a band of people in distress, debt, and other conditions of discontent (1 Sam 22:2). They hired themselves out as mercenaries (1 Samuel 18), claimed protection money (1 Sam 25:4–8), and made raids on enemy settlements (1 Sam 27:8–9). Though the description is part of the official historiography, it does convey a picture of the "Hebrews" (1 Sam 29:3) that matches the information from contemporary extrabiblical sources.[13]

The ancestors of the Israelites, then, were ethnically mixed and had various ways of life. They *became* Israelites, over the course of generations, in the Palestinian highlands. How does this reconstruction of the "emergence of Israel in Canaan" relate to the biblical tradition of the exodus and the conquest?[14] At first sight, the narratives clash. Whereas the archaeological analysis reveals a process by which a distinct Israelite ethnic and cultural identity developed within Palestine, the exodus narrative tells the story of a fully formed Israelite people that was led out from Egypt and then took possession of Palestine. The careful analysis of the biblical sources shows that the exodus-and-conquest model was developed, originally in the Northern Kingdom, as a national narrative to provide the different population groups with a putative common history. The link with the historical realities of the late second millennium BCE is tenuous at best.[15] The exodus tale is fiction, yet like all good fiction, it is full of truth as well. It actually combines two cultural memories that each possess considerable historical plausibility. The one is about a *migration* from the southern wilderness; the other, about fugitives who had experienced a *liberation*. In the earliest layer of the tradition, the exodus was not a story of liberation but of migration from Egypt, or more specifically, the southern wilderness that bordered on Egypt.[16] The ancestors had "come up" (*'ālâ*) from Egypt. This was true of some of the proto-Israelites, namely the pastoralist tribes from Edom, Midian, and the Negev. The element of liberation from slavery—with YHWH as the one who "brought you out from the land of Egypt" (here the verb is *hôṣî'*)—originally had a different background without any link to Egypt.[17] It referred to the historical experience of those proto-Israelites who had been "Hebrews" in the sociological sense of the term. The historical background of two distinct groups that eventually became, along with several others, the people of Israel was adopted and adapted to create a narrative that could serve as the imagined past of the nation as a whole.

The Gods of the Territory in the Early Iron Age

The archaeological evidence shows that the Israelites originated inside Palestine as a conglomerate of various ethnic groups that eventually called themselves by the name Israel. That name originally belonged to the inhabitants of the central hill country (Merenptah stela, ca. 1200 BCE) but was extended to the population of the entire Palestinian hill country plus part of Transjordan.[18] The three principal ethnic groups that would, over time, constitute the nation of Israel were native Canaanites, Arameans from the north, and an assorted mix of pastoralist nomads from the south. Each group had its own god. The Canaanites worshipped Baal; the Arameans, El; and the Edomite and Midianite nomads, the little-known deity YHWH. In order to understand the dynamics of the process that eventually led to the adoption of YHWH as god of the nation, it is helpful to know a bit more about Baal, El, and YHWH. Where did they come from, and what were their profiles?

Baal was familiar to the land (fig. 10). The Canaanite settlers of the Palestinian highlands were the descendants of the population of such city-states as Hazor, Megiddo, Taanach, Beth-Shan, and Gezer. Personal names of people from these places reflect the popularity of the gods we have come to know quite well owing to the thousands of tablets from the city of Ugarit. The storm god Baal (originally a title of Addu, Hadad) and his consort Anat (Ḥanat, the Hanean goddess) are chief among them.[19] The Canaanite cities had flourished during the Middle Bronze Age, but the Late Bronze ecological crisis had led to their abandonment and impelled those who left to adopt a nonurban lifestyle. When their descendants founded new settlements in the Early Iron Age, they called the places where they lived after topographical features (Geba, Gibeah, Ramah, Mizpah—height, hill, vista), by the function of part of the settlement (Ataroth, Gederah—enclosures, sheepfold), or after the god they worshipped. The Baal toponyms belong to the third category.[20] They are compound names, such as Baal-Meon and Baal-Shalisha, in which the second element is usually a family name. In view of the variant Beth-Baal-Meon (Josh 13:17; Mesha stela, line 30) for Baal-Meon (Num 32:34; Josh 13:17; 1 Chr 5:8; Mesha stela, line 9), the reference is to a sanctuary (a "house") for the family god.[21] That family god was none other than a local form of Baal, the god of rain and fertility.[22]

The proto-Israelites of Aramean descent worshipped *El* (fig. 11). According to a tradition preserved in the Bible, their ancestor was Jacob, the

Fig. 10. Statue of Baal from Late Bronze Age Ugarit. Louvre, Paris, AO 17329. (Wikimedia Commons.)

"fugitive Aramean" (Deut 26:5). Jacob's name is indeed more Aramean than Israelite.[23] It is short for *ya'ăqōb-'ēl,* "El-has-protected," a personal name not uncommon among the Amorite tribes mentioned in texts from Mari (Yaḫqub-El, Yaqub-El).[24] Geographically, the Aramean tribes for whom Jacob stood a symbol came from the area of Haran (Gen 27:43, 28:10, 29:4). Their religion displays a remarkable continuity with the religion of the Amorites who inhabited the area in the early second millennium BCE.[25] In the patriarchal narratives, Jacob is a worshipper of El. The altar at Bethel is dedicated to El (Gen 35:1, 3, 7), which suggests that the town derived its name from the temple (the "house") of El, on the analogy of such place-names as Beth-Shemesh ("Temple of the Sun God"). Jacob gave the altar at Shechem the name "El, god of Israel" (Gen 33:20). Who is this El? Is he the god El as evoked in the mythology from Ugarit, the bearded patriarch whose position of leadership has been passed on to Baal? It is true that some biblical poems and other passages use images and titles that in Ugaritic texts apply to El.[26] Yet there are aspects of the Aramean El that depart from the profile of the god we know from Ugarit. An important lead in this respect is his title Shaddai (El Shaddai). There is one Ugaritic occurrence of this title, but the correct rendering and significance is problematic.[27] Whereas in the biblical tradition Shaddai is a common title of El, it is uncommon in the Ugaritic texts—if it really occurs as a title at all.

Fig. 11. Gold-coated figu-
rine of the god El from the
Late Bronze Age, Megiddo.
Museum of the Institute for
the Study of Ancient Cultures
(ISAC), University of Chicago.
(Wikimedia Commons.)

Even though Shaddai occurs mostly in relatively late biblical texts (often ascribed to the Priestly source), the Balaam inscription from Deir Alla
shows that the term is ancient. The text depicts El in his role as president of
the assembly of the gods (*'lhn*). These gods are twice referred to as Shaddai deities (*šdyn*).[28] In light of this inscriptional evidence, there is reason to
surmise that the occurrences of Shaddai in Gen 49:25 and Ps 68:15 are relatively early, too.[29] What is the meaning of Shaddai? The traditional translation "the Almighty" goes back to the various renderings of the name in the
Septuagint (often *pantokratōr*) and the Vulgate (*omnipotens*), which drew
their inspiration from the popular understanding of Shaddai as *ša-day*, "who

suffices" (as reflected in *ho hikanos*, "who suffices, is powerful," as Greek translation of Hebrew *šadday* in Ruth 1:20–21 LXX).[30] This folk etymology is not very helpful. A more promising avenue of approach looks at a connection with Akkadian *šadû*, which has the related meanings of "mountain (region)" and "open country, steppe." Shaddai would then be the Aramaic equivalent of Akkadian *šaddû'a*, "mountain dweller."[31] At first sight, that title may not seem very illuminating for there are many gods who were believed to dwell on a mountain. But a closer inspection points in the direction of a deity quite familiar from Old Babylonian sources. This is Amurru, the chief god of the Amorites, who carries the title *bēl šadê*, "lord of the steppe" (cf. the variant title *bēl ṣēri*, with the same meaning). In the very image of his worshippers, Amurru is a steppe dweller.[32] Now the full name of Amurru is El-Amurru, the "Amorite El."[33] The El connection fits with the fact that Amurru has as his consort the goddess Ashratu (biblical Asherah).[34] She is the Lady of the Steppe (Bēlet-ṣēri) and the "bride" of El.[35]

The Aramean El, then, is an avatar of Amurru, that is, the El worshipped by the Amorite tribes.[36] This has implications for his profile. The Amorite El comes across as far more combative than the El of the Ugaritic texts. He has traits of a storm god and is described, in a royal hymn, as a heroic and terrifying warrior equipped with bow and arrows, helper of the king in battle.[37] An ancient Hebrew inscription from Kuntillet Ajrud, at a crossroads in the northeastern Sinai, also casts El in the role of divine warrior: "When El shone forth in [. . .] And mountains melted, and peaks grew weak [. . .] Baal on the day of battle [. . .] on the day of batt[le . . .]."[38] The inscription is from the end of the ninth century BCE, but the composition may be older. It is a classic theophany text that could go back to the Early Iron Age. The site at Kuntillet Ajrud served as a port of call for Israelites from the Northern Kingdom, witness the reference to "Yhwh of Samaria" in another inscription.[39] It makes sense. The Jacob tradition is from the Northern Kingdom (Hos 12:3–15), and the findspot of the Balaam inscription was Israelite territory too (Succoth in the land of Gilead). The meeting of Canaanite Baal, Aramean El, and the southern god Yhwh took place in northern Palestine.

It is time to take a closer look at *Yhwh*, the god who eventually became the god of Israel, just as Israel would come to be "the people of Yhwh" (*'am yhwh*). The worship of Yhwh is not indigenous to Canaan. A quite compelling indication to this effect is the total absence of Yhwh in Palestinian place-names. These toponyms often refer to a god, such as Baal or El, but never to Yнwн.[40] Indeed, Yнwн was not a member of any of the traditional pantheons of Syria or Palestine. The place from which his cult would spread lies to the south of Israel.[41] The earliest extrabiblical occurrence of the divine name is in an Egyptian survey of bedouin lands. The inscription is from the time of Pharaoh Amenophis III (r. 1425–1400 BCE). Alongside Mount Seir and (perhaps) Mount Paran, the text lists "the Shosu-land Yahu" (*t3 š3św yhw3*). The divine name occurs here as the name of a mountain west or east of the southern Arabah, the rift valley that extends to the Gulf of Aqaba.[42] Apparently, then, Yнwн was named after the mountain where he was thought to dwell.[43] The association of Yнwн with a mountain in the vicinity of the southern Arabah is echoed in several Hebrew theophany texts. Three of them deserve special attention (translation by P. Kyle McCarter):[44]

Deut 33:2
> Yahweh came from Sinai,
> He dawned from Seir,
> He appeared from Mount Paran.

Judg 5:4–5
> Yahweh, when you went out from Seir,
>> When you marched from the fields of Edom,
> The earth shook,
>> Yes, the skies poured,
>> Yes, the clouds streamed with water.
> The mountains flowed before Yahweh, the one of Sinai,
>> Before Yahweh, the god of Israel.

Hab 3:3, 7
> A god came from Teman,
>> A holy one from Mount Paran.
> His "splendor" covered the sky,
> His "praise" filled the earth. . . .
> The tents of Cushan quivered,
>> The curtains of the land of Midian shook.

Leaving aside Mount Sinai, whose location in antiquity is still under debate, all of the places here mentioned are in Edom or in territory adjacent to Edom.[45] Yнwн, according these texts, came from the south.[46] This is consonant with the extrabiblical evidence from Kuntillet Ajrud (ca. 800 BCE), which has various fragments that mention "Yнwн of the Southland" (*yhwh tmn, yhwh htmn, yhwh tymn, yhwh htymn*).[47] On the basis of these data, there is an emerging consensus that Mount Sinai should be located in southern Edom or northern Midian.[48]

Toward the end of the nineteenth century, as scholars began to realize that historically the cult of Yнwн had originated in Edom or Midian, the theory of Yнwн's southern origins came to be known as the Kenite or Midianite hypothesis. In its classical form, this hypothesis argues that Moses was related to a Midianite priest of Yнwн (Exod 2:16–22, 3:1, 18:1). This man—a member of the Kenite branch of the Midianites (Judg 1:16, 4:11)—initiated Moses and the Israelites into the cult of Yнwн (Exod 18:10–12). After that, the Israelites took Yнwн to Palestine. Looking at the Kenite hypothesis in retrospect, it comes across as a delicate balancing act between critical scholarship, on the one hand, and confidence in the biblical narrative, on the other. The idea that the Israelites, liberated from the Egyptian "house of servitude," became worshippers of Yнwн in the desert and then took their new religion to the land of Canaan does not persuade modern historians. The historical tradents of the cult of Yнwн were far more likely the Kenites and Midianites themselves. They were nomads (Shasu, as the Egyptian texts have it) and tent-dwellers ("the tents of Cushan . . . , the curtains of Midian") whose wanderings would also take them to Palestine. There were Kenite clans living around Arad in south Palestine (Judg 1:16) and around Kedesh in the north (Judg 4:11). Midianites, too, had reached Palestine, witness the reports about military encounters with them (Judges 6–8). Other Edomite or Midianite tribes, such as the Rechabites, were integrated in the population of the highlands and regarded themselves as Israelites (2 Kgs 10:15–17; Jeremiah 35; 1 Chr 2:55).

The profile of Yнwн in the archaic theophany texts is essentially that of a divine warrior.[49] He is, as later texts say, a "man of war" (Exod 15:3), "mighty in battle" (Ps 24:8). His appearance sets heaven and earth in turmoil: bursts of clouds start pouring water, mountains move from their places, and human habitations quiver in fright. This is the language of poetry. It does not define Yнwн as a storm god, though he definitely has the powers of a storm god. Nor does it define Yнwн as a sun god, though the language that is used indicates he is not lacking in solar aspects.[50] Yнwн is not part of a pantheon with a labor division. He does have an entourage of helpers—Hab 3:5 mentions Pestilence (*deber*) and Plague (*rešep*), terms that occur as divine names outside the Bible—and the goddess Asherah as his consort, but his tribal worshippers would invoke his help in a wide variety of situations.[51] The likeness of Yнwн to Aramean El is striking. Both are divine warriors with traits of a storm god. As such they are also similar to the Canaanite god Baal. Although the Baal polemics of the Hebrew Bible might suggest otherwise, Yʜwʜ and Baal were nearly identical twins. Thus the contest between Yʜwʜ and Baal on Mount Carmel does not oppose two gods with different profiles: these gods were both expected to bring rain, but the one delivered where the other failed (1 Kings 18). If Yʜwʜ rose to the position of national god, it was not because his profile was very different from that of his competitors. One religion does not supplant the other because it is intrinsically superior, but because its human adherents manage to gain some form of ascendency over others.

To round off the discussion of Yʜwʜ, there is the issue of his name. The four-letter name—the Tetragrammaton, as the scholarly term has it—follows an old orthographic convention, as demonstrated by the Mesha stone and the texts from Kuntillet Ajrud. Its pronunciation is a bit of a guess. Out of religious scruple, Jewish tradition avoids pronouncing the proper name of God and prefers to call him Adonai, "my Lord." When vowels were added to the biblical text (the Masoretic vocalization), the name *yhwh* was given the vowels of *'ădōnay*, which led to the pronunciation Jehovah. This is the transcription of the divine name found in older scholarly publications, but it is now mostly abandoned. Today, the conventional hypothesis says the god was called "Yahweh," though many scholars admit it is far from certain this is how the Israelites pronounced it. The Elephantine papyri (fifth century BCE) write God's name as *yhw* or *yhh*, which yields the pronunciation Yaho.[52] It is the standard form of the name in Greek transcriptions.[53] Also, it tallies with the cuneiform writing of the divine name as it occurs in Hebrew proper names: *yahu, yaḫu, ya'u* (note that there is no *o*-sound in cuneiform).[54] Yaho or Yahu is historically the most likely pronunciation of the Tetragrammaton.[55] The pronunciation Yahweh goes back, ultimately, to the name etymology given in Exod 3:13–15. There is no reason to assign any historical value to the theological speculation in this late biblical passage.[56] The orthography of the name, with *-wh* instead of a mere *-w* or *-h* as in Elephantine, may be due to the length of the final vowel.[57] An alternative explanation could be that the spelling *yhwh* preserves the memory of a toponym, since Hebrew toponyms more often have a final *-ōh*, as in Jericho (written as *yryḥw* or *yryḥh*), Mount Nebo (written as *nbw* or *nbh*), and Shiloh (written as *šylw, šlw,* and *šlh*).[58] There is no way to recover the original meaning of the name Yʜwʜ. The many proposals that have been made are in the end all guesswork, some of it based on very questionable assumptions. It is best to admit that the meaning of the name eludes us. It probably does not matter. To believe that the name reveals the true nature of the deity is a form of magical thinking. A name is just a name, even if it is the name of the Almighty.

Family and Kinship

After the collapse of the Canaanite city-states, Early Iron Age Palestine had acquired characteristics of a tribal society. In the absence of a state with a formal political apparatus to enforce law and order, the lineage group was the social institution that disciplined and protected the individual members. Family was everything. Family—that is, the kinship group of related families that traced their lineage to a common ancestor—was the social institution that protected its members against physical aggression from outside, material destitution, and social isolation. The members, for their part, were expected to be committed, 100 percent, to the perpetuation of the family name and the preservation of the family honor. Referred to as *mišpāḥâ* ("extended family") or *'am* ("people, clan"), the family had shared ownership of the family land (its *naḥălâ*, "inheritance") and the mutual obligation to defend each other's life. They were "brothers." Should a man lose his parcel of land, on account of unpaid debts or some other form of hardship, it was up to his next of kin to "redeem" (*gā'al*) the land to make sure it remained within the family (Lev 25:23–55).[59] Revenge of a brother killed by an outsider was another sacred duty. The family had to "redeem the blood" (see, e.g., Num 35:9–28; Deut 19:12; 2 Sam 14:11). Along similar lines of reasoning, a brother had to marry his sister-in-law if her husband had died without offspring (the so-called levirate marriage; Deut 25:5–10; cf. Gen 38:8–11; Ruth 2:20; 3:9, 12; 4:1–14). These mutual responsibilities did not spring purely from feelings of affection but were based on the fact that the brothers were of one "bone" and one "flesh" (Gen 29:14; Judg 9:2; 2 Sam 5:1; 19:13, 14; cf. Gen 2:23). They constituted what has been called a "corporate personality."[60]

Though women could have decisive influence in family matters, the formal authority within the family lay with the men, and more especially with the paterfamilias. He was, among the "brothers," the president of the family council and the officiant at major family ceremonies. This position befell the oldest male member in full possession of his mental capacities. The ideology that determines the logic of the family as a corporation is one of male dominance. True enough, some Israelite women acquired fame as heroines or matriarchs, their graves being revered as places of pilgrimage (Gen 35:8, 16–20; 1 Sam 10:2; Jer 31:15; Matt 2:16–18; Judg 4:5), but family was the business of men.[61] The family was patrilineal and patrilocal.

Descendance from the fathers determined membership and position in the family. Girls would leave their family when they married, joining the family of their husband. When the woman from Shunem where Elisha was staying told the prophet she needed nothing because she was living "among [her] own people" (the Hebrew word is *'am*; 2 Kgs 4:13), she was referring to her husband's family. In most cases, the transfer from the family of the father to the family of the husband was not a complete break with the past because people were expected to marry outside their own family (in the more restricted sense, the *bêt 'āb*, "father's house") but inside the clan (*mišpāḥâ*). And since the clan would often live in the same area (village, city quarter), close to the family land, women who married would not necessarily end up miles away from their father's house.

Since the early Israelite family functioned in more or less the same way as families in other tribal societies in the area (such as those of the Amorites, the Arameans, the population of Emar), study of the unwritten rules that governed family interaction outside Israel may shed some light on aspects of the Israelite concept of family that are not immediately clear from the Bible. Whereas the dominant metaphor for family in the Bible is "bone and flesh," the Amorites preferred to speak of "flesh and blood" (*šīru u dāmū*).[62] The social reality was by and large the same. The family was a corporation with a shared title to land.[63] Disobedience to the paterfamilias, whether by a man or a woman, entailed excommunication from the family, symbolized by rites of divestiture. It was the reverse of the rites of investiture on the incorporation into the family, as when the groom "covered" the bride with clothing.[64] The garments stood for the protection the husband's family would henceforth afford her; to go out "naked," as the consequence of divestiture, meant the complete lack of protection.[65] There was a strong sense of boundary between in-group and out-group. Those who did not belong to the family were *aḫû*, "outsiders," or more strongly, "strangers," a term with overtones of enmity (*nakrum*; in Emar Akkadian *nikaru*; cf. Hebrew *nokrî* and *nēkār*).[66]

One element of the family that comes to the fore more clearly in extrabiblical texts than in the Bible is the role of family religion. In Mesopotamian society, young women were devoted to the god of their father, but after their marriage they would redirect their religious loyalty to the god of their husband. This "conversion" follows from the fact that families venerated their particular family god whom they referred to as "the god of our father" or "the god of our ancestor."[67] The cult of the family deity— usually a well-known god rather than an anonymous divine agent—is to be distinguished from the cult of the ancestors. Though the latter could on occasion be referred to as "gods," the spirits of the ancestors were invoked as a plurality whereas the family god is always in the singular. The family has only one god. Such must also have been the case in early Israel, in view of the survival of a number of stereotypical phrases. On several occasions the patriarchal narratives refer to El or YHWH as "the god of my/your father," where the term "father" might also be translated as "ancestor" (e.g., Gen 31:5, 16, 29–30, 51–53; 32:10–11 [32:9–10]; 43:23; 50:16–17). The "god of the father" is linked to "the house of the father," that is, the family. After they have been sold into marriage to Jacob, Rachel and Leah conclude they have become "strangers" (*nokriyyôt*) in their father's house, without a title to its inheritance, and shift their loyalty to the god of their husband (Gen 31:10–18). A distant echo of religious transfer due to marriage is the formula a later author has put into the mouth of Ruth: "Your family [*'am*] is my family, and your god is my god" (Ruth 1:16, my translation). Likewise, the qualification of a non-Israelite spouse as "the daughter of a foreign god" (*bat 'ēl nēkār*, Mal 2:11) preserves the memory of customs and views that were common during Israel's tribal era. Every kin group or family had its own god, and a wife from a foreign tribe belonged to a foreign god.[68]

Though rooted in the biological realities of kinship and descent, family is in the last resort a social institution. The practices of incorporation and excommunication show that the boundaries of the family were negotiable. Marriage and adoption were the principal means to incorporate outsiders. Wedding rites changed from place to place, but the common core was the same in all tribal cultures of the time. The transfer of a woman from one family to another consisted of a performative speech act ("You are my wife, I am your husband") and a number of symbolic acts (the groom anointed the bride, put a veil over her, covered her with the hem of his garment, or "tied the garment's hem"), followed by a ceremonial meal to which all family members were invited, ancestors included.[69] The ritual of adoption was less elaborate but followed a similar procedure. Early Israelite law determines that the slave who relinquishes his right to be released—his wife and children would stay behind with his master—is to receive a piercing in his ear as token of his perpetual appurtenance to the master's family. The master is to perform the piercing before the gods (*hā'ĕlōhîm*) located "near the door or the doorpost" of the main family house (Exod 21:2–6; cf. the abridged and purged version in Deut 15:17). The "gods" in question are the ancestors, represented by statuettes known in the Bible as the teraphim.[70]

The most common instance of excommunication was divorce. The ex-wife had to leave the house "naked," symbolically stripped to the skin by the deposition of the family garments or by the "cutting of the garment's hem."[71] Sons or daughters who put the family to shame could count on a similar treatment.[72]

The rites of incorporation and excommunication exemplify the important role of ceremonial acts in the constitution of the family and the delineation of its boundaries. In early Israel, the annual family sacrifice fulfilled a similar role in the family's perpetuation. At least once a year the family celebrated the sacrificial feast in honor of the ancestors. All adult males were expected to attend. These were the circumcised men of the family, for the ancient rite of circumcision, later performed on male infants, was originally a rite of passage marking the beginning of adulthood. It made a boy a man, full member of the tribe, and fit for participation in its rituals.[73] In the History of David's Rise, part of the Deuteronomistic History but once an independent document, David uses "the yearly sacrifice for all the family" (*zebaḥ hayyāmîm lĕkol-hammišpāḥâ*) as pretext for his absence at the new moon banquet of King Saul (1 Sam 20:6).[74] His older brother—David was the youngest of the family (1 Sam 16:11)—has allegedly summoned him to come to Bethlehem (1 Sam 20:28–29). This is fiction, but it shows that the annual family feast coincided with the new moon period, took place at the hometown of the family, and was presided over by the elder brother. The latter detail explains why the young man Saul, in a very similar setting (cf. 1 Sam 9:12, where *zebaḥ hayyôm* is to be read as *zebaḥ hayyāmîm*, "the annual sacrifice for the family [literally, people] at the shrine"), asks to be excused by his uncle, that is, the elder brother of his father (*dôd*, 1 Sam 10:14–16; cf. 1 Sam 14:50–51). This uncle was the acting paterfamilias. The annual celebration was a reaffirmation of the family ties. By participating in the sacrificial meal, all those present renewed their allegiance to the family god, the ancestors, and the paterfamilias. At the time it was a men's affair (cf. 1 Sam 9:11–14, 22–25); but over time customs changed, and it became common for the entire family to participate.[75]

Tribal Covenants and Tribal Warfare

As we have seen, the three principal ethnic groups that would come to constitute the nation of Israel over the course of two or three centuries were native Canaanites, tribal Arameans from the north, and an assorted mix of pastoralist nomads from Edom, Midian, and the Negev. Both the Aramean tribes and the southern nomads were new to Palestine. So were, in some ways, the Canaanites: they were the descendants of city-dwellers who had been forced to find new means of survival in the country. For each group, then, it was a new beginning, fraught with the uncertainty and insecurity that belong to new beginnings. The encounter between the three groups set in motion a process in which each had to negotiate the nature of its relations with the others.

The outcome of this process is well known. At the beginning of the first millennium BCE, Saul and David would turn a loose coalition of clans and tribes into a polity. It would call itself Israel. Concomitant with these developments, YHWH would rise to the position of national patron deity. The outcome is known, but the story of the events that led there is yet to be told. The encounter of the three ethnic groups in Early Iron Age Palestine was also an encounter of deities. The ties among the various tribes and their gods were strong. Even though these tribes consisted of multiple families and clans, their gods were conceptually similar to family gods. A tribe could have many ancestors, but only one tribal god—even if that god had a consort and an entourage. It is not by mistake that a prophet like Amos could refer to the Israelites as a "family" with one god to lead them (Amos 3:1). In tribal thinking, tribal gods were family gods. Conceptually, they embodied the identity of the tribe. For the tribe, the worship of its god was essential for survival. Should the tribe give up its god, it would lose its identity and be absorbed by competitors. So if one of the three gods ended up being the god of the new nation, what happened to the two others? What mechanisms informed the political dynamics before the monarchy?

In the process that led to the formation of the Israelite nation, both tribal *covenants* and tribal *warfare* played an important part. The two are closely related. Tribes might agree not to attack each other. To that end they swore an oath, had a common meal, and erected a boundary stone as a perpetual reminder of their pact (Gen 21:22–32, 26:28–30, 31:43–54). They had a *běrît*, a covenant, to which they made their gods a witness. Names such as Baal-berith and El-berith may preserve the memory of such a pact involving the population of Shechem (Judg 8:33; 9:4, 46). Covenants warded off the danger of warfare between the partners. At the same time, they committed the two parties to come to each other's aid when one of them would attack or be attacked. So while covenant making creates conditions of peace—the term *šālôm*, "peace," can refer to a covenant—the partners understand that they must fight each other's fights when the need arises.[76] Through the covenant rites, they have created ties of kinship. They are brothers. When the hour has come for tribal warfare, they will have to be brothers in arms. They were already one people in theory, but the battlefield violence against a common enemy will give new meaning to the term. Warfare is a nation-builder.[77]

The oldest nucleus of the Song of Deborah (Judg 5:14–22, 24–30) illustrates the ethos of tribal warfare in the premonarchic era.[78] It is hardly a coincidence that this archaic piece of poetry is about the battlefield. Although the song highlights the cosmic dimensions of the battle ("The stars fought from heaven, / from their courses they fought against Sisera," Judg 5:20 NRSV), it refrains from attributing the victorious outcome to any god in particular, preferring instead to focus on the cold-blooded killing of Sisera by the hands of an intrepid woman. In the background, the song assumes the existence of a coalition of tribes and/or territories—the distinction is not so easy to make (2 Sam 15:2).[79] They are ten in all: Ephraim, Benjamin, Machir, Zebulon, Issachar, Reuben, Gilead, Dan, Asher, and Naphtali (Judg 5:14–18). It comes across as a rather loose confederation. The four of them that did not participate in battle (Reuben, Gilead, Dan, and Asher) are chided and derided but not cursed (Judg 5:15–17). This is poetry in the key of shame and honor, not a hymn on divine retribution. The poem is witness to intertribal coalition formation for military purposes, not to a commitment to one god to the exclusion of others. Nevertheless, a major battle against a common enemy is likely to have instilled a sense of purpose and unity that might, at some point, stimulate state formation.

Warfare and covenant making are opposites in the service of the same goal. Both are instruments of nation building, the one by the collective exercise of violence against a common enemy and the other by the creation of artificial ties of kinship. An important consequence of both was the extension of the number of young women available for marriage and procreation. The warriors who won the battle killed their opponents and captured the women, after which the latter were forced to join the group of the victors and contribute to its survival (Deut 20:14, 21:10–14; Judg 5:30). Covenant making was the peaceful way to increase the number of potential marriage partners. The groups that concluded a covenant could henceforth intermarry, since they had become one family (Gen 34:16). Warfare and covenant making were essential to the genesis of Israel as a nation, as well as to the making of Israelite religion. To properly understand the role of these social institutions, it is necessary to study their ideology and the way it was put into practice.

Kinship by Covenant

Few concepts are as crucial to Israelite religion as covenant. Over time, covenant became the dominant metaphor to define the nature of the special bond between YHWH and the people of Israel. God had, so the biblical tradition says, concluded a covenant with the Israelites that they be his people and he their god. The covenant concept continued as a theological paradigm in early Christianity. Whereas the Jews were the people of the "old covenant" (the old "testament," in the Greek rendering), the followers of Jesus were the people of the "new covenant" (the new "testament"). Many scholars have emphasized that this notion of a covenant between a god and his worshippers is uniquely Israelite. Perhaps it is. But the task of the historian is not simply to dwell on unique features but to explain them. How did the religious leadership of Israel come up with the idea of conceptualizing the relationship with the national deity as a covenant? Although the answer to this question has to wait for the discussion in the next chapter, it has to take into account the dynamics and the effects of covenant making in the ancient world, a central element being that covenant making created ties of kinship.

Kinship is both a biological reality and a social construct. The annual family sacrifice celebrates the family and thus renews the ties of lineage kinship. The ritual makes the family real again. Marriage and adoption illustrate the possibility for the family to extend itself by rites of incorporation. The latter create kinship between people not related by blood. Through marriage, the partners become one bone and one flesh (Gen 2:23). This special bond, by which a woman is joined to the family, is on occasion referred to as a "covenant" (*běrît;* Prov 2:17; Mal 2:14). The choice of the term is telling because the covenant was at the time the principal means to create ties of kinship between groups that had no consanguinity. Covenants have been crucial in the making of Israelite religion. To put the practice in context, we need to look at the place of covenants in the tribal societies of the ancient Near East.

This focus on covenant making in tribal societies avoids the pitfall of using the political treaties of Hittites (fourteenth to thirteenth centuries BCE) and Assyrians (seventh century BCE) as the model for understanding covenant making in Israel. It is true that the book of Deuteronomy conceptualizes the bond between God and Israel along the lines of a treaty between a king and his vassals. The correspondences with

Neo-Assyrian treaties, in both ideology and terminology, are too striking to be fortuitous.[80] But the authors of Deuteronomy did not invent the notion of covenant. They gave a new twist to an institution the Israelites had long been familiar with. In the tribal past of Israel, however, the covenant had a purpose that differed from that of a vassal treaty. It was meant to create ties of kinship—a purpose totally absent from the Neo-Assyrian treaties. A reference to a covenant between two tribal chiefs in a letter from Mari illustrates the nature of the tribal agreement. The covenant is a "pact of blood and a solemn engagement" (*damū u dannātum*), sealed by an oath (*nīš ilim*), as a consequence of which those who have entered the covenant have become "brothers." Henceforth, they are under obligation to help one another as brothers should: "Are you not of my blood? . . . You are of my blood!"[81] The covenant creates *damuttum*, "blood ties, consanguinity."[82]

Among the tribal societies of the Near East, the covenant ceremony exhibits local and historical variations. Three elements are almost universal, though: (1) the killing of a domesticated animal by cutting it in two, (2) a solemn promise under oath (*nīš ilim*), and (3) a festive meal at which the covenant partners share the same food and drink. Among the Amorite nomads, the animal that is cut up is a donkey (*ḫayaram qaṭālu*, "to kill a donkey," said *imēram dâku* in proper Akkadian). This "donkey of the covenant" (*ḫayarum ša salīmim*) is not meant to be eaten but to serve as a warning of what could happen to the covenant partners if they do not live up to their mutual obligations. The treaty between Bargayah and Matiel (mid-eighth century BCE) is quite explicit: "[Just as] this calf is cut in two, so may Matiel be cut in two [should he fail to fulfil the covenant obligations]."[83] The citation shows that a calf (*ʿgl*) could take the place of a donkey, without affecting the meaning of the act. The animal was not sacrificed but "cut in two" (*gzr*).[84] The very same practice with the very same kind of animal is referred to in Jer 34:18. The Hebrew verb is *kārat*, "to cut," the equivalent of Aramaic *gĕzar*. Other domesticated animals, such as oxen, could be used to send the same signal (Gen 15:9; 1 Sam 11:7). It is this part of the ceremony that has given its name to the making of a covenant. The Hebrew expression is *kārat bĕrît*, "to cut a covenant."

The covenant oath and the covenant meal are inextricably linked. The oath invokes the god of the covenant as witness to the solemn engagement of the parties and as ultimate instance to punish infractions. The covenant meal is a rite of communion but at the same time an ordeal in installments. The partners sat down and "ate from the same platter and drank from the same goblet," after which they anointed each other.[85] The meal created community, but the ingested substances (food and drink) and the oil that had soothed the skin also lodged the threat of divine retribution in the very body of the participants, where it was bound to cause physical harm if one of them would break the oath.[86] These covenant practices inform the biblical comparison of the curse with water entering the body and oil penetrating the bones (Ps 109:18). Various other symbolic acts could be part of the proceedings, one of them also familiar from wedding rites. A covenant ceremony could be referred to as "tying the hem" (*sissiktam rakāsu/kaṣāru*), which suggests that the partners, to demonstrate they had become family, tied the hems of their clothing together, though at some point the practice may have survived as a phrase only.[87] Marriage contracts also mention the tying of the hem. In a similar manner, divorce and expulsion from the family were symbolized by "severing" the hem (*sissiktam batāqu*).[88]

Since we are looking at covenant procedures in the Near East in view of the role of covenant making in the early history of Israel, there is reason to mention a few aspects that may be helpful in illuminating Israelite practices. (1) Most covenants bring together kings, whose solemn promise is automatically binding for their subjects. There are situations, however, in which tribal groups enter a covenant collectively: "Asdi-Takim and the kings of Zalmaqum and the sheikhs and elders of the Benjaminites killed donkeys in the temple of Sin in Haran."[89] As we have seen, "killing donkeys" (*ḥayarī qatālu*) is the central rite in covenant making, here performed by tribal leaders and elders. In some cases, about a hundred of them would be present at the ceremony.[90] (2) The engagement that the covenant solemnized consisted of a loyalty oath in which the partners promised nonaggression and mutual aid, the latter especially military. An oral engagement sufficed. Over the course of the centuries, especially after 1500 BCE, written covenants became the norm. Often inscribed in stone or on metal, the texts were kept and displayed in temples.[91] (3) Various texts, all from the first half of the second millennium, mention the renewal of the loyalty oath.[92] One king writing to another reminds him that "each year the oath needs to be renewed."[93] It is not clear whether this was common practice, but it does provide an interesting parallel to the annual sacrificial meal for the clan, which functioned as the ritual renewal of family ties.

Tribal Warfare

In ancient times, warfare was religion. A military encounter was a battle between gods. Was it therefore a "holy war," as scholars have called it?[94] That phrase is infelicitous because it elicits associations with a struggle against unbelievers. Warfare in antiquity was not inspired by missionary zeal but was a means to improve the prospects of survival for one's own group. Nevertheless, the ideology of warfare was thoroughly religious, in Israel and throughout the ancient Near East.[95] In the "wars of YHWH" (1 Sam 18:17, 25:28), the human warriors came "to the help of the LORD" (Judg 5:23). At the end of the battle, symbols of the defeated deity—statuettes, the ark, holy vessels—were carried to the temple of the god who had prevailed (fig. 12). There they were put on display as victory trophies and in commemoration of the humiliation of the enemy (1 Sam 5:1–2).[96] This is what the Israelites did, and the Assyrians as well—much like everybody else at the time. The Assyrians did not impose a new religion in conquered territories but deported the religious symbols of the enemies back home for display and left the "weapon" of their own god Assur in the temple of the defeated.[97]

Since the soldiers were waging war in the name of their god, it was essential that he should go to war at their side. To the ancients this meant a visible presence of the deity had to be in the military camp. In most cases the troops brought statuettes of their gods with priests to prepare the offerings and to consult the deity about the appropriate military action. When the Philistines went out to war, they took their "idols" with them (2 Sam 5:21). The Israelite army came with the ark, a portable shrine that embodied God's presence (1 Samuel 4–6).[98] When they were in the camp, the ark was placed in a tent known as the tabernacle (miškān; literally, "dwelling place") or the "tent of meeting" ('ōhel mô'ēd). Later tradition took the military campaign as model for the description of Israel's wanderings in the desert. It thereby turned the tent sanctuary into the movable forerunner of the temple, an idea informing much of the Priestly descriptions of the tabernacle (Exodus 25–31). In reality, temple and tabernacle existed side by side, the latter doing duty as divine accommodation when God went out to war.[99] The original setting of tabernacle and ark echoes in parts of the wilderness tradition:

Whenever the ark set out, Moses would say,

"Arise, O LORD, let your enemies be scattered,
and your foes flee before you." (Num 10:35 NRSV; cf. Ps 68:2 [68:1])

Fig. 12. Assyrian troops carrying off divine images from defeated cities; artist's impression after Tiglath-Pileser III palace relief from Nimrud. (Drawing by Willem Zijlstra.)

These words, allegedly spoken in the desert, are at home in situations of warfare. Yhwh is the divine warrior who marches out at the head of his warriors (Ps 44:10 // 60:12 // 108:12).

The ideological interpretation of warfare as a contest between gods had important psychological effects on the soldiers. The call to battle and to engage in combat typically came from the god: "And Chemosh said to me: 'Go, take Nebo from Israel'"; "And Chemosh said to me: 'Go down, fight against Horonaim!'"[100] In these instances, gods speak through prophets.[101] Barak had started the legendary battle against Sisera at the summons of the prophetess Deborah (Judg 4:4–10). Soldiers, it is intimated, were doing the work of God. If they died, they would die for God. To incite the warriors to the point where they would willingly give their lives for the higher cause, prophets would work themselves into a collective frenzy. Dancing like dervishes, they held out promises of victory, performing various symbolic acts to get the message across (1 Kgs 22:5–12). The purpose was to put the soldiers in a state of intoxication that would make them rise above themselves. The warriors, for their part, took the rush of adrenalin at the departure for battle as a sign that the spirit of God had come over them. They were looking forward to a spree of violence. In the image of the God who shattered the heads of his enemies (Ps 68:22 [68:21]) and whose sword was "sated with blood" (Isa 34:6), warriors had to be ruthless. To do battle was to surrender to the power of the spirit of God to the point where one no longer cared whether one was dead or alive; victory was the only thing that mattered.

Victory was the goal, and victory meant the annihilation of the opponent. It was known as *ḥerem*-warfare. The Hebrew term *ḥerem* is related to the common Semitic root *haram* (*ḥaram*), "to be consecrated." The military opponents were consecrated to God, which was understood to mean that they were to be offered up as holocaust (Deut 13:17). It was the ultimate human sacrifice. Those who did the killing were acting like priests, the killing fields being their altar grounds. The underlying logic has to do with the ban on spilling blood (Gen 9:5). Blood is sacred. The only way to circumvent the taboo on slaughter is by turning the victims into offering material. This had the practical consequence that soldiers were "consecrated" (Isa 13:3) and had to observe strict rules of ritual purity. As long as they were under arms, no razor was to touch their hair (Judg 5:2) and no woman was to lie in their embrace (Deut 23:10–15; 1 Sam 21:2–8). The concept was not restricted to Israel. Mesha, too, says he had devoted his Israelite opponents to complete destruction: "I killed [*hrg*] all the people of the city as a sacrifice [*ryt*] for Chemosh"; "I killed the whole population . . . for I had consecrated them [*hhrmth*] for Ashtar Chemosh."[102] In *ḥerem*-warfare, there is no room for compromise. It is all or nothing.

Since a military confrontation was ultimately a battle between gods, the outcome could have an impact on the religious loyalties of the warriors. The god who had led his troops to victory was obviously worthy of worship, whereas the gods who had failed were likely to inspire some doubt about their powers. True believers will always find an explanation for such disappointments, for the designs of the gods are impenetrable and the possibilities of human error are endless. People will not abandon their god on account of one lost battle. But the god who had secured victory for his worshippers was bound to be rewarded by their enduring devotion. In the early history of Israel, this is an element that must have played a role. Although there is no equivalent in the Hebrew Bible to the tale of Emperor Constantine, who allegedly converted to Christianity after the battle on the Milvian Bridge because he believed Christ had brought him victory (owing to the famous *in hoc signo vinces* dream), the successful tribal warlord could legitimately aspire to political leadership and his god could lay claim to the devotion of his subjects. As we shall see in the cases of Saul and David, success in warfare was a way to achieve a rulership position. It is to be expected that the god in whose name they had won the battle would be more or less predestined to become the god of their chiefdom or state.

Saul and David and the Rise of a State

At the turn of the first millennium BCE, the tribal society of Palestine went through a series of transitions that ultimately led to the rise of a patrimonial state. The historical details of this process are elusive. The two main sources available for a reconstruction are the books of Samuel and the archaeological record. They allow us to discern the mechanisms behind the state formation and its general effects on the demographic situation.[103] The more we focus on details of the reconstruction, however, the greater the amount of speculation involved. Critically following the biblical data, the reconstruction here proposed gives a crucial role to the figures of Saul and David. In view of the reference to Judah as "the house of David" in the Tel Dan inscription, there is some justification for this.[104] Also, the negative framing of Saul in the History of David's Rise lends historical plausibility to his positive achievements. Nevertheless, under the circumstances, every historical reconstruction is fraught with a fair amount of uncertainty. Some events set in the lifetimes of Saul and David may be retrojections of a later period. What matters most in the present context, however, is to come to grips with the historical dynamics at work in the transition from a tribal society to a territorial state, on the one hand, and the rise of YHWH to the position of divine patron of that state, on the other.

This is the story of the coming about of an Israelite state in a rough outline based on the biblical record. Because of the military successes of Saul as a warlord, and his rise to political leadership in their wake, the inhabitants of the central hill country came to be incorporated in a new polity. After a number of victories, Saul expanded his chiefdom with the Jordan valley and the Transjordanian plateau of Gilead.[105] When he died, his son-in-law David took possession of the throne and succeeded in extending the southern border of the kingdom all the way to Judah. During the first half of the tenth century BCE, much of the territory of Israel and Judah had been brought under the authority of a single ruler. It was the beginning of the monarchic period.

Although Saul and David succeeded in building a state, they did not build a nation. Their state was a patrimonial state, not a nation-state. The cohesion of the state was based on personal loyalty to the ruler, similar in some ways to the loyalty to a paterfamilias. Over the course of the preceding two centuries, the population of Palestine had, for the most part, settled in towns and villages. Apart from some clans, they had abandoned the migratory mode of existence and turned to agriculturalism. Hills had been deforested and terraces had been laid out, as a result of which the hill settlements found themselves close to arable land. Their inhabitants had become peasants. However, these changes in the way of life had done little to erode the tribal structures of society. Lineage groups continued to be the prime social units. The population of a village rarely exceeded three hundred people, and nearly all of them were related by blood. Settlement (ʿîr) and clan (mišpāḥâ) nearly coincided, just as names of regions and names of tribes were hard to disentangle (2 Sam 15:2).[106] Both Saul and David were firmly rooted in the tribal society of their day. The kingdom they painstakingly put together had its base in Benjamin, the tribal territory to which Saul's ancestral clan belonged. This was central hill country, the area where the stela of Merenptah had located "Israel." The name "Israel" was transferred to the incipient kingdom, but the subjects of the kingdom were still a long way removed from a nation.

Among the different segments of the population in Saul's kingdom, the sense of unity was weak. Even in the days of Hosea (eighth century BCE), the fault lines between the various ethnic components of Israel were still in evidence. Hosea or one of his disciples puts the tradition of Jacob the patriarch in contrast with the Moses tradition (Hos 12:3–15), the one being the master narrative of the Aramean component of the population, and the other, the proud heritage of the southerners. The critique against those who call YHWH their Baal (Hos 2:18) could be interpreted as a sneer in the direction of the Canaanite branch of the population. The religious diversity has a parallel in linguistic diversity and the coexistence of different scripts. The Hebrew dialect in the north differs from that in the south (Judg 12:5–6). In both its vocabulary and grammar, the former has elements of Aramaic, a language still in use in Gilead in the ninth century

BCE (witness the Balaam inscription).[107] Most visitors from the North-ern Kingdom in Kuntillet Ajrud used the Hebrew script, but some the Phoenician.[108] Other cultural differences include the customs with respect to the disposal of the dead. Whereas the predominant practice in the hill country was burial, the inhabitants of Jabesh-gilead followed the Aramean custom of cremation (1 Sam 31:11–13).[109] The geomorphological features of Palestine favor the persistence of regional difference. Many people hardly ever traveled beyond the confines of their native village. Local autono-my was the rule. Isolated areas could preserve their local culture—religion included—for centuries.

The state that Saul founded and David developed was a patchwork. It consisted of an assortment of largely autonomous tribal areas and clan groups, held together by their common allegiance to the monarch. The way in which Saul and David built this patrimonial state was by the clever use of covenants and warfare. It is impossible to reconstruct the detailed history of the events that led to the formation of the first Israelite state. Almost all we have is the biblical record, which is both fragmentary and biased. Yet the Bible does allow a few glimpses into the dynamics of the process. The story of Saul's deliverance of Jabesh-gilead gives some clues. On the eve of the campaign, Saul reportedly performed a symbolic act: "He took a yoke of oxen, and cut them in pieces and sent them throughout all the territory of Israel by messengers" (1 Sam 11:7 NRSV). The meaning was hard to miss. The dismemberment of animals was a common covenant rite to demon-strate what would happen to disloyal partners. Saul sent the tribes a dra-matic reminder of their covenant oath. That oath had been sworn by YHWH, as implied by the effect of Saul's action: "Then the dread of the LORD fell upon the people" (1 Sam 11:7 NRSV). When Nahash the Ammonite had laid siege to Jabesh-gilead, the population had offered him a pact ("cut us a covenant," 1 Sam 11:1). Their proposal was turned down. In search for an ally against the Ammonites they came to Saul. He accepted, mustered an army, and delivered the town. The inhabitants, on their part, demonstrated their loyalty many years later by a risky rescue operation to save the bodies of Saul and his sons from further desecration (1 Sam 31:11–13). Although the text does not mention a formal covenant between Saul and Jabesh-gilead, it must have formed the basis of Saul's military intervention. In fact, the intermarriage of Benjaminites with young women from Jabesh-gilead wit-nesses to the existence of such a covenant—even if the story that speaks of this connubium may have erred in its timeline (Judg 21:8–14).

Covenants created kinship where no blood ties existed. "Look, we are your bone and flesh," is the message of the tribes to David at Hebron (2 Sam 5:1 NRSV). They are not implying they already are kin, but soliciting David to treat them as kin by virtue of a covenant: "So all the elders of Israel came to the king at Hebron; and King David made a covenant with them at Hebron before the LORD, and they anointed David king over Israel" (2 Sam 5:3 NRSV). Covenants made between individuals—such as those between David and Jonathan (1 Sam 18:3–4, 20:8, 23:18; 2 Sam 21:7) or between David and Abner (2 Sam 3:21)—were binding for everyone under their authority. For Saul and David, covenant making was a way of extending their sphere of influence. Whether people entered a covenant voluntarily or by force—both Saul and David were successful army leaders—did not really matter: the loyalty oath sworn by YHWH made covenant partners think twice before trying to get out of their obligations. In addition to these political pacts there were also covenants of a seemingly more personal nature. These were the marriages of Saul and David to women from different clans and families (1 Sam 14:49–50, 25:39–43; 2 Sam 5:13–14). But here, too, the personal is political. Marriage with a Calebite woman creates kinship with the Calebites (1 Sam 25:2–42), just as marriage with a woman from Jezreel draws the Jezreelites into one's orbit (1 Sam 25:43).

Toward Religious Unification

By warfare and covenants, Saul built a state, which David, by similar means, would later enlarge. Neither of them ever tried to build a nation. They ruled over different population groups with different group identities. But if they could not hope to forge national unity, they did set in motion a process that would lead to greater religious unity. The state over which Saul ruled had YHWH as divine patron. For Saul the choice of this god was hardly a choice, because YHWH was his ancestral deity, as witnessed by the name of his son Jonathan.[110] Saul's family had Edomite roots. They lived in the area of Gibeon. There is a striking overlap of names that ran in Saul's family, names of people from Gibeon, and Edomite names.[111] The family worshipped YHWH as its divine patron, presumably at the "high place" (bāmâ) of Gibeon (1 Kgs 3:4). Gibeon was known for having the greatest YHWH temple of the land (1 Kgs 3:4; cf. 2 Sam 21:6, 9, where "Gibeah" stands for Gibeon; cf. LXX Gabaōn). When David by deft maneuvering inherited Saul's kingdom, he did not change the religion of the state. For the first seven years of his reign, David ruled from Hebron (2 Sam 5:5).

The temple at Hebron was a sanctuary for a local form of YHWH (2 Sam 15:7–8).[112] As commander of a band of warriors, David fought "the battles of YHWH" (1 Sam 18:17, 25:28; cf. Num 21:14). And in keeping with the religious ideology of the time, the state's territory was "YHWH's estate" (1 Sam 26:19).[113]

What was the consequence for the worship of other gods of the rise of YHWH to the position of divine patron of the state? The early Israelite state was patrimonial. It had come into being through covenants by which various population groups had pledged loyalty to the head of state. In a way, they had joined the family of which the king was the acting paterfamilias. Since families could have many ancestors but only one family god, incorporation into the family arguably required one to renounce other gods. But that is theory. In actual practice, the early Israelite kings did not pursue a policy of religious reform by which they sought to eradicate the cult of other gods. Their subjects were free to direct their devotion to El or Baal.[114] However, something did change. The rise of YHWH as patron deity of the state sparked a dynamic that over the course of the next century did affect the positions of El and Baal. Perhaps the treaties made by Saul and David had been sworn by YHWH and the god of the treaty partner—even though the Bible tells it differently. But over time, as covenants were renewed, the oath came to be by YHWH alone. He was the divine head of state, and the subjects of the state had to pledge their allegiance to him and by him. It did not mean that Baal and El were no longer part of the picture. They continued to be worshipped but were reconfigured as manifestations of YHWH. Their names were transformed into titles, as indeed they had been in the beginning. YHWH was "God" (El) and "Lord" (Baal). What facilitated the process was the fact that the profiles of YHWH, El, and Baal were rather similar. Whether the identification of the gods was ever completely successful is questionable. The polemics against Baal by the prophets and the Deuteronomistic authors suggests a protracted rivalry between YHWH and Baal. But this may be due to the circumstance that in the northwest, Israel bordered on the territories of Tyre and Sidon, places that venerated Baal as patron deity. In that sense Baal was a political rival of YHWH. The treaties with Tyre and Sidon that the Omride dynasty concluded stirred up hostility against Baal among some of the traditionally Yahwistic groups of the population (such as the Rechabites).

The identification of El with YHWH, on the other hand, succeeded almost seamlessly.[115] In this merger of deities, YHWH remained the proper name and El became a title. The inscriptions from Kuntillet Ajrud provide extrabiblical evidence of the usurpation of El by YHWH. A number of times they refer to YHWH and "his Asherah."[116] A later echo of Asherah as YHWH's consort occurs in a collection of Aramaic religious texts from Egypt (papyrus Amherst 63). It mentions "Throne-of-Yaho and Asherah . . . from the Negev."[117] Asherah is the name of the Amorite goddess Ashratu, the consort of Amurru, the Amorite El. Also in the Ugaritic mythology, El and Asherah are a pair. The Aramean tribes who settled in Transjordan and the northern highlands brought along the cult of El and his Asherah. In the process of conflation with El, YHWH inherited the latter's female consort.[118] There is another piece of evidence for the fusion of deities. An Israelite psalm preserved in papyrus Amherst 63 refers to Yaho as "our bull" (12:17). "Bull" was the traditional epithet of El, familiar from the Ugaritic texts.[119] The bull statues of Bethel and Dan were originally symbols of El. They probably had a history that reached back further than the time of Jeroboam I (r. 922–901 BCE), who allegedly introduced their worship (1 Kgs 12:26–30). The bull-shaped icon was present in Palestine well before the first millennium BCE. The archaeological evidence includes a bronze bull from the Late Bronze temple at Hazor and one found near the so-called Bull Site (twelfth century BCE) (fig. 13).[120] In keeping with the takeover of El by YHWH, the bulls were reinterpreted as symbols of YHWH: "This is your god, O Israel, who brought you up from the land of Egypt" (1 Kgs 12:28 NJPS; cf. Num 23:22).[121] In the reconstruction of a later editor of the Pentateuch, YHWH had appeared to the patriarchs as El Shaddai and had revealed his true name only to Moses (Exod 6:3). This speculation from the postexilic period gives a theological twist to the result of the religious policy of the early Israelite kings.

In the long run, the state-sponsored process of religious unification stimulated the development of a national identity. Saul and David did not build a nation. Their patronage of YHWH as divine head of state, however, would eventually turn the Israelites into "the people of YHWH" ('am yhwh; Num 11:29; 1 Sam 10:1 LXX). The latter expression may originally have applied to the warriors who did battle on the side of YHWH.[122] They came to the help of YHWH (Judg 5:23), fought the battles of YHWH (1 Sam 18:17, 25:28; cf. Num 21:14), achieved the "triumphs of YHWH" (Judg 5:11)—in short, they were "the people of YHWH" ('am yhwh; Judg 5:3, 5, 11, 13; cf. 2 Sam 1:12). The Hebrew term 'am, conventionally translated as "people," is originally a term of kinship. When the expression was used to designate

Fig. 13. Bull statuette found near the so-called Bull Site. (Wikimedia Commons, CC-BY-SA-4.0, https://creativecommons.org/licenses/by/4.0/deed.en.)

the population of the kingdom, it was based on the notion that the subjects of the king formed, in theory, one family. By the covenant they had entered, they had become one kin. And since YHWH was the ancestral god of the family, they were "the kin group of YHWH." The term referred to a political reality. The Israelites were "the people of YHWH," just as the Moabites were "the people of Chemosh" (*'am-kĕmôš*; Num 21:29; Jer 48:46). In due course, though, the god of the state would become a national symbol. Despite the different ethnic roots of the population, the inhabitants of the hill country, the Jordan valley, and Gilead came to think of themselves as Israelites and of YHWH as their national god. In the end, religion would turn them into one nation.

2 Royal Religion

Sometime in the early stages of human history, says the Sumerian King List, kingship came down from heaven.[1] It had been invented by the gods. Most early Israelites did not take the same lofty view of the institution. The antimonarchic sentiment that surfaces at times in the historical books (e.g., Judg 9:8–15; 1 Sam 8:11–18, 10:17–19) and resonates in Hosea (Hos 8:4, 9:15, 12:12, 13:9–11) has old roots. It goes back to the spirit of proud independence of the pastoralist tribes that had found their way to Palestine. But since the days of Saul and David, kingship was a fact of life. Its impact was tremendous. Outside the capitals of Israel and Judah, in places that had little communication with the rest of the world, life seemed to continue much as before, but one way or another the new political reality affected everyone. Taxes, conscription, and the rise of new elites changed the social landscape. But also religion did not stay the same. Since the religious imagination draws its metaphors from the social and political realities of its time, it comes up with new metaphors when those realities change. Though the metaphor of God as valiant warrior was never discarded, during the monarchic period God became king, and the place where he lived, in heaven as on earth, became a palace. The new metaphor also influenced the popular perception of the daily temple cult as the feeding and humoring of the deity by a staff of servants.[2]

The psychological roots of religion run deep. Few cultural phenomena have the power to steer human behavior the way religion does. In a civilization where a separation between politics and religion was unthinkable, a monarch had to be careful to pursue a religious program that would win him the support of the population—preferably not just one segment, but the entire population—and be conducive to the rule of law and order in the kingdom. This does not mean that the king was somehow above religion and used it merely as an instrument of social engineering. The king was just as religious as his subjects. He believed he had a divine mission. It was his duty to extend the realm of the deity by temple building and warfare, and to take care of God's people by providing justice and protection. This chapter looks at five aspects of royal religion: rituals that celebrate the divine mandate of the human ruler; the role of the king as temple builder and provider of the gods—YHWH first of all, but also his entourage and often additional gods; the place of priests as civil servants; the role of prophets; and the king as head of the army and as supreme judge.

The Divine Mandate of the King

In the early beginnings of Israelite monarchy, kingship had not descended from above but came about by a pact between a successful warlord and tribal elders. The book of Judges tells the story of Jephthah. He owed his position as "head and commander" over Gilead to an oath by the elders that he would rule over them if he defeated the Ammonite enemy (Judg 11:1–11). The narrator avoids the word "king," but the pattern of the agreement is very similar to the story of Saul's rise to kingship. After Saul's victory over the Ammonites, the Israelites "made him king before the LORD" (1 Sam 11:15). The ceremony included a sacrificial meal, which suggests it was a covenant, since the šĕlāmîm sacrifice is a covenant sacrifice.[3] In both cases—Jephthah's and Saul's—the agreement is formalized "before the LORD" (Judg 11:11; 1 Sam 11:15). There is no divine mandate of the king but an agreement between human parties sealed by a religious oath. This is also the scenario behind the offer of rulership to Gideon (Judg 8:22) and, later, David's rise to kingship (2 Sam 2:4, 5:3). Once the warlord has defeated a common enemy, the people's representatives acclaim him as their king. The myth of Marduk's rise to kingship, as told in the Babylonian Story of Creation, follows a similar pattern: because the god of Babylon has been successful in the battle against Tiamat and her army, the other gods bow to him as their king. The myth mirrors the ways in which the human institution of kingship originated.[4]

In the course of the tenth and ninth centuries BCE, a new view of kingship emerged in Israel, perhaps in connection with the rise of royal dynasties and surely under the influence of the royal ideology in surrounding countries. The change is visible in the *anointment* ceremony.[5] In the ancient Near Eastern practice of covenant making, the anointment created family ties between the partners. To ratify a sale of land—land that theoretically could not be alienated from the family—buyer and seller "ate from the same platter, drank from the same cup, and anointed each other with oil."[6] The buyer had become family. Anointing also was a wedding rite: the groom anointed the bride and thereby incorporated her into his family.[7] When the northern tribes wanted David to be their king, "King David made a covenant with them at Hebron before the LORD, and they anointed David king over Israel" (2 Sam 5:3 NRSV; same rite in 2 Sam 2:4; cf. 1 Kgs 5:15). Anointment by the people, represented by the elders, was the norm, as is clear from the fable of Jotham. In this satire on the institution of kingship, "The trees once went out / to anoint a king over themselves" (Judg 9:8 NRSV). Although the anointment by popular representatives continued to be practiced throughout the monarchic period (2 Kgs 11:12, 23:30), the formal enthronement ceremony put in place a new scenario of anointment. In this rite it was a representative of YHWH—normally the high priest (e.g., 1 Kgs 1:39)—who did the anointing, which made it a symbol of the divine mandate of the king. It was the expression of a new paradigm. In the new conception, the covenant was between God and the king, rather than between the people and the king. Because covenant creates kinship, the ritual anointment made the king a son of God (cf. 2 Sam 7:14). Behind the scenes, the competition between candidates for the royal succession was often fierce, each woman of the royal harem trying to win support for her own son, but the anointment ceremony decided the matter. To raise a hand against the LORD's anointed was taboo (1 Sam 24:7, 11; 26:9–11; 2 Sam 1:14–16). God had made him king—a claim made by monarchs throughout the Near East.[8]

The new paradigm comes to the fore most clearly in some of the songs composed for public celebrations in which the king stood center stage.

> Ps 45:7–8 [45:6–7, author's translation based on the NRSV]:
> Your throne, O God [the king], endures forever and ever.
>> Your royal scepter is a scepter of equity;
>> you love righteousness and hate wickedness.
> Therefore *YHWH, your God, has anointed you
>> with the oil of gladness beyond your companions.

> Ps 89:19–20 NRSV:
>> I have set the crown on one who is mighty,
>> I have exalted one chosen from the people.
> I have found my servant David;
>> with my holy oil I have anointed him.

Ps 2:2, 7–8 NRSV:
The kings of the earth set themselves,
    and the rulers take counsel together,
    against the LORD and his anointed . . .
. . . .
I will tell of the decree of the LORD:
He said to me, "You are my son;
    today I have begotten you.
Ask of me, and I will make the nations your heritage,
    and the ends of the earth your possession."

The first text comes from a royal wedding song and goes back to the (early) monarchic period. The reference later in the psalm to the bride as "daughter of Tyre" (Ps 45:13 [45:12]) might well be an indication of its setting in the Northern Kingdom.[9] This is one of the few texts that has preserved the notion of divine kingship: the king is addressed as "God" (*'ĕlōhîm*, Ps 45:7 [45:6]).[10] The idea was offensive to many later interpreters of the Bible, who endeavored to come up with translations that gave a more innocent twist to the phrase.[11] All over the Near East, however, especially on occasions of great pomp, kings bathed in a supernatural glow.[12] They were sons of the gods. Hence the royal title Ben-Hadad (in proper Aramaic, Bar-Hadad, "son of Hadad,"), carried by various Aramean kings; hence also Assurbanipal's claim he was born of, and raised by, the gods.[13] Similar statements with respect to the divine nature of the king were common in Egypt and Syria, both in poetic utterances and in the form of iconographical motifs.[14] In both life and death, kings were not like ordinary mortals.[15] People knew of course that kings were also human, at times all too human, yet nevertheless acclaimed them as gods. No one at the time cared to write a treatise on the two natures of the king, for the two of them seemed perfectly compatible. The king reigned with the approval of the people, in token of which he had been anointed by the people's representatives. At the same time, the king had been chosen and anointed by God, and reigned, as son of God, with full divine mandate.[16]

The proclamation of the king's election by God, his ritual anointment by the high priest, and the celebration of his divine sonship were all scheduled to happen during a grand public ceremony. It is unlikely this occurred only at the beginning of the king's reign. Just as in Babylon, where a royal reinvestiture with attendant oracles of victory took place every New Year festival in spring, there is good reason to assume that also in Israel the installation of the king was annually celebrated, most likely at the New Year festival in autumn.[17] The songs of which excerpts were given above all contain divine promises of victory. Texts from Mari have yielded an illuminating parallel to this Israelite enthronement ritual. A prophet of the god Adad has delivered an oracle for King Zimrilim that looks back at his investiture:

> I have brought you back to your father's throne and I gave you the weapons I used to defeat the Sea [têmtum, i.e., Tiamat]. I anointed you with my awe-inspiring oil so that nobody could stand in your way. Now hear this one word of mine. When someone with a lawsuit calls upon you, saying "I have been mistreated," take your stand and judge his case. Render a just verdict. That is what I ask of you.[18]

Here, too, the anointment is by the god. The presentation of the divine weapons and the demand for justice refer to the two most significant duties of any Near Eastern king: to fight the battles of the deity, and to make justice prevail in the land. It was no different in Israel. The oracles in the biblical royal hymns quoted above focus on divine support in battle. Yet there is also the occasional allusion to the king as supreme judge (Ps 45:4–8). More explicit with respect to the latter is Psalm 101, which reads like an inaugural address by the new king, promising he will walk "with integrity of heart" (v. 2) and shall "destroy all the wicked in the land" (v. 8).

One of the perhaps unforeseen consequences of the shift in the mandate of the monarch—originally appointed by the people, later by God—was a new development in the religious ideology of the covenant. From its earliest beginnings, kingship in Israel had been closely linked to the practice of covenant making. The ruler and the people made a solemn agreement that he should be their king and they his subjects; the oath by Yhwh made the pact binding. It was a covenant between two human parties before God. When the enthronement ceremony came to include an anointment of the monarch by God—represented, on the occasion, by the chief priest—the covenant was between God and the king. The natural complement to this new concept of the covenant—in which Yhwh was not merely witness but actual covenant partner—was an additional covenant between Yhwh and the subjects of the king. Yhwh made a covenant with the king and another covenant with the people. As God's chosen people they owed obedience and loyalty to God's chosen king.

Perhaps the earliest expression of this new triangular covenant model is preserved in the story of the investiture of King Joash of Judah (r. 836–796 BCE). The high priest Jehoiada masterminded the ceremony:

> [Jehoiada] then brought out the king's son, and placed on him the crown and the insignia. They proclaimed him king and anointed him. They clapped their hands and shouted, "Long live the king!" . . . Jehoiada made a covenant between YHWH and the king; as well as with the people that they should be a people for YHWH; also between the king and the people. (2 Kgs 11:12, 17)

The English translations of verse 17 struggle with the syntax. The Hebrew has the usual expression for covenant making—*kārat běrît*, "to cut a covenant"—followed by the preposition *bên*, "between," to introduce the covenant partners. It is a triple covenant: one between YHWH and the king, one between YHWH and the people, and one between the king and the people. The real innovation is the second covenant, by which the people become "a people for YHWH" (*'am lěyhwh*). It introduces a concept that would become a central tenet of Israelite religion and lead to the narrative of the covenant at Mount Sinai. The new conception of kingship—new for Israel, because the idea of sacral kingship had long been common to much of the Near East—existed side by side with the older practice of kingship by covenant. But in the cultic celebrations of kingship—the enthronement rites, annually repeated at the New Year festival—the position of the people had been altered. Formerly the covenant had been made between the people and the king with the deity as witness ("before YHWH"). Now YHWH had become the principal actor: "I have made a covenant with my chosen one" (Ps 89:4 [89:3]).

YHWH's Enthronement Festival in Autumn

The advent of kingship had a profound impact on Israelite religion. Saul and David and their successors, both in Judah (the Southern Kingdom) and in Israel (the Northern Kingdom), were actively involved in the promotion of YHWH as patron god of the state. In the new coronation rituals, YHWH had taken the place of the people as the performer of the anointment as a sign of the royal investiture. This emphasis on the divine mandate of the king undoubtedly had the approval of the monarch and ultimately must have been devised by the clergy at court. For the coronation rite to have its full public effect, however, the position of the deity who appointed the king had to be beyond dispute. It was in the interest of the monarchy, then, to persuade the population of the supremacy of YHWH. In the religiously divided realm over which they ruled, the means to unite the nation was the proclamation of YHWH's kingship, relegating the other gods to subservient positions. It was a classic solution. All over the Near East, kingship had long been the dominant metaphor to express divine superiority. Kingship was not a theoretical attribute of the god, but the central theme of the biggest festival of the year. At Ugarit, the New Year festival in autumn celebrated Baal's rise to kingship. The custom had a counterpart in Babylonia, where the Akitu festival included a recitation of the Enuma Elish in memory of Marduk's defeat of Tiamat and his ascension to kingship. In the presence of delegations from surrounding cities, the annual celebrations reaffirmed the primacy of the god of the royal capital, without dismissing the reality of other gods. The god of the king was simply the king of the gods.

In analogy with the festivals in Ugarit and Babylon, then, the kings of Israel and Judah organized the enthronement festival of YHWH. They borrowed elements of the Canaanite tradition—such as the timing of the festival in autumn and references to the combat myth against Yamm and his helpers (Ps 74:12–17, 89:10–15)—but framed it in a new way. The New Year festival in autumn celebrated YHWH's ascent to kingship, both over the other gods and, more significantly, over the people of Israel. He became their king and they became his people—the *'am yhwh*, "the people of the LORD." The obvious places for the cultic celebration of YHWH's enthronement were the royal temples, located in Jerusalem in the south and Bethel in the north. Both temples had long been major religious centers. Their new status as "royal sanctuaries" and "temples of the kingdom" (paraphrased after Amos 7:13) came about in the time of the monarchy as the kings elected these venerable holy places to serve as central state temples. The tale of the solemn transfer of the ark, from Kiriath-jearim to Jerusalem, documents King David's choice of Jerusalem as religious capital (2 Sam 6:1–19; Psalm 132).[19] In a similar vein, the story of King Jeroboam I's introduction of the official New Year festival of the Northern Kingdom at Bethel (1 Kgs 12:32) implies a choice for Bethel as central sanctuary.[20] Though it is possible to give a fairly reliable outline of YHWH's enthronement festival in these royal temples, we cannot be sure that all local sanctuaries of Judah and Israel staged similar celebrations, even though the official festivities in the capitals are bound to have had repercussions elsewhere in the country.

Just as Bethel and Jerusalem had been important temple cities prior to the monarchy, so the New Year festival in autumn had been in existence for a long time before the royal administration turned it into a celebration of Yhwh's kingship. The festival took place at the "turn" of the year (Exod 34:22) and thus inaugurated the new annual cycle (cf. the Gezer calendar, which puts the "ingathering" [*ʾsp*] at the beginning of the year).[21] In origin it was a celebration of the grape harvest and the new wine. The tradition was older than the Israelites. The book of Judges describes a wine festival of the inhabitants of Shechem: "They went out into the field and gathered the grapes from their vineyards, trod them, and celebrated. Then they went into the temple of their god, ate and drank" (Judg 9:27 NRSV). Deuteronomy says that the festival is to take place "when you have gathered in [*ʾāsap*] the produce from your threshing floor and your vat" (Deut 16:13). This is the time of the vintage. There were songs and shouts of joy in the vineyards and in the presses (Isa 16:10). Many people spent the night close to the fields in makeshift huts, a custom to which the festival owes one of its names (Succoth, meaning "huts, booths").[22] "Ingathering" (*ʾāsîp*) was another name (Exod 23:16, 34:22). The ingathering included cereals, but the recent grape harvest loomed larger. Young women would go out and dance in the vineyards (Judg 21:19–21), the new wine flowed freely (1 Sam 1:9–14), and people might behave a little less decorously than they ordinarily would (Judg 9:27). Religion can be serious and solemn. The wine festival was serious but hardly solemn: a mood of permissiveness permeated the celebrations.

Over time, the autumnal festival came to be known as "the Yhwh festival" (Judg 21:19, Hos 9:5). Grafted upon the older wine festival, the New Year festival's new style celebrated Yhwh's ascent to kingship. Echoes of the celebrations are present mostly in the book of Psalms. Many of those songs were composed for use in the temple liturgy and provide witness, even if oblique, to cultic events. The "Yahweh-kingship psalms" (Psalms 47, 93, 96–99) are a case in point.[23] Many of them contain the traditional formula *yhwh mālak*, "Yhwh has become king."[24] These songs celebrate the ritual reenactment of Yhwh's enthronement rather than his everlasting rule. The principal means to visualize the event was by a procession of a symbol of the deity—a portable shrine like the ark or, as in Bethel, a bull image—leading up to its entry into the throne room of the temple: "Your solemn processions are seen, O God, / the processions of my God, my King, into the sanctuary" (Ps 68:24 NRSV). The central event is the enthronement of the deity, referred to in Ps 47:6 with the verb *'ālâ*, "to ascend": "God ascends midst acclamation; the LORD, to the blast of the horn" (Ps 47:6 [47:5] NJPS).[25] Once YHWH has seated himself on the throne (the *kissē*; Ps 47:9, 89:15, 97:2), his reign as king has begun. All the other gods must recognize his ascendency (see, e.g., Ps 89:6–9, 95:3, 96:4, 97:7), and the worshippers hail him as their king (Ps 47:7, "our King"; 68:25 [68:24], "my King").

For the historian, the use of the biblical psalms as a source of information is not without problems. The songs are unprovenanced, carry no date, and have often been subject to a process of editing and reediting due to which the original is either irretrievable or a matter of conjecture.[26] As luck would have it, however, three early extrabiblical New Year psalms from the Northern Kingdom, preserved in a papyrus from Egypt (Amherst 63), provide an uncensored glimpse into the festivities.[27] It was still a wine festival, as it had been among the Canaanites, but the focus had shifted. The three songs celebrate the ascendency of Yaho (this is how they pronounced YHWH) over all other gods, his power to determine destinies and punish evildoers, and the privileged bond he had with Israel. There was animal sacrifice (Amherst 63, 13:1) and a banquet with wine to which the deity was invited (Amherst 63, 13:5): "They have mixed the wine in our jar, in our jar at our new moon festival. Drink, O Yaho, from the bounty of a thousand bowls!" (Amherst 63, 13:6–7). Songs to the sound of harp, lyre, and flute contributed to what must have been an ebullient mood (Amherst 63, 13:8–10). At the same time, the festival acclaimed Yaho as ruler over all the other gods. Under the light of the rising moon, Yaho had no equal among the gods (Amherst 63, 13:11–12). The "host of heaven" under him—that is, the multitude of stars beneath the moon—proclaimed his rule (Amherst 63, 13:14–15). This was the time when Yaho lifted some and humiliated others (Amherst 63, 13:5–6) and would "take vengeance on [his] adversaries" (Amherst 63, 13:12; cf. Nah 1:2; Ps 94:23).[28] The worshippers declare he is their god and that they are his people: "Some by the bow, some by the spear—behold, as for us, our lord and our god is Yaho. May our Bull be with us!" (Amherst 63, 12:16–17). Yaho, indeed, is sure to "arise to the rescue" of his people (*'mk*, "your people"; Amherst 63, 13:16).[29]

These three songs show that the New Year festival was indeed "the enthronement festival of Yahweh."[30] Though the songs have no explicit reference to an enthronement, the fact that Baal-shamayin and Baal-zaphon are said to offer congratulations to Yaho (Amherst 63, 12:18–19, 13:15–16) implies that his rulership was recently acquired. These songs see Yaho's rise to kingship figured in the nightly skies, in which the new moon makes its appearance (Amherst 63, 12:12–13), waxes to full moon, and then makes the other stars look pallid because of its brilliance (Amherst 63, 13:13–15). Submitted to a close reading, the three extrabiblical songs do betray several departures from the impression conveyed by the biblical psalms. Nowhere do the latter picture YHWH reveling in a feast of wine, nor do they suggest that the rise of the moon figures his ascent to kingship. But a northern prophet like Hosea does mention libations of wine for YHWH on the day of his festival (Hos 9:4–5), and Amos, speaking about rituals performed in the Northern Kingdom, alludes to a procession in which the participants carry astral symbols (Amos 5:26).[31] These elements likely offended the religious scruples of later scribes and were edited out in the official anthology of liturgical texts. Historically, celebrations of the New Year festival are bound to have displayed differences according to period and place. Yet in the midst of diversity, a number of elements constituted the common core: the celebration of YHWH's kingship, over the other gods and over Israel, is the central one.

In the transition from tribal leadership to a monarchic regime, kingship was conferred by covenant between the people and their chosen ruler. It was a form of constitutional monarchy, the covenant serving as a constitution (cf. 1 Sam 10:25). The biblical records suggest that public endorsement of the new ruler, formalized by covenant, remained a foundational aspect of the monarchy even as the focus shifted to the divine mandate. YHWH's ascension to the throne, celebrated every autumn, was based on a covenant too. The enthronement festival was also a covenant festival. Most of the psalms composed for the occasion have no explicit reference to this covenant, but one does. Psalm 50 opens with a theophany followed by a direct divine speech addressed to "my devotees who make a covenant with me over sacrifice" (Ps 50:5). Nowhere in the psalms is the reference to covenant renewal more explicit. The dramatic effect is heightened by a first-person address by the divine king:

> Hear, my people, and I will speak;
> Israel, and I will admonish you:
> I am the *LORD your god." (Ps 50:7)

This divine speech has a close parallel in Psalm 81:

> Hear, my people, and I will admonish you;
> Israel, if you would but listen to Me:
> You shall have no foreign god,
> Nor shall you bow down to an alien god.
> I am the LORD your god
> Who brought you up from the land of Egypt. (Ps 81:9–11 [81:8–10])

The opening section of Psalm 81 refers quite explicitly to the time of the autumnal festival: "Blow the horn at the new moon, at the full moon, for the day of our festival" (Ps 81:4 [81:3]). The full moon, that is, the fifteenth day of the month, marked the beginning of the Festival of Booths in Judah in the seventh month (Lev 23:34) and the day of the annual festival at Bethel a month later (1 Kgs 12:32).

The parallel between Ps 50:7 and Ps 81:9–11 shows that these verses were not a spontaneous creation of a Hebrew poet but part of the established liturgy of the festival, even if the ritual performance did allow some variation and paraphrasing. The references to the covenant with a view to its renewal had their setting in the enthronement festival, as demonstrated by Psalm 95. There, the reference to YHWH as the "great king over all the gods" (Ps 95:3) is followed by a divine speech very much in the spirit of Psalm 81. The introduction to this divine speech echoes the phraseology of Psalms 81 and 50: "Today, if you would but listen to his voice . . ." (Ps 95:7). As Sigmund Mowinckel noted, Psalms 50, 81, and 95 belong to the same festal complex, in which YHWH's enthronement entails a rite of covenant renewal.[32] Part of this covenant renewal required the solemn commitment to the terms of the covenant (Ps 50:16)—the latter stipulating undivided loyalty to YHWH ("you shall have no foreign god, nor shall you bow down to an alien god," Ps 81:10), as well as the observation of a small set of social taboos. These moral prohibitions are alluded to in Ps 50:18–20 (theft, adultery, defamation) and read like a forerunner of the Decalogue ("You shall not steal," "You shall not commit adultery," "You shall not bear false witness against your neighbor"; see Exod 20:13; Deut 5:17).

The correspondences between some of the enthronement festival psalms and the narrative of the covenant at Sinai (Exodus 19–20; Deuteronomy 5) are anything but fortuitous. The background of the Sinai covenant and the Ten Commandments is not a remote event from the early history of the Israelites but the annual performance of YHWH's enthronement. The story is rooted in ritual. In the Northern Kingdom, the celebration of YHWH as "the god who brought you up from Egypt" included this established liturgical phrase on the occasion of the festival procession (1 Kgs 12:28). Over time, this narrative nucleus bloomed into the national myth of deliverance from Egypt and the covenant at Sinai. This covenant formalized the exclusive bond between Yʜᴡʜ and Israel. In the cultic celebrations, the covenant was closely correlated to Yʜᴡʜ's rise to kingship. The forerunner of the Decalogue is to be viewed as the first act of God as king. It is a speech act that establishes Yʜᴡʜ as lawgiver and supreme judge—both eminently royal functions. Once again: the ritual is first, the story comes after.

Temples and Territory

With the rise of territorial states in Iron Age Palestine and Transjordan, many of the formerly tribal gods turned into territorial deities. After they were promoted to the rank of patron gods of the new states, their connection with their devotees came to be based on territorial claims. The inhabitants of the state were to worship the god who owned the land. When Saul elevated his family god to the position of patron deity of his kingdom, Yʜᴡʜ became the divine king of the territory of Israel. David, too, worshipped Yʜᴡʜ as the tutelary deity of his realm. It was a position that would define the deity for a long time to come. In the image of the human monarch, Yʜᴡʜ "became King in Jeshurun," Jeshurun being an archaic name for Israel (Deut 33:5 NJPS). It meant that from then on, the "inheritance" or "estate" of Yʜᴡʜ (both terms translations of Hebrew naḥălâ) was a territorial state rather than a people (1 Sam 10:1 LXX, 26:19; 2 Sam 14:16, 20:19). The territory of the state was the "land" ('ereṣ; Hos 9:3; Joel 1:6), "soil" ('ădāmâ; Isa 14:2; Zech 2:16), or "house" (bayit; Hos 8:1, 9:8) of Yʜᴡʜ, and the cities in the land were "the cities of our God" (2 Sam 10:12 NRSV). The link was very tight. Foreigners who came to settle in the land had to learn "the law of the god of the land" (2 Kgs 17:26 NRSV), while those driven out of the land were forced to "serve other gods" (1 Sam 26:19).[33] A foreigner who wanted to worship Yʜᴡʜ abroad would preferably do so on earth ('ădāmâ) that came from the land of Israel (2 Kgs 5:17).

The new conception of God as the lord of a territory was common to much of the ancient Near East.[34] It informs the stone inscription of Mesha, king of the Moabites, which commemorates the victories of Mesha over the Omride kings of Israel (ca. 850 BCE).[35] The monument explains that King Omri had oppressed Moab for many days "because Chemosh was angry with his land [Moab]" ('rṣh, line 6). With Chemosh on his side, Mesha was able to recover much of the lost territory for the god. To materialize the Moabite claims on the reoccupied land, the king launched an intensive building program. He built (or rebuilt) cities, water reservoirs (*ʾšwḥ*, lines 9, 23), palaces (*bt mlk*, line 23), and sanctuaries (*bmt*, lines 3, 27). Building was an act of possession. By creating new realities on the ground, the monarch materialized his claim on the land. The king did not do so as a private individual but in his capacity as steward of the god who had ownership of the land. Hence the special mention of sanctuaries for Chemosh, referred to in Mesha's inscription as "high places" (the traditional rendering of Hebrew *bāmâ*—*bmt* and *bt bmt* in the Moabite text, lines 3, 27) and "temples" (literally, "houses," lines 30–31).[36] These state-sponsored sanctuaries were located mostly along the border, often in combination with fortresses garrisoned by soldiers to protect and defend the god's domain. The borders were not the straight lines familiar from the map of the modern Middle East. Should you draw a line from one border fortress-cum-sanctuary to the next, you would likely end up with saw-shaped boundaries.

Fortresses also marked the borders of Judah and Israel, most of them with attendant cult installations (fig. 14).[37] Some have been found by archaeologists, whereas others occur only in the biblical record. Along the borders of the Southern Kingdom (Judah) there were fortresses in Michmash, Geba (1 Kgs 15:22; 2 Kgs 23:8), and Mizpah of Benjamin (Judg 20:1; 1 Sam 7:5–6, 10:17–25; 1 Kgs 15:22; Jer 41:1–7);[38] in Vered-Jericho to the east;[39] and on the southwestern and southern borders in Lachish, Beersheba, Horvat Uza, Horvat Qitmit, Horvat Radum, and Arad (Amos 5:5, 8:14).[40] Fortresses-with-sanctuary on the borders of the Northern Kingdom (Israel) included Megiddo, Mount Carmel, Dan, and perhaps Bethsaida in the north (1 Kgs 12:29, 30; Amos 8:14) and Bethel, Ramah, Mizpah, and Gilgal in the south (1 Sam 7:16–17; 1 Kgs 15:17 [Ramah]; Amos 5:5).[41] Traditions preserved in the Hebrew Bible suggest there were also Israelite border fortresses in Transjordan, such as Mizpah in Gilead (Gen 31:43–54; Judg 11:11). The Mesha stone, too, implies as much for the cities of Ataroth (lines 10–13) and Nebo (lines 14–18).[42] Most if not all of these border sites had a sanctuary of sorts, plus a territorial marker in the form of one or more stelae. Their meaning was unmistakable: you are now entering the territory of Yнwн. The boundaries of the state were religious demarcation lines (cf. Gen 31:51–53).[43]

It would be an error to think of these border temples as political statements only. The cult installations were equipped with incense burners and

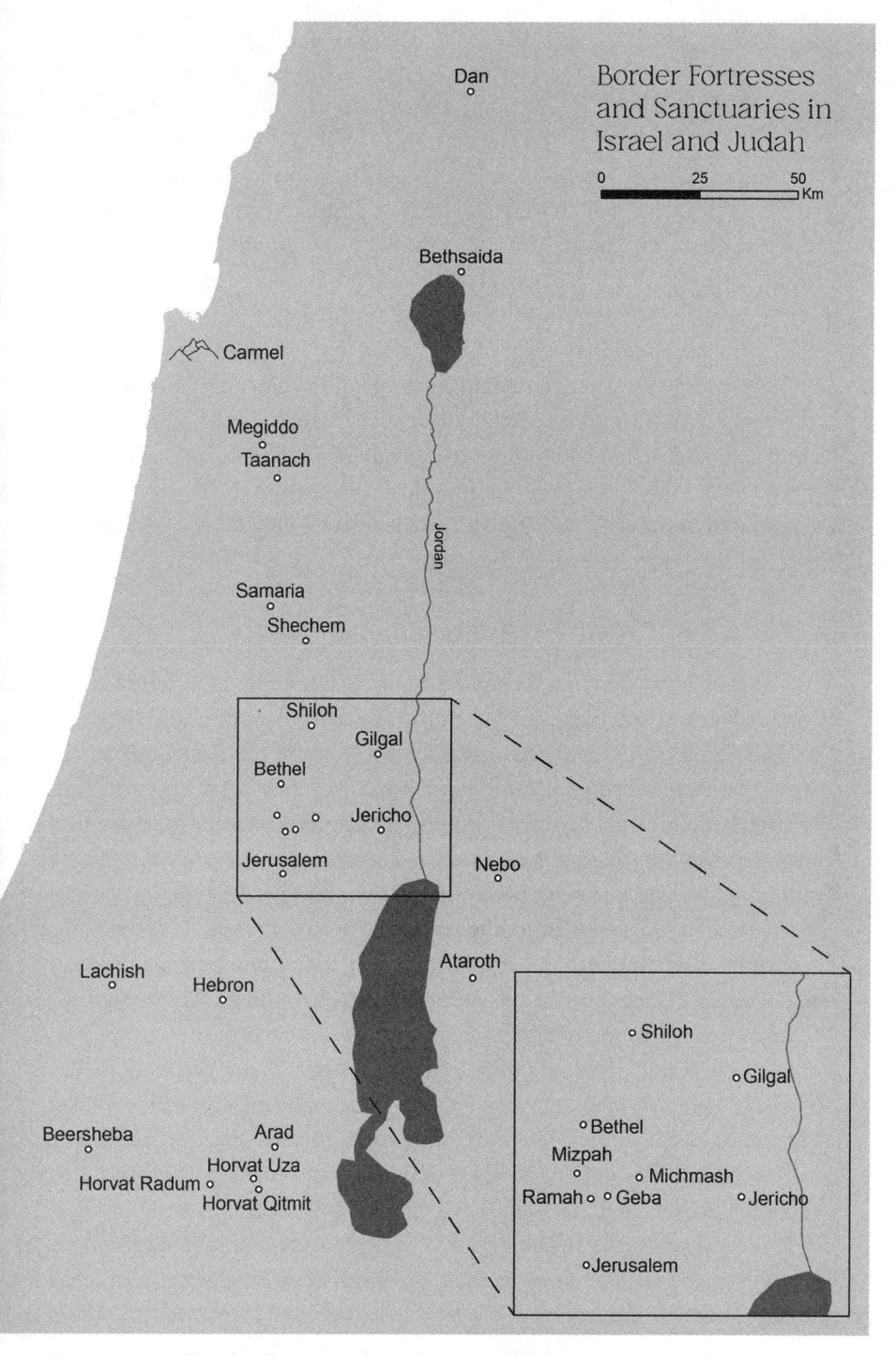

Fig. 14. Map of border fortresses and sanctuaries in Israel and Judah. (Map created by Jip Zinsmeister.)

altars. In combination with the god's symbol, the cult at these sanctuaries was designed to guarantee the effective presence of the deity. Military men guarded the border, but ultimately God protected the realm. Alongside a string of border sanctuaries, the states of Israel and Judah each had one central sanctuary—Jerusalem in Judah, and Bethel in Israel (1 Kgs 12:32–33; Amos 7:13), both of which were also, at least at some point during their history, temples at the border.[44] In keeping with the dominant Near Eastern royal ideology, the kings of Israel and Judah are bound to have contributed to the regular cult in various other local and regional centers. For rulers it was the accepted way to secure popular support, as evidenced by the self-presentation of Hammurabi in the prologue to his code.[45] But the royal involvement in the cult focused on the central temple of the kingdom. The temples of Bethel and Jerusalem were truly state temples under the auspices of the king. They were the principal settings for all the formal royal ceremonial, from enthronement to marriage, including all the annual rites that required the presence of the king.

The Royal Temples of Jerusalem and Bethel

The temples of Jerusalem and Bethel were border temples raised to the status of central sanctuary, the one of the Southern Kingdom and the other of the Northern. The two were rivals, as the story of the institution of the New Year festival at Bethel by Jeroboam I intimates (1 Kgs 12:25–33). These central temples were the most prominent religious places in the political infrastructure by which the monarchy secured the integrity of the territory and its hold on the population. Whereas the other border temples defined the perimeter of the kingdom, the temples at Jerusalem and Bethel defined its center. They were at the ideological rather than the topographical center, because in fact they were situated close to the border. Mythologically speaking, however, the national sanctuary was "the navel of the earth" (Judg 9:37; Ezek 38:12).[46] This was the place where the national god had his domicile, where the king came on solemn occasions and moments of crisis (such as a national fast, Jer 36:9), and where thousands of people would visit, some almost daily to do their devotions, and many more during the religious high holy days, when the population of the city saw a considerable increase.[47] Prophets like Amos, at Bethel, and Jeremiah, in Jerusalem, would use the temple court as their platform when they wished to reach a large audience (Jeremiah 7, 26; 36:10; Amos 7:10–17). The temple was a meeting place. Religious center (temple city) and political center (palace city) need not coincide. In Jerusalem they did, for the temple was located next to the royal palace (Ezek 43:8), the two monumental buildings being demarcated from the rest of the city by a shared wall (1 Kgs 7:12).[48] But in the Northern Kingdom, political center and religious center were separate since the Omrides built the city of Samaria as the administrative center of the kingdom (1 Kgs 16:23–24), while Bethel continued to be its religious center. There was a state temple at Samaria, too, but it never achieved the status of central sanctuary (1 Kgs 16:32; 2 Kgs 10:18–29).[49]

Both Jerusalem and Bethel are cities with a long history. Their temples had a venerable past as well, even though they had suffered serious damage during some periods—as Bethel did toward the end of the Bronze Age (ca. 1300–1200 BCE). Such was the renown of these old sanctuaries that their origins were the subject of popular legend. The Bethel temple, located on a hill a little outside the city wall (Gen 12:8, 13:3–4), was known for the stone stela and the monumental oak within its precinct. These features had given rise to foundation stories involving the patriarch Jacob—who had supposedly used the stone as a headrest and in his dream was visited by angels (Gen 28:10–22; cf. 31:13, 35:7)—and the matriarch Deborah—was this the wet nurse of Rebekah buried underneath the "oak of weeping," or Deborah the prophetess, who used to sit under the tree? The traditions did not agree (Gen 35:8; Judg 4:4–5; cf. Josh 2:1–5 LXX; 1 Kgs 13:14). The Jerusalem temple, built on the acropolis of the city, was believed to be situated at a very special place too—either on the hill where God had miraculously provided an offering ram as substitute for Abraham's son (Gen 22:1–19; 2 Chr 3:1) or at the threshing floor where God had put an end to an epidemic (2 Sam 24:15–25, based perhaps on the association between the words *deber*, "plague," and *děbîr*, "inner sanctum," "cella"). Who could tell which tale was true? Perhaps it did not matter because the point was that the temple stood on hallowed ground. It is true that these YHWH temples were located in places where earlier temples had stood. Neither the state temple at Bethel nor the one at Jerusalem was a completely new creation. Although kings proudly presented themselves as the builders of the temples, they had in fact been rebuilding, adding, renovating, and redecorating.[50]

The YHWH temples at Bethel and Jerusalem had a pre-Yahwistic past. That past was not simply wiped out the moment the authorities claimed and reconfigured these temples for the worship of YHWH. Bethel had been a temple of El, as the name of the city ("House of El," meaning "Temple of El") still intimates. Had the stone and the oak been embodiments of El and his Asherah? Stone and tree were worshipped among the Israelites as though they were divine father and mother (Jer 2:27), and the identification with El fits with his father title ("El your father," Gen 49:25).[51] But they also could have been grave markers. The so-called golden calf—in fact a bull statue with a plating of precious metal—was originally a symbol of El, known as Bull El in Ugaritic texts. When Jeroboam presented this bull as "your god, O Israel, who brought you up from the land of Egypt" (1 Kgs 12:28), he boldly identified Yhwh and El, thereby claiming the El temple as an official place of worship for Yhwh.[52] The identity of the god to whom the pre-Yahwistic temple at Jerusalem was devoted is less easy to establish. The name of the city is too old to offer a reliable clue—Shalem was a faded astral deity by the later Iron Age.[53] Two implements of the temple furnishings provide a more promising lead. Located in the temple court for all temple visitors to see stood the bronze Sea (1 Kgs 7:23–26, 44; 2 Chr 4:2–10) and the bronze Serpent known as Nehushtan (2 Kgs 18:4). The Serpent embodied Leviathan, "the fleeing serpent [nāḥāš bārīaḥ], . . . the twisting serpent [nāḥāš ʿáqallātôn]" (Isa 27:1), the mythological adversary defeated by Baal (see the Ugaritic Baal Cycle, where we find the exact same titles: bṯn brḥ bṯn ʿqltn).[54] The bronze Sea stands for Yamm, another enemy who lost the battle against Baal. In conformity with a common Near Eastern practice, the Jerusalem temple displayed images of divine enemies as a reminder of the power of the god who defeated them.[55] Apparently, then, the sanctuary had once been devoted to Baal. When the place was converted into a Yhwh temple, Baal's mythological exploits were transferred to Yhwh (see, e.g., Isa 27:1, 51:9–10; Ps 74:12–17, 89:10–12 [89:9–11]), as was the poetical identification of Mount Zion (the elevation on which the temple was built) with Baal's abode Mount Zaphon (Ps 48:3 [48:2]). Both at Bethel and in Jerusalem, then, the profile of Yhwh had inherited traits of other gods.

Was Yhwh the only god worshipped in the central sanctuary? So much would seem to be implied by the designation bêt yhwh, "temple of Yhwh," familiar from the Bible and found once or twice in ancient inscriptions.[56] The impression may be deceptive. In the fifth century BCE, the Jews at Elephantine (southern Egypt) also referred to the temple on their island as the "temple of Yaho."[57] Yet the Elephantine papyri make it clear that the temple also offered room to a number of other deities: Yaho's consort, known as Anat-Yaho or Anat-Bethel, plus the god Eshem-Bethel.[58]

Fig. 15. Figurine of the goddess Asherah. Reuben and Edith Hecht Museum, University of Haifa. (Wikimedia Commons, CC-BY-SA 3.0, https://creativecommons.org/licenses/by-sa/3.0/deed.en.)

This is not the place for an in-depth discussion of the "polytheism" of the Elephantine Jews, but the evidence from Persian Egypt shows that it is quite possible that the YHWH temples in the Northern and Southern Kingdoms housed symbols of other gods. Those gods were not regarded as "foreign" (*zār, nēkār*) but as members of YHWH's entourage. The principal other god in the state temples of Israel and Judah was a goddess, that is, YHWH's consort, Asherah (1 Kgs 15:13, 16:33; 2 Kgs 18:4, 23:6–7) (fig. 15).[59] Her cult stood under the official patronage of the queen mother (*gĕbîrâ*).[60] This division of responsibilities between king and queen mother mirrors the prominent role of women in the cult of the goddess (2 Kgs 23:7; Jer 44:15–19). Next to YHWH and his Asherah, there were, at least during some periods, other gods (2 Kgs 21:5, 23:4). Perhaps the prohibition to have no other gods *'al pānay* (Exod 20:3; Deut 5:7), literally, "across from me, facing me," refers to symbols or images of such other gods.[61] Many worshippers of the time would have said that those "other gods" were not really other gods but part of YHWH's entourage (consort, servants) or alter egos (El, Baal). It seemed only natural. Who has ever heard of a king living in his palace all by himself?

At times there were also political considerations that would lead the authorities to have the state temples offer hospitality to other gods. Treaties and alliances with other states were an important instrument in international politics. The advantages were similar to those offered by tribal covenants. In addition to vows of nonaggression and military aid, there was the obligation to mutually extradite fugitive slaves or culprits and to provide justice for each other's merchants and expatriates.[62] Elijah stayed in Sidonian territory (1 Kgs 17:7–10), and the woman from Shunem lived in Philistea (2 Kgs 8:1–6), because there were treaties between Israel and Tyre (sealed by a marriage with a Tyrian princess, 1 Kgs 16:29–33) and between Israel and Philistea (cf. 2 Kgs 1:2). Such treaties were ratified by the national gods, in commemoration of which the national temples would often have a copy of the treaty and a token presence of the other nation's god (1 Kgs 16:32–33).[63] In the royal temples, then, the national god YHWH would be accompanied by his consort, some divine servants and companions, and the politically opportune gods-in-residence.[64]

Temple: Function, Architecture, Organization

The temple was the domicile of the deity. It was the residence (*miškān*, Lev 17:4) where he dwelled (*šākan*, Zech 2:14–15, 8:3). The principal metaphors were "house" and "palace." The Jerusalem temple was known as "the house of YHWH" (*bêt yhwh*) or "the palace of YHWH" (*hêkal yhwh*).[65] The phrases were so much part of everyday language that few speakers realized they were using metaphors. But in reality, of course, the temple was *like* a house, or *like* a palace. What the temple in Jerusalem actually looked like has to be imagined on the basis of biblical and extrabiblical (Josephus) descriptions and contemporary Levantine temples such as those of Ain Dara and Tell Tayinat (fig. 16).[66]

Archaeological remains of the temples at Bethel and Jerusalem are lacking or inaccessible. The Jerusalem temple's architecture and its plan corresponded to the setup of a house (especially an elite house) or a palace, which meant it was divided into zones of graded seclusion (fig. 17).[67] The temple area as a whole was demarcated by an enclosure or precinct—what in Greek would be called a *temenos* (from the verb *temnō*, "cut off," i.e., cut off from the secular domain) and in Arabic a *haram*, a "sacred place" (*OED*).

Fig. 16. Remains of Iron Age temple from Tell Tayinat. (Wikimedia Commons, CC-BY-SA-4.0, https://creativecommons.org/licenses/by-sa/4.0/deed.en; photograph by Stephen Batiuk, Tayinat Archaeological Project.)

Inside the enclosure there was the "court" (*ḥāṣēr*), which was open to all worshippers. Here was the large altar for animal and vegetal sacrifices. The temple building itself consisted of three parts: an entry hall or anteroom (the *'ûlām;* in Jerusalem, ca. thirty-three feet wide and sixteen feet deep), leading up to the sanctuary proper (the *qōdeš* or *hêkāl;* in Jerusalem, ca. sixty-six feet deep), and, at the very back, the private chamber of the god (the *děbîr,* or "holy of holies"; in Jerusalem, ca. thirty-three feet deep). Inside the sanctuary was a table permanently provided with bread, ten lampstands, and a small incense altar (1 Kgs 7:48–49; Josephus, *J. W.* 5.216–218). In addition, there were several rooms to the sides of the building (Josephus, *J.W.* 5.220–221), used for a variety of purposes (offices, storage facilities, dining rooms, bedrooms).[68] To reach the innermost part of the temple—in the actual floor plan the very hind part—one had to pass four entrances: first one of the gates in the enclosure wall, then a flight of steps to the entry hall (Josephus, *J.W.* 5.207), the doors that gave access to the actual temple (1 Kgs 6:33–35), and finally the curtain and/or door that separated the holy of holies from the main room of the temple (Exod 26:31–34; Lev 16:12; 1 Kgs 6:31–32; Ezek 41:3; Josephus, *J.W.* 5.219). The spatial division represented a mounting order of intimacy with the deity. Whereas the court was open to all worshippers, only the high priest was allowed to enter behind the curtain, and then only once a year (on the Day of Atonement or Yom Kippur, Lev 16:11–17).

The various thresholds of the temple—whether marked by a gate, a flight of steps, a door, or a curtain—separated successive zones that each had its rules of entry. Guardians of the threshold (*šōmĕrê ḥassap*), a prestigious priestly function, were responsible for their observance (2 Kgs 12:10, 22:4, 23:4, 25:18; Jer 35:4, 52:24).[69] In this respect, the temple compares to a Persian palace (Esth 2:21, 6:2). The separation principle that informs the Near Eastern purity laws was fully operative. During the Hellenistic period, the inner court of the temple (referred to in Jer 36:10 as the "higher court" to distinguish it from the adjacent palace court) was inaccessible to non-Jews on account of its holiness (Acts 21:28–31; Josephus, *J.W.* 5.193–194).[70] Before the exile, the gate to this court was a public meeting place, where prophets might take their stand to address the crowd (Jer 7:2, 19:14, 26:2, 36:10) and where officials gathered for a public session (Jer 26:10).[71] Traders here sold sacrificial animals to temple visitors from out of town (Zech 14:21; Jer 7:21; Matt 21:12–13).[72] The temple court was the place where people came to pray, especially at the time of the morning and evening incense offerings (Luke 1:10). The temple building was accessible only to priests, who had to observe strict rules of purity. In keeping with the rule that on holy ground sandals had to be removed (Exod 3:5; Josh 5:15), the priests performed their duties barefoot.[73] Also, they wore clean linen garments, supplied to them by the guardian of the wardrobe (2 Kgs 22:14; cf. 10:22). The ultimate degree of holiness obtained in the private chamber of the god. The rare priest who was allowed inside felt inevitably inadequate and impure in the presence of the deity, even when every precaution had been taken (Isa 6:5).

Being the "house of God," the Jerusalem temple, just like the temples of Mesopotamia, Syria, and Egypt, was "holy" (e.g., Ps 5:8, 65:5, 93:5, 138:2).[74]

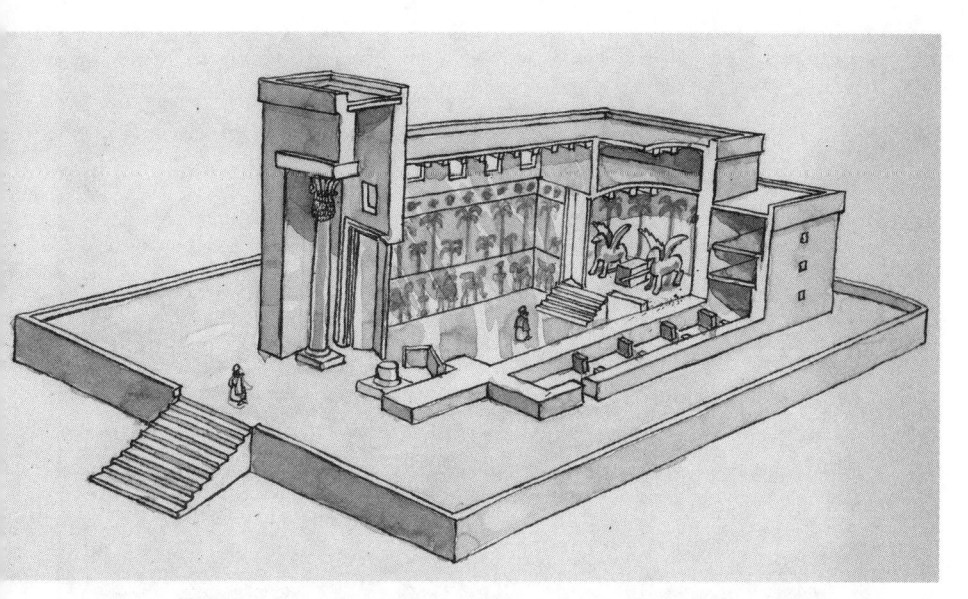

Fig. 17. Artist's impression of Solomon's Temple. (Drawing by Willem Zijlstra.)

The divine presence made it a sanctuary, also in the sense that it was a place of refuge and safety. Any worshipper who came and stayed in the temple court enjoyed, at least for a time, asylum. Temple visitors stood under the immediate protection of God, as many of the individual prayers in the book of Psalms proclaim: "Let me abide in your tent forever, / find refuge under the shelter of your wings" (Ps 61:5 [61:4], trans. NRSV). The "tent" is a poetic designation of the temple, with resonances of the archaic "tent of meeting" from the premonarchic period, and "the shelter of your wings" is an expression from the realm of family law. The man who "spread his wings" over a woman indicated by this gesture that he took her in marriage and, by the same token, under his protection (Ezek 16:8; Ruth 3:9). The "wings" are the fringes of the garment. Metaphorically, God spread the skirts of his robe (Isa 6:1) over the worshippers; they found themselves "in the shadow of his wings," that is, under his protection (Ps 17:8, 36:8, 57:2, 63:8), just as a wife stood "under the protection of" (*ina ṣilli;* literally, "in the shadow of") her husband, as Mesopotamian texts put it.[75] The sanctuary provided by the temple had a special meaning for those who went there for shelter from opponents. By grasping the horns of the altar in the temple court, the alleged offender enjoyed temporary immunity (1 Kgs 1:50–53) (fig. 18). Temporary, for God would not allow real offenders to go free. The temple administration would require the refugee to take an oath, after which the

Fig. 18. Horned altar, limestone, Beersheba, eighth century BCE. Israel Museum, Jerusalem. (Wikimedia Commons.)

priestly oracle by Urim and Thummim (to be discussed below) would bring a verdict of guilt or innocence (Exod 21:13–14; 1 Kgs 8:31–32).

Palace and temple have been described as the two "great organizations" of ancient Mesopotamia.[76] Though in Israel and Judah the scale of the temple was significantly smaller than that of the palace, the various functions of the temple and the volume of its staff justify the use of the phrase "great organization." In essence the temple is the household of the deity, just as the palace is the household of the king. But in addition to its main function of catering to the needs of the god, the temple had a number of secondary functions. Being the safest place of the kingdom, the temple also served as the national treasury and bank of savings (the *ʾôṣār*; 2 Sam 8:9–12; Josh 6:19, 24; 1 Kgs 7:51, 15:18; 2 Kgs 12:19; 2 Macc 3:10–15; 4 Macc 4:3; Josephus, *J.W.* 6.282).[77] Owing to the economic role of the temple, its staff included accountants (2 Kgs 12:11), money weighers (*šôqēl*; Isa 33:18, 46:6), "merchants" (*makkār*; 2 Kgs 12:6, 8), and clerks (Jer 36:10).[78] At times the temple was a court of law where the judicial role of the deity translated in a priestly verdict on the basis of an evaluation of the evidence in conjunction, if need be, with the administration of the oath and trial by ordeal (Deut 17:8–13, 21:5; 1 Kgs 21:8–14; Joshua 7; Psalm 17).[79] Some temples were also production centers of cold-pressed oil and woven textiles.[80] In addition, the temple served as armory (1 Kgs 14:28; 2 Kgs 11:10),[81] tax collection center (Mal 3:10; Neh 10:39–40, 13:12),[82] seat of the temple police (2 Kgs 11:1–20; Jer 29:26), prison ward (Jer 20:1–3, 29:24–28, 37:15–16), and place of asylum (Exod 21:13–14; 1 Kgs 1:50–53). It also offered facilities for dining (1 Sam 1:9 LXX, 9:22; Ezek 42:13), drinking (Jer 35:2), and staying overnight (2 Kgs 11:1–3). All those employed by the temple were "priests," but it is clear, from the variety of services they performed, that a narrowly spiritual understanding of their role is inadequate.

Images of YHWH?

YHWH resided in the temple—no doubt about it. But what was the mode of his presence, and how did it manifest itself? Since God was to be found in his private chamber, the holy of holies, the question boils down to the issue of the furnishings of the inner sanctum. Josephus (*J.W.* 5.219) bluntly says that "there was absolutely nothing inside." Perhaps that was true in his day, but in the monarchic period the cella did house several objects. Their identity, function, and form are not completely certain and may have changed over the course of four centuries.

The principal object housed in the cella was the ark (1 Kgs 8:1–9). It was a wooden chest (*'ărôn*, cf. Akkadian *arānu*, "chest, coffer, cashbox, coffin"), allegedly made by Moses and kept in a succession of tribal sanctuaries until David took it to Jerusalem. Careful analysis of the biblical record points to the historical existence of multiple arks.[83] Those were used as shrines of divine images, carried out in procession on religious high holy days, on which occasion the god might be invited "to open [his] shrine" and partake of the offerings.[84] We do not know what was in the ark at Jerusalem. Later tradition says the ark contained nothing but the stone tablets of the Ten Commandments (1 Kgs 8:9), but that is a theological speculation based on the idea that the Torah is the true embodiment of God. Though at one time the ark may have contained a sculpted stone, chances are it was empty. Elements in the biblical tradition intimate the ark served as God's throne (Jer 3:16–18) or footstool (1 Chr 28:2; Ps 99:5, 132:7). The description of Solomon's Temple says the ark was flanked by two huge cherubs (1 Kgs 6:23–30, 8:6–8)—winged fantasy animals modeled upon the *kurību*

Fig. 19. Cherubim throne from Cyprus, sixth century BCE. Kunsthistorisches Museum, Vienna. (Wikimedia Commons, CC-BY-SA-4.0, https://creativecommons .org/licenses/by-sa/4.0/deed.en.)

from Mesopotamia (fig. 19).[85] The standard liturgical phrase saying Yhwh is the one "seated upon the cherubim" (see, e.g., 1 Sam 4:4; 2 Sam 6:2; Isa 37:16) is best interpreted as a reference to the invisible presence of the deity. In this respect, a tenth-century BCE cult stand from Taanach having one register with cherubs flanking an empty space is suggestive (figs. 20 and 21).[86] Larger than life, the god did not fit the dimensions of the sanctuary. In Isaiah's vision, the hem of Yhwh's robe alone was enough to fill the temple (Isa 6:1). The king of the gods was the greatest of all—his throne was too big for a lesser deity.[87]

Figs. 20 and 21. Taanach cult stand. Israel Museum, Jerusalem. (Wikimedia Commons, CC-BY-SA-4.0, https://creativecommons.org/licenses/by-sa/4.0/deed.en [*left*]; drawing [*right*] by Willem Zijlstra.)

Most probably, then, the temple of Jerusalem symbolized Yhwh's presence by an empty throne in the cella. The practice was not without parallels outside Judah. Excavations around the cities of Tyre and Sidon, situated in the coastal zone the Greeks came to refer to as Phoenicia, have yielded several miniature divine thrones. They were votive objects. Most of them were "sphinx thrones," so called because winged lions flanked the seat on both sides. Some of them may have once held a divine image or symbol. Others, though, were clearly meant to remain empty.[88] The role of the throne as a kind of substitute of the divine image might be reflected, too, in the designation "Lord of the throne" (*mr' myt*[*b'*]), used in a Palmyra inscription to refer to the otherwise anonymous "good and merciful" god.[89] Another

Fig. 22. Storm god riding a bull; stela from Arslan Tash. Louvre, Paris.
(Wikimedia Commons, CC-BY-2.0 FR, https://creativecommons.org/
licenses/by-sa/2.0/fr/deed.en.)

parallel comes from Nabatea, Jordan, where the divine throne (*mwtb*) was an object of special veneration.[90] Though it is quite possible that images of YHWH were also in Judah and Israel, there is no evidence that the royal temple at Jerusalem had one.[91] To worshippers, YHWH's presence was real—in their eyes the throne was not empty—but the furnishings of the inner sanctum *suggested* divine presence without actually *representing* it by a statue.[92]

The tradition in the Northern Kingdom was different. The gold-plated "ephod" that Gideon had set up in his hometown Ophrah (Judg 8:27) was, as commentators generally agree, a statue (for another occurrence, see 1 Sam 21:10).[93] The context suggests it was devoted to YHWH (Judg 8:23). What the object of worship actually looked like is unknown, but its size was serious since seventeen hundred shekels of gold were used for its production (Judg 8:22–27). A less sizable amount of silver—two hundred shekels—went into the production of the image in the domestic chapel (a *bêt 'ĕlōhîm*) of Micah, a man from the hill country of Ephraim (Judg 17:1–6). Here, too, the statue functioned in the context of the cult of YHWH (Judg 17:3, 13). According to the biblical narrative, Micah's statue ended up in Dan—which turns the tale into another origin story of the bull image of Dan (Judg 18:29–31; 1 Kgs 12:29–30; cf. Amos 8:14). In the royal temple at Bethel, worshippers venerated YHWH by focusing their devotion on a gold-plated bull image (1 Kgs 12:28–29; Exod 32:1–6). The bronze bulls from Hazor and northern Manasseh show that the icon was not new to the area.[94] Did it represent YHWH? In the Canaanite iconographic repertoire, there are images of Baal riding on a bull (fig. 22). This suggests to some scholars that the bull images of Bethel and Dan represented YHWH's vehicle rather than the god himself.[95] It is an interesting theory that suits the aniconic ideology that became the norm in Judah, but the interpretation lacks a solid basis. In the Israelite tradition, YHWH was "the Bull of Jacob" (*'ăbîr ya'ăqôb;* Gen 49:24–25; Ps 132:2, 5; Isa 49:26, 60:16) or "our Bull."[96] Those who were kissing the bull icon (Hos 13:2; cf. 1 Kgs 19:18) were expressing their devotion to YHWH, not to his vehicle. Eventually, voices would be raised against the cult of images (Hosea). But until the mid-eighth century BCE, in the Northern Kingdom the veneration of images was apparently uncontested.[97]

Priests and Prophets

As God's son by covenant, the king had to serve and honor the deity the way a son was to serve and honor his father (cf. Mal 1:6). The duties of a king were many, but his first responsibility was to see to it that "the table of Yhwh" was well-provided.[98] The sacrificial cult was the province of priests (Mal 1:7), but they brought the offerings in the name of the king. The monarch was the head of the priests. This was the rule in Israel and Judah, just as it was in all the surrounding countries. In certain parts of the Near East, the king claimed the priestly title. Assyrian kings, for instance, referred to themselves as šangû, "chief administrator of the temple."[99] It was an honorific title meant to convey that the king organized and carried out the cult of the gods of the nation.[100] At Sidon, kings presented themselves as "priest" (khn) of Astarte, chief goddess of their city-state.[101] On solemn occasions, the Israelite king could be called a priest too. As the enthronement oracle says, "You are priest forever, a rightful king by My decree" (Ps 110:4 NJPS). But on the whole, "priest" is rarely used as a royal title. Only on special occasions would kings themselves act as priests. Examples include David, clad in a priestly garment and bringing sacrifice when he led the ark to Jerusalem (2 Sam 6:12–18); Solomon, at the dedication of the temple (1 Kgs 8:63); Jeroboam I, who ascended the Bethel altar at the institution of the northern New Year festival in autumn (1 Kgs 12:32–13:6); Jehu, who offered sacrifice in the Baal temple at Samaria (2 Kgs 10:25); and Ahaz, who inaugurated a new altar by bringing the offerings himself (2 Kgs 16:10–18). Ordinarily, however, the priestly functions of the king were delegated to professional priests. These "priests"—kōhănîm is the Hebrew term (singular kōhēn)—constituted the main personnel of the sacred premises.[102]

The priests at the state temples (border sanctuaries and central temple) were civil servants. Those in the highest ranks—most notably the high priest—owed their position to a royal appointment and could be dismissed by the king as well (cf. 1 Kgs 2:26–27, 4:4, 12:31–32). By their very office priests stood in the service of God, but they were also "servants" of the king, as Babylonian priests candidly said on their personal seals.[103] The high priest took his orders from the monarch (1 Kgs 1:32–40; 2 Kgs 16:10–16) and was expected to report to the monarch when anything irregular happened in the temple, such as a prophecy that could be interpreted as a call to insubordination (Amos 7:10). The leading priest's family and the royal house were often connected by marriage (e.g., 2 Kgs 11:1–8), a fact that illustrates both the powerful position of the high priest and his close ties with the king. Though priests were remunerated with a portion of the sacrifices (Josh 13:14; 1 Sam 2:12–14; Hos 4:8) and a percentage of the temple taxes (the tithes, Deut 26:12), those in the employ of state temples also had the usufruct of a parcel of the royal lands (1 Kgs 2:26–27; Jer 32:6–15, 37:12; Amos 7:17; cf. Gen 47:22 for Egypt).[104] There was no real separation of powers between the sacred and the secular. Clergy and monarchy were often as close in early Israel and Judah as they were in late medieval Europe. The dependence between priests and king was mutual, although the absolute authority of the monarch was not in doubt. It made it very difficult for a priest to speak out against the king to whom he owed his office.

In the view of later historians—more specifically the editors of the Deuteronomistic History, running from Joshua to the books of Kings—the priests who served in the state-sponsored temples came from different backgrounds:[105] "And [King Jeroboam] made sanctuaries and appointed priests from the general population, who were not Levites" (1 Kgs 12:31, cf. 13:33). This is a biased presentation of the past. In the eyes of the Deuteronomists, the practices allegedly introduced by Jeroboam I were a deviant form of religion whereas Levites were legitimate priests, so they concluded Jeroboam must have appointed non-Levite priests. He possibly did, but there is no reason to assume he vetoed Levites. On the contrary, Levites were known as ritual specialists and in that capacity were highly appreciated as temple personnel. Micah from the hill country of Ephraim had appointed one of his sons as priest in his private temple but did not hesitate to engage a Levite when the occasion presented itself (Judg 17:5–13, 18:14–20).[106] One of the oldest, if not *the* oldest, characterization of the Levites calls them "devoted" (*ḥāsîd*, which could also be translated as "loyal") to Yhwh and in possession of the Urim and Thummim (Deut 33:8)—the oracular means by which Levites could establish guilt or nonguilt and, by extension, elicit information about hidden things in general, such as the future. The Levites were also staunch Yahwists, and as such, supporters of royal religion in Judah and Israel, which promoted Yhwh as the god of the territory. In fact, it is likely the Levites played a significant part in the spread of the worship of Yhwh.[107] They could be found throughout Palestine, without a tribal territory of their own, for which reason some scholars like to speak of a "Levitical diaspora."[108] The striking prominence of Egyptian names among members of their lineage (Moses, Aaron, Hophni, Phinehas, Hur, Merari, Pashhur) suggests they had a background in a region within the orbit of Egyptian culture—such as the wilderness of Edom. They could well have been the channel by which the wilderness traditions came to be part of Israel's historical narrative.[109]

Historically, the Levites were not a tribe but a priestly guild or a religious order. Over time, however, they came to be assimilated to a tribe. The gradual transformation of the Levites into a lineage group is in line with the prevalence of the principle of hereditary priesthood in Israel and Judah. Though in antiquity many professions were passed on from father to son, the case of priests is different from normal family traditions. The purity that was mandatory for the holder of the priestly office came to be ascribed to the lineage. Purity became inherited by birth, and the priests developed into a social caste much like the Indian Brahmins. There were various priestly lineages, the Levites and the Zadokites being the more familiar but certainly not the only ones. It is to be expected that different priestly families had different family traditions, some of which must have pertained to matters of religion and ritual.[110] Conflicts between different priestly houses left traces in the biblical record, but the reconstruction of their historical disputes is a delicate affair (Exodus 32; Numbers 12; 1 Sam 2:27–36). One consequence of the heredity of the priesthood was a surplus of priestly candidates, leading to the practice of priestly duties being performed by turn (Luke 1:8); rotation rosters of priestly personnel were not unknown in Babylonia either.[111] Some men who came from priestly families were better known for other activities than for their role as priests (the prophet Jeremiah is an example).

Another category of religious functionaries that would regularly perform at royal temples consisted of prophets. Since most of these men and women have their historical background in local religion, a more extensive discussion of their activities is given in the next chapter. Here, however, it is necessary to point out the significant role that prophets often played in the life of an Israelite king—in both the Northern and the Southern Kingdoms. Many prophets would show up at state temples to speak "the word of God," as they themselves would say. Some of them were likely temple prophets (Habakkuk may well have been one), some made the rounds of sanctuaries (Samuel, Elisha), and some would occasionally go there to deliver their message (Amos, Jeremiah).[112] For the king, it was essential to have the support of prophets. Alongside revelatory dreams and the priestly oracle, prophets were a major channel of communication with God (1 Sam 28:6). At the same time, the prophet's stance toward the king and his actions would often give an inkling of public opinion. Unlike priests, prophets were independent. Some had their own sources of income, and some lived from gifts (Num 22:7; 1 Kgs 13:7, 14:3; 2 Kgs 5:15, 8:8), but it was unusual for an Israelite prophet to "eat at the table" of the king (as is said about the "prophets" of Baal and Asherah, "who eat at Jezebel's table," 1 Kgs 18:19; for the expression, see also 1 Kgs 2:7). Dissent and contestation, and other forms of criticism of the king's politics or behavior, hardly ever penetrated the walls of the palace unless they were voiced by a prophet (see, e.g., 2 Sam 12:1–14). In the latter case, it was hard to distinguish the voice of God from the voice of the people.[113] At court and in circles tied to the court, feelings about prophets were ambivalent. Officials might speak disparagingly about the prophet as a "madman" (2 Kgs 9:11; Jer 29:26) but also feared his influence and the impact of his words. Owing to his status, a prophet of fame might have direct access to the king and his army commander (2 Kgs 4:13).

On two kinds of occasion especially, prophets played a prominent part in the affairs of the state. The one concerns the proclamation of the divine mandate of the king, both during the period leading up to his ascension to the royal office and during the annual renewal of his rule; the other was in situations of warfare. When several pretendants were vying for the throne, endorsement by a prophet of influence could make all the difference (2 Kgs 9:1–14). All over the Near East, kings claimed that the gods had elevated them to the throne.[114] Such royal propaganda echoed the prophetic oracles that the king had received on his way to kingship, and that were recycled and updated at national celebrations of the New Year festival. In the Bible, some of those oracles survive as "frozen prophecies" in the Psalms (Ps 2:7–9, 89:20–38, 110:1, 132:11–18). Considering the close connection between the royal mandate and success in warfare, it comes as no surprise to find that many of these oracles addressed to the king cast him in the role of warrior (Ps 2:9, 89:20–26, 110:1). Oracles of encouragement and divine promises of victory were a fixed ingredient of Near Eastern warfare, as is clear from references in the inscriptions of King Zakkur of Hamath, Neo-Assyrian prophecies, and royal inscriptions, as well as a host of biblical passages.[115] Prophetic performances holding out the prospect of victory, with a choice of rhetoric designed to galvanize the troops, were likely to occur on the eve of a campaign (see, e.g., 1 Kgs 22:6–28) or just before a particular battle (2 Kgs 3:11–20). Kings might have mixed feelings about prophets, but they could not do without them. They were, in a way, the real "chariots and horsemen of Israel" (2 Kgs 2:12, 13:14).

The Life of a Priest

All priests at the state temples served under the authority of the high priest, his adjunct, and the triumvirate of the "guardians of the threshold" (2 Kgs 25:18 // Jer 52:24). Since they worked on the premises of the god's palace, they had to observe a strict etiquette. Its rules, written and unwritten, are customarily referred to as purity prescriptions. That term echoes the biblical terminology but fails to convey the notion of propriety. Priests had to be clean, well-groomed, dressed in proper clothes, and in possession of a pleasant appearance because otherwise the deity might take offense. The purity rules are court etiquette. Servants of the god had to be physically unblemished (Lev 21:16–23). Their heads were not to be shaven, but their hair had to be properly trimmed (Ezek 44:22); the rule was similar in Mesopotamia, where it led to the presence of temple barbers.[116] Priests wore light garments, normally linen, so they would not sweat (Exodus 28; Ezek 44:18). These clothes were provided by the temple wardrobe, whose supervisor was likely responsible for their cleaning as well (2 Kgs 10:22, 22:14).[117] Priests did not need to be celibate. The married state was compatible with their professional purity, though they had to be circumspect in their choice of marriage partner (no prostitutes, no divorcees; Lev 21:7). While priests were on duty, alcohol was not permitted—not so much for reasons of purity, it seems, but so their ability to distinguish between sacred and profane was not impaired (Lev 10:8–11; Ezek 44:21).

Though priests performed a wide variety of tasks, consonant with the wide array of secondary functions of the temple, their primary duties were twofold: (1) they had to provide the patron god of the state with all the services that would secure his continued presence at the sanctuary and benevolent patronage of the king and his realm, and (2) they had to provide instruction to the population and the king about the will of God, in matters of both general conduct and strategic choices. The first duty required the scrupulous performance of the sacrificial cult, which included all kinds of offerings to be presented in the proper ways and at the proper times. The second duty required the priests to give *tôrâ*, "instruction," for which they could rely on traditional lore about morality and purity rules, on the one hand, and on consultation of the deity by means of the Urim and Thummim, on the other. Priests were religious specialists. They had been trained in the performance of ritual, in knowledge about correct and incorrect behavior, and in the technique of oracular inquiry. In what follows we discuss the role of priests in the performance of sacrificial cult, the communication of torah, and the consultation of the oracle.

The essence of the sacrificial cult in the Near East has been defined as "the care and feeding of the gods."[118] The underlying idea is that the worshippers of the time thought of their gods, in an anthropomorphic manner, as though they were human potentates whose every will had to be satisfied so as to keep them in good spirits. To modern ears, this may sound like a rather crude conception of divinity. It may be helpful here to distinguish between the inherent logic of the sacrificial cult, on the one hand, and the meaning it could assume in the perception of worshippers, on the other. As for the logic, the use of such terms as *lehem*, "food," and *rêaḥ nîḥōaḥ*, "soothing odor," both frequent in sacrificial prescriptions (see, e.g., Leviticus 21; Lev 22:25; Num 28:1–6), indicates that the offerings of meat, salt, wine, and bread were designed to serve as food for the deity, whereas the burning of incense was to put him in a pleasant mood (cf. Prov 27:9; Tob 6:17). Also the rhythm of the sacrifices—once in the morning, once in the evening (see, e.g., Num 28:3–8)—corresponds to the Mediterranean custom of two meals a day. The metaphor that informs the proceedings is that of the ceremonial meals at the royal court. In this respect, the sacrificial cult in Israel is at home during the monarchic period. On the principle *do ut des* ("I give so that you will give"), the offerings were meant to create reciprocity, so as to obtain the continued presence and benevolence of the deity. Sacrifice on the principle *do ut abeas* ("I give so that you will go away") was not at home in the royal temples. As for the feelings the sacrificial cult inspired in worshippers, they are bound to have been diverse. To some the burning of incense was a means to dispel the foul mood of the deity (1 Sam 26:19), while others thought of the fragrant smoke as a symbol of their prayers ascending to heaven (Ps 141:2; cf. Rev 8:4–5). In general we have no way of knowing what went on in the minds of those who performed the sacrifices nor of those who watched. What we do know is that, in spite of the critique of primitive conceptions of sacrifice (e.g., Amos 5:21–25; Ps 50:8–13), the dutiful performance of the prescribed offerings continued to be a major concern in postexilic Judah and early Judaism (e.g., Mal 1:6–14). In the end, what mattered was the scrupulous observance of the commandments— whatever the original meaning of the act.

One aspect of the sacrificial regime deserves separate mention. It concerns the occasional offerings brought to purify individuals or the community, including inanimate objects contaminated by impurity, especially the temple and its furnishings (e.g., Exod 29:35–37). The most common term for the relevant sacrifice is *ḥaṭṭā't*, derived from *ḥiṭṭē'*, "to purify," whereas the term for the ritual operation is *kippēr*, "to wipe away, to wipe clean." The ceremony of Yom Kippur (Day of Atonement) owes its name to this verb. An old tradition, already found in the Septuagint, interprets the *ḥaṭṭā't* as "sin-offering" (Greek *hamartia*) because the word also has the meaning "sin" (from the verb *ḥāṭā'*, "to miss, to go wrong, to sin"). The fact that the *ḥaṭṭā't* is prescribed upon recovery from childbirth (Leviticus 12), at the termination of the Nazirite vow (Num 6:13–20), or at the dedication of a new altar (Lev 8:15; Exod 29:36–37) shows that the offering has little to do with the cultic reparation of a moral or religious fault. It confers or restores purity.[119] Impurity originates in liminal situations. It is intimately connected with the separation principle. Birth is a moment of passage, and so is death; the end of a period of consecration and the reinsertion into ordinary life are moments of passage (e.g., Num 6:13–20; Lev 14:19); inauguration of a sacred object is by definition a moment of passage; and so is the transition from the profane to the sacred (Isa 6:1–7). In all of these cases there is a need for ritual cleansing. In the temples of Israel and Judah, this cleansing was performed by priests, occasionally as the need arose and annually at the beginning of the New Year (Yom Kippur, Leviticus 16; Lev 23:27–28, *yôm kippurîm*).[120] The rite normally involved aspersion with the blood of the sacrificial victim because its blood was believed to have the power to purify. This kind of sacrifice, then, had little to do with the daily offerings or the killing of a domesticated animal in covenant ceremonies.

The priestly concern for purity might seem a bit like a collective and irrational fear of dirt and defilement (mysophobia). That, however, would be a misleading association. Purity is about boundaries and their transgression, compartments and their blurring, and the principle of separation—everything in its proper place. Similar principles underlay the moral and religious instruction the priests had to impart. The priestly *tôrôt* (*tôrâ*, "instruction," is the singular) could concern technicalities of the purity rules, such as the way in which impurity was transmitted (Hag 2:11–13); but the main body of this teaching consisted of variations on a handful of basic moral concepts. We know these moral rules as prohibitions from the Decalogue: "You shall not murder. You shall not commit adultery. You shall not steal. You shall not bear false witness against your neighbor" (Exod 20:13–16; Deut 5:17–20). These commandments are very similar the so-called temple *tôrôt*, that is, the priestly moral instructions for admission to the temple.[121] Echoes of such instructions are found in a number of liturgical texts (Psalm 15; Ps 24:3–6, 50:18–19, 81:9–11) and prophetic texts (e.g., Isa 33:14–16; Hos 4:2; Jer 7:9). Was a written summary of this priestly torah on display in Israelite temples, as a warning to visitors? An early reference to God's handwritten Torah, made in connection with places of worship, suggests as much (Hos 8:12).[122] But to most men and women who worshipped in the temple, torah was an oral genre. Their reading skills were often rudimentary, and they came to seek torah "from the mouth" of the priest (Mal 2:7).

The moral instruction that priests were expected to give could be summed up in a small set of apodictic prohibitions ("You shall not . . ."). Those prohibitions were the core of what would become, in the course of the literary tradition, the "Ten Words," the only part of the Torah purportedly "written with the finger of God" (Exod 31:18, cf. 32:15–16; Deut 4:13; 5:19; 9:10; 10:2, 4).[123] A literary analysis of the Decalogue suggests that its precepts go back to old tribal wisdom sayings.[124] The Ten Commandments might indeed be said to reflect tribal ethics in the sense that they provide rules of conduct valid only within the tribe. Within the tribe, murder, adultery, theft, and false accusations—especially allegations under oath—are totally out of place, for they would be a breach of trust among brothers and erode tribal unity. Outside the tribe, matters are different. In intertribal warfare, killing was the purpose and plunder was the rule. Also the prohibition to worship "other gods" fits the tribal context. Originally formulated as an interdiction to have a "foreign" god (*'ēl nēkār, 'ēl zār;* see Ps 81:10 [81:9]), it is a condemnation of the cult of gods from other tribes. All of these moral and religious interdictions are based on a logic similar to the one that informs the purity rules. Everything in its proper place. Within the tribe the invisible boundaries—created by ties of blood, covenant, and inheritance—are not to be transgressed, nor is the boundary separating the tribe from the rest of the world. In the monarchic period, the tribal ethics were elevated to the status of a national constitution, placed under the authority of the patron god of the state, and taught by priests in the royal sanctuaries. The nation was the new tribe.

The role of the priests as instructors was not limited to the teaching of moral torah and purity rules. Priests also dispensed oracular responses. Whereas their knowledge of torah was the fruit of training in principles of morality and the logic of contamination and cleansing, their ability to provide answers to queries about hidden things (blame or innocence, the future, the cause of misfortune, and the like) had been acquired by learning how to read the oracle. It was not a gift but a technique. The oracle involved the manipulation of several small objects kept in a pouch stitched to the garments of the priest. It was known as the Urim and Thummim (at times, for short, as "Urim"), and the pouch for the Urim and Thummim was called the ephod (the linen ephod, to be distinguished from the solid ephod).[125] Although the particulars of the Urim and Thummim oracle are yet to be elucidated, it is clear that its outcome could be only one of three possibilities: "yes," "no," or "inconclusive." This has several implications. One is that the clients who came for an oracle had to phrase their questions in a way that allowed a "yes" or "no" answer (for examples, see 1 Sam 23:9–12, 30:7–8). Another is that the priest must have performed the oracular inquiry a number of times in order to be sure that a "yes" was really "yes," and a "no" really "no." If there was no consistency in the outcome, the result was inconclusive, which was taken to mean that God refused to answer the inquiry (1 Sam 28:6). The technique of the oracle was a variation on the more popular practice of casting the lot (*gôrāl*, Greek *klēros*), where the outcome was also interpreted as a decision from Yhwh (Prov 16:33).[126] The most instructive passage on the Urim oracle is found in 1 Sam 14:41–42 (reading based on the LXX):[127]

> Then Saul said, "O Lord God of Israel, why have you not answered your servant today? If this guilt is in me or in my son Jonathan, O Lord God of Israel, give Urim; but if this guilt is in your people Israel, give Thummim." And Jonathan and Saul were indicated by the lot, but the people were cleared. Then Saul said, "Cast the lot between me and my son Jonathan." And Jonathan was taken. (NRSV)

The outcome of the oracle, then, is either Urim or Thummim—those are not the names of the lots but designate the result.[128] Apparently, the original use of the oracle was to determine guilt or nonguilt, which is why priests spoke of the "verdict [*mišpāṭ*] of the Urim before the Lord" (Num 27:21).[129] Arguably, "Urim" stood for guilt (derived from the verb *'ārar*, "to accurse," the curse being triggered by an untruthful oath of innocence; cf. Num 5:11–31), whereas "Thummim" stood for blamelessness (from the verb *tāmam*, "to be whole, blameless"). Because the priest "cast" (*hippîl*) the lots, the procedure is usually thought to have involved two stones. But no text in the Bible says the Urim and Thummim were stones. It is just as possible that the procedure required the use of a dice or the throwing of ankle bones (astragali) of sheep or goats.[130]

Compared to the oracle practice in Mesopotamia—where divination manuals show that the reading of portents had become an arcane science—the oracular consultation in Israel was almost primitive.[131] It reflects a society in which the royal bureaucracy was still in its infancy. For all really important matters, the "inspired decisions" came from the lips of the king (Prov 16:10 NRSV). The Hebrew term is *qesem*, which normally refers to the oracle (NJPS translates "magic"). Projected onto the divine realm, it was YHWH who gave the yes/no verdict, without the intervention of scholars specialized in divinatory lore. The fact that priests performed the oracular inquiry merely shows that their instruction (torah) embraced both knowledge from tradition and knowledge obtained by direct consultation of the deity.

The King as Army Commander and Defender of the Oppressed

In the image of God, peerless warrior, and supreme judge, the chief duties of the king, next to his responsibility for the temple cult, required him to lead the troops into battle and to provide justice for his people. He was, by virtue of his office, commander-in-chief and chief justice. The parallel between king and god is striking. Just as YHWH "goes out before" the warriors to "fight" for them (Deut 1:30; 2 Sam 5:24), so the king is to "go out before" his people to "fight" their battles (1 Sam 8:20). And just as God "judges his people" (Ps 50:4, 135:14), so the king is to "judge [God's] people with righteousness" (Ps 72:2). Royal propaganda and rhetoric? Only in part. While many kings spent most of their time in the palace, their schedule dictated that, come spring, they went out to do battle (2 Sam 11:1; cf. 1 Kgs 20:22, 26; 2 Kgs 13:20). And in their daily routine, the morning was the time they would receive people in the audience hall and arbitrate in cases brought to them for a final verdict (Ps 101:8; Jer 21:12). Both warfare and the administration of justice were sacred duties, in which the king acted as deputy of God. God was the ultimate shepherd of his people, and his anointed king was to be the manifestation and incarnation of God's rule. As might be expected, the reality was often more prosaic than the lofty language of royal ideology suggests.

The king's role as commander-in-chief is intimately related to the origins of royal rule in Israel. The monarchy came about because tribal leaders elected a successful warlord from their midst to be their leader in battle. When warlords became kings, military prowess and victories continued to be a cornerstone of their rule. Competition for land and resources was deemed to be the natural state between nations, the way it formerly had been between tribes. Those that were not allies by covenant were enemies—potentially if not in fact. As in earlier times, military conflicts had a religious dimension because the patron gods of competing states were waging a battle for supremacy. Also, for the king, warfare was a duty not only for the protection of the realm but for its extension. Battles were still "battles for YHWH" (1 Sam 25:28; Num 21:14), and the incorporation by force of foreign territory meant an addition to the realm of the deity. With God's help, the king was to push the borders of his domain ever more toward the horizon, as the oracles delivered at his enthronement proclaimed (Ps 2:8, 110:2).[132] The notion that warfare in Israel was only defensive, though often true in practice, should not be taken as its programmatic purpose, since ideologically wars were waged to conquer new territory for God.

One of the innovations of the monarchy was the creation of a standing army, not in lieu of but to complement the people's militia (2 Sam 11:1, 24:9).[133] Led by a professional army commander (*śar haṣṣābā*; see, e.g., 1 Sam 14:50; 2 Sam 8:16; 1 Kgs 1:19; 2 Kgs 4:13), the soldiers owed absolute loyalty to the king. They were his personal guard and often had their living quarters close to the palace, in the city's citadel (2 Sam 11:1–13). Every one of them had to take a loyalty oath to the king, a practice known from other places in the Near East.[134] The conditional curses of this oath are echoed in the curse King David uttered against his army commander Joab, after Joab had betrayed his trust: "may the house of Joab never be without one who has a discharge, or who is leprous, or who holds a spindle, or who falls by the sword, or who lacks food" (2 Sam 3:29 NRSV). Impurity brought about by a physical ailment—a morbid discharge or a skin disease—disqualified one for battle (Num 5:2); an effeminate—a spindle is typically a woman's attribute—is a horror to soldiers (the same curse in the Hittite soldiers' oath).[135] Dishonor, shame, defeat, and starvation are the lot of the deserter or defector—the very opposite, that is, of the ideals of masculine warrior culture. The curse throws into relief the almost obsessive concern with honor in warfare, quite in keeping with the shame culture of the time. To find death at the hands of woman was much worse than an honorable defeat (Judg 5:24–27, 9:53–54; Jdt 13:15). And perhaps it was preferable to have died rather than to be maimed or turned into an object of ridicule (Judg 1:4–7; 2 Sam 10:4–5).

Although the king was the army's commander-in-chief, he would often not participate in the battle in person, preferring the pleasures of the palace to the discomforts of the military camp (2 Sam 11:1).[136] When he did go out with the troops, the hardships he had to endure were usually more bearable than those of ordinary soldiers. Like the rest of the military, the king would spend the night in a tent, but his accommodation was more luxurious than the standard-issue tent. In his tent, Holofernes had a bed with a canopy woven with purple and gold, decked with emeralds and other precious stones. There were silver lamps and silver tableware, and on the menu were delicacies and wine (Jdt 10:20–23, 12:1). Though the tale of Holofernes and Judith is fiction from a later period, it does reflect old customs. The description of an Aramean king having a drinking party with his allies on the very eve of battle (1 Kgs 20:12) is bound to reflect a common reality. It conveys a rather different image than that of the king restoring his strength by "drinking from the stream by the path" (Ps 110:7)—the idealized portrait of the warrior who prefers clear water to beer or wine.[137] At times, the king put in an appearance at the last moment when it was clear the battle had been won and the beleaguered city was about to surrender (2 Sam 12:26–31). Dressed in royal attire—a diadem (*nēzer*) on his head and a metal clasp (*'eṣ'ādâ*) on his arm (2 Sam 1:10, cf. 2 Kgs 11:12; read *'eṣ'ādôt* for *'ēdût*)—the king made a solemn entry and so claimed the victory for himself.[138] The ideology of royal warfare did not always match the realities of the battlefield.

Aside from his role as commander-in-chief, the king was also the highest judicial authority. He stood at the pinnacle of the judiciary system, to which the lower courts—such as that by the elders at the gate—were subordinate.[139] The king's office obliged him to destroy "all the wicked in the land" (Ps 101:8) and to champion the cause of the poor and the needy and those with no helper (Ps 72:12–14). In his capacity as judge, the king was believed to pronounce God's judgments (Ps 72:1). The ideology was common to the Near East.[140] The reality differed from place to place. In popular legend, the kings of Israel and Judah tended to listen with a willing ear to all those who came to them for help (2 Sam 14:1–11; 2 Kgs 6:26–30, 8:1–6). Did people come to the palace for an audience? The Ugaritic Aqhat legend says the king gave his verdicts "at the entrance of the city gate, among the leaders sitting on the threshing floor."[141] The very same location "on the threshing floor at the entrance of the gate" is mentioned as audience place of the Israelite king (1 Kgs 22:10; cf. Jer 38:7). It is likely that both the audience hall in the palace and the entrance of the city gate could serve as the place where the king rendered justice.[142] Whether he normally did so in person is unclear. The monarch could send deputies to hear the cases of his subjects; the passage that mentions them suggests this was standard procedure (2 Sam 15:3).[143] But whether in person or through delegates, the king was to assure there was justice for all those who had a suit (2 Sam 15:4). This was a foundational aspect of his rule. His throne was a "throne of judgment" (*kissē' dîn*, Prov 20:8).

The legal basis for the royal verdicts, just as for the jurisdiction by the lower courts, was the common law. Not in a single case is there reference to a law code that the king or his advisors might consult. The king consulted with himself, and his verdicts were taken to be proof of his extraordinary wisdom. Because of the insight God has granted him, the king "cannot err in judgment" (Prov 16:10 NJPS). To demonstrate his legal acumen, the Babylonian king Hammurabi had his verdicts set in stone to serve as a reference for future generations. Though not a legal code in the Roman sense of the term, it was a step toward the codification of casuistic law.[144] Scholars have claimed that in Israel, too, the role of the palace in the administration of justice led to the creation of law codes. There is no indication, however, that the texts in question (such as Exod 21:18–22:16) were designed as law codes or ever used as such. What they more likely attest to is the scholarly study of customary law, as part of the training of royal and temple officials.[145] Law was a scribal genre that flourished in the shade of the palace. As such, it offers an illustration of another facet of the cultural impact of the monarchy. Owing to the accumulation of capital by the palace, in combination with the need for educated civil servants, the scribal training was institutionalized. In addition to such subjects as formal letter writing and bookkeeping, the curriculum included wisdom (Prov 25:1) and law—itself a branch of wisdom. Nobody liked the taxes imposed by the palace (1 Sam 8:11–18), but the institution of the monarchy did undeniably contribute to the further development of the legal culture of the time. Although the antimonarchic sentiment in Israel never fully subsided, nobody really wanted a return to the days when "there was no king in Israel and all people did what was right in their own eyes" (Judg 17:6, 21:25).

3 Local Religion

After the advent of the monarchy, the vast majority of the population lived in towns and villages, where family and neighborhood were the anchors of identity, and where the necessity to make a decent living was the dominant concern. Most of the time, the palace felt far away. People spent their lives within a perimeter of a mile or two around their homes, moving every day between their houses inside town and their fields outside town. Only on special occasions did they travel longer distances—when they were drafted for military service, or to visit a regional fair or a famous prophet, or to make a pilgrimage to some holy place. But most of the time they stayed home or close to home. What mattered to them was their position in the local community. With an average population of between three hundred and five hundred people, the towns of Israel and Judah were small.[1] Nobody was anonymous, and every face was familiar. When the city was large enough to have neighborhoods, those were mostly inhabited by related families. Though society no longer qualified as tribal, some of the tribal values continued to regulate social interaction—just as the nomadic lifestyle, for example, left a legacy of set phrases and expressions ("to your tents, O Israel!," 1 Kgs 12:16). Blood solidarity and family honor were important. Not everybody was a friend. The rule that you should bring back your enemy's ox or donkey that had gone astray (Exod 23:4) implies that neighbors could be enemies. Some of the individual complaints in the book of Psalms give an inkling of the slander and backbiting that could be going on: "How long, you people, shall my honor suffer shame? / How long will you love vain words, and seek after lies? (Ps 4:3 [4:2] NRSV).[2] The language may seem a bit too grandiloquent for a dispute between neighbors, but loss of social status in a small community could be dramatic for the victim.

Local religion is not a separate phase of Israelite religion but offers a picture of what religion consisted of and meant for the peasant population of the many towns and villages that dotted the Palestinian countryside. The people were citizens of a state and owed loyalty to the monarch. To them, however, the state was almost an abstraction, and the king a figure of fairytales. Their concerns were this year's harvest, the future of their family, the way the neighbors spoke of them, and whether or not they would be able to pay off their debts. Though they did not really think of religion as an instrument, they practiced it as a means to protect themselves against the vagaries of the climate, to enhance their chances of having offspring, to keep away disease, to promote their standing in the community, to streamline and smoothen the transitions of human life, and to keep in touch with the ancestors below. Those and a host of smaller concerns informed religion at a local level. This was domestic religion, family religion, folk religion, popular religion—the one label is perhaps not as fortunate as the other, but the common thrust is clear. Because of the nature of the written sources, local religion has suffered from the stigma of superstition and deviancy. In historical reality, however, it was as much part of the bigger picture of Israelite religion as royal religion was. There is no good reason to relegate it to the margins.

Towns and Local Sanctuaries

In order to obtain an accurate image of local religion it helps to keep in mind the living conditions of the bulk of the population. Most of them were peasants.[3] The towns where they lived were surrounded by fortified walls. Unwalled hamlets were an easy target for raiders; especially in times of warfare, the walls were an important line of defense against invaders.[4] Because of the presence of a wall, the Israelite settlements are often referred to as cities. Terminology can be tricky, though. In Biblical Hebrew, the word *'ir* designates a settlement of any size, running from a city to a village.[5] When it comes to size, most walled settlements of the highlands had the dimensions of a town or a village. Since the arable land lay outside the walls, often in the form of agricultural terraces, the men who worked the fields had to make a daily commute. They left in the morning and returned in the afternoon, each time passing through the city gate—hence the blessing says that "the LORD will keep / your going out [in the morning] and coming in [in the early evening]" (Ps 121:8 NRSV). Since the distance had to be covered by foot, their plot of land was rarely more than two miles away. The limited availability of arable land within a two-mile radius put a constraint on the number of people a town could sustain: five hundred inhabitants was a maximum. Most towns were smaller. To shore up its defensive position, the typical Israelite town was "a city built on a hill" (Matt 5:14)—or more accurately, for most Israelite towns, built against a hill (fig. 23). Visitors had to "go up" (*'ālâ*) to the town. What would they encounter during their visit? The story of the wanderings of the young man Saul and his servant in search of the lost donkeys of Saul's father gives an idea (1 Sam 9:1–10:16). When the two men are about to resign themselves to a failed mission, the servant persuades Saul to pay a visit to a prophet (a "man of God") in a town they are passing—which turns out to be Ramah (or Ramathaim) of the Zuphites, the hometown of Samuel.[6] We will follow them and dwell a while on the various features of the built landscape.

As they are making their ascent to the town, they encounter a group of girls who have come out to draw water (1 Sam 9:11). This is exactly the same scenario as in the tale of Abraham's servant, sent on a mission to Aram-naharaim in order to find a suitable girl for his master's son (Gen 24:10–27). This classic motif is based on the common circumstance that the spring that supplied the city with water was located outside the gate, at a lower point on the slope of the hill. In the late afternoon ("at evening time," as Gen 24:11 says) the girls of the town would come out, always in groups, each carrying a jar, to draw water for their families. The well provided "living water," as opposed to the stagnant water gathered in cisterns (a *bôr;* most town houses had one) and in rectangular pools (the Hebrew term is *bĕrēkâ*), found both inside and outside towns and cities. The significance of the difference comes to the fore in the use of the pool of Samaria where, according to the wry observation of a biblical author, blood was washed off war chariots, prostitutes bathed, and dogs would quench their thirst (1 Kgs 22:38). Unless connected to a source, pool water was impure. Well water, on the other hand, had the power to purify and was therefore essential, not only as fresh drinking water, but also for the performance of all those daily rituals that required ablutions. There is no indication of the veneration of wells as sacred sites, even though they might serve on occasion as the scene of a public ritual (1 Kgs 1:33). But the source was an important meeting point, and one of the few places where a man might speak to a woman without raising suspicion (Gen 24:10–20, 29:1–14; Exod 2:15–22; 1 Sam 9:11; John 4:1–15).

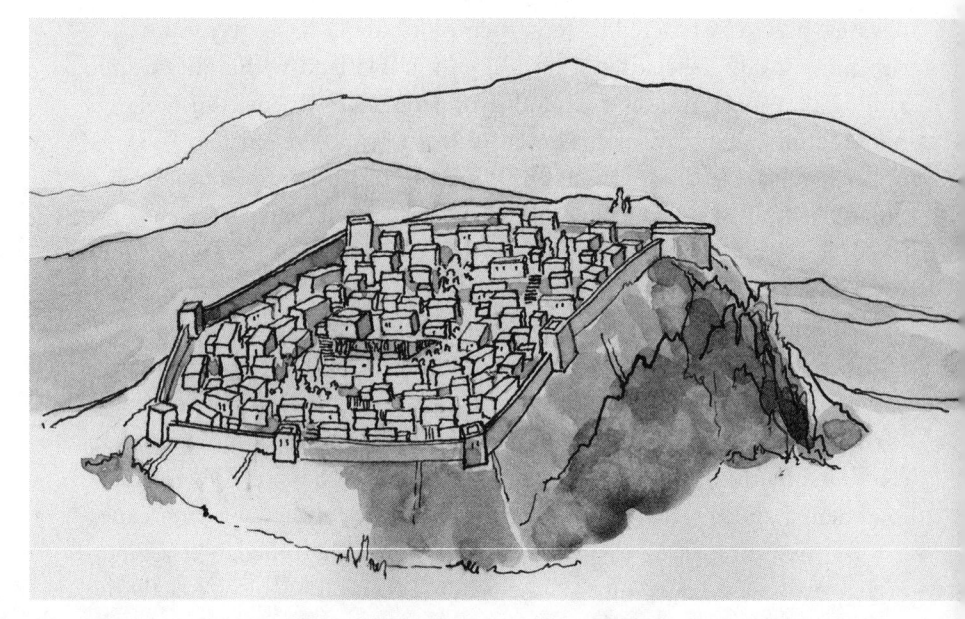

Fig. 23. Artist's impression of an Israelite town. (Drawing by Willem Zijlstra.)

Back to Saul and his servant. Following the instruction of the girls, the two of them "went up to the town. As they were entering the town, they saw Samuel coming out toward them on his way up to the shrine" (1 Sam 9:14 NRSV). Their meeting took place "inside the gate" (1 Sam 9:18). The phrasing reflects the fact that the gate was a building rather than a mere opening in the wall (fig. 24).[7] As a rule, the city gate had open chambers or recesses with benches facing the passageway that led to an open area within the city (the *rĕḥôb*, literally, "broad place," a kind of plaza; 2 Chr 32:6). This was the city center. Here, in or close to the gate, vendors sold their wares (2 Kgs 7:1);[8] men met for gossip, consultation, and the settlement of disputes (2 Sam 3:27; Ps 69:13 [69:12]; Amos 5:15; Prov 24:7, 31:23; Job 29:7; Ruth 4:1–2);[9] and prostitutes plied their trade (Prov 7:12).[10] This also is where visitors went for a place to stay (Judg 19:15–21), because the inn was never far from the gate (Josh 2:1, 15). Though often an impressive construction, the gate was the liminal point of town and city, the transit between inside and outside. Outside the gate were those deemed unfit to dwell within, on account of a repellent disease or some other affliction associated with impurity (2 Kgs 7:3–4); outside was the dung heap and the pit for waste disposal (the *madmēnâ,* covered with straw to mitigate the stench; Isa 25:10);[11] outside was the haunt of evil spirits, robbers, and scavengers.

Fig. 24. Remains of Megiddo city gate. (Wikimedia Commons, CC-BY-SA-4.0, https://creativecommons.org/licenses/by-sa/4.0/deed.en.)

As the most vulnerable part of the wall, the gate needed special protection. The reference to the "high places of the gates" (2 Kgs 23:8 NRSV; NJPS, "shrines of the gates"), reportedly destroyed by King Josiah, is intriguing. The correct interpretation of the text is debated: although the term *bāmôt* must refer to shrines—their size is a matter of conjecture—the term *š'rym*, though usually read as "gates" (*šĕʿārîm*), might be emended as *šōʿărîm*, "gatekeepers," or *šĕʿîrîm*, "goat-demons."[12] Though there is evidence for a cult at the city gate, both textual and archaeological (Judg 5:8; Deut 32:17), its exact configuration and importance seem to have varied.[13] Representations of evil-averting spirits, comparable to the Humbaba masks at Babylonian gates, are likely to have been a common feature (fig. 25).[14]

According to the story of Saul's encounter with Samuel, the more significant cultic place was outside the gate. The girls tell Saul that Samuel "has come just now to the town, because the people have a sacrifice today at the shrine" (1 Sam 9:12 NRSV). On his way to this shrine, Samuel leaves the town and goes up the hill. At Samuel's invitation, Saul and his servant join him, and they go to the town's *bāmâ*, traditionally rendered as

Fig. 25. Humbaba mask, from the Old Babylonian period. Slemani Museum, Sulaymaniyah, Iraq. (Wikimedia Commons, CC-BY-SA-4.0, https://creativecommons.org/licenses/by-sa/4.0/deed.en.)

"high place." The term occurs also in the Moabite stela of King Mesha as a designation of a cult place, without any derogatory connotation.[15] Ancient texts use the words *bāmâ*, "high place," and *miqdāš*, "sanctuary," as variants (Isa 16:12; Amos 7:9). Its out-of-town location, on a more elevated place, suggests it was a hilltop shrine. This topographical setting fits the tendency, in Israel as elsewhere in the Near East, to construct temples at the more elevated points in the landscape (1 Kgs 14:23; Hos 4:13). When the local temple is inside the city walls—as it likely was at times—it is normally on the acropolis, the highest and safest part of town.[16] Historically, the temple—"sanctuary" and "shrine" are the more modest terms—was often the nucleus around which the city had aggregated.[17] Situations where the temple was outside the city—as in Ramah, according to the biblical narrative—were most likely due to the practical necessity to have the settlement in proximity of a source of water. An additional consideration might have been the wish to maintain a respectful distance between the human settlement and the "house of God," on the basis of the separation principle (cf. Exod 33:7–11).

The shrine Samuel was going to for a sacrificial meal served the needs of "the people" (*'am*) of the town (1 Sam 9:12). Since some thirty men participated in the sacrifice (1 Sam 9:22), the population presumably consisted of some thirty families or extended families. If a relatively small town like Ramah had its own shrine (though shared perhaps with a few other settlements in the vicinity), is seems warranted to assume that "any settlement the size of a village and upwards would have contained a cultic complex of some sort" (cf. Jer 11:13).[18] The discovery of an Iron Age temple in modern Moza, some three miles from central Jerusalem, is indicative of the sanctuary density in Judah (and, by extrapolation, in Israel).[19] The inhabitants of an Israelite town—in larger settlements, the neighborhood—were not merely a civic community, but also a cultic community. Based on real or putative ties of kinship, they conceived of each other as family, devoted to the same god and the same ancestors.[20] The sanctuary they used for their periodical sacrifices, prayers, fasts, and other religious ceremonies belonged to the community, even if in practice the more affluent and powerful families were the actual owners and providers. The clan sanctuary for Baal at Ophrah of the Abiezrites belonged to Joash the father of Gideon— apparently a leading figure among the townspeople (Judg 8:25–32).[21] In a similar manner, the "house of God" (*bêt 'ĕlōhîm*) of Micah from the hill country of Ephraim (Judg 17:1–6) also served the families from "the houses near Micah's house" (Judg 18:22, cf. 18:14).[22] From a rather later period and a rather different place, but nonetheless pertinent to the subject, is the evidence from Elephantine where the Jewish community had its own "temple of Yaho." After its destruction, the heads of five leading families of the community offer the Persian governor a substantial bribe for permission to rebuild.[23] The temple served the needs of the community, but they were its principal sponsors.

The Furnishings of Local Sanctuaries

Having established that every town in Israel and Judah had access to a sanctuary, either inside or outside the walls, we must determine what it looked like.[24] The basic rule is that its ground is sacred and inviolable, and therefore separate from the surrounding area. To mark the boundary between sacred and profane, there is always an enclosure. It can be an oval of assembled boulders, such as the ones discovered at Horvat Qitmit (Edomite) and at the so-called Bull Site, but more frequently the sacred area is hedged off by a regular wall (fig. 26).[25] In the case of the almost symbolic boulder boundary, the sanctuary is likely to have been in the open air, as at the Bull Site. The words *miqdāš* and *bāmâ* do not necessarily imply there was a building.[26] The one indispensable feature of an Israelite sanctuary is an altar for animal sacrifice (*mizbēaḥ*, at times specified as *mizbaḥ hā'ōlâ* to distinguish it from the incense altar, *mizbaḥ haqqĕṭōret*; Exod 30:27–28).[27] Samuel is said to go up to the shrine because the people have a "sacrifice" (*zebaḥ*), which—as becomes clear when the story unfolds—is a communal meal around a dish of meat (1 Sam 9:22–25). The full term for this kind of sacrifice is *zebaḥ šĕlāmîm*, often rendered somewhat bleakly as "offering of well-being," but actually it is a community sacrifice, consecrated to the deity but to be divided among, and eaten by, the participants—the "guests," as they are called (1 Sam 9:13, 22; cf. 2 Sam 15:11; 1 Kgs 1:41, 49; Zeph 1:7; Prov 9:18). At a local level, there was no need for a priest to perform this ritual. Samuel was to "bless" the sacrifice before its consumption, but he spoke the dedicatory phrases in his capacity as the leading man of the clan—not because he was a prophet or a priest (1 Sam 9:13). The one professional involved is the cook (*ṭabbāḥ*, 1 Sam 9:23, 24). Does this mean the shrine was a dining hall rather than a sanctuary? Not exactly. It was essential that the animal to be slaughtered and eaten was consecrated to God first, because no living being could be killed unless it be as sacrifice for the deity. That was one of the reasons the battlefield was conceived of as a holocaust (the notion of *ḥērem*-warfare). Secular slaughter was an innovation of later times (Deut 12:15–16, 20–25). So the banquet to which the men of the clan had been invited was a religious occasion, including an invocation of the deity and the presentation to the god of part of the sacrificial victim.

Though the sacrificial meal could take place in the open air, the shrine near Ramah had a hall (*liškâ*) where the guests could sit and eat. We must probably visualize this as a room with benches and a roof, one of the four sides open for light and air. According to the narrative of the annual sacrifice of Elkanah and his wives at Shiloh, the temple there had a dining hall too. Hannah "went into the hall [Greek *katalyma*, which renders Hebrew *liškâ*] and she ate with her husband and drank" (1 Sam 1:18 LXX, same expression as in 9:22).[28] In the Deuteronomic ideology, the temple of Shiloh was the forerunner of the temple of Jerusalem (Jer 7:12–15), so the description of the Shiloh temple is likely to have been a projection upon the past of the situation at Jerusalem that the authors were familiar with. The Jerusalem temple had several "halls" or "chambers" (another possible translation of *liškâ*), some of which were used for dining (Jer 35:2). But it stands to reason that many local sanctuaries had a dining hall of sorts, seeing that it was one of the main purposes of a *bāmâ* to accommodate a party for a communal banquet.

An altar and a dining hall were hardly the only features of a local shrine. Another characteristic was the presence, either in or near the sanctuary, of one or more erected stone slabs (fig. 27). The standard term is *maṣṣēbâ*, from the verb *nāṣab*, "to set up, erect." References to such stelae abound in the Hebrew Bible, mostly in a polemical context because to later biblical writers the worship of stone and wood seemed pure idolatry.[29] In reality, these stones served as signals of superhuman presences without actually embodying them. The use of these erected stones, chiseled to obtain a smooth oblong stela of sometimes imposing height, was an old tradition in the Eastern Mediterranean and western Mesopotamia.[30] The Israelites continued the practice until the late monarchic period.[31] Their stone stelae stood for YHWH, Baal (2 Kgs 3:2, 10:26–27), or El (to whom the object owed its name "bethel," Greek *baitylion*, literally, "house-of-El").[32] As the material token of the divine presence, the *maṣṣēbâ* was an object of worship, with rites involving libations and frictions with oil (Gen 35:14), and various types of offerings and sacrifice.[33] The veneration of these stones could be intense—so intense, in fact, that these aniconic objects came to be deified in their own right, as the divine names Bethel, Sakkun (variant, Sikkanu, "stela"), and Abnu ("stone") indicate.[34]

Fig. 26. Hilltop cult installation surrounded by a circle of boulders, from the Bull Site in the Samarian highlands. (Wikimedia Commons, CC-BY-SA-4.0, https://creativecommons.org/licenses/by-sa/4.0/deed.en.)

In the context of a local sanctuary, the typical companion item of the stone stela was the tree or the wooden pole stylized as a tree, known in the Bible as the *'ăšērâ* (fig. 28).[35] Asherah is the name of the great goddess, consort of El and mother of the gods ("the seventy sons of Asherah").[36] Since this goddess gave her name to the tree or tree symbol in the sacred precinct, the asherah originally embodied the presence of this mother goddess.[37] Also outside Israel there are references to the veneration of wooden poles styled as trees.[38] As in the case of the stone stela (*maṣṣēbâ*) and the god, the tree symbol and the goddess did not coincide; the male plural *'ăšērîm* marks the distinction. The stone and the tree could be standing close to each other. In Shechem, the "great stone" (*'eben gĕdōlâ*) was located "at the foot of the oak in the sacred precinct of the LORD [*miqdaš yhwh*]" (Josh 24:26 NJPS).[39] This "oak" (*'allâ*) at Shechem is likely identical with the "terebinth" (*ēlâ*) of Shechem where Jacob supposedly buried all the alien gods of his household (Gen 35:4). The tree was also known as "the terebinth of the soothsayers" (*ēlôn mě'ōnĕnîm*, Judg 9:37), which suggests it once was used for the purpose of dendromancy (divination by trees, Hos 4:12).[40] Once upon a time,

Fig. 27. Standing cult stones (*maṣṣēbôt*) in Arad sanctuary. (Wikimedia Commons, CC-BY-SA-4.0, https://creativecommons.org/licenses/by-sa/4.0/deed.en.)

people also visited the local shrine to obtain "word of tree, and whisper of stone," as the Baal Cycle puts it.[41] In the monarchic period those were mostly distant memories. Tree and stone still survived, but mainly as traditional markers of a divine presence.

Fig. 28. Sacred tree representing Asherah incised on a rectangular altar from Tel Rehob. Israel Museum, Jerusalem. (Wikimedia Commons, CC-BY-SA-4.0, https://creativecommons.org/licenses/by-sa/4.0/deed.en.)

The divine presence signaled by stone stelae and sacred trees may have been associated also, in the mind of the worshippers, with the presence of the ancestors. The dead (*hammētîm*) were deities (*'ĕlōhîm*) too (Isa 8:19–20). In fact, both the erect oblong stone and the evergreen tree occur quite explicitly in the context of funerary rites and the ancestor cult. It belonged to the duties of a son to set up a stela (*skn;* Akkadian *sikkanu*) for his father at the latter's death (2 Sam 18:18). A husband could do the same for his wife when she died (Gen 35:20). The Ugaritic Aqhat legend says that the son has to erect the stela of his deified ancestor "in the sanctuary" (*bqdš*).[42] There is good archaeological evidence to show that ritual practice meshed with the literary imagination. Around 700 BCE, a citizen of Sam'al (modern Zincirli in southeast Turkey) by the name of Katumuwa commissioned a stone monument for himself that was to serve as a place for funerary offerings by his sons. He had the stela set up in a mortuary chapel next door to the temple of Hadad.[43] The ancestors were believed to partake of the offerings in the company of the gods.[44] Unless the funerary stela was erected in a specially designed necropolis, the local chapel was a natural location.[45] Apparently, then, the local shrine was at once a place of worship for the clan deities (or the clan deity and his consort) and for special offerings to the ancestors. This makes the identification of the *maṣṣēbôt* with particular gods a hazardous affair. The same is true for the sacred trees (the asherim), since trees were also used as grave markers (Gen 35:8; 1 Sam 31:13; 1 Chr 10:12; cf. Gen 23:17–20).

At this point, it is relevant to compare what we know about the furnishings of a local sanctuary out of town with those of one inside the walls. One instance of a shrine inside town is "the house of God" (*bêt 'ĕlōhîm*) of Micah from the hill country of Ephraim (Judg 17:5). We know it only from written sources (Judges 17–18). The expression "house of God" might also be translated as "temple." It implies the existence of a building in which the deity was present through a symbol, which in most parts of the Levant would have been an anthropomorphic image. As it so happens, the biblical tale tells the origin story of Micah's "idol of cast metal" (NRSV's translation of the hendiadys *pesel ûmassēkâ;* Judg 17:4, 18:18). It was made from accursed silver (Judg 17:2–4), was later stolen by Danites, and eventually was set up and worshipped in the temple at Dan. Apparently, this tale of origins is a critique of the cult of the bull image in Dan (Amos 8:14; 1 Kgs 12:25–31). At an earlier point of the story, however, the author says that Micah's temple was furnished with "an ephod and teraphim" (Judg 17:5). Hosea 3:4 mentions the same objects in the context of cultic worship (note the preceding reference there to "sacrifice" and "cult stone," *maṣṣēbâ*). This ephod must have been a metal-coated divine image, as in Judg 8:27 and 1 Sam 21:10.[46] The word "teraphim," often rendered as "household idols," refers more specifically to one or more ancestor images (the Hebrew term occurs only in the plural but can designate a single object, as in 1 Sam 19:11–17). They represent the deified dead, which is why teraphim can occur in synonymous parallelism with the "the gods" (*'ĕlōhîm*, Gen 31:30) and "the dead" (*mētîm*, 2 Kgs 23:24 // Deut 18:11). Consultation of the teraphim (1 Sam 15:23; Ezek 21:26 [21:21]; Zech 10:2) was a form of necromancy.[47] Perhaps the story of Micah's idol conflates two originally independent traditions, the one about Micah's temple with its ephod and teraphim and the other about Micah's silver idol.[48] It does not really matter. The presence of teraphim in a sanctuary inside the town walls points to the coexistence of worship of the deity (represented by the ephod) and the cult of the dead (represented by the teraphim).

On the basis of their furnishings, both the *bāmâ* outside of town and the sanctuary within were places for communal worship of the clan god and the ancestors, often in the context of sacrificial feasts. A rite that did not require the presence of a group was the burning of incense (Hebrew *qĕtōret*, with the verb *qattēr*, "to burn incense"). This was a very common ritual practice, performed both at the hilltop *bāmâ* (1 Kgs 22:44; Jer 48:35) and at the shrine or temple in town (2 Kgs 23:5). Incense offerings filled the air with a rather heavy but pleasant smell. They produced, as the texts say, a "soothing scent" (*rêaḥ nîḥōaḥ*). Incense was valued as a social amenity (Prov 27:9). Its cultic purpose was to put the gods in a good mood and to induce them to accept prayer and supplication (Jer 11:12). Some people associated the smoke of incense with the way prayers and laments were supposed to rise to heaven (Ps 141:2). But even though the smoke would rise upward, incense offerings played a role in the ancestor cult too. Toward the end of "The Descent of Ishtar," there is an unmistakable allusion to incense used to summon the dead: "Let the dead come up and smell the incense [*qutrinnu*]."[49] More usually, though, offerings of incense were directed at the gods in heaven, and especially such astral deities as the Queen of Heaven—the goddess of the morning star (Jer 44:17). To burn the various substances—incense, at times cannabis, and also the fat of sacrificial victims, or aromatic preparations of flour—people used a special altar, referred to at times as the "incense altar" (*mizbaḥ haqqĕtōret*) to distinguish it from the larger "burnt offering altar" (*mizbaḥ hā'ōlâ*; Exod 30:27–28).[50] The typical Israelite incense altar was the four-horned altar, often made from stone but sometimes from cheaper materials such as clay or limestone (fig. 29).

Though most of the Iron Age Palestinian incense burners bear only a faint resemblance to a tower, their model goes back to the Syrian ceramic

Fig. 29. Artist's impression of Israelite incense altars. (Drawing by Willem Zijlstra.)

altars that were shaped like miniature towers. The rectangular top of these incense altars imitated the top of a tower, the four horns at the corners representing the tower's battlements.[51] The form reflects the ancient tradition to choose elevated places in the built landscape for the performance of sacrifice and incense offerings. Towers qualified as such, but at a more modest level, so did the roofs of houses. Roofs were flat. In the warm season, people spent the night there (1 Sam 9:25–26). The roof allowed an unencumbered view of heaven where, in a time with no city lights, the stars shone brighter than today. It was a natural spot for incense offerings to the gods of heaven. Compared with the Israelite incense burners, the clay and limestone cult stands, often fenestrated and finely decorated, are far more eloquent in their use of religious imagery (see figs. 20 and 21, above, in Chapter 2, and fig. 28 in this chapter). Found in temples, tombs, and houses, these cult stands draw from a rich repertoire of mythological and architectural motifs. Some of them have the shape of a tower.[52] Though the interpretation of their iconographic program is fraught with speculation, they do show that Israelite religion was certainly not without images. How much these images reflect actual temple decorations is uncertain. The stands were used to support bowls for vegetal offerings and perhaps, on occasion, as incense burners.

Local Rituals

Whereas *royal* religion was concerned to preserve the integrity of the realm, the popular support of the monarch, and a sense of national solidarity, *local* religion sought to foster unity among members of the local community. After they had settled the hill country and adopted an agricultural mode of life, the Israelites continued to live by the norms and values of a tribal society. When inhabitants of an Israelite or Judean town spoke of their "people" (*'am*), they were thinking of their local community rather than of the nation (1 Sam 9:12; 2 Kgs 4:13). The *'am* was the clan they belonged to. The local population consisted of families and extended families, related to each other by ties of kinship and intermarriage.[53] The men of the town were "brothers." The economic system they lived by was an early form of capitalism regulated by certain rules designed to mitigate excesses. Though barter was the predominant mode of economic transaction, it had some traits of a money economy because everything could be converted to silver—a term one is sometimes tempted to translate as "money." One unwritten rule said that the land surrounding the town—arable land and pasture ground alike—belonged to the clan as a whole.[54] While individual families could sell the land that was their inheritance, it could not be alienated, that is, sold to parties outside the clan. In a somewhat similar vein, if a father "sold" his daughter to another man—meaning, he gave her in marriage without a bride price, usually in payment of a debt—the latter was not permitted to sell her off to "a strange clan" (*'am nokrî*, Exod 21:7–11). The system allowed individual accumulation of capital but put a rein on the ensuing social disparity through periodical remission of debts, manumission from slavery, and the return of sold land holdings to the family (Exod 21:2–6; Lev 25:13–18, 23–24). The concern for the integrity of the clan group and its land prevented any unbridled capitalism—at least in theory.

In many ways, local religion fostered the cohesion of the clan. Most of the celebrations at the local shrine (*bāmâ, miqdāš, bêt 'ĕlōhîm*) involved the clan as a whole. Saul and his servant met Samuel on his way to the hillside *bāmâ* for a sacrificial meal of the clan (*'am*), represented by some thirty men. Since the local shrine was consecrated to the clan god and the ancestors, participation in the *zebaḥ* consolidated the community among the living members of the clan, between the clan and its god, and between the clan and the ancestors. If the *zebaḥ* to which Saul was invited was the *zebaḥ hayyāmîm*, the annual sacrificial meal, as a slight textual emendation suggests (1 Sam 9:12, haplography of the Hebrew letter mem), Samuel officiated in his capacity as the paterfamilias of the town. But a community *zebaḥ* could also be nonperiodical (1 Sam 16:1–5). At times, there was simply a good reason for a spontaneous celebration, such as a military victory or the birth of a child. Less festive occasions would also bring out the entire clan. When the elders and the nobles of a city proclaimed a fast (*ṣôm*), the entire clan was invited to the sanctuary (1 Kgs 21:9, 12).[55] All of the adult men were expected to join in the case of a verdict of death by stoning (1 Kgs 21:13). Sacrificial meals, public fasts, and execution by collective stoning: irrespective of their primary purpose, they were also means of building community. In this respect, the repeated injunction not to have other gods (Exod 22:19, 23:13) is not so much a harbinger of monotheism as an urgent warning against scissions in the local community that the worship of new gods would inevitably entail.

It seems unlikely that these community rituals were occasions in which the men and women of the town participated in like manner. In fact, the biblical narratives convey the impression that these were "men only" celebrations. The guests at the sacrificial meal that Samuel presided over in Ramah numbered "about thirty men" (1 Sam 9:22). There is no reason to suppose women were included. At the sacrificial meal organized at Bethlehem, too, only men were present (1 Sam 16:1–13). Same story for the fast proclaimed in the city of Naboth (1 Kgs 21:8–16). The one counterexample that could be cited is the annual sacrificial meal at Shiloh to which Elkanah went with his wives Hannah and Peninnah, plus the children (1 Sam 1:1–8). That story, however, projects the custom of a much later period—of the annual pilgrimage to Jerusalem by families (Luke 2:41–42)—upon a time with different manners, on the strength of the Deuteronomistic doctrine that the temple at Shiloh (note the expression *hêkal yhwh*, 1 Sam 1:9, to be compared with Jer 7:4) was the precursor of the Jerusalem temple (Jer 7:12–15). The Israelite clans and tribes were patrilineal and patriarchal, and the rituals that sought to reinforce and perpetuate the cohesion and authority structures of the clan were by and large the business of men.

Domestic Religion and Ancestor Cult

The story of Saul's meeting with Samuel says that the two men, at the end of the celebration, went back to town: "When they came down from the shrine into the town, a bed was spread for Saul on the roof, and he lay down to sleep" (1 Sam 9:25 NRSV). It must have been the warm season. Aside from the reference to the roof, nothing is said about the setup of Samuel's house. Assuming it resembled the majority of Israelite houses at the time, the ground plan was rectangular (fig. 30). Its outer doorway, in the middle of the broad front wall, led directly into a roofed courtyard flanked, on both sides, by elongated rooms used as storage facilities and as stables for a few domestic animals, such as the "ox and ass" (Exod 20:14) and perhaps a lamb (2 Sam 12:3) or a calf (1 Sam 28:24).[56] At the back of the courtyard was another doorway, which gave access to a perpendicular backroom running the width of the building. This was the *heder* or *hadar miṭṭâ*, the bedroom, the most private part of the house. In the *heder* a man could show tears (Gen 43:30), spouses slept together, women gave birth to their children (Cant 3:4), and people spoke without fear of being overheard (2 Kgs 6:12; Eccl 10:20). Many houses had a second floor (*'aliyyâ*) with rooms for family and guests (cf. 2 Kgs 4:8–11).[57] All this might suggest that the Israelite house was a building designed for purely mundane purposes. That, however, is not entirely true. The house was also the place where the inhabitants conducted a domestic cult addressed to the house "gods," that is, the family ancestors represented by anthropomorphic statuettes (the teraphim).

The presence of the family's gods within the house is alluded to in a ruling about the manumitted servant who decides he wants to remain a member of the household. In that case "his master shall take him to the gods, and he shall take him to the door or the doorpost, and his master shall pierce his ear with an awl; and he shall be his servant for life" (Exod 21:6). A comparison of this passage with its reformulation in Deut 15:17

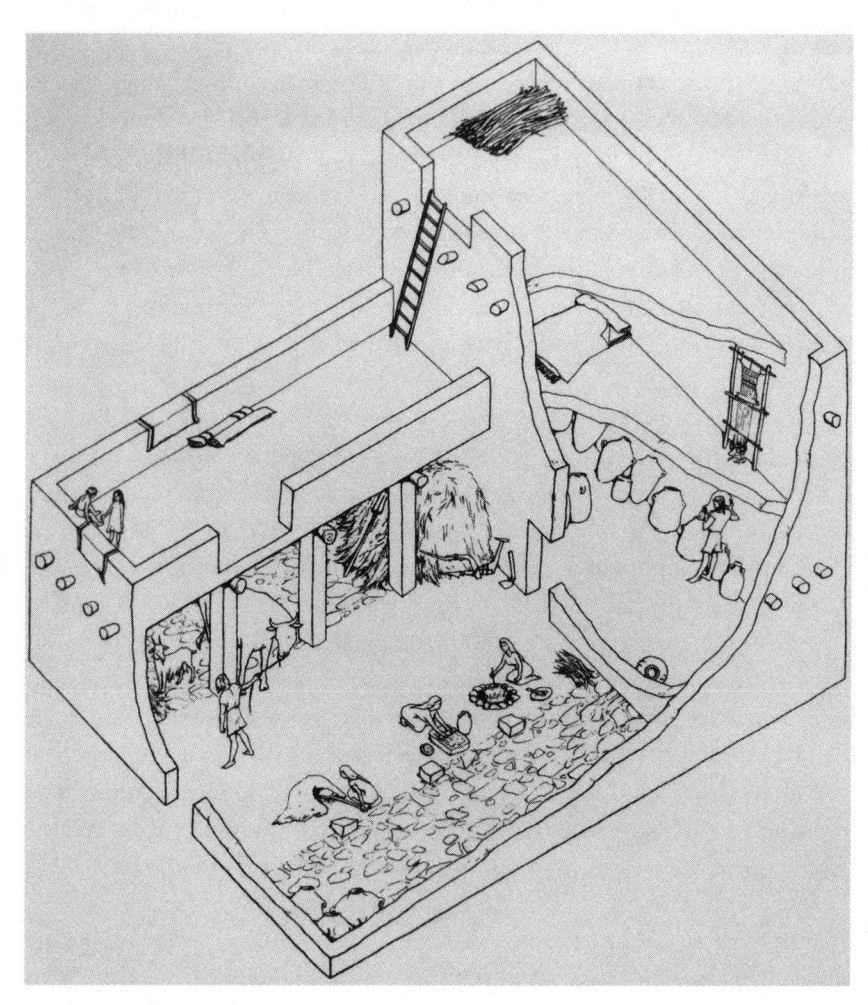

Fig. 30. Four-room house; artist's impression of diorama in Israel Museum, Jerusalem. (Wikimedia Commons, CC-BY-SA 3.0, https://creativecommons.org/licenses/by-sa/3.0/deed.en.)

shows that the reference to "the gods" is old. The Deuteronomic scribe suppressed it. These gods were located next to "the door or the doorpost." Not all houses had a real door, but every house had a wooden doorpost at its main entrance.[58] This must have been where the ceremony took place: the awl pierced the new household member through the ear and went into the wooden doorframe. Israelite houses did not, as a rule, have a separate cult room as Mesopotamian houses sometimes had.[59] A corner of the house, often in the bedroom, served as such. The bedroom felt like a natural setting for the images representing the ancestors of the house. A subtle reference in the standard version of the Gilgamesh Epic indicates that in Mesopotamia, too, it was not unusual to have an ancestor statuette in the bedroom.[60] Women gave birth in the bedroom. Newborn babies entered the world before the deified ancestors and stood under their protection from day one.[61] Also the rite of passage that turned nonfamily into family (the case of the manumitted slave) took place before the ancestors who embodied the family's identity and authority. It left an indelible mark in the servant, who had literally been pierced to the house—the house that stood for the family.

It makes sense to have the ancestors—the house "gods," represented by the teraphim (Gen 31:30–35)—be witness to the entry into the family of a new member. Their tacit presence was a form of approval. It should not come as a surprise to find that they had a similar role when a woman joined the family through marriage. Mesopotamian texts have several references to the presentation of the bride to the ancestors.[62] The newlyweds were to spend the first night "before" or "in the presence of" the domestic gods, that is, the ancestors.[63] The Israelites observed a similar practice. When David married Saul's youngest daughter Michal, the couple spent their honeymoon night in the presence of the teraphim. That is why, the morning after, when David was forced to flee because his father-in-law was plotting to have him killed, Michal could put the teraphim underneath a blanket in order to suggest the presence of her allegedly ill and bedridden husband (1 Sam 19:13–16).[64] Both Michal and David were the youngest of their respective families (1 Sam 14:49, 16:11–13). Normally, the ancestor statuettes were in the possession of the oldest heir, who was the first in line to become the paterfamilias.[65] But a wedding was special. Whatever the age of the marriage partners, irrespective of their positions in the family line, their union needed the blessing of the ancestors. The silent presence of the latter signified acceptance and, it was hoped, the promise of offspring, since children were customarily viewed as a gift of the ancestors.[66]

Apart from the role of the ancestors in these rites of passage, it is likely they were the object of daily devotions in the form of regular offerings of bread and water (Deut 26:14; Jer 16:6–8; Ps 16:3–4; Sir 30:18 LXX; Tob 4:17). But though the ancestors were believed to be like gods, they did not take the place of God. The respective responsibilities of the ancestors as opposed to those of God comes to the fore, in a subtle yet unmistakable fashion, in one of the oldest pieces of Israelite jurisprudence.

The Covenant Code—a misnomer, because it is not a legal code but a series of paradigmatic verdicts—determines that cases of suspected misappropriation in the home are to be adjudicated by "the gods" (Exod 22:6–8), whereas contentions about the disappearance of animals outside the house should be brought to Yhwh (Exod 22:9–12). In both cases, the suspected offender had to take an oath of innocence. In the first case, it is "the gods" who will establish innocence or guilt—presumably through an oracle like the Urim and Thummim—after which the convict is to pay a double indemnity. In the second case, the oath by Yhwh is to bring clarity in the matter. The disparity between the two cases does not reflect a different theological bias, but follows from the place where the presumed offense had been committed. In the house, the ancestors keep watch, witness every event, and can identify the perpetrator of a secret theft. Everything outside the house falls under the purview of Yhwh, for he is the Lord of the land.

Daily acts of devotion performed in a domestic context were not limited to the cult of the ancestors. Archaeologists have discovered a few model shrines in a domestic context (fig. 31). Most of them are from the Late Bronze or Early Iron Age and come from Philistia and Transjordan, but some are from Israel of the monarchic period (Tirzah, Tel Rehov). Such house shrines were common in the Levant. They have the form of a cubicle with an opening in front and may at one time have contained divine images or symbols, or simply served as receptacles for small offerings. They are not miniature reproductions of major temples but seem to have been designed specifically for the domestic cult.[67] Some of the most prevalent forms of domestic religion had no need for a miniature shrine or a cult niche, since they took place on the roof. This was the place where, at daytime, the sun was near and, at night, the moon and the stars. Upon hearing about Gilgamesh's plan to travel to the distant and dangerous cedar forest, his mother Ninsun bathes, puts on a fine dress, and climbs the staircase up to the roof: "On the roof she set up a censer to Shamash. Scattering incense she lifted her arms in appeal to the Sun God." A prayer follows in which she asks Shamash to protect her son and bring him back alive.[68] Similar scenes must have been common in Israel. The rooftop was typically the place to burn incense to the host of heaven, to bow down, and to bring libations to the gods (Jer 19:13, 32:29; Zeph 1:5; cf. 2 Kgs 23:12).[69] It did not seem incompatible with the veneration of Yhwh, since he was "the Lord of hosts" (*yhwh ṣĕbā'ôt*), the leader of the heavenly army.[70]

Fig. 31. Model shrine from Tel Rehov. Israel Museum, Jerusalem. (Wikimedia Commons, CC-BY-SA-4.0, https://creativecommons.org/licenses/by-sa/4.0/deed.en.)

Women and Local Religion

In view of the male-dominated celebrations at the local shrine and the patrilineal transmission of the family gods, local religion might easily come across as a man's world; however, that is a misleading impression. It is true that women were less visible in an Israelite town than men. After all, women had to be chaste and stayed indoors much of the time. When a married woman left the house, she put on a scarf (Isa 3:18–23).[71] It covered most of her head, leaving only the eyes and brow exposed (Cant 4:1, 6:7). She was practically unrecognizable (Gen 38:14). Girls had greater liberty. Until the time they were betrothed—usually at the age when they entered puberty— they could move around freely, though they rarely left town alone. But the time of carefree play was short. Soon their fathers would become anxious about them, keeping them behind closed doors lest they become pregnant by some smooth-talking stranger (Sir 42:9–14). Family honor was a delicate matter, and a scandal had to be avoided at all costs. This moral climate left women only limited room to have a public role in religious activities. Somewhat ironically perhaps, though, religious causes and rituals also provided them with opportunities to temporarily step outside the ordinary social conventions.

We know relatively little about life-cycle rituals in Israel—probably because they were so common that nobody cared to keep a record.[72] But the Bible does mention one annual ritual for unmarried girls. The story of Jephthah's anonymous daughter, said to have been burned by her father in fulfillment of a vow, concludes with a reference to a four-day "custom" (*hōq*) for "the daughters of Israel" (Judg 11:39–40). Once a year they would go out "to sing antiphonic songs" for the daughter of Jephthah. Though the usual Bible translations interpret the annual rite as a collective mourning ("chant dirges," NJPS; "lament," NRSV), the Hebrew verb (*lĕtannôt*, from *tānâ*, with reduplication of the middle consonant) refers to antiphonal singing, in which a lead singer chants a phrase that is then repeated by a choir.[73] There is no compelling reason to think that the four days were spent in tears. On the contrary, the reference is most likely to an annual festival such as that of the grape harvest, during which the girls came out to the vineyards "to dance in the dances" (Judg 21:21 NRSV). On that joyful occasion, they came out and acted the way Jephthah's daughter had, when she had been "coming out to meet [her father] with timbrels and with dancing" (Judg 11:34 NRSV). The girls who participated were on the brink of a new phase in their lives. The years of innocence were almost over, and soon they were to embark on the life of married women (Judg 11:37, 21:21; m. Ta'an. 4.8). As such, this was a rite of passage, but one that was playful and very common in the culture of those days.[74] The "city festival" (*isinni āli*), as Mesopotamian texts say, was typically the occasion for adolescent women to dress up, have fun with other girls, and drive the boys crazy.[75] Figurines of a woman with a tambourine, popular in ancient Judah, were like mementos of those fleeting moments (fig. 32).[76] One may wonder about how far such life-cycle

Fig. 32. Votive figurine of girl with tambourine from Astarte temple on Cyprus. Ashmolean Museum, Oxford. (Wikimedia Commons, CC-BY-SA-4.0, https://creativecommons.org/licenses/by-sa/4.0/deed.en.)

rites were religious, but that is a question the people involved would never ask themselves; to them, religion and culture were as good as one.

For most girls, marriage was the way to motherhood, which, in their idea of the good life, was a woman's destiny. To be married and not have children was a disgrace; the shame seemed worse than death: "Give me children, or I shall die!" (Gen 30:1). When a man had two wives, the competition could be fierce. The other woman was the "enemy" or the "rival."[77] Even if a woman was her husband's favorite, nothing could take the place of children (1 Sam 1:1–8). If she did not get pregnant, she felt as though something was wrong with her. At times, the fear of childlessness drove women to special acts of devotion. To move the deity to bless her with offspring, a woman might take vows, promising God-knows-what if only her wish would be granted. If she was lucky, she would bear the "son of [her] vows" (Prov 31:2). But vows were a serious matter. The temple where they had been taken kept a record. Once God had answered the vow, it had to be fulfilled by a gift or a payment to be delivered at a set date—usually the day of a festival (Eccl 5:4–6; cf. 1 Sam 1:24–28). Unpaid vows could kill the baby.[78] In most cases, it was up to the husband or the woman's father to come up with the money (Num 30:4–17). But if the woman's vow had been made in secret, she might be forced to resort to unorthodox means to honor her obligation. Prostitution in payment of vows was perhaps less unusual than we would like to believe.[79] Faced with the choice between childlessness and prostitution, the latter might well seem the lesser evil (Gen 19:30–38, 38:12–26; Num 5:11–31).

Vows, one might say, are an intensified form of prayer, the petition deriving extra urgency from the promise of a conditional gift. In Israel, as in many other cultures, prayer was (and is) perhaps the most common religious act performed by ordinary people. Is it a coincidence that the ancient texts refer so often to women praying? From Hannah at Shiloh (1 Sam 1:10) to Judith in Bethulia (Jdt 9:1, 13:3); from the women praying to the Queen of Heaven in Egypt (Jer 44:15–19) to the women gathered at the place of prayer by the river in Philippi (Acts 16:11–15)—there are no statistics, but prayer seems to have been the special province of women.[80] To whom did they pray? Presumably to the gods they believed were most likely to answer their prayers. At the local shrine they could turn to the local god, Asherah, or the ancestors. The local god was generally a manifestation of YHWH— perhaps originally an El figure, perhaps a local Baal. YHWH was the most prominent Israelite deity—a fact reflected in the personal names of the period—even though his worshippers made a distinction between YHWH venerated in one temple or another.[81] A vow taken by YHWH of Hebron could not be redeemed in any other place than in Hebron (2 Sam 15:7–9).[82] Many worshippers, men as much as women, preferred to present their petition to Asherah rather than YHWH. As the divine consort, the goddess had privileged access and could put in a good word on behalf of those in distress.[83] A Judean burial inscription from the monarchic period says that YHWH saved the interred individual "by his Asherah" (*l'šrth*), meaning "through" or "by the intercession of" Asherah.[84] The text casts Asherah in a role familiar from Mesopotamian prayers, which often ask a goddess to intercede with her husband.[85] At home one could ask the teraphim for their blessing. Or one could go up to the roof and present a small offering to the gods of the night—most often the moon and the morning star, commonly known as the Queen of Heaven.

How did people pray? Normally aloud. Silent prayer was rare and probably mainly a feature of devotion in later periods (1 Sam 1:13; Jdt 13:4–5). Most of the prayers were rudimentary. The gestures counted as much as the words. People touched or kissed the symbol of the deity, made a genuflexion, murmured a few words of devotion, and presented their request. The prayer that Hannah is said to have spoken in thanksgiving at the Shiloh temple is hardly representative (1 Sam 2:1–10). The words the narrator puts in her mouth resemble the prayers from the book of Psalms. Those are texts that required the assistance of a cult specialist. He read the prayer line by line, after which they were repeated by the worshipper.[86] That is what happened at major sanctuaries that had competent staff members to assist those who came to pray. It is questionable whether local sanctuaries could provide this service. Prayers there consisted mostly of a few standard phrases. Incense was the most common offering to go with prayer, although the cult stands that have been found in Palestine, in both domestic and temple contexts, suggest that less costly offerings also occurred.[87] Prayer was petition, not a way to achieve union with the deity: women prayed for the welfare of their children, for the health of their husband, and for food that would last them until the next harvest.

Special needs could impel people to undertake the journey to a famous shrine elsewhere or to some man of God whom they revered (1 Kgs 14:1–18; 2 Kgs 4:17–30; cf. 2 Kgs 1:2–4). During the period of the monarchy, pilgrimage was not yet the annual duty it became in later times, but that does not mean it did not happen (Amos 5:5, 8:14). As in many other places in the Near East, religious high holy days were for many people an occasion to visit a renowned temple at some distance from where they lived. There they could consult religious specialists who were not available at the local sanctuary.[88] Some of such visits may have been made to a place considered to be imbued with a special degree of holiness on account of its past (as Elijah's journey to the mountain of God in the desert by way of Beersheba, 1 Kgs 19:3–14; cf. Gen 21:33–22:19).[89] For most women, the purpose of pilgrimage was to pray for pregnancy, a safe delivery, untroubled lactation, or the healing of disease. Most of the so-called pillar figurines of women—handmade in series, some of them with heads cast in molds—are best interpreted as votive gifts in connection with health and fertility issues.[90] It is quite possible that these almost schematic female torsos supporting their breasts or holding an infant represent the goddess Asherah, as various scholars have argued (fig. 33). Women identified with the goddess. The pillar figurines might then be connected with the cultic wooden pillars in local shrines (the *asherim*). Whether other small statuary, such as the plaque figurines (representing a woman lying on a bed or standing in a cult niche) and the horse-with-rider figurines (related to the solar cult? representations of a death-dealing demon?), are also witness to the visit of sanctuaries, whether close-by or at a place of pilgrimage, is uncertain.[91]

Another area where women figured prominently are the rites that attend the transition of the deceased from this world to the underworld. Women knew the pains of birth as well as the sorrows of death. They were present at the very beginning and the very end. Quite tellingly, in this respect, is the fact that "wise woman" (*ḥăkāmâ*) designates both a midwife (the *sage-femme*, as the French say) and a mourner (Jer 9:16).[92] Men were certainly present at funerals, but the real professionals of mourning were women. Also in religious rites that involved mourning—such as the summer burial of Tammuz, a Mesopotamian fertility god expected to return to life with the autumn rains—it was women who wept for the dead (Ezek 8:14).[93] It bears stressing that mourning for the dead was a public display of grief. Following an unwritten choreography, professional female mourners, often bare-breasted, would moan and wail, moving to and fro, and beat themselves so hard that it hurt (Isa 32:11–12; Jer 49:3).[94] This was a way to turn an unassimilated physical fact into a social and psychological reality for all. Everyone had to make a journey. The departed had to be buried, and their spirits were to find a place in the netherworld; the survivors had

Fig. 33. Judean pillar figurines, eighth to sixth centuries BCE. Israel Museum, Jerusalem. (Wikimedia Commons, CC-BY-SA 3.0, https://creativecommons.org/licenses/by-sa/3.0/deed.en.)

to make the transition to a social world in which the dead no longer participated. Mourning was an outburst of emotion, but it was deliberate and channeled in the service of a collective rite of passage.[95] The ritual is another illustration of the importance of the separation principle. The special involvement of women was based on the intuition that they were closer to the boundary between life and death than most men; they were more susceptible to identify with the dead. It is probably for the same reason that the consultation of the dead (necromancy) was often the business of women, both in Israel and elsewhere in the Near East (1 Sam 28:3–25; Ezek 13:17–23).

Seers, Prophets, Necromancers

On their search for the lost donkeys, Saul and his servant decided to visit Ramah because the town had a prophet, and "everything he says, will certainly come about" (1 Sam 9:6). In fact, the servant does not call him a prophet but a "man of God" (1 Sam 9:6, 8). In an aside, the narrator of the story explains: "Formerly in Israel, anyone who went to inquire of God would say, 'Come, let us go to the seer'; for the one who is now called a prophet [*nābi'*] was formerly called a seer [*rō'eh*]" (1 Sam 9:9 NRSV). The comment shows that prophecy has a history and that what many people nowadays regard as perhaps the most quintessential biblical figure was once something slightly different. The prophet (or "seer," or "man of God") Saul and his servant went to see is Samuel. According to the biblical biography of Samuel, he started out as a priestly servant. Dedicated by his mother to the Shiloh temple (in fulfillment of her vow), the boy "entered the service of the LORD under the priest Eli" (1 Sam 2:11 NJPS). Dressed as a priest with a linen ephod (1 Sam 2:18), the young boy Samuel used to sleep in the temple to keep watch over the ark of God (1 Sam 3:3). It is in the temple that he had his calling as a prophet. In his sleep, God called him by name. Samuel took the voice to be Eli's; without the instruction of the priest he would not have understood God was talking to him (1 Sam 3:1–14). In other words, Samuel became a prophet in the temple and was initiated in the art of prophecy by a priest. The story illustrates the close ties that once existed between priests and prophets.

Those ties are not merely historical, for some of the best-known biblical prophets were priests. Jeremiah was "one of the priests who were in Anathoth" (Jer 1:1), and Ezekiel was "the priest Ezekiel" (Ezek 1:3). Other names may have to be added to the list. Isaiah had his calling in the temple and was apparently familiar with the furnishings of the inner sanctum (Isa 6:1–8). He had good relations with the high priest Uriah whom he asked to cosign the deed to his son Maher-shalal-hash-baz (Isa 8:1–2; cf. 2 Kgs 16:10–16). Moses, whom certain circles in the Northern Kingdom regarded as the ancestor of all prophets (Num 12:1–9; Hos 12:14), could also be counted among the priests (Ps 99:6). And as late as the time of Jesus, there was a popular belief that the high priest had the gift of prophecy (John 11:51; cf. Josephus, *Ant.* 13.282–283). Conversely, certain men whom the biblical tradition calls "prophets" behaved very much like priests (1 Kgs 18:20–46, 19:10). Add to all this that the Arabic etymological correspondent of Hebrew *kōhēn*, "priest," is *kâhin* and means "prophet" and it will be clear that the oft-posited contrast between priest and prophet is quite misleading.[96] The once popular view, still found in some quarters, that priests represented the establishment and prophets the antiestablishment, is based on a false dichotomy. According to a later tradition, kings had prophets on their payrolls, too (such as the court prophets Gad and Nathan, both in the service of King David according to 2 Chr 29:25). At some point in the history of Israelite religion, priests and prophets developed their own distinctive profile, but there never was a complete split.

Judging by the biblical presentation of the prophets, they were national figures sent by God to urge the Israelites to repent and bring their lives in conformity with the divine commandments. Historically, however, most men and women posthumously labeled "prophets" were active locally, even though their renown might spread well beyond the place where they lived. Saul's servant knew about the man of God in Ramah by reputation. They decided to consult the "prophet"—an anachronism, as the narrator explains—and deliberated about the fee they should give (1 Sam 9:7–10). The prophet provided a service, and the client was expected to pay (Num 22:7; 1 Kgs 13:7, 14:3; 2 Kgs 5:15, 8:8). Prophets—men of God, seers—had a special gift: "Everything he says, will certainly come about" (1 Sam 9:6). This wording is striking: the way Saul's servant put it, Samuel did not have the gift of foreknowledge but the power to predict. His word produced the future. The curse of a prophet could kill, as illustrated by the story of the forty-two boys mangled by two she-bears (2 Kgs 2:23–24). In like manner, the intercessory prayer of the prophet had special efficacy (see, e.g., Gen 20:7; Exod 8:8–9; 1 Sam 12:23; 1 Kgs 13:6; Isa 37:4; Jer 42:1–12). It is one reason why prophets played a prominent role in warfare; their blessing or curse spelled victory or defeat (Numbers 22–24; 1 Kgs 21:10–13; 2 Kgs 3:9–20). But ordinary people cared less about the outcome of military campaigns than about their own lives, their property, and the welfare of their loved ones. They consulted a prophet to find out whether they would recover from disease—they themselves, their spouses, or their children (1 Kgs 14:1–3, 17:17–24; 2 Kgs 1:2, 4:17–37, 5:3, 8:7–8). Many prophets did not limit themselves to a prognosis but acted as healers as well, prescribing various treatments to reinvigorate their patients (2 Kgs 4:24–37, 5:1–19; Isa 38:21). Some of those healings became the stuff of popular legend, such as the tales about Elisha, in which the prophet comes across as a true miracle worker.[97] Most prophets, however, had more modest careers and remained anonymous (1 Kgs 13:11).

The books of the biblical prophets—that is, the books that carry the name of a prophet—leave readers with the impression that the prophet was a lone and tortured genius. Some prophets may have been that way, but historically many prophets operated in groups and lived in prophetic communities. To corroborate his prophecy that Saul would be king, Samuel gave Saul three "signs" (*ōtōt*), that is, three remarkable events that would occur to him on his way home (1 Sam 10:7). One of them involved an encounter with "a band of prophets coming down from the shrine with harp, tambourine, flute, and lyre playing in front of them; they will be in a prophetic frenzy" (1 Sam 10:5). Their enthusiasm was contagious, for Saul joined in their frenzy and was, for a while, "among the prophets" (1 Sam 10:6, 9–13; cf. 19:18–24). Such bands of prophets had a leader (their "father," 1 Sam 10:12; 2 Kgs 2:12; cf. 2 Kgs 6:21, 13:14) and were apparently to be found in the vicinity of local shrines ("coming down from the shrine"). One story presents Samuel as the leader of a company of prophets living in an encampment outside Ramah (1 Sam 19:19–20).[98] Other such groups are the "sons of the prophets" living on the outskirts of Jericho (2 Kgs 2:4–15, 6:1–7), at Gilgal, and in Bethel (2 Kgs 2:3, 4:38). The NJPS translates the expression "sons of the prophets" as "disciples of the prophets," thereby suggesting they were followers and apprentices. Indeed, the sons of the prophets are said to be sitting before Elisha, a phrase that qualifies their interaction as that of students and teacher (2 Kgs 4:38, 6:1; cf. 6:32; Ezek 8:1, 14:1, 20:1; Acts 22:3). Isaiah's reference to his "disciples" (*limmûday*, Isa 8:16) suggests that these prophetic "schools" also existed in Judah.

Prophecy is a cultural phenomenon, and as such, it was something that could be learned—at least, up to a point.[99] Prophetic experience and prophetic behavior were not completely spontaneous but used established techniques and followed conventional patterns. Those came in a wide array. One venerable technique, known and practiced in the Near East since time immemorial, was that of spirit possession. To the sound of rhythmic music, prophets worked themselves up into a trance, as they shouted and sang, all the while dancing like dervishes (1 Sam 10:5–6, 10–13; 1 Kgs 18:28–29). The men sought to become like empty vessels so that the divine spirit might fill them and use them as its mouthpiece. Though single prophets might use this technique for an oracle (2 Kgs 3:15–20), prophetic trance was mostly a group phenomenon. Young men would sometimes take a temporary vow and join such groups, as though it was a rite of passage from adolescence to adulthood (Amos 2:11). But possession was a primitive technique compared with the higher arts of prophecy. A more respected way to elicit an oracle was the dream. Prophetic dreams were of two kinds: the spoken message dream and the vision. In the former, the prophet heard God—or a messenger of God—speak and say what he had to say. In the second type of dream, the prophet saw something he knew was a sign from God. Both kinds of dream required skills of memory and interpretation in order to translate the dream into a prophecy. Everybody dreams, but prophets are rare. The prophetic dream was a creation of prophets while awake looking back on the things they believed they had heard or seen while asleep.

One of the means to elicit prophetic oracles was by association, not only through dreams but from objects and events visible to everyone. While he was in the Jerusalem temple, Jeremiah saw the branch of an almond tree and a boiling pot (Jer 1:11–14). Those were not visions in the usual sense of the term but things he simply saw. Freely associating, he discovered their meaning. The branch of almond (*šāqēd* in Hebrew) meant that YHWH was watching (*šōqēd*) over his word in order to bring it to pass; and the boiling (*nāpûaḥ*) pot stood for the eruption (*tippātaḥ*) of violence that would sweep over the country. In like manner, Amos observed a basket of summer figs (*qayiṣ*) and prophesied that the "end" (*qēṣ*) was near (Amos 8:1–2; cf. Jer 24:1–10). When the mind of the prophet is properly attuned, everything he sees bears a deeper meaning. Much of the Mesopotamian omen literature is based on similar principles of interpretation: analogy, association, and paronomasia.[100]

While prophecy was a characteristic phenomenon of Israel and Judah— and even more so in the Hebrew Bible—it was by no means unique. All the divinatory techniques used by the Israelite prophets have their counterparts in the surrounding civilizations.[101] Written oracles and reports on prophecy from Mesopotamia are particularly profuse in two periods: the Old Babylonian period (ca. 1800–1550 BCE), preserved mainly in the archives of the kingdom of Mari;[102] and the Neo-Assyrian period (ca. 900–600 BCE), addressed mostly to the Assyrian monarchs of the time.[103] These texts show that the phenomenon of "inspired divination"—as distinct from "deductive divination"—was flourishing in Mesopotamia. Prophecy was familiar in Syria too.[104] It was, in a way, the most egalitarian type of communication with the divine. Prophecy was a gift that could manifest itself in people from all social classes, women and men alike. The modus operandi was the same as in Israel: prophetic frenzy, messages received in dreams and visions, and revelations obtained in ways that only the prophets understood. In a strongly hierarchical society, prophecy was one of the rare means for popular dissent to manifest itself.[105]

For the general population, prophets were heroes. Their popularity made it difficult for the authorities to simply suppress their critique. The Gospel says that Herod put John the Baptist in prison because he had publicly condemned Herod's marriage to his sister-in-law: "Though Herod wanted to put him to death, he feared the crowd, because they regarded him as a prophet" (Matt 14:5 NRSV). Though these events are from the Roman era, centuries later than the monarchic period, the desire of autocratic regimes to silence voices of dissent exists in all times. In ancient Israel, prophets were a standard target. Both King Ahab and his successor Ahaziah tried to arrest the prophet Elijah (1 Kgs 18:6–14; 2 Kgs 1:9–14); and the high priest Amaziah summoned Amos to leave the Bethel temple because he feared the prophet's inflammatory speeches would undermine the authority of King Jeroboam II (Amos 7:10–17). The desire to exert control also affected other channels of divination such as necromancy. The story of Saul's consultation of the medium at Endor says that the king had "expelled the mediums [*hā'ōbōt*] and the wizards [*hayyiddĕ'ōnîm*] from the land" (1 Sam 28:3 NRSV; cf. v. 9). This had been a measure to limit possible sources of popular unrest, rather than an attempt to eradicate superstitious practices. In his hour of need, Saul himself had no overriding qualms about invoking the help of a necromancer.

The story of Saul and the necromancer of Endor is the only narrative about a spiritualist séance in the Bible. This observation, however, does not warrant the conclusion that necromancy was a marginal phenomenon. The many references to the consultation of ghosts—the Hebrew word is *'ōb* (plural *'ōbōt*), linguistically a close relative of *'āb* (*'ābōt*), "ancestor(s)"—indicates otherwise (Lev 19:31, 20:27; Deut 18:11; 1 Sam 15:23; Isa 19:3, 29:4; Ezek 21:26; Zech 10:2). The fact that most of these references are polemical attests to the persistence of the practice. Many necromancers were women.[106] Assuming they were like the medium of Endor, people went to them for a consultation in the privacy of their home. During the session Saul became unwell and sat on the bed; in the meantime, the woman prepared him a meal. The context is entirely domestic (1 Sam 28:20–25). How necromancers proceeded to bring up a ghost, and how they conversed with the spirit, is not clear. Mesopotamian necromancers such as the *šā'iltu*—literally, "the woman who consults, who inquires," a term reminiscent of the Hebrew expression *šā'al* (*bā*) *'ōb*, "to consult a ghost" (Deut 18:11; 1 Chr 10:13)—burned incense to draw the ghost from the underworld; there is also the stray reference to the use of skulls.[107] Whether Israelite practice was similar is unknown.[108] The woman of Endor saw "a divine being [*'ĕlōhîm*] coming up out of the ground" and is asked why she has "disturbed" (*rāgaz*, Hiphil) him by bringing him up (1 Sam 28:13–15). Resting in the underworld, the dead don't like to be woken from their slumber.[109] Also in that respect they are similar to gods.[110]

In view of the importance in local religion of the ancestor cult, the practice of necromancy should come as no surprise. In spite of the

Deuteronomistic censure of the phenomenon, many people found it entirely legitimate to ask a prophet to consult ghosts: "should not a people consult their gods, the dead on behalf of the living?" (Isa 8:19 NRSV). With the synonymous parallelism between the gods (*'ĕlōhîm*) and the dead (*mētîm*), the question is another indication of the divine status of the ancestors. In addition, the circumstance that the question is addressed to prophets—the disciples of Isaiah, according to Isa 8:16—proves that the professional activities of prophets did, at least on occasion, include necromancy. The Deuteronomistic portrait of the prophets as preachers of true religion is misleading. Historically, both male and female prophets were active in the entire spectrum of inspired divination—as distinguished from the more technical form of divination practiced by priests. In local religion, those with a gift for divination used many ways to get in touch with the divine: from spirit possession and visionary experience to necromancy and the interpretation of dreams. To those who came for an oracle of God or a word from the ancestors, it did not matter. As long as they got an answer that would allow them to go on with their lives, they were unlikely to question the divinatory method.

4 Diaspora Religion

Samaria's defeat by the troops of Shalmaneser V (722 BCE) and Sargon II (720 BCE) brought an end to the Northern Kingdom.[1] It became a province of the Assyrian Empire. Many of the Samarian soldiers were incorporated into the Assyrian army, part of the population went into exile, and deported people from abroad were resettled in what had once been Israelite territory. The events could have spelled the end of Israelite religion, but instead, they produced a phenomenon that inaugurated a new phase. Israelite religion became diaspora religion. Tribal religion had come to an end with the rise of the monarchy; royal religion ended with the last kings; local religion changed under the impact of forced migration. All of these earlier phases of Israelite religion left a legacy, but the diaspora experience initiated a process that would change the face of Israelite religion.

"Diaspora" is a Greek term, borrowed from the Septuagint, where it translates various Hebrew words understood to refer to Israel's "dispersion" (see, e.g., Jer 15:7). Through deportation or forced migration, people ended up as exiles and refugees in places far from home. Because the migration was by coercion, it is often called an exile—as reflected in the traditional distinction between the "preexilic" and "postexilic" periods (where the reference is to the Babylonian exile of the Judeans). By focusing on diaspora religion, this chapter approaches the phenomenon from a slightly different angle. It does not make a sharp distinction between enforced and voluntary migration. Voluntary migration was hardly ever totally voluntary because very few people left their land spontaneously in search of a change of scenery. Circumstances such as famine, violence, or economic distress usually forced the decision upon them. Perhaps they went abroad hoping they might return one day. In many cases, however, their diaspora proved to be permanent. Bereft of the traditional beacons of their inherited identity, the

Israelite migrants had to somehow reinvent themselves, just like the Judean exiles in Babylonia more than a century later. It meant coming to terms with a new homeland, while at the same time holding fast to the past. The diaspora community developed a diaspora identity and a diaspora religion.

In the centuries that followed the fall of Samaria, a series of diasporas came to shape the history of Israelite religion. There was a Samarian diaspora in Assyria—about which we know next to nothing except for the fact that it happened, with some distant echoes in the diaspora novella of Tobit.[2] There was another Israelite or Samarian diaspora in Judah. Textbooks rarely mention it because they assume that Israel and Judah had more or less the same language and the same religion. But for those involved it was a real diaspora. They had found refuge from violence and famine, but separated from their ancestral lands they found themselves in the position of second-rate citizens. The Judean diaspora in Babylonia (which included descendants of the northern refugees) originated in the early sixth century BCE as the army of Nebuchadnezzar II deported significant sections of the population of Jerusalem and surroundings—in 597, 586, and 581 BCE. Around the same time, groups of Judeans decided not to wait for a further deterioration of the situation and made their way to Egypt, where they joined diaspora communities throughout the land, from places in the Nile delta (Migdol, Tahpanhes, Memphis) to the deep south (Elephantine in the "land of Pathros"; Jer 44:1, 15). The four diasporas here mentioned do not exhaust the list, but they are the major ones. This chapter takes a closer look at three of them: the Israelite diaspora in Judah; the Judean diaspora in Babylonia; and the diaspora in Egypt, which involved both Samarians and Judeans.

The Israelite Diaspora in Judah

One of the most remarkable stories in the books of Kings deals with the unexpected discovery of the "book of the law" in the Jerusalem temple (2 Kings 22–23). The report dates the event to the eighteenth year of King Josiah, that is, 622 BCE. The king was still in his twenties. He had decided that the time had come for a thorough renovation of the "house of YHWH." The royal secretary Shaphan was sent to the high priest Hilkiah, the temple administrator.[3] The two of them were to draw the balance of the temple funds and make the money available for the acquisition of the necessary construction materials. During the perquisition of the temple treasury, the "book of the law" had come to light (2 Chr 34:14). Hilkiah gave it to Shaphan, who read it and immediately realized its importance. He informed the king, read the book to him, and was ordered to make a divinatory inquiry, together with Hilkiah and three other officials. The prophet they chose to consult was a woman: Huldah the wife of Shallum, keeper of the temple wardrobe. She confirmed the authenticity of the book and the seriousness of the situation, since for many long years no one had paid any heed to this divine law from the time of Moses. The book, most modern scholars agree, must have been an early version of Deuteronomy. It was at the basis of Josiah's reform— assuming the reform was more than just a story.

The miraculous discovery of a hidden book is a classic folklore motif, usually employed to endow a recent piece of writing with an aura of antiquity and, hence, authority. Deuteronomy is a pseudepigraph, with Moses as its fictitious author. It was in fact a product from the time of Josiah. Those involved in its conception and propagation were descendants of Israelites who had come to Judah after the fall of Samaria.[4] Deuteronomy was a creation of the Israelite diaspora. One indication to this effect is the role of Huldah. She and her husband lived in a Jerusalem neighborhood known as the Second Quarter (the Mishneh, 2 Kgs 22:14). It was a suburb on the Western Hill that had developed in the days of Hezekiah to accommodate refugee families from the north.[5] The extension of the city ran parallel to a expansive growth of settlements in Judah as its population almost doubled under the impact of the Israelite migration (cf. 2 Chr 30:25).[6] Historically, then, Huldah and Shallum had their roots in the north.[7] The same is true of the chief temple administrator Hilkiah, who belonged to the priests of Anathoth, the original core of whom descended from the priesthood that had served in Shiloh and, later in the days of King Saul, at Nob.[8] Some of the "men of Anathoth," as they are called in the book of Jeremiah (Jer 11:21–23), were from families that had settled in Anathoth well before the fall of Samaria. Others are likely to have joined them after, in search of a safe haven. They constituted the milieu that shaped the religious ideology of Deuteronomy.

The book of Jeremiah provides an intriguing insight into the connections that existed between leading families of the Israelite diaspora in Judah. While the redactional activity of later scribes is in evidence throughout the text, the abundance of names and surnames is hardly to be explained as mere invention. They preserve the memory of a time of political and religious turmoil in which it mattered to be able to distinguish fellow travelers from opponents. Jeremiah himself was from the priests of Anathoth (Jer 1:1, 32:6–15). He was the son of Hilkiah (Jer 1:1) and the nephew of Shallum (Jer 32:6–15)—the former presumably no other than Hilkiah the high priest and the latter likely the husband of Huldah.[9] Shallum had been keeper of the wardrobe in the temple. His son was one of the "guardians of the threshold" (Jer 35:4), and his grandson rose to the position of deputy high priest ("the second priest," Jer 52:24).[10] Both were in sympathy with Jeremiah (Jer 29:25, 35:4). Jeremiah's closest collaborator was Baruch, presented in the text as his private secretary (Jer 32:12; 36:4, 32). Baruch's brother Seraiah reportedly carried an early collection of Jeremiah oracles—mostly oracles of doom for Babylon—to the city of Babylon in 594 BCE, when he went there for the payment of the annual tribute (Jer 51:59–64; cf. 32:12 for the genealogy).[11] Was this Seraiah the high priest, taken to Babylon by force in 586 (Jer 52:24)? Nothing is known about the background of Shaphan the royal secretary, ally of Hilkiah in the alleged discovery of the law.[12] His sons and grandson took Jeremiah's defense on more than one occasion (Jer 26:24, 36:25; cf. LXX 43:25, 39:14). One son allowed Baruch to use his temple office for a public reading of the Jeremiah scroll (Jer 36:10). Another son of Shaphan, together with a son of Hilkiah, agreed to carry a written message from Jeremiah on their royal mission to King Nebuchadnezzar of Babylon (Jer 29:3). These were men from powerful families.

More than a hundred years separate Josiah's reform from Samaria's fall and the beginning of the Israelite diaspora. Clearly some of the migrated families had done well and achieved positions of influence in the Judean administration.[13] They were part of a new elite, perhaps propelled to power in the aftermath of the palace revolution as well as the popular insurrection preceding the reign of Josiah (2 Kgs 21:23–26).[14] But even though—over the course of several generations—they had successfully adapted to their new homeland, these families had not forgotten their northern inheritance. Both Deuteronomy and the book of Jeremiah bear witness to some typically Israelite religious tenets. Cases in point are the exodus tradition (absent from the original core of Micah and Isaiah, but well-known to such northern prophets as Amos and Hosea);[15] the sanctuary of Shiloh as the forerunner of the Jerusalem temple (Jer 7:12–15; 26:6, 9); the prominence of Mount Ebal and Mount Gerizim (Deut 27:4, 12); and the antimonarchical tendency of Deuteronomy (Deut 17:14–20). Deuteronomy is indeed, as a string of scholars have observed, a document full of northern ideas used to promote a religious reform in the south.[16] The historical scope and impact of that reform are a matter of debate, but the transfer of ideas was to have a lasting effect.[17]

The fact that several Israelite families had made it into the Judean elite is no reason to overlook the diversity within the northern diaspora in the Southern Kingdom. The pro-Babylonian stance of Jeremiah, to mention just one point, was cause for concern in his own social circles. After all, patriotism for the new home country is like the first commandment for any diaspora community, and the attitude of Jeremiah struck many as highly unpatriotic. Also, the northern families that had experienced upward social mobility were a minority. The Rechabite community was in a different situation. Like Jeremiah and many of his connections, they had their roots in the Northern Kingdom too (2 Kgs 10:12–17), came to Judah after the fall of Samaria, and had moved to Jerusalem under the impact of Nebuchadnezzar's military campaigns (Jer 35:11). The Rechabites cultivated the memory of their nomadic past. Life then had been simple, and religion had been pure. These ideas led them to cling to the lifestyle of desert nomads: they dwelled in tents, avoided alcohol, and shunned the practice of agriculture (Jer 35:6–10). In the Judean society they had their own niche, but as a somewhat sectarian group from the north they remained socially marginal. Part of the internal diversity was religious. The strong devotion to YHWH of the priests from Anathoth and the Rechabites is unlikely to have characterized the entire Israelite diaspora in Judah. The cult of the Queen of Heaven, performed by women and their families, in Jerusalem and the towns of Judah as well as in the diaspora in Egypt (Jer 7:16–20, 44:15–25), was most likely a practice imported from the north. Letters addressed to the Aramean community of Syene (modern Aswan), just across from Elephantine, indicate that the Queen of Heaven is to be identified with Anat-Bethel, the consort of Bethel, and it seems Bethel was venerated by Israelites rather than by Judeans (Jer 48:13).[18] The Northern Kingdom had a mixed population, and it was to be expected that the Israelite diaspora had mixed religious practices as well.

Owing to the nature of the meager written evidence for the Israelite diaspora in Judah, it is not really possible to get a picture of its earlier phases. The archaeology suggests that the newcomers in Judah were not completely dispersed since they lived in separate neighborhoods (such as Jerusalem's Second Quarter) and towns. In that respect, their experience mirrored the Judean diaspora in Babylonia and in Egypt. The life in Israelite "colonies" facilitated the people's continued attachment to their cultural traditions and explains the preservation of those traditions. Was the first generation of migrants hoping for a return? Most of their descendants no longer did. As the northern diaspora was becoming more and more integrated in the social and cultural fabric of Judah, their diaspora identity slowly merged into a Judean one. The desecration of the Bethel temple—perhaps the principal event of Josiah's reform (2 Kgs 23:15)—brought an end to the only serious Yahwistic rival of the Jerusalem temple. Henceforth Jerusalem was the uncontested religious center (Jer 41:5). Judah became the repository of the religious traditions of Israel. The books of Hosea and Amos entered the collected scriptures of the south, just as did a fair number of northern psalms. "Israel" and "Jacob" ceased being names for the Northern Kingdom only and came to be applied increasingly to inhabitants of Judah too. The Babylonian oracles of Second Isaiah (found mostly in Isaiah 40–48) address the Judean diaspora community all the time as "Jacob" and refer to Yhwh as "the Holy One of Israel."

The Judean Diaspora in Babylonia

One major difference between the Israelite diaspora in Judah and the Judean diaspora in Babylonia is the fact that very few, if any, of the Judeans left home on their own initiative. They had not gone to Babylonia to escape persecution or in pursuit of a better life. The Babylonian military had deported them against their will in order to break the resistance of a refractory vassal state. There were three deportations. The first one occurred in 597 BCE, after the defeat of "the city of Judah" (*āl Yahudu*), as Babylonian sources called Jerusalem.[19] King Jehoiachin was deposed, and he and his entourage, thousands of warriors, and hundreds of artisans were taken to Babylon (2 Kgs 24:8–17; Jer 24:1, 29:1–2, 52:28). The second deportation took place in 586. It involved fewer people than the first one, but the numbers were still substantial (2 Kgs 25:11–12; Jer 52:29). A third deportation followed in 581, in the aftermath of the murder of Gedaliah and Judean migrations to Egypt (Jer 41:16–43:7). It differed from the two previous ones because it also involved Judeans who had moved to Egypt.[20] This exile in three installments brought a substantial number of Judeans to Babylon. How many in all? Estimates are precarious, but the total figure was probably closer to five thousand (Jer 52:28–30) than ten thousand (cf. 2 Kgs 24:16, 25:11–12).[21] Many inhabitants of Judah stayed behind (Jer 39:10; Neh 1:1–3); the land was not emptied of its population.[22]

History is, by definition, written in hindsight. As such it is liable to present a skewed picture of the experience of those who were actually living in past times. We know the outcome, so to speak, and because we know the end of the story, we tend to read the beginning and the middle from that perspective. The first generation of Judean exiles had no idea the Babylonian dominance would ever end. Nor, for that matter, did the second generation. For all they knew, their diaspora was permanent. For many of them, it would indeed turn out to be so, for when the Persians—as the new masters of the Near East—decreed that at least some Judeans were free to return to the land of their ancestors, most of them chose to stay. It is, in other words, misleading to describe the Judean diaspora in Babylonia as a temporary situation. To most of those involved, it was not. A second optical illusion, induced in no small measure by the biblical account of the facts, is the belief that history had come to a halt in Judah. In the minds of those who had been taken to Babylon—the "children of the exile" (běnê haggôlâ), as they called themselves—they were the chosen people, whereas those who had been left to stay in Judah were more or less irrelevant. But the exile had not depleted Judah of its traditional population. Even if it is impossible to write about the period by adopting *their* perspective—we have nearly nothing to go on—it is helpful to be aware it was just as real as that of the diaspora returnees who ended up on what they considered the good side of history.[23]

In order to get a realistic view of life in the Babylonian diaspora, we need to distinguish three phases. The first phase began with the deportation of King Jehoiachin (also known as Jeconiah), members of his administration, and a large contingent of soldiers and artisans. It was a national disaster, but the Jerusalem temple was still standing; and in the beginning some Judean prophets, both in Jerusalem and in Babylon, predicted an imminent return of the exiles and the restoration of Jeconiah's kingship (Jer 28:1–4; 29:8–9, 15, 20–23, 31–32). They were still in denial. The second phase started with the razing of Jerusalem and the sack of its temple (586 BCE). For all those deported to Babylon, there was no longer any realistic hope of a swift return. They had to make the best of a situation that might last for a long time indeed. The Persian conquest of Babylonia initiated the third phase (539 BCE). Some years after their victory, the new emperors adopted a policy that allowed groups of exiles to go back to the lands their families had come from. Even though only a minority of the Judean exiles left Babylonia, those who continued to live there felt they had been granted some sort of recognition as a separate ethnic and religious community. The temple reconstruction project in Jerusalem may have strengthened their self-awareness as a nation, but the new self-perception had already set in before. It is reflected in the renaissance of Hebrew Yahwistic names, as opposed to the trend during the previous period, especially in the cities and among the elite, to adopt Babylonian personal names.[24]

Cuneiform archives from the Neo-Babylonian and Persian periods attest to the presence of a significant number of Judean exiles in southern Mesopotamia, where they lived in the vicinity of Nippur.[25] A major settlement was Al-Yahudu ("Judah-town"), echoing the name the Babylonians used to refer to Jerusalem. Such "mirror towns," as they have been called, were not unusual.[26] Not too far from Al-Yahudu were the towns of Ashkelon, Gaza, Sidon, and Tyre, created as rural settlements for deported Philistines and Phoenicians.[27] The various diaspora communities in the Neo-Babylonian Empire lived, for the most part, as separate colonies, often named after cities where the people had come from or after their ethnicity. The ethnic profile of these diaspora towns differed from place to place, but the general picture is the same. Al-Yahudu was first known as the "town of the Judeans" (*ālu ša Yahudayya*, 572 BCE), and the fields that the inhabitants cultivated were "the fields of the Judeans."[28] Not everybody was from native Judean stock, though. In the town there also lived Arameans, whose names suggest a particular veneration for the gods Bethel, Nanay (also referred to as Banitu, "Beautiful One," or Urkittu, "the One from Uruk"), and Nabu.[29] Their presence was hardly due to a deliberate policy of mixing populations, which was not the Babylonian practice. Did they come from the Aramean diaspora in Egypt, and had they been brought to Babylonia in 581 BCE?[30] That would explain why the Aramean woman Nanay-biḫi, slave in the household of the powerful Judean Ahikam, is said to be from Egypt.[31] To judge by the name-giving patterns over the generations, people with Yahwistic names and people with Bethel names did not intermarry—or if they did, only sporadically. Their interactions were frequent, though. The presence of one Bethel-sharezer (Bethel-šar-uṣur) among the returnees in Jerusalem (Zech 7:2) suggests that some of these Bethel worshippers came to identify themselves as Judeans.

It would be mistaken to suggest that the entire Judean diaspora lived in the Nippur countryside. During the reign of Nebuchadnezzar II (r. 605–562 BCE), the city of Babylon offered employment to a significant number of dignitaries, artisans, and specialized laborers from conquered territories.[32] Some Judeans made a career as merchants and lived in such cities as Sippar.[33] Nevertheless, the vast majority of exiles lived in conditions that were very much like those reflected in the archives from Al-Yahudu. Agriculture was the dominant mode of subsistence, with barley and dates as the main crops (fig. 34).[34] This does not mean the Judean inhabitants had been farmers and peasants in their previous lives. On the contrary, they—or their ancestors—had been part of the upper class back home—as administrators, priests, judges, prophets, artisans, and the like. In their new surroundings, however, they found themselves in occupations the Babylonian authorities had deemed suitable. The system under which they lived was "land for service," which meant they were settled in little-developed territories where they worked the soil for their own subsistence and profit, in return for rent, taxes, and the performance of service obligations. Rent and taxes were unavoidable.[35] Service obligations (referred to as *ilku*, from the Akkadian verb *alāku*, "to go"), on the other hand, could be bought off if one had the means to do so.[36] For some, it was not a bad life. They had land they could lease out to others, rented out houses, owned oxen and sheep, made loans, held one or more slaves, and were active in various profitable business ventures.[37] These are the people who kept archives, which is why we know more about them than about others. But most Judeans were less fortunate. They were unable to buy off their corvée duties, which meant they spent two months a year away from home.[38] They had to go "to Elam," as the conventional phrase had it, working for imperial projects wherever they were needed.[39] The living conditions of some Judeans forced them to hire out their own children.[40] Debt slavery was not unknown among the Judean exiles either.[41] It was not happiness for all.

In towns like Al-Yaḫudu, most Judeans lived in relative seclusion from the rest of Babylonian society. A handful of them acted as intermediaries with the Babylonian and, later, Persian administration. Ahikam, for instance, collected taxes from his fellow Judeans and dealt with the fiscal authorities. He and his family were in regular contact with non-Judeans. Such contacts were also common for the Judean merchants of Sippar and the Judean artisans in Babylon. It is mostly among this class of Judeans that mixed marriages occurred.[42] But the vast majority of Judeans in the Nippur countryside married their sons and daughters to partners from other Judean families. The rare intermarriage that did happen in Al-Yaḫudu involved a fatherless bride without a dowry who married a lower-class Babylonian.[43] A form of partial self-government contributed to the relative insulation of these Judean diaspora communities. The specific competencies of "the elders of Judah" (*ziqnê yĕhûdâ*) are unknown (Ezek 8:1).[44] However, the cuneiform reference to the "assembly of the elders of the Egyptians" (*puḫru ša*

Fig. 34. Date palm grove on the Euphrates River near the location of the ancient city of Babylon (Hilla, Iraq, 1932). (Library of Congress, Prints & Photographs, LC-DIG-matpc-16123.)

šībūti miṣirāyī) overseeing a decision about land division among Egyptian soldiers in Babylonia suggests the Judean elders were authorized to regulate internal Judean affairs.[45] What language did the Judean exiles speak? The presence on a 550 BCE tablet of the personal name Shelemiah (*šlmyh*, Šalam-yāma in the cuneiform text), handwritten in ancient Hebrew characters, suggests they initially continued to speak Hebrew.[46] At some point, though, they shifted to Aramaic. While the language of their official documents is Akkadian, the tablets regularly carry an annotation on the side in Aramaic.[47] Already widely used in the later Neo-Babylonian Empire, Aramaic became the international language of choice during the Persian era.[48]

The Judean Diaspora and Babylonian Religion

The cuneiform sources relating to the Judean diaspora say little about religious life, but the personal names they contain reveal a rather liberal attitude. There is no indication that names that mention a Babylonian god were taboo among the Judean exiles. The royal merchant Hosea of Sippar gave Babylonian names to his sons Bel-iddin, Bel-uballiṭ, Nabu-ittannu, and Šamaš-iddin.[49] And in Al-Yaḫudu, the Judean Neriah (Nir-Yāma), son of Ahikam, called one of his sons Aqabi-Yāma and the other Nabû-aḫ-uṣur.[50] Up to a point, names may have been just names; the reference to a foreign deity could be considered harmless and insignificant.[51] Yet the alternate names Bēl-šar-uṣur and Yaḫu-šar-uṣur, carried by one and the same man around 550 BCE, suggest some Judeans took Bel and Yahu to be names of the same god.[52] The book of Daniel mentions the practice of double names: Daniel has Belteshashazzar (Bēlet-šar-uṣur) as his Babylonian name, just as his companions have both a Hebrew and a Babylonian name (Dan 1:7). Though Daniel is a fictive diaspora tale of later times, the phenomenon of double names did have some currency at the time.[53] But the case of Bēl-šar-uṣur and Yaḫu-šar-uṣur is different: it is the same name, only the god differs. It shows that the Judean exiles, or at least some of them, were open to the idea that the main Babylonian god Bel and their god Yaho differed in name only. They may have been more willing to embrace Babylonian religious ideas and practices than sometimes assumed.

There is indeed evidence that the exiles joined in some of the Babylonian religious ceremonies. The principal Babylonian festival was the Akitu, celebrated twice a year, once in spring (in the month of Nisan) and once in autumn (in the month of Tashritu, which literally means "renewal").

The reference in Second Isaiah to the procession of Bel and Nabu, the two main deities of the festival (Isa 46:1–3), shows that the Judean exiles were familiar with this ritual.[54] Those who were in the city of Babylon at the beginning of Nisan or Tishri (Tashritu) could hardly have missed the festivities.[55] During the first years of his exile in the city, King Jehoiachin was given special treatment. Though in fact a hostage, he received daily rations from the palace and still enjoyed royal dignity.[56] All this obviously on condition that there be no doubt about his loyal recognition of the Babylonian king as the king of kings. In practice, this must have meant attendance at the Akitu festival, one of the political objectives of which was to proclaim the divine support of the Babylonian king. At some point, Jehoiachin was imprisoned. His release on the eve of the Babylonian New Year festival in spring (month XII/day 27, 2 Kgs 25:27–30 // Jer 52:31–34), just before Amel-Marduk (r. 562–560 BCE) officially acceded to the throne, must have entailed the formal duty to be present at the spring Akitu festival to honor the new Babylonian king.

All this, one might say, belongs to the conventional rules of diplomacy and correct behavior. But the case of a Judean prophet speaking oracles of victory for Nebuchadnezzar on the occasion of the Akitu festival is something else. It goes beyond the demands of duty. Yet this is precisely what Ezekiel must have done. He was a priest and a prophet, and a leading figure in the early Judean diaspora (Ezek 1:1–2, 8:1, 14:1, 20:1). Living among the Judean exiles in Tel Abib by the river Chebar (Ezek 3:15), Ezekiel is likely to have been familiar with other Judean diaspora settlements in the Nippur countryside.[57] The book that carries his name contains a number of prophecies delivered on some of the main festival days of the Babylonian calendar. On New Year's day of 586 ("in the twelfth year, on the first day of the first month," Ezek 26:1 LXX[A]), Ezekiel publicly predicted that Nebuchadnezzar would lead a successful military campaign against the city of Tyre (Ezek 26:1, 7–14). Fifteen years later, again on New Year's day ("in the twenty-seventh year, in the first month, on the first day of the month," Ezek 29:17), Ezekiel admitted that the Tyrian campaigns had been difficult and the outcome disappointing: "King Nebuchadrezzar of Babylon made his army labor hard against Tyre . . . ; yet neither he nor his army got anything from Tyre to pay for the labor that had been expended against it" (Ezek 29:18 NRSV). To redeem his earlier overly optimistic prediction, the prophet then delivered an oracle promising Nebuchadnezzar victory against Egypt: "I have given him the land of Egypt as his payment for which he labored, because they worked for me, says the Lord GOD" (Ezek 29:20 NRSV). The campaign against Tyre lasted thirteen years.[58] Several campaigns against Egypt followed, leading to Egypt's defeat in 568 BCE. So here was a Judean prophet who, on the occasion of the Akitu festival in spring, pronounced oracles of victory for the Babylonian king in the name of the ancestral god of the Judeans. This should not come as a surprise. If the exiles could be expected to pray for the Babylonian (and later Persian) authorities (Jer 29:7), Judean prophets might well deliver favorable oracles to the same authorities.[59] By speaking those oracles at the Babylonian New Year festival, Ezekiel conformed to a practice attested already for the Neo-Assyrian Empire: the celebration of the city god's victory over his opponents went in tandem with prophecies of divine support for the king against his enemies.[60] Two of Ezekiel's other oracles against Egypt were delivered on Babylonian festival days as well.[61] Hardly a coincidence. This Judean prophet demonstrated his loyalty to the Babylonian ruler by oracles of victory, delivered in the name of YHWH, which he spoke on public Babylonian holidays.[62]

Worshipping YHWH in Babylonia

Though the Judean exiles may have been more open to the religion of the Babylonians than has often been assumed, most of them did not abandon the religion of their forebears. Their situation resembled that of the foreigners whom the Assyrians had deported to Samaria. Those people "worshiped the LORD but also served their own gods," as the Deuteronomist writes (2 Kgs 17:33 NRSV). The underlying logic is clear. In a foreign land you have to pay respect to the god of the land—YHWH in Samaria, Bel in Babylon—even as you continue to worship your own god. Little is known about the Yahwistic cult in the Babylonian diaspora. It existed, but what it exactly looked like is mostly guesswork. Did the Judeans have a YHWH temple they could visit? The Arab migrants in the Nippur region had a temple for the moon god in their town ("the Temple of Sin in the town of the Arabs").[63] And in fifth-century BCE Egypt, the Jewish community at Elephantine did have a local "temple of Yaho." It is unclear whether the Babylonian Judeans had one, though scholars have surmised there was a YHWH temple of sorts at Casiphia in northern Babylonia (Ezra 8:15–20).[64] In the absence of unambiguous evidence, however, it seems safer to err on the side of caution and to assume the Judean exiles worshipped YHWH without a temple. This probably means there was no sacrificial cult, either. There must have been places of prayer, likely on river banks where people could perform ablutions and pray "with washed hands."[65] Incense offerings were likely part of the ritual (cf. Mal 1:11). Would the Judeans periodically get together for scriptural readings? It is a popular suggestion in the scholarly literature, but such synagogue-like meetings sound very much like a retrojection of later customs onto an earlier period we know little about.[66]

Whereas the first generation of exiles had vivid memories of Jerusalem, most of the second and third generation had never set eyes on the city. To them, it was mostly the subject of stories. They were born in Babylon—as the personal name Zerubbabel ("offspring of Babylon"), grandson of King Jehoiachin, says.[67] Nevertheless, the name of Jerusalem continued to resonate with them. Four periodical fasts made sure they would not forget (Zech 7:1–7, 8:18–19).[68] In chronological order, the annual fasts preserved the memory of the beginning of Jerusalem's siege in the tenth month (Tebeth, day 10; 2 Kgs 25:1; Jer 39:1, 52:4); the breaching of the wall in the fourth month of the next year (Tammuz, day 9; 2 Kgs 25:3–4; Jer 39:2–3, 52:6–7); the destruction of the city, including temple and city walls, in the fifth month (Ab, beginning on day 7; 2 Kgs 25:8–12; Jer 52:12–14); and the murder of Gedaliah in the seventh month (Tishri, 2 Kgs 25:22–26; Jer 41:1–3).[69] We do not know since when or how widely these fast days were observed, but those who returned to Jerusalem around 520 BCE believed the custom had been in existence for more than seventy years (Zech 7:5). The practice, then, must have developed in the diaspora.

There is something peculiar about these fasts. While a fast day in commemoration of the temple desecration could have been a popular response to a national trauma, the collective observance of four days of fasting seems too contrived for it to be accounted for as a spontaneous initiative. Especially the fast for Gedaliah is striking. He was the pro-Babylonian grandson of the royal secretary Shaphan, appointed by Nebuchadnezzar as governor of Judah, and could be viewed as a Babylonian puppet.[70] Unlike Jeconiah, released from his Babylonian prison in 562 BCE (2 Kgs 25:27–30), he was not of royal lineage. Why should the exiles continue to mourn his death? The most plausible explanation is that the four fasts were designed not merely to commemorate historical events but to bring together different factions among the Judeans of Babylonia—also those who had been deported to Babylonia in the aftermath of Gedaliah's murder. The fasts fostered a sense of collective history that the entire Judean community could embrace.[71]

These calendrical fasts also throw into relief a change in the appreciation of time among the exiles. Their ancestors used to date events by referring to the main phases of the agricultural calendar ("once, at the time of the barley harvest . . ."). In Babylonia, the Judeans became calendar-conscious. One indication to this effect is the practice to date oracles by year, month, and day of the month, first found in the book of Ezekiel and later also in Haggai and Zechariah.[72] There is no parallel in the preexilic prophets. The timely observation of the four fasts suggests that the administrative calendar, current in Babylonia and consistently employed in the archives of Al-Yaḫudu and other Judean settlements, was adopted by the diaspora community as the proper means of measuring time. Along with the Babylonian calendar, the Judeans also adopted the Babylonian month names (Zech 1:7, 7:1; Esth 2:16; Neh 1:1, 2:1, 6:15; 1 Macc 7:43; 2 Macc 15:36; cf. the Aramaic ostraca from Beersheba).[73] Another sign of the new calendar awareness is the introduction of a formal period of rest every seventh day (the Sabbath). During the monarchic era, the Hebrew word *šabbāt* referred to Full Moon (day 15 of the month); during the Persian period, it referred to the seventh day of the week (Neh 10:32, 13:15–21). The shift in meaning is likely to have occurred among the Judean exiles in sixth-century BCE Babylonia, presumably under the influence of the local cultic calendar (Ezek 46:1).[74] Over time, Sabbath observance became a hallmark of Judaism. Its Babylonian background is hard to ignore, though, even if it is less explicit than the adoption of Babylonian month names.[75]

It is highly questionable whether the average Judean exile in Babylonia actually observed the Sabbath. The available cuneiform documents contain no hint that people took a rest every seventh day. Then again, there is also no evidence that the common Babylonian avoided professional activities on the various "evil days" of their cultic calendar. These speculations on the special character of particular days of the month originated among scholars and had little effect outside their circles. Likewise, the doctrine of the seventh-day Sabbath was a priestly innovation with, at least initially, little popular appeal. To the priestly elite it was important, though. The rhythm of the seven-day week, with a rest on every seventh day, provided the framework of the priestly account of creation, now found as the opening chapter of the book of Genesis. God created the world in six days and rested on the seventh, thereby setting an example for all the faithful to follow. Those who belonged to the priestly school that produced this creation account presumably did. But priests were special, and not everybody could be expected to live by their rules. Yet even if the priestly doctrine of the seventh-day Sabbath may have been unfamiliar at first, there is no reason to underestimate its significance. Eventually it would have tremendous impact. Its elaboration in the diaspora points to a fair degree of familiarity among Judean intellectuals with the lore of their Babylonian counterparts.[76] This is yet another indication of the acculturation of the exile community, even as it sought to hold on to—or reinvent—its distinctive identity.

The development of several new traditions in the Judean diaspora in Babylonia, such as the annual fast days, indicates that the various Judean settlements were in communication. Individual Judean entrepreneurs and traders moved around and were in touch with compatriots. After the death of Ahikam from Al-Yaḫudu, his five sons divided part of the paternal estate in the city of Babylon, in the presence of several Judean witnesses. The trip from the Nippur region to Babylon was apparently no problem for them.[77] Other Judeans, such as the merchant family of Hosea in Sippar, were used to long-distance travel in the line of business.[78] These were commercial and more or less informal contacts. The meetings of Ezekiel with "the elders of Judah" (*ziqnê yĕhûdâ*) were more formal (Ezek 8:1; cf. 14:1, 20:1; cf. Jer 29:1). Assuming the assembly of the elders of Judah was competent to rule on internal Judean affairs (in the likeness of the "assembly of the elders of the Egyptians"), they must have come together with some regularity. But meetings in person were not the only way to stay in touch. Letters were another line of communication. Jeremiah is reported to have sent written messages to the Babylonian diaspora on two occasions (Jer 29:1–3, 51:59–64). Fact or fiction? The phenomenon as such was familiar at the time (Jer 29:25). Other prophets, too, resorted to epistolary communication when the circumstances so demanded.[79] Against this background, it is not so strange to see that the prophetic call of Ezekiel consisted of the ingurgitation of a written scroll (Ezek 2:8–3:3). Writing as a means of dissemination and epistolary communication grew more important in the diaspora.

The Zionist Movement and the Migration to Jerusalem

According to the official version of the history of the Jewish people, the Persian conquest of Babylonia brought an end to the exile. During the first year of his reign, King Cyrus of Persia decreed that all of the exiles from Judah were permitted to go up to Jerusalem to rebuild the house of the LORD (Ezra 1:1–4). Assuming that "the first year" refers to Cyrus's kingship over Babylon, it was 539 BCE. The royal announcement allegedly met with a massive response: more than forty-two thousand exiles would have made the journey back to Judah (Ezra 2:64–67). On more than one count, this version of the facts is hard to believe. The cuneiform archives from Al-Yaḫudu and other towns with Judean families cover the period between 572 and 477 BCE. There is no trace of a Judean exodus after 539; everything continues much as before, though the Judeans now fall under the authority of a Persian governor.[80] There is no trace in the texts of Judeans migrating back, and certainly not of a massive return. References to more than sixty Judeans in the fifth-century BCE administration of a Babylonian banking house in Nippur (the Murašu tablets) leave a similar impression.[81] And in what remains of the Persian royal inscriptions of the period, nothing like the Cyrus edict has been found. The Cyrus Cylinder that celebrated the Persian conquest of Babylon does speak about the return of Babylonian gods to their original sanctuaries but says nothing about migrant communities going home.[82] These are arguments from silence, one might say, but they carry a real weight nonetheless.

Still, it would be an error to dismiss the biblical presentation as pure fiction. There is evidence for the return of at least one other diaspora community to the land of its ancestors. In Neirab (modern Al-Nayrab), a town in the vicinity of Aleppo, French archaeologists discovered an archive of some thirty cuneiform documents written between 560 and 520 BCE. They mention Neirab as their place of origin, but it is clear that the tablets are from Babylonia. The Neirab they refer to is the mirror town of that name, also known as "the town of the Neirabians," situated in the Nippur countryside. Around 520 BCE the Neirab exiles returned home—or some of them did—and took their family records with them.[83] They made their homeward journey during the reign of Darius I (r. 522–486 BCE) rather than that of Cyrus (r. 559–530 BCE). Interestingly, the dated oracles from Haggai and Zechariah, delivered in Jerusalem, are nearly all from the second year of Darius.[84] This suggests a scenario in which groups of Judean exiles went to Jerusalem about the same time the Syrian exiles returned to Neirab.[85] Work on the rebuilding of the temple had yet to be started, and some of the returnees were wondering whether they should continue to observe the fast days they had kept in Babylon (Zech 7:1–3).[86] Clearly, these were still the early days of the Judeans from Babylonia in Judah.[87]

The reason why the biblical tradition credits Cyrus with the formal permission for the exiles to return is related to the idealized image of that king in the oracles of Second Isaiah. Second Isaiah (or Deutero-Isaiah) is the name of an oracle collection (Isaiah 40–55) rather than a prophet. We do not know who wrote these texts. It is clear from their language and content that some of them are from Babylon (most notably those found in Isaiah 40–48).[88] A case in point is the main victory oracle for Cyrus (Isa 45:1–7). It addresses the king by name (Isa 45:1; cf. 44:28) and calls him Yнwн's "anointed one" (Isa 45:1; cf. 44:28, "My shepherd"). It looks as though the Persian ruler is still to conquer Babylon:

> I [Yнwн] will march before you
> > and level the city walls,
> I will break in pieces the doors of bronze
> > and cut through bars of irons. (Isa 45:2)[89]

Such violence proved unnecessary, for Cyrus had the support of much of the Babylonian clergy. The city gates were wide open when he arrived.[90] The language of Second Isaiah's victory oracle for Cyrus has close correspondences in the Cyrus Cylinder, the latter being a composition by Babylonian scholars to celebrate the Persian king as the one whom Marduk (Bel) himself had taken by the hand (fig. 35).[91] Just as Ezekiel had joined the chorus of prophets promising victory to Nebuchadnezzar in the first half of the sixth century BCE, so Second Isaiah sided with the propagandists for Cyrus in the second half. Little danger was involved. Toward the end of Nabonidus's reign (r. 556–539 BCE), Babylonian scribes composed a scathing parody on the unpopular monarch.[92] From a Babylonian perspective, Deutero-Isaiah was just another voice in support of Cyrus.[93] But to Second Isaiah, Cyrus was much more than just a welcome change. Cyrus was a messiah. He would carry out all of God's purposes: "He shall build my city, and set my exiles free" (Isa 45:13; cf. 44:28). It was enough for later Judean historians to antedate the decision of Darius and present it as a decree by Cyrus. Although a few of the Judeans in Babylon migrated back to Judah shortly after Cyrus had conquered Babylon, most of the returnees made the journey under Darius and his successors.

The hope that Cyrus would order the restoration of Jerusalem is one manifestation of a Zionist awakening among some of the Judean exiles. We have no idea about the numerical significance of the movement nor when it started. But it is clear that the change of rule in Babylonia sparked a sentiment that may have been gestating for a while. Some of the exiles were dreaming of Jerusalem. As the actual memories of Jerusalem faded, the city and its temple grew ever more beautiful in the imagination. Jerusalem became the symbol of everything desirable yet out of reach.

Fig. 35. Cyrus Cylinder. British Museum, London. (Wikimedia Commons; photograph by Mike Peel, www.mikepeel.net.)

It had been "the splendor of Israel" and the "perfection of beauty" (Lam 2:1, 15). In the minds of the exiles, Jerusalem was "the holy city." That expression, common in later times, first occurs in Second Isaiah (Isa 48:2, 52:1). To the Zionists—who called themselves after the holy city (Isa 48:2)—it was much more than a nice turn of phrase. If Jerusalem was the holy city, it was a sacred duty to rebuild it. It was the geographical heart of their religion. Not to go there, if the chance arose, would betray a lack of commitment. In the spiritual milieu of Second Isaiah, these ideas went in tandem with an unmitigated critique of Babylonian religion (Isa 44:9–20; 46:1–2, 6–8; 47:13). It was either/or. Religious assimilation, as encountered among sections of the Judean diaspora, was unacceptable (Isa 48:5). You had to leave Babylon to go to Jerusalem: "Go out from Babylon, flee from Chaldea" (Isa 48:20 NRSV);

> Depart, depart, go out from there!
>> Touch no unclean thing;
> go out from the midst of it, purify yourselves,
>> you who carry the vessels of the LORD." (Isa 52:11 NRSV)

The exiles were to follow in the footsteps of Abraham and leave the land of the Chaldeans (Isa 41:8–9, 51:1–2). Do these calls date to the time of Cyrus? There is reason to suspect they are later. The reference to Egypt as ransom for the Judeans (Isa 43:3) becomes meaningful against the background of the Persian conquest of Egypt in 525 BCE. When Darius eventually granted Judeans permission to leave, a few years after Egypt's submission, most of them chose to stay. The Zionists were a minority.[94]

One of the spiritual sources of the Zionist party was the book of Jeremiah—or rather a forerunner, consisting of assorted oracles and perhaps some biographical stories. When and how this early Jeremiah scroll came to Babylon is a matter of speculation. Jeremiah himself had been in written communication with the exiles, and several of the Judean deportees, taken to Babylonia between 597 and 581 BCE, had supported him. They remembered the prophet and his preaching. Jeremiah may have died in Egypt, but his words circulated in Babylon.[95] Second Isaiah knew them.[96] Among the authors who wrote Isaiah 40–55, the figure of Jeremiah, whom many had thought of as a collaborator during his lifetime, rose to the status of a martyr. For all the opposition he had endured, his predictions had come true. There was good reason, therefore, also to believe in his promise that the exile would be limited to seventy years (Jer 25:11–12, 29:10). God's "good word" (Jer 29:10) would not pass away unfulfilled (Isa 40:8). There would be an end to the dispersion. One day soon the people would all be gathered from among the nations and return to Zion (Isa 49:14–26). This hope led some of the Zionists in Babylon to look at Jeremiah as a man whose unwavering commitment to his mission had opened the door to atonement. He had experienced suffering, more so perhaps than any prophet before him, but his suffering was ultimately their salvation (Isa 53:4–6).[97] It was a new view of martyrdom, first expressed in Second Isaiah and destined to have great influence on later Judaism and Christianity.[98]

The Egyptian Diaspora

A chapter on diaspora religion would be tendentious by omission if it failed to discuss the Samarian and Judean diaspora in Egypt. This Egyptian diaspora is best known for what used to be referred to as the Jewish military colony of Elephantine.[99] The island of Elephantine, close to the Egyptian border with Nubia, was the findspot of hundreds of papyri and ostraca (potsherds used as writing material) in the early twentieth century. The texts cover the entire fifth century BCE and document the existence on the island of a community of people with Hebrew names and a local temple for Yaho. Did that make them Jews? Where did they come from? And when? Simple questions, not so easily answered. They touch upon some very relevant issues for the history of Israelite religion, however, and merit the effort of a modest investigation.

Were these people Jews? If the term "Jews" is understood to refer to those who observed the rituals and tenets of Judaism, they were not, for "Judaism" as the world knows it did not see the day before the second century BCE.[100] Judeans then? After all, the Elephantine papyri regularly call them yĕhûdayyē' (singular yĕhûday). But the evidence is a little more confusing than that, for the texts identify the inhabitants of the community just as often as Arameans ('ărāmayyē', singular 'ărāmay). In fact, one and the same person can identify both as a "Judean" and an "Aramean."[101] And though the personal names are classic Hebrew names, many of them familiar from the Bible, the people who carried them spoke Aramaic among each other. They were part of the wider Aramaic-speaking diaspora in Egypt. In recent years, the cultural background of this diaspora, including the Elephantine community, has come into sharper focus owing to the discovery and decipherment of a multicolumn papyrus with Aramaic literary texts. The Amherst papyrus—so called after its collector, Lord Amherst of Hackney—was found in Egypt and is written in Demotic (late-Egyptian) characters, but it uses the Aramaic language. It is a compilation of texts from different diaspora communities in Egypt that, at least in the mind of the compilers, were closely associated.[102] This cultural constellation—distinct diaspora communities, yet in close contact—resembles very much the historical situation in and around Elephantine, where just across from the island, in the town of Syene, there were two Aramean communities, one group devoted to Bethel and the Queen of Heaven and the other to Nanay (often invoked by her title Banit, "Beautiful One") and her consort Nabu.[103]

Two sections of the Amherst papyrus have a direct bearing on the identity of the Elephantine community. One contains three religious songs to Yaho, one of which has a striking resemblance to Psalm 20 and two others with clear affinities to a variety of psalms yet without a specific correspondent in the Bible. The other section has a historical narrative of the arrival of a group of Samarians, led by a man from Judah, who mentions that they are also bringing his sister (wife?) from Jerusalem. The Amherst papyrus is a difficult text, as the discrepancies between the available translations show.[104] But these passages establish some facts beyond a reasonable doubt. The text describes the arrival of a mixed group of migrants, consisting of Samarians (apparently the majority) and Judeans (in a position of leadership).[105] The presence of a Samarian element in the Egyptian diaspora comes to the fore as well in the three songs to Yaho. They call Yaho "our Bull" and identify him with the god Bethel.[106] "Bull" as a divine title fits the religion of the Northern Kingdom (Samaria) in which the "golden calf" was a symbol of YHWH. Also, the book of Jeremiah implies that the veneration of Bethel was specifically Israelite (Jer 48:13). At Elephantine too, at least some of the inhabitants identified Yaho and Bethel, since at times they refer to his divine consort Anat-Yaho as Anat-Bethel.[107]

But despite the presence at Elephantine of inhabitants with Samarian roots, there is not a single reference to Samarians in the papyri. This can only mean that the ethnic designation "Judean" had come to include Samarians. We know this to have been the case during the Hellenistic period. The inhabitants of the village of Samareia in the Fayum are called *Ioudaioi* in Greek papyri of the third and second centuries BCE.[108] This process of inclusion had apparently been well under way, if not come to term, in the Persian period. It must have started with the Samarian diaspora in Judah, owing to which Samarians eventually became Judeans, and Judeans could refer to themselves as "Israel" and "the house of Jacob." The fact that both the Samarian and the Judean migrants to Elephantine could be called Arameans has a number of possible explanations. It could refer to their language or to their identity in the Persian administration—either because they were all from the province of Ebir-nāri (which covered northern Mesopotamia, Syria, and Palestine), and therefore by definition "Arameans" or "Syrians," or because they administratively fell under the Aramean contingent of the Persian armed forces in Egypt. None of these solutions has gained undivided adherence.

Though ethnically speaking the Elephantine community was not Aramean, its members were culturally very close to their Aramean neighbors on the east bank of the Nile. At Elephantine, people took the oath by Yaho, but also by Anat-Yaho and by Herem-Bethel.[109] One document from the Elephantine archives is a cumulative record of monetary contributions to the temple of Yaho. The total amount is distributed over three gods: some of the money goes to Yaho, the rest to Eshem-Bethel and Anat-Bethel.[110] Eshem-Bethel and Herem-Bethel, both also mentioned in the Amherst papyrus, belonged to the entourage of Bethel as their names indicate.[111] Bethel and his consort were the main gods of many Arameans in Egypt, not only in Syene, but also at Memphis and other places.[112] Clearly, the religion of the Elephantine community intersected with the religion of these Arameans. This is all the more striking because they did not inter-marry, or only very seldom.[113] Intermarriage was not unknown at Elephan-tine, but the couples usually consisted of a Judean man and a lower-class Egyptian woman, or a Judean woman and a high-ranking Egyptian man.[114] The occasional reference to Egyptian gods—greetings by Khnum, an oath by Satet—normally occurs in the context of these mixed marriages.[115] The general impression conveyed by the papyri and potsherds is that of a self-contained community, cultivating good relations with the neighbors but devoted to its own god and its own religion. The people did not think of their religion as a form of syncretism at all.

The Elephantine documents open a window onto the historical reality of the Judean diaspora in Egypt. Up to a point they confirm the witness of the Bible. The book of Jeremiah speaks about a Judean migration to Egypt in the aftermath of the fall of Jerusalem. Military commanders led this movement and forced Jeremiah to go along (Jer 43:4–7). The places where the Judeans settled were the Nile delta (Migdol, Tahpanhes), Mem-phis (Noph), and the southern province to which Elephantine belonged (Pathros).[116] These various toponyms and some more occur in the Aramaic texts from Elephantine as places with diaspora settlements. Whether the contemporaries of Jeremiah founded these settlements or joined existing ones is unclear. Jeremiah 44 situates the worship of the Queen of Heaven specifically in the southern province (Jer 44:15, Pathros). Though the title Queen of Heaven does not occur in Elephantine texts, the Arameans of Syene used it as the name of Bethel's consort. She is likely to have been identical with Anat-Bethel. What one would not have suspected on the basis of the biblical texts is the presence of a Yaho temple on the island. The inhabitants were unaware of any rule against it. After its destruction in 410 BCE, they wrote to the authorities in Samaria and Jerusalem to win their support for its reconstruction—which they obtained.[117] The religious situation at Elephantine is unlikely to have been the exception to the rule. Aramaic documents from the Judeans at Edfu, some sixty miles to the north, attest to the presence of several "priests." This could mean the dias-pora community there had a temple too.[118] Judeans (including Samarians) in the Egyptian diaspora kept their traditional religion, but that did not mean they lived by the Bible. How could they? There was no Bible—just religious tradition and cultural memory, most of it handed down orally, and only some in writing.

From Babylonian Exile to Jewish Diaspora

According to the book of Jeremiah, the time of Judah's exile in Babylonia would be seventy years (Jer 25:11–12, 29:10). This became a classic reference among the returnees in Judah and their descendants (Zech 1:12, 7:5; Ezra 1:1; 2 Chr 36:22; Dan 9:2). It was not the first time someone had announced a seventy-year period of desolation for a Near Eastern city. Well before Jeremiah was born, the city of Babylon had been sacked by the Assyrians (689 BCE). Marduk had become angry with the inhabitants and had vowed, according to an Assyrian inscription, to abandon his city "for seventy years." In his mercy, however, he had inverted the cuneiform signs for "seventy," thereby reducing the sentence to "eleven" years.[119] "Seventy years," apparently, was a figure of speech for "a long time" (Jer 29:28). It was about the lifespan of a person (Ps 90:10). In the minds of later generations, however, the seventy years came to stand for a precisely delimited period of divine punishment. For seven decades the people had suffered God's wrath. But from their perspective, it had been an interruption—a major interruption, lasting a lifetime, but in the bigger scheme of things a transition between the time before and the time after. Modern scholarship has mostly adopted the same perspective, distinguishing preexilic, exilic, and postexilic periods. Clearly, such chronological references are not entirely neutral. Though the terms will continue to be used, they should not obfuscate the fact that the diaspora experience became an abiding feature of Israelite religion and its various successors. There was, in a way, no end to the exile.

There was no end to the exile for all those who remained in Babylonia, even though the Persian authorities had granted them permission to leave. Most of the exiles preferred to live in circumstances that were not ideal but bearable rather than to go on a journey to a destination they had never seen. Why jump into the great unknown? The adventurers who left were a minority. Some went for religious reasons, some because of patriotic zeal, some simply to try their luck in a different place. Their return to the homeland also had an effect on those who stayed. It showed that their "captivity" was over, which meant that their presence in Babylonia was more or less by their own consent. Also, the Persian policy with respect to the Judeans implied their recognition as a distinct ethic group, reinforcing the cohesion of the Judeans in the diaspora as a distinct ethnic-religious community. All through the fifth century BCE, the eastern diaspora Judeans lived in their own colonies and neighborhoods, married into Judean families, and venerated the god of their Judean ancestors. Regular contact between the Judean diaspora and the authorities in Jerusalem contributed to a rudimentary form of religious unity. Similar developments occurred in Egypt. During the Persian period, the Judean and Samarian colonies there continued to flourish, and nothing indicates there was a widespread desire to return to Judah. Rather the contrary. At Elephantine, the destruction of the Yaho temple by Egyptian opponents (410 BCE) was no incentive for people to leave the island. The community stayed and rebuilt the temple, with the moral support of the authorities in Samaria and Jerusalem. Clearly, the Egyptian diaspora felt a connection to the homeland, even though they had no intention of leaving. Another indication of a nascent transterritorial religious identity was the introduction in the Egyptian diaspora of a common religious calendar.[120]

The historical developments of the Babylonian and Egyptian diaspora during the Persian period prefigure the transformation of the Judean and Samarian dispersion into the Jewish diaspora. The use of the term "Jewish" here is a delicate matter. It could be argued, as many authors have done, that "Jewish" is an anachronism before the birth of Judaism in the second century BCE.[121] When it comes to ethnicity, however, there are also drawbacks to the rigid translation of Aramaic *yĕhûday* (or Greek *Ioudaios*) as "Judean," since the evidence from Elephantine shows that Samarians were included in that category. In fact, one of the unanticipated consequences of the diaspora experience was the development of a sense of common identity among people despite their different origins. Thrown together in a foreign and potentially hostile environment, people discovered that they were a community through ties of language, race, and religion. Back home the predominant pattern may have been one of religious localism, but abroad the situation was different. Are we to call this newly discovered—or invented—identity "Judean" or "Jewish"? Neither term is entirely felicitous. Most scholars today feel that the term "Judean" is to be preferred. Let us go with the flow, as long as we are fully aware that the Judean diaspora included Samarians and would eventually turn into the Jewish diaspora.

5 Ethnic Religion

In 539 BCE, Cyrus the Great made a triumphal entry into the city of Babylon and proclaimed himself its new king, in token of which he made the rounds of the local sanctuaries to pay his respects.[1] With the apparent approval of the local god Bel, the city and with it the entire Babylonian Empire passed into the hands of the new master. It was the beginning of the Persian era (fig. 36). More than two hundred years later, in 333 BCE, Alexander the Great would defeat Darius III in the battle at Issus and bring an end to the Persian hegemony. But for two long centuries, the peoples of the Near East would be living in a world where the Persians ruled. No one could ignore their presence. The empire change was also the beginning of a new chapter in the history of Israelite religion—not only because the Persian kings gave permission for a repatriation of some of the Judeans from the Babylonian diaspora, but also on account of the way in which the Persian supremacy influenced the course of Israelite religion in the long term. Textbooks on Israelite religion tend to describe the Persian period as a time of restoration.[2] While it is true that the population of Judah built a new temple and restored the walls of Jerusalem, these reconstruction projects did not entail a return to the situation as it had existed before the Babylonian capture and destruction of the city. During the Persian period, Israelite religion went through a major transformation and developed a new profile. Diaspora religion did not disappear but contributed to the emergence of what is best described as ethnic religion. Israelite religion became ethnic religion in the sense that the religious community coincided no longer with the population of a particular state (as it had under royal religion) or topographical area (as was the case in local religion) but with a specific ethnic group. Its members were known as Yehudim, "Judeans," even though their number included many people who lived outside the Persian

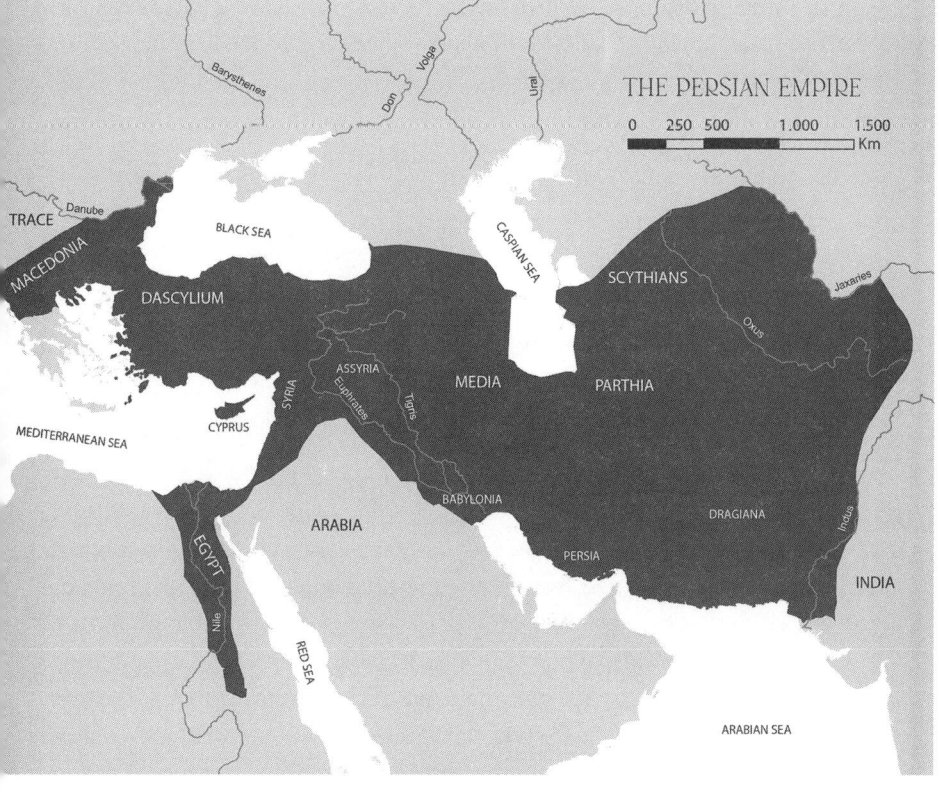

Fig. 36. Map of the Persian Empire. (Map created by Jip Zinsmeister.)

province of Yehud. These Judeans shared the worship of Yʜwʜ and the observance of a common set of religious festivals. Religion and ethnicity became inextricable to the point that the one became a defining feature of the other (and vice versa).

To measure the Persian impact on Israelite religion it is helpful to distinguish between indirect and more direct influence. The indirect influence did not become visible until the later Persian and the subsequent Hellenistic periods. It affected primarily the religious imagination. The experience of Persian imperialism changed the way the Judeans thought about God, angels, and their own position with respect to the supramundane realities. This is the subject of the first section of this chapter. The more direct influence of the Persians was tangible in the partial repatriation of the Babylonian Jews, the creation of Yehud as a separate Persian province, and the Persian authorization and endorsement of several missions to Yehud and the Judean diaspora by prominent Judean men from Babylonia. One of the consequences of this Persian policy was the official promulgation of the Pentateuch as the law of the God of heaven for the entire Judean community, throughout the southern Levant as well as in the diaspora. The enforcement of this Torah as "the law of the (Persian) king," moreover, had implications for the Israelite and Jewish conceptualization of the Torah as a law book. Henceforth, all members of the ethnic community were to observe the religious festivals "as written" (*kakkātûb*), on the dates and in the manner as prescribed in the law. The ethnic religion that took shape under Persian influence is the link between the diaspora religion of the Babylonian era, on the one hand, and the scriptural religion as it developed during the Hellenistic period, on the other.

Persian Imperialism and the Religious Imagination

For "the children of the Golah"—the self-designation of the Judean repatriates—the migration from Babylon to Judah occurred in the wake of the transition from Babylonian to Persian supremacy. The change of rule threw a large shadow. Like many peoples in the ancient world, the Judeans were in awe of the Persians—the efficiency of their military machine, their smooth communications network, the rumored opulence of their palaces, and the secrets of their sumptuous court life.[3] This did not mean, however, that they hastened to adopt Persian culture. Though some aspects of Israelite religion in its later stages seem to echo certain Zoroastrian notions (such as its dualism), the Persian influence was in general more subtle—though not, for that reason, any less pervasive.[4] The presence of Persian loanwords, in both Hebrew and Aramaic, bears witness to the impact of the new masters. Some of those terms—like *rāz*, "secret"; *pardēs*, "park, paradise"; and *dāt*, "law"—would play a considerable role in later Jewish writings.[5] Under the Persians, the world had entered a new era.

The Judean experience of the Persian hegemony left a mark on the collective religious imagination too. This was to be expected. People have always borrowed their religious metaphors from the world they are familiar with, looking to asymmetric and hierarchical relations as models to conceptualize their position vis-à-vis the gods. That is why, during the time of the monarchy, the Israelites thought of God as their king and themselves as his subjects. During the Persian era, God came to be modeled after the Persian emperor, and the heavenly court came to resemble a Persian palace. One unmistakable indication of the Persian influence upon the new religious speculations is the notion of the seven "angels of the presence." Though found foremost in texts from the Hellenistic period, the Persian background of the idea is not in doubt. The topic merits a slightly longer demonstration since it throws additional light on some of the major transformations in the way in which the Israelites—Judeans *and* Samarians—thought about God and the world of the gods. So let us first take a closer look at the emergence of these seven angels, and follow up with a discussion of the burgeoning monotheism of the time.

In most English Bibles, the book of Tobit has a place in the section of the Apocrypha. Written around 200 BCE, the book tells the story of Tobias son of Tobit and his journey from Nineveh to Ecbatana, where he ends up marrying his cousin Sarah.[6] Tobias has a mysterious travel companion who eventually reveals his true identity: "I am Raphael, one of the seven angels who stand ready and enter before the glory of the Lord" (Tob 12:15 NRSV). The theme of the seven angels who have privileged access to God originated in the Persian era. An early occurrence is in the Astronomical Book preserved in 1 Enoch (1 Enoch 72–82). Many scholars hold that this section is the oldest stratum of the Enoch literature and may stem from the late Persian period.[7] After his tour of heaven, Enoch returns to earth: "Then the seven holy ones brought me and placed me on the ground in front of the gate of my house." (1 En. 81:5). These seven "holy ones" are the seven angels.[8] They are still there in the book of Revelation: "When the Lamb opened the seventh seal, there was silence in heaven for about half an hour. And I saw the seven angels who stand before God, and seven trumpets were given to them" (Rev 8:1–2 NRSV).

Both the figure of the seven archangels (1 Enoch 20, in the Greek text from Akhmim; 1 En. 90:21; T. Levi 8:2) and their designation as "angels of the presence" (Jub. 1:27, 29; 2:1, 18; 15:27) go back to the organization of the Persian court.[9] All major political decisions were made by the king in consultation with his inner circle, consisting of "seven counselors" or "officials." An early reference to this political body occurs in the Artaxerxes edict concerning the mission of Ezra: "You are commissioned by the king and his seven counselors" (*šibʿat yāʿăṭōhî*, Ezra 7:14).[10] The book of Esther gives the names of the seven men at the court of Xerxes (Ahasuerus) who were "the seven officials [*śarîm*] of Persia and Media, who had access to the king [*rōʾê pĕnê hammelek*], and sat first in the kingdom" (Esth 1:14 NRSV). Xenophon (*Anab.* 1.6.4) refers to these officials as "seven of the noblest Persians," and Herodotus (*Hist.* 3.84, 118) offers an historical explanation for why they had free and unannounced access to the king. Though the historical relationship between the Persian king and his counselors will have varied over time—the number seven may have included the king himself, and their specific office is uncertain—it is clear that in the popular perception, as reflected in the writings of Greek and Judean authors, the Persian monarch had seven advisors with privileged access.[11]

The Hebrew word for angel is *mal'ak*. Its literal meaning is "messenger," which is indeed one of the main roles attributed to angels. In a world where God's transcendence was increasingly conceptualized as distance and inaccessibility, contact with the divine required mediation. As God was cast in the likeness of a Persian monarch, there arose the need for messengers, go-betweens, and intercessors. The older notion according to which one could say a prayer expecting that God heard one's voice—the view that informs many of the individual prayers in the book of Psalms—gave way to a different metaphor. The new metaphor was based on the analogy with the Persian postal system, with letter bearers and couriers, much admired by the Greek authors.[12] Once again, the book of Tobit offers an illustration. Before Tobias had begun his journey, his father Tobit and his cousin Sarah, the one in Nineveh and the other in Ecbatana, had each said an individual prayer, simultaneously yet unbeknownst to the other: "At that very moment, the prayers of both of them were heard in the glorious presence of God" (Tob 3:16 NRSV). This looks like the old conception. But another passage in the same book shows otherwise: "So now when you [Tobit] and Sarah prayed, it was I [the angel Raphael] who brought and read the record of your prayer before the glory of the Lord" (Tob 12:12). The speed of transmission remains miraculous, but the mechanics are new. Angels make a record of the spoken prayer and transmit the message to the inner circle of God, where it is read aloud in his glorious presence. This is how petitions were supposed to reach the Persian emperor.

Under the impact of the Judean experience with the Persian superpower, the Judean unease with "other gods" turned into a form of monotheism. Though the Elephantine papyri show that Judean communities long continued to venerate divine companions of Yaho, the Persian period also witnessed the gradual demotion of other gods to the rank of angels. Up to a point, it was a matter of semantics. The Sons of El who once constituted the council of the gods became the council of the holy ones—the latter now a term for angels.[13] But in the minds of the worshippers, the difference between gods and angels was real. There was only one true God. This made the Judeans monotheists, also in the eyes of their contemporaries.[14] Angels were not gods but beings of a lower rank and a different nature. From colleagues and peers, the other gods turned into God's servants, leading to a host of angels—thousands and thousands of them. Some texts simply say that their number is beyond counting. Why these exorbitant figures? On the one hand, because the angels are as numerous as the stars, the celestial luminaries traditionally associated with gods.[15] On the other hand, however, the innumerable angels reflect the experience with the Persian bureaucracy. Within the Persian Empire were countless officials, of varied authority and rank, who stood between the simple subject and the emperor. There surely were not fewer servants at the heavenly court. Though every class of angels had its own role to perform, all of them were links in the chain that ultimately connected the individual to God.

It is as good as impossible to separate the Judean turn to monotheism from the rise of a more universalistic outlook on the world. The Persian monarch ruled over an empire of many nations, tongues, and customs. His reign embraced the world as people knew it. Since the Judean god was imagined to be like the emperor, his rule had to be universal too. God came to be viewed as the king of the world, entitled to the tribute of every nation. Just as Cyrus claimed that "all the kings who sit upon thrones throughout the world . . . brought their heavy tribute before me and . . . kissed my feet," so a psalm from this period says,

> All the nations you have made
>> shall come and bow down before you, O Lord,
>> and shall glorify your name. (Ps 86:9 NRSV)[16]

Another element that contributed to the rise of Judean universalism was the significant growth of international trade and travel during the Persian period. Contacts between Judah and the diaspora Judeans in Babylonia, Egypt, and Syria were another incentive for a more global consciousness: "For from the rising of the sun to its setting my name is great among the nations, and in every place incense is offered to my name, and a pure offering" (Mal 1:11 NRSV).

Transformations in the collective way of thinking about the universe and the gods are usually slow and barely perceptible to the people involved in the process. Most gods retain their names and their titles. Revisions of the traditional mythology are very rare too. On the surface, therefore, the human perception of the gods may seem as changeless and eternal as the gods themselves. From a distance, however, mutations in the religious sensibility do not go unnoticed. One manifestation of the new religious climate is the prominence of "the God of heaven" as title of YHWH, occurring both in apposition to the divine name ("the LORD, the God of heaven," Ezra 1:2) and as substitute for the divine name ("the law of the God of heaven," Ezra 7:12). Letters and letter drafts from the archives of the Judean community at Elephantine show that both types of reference, that is, with or without the proper divine name (mostly written as *yhw* in Elephantine), were indeed common in the fifth century BCE. In view of the frequent references to the proper name Yaho in the Elephantine papyri and potsherds, there is no reason to speculate that "the God of heaven" (at times, "Lord of heaven," in Elephantine texts) is a pious locution to avoid the god's proper name. In this respect, the popular title is to be distinguished from the later use of "heaven" as code for "God," common in books like 1 Maccabees (e.g., 1 Macc 3:50, 4:10, 9:46), the works of Josephus, and the Gospels (Luke 15:18, "I have sinned against heaven"). Close study of the use of the appellation "God of heaven" indicates it served as a conventional title for the highest god. Everybody could understand it, Judeans and non-Judeans alike. The common Near Eastern image of the winged sun disk, widely used during the period throughout the Persian Empire, may be seen as the iconographic counterpart of the phrase.[17]

The Judean Repatriates and Their Neighbors

Whereas the Persian influence on the religious imagination was largely indirect and perceptible only in the long term—it comes to the fore most clearly in texts from the Hellenistic period—the political decisions of the Persians impacted the course of Judean history in more direct and immediate ways. Over the course of the late sixth and much of the fifth centuries BCE, various Persian monarchs allowed groups of Judeans in Babylonia to return to the land of their ancestors. Even though the Judean diaspora was not as gloomy as the term "captivity" (*šĕbî, šibĕyâ, šĕbît*) suggests (e.g., Ezra 2:1, 3:8, 8:35; Neh 1:2, 3), Judeans could not simply leave Babylonia without authorization. The permissions that were granted served a Persian cause. While the repatriation diminished the labor force in Babylonia, the installation of a reliable leading class in Judah facilitated the profitable administration of the Persian province of Yehud. Several Babylonian Judeans served as governors of Yehud. Commissioned by different Persian kings, each of them went to Judah in the company of a group of returnees: the otherwise unknown Sheshbazzar in the time of Cyrus (Ezra 1:8–11, 5:14; 1 Esd 2:10–15),[18] Zerubbabel under Darius I (Ezra 2:2; Hag 1:1, 2:1–2; cf. 1 Esd 4:13–63), and Nehemiah in the days of Artaxerxes (Neh 2:1–9, 5:14). Another wave of Judean migrants arrived with Ezra (Ezra 8:1–20), whose mission as lawgiver had a broader topographical scope than Judah (Ezra 7:25) but whose seat of office was in Jerusalem (Ezra 8:32). Some passages in the books of Ezra-Nehemiah telescope these successive waves and wavelets of migration to Yehud into one massive return during the first year of Cyrus (Ezra 1–2), even though the first substantial repatriation of Judean exiles occurred under Darius I (r. 522–486 BCE), about the same time the diaspora from Neirab was allowed to go back to Syria.[19] In 525 BCE Egypt had been incorporated into the Persian Empire, and from that moment on the provinces in the southern Levant gained greater political relevance.[20]

The particular perspective of Ezra-Nehemiah focuses on Judah and seeks to demonstrate how Cyrus's subjugation of Babylonia inaugurated the period during which the Judean returnees came to live around the new temple in Jerusalem as the legitimate *qāhāl*, the religious community.[21] There was no place in this perspective for the sanctuary at Mount Gerizim in Samaria, the oldest remains of which go back to the mid-fifth century BCE at the latest (fig. 37).[22] Located about thirty miles from Jerusalem, this hilltop altar place near Shechem was larger and more monumental than the rather modest Second Temple in Jerusalem (Hag 2:3; Ezra 3:12).[23] There is no word of it in Ezra-Nehemiah. In the vision of its authors, Samarians practiced a deviant form of Yahwism. They were not really Israelites (Ezra 4:2). When the Samarian leadership offered to participate in the rebuilding of the Jerusalem temple, their help was firmly rejected (Ezra 4:1–3). Even though the Samarians worshipped the same god as the Judeans (Ezra 4:2), they were not regarded as brothers but as "adversaries" (*ṣārîm*, Ezra 4:1). The literary references to the Samarians as opponents, alone or alongside Ammonites ("Tobiah the Ammonite servant") and Idumeans ("Geshem the Arab"), hint at a geopolitical context of the Judean restoration project that merits closer scrutiny (Neh 2:19, 6:1). It is clear that the small province of Yehud, which covered an area of some thirty by thirty miles, was bordered on all sides by provinces or districts whose populations had religious practices that were, from the perspective of the authors of Ezra-Nehemiah, incompatible with the correct worship of YHWH. Once we step outside this ideological frame, however, the situation presents itself in rather different terms.

Fig. 37. Mount Gerizim seen from Mount Ebal, circa 1915. (Wikimedia Commons, OSU Special Collections & Archives: Commons@Flickr Commons.)

Let us begin with Samaria. In the days of Ezra and Nehemiah—roughly around 450 BCE—the split between Samaritans and Jews was still some three centuries away. The distinction Samaritan/Samarian resembles the one between Jew/Judean. In both cases the Hebrew or Aramaic term refers originally to the inhabitants of a geographically delimited area (Samaria, Judah) and developed secondarily into a reference to a religious community (Samaritans, Jews). Only under the rule of the Hasmoneans in the second half of the second century BCE is there evidence of a growing gap between Samaritans and Jews. The destruction of the Gerizim temple by John Hyrcanus in 112 BCE meant a definitive parting of the ways.[24] But in 450 BCE, there were no Samaritans—only Samarians. Though Ezra-Nehemiah refers to political tensions between the provinces of Judah and Samaria, the fact that in the late fourth century BCE a brother of the Jerusalem high priest accepted the offer of Sanballat the governor of Samaria to serve as high priest at Gerizim suggests a fair degree of affinity between the respective priesthoods of Samaria and Judah.[25]

After the fall of Samaria in 722/720 BCE, the former Northern Kingdom had become an Assyrian province. Owing to the Assyrian policy of mass deportations, non-Israelite groups had come to live alongside a great many Israelites who did not leave the land. The cult of YHWH continued to dominate the religious landscape, though, owing in part to the missionary activity of a number of Israelite priests who had been repatriated from Assyria at the order of the king to teach the new population the proper cult of "the god of the land." They settled at Bethel, the venerable temple town of the Northern Kingdom (2 Kgs 17:27–28).[26] Until the destruction of the Bethel altar by Josiah around 620 BCE (2 Kgs 23:15), then, the Bethel temple continued to be an important center of YHWH worship—even if some Judeans rejected it as idolatrous.[27] We are poorly informed about the religious situation in Samaria through the late seventh and sixth centuries BCE, but the reference to a delegation from Shechem, Shiloh, and Samaria bringing offerings to the Jerusalem temple in 586 shows that YHWH worship had not ceased in Samaria (Jer 41:5). Also, the Gerizim sanctuary of the fifth century BCE was consecrated to YHWH and no other god.[28] The prominence of Yahwistic names in the Samaria papyri from Wadi Daliyeh has led scholars to conclude that during the Persian period Samaria was predominantly Yahwistic, even more so perhaps than during the Iron Age.[29] Throughout the fifth century, then, both Samaria and Judah were Persian provinces with a population whose majority worshipped YHWH.

Across the Jordan was the territory of Ammon. In the time of Nehemiah, it was ruled by a man named Tobiah. Was he the founder of the Tobiad dynasty from Hellenistic times (Josephus, *Ant.* 12.160–236)? The name Tobiah is Yahwistic ("Yah is good"), as is the name of his son Jehohanan ("Yaho has been gracious," Neh 6:18). Also the Judean high priest Eliashib had permitted him to use a room in the Jerusalem temple (Neh 13:4–9), all of which facts are strong indications that Tobiah was a YHWH worshipper. The historical explanation for the existence of the cult of YHWH in Ammon is the Ammonite conquest of the Israelite territory of Gad in Transjordan in the wake of Israel's defeat by Tiglath-Pileser III in the late eighth century BCE (2 Kgs 15:19–22, 29; Jer 49:1–2).[30] Ammon thereby absorbed a significant Israelite population. The latter was able to maintain its traditional religion and to preserve connections with Yahwists on the other side of the Jordan (cf. Jer 41:10, 15). It was out of their midst that Tobiah at some point must have gained a position of leadership. Judah's neighbor to the east, then, had a mixed population that included a fair number of Yahwists of Israelite stock.[31]

The third "adversary" of the Judeans that Ezra-Nehemiah mentions is Geshem (or Gashmu, Neh 6:6) the Arab. The reference is most likely to the ruler of Idumea, a territory that during the Persian and Hellenistic periods stretched from the southern Judean hill country to the northern Negeb, and from the Dead Sea to the port cities of Ashkelon and Gaza.[32] It incorporated the land of Edom (from which name Greek "Idumea" most likely derives), but included such formerly Judean areas as the Arad and Beersheba valleys, the southern Shephelah, and the southern Judean hills.[33] Idumea is the expanded version of the former state of Edom, owing to its annexation of Judean and Philistine territory (1 Esd 4:50; cf. Ezek 25:12, 36:5; Obad 1:12–15; Joel 4:19 [3:19]; Mal 1:2–5).[34] It seems to have been a Persian protectorate rather than a province, perhaps in recognition of the logistic and material assistance it had given to the Persian army during the Egyptian campaign (Herodotus, *Hist.* 3.4–9).[35] "Geshem the Arab" belonged to the Qedarites, an Arab group active in the area between the Syrian desert and North Arabia. After the decline and fall of the Assyrian and Babylonian empires, they had gained control of southern Palestine.[36] The area had a mixed population. Names on the Idumean ostraca of the period reflect worship of Qos (the old Edomite deity Qaush), Arab deities like Il and Manat, and such originally Babylonian gods as Shamash, Nabu, and Sin.[37] Owing to the incorporation of formerly Judean territories, however, Idumea also had worshippers of YHWH within its borders, witness the occurrence of the tribal name Yehôkal. In fact, one of the ostraca bears a reference to a "temple of Yaho" (*byt yhw*), apparently located at Khirbet el-Qom (ancient Makkedah, west of Hebron).[38] Though the Yahwists must have been a minority, they apparently did have their own temple, about twenty miles south of Jerusalem.

Surrounded by three provinces or polities with a sometimes sizable population of Yahwists, the Babylonian Judeans who had repatriated to Judah in order to help rebuild and administer the "holy city" in the land of their ancestors had to determine what was to be their attitude toward the non-Judeans— at least in terms of provincial boundaries—who worshipped the same god as they did. Could they be counted as "Israelites" too? The issue was all the more pressing since the Persian authorities, in line with a long-standing tradition in the Near East, tended to identify ethnic divisions with religious boundaries. In a way, the situation of these Yahwists outside the borders of Judah was similar to that of the Judean diaspora in Babylonia or Egypt. Didn't the Judean community on Elephantine Island have its own "temple of Yaho"? The presence of these pockets of Yahwists, whether in Egypt or Babylonia, or closer to home in Samaria, Ammon, and Idumea, gave urgency to the issue of the boundaries of the *qāhāl*, the religious community—and also, more or less by the same token, of the ethnic community. Did this community consist of true-blooded Judeans only, or were all worshippers of YHWH in a way Judeans, whatever their genealogical pedigree?

A further complicating factor in the debate about Judean ethnicity and religion was the circumstance that the recent migrants to Judah—having come from Babylonia, they were the "new" Judeans—were not masters of their own land. They were, in a way, "slaves" serving foreign kings whom God had set over them (Neh 9:36–37; cf. Ezra 9:9). The Judeans who had been deported to Babylon in the early sixth century BCE had been forced to leave the kingdom of Judah. When some of their descendants returned, many years later, they came back to a Persian province. The world had changed. Instead of a king in Jerusalem, there was a provincial governor ruling from a palace south of Jerusalem adorned with a Persian garden.[39] It stood for the new culture. The governor's palace in Samaria had a similar ornamental garden—a "paradise," as Greek authors called it, using a term borrowed from the Persian.[40] The governor himself might be Judean (Zerubbabel, Nehemiah), but he was subordinate to the Persian satrap in Damascus. Persian judges provided law and order, aided by the armed force of police and mercenaries.[41] A system of taxes on land, produce, and people put a heavy burden on the population (Neh 5:4, 15).[42] Many people had lost their land and were forced to hire themselves out as day laborers (Neh 5:1–5).[43] Judah had become Persian property. The palace of the king of kings was far away, yet there was no escaping his presence. The emperor had his eyes and ears everywhere.[44] For the new Judeans, then, there were at last three capacities in which they had to negotiate their identity: as Persian subjects, as members of the Judean ethnic community, and as adherents of a religion focused on the cult of YHWH in the temple at Jerusalem.

The Boundaries of the Community and the Mission of Ezra

The books of Ezra-Nehemiah document the existence of different positions about the boundaries of the Israelite ethnic-religious community. In view of the anti-Samarian stance of the books, its composers subscribed to the narrow definition.[45] Only "those of Israelite descent" who had "separated from all foreigners [*bĕnê nēkār*]" belonged to the legitimate community (cf. Neh 9:2). Yet the books also contain evidence showing that at least several high-placed Judeans of the time advocated a broader understanding of Israelite identity. Some Jerusalem-based prophets collaborated with Tobiah and Sanballat (Neh 6:10–14), and leading circles of Jerusalem were sympathetic to Tobiah (Neh 6:17–19, 13:4–9). Moreover, Tobiah the Ammonite "servant," his son Jehohanan, and Sanballat the Samarian governor all had Judean ties by marriage (Neh 6:18; 13:4, 28; cf. 13:23; Josephus, *Ant.* 11.306–312). There was a Judean faction, then, that did not think of Samarians and Ammonites as "foreigners."

Ezra-Nehemiah is not a neutral record of events as they occurred in fifth-century BCE Judah, so its use as an historical source requires some circumspection. Doubts have been raised against the authenticity of some of the official documents from which the authors quote, and also about the actual significance of narrated events as well as their relative chronology.[46] Before we focus on specifics, however, it is helpful to highlight the narrative pattern that frames the particular episodes. The recurring cycle of similar events begins with the request to the Persian authorities by Babylonian Judeans for permission to go to Judah in order to contribute somehow to the restoration (Ezra 7:6; Neh 2:4–5); permission is granted, at times in combination with a commission by the Persian king (Ezra 1:2–4, 8–11; 3:7; 7:11–26; Neh 2:7–9); a cohort of Judeans makes the journey to Judah (Ezra 2:1–70, 8:1–36; Neh 7:5–72, 12:1–25); upon arrival in Jerusalem, the Judean repatriates begin to carry out the task they have come to perform (Ezra 3:1–3, 8–13; 5:1–2; Neh 2:11–18, 3:1–32, 8:1–12 [Ezra's mission]); the work of restoration elicits opposition from the rulers of Samaria and other places in Ebir-Nari (Ezra 4:1–5, 5:3–5; Neh 2:10, 19; 3:33–35; 4:1–8; 6:1–14); the conflict is brought to the attention of the Persian authorities (Ezra 4:6, 7–24; 5:6–17), who, in the end, reiterate their support of the Judean cause (Ezra 6:1–12). To mark the completion of the work, in part or in full, the Judeans celebrate one of the festivals of their religion (Ezra 3:4–6, 6:19–22; Neh 8:13–18). This pattern served as a model for the authors to frame and edit their material, which they took from a variety of sources.[47]

The presence of this narrative pattern elicits the question of whether it is primarily a literary device serving the strategy of the authors or a faithful reflection of the realities of the late sixth and fifth centuries BCE. Since the pattern clearly suits an ideological concern, there is reason to submit individual episodes to a critical analysis. There are some instances where a reported event is evidently a doublet inserted in the narrative to provide an element of the literary pattern. The celebration of Succoth (Festival of Booths) by Jeshua and Zerubbabel "as is written" (Ezra 3:4) is a doublet of the Succoth celebration by Ezra (Neh 8:13–18) and impossible to reconcile with the observation in Neh 8:17 that Succoth had not been celebrated this way "since the days of Joshua son of Nun."[48] But while individual instances of patterned elements may have been a literary fiction or a doublet, there can be little doubt about the fact that the pattern as such is based on real events. In other words, Babylonian Judeans did ask for permission to migrate to Judah, and Persian authorities commissioned some of them to perform specific tasks. The opposition they encountered, from Samarian authorities and others, was real enough as well. If the new Judeans nevertheless succeeded, it was also due to the explicit support of the Persians. And the references to the correct and timely celebration of festivals do reflect one of the significant innovations of the time.

A central element in the narrative of Ezra-Nehemiah is the opposition the returnees and their leaders experienced from the side of Samarians, Ammonites, Arabs, and other "people of the land." The main concern of the adversaries was that the monumental building projects of the new Judeans were political statements in support of a program for greater autonomy. The Judean refusal to partner with the Samarians in the temple reconstruction (Ezra 4:1–5) led to an official inquiry about the formal building authorization (Ezra 5:6–17). By the sixth year of Darius (516 BCE), however, Yehud had become a separate Persian province with a new temple symbolizing its new status.[49] The reconstruction of the city walls some seventy years later seemed another step toward independence. The Judeans might just as well cease paying taxes and proclaim their own kingdom (Ezra 4:11–16; Neh 2:19, 6:5–7).[50] How far these fears were real or merely insinuations is unclear. But there can be little doubt that the Samarians and their allies suspected the Judeans of a separatist agenda. The hostile attitude of the Judean leadership (Zerubbabel, Nehemiah) seemed to confirm their suspicions. In all likelihood, the hostility on the part of the Judeans had a variety of motives. During the years of the temple reconstruction, in the early reign of Darius I, some circles entertained hopes for a restoration of the monarchy, with Zerubbabel as the new branch on the trunk of the Davidic dynasty (Zech 6:9–15; cf. Hag 2:20–23; Zech 4:6–10). In the time of Nehemiah such aspirations had lost their plausibility. What mattered to Nehemiah and his supporters was the purity of the "holy race" (*zera' haqqōdeš*, Ezra 9:2). His concern was to keep the religious community intact and free from "admixture" (*'ēreb*, Neh 13:3) of non-Judean elements.

In view of the negative reactions of the Samarians and their allies against the missions of Zerubbabel and Nehemiah, the absence of any animosity toward Ezra is striking. It is true that the Ezra narrative mentions the potential threat of "enemies" (Ezra 8:22, 31), but that term refers to gangs of robbers and brigands that might attack Ezra's caravan on the way to Judah. The report on Ezra's activity does not mention any Samarian opposition. Also in other respects, it is necessary to make a clear distinction between the missions of Zerubbabel and Nehemiah, on the one hand, and that of Ezra, on the other.[51] Ezra did not come to build, like they did, but to investigate and instruct. Zerubbabel was the grandson of King Jehoiachin, and Nehemiah a high official at the court of Artaxerxes I (Neh 1:11), whereas Ezra was a priest and "a scribe skilled in the law of Moses" (Ezra 7:1–6; cf. 1 Esd 8:9).[52] According to the Aramaic text of the Persian edict that describes Ezra's mission, he was to "make inquiries about Judah and Jerusalem according to the law of your God, which is in your hand" (Ezra 7:14 NRSV) and "to appoint magistrates and judges who may judge all the people in the province Beyond the River who know the laws of your God; and you shall teach those that do not know them" (Ezra 7:25 NRSV). "Beyond the River" (*'ăbar nahărāh*; Hebrew *'ēber hannāhār*) translates Akkadian Ebir-Nāri, the customary designation of the satrapy that covered all of Syria-Palestine south of the Euphrates. In Ezra-Nehemiah this satrapy is consequently referred to as a "province." Though at times "the province Beyond the River" seems to designate specifically the southern Levant (cf. Ezra 4:16), the designation always includes Samaria (Ezra 4:11, 17). Ezra's activity was to have an impact in Samaria too, then. In fact, he had a double mission. One, he was to reorganize the temple cult in Jerusalem and Judah in conformity with the law of God; and two, he was to take measures to ensure that Yahwists in Judah and the neighboring provinces ("all the people in the province Beyond the River who know the laws of your God") would observe the precepts of the law of his God.

The second part of Ezra's mission acknowledges the presence of YHWH worshippers outside Judah. Whereas the activity of Zerubbabel and Nehemiah was limited to Judah, the commission of Ezra extended beyond the borders of Judah and included Samarians and other Yahwists. They too would have to fall in line with the divine law (the Aramaic term used is *dāt*, a loan from Persian *dāta*).[53] Whether the law in question was completely new to them is unlikely since the non-Judean Yahwists are referred to as "those who know the laws [*dātē*] of your God." Nevertheless, the law Ezra brings with him—"the law of your God, which is in your hand" (Ezra 7:14)—is, at least in part, an authoritative innovation to Yahwists both inside and outside of Judah, for it is to be used to reorganize the Jerusalem temple cult (Ezra 7:15–24) and has to be taught to those who do not know it (Ezra 7:25). Most of the discussion about Ezra's mission has focused on the identification of the law he was to promulgate (Deuteronomy, the Priestly source, the Pentateuch, or some unknown law?), but the fact that he brought one law that would apply to all YHWH worshippers throughout Beyond the River, both inside and outside Judah, deserves as much attention. It means that the mission of Ezra was intended to unify and homogenize, at least up to a point, the Yahwistic community regardless of the particular province where its members lived. In this respect, the mission of Ezra was designed to have the opposite effect of the division that Zerubbabel and Nehemiah had caused between Judean and non-Judean Yahwists. Seen from this perspective, Ezra most likely came to Judah after Nehemiah, though the dating of his mission remains a thorny issue.[54]

Though the initiative of Ezra's mission came from Ezra himself ("his request," Ezra 7:6), the Persian king had given his approval. Owing to his authorization, the law of God that Ezra brought would be as binding as "the law of the king" (*dātā' dî malkā'*, Ezra 7:26). Ezra's Torah had "imperial authorization" (*Reichsauthorisation*), as scholars have called it.[55] Such, at least, is the message of Ezra-Nehemiah. But just how plausible is this scenario from a Persian perspective? One preliminary observation concerns the absence of any religious proselytization on the part of the Persians. Although the Achaemenid rulers were committed Zoroastrians, they did not try to implant their religion in the territories they had conquered. The monumental rock inscription of Darius I at Behistun is replete with references to Ahuramazda ("Wise Lord"), the one true god and divine patron of the Achaemenid kings (fig. 38). His worship, so the text claims, will bring happiness in life and in death.[56] The royal chancellery produced an Aramaic version of the inscription, copies of which were dispatched throughout the empire.[57] A copy of this text also found its way to the Judean community at Elephantine. Besides the Life and Words of Ahiqar, it was the only Aramaic text of a literary nature discovered in their archives. Its presence was a reminder of the importance of unquestioned loyalty to the Persian emperor and his successors.[58] That was a virtue the Judeans claimed time and again, but that fact did not impel them to abandon their own religion for the religion of Ahuramazda. Nor were they expected to. Like the Assyrians and the Babylonians before them, the Persians believed the nations should follow their own religious customs.

The pitfall for anyone attempting to make sense of the Persian policy toward the religion of their subjects is to project modern notions of religious freedom on a people that lived in a premodern world. The Persians did not believe in the free exercise of religion as a fundamental human right. To them, religion was not a private matter, nor was its practice optional. At the time, religion and ethnicity were like Siamese twins. To be a Babylonian meant one worshipped Babylonian gods and followed Babylonian religious customs, just as the Egyptians were devoted to Egyptian gods and kept Egyptian rituals. This principle led Persian authorities to adopt a policy that tended to actively facilitate the observance of the religious practices that defined the various ethnic communities in their empire. Recognition as a distinct ethnic community entailed the right to practice the community's religion. In this respect, the Persian policy vis-à-vis the religions of non-Persians under their rule was not so much one of permissiveness as one of regulation. They considered it to be in the interest of the state that the formal worship of the many gods in their kingdom continue undisturbed and in accordance with the proper rules. The Cyrus Cylinder celebrates the first Persian ruler of Babylon as exemplary in his zeal for the welfare of Babylon and all its sacred centers. Mesopotamian gods whose images had been carried off he returned to their sanctuaries, just as he took measures to ensure regular provisions for the temple cults.[59] The propagandistic bias of the inscription is undeniable, but the Persian policy was more than a show of goodwill. It aimed at obtaining the goodwill of the gods who would then bless Cyrus, his son, and his army.[60] Intercession for the Persian emperor and his son is a standard theme in documents about Persian sponsorship of local cults (Ezra 6:10; cf. 7:23). Cynics who would view this as empty rhetoric are missing the point. To the Persian authorities, good statesmanship entailed the duty to facilitate the orderly performance of the rites of religion throughout their domain. It would be foolish to incur the displeasure of the gods by not observing the proper forms of worship (Ezra 7:23, "or wrath [qĕṣap] will come upon the realm of the king and his heirs," NRSV; cf. Zech 7:12 for a similar use of the notion of divine wrath, qeṣep). Their worship of Ahuramazda did not mean the Persian

Fig. 38. Rock inscription of Darius I at Behistun showing the emperor punishing adversaries. (Wikimedia Commons, CC-BY-SA-4.0, https://creativecommons .org/licenses/by-sa/4.0/deed.en.)

kings refused to acknowledge other gods. As Darius says in the Behistun inscription, "Ahuramazda helped me, and the other gods who are."[61]

The most illuminating texts on the Persian policy toward local cults come from Egypt. Cambyses II, son of Cyrus the Great, conquered Egypt in 525 BCE. He had a high-ranking priest from the city of Sais in his Egyptian administration. Udjahorresnet had previously served two Egyptian pharaohs and spent the second part of his career at the courts of Cambyses II and Darius I. In his autobiography, inscribed on a funeral statue, this Egyptian scribe and scholar commemorates some of his achievements (fig. 39).[62] At his advice, Cambyses restored and purified the temple at Sais, instituted regular offerings, and participated himself in acts of worship.[63] This fits with other inscriptional evidence on Cambyses's performance of major Egyptian rituals and his regulations on provisions for the Egyptian temples.[64] Under Darius I (r. 522–486 BCE), Udjahorresnet lived for a time at the Persian court in Elam but was later sent back to Egypt commissioned by the king to restore and reorganize "the office of the House of Life." The "House of Life" (Egyptian *pr 'nḥ*) refers to a locality near the temple and, by extension, the body of scholars and specialists attached to it.[65] Udjahor-resnet made the journey, executed his task as instructed, and so endowed the Egyptian temples again with the relevant scholarly infrastructure: "His majesty [Darius] did this," he observes, "because he knew the usefulness of this art . . . , for preserving the names of all the gods and their temples, their offerings and their rituals forever."[66]

The mission of Udjahorresnet shows that Darius I authorized an Egyptian priest, presumably at the latter's own request, to go to Egypt to organize the proper performance of local religion. The efforts to facilitate and regulate religion in Egypt also led Darius to ask the Persian satrap there to send him "scholars [from] among the soldiers, priests and scribes of Egypt." These men were "to write the law of Egypt" that had been valid from olden days until the last Egyptian dynasty. The Egyptian papyrus that relates the event is not in mint condition, but it is still possible to read that the law in question was also about proper procedure in the temples. The scholars came and produced the law:[67] "They wrote a copy on papyrus in Assyrian writing [i.e., Aramaic] and in documentary writing [i.e., Demotic]. . . . They wrote in his [the king's] presence; nothing was left out."[68] This report spells out the importance the Persian emperor attached to a body of written law that would be comprehensive ("nothing was left out") and accessible to him and his experts.[69] The Egyptian scholars prepared the text at the Persian court ("they wrote in his presence"). This Egyptian "law" commissioned by Darius is likely to have covered more realms than the traditional rules for religious rites and ceremonies.[70] But the explicit mention of "temples" indicates that religion was a central subject.[71] Normative guidelines were to prevent a situation where private prejudice, sloppy procedure, or mere improvisation would be detrimental to the correct performance of religious ritual. There was to be law and order, also in matters of religion.

In view of the Persian policy with respect to the religion of their subjects as reflected in historical documents outside the Bible, the account of the mission of Ezra has a high degree of plausibility. Following in the footsteps of the Assyrians and the Babylonians before them, the Persians pursued a policy of religious tolerance—which, it should be stressed, was not tantamount to religious permissiveness or laissez-faire. They were not averse to actively contributing to the regulation of native religions by

Fig. 39. Statue of the Egyptian priest Udjahorresnet. Vatican Museum. (Wikimedia Commons, Creative Commons .)

authorizing native priests to organize the religion of their own people. In this respect, there is a parallel between the mission of Ezra and the mission of Udjahorresnet. Nor were the Persians the first to take measures that would promote religious unity in the territories under their control. More than two centuries earlier, the Assyrian king sent Israelite priests in exile back to Samaria to teach the new population the worship of the god of the land (2 Kgs 17:27–28). It seemed sound politics because it would be beneficial to social cohesion in the province. Similar considerations may have moved the Persian king to authorize and endorse the mission of Ezra. Since the divine law Ezra came to promulgate was to apply to Samarian and Judean Yahwists alike, it could serve as a basis for religious unity transcending provincial division. Considering the interprovincial conflicts that had plagued the region, the authorities had reason to support measures that would foster a more peaceful coexistence.

The Law of Ezra

Since Ezra's mission was aimed to impact the lives of Yahwists inside the borders of Judah and beyond, the identification of the law he was commissioned to proclaim and disseminate has naturally been the subject of intense debate. Let's see where the evidence leads us. The terminology of the Ezra-Nehemiah account provides a first clue. The law that Ezra brought is "the torah of Moses," also known as "the torah of the LORD," because Moses had received the torah from "the LORD the God of Israel" (Ezra 7:6, 10). This torah is a written document, referred to in Hebrew as a *sēper*, "book" (Neh 8:1, 3), which at the time had the form of a written scroll made of skin (leather, parchment).[72] Though originally torah was an oral genre (Hag 2:11–13; Mal 2:6, 7; Prov 28:9), the "torah of Moses" that Ezra promulgated was "the book of Moses" (Neh 13:1). This leaves us with two possible identifications. In the narrow sense of the term, "the book of Moses" refers to Deuteronomy, which refers to itself as a book (*sēper*) written by Moses (Deut 31:24–26; cf. 31:9, 10–13; 17:18–19). The other option is to take "the book of Moses" in the broad sense of the term and to identify it with the Torah, that is, the five books of Moses or the Pentateuch (the latter term is Greek and means "the five-volume [book]").[73] In the minds of the authors of the books of Ezra and Nehemiah the torah of Moses was most likely identical with the entire Torah, meaning the Pentateuch. Its public reading was reportedly spread over seven days (Neh 8:18), and the communal lamentation elicited by that event is full of echoes from the books of Genesis and Exodus (Neh 9:6–37). Among modern scholars, opinions are divided;[74] however, there are good reasons to assume that the law Ezra is said to have brought, in the latter half of the fifth century BCE, was indeed the Pentateuch.

In order to make a case for the Pentateuch as composed and promulgated around the middle of the Persian period, three sets of data are particularly relevant: (1) the nature of the Pentateuch as literary document, (2) the way it reached its status as sacred scripture, and (3) its textual history. Let us first consider the nature of the Torah as a literary document. Within ancient Near Eastern literature, the Pentateuch stands out as a rather uncommon document. It is true that there are parallels to every separate literary genre encountered in the Pentateuch: stories of the beginning (creation, the flood), patriarchal epics, law collections, liturgies, blessings and curses, covenant texts, and more of the like. But the compilation of all that material into one reasoned composition was unusual, to say the least. Moreover, the technique of interweaving variant versions into one composite narrative or argument, as in the flood story (Gen 6:9–9:19) or the call for cult centralization (Deuteronomy 12), is without parallel.[75] And so is the presence of two or more variant versions, as in the two creation stories (Gen 1:1–2:4, 2:4–3:24) or recurrent episodes in the patriarchal narratives (such as the spouse-sister motif in Gen 12:14–20, 20:1–18, 26:6–11). Clearly the aim of the composers was to be comprehensive rather than consistent and coherent.[76] They did not want to choose one tradition at the cost of another. In this respect it is also significant they refrained from identifying the one place that Yhwh would choose as the sole legitimate site for worship; it could be Gerizim just as well as Jerusalem. Some would call this editorial strategy a compromise. Others might say the authors tried to create a document that could serve as a platform for different constituencies to come together as one community.

The editorial method that produced the Pentateuch was to stitch together and interweave distinct literary materials into one text that could serve as charter document for Israel as one nation, embracing both Judeans and Samarians. Beginning with the creation of the world, the Pentateuch has a universalist outlook. The foundational story it tells focuses on Israel as God's chosen people amidst the nations (Deut 33:29). Since the text envisions a return from the diaspora (Deut 30:1–10), the composition as a whole cannot be earlier than the Persian period. Was it a legacy from the eastern diaspora? That is a plausible scenario. Both the sense of a collective group identity and the presence of a universalist perspective were characteristic elements that developed in the Judean diaspora community in Babylonia. The impetus for the Pentateuch project was likely the wish to consolidate the new-won national awareness and extend it to all of Israel (Samarians included). Its execution presupposes access to earlier Hebrew literature. This was probably easier in the city of Babylon than elsewhere. Written scrolls were part of the Jerusalem temple archives carried off to, and stored in, the Babylonian capital.[77] Although it is impossible to identify the individuals who acted as compilers and editors, they must have come from circles of Judean priestly scribes. One need not embrace classical source theory to acknowledge that the passages traditionally assigned to the Priestly source (P) constitute the framework of the Pentateuch.[78] The Priestly account of creation opens the composition (Genesis 1) and thereby determines its perspective. Another significant Priestly intervention was the insertion of a theological explanation to link the patriarchal narratives with the Moses tradition (Exod 6:2–7:7).[79] In terms of composition, content, and redactional intent, the Pentateuch bears the marks of a Priestly redaction during the Persian period.

This brings us to the Pentateuch's promulgation as "law," that is, as authoritative textual corpus for the entire Yahwistic community. In the eyes of rabbinical Judaism the Torah is the most sacred part of the Bible, the Prophets (Neviim) and the Writings (Ketuvim) serving as complement and commentary. The Samaritan community recognizes only the Torah as their sacred scripture. It is the common foundation of the two religions, if Judaism and Samaritanism may be so called. The five books of Moses must have reached this uncontested status of sacred literature well before the split between the Jewish and the Samaritan communities. That this occurred as the result of a natural, gradual process seems very unlikely.[80] Though many of the materials out of which the Pentateuch has been built are the product of a long oral and/or literary history, the composition as a whole bears the marks of a deliberate editorial creation. Soon after it came into public circulation it was widely accepted as an authoritative body of literature, as references in Chronicles and the Pentateuch's own textual history illustrate.[81] The Pentateuch's promulgation as binding rule required the intervention of an agent with sufficient authority to impose the text on the community. Though Ezra was the mediator of this law of God, it was the Persian authorization that compelled both the Judean and the Samarian communities to recognize the authority of the text.

The Pentateuch is sacred scripture for both the Jewish and the Samaritan communities. Its recognition as holy writ preceded the schism between the two. The deliberately composite nature of the Pentateuch means that the original Torah was a single master text. There were no textual variants, because the variants had been incorporated into one single "compromise" text. The process of dissemination and copying began after the Torah's promulgation. It was the scribal counterpart of the oral dissemination and interpretation of Torah (cf. Neh 8:4–8). In the course of the copying process all sorts of variants crept into the text—some inadvertently, others by design. At the time of the schism between Samaritans and Jews, in the aftermath of the destruction of the Gerizim temple by John Hyrcanus (r. 134–104 BCE), there was the Jewish Pentateuch (as transmitted by the Masoretic Text [MT]) and the Samaritan Pentateuch (SP). The two differ in about six thousand places, though most of those differences are minor or minimal. Before the bifurcation of the two texts, however, there was the Old Greek translation of the Pentateuch (OG), from the third century BCE, later incorporated in the Septuagint. On the whole, the OG is closer to the MT than to the SP, but in more than 30 percent of the cases, the OG and SP align against the MT. This fact refutes the hypothesis of an early parting of the ways between two textual communities. Rather, it is evidence of a lively process of transmission attended by small editorial interventions that must have taken place in a variety of scribal environments over a longer period of time—centuries rather than decades.[82] As the Pentateuch copies among the Dead Sea Scrolls demonstrate, the process continued after the OG. These facts are best explained by assuming that the Pentateuch was in circulation as one unified composition since the Persian period.

Though the role of the Persians in the promulgation of the Torah was indirect—the initiative lay with a group of Judean Babylonians represented by Ezra—it was nonetheless crucial. Without their authorization, it is not certain the five books of Moses would have achieved the status of sacred scripture in so short a period. Another effect of the Persian involvement was the conceptualization of the Pentateuch as "law." In the older literature it is not unusual to read that "law" is a mistranslation of Hebrew *tôrâ* to be blamed on the latter's equation with Greek *nomos*.[83] It is true that the literal meaning of *tôrâ* is "instruction, teaching," and that the term thus has a broader sense than the word "law" conveys.[84] But rather than blaming the translators of the Hebrew Bible into Greek (the Septuagint), we should be looking at the Persians. The edict that formulates Ezra's mission translates "the torah of the LORD" (Ezra 7:12) as "the law of the God of heaven" (Ezra 7:14). The edict is written in Aramaic, and the term for "law" is *dāt,* a loan from Old Persian *dāta.* The Persian term also entered the Akkadian language as *dātu.* It has a rather specific meaning. The *dāt* is a royal ruling, laid down in writing, and as such unalterable. So the *dāt* is normally "royal *dāt*" (*dātu ša šarri* in Babylonian). One of the most illuminating passages on *dātu* occurs in a record of a legal decision from the twenty-fifth year of Darius I, that is, 497 BCE.[85] The case concerns the illegal appropriation of a slave girl by a man who claims she is his sister. Submitted to an interrogation (*maš'altu*) he admits he lied, and he loses the case. The verdict is based on the *dātu:* "The simmagir and his colleagues the judges opened the dātu. On the basis of the dātu they imposed on PN (a penalty of) four slaves." As one of the editors of the text comments, "Thus we may postulate the existence of a royal 'rule book' for regulating different cases of disputes over the status of slaves."[86] Or, in the words of another scholar, the *dātu* here refers to a "compendium" that was "consulted" to determine the correct penalty.[87]

Owing to the Persian authorization, the Torah had the force of "the law of the king" (*dātā' dî malkā',* Ezra 7:26, the Aramaic equivalent of Akkadian *dātu ša šarri*). It was a "book" (*sēper*) that could be "opened" (Neh 8:5), and the rules it contained were binding for all time (Neh 8:13–18; Ps 119:144). Henceforth, rules had to be followed and rituals to be performed "as it is written" (*kakkātûb*), as the standard phrase has it in Ezra-Nehemiah and Chronicles.[88] After the promulgation of the *dāt* of the God of heaven, everything had to be by the book. Whether actual practice always conformed to this principle is an open question. In many a case where texts say that everything was performed "as it is written" (*kakkātûb*), the reference to the codified law may well have been part of a rhetorical strategy.[89] Nevertheless, the reconceptualization of torah as *dāt* imparted unprecedented authority to the written text of the Torah. It would put the art of reading and interpretation at the heart of many later developments of Israelite religion.

The Practical Effects of Ezra's Mission

According to the conventional terminology, the objective of Ezra's mission was the "promulgation" of the law of the God of heaven. Assuming this law is to be identified with the Pentateuch, what did its promulgation entail and what were its practical effects? The term "promulgation" implies publication and dissemination of an officially authorized text.[90] The text in question was a book, or more precisely a written scroll. Ezra, quite literally, had the law "in [his] hand" (Ezra 7:14). Its publication had to take place in a society that still had many characteristics of an oral culture. Publication, then, consisted first of all of oral dissemination. This is consonant with the description of Ezra giving public readings from "the book of the Torah of Moses" to an audience of men and women gathered for the occasion (Neh 8:1–3). A more detailed account of the event says that Ezra stood on a raised platform, while several Levites "explained" (*mĕbînîm*) the Torah (Neh 8:7): "So they read from the book, from the law of God, with interpretation. They gave the sense so that the people understood the reading" (Neh 8:8 NRSV). A mere public reading of the text was insufficient. For the promulgation of the Torah to be effective, the participation of a class of temple personnel with scribal training was essential.[91] These Levites were likely also responsible for the dissemination of the Torah in the wider area of Judah (cf. 2 Chr 17:9).

Since the promulgation of the Torah was essentially by word-of-mouth, the general population could hardly develop an intimate knowledge of the text. To most people, the book of the law of God was more like a symbol they could venerate than a text they could read. The interpretations and explanations that the Levites offered would often end with practical instructions to the audience. In this respect, the report on Ezra's public reading of the Torah is quite characteristic. It culminates in a collective celebration of the Festival of Booths "as it is written," with people dwelling in booths made of branches "on the roofs of their houses, and in their courts and in the courts of the house of God, and in the square" (Neh 8:15–16 NRSV). The text pays attention both to the correct dates of the festival and to the correct procedures (Neh 8:13–18; cf. Ezra 3:4–5). Though presented as a return to the festival as it was originally celebrated (Neh 8:17), the erection of temporary booths around the house and in the temple was an innovation. Succoth ("booths") was the traditional harvest festival in autumn, and the booths were makeshift dwellings near the fields. In the new version of the festival, the booths were a reminder of the exodus and the wilderness wanderings, when God made the people of Israel live in booths (Lev 23:39–43, esp. vv. 42–43). The festival's reinterpretation links the ritual to Israel's history as laid down in the Pentateuch. This was probably how most people in Judah and other places became familiar with the national narrative: the religious high holy days of the calendar became reenactments of moments of the exodus.[92] Even the weekly Sabbath was a reminder of their liberation from Egyptian slavery (Deut 5:12–15).

Aside from the new-style celebration of Succoth, the books of Ezra-Nehemiah describe a number of other practical effects of the promulgation of the "law of the God of heaven." The various as-it-is-written (*kakkātûb*) passages in the books highlight official measures taken in conformity with the new law. Perhaps the most striking fact about these measures is that they all pertain to either the temple cult (Ezra 3:2–3; Neh 10:35, 36–37) or the celebration of the festivals of the religious calendar (Ezra 3:4–7; Neh 8:13–37, both Festival of Booths; cf. Ezra 6:19–22, Passover and the Feast of Unleavened Bread). Other passages do not employ the *kakkātûb* formula but refer to the "book of the law" or the "book of Moses" as ground for action (Ezra 6:18, 10:3; Neh 9:3, 13:1–3). They concern measures to ensure the regular performance of the temple cult (Ezra 6:18; Neh 10:33–40), the observance of Sabbath and other holy days (Neh 10:32, 13:15–22), and the ban on intermarriage (Ezra 10:1–44; Neh 9:1–3, 10:31, 13:1–3). By the witness of Ezra-Nehemiah, then, the application of the law that Ezra had come to promulgate was restricted to the domains of cultic law and family law. Confirmation of this particular focus in the application of the law can be found in the description of Nehemiah's reform measures to redress social injustice (Neh 5:1–13). Although the authors—or Nehemiah himself, if we assume the passage is part of the document conventionally known as Nehemiah's Memoir—could have pointed out that there is a basis for such measures in the Torah, they did not do so and limited themselves to a general reference to "fear of our God" (*yir'at 'ĕlōhênû*, Neh 5:9) as moral guideline.[93] Apparently, then, the domain of property law fell outside the purview of Ezra's law as it translated into practice.

The introduction of the Torah did not turn Judah into a theocracy. Even though Ezra had been commissioned by King Artaxerxes, the Persian patronage of his mission did not mean the Persian authorities in Yehud were going to use the law of Moses as their own code of law. The governance of the provinces was based on a dual system. By appointment of the Persian authorities, there was a provincial governor. Directly under the governor were several prefects to maintain public order, plus a number of "royal" or "provincial" judges.[94] Most of the time, both the governors and the judges carry Persian names.[95] It does not mean all of them were Persians, but most of them probably were.[96] These royal judges were responsible for the adjudication of all disputes in matters of civil and criminal law. As a rule, family law did not fall under their purview, since that domain was too closely associated with the realm of religion. The second tier of governance in the province consisted of local institutions and varied from place to place as local tradition had it. In Judah, in Samaria, and in the Judean community at Elephantine, the local leadership consisted of the high priest and his priestly colleagues, on the one hand, and a council of laymen—usually the heads of prominent families in view of the titles "elders" (Hebrew *zěqēnîm*, Aramaic *śābayyāʾ*) and "nobles" (*ḥōrîm*)—on the other. They were responsible for the internal affairs of the community.[97]

Even in Judah, then, the practical effects of Ezra's mission were limited. Outside of Judah, in Samaria and in the diaspora, the impact of the newly promulgated law on the general population is unlikely to have been more comprehensive. Although the priestly elite of Samaria must have embraced the new charter document as a foundational text that legitimized the Gerizim sanctuary, there is no evidence that the book of Moses found a wide following outside scribal circles connected with the priesthood. This may be in part due to lack of pertinent evidence from the fifth century BCE, but the fourth-century Samarian papyri from Wadi Daliyeh attest to a tradition of local common law uninfluenced by Pentateuchal prescriptions.[98] The "one God, one temple" ideology of Deuteronomy remained without effect outside Judah. In addition to Mount Gerizim in Samaria,[99] there was a "house of Yaho" at Makkedah (Khirbet el-Qom) in Idumea[100] and a "house of Yaho" on Elephantine Island. The Judean leadership knew about these temples and saw no reason to object. In fact, around 410 BCE, the Judean governor endorsed the plan of the Elephantine community to rebuild their local temple.[101] In the Egyptian and Babylonian diaspora, intermarriage between Judeans and non-Judeans was certainly not taboo.[102] And in both Egypt and Babylonia, the Judeans regulated their affairs by local law, not by the law of Moses.[103]

The one area where Ezra's mission did have a visible effect outside Judah concerns the religious calendar and the celebration of the Judean festivals. The most revealing text in this respect is the "Passover papyrus" from Elephantine. It is a letter addressed to the leadership of the Judean community on the island ("my brothers") by a fellow Judean called Hananiah ("your brother Hananiah"). The message opens with a reference to an order sent by the Persian king to the Egyptian satrap Arsames: "This year, year 5 of Darius, [word] has been sent from the king to Arsam[es . . .]."[104] This is Darius II (r. 424–404 BCE), so the year is 419 BCE. Because of the damage the papyrus has suffered, the content of the royal order has been lost. But in the rest of the letter, Hananiah explains the consequences of the order for the Elephantine community:

> So now, you, thus count four[teen days in Nisan and on the 14th at twilight ob]serve [the Passover!] And from the 15th day until the 21st day of [Nisan observe the Festival of Unleavened Bread. Seven days eat unleavened bread! Now,] be pure and take heed. Do n[ot do] any work [on the 15th day and the 21st day of Nisan.] Do not drink [any fermented drink. And do] not [eat] anything of leaven [nor let it be seen in your houses from the 14th day of Nisan at] sunset until the 21st day of Nisa[n at sunset. And b]ring into your storerooms [any leaven which you have in your houses] and seal (them) up during [these] days.[105]

This translation has restored damaged passages (everything between square brackets), including the speculated reference to Passover. But erase every bracketed restoration, and it is still perfectly clear that Hananiah gives instructions about a religious practice to be observed through Nisan 15–21, which requires ritual purity ("be pure," *dkyn hww*), abstention from work, avoidance of certain beverages, and the removal of leaven (*ḥmyr*, in the phrase *mnd'm zy ḥmyr*, "anything of leaven"). The connection with Matzoth (Feast of Unleavened Bread) is unmistakable.[106] Though it has become commonplace to stress that the Passover papyrus does not actually mention Passover, the immediate context and structure of the letter hardly allow any other restoration in line 4 than *psḥ'*.[107]

The Passover papyrus is one of the rare pieces of extrabiblical evidence to show that the promulgation of the Torah did have repercussions outside Judah. Like Ezra, Hananiah was a Judean. Whether he came from Judah or Babylonia is unclear, but his mission to Egypt had the authorization of the Persian king.[108] Was he an advisor to the king in matters of Judean affairs, like Ezra and the otherwise unknown Pethahiah son of Meshezabel (Neh 11:24)?[109] Even though the order of Darius II has not been preserved, it is clear that the instructions by Hananiah derive their authority ultimately from the king—as the word *kn*, "thus, so" subtly conveys (line 3). From references in the Elephantine ostraca, we know the community was already familiar with Passover.[110] Hananiah's instructions do not introduce a new festival but focus on the correct days and the proper procedure. The letter he sent to the Elephantine community seems designed to ensure that the Egyptian diaspora would celebrate Passover and Matzoth on the same dates and in the same manner as the Judeans of Jerusalem (Ezra 6:19–22; cf. 1 Esd 7:10–15).[111] All those of Israelite stock who worshipped the Israelite god, wherever they found themselves in the Persian Empire, were to synchronize their celebrations and to observe a uniform ritual.

The mere fact that Hananiah wrote to the Elephantine Judeans about the proper celebration of Passover and Matzoth does not mean they actually followed his instructions; but since they kept his letter in the communal archive, chances are they did honor his directives. Almost ten years after Hananiah's letter, members of the Judean community were complaining that the local Egyptians had been harassing them "since Hananiah came to Egypt until now."[112] His mission had made an impact, apparently. It is quite possible that the introduction of a uniform festival calendar in the later fifth century BCE had only a temporary effect. It may have fallen into abeyance, with the exception of certain priestly circles. There simply is no evidence that would warrant an argument for or against such a hypothesis. But there is no good reason to underplay the significance of the Passover papyrus of Elephantine.[113] Its unedited evidence underscores the significance of the religious festivals as markers of Jewish identity in the aftermath of Ezra's mission. Being part of the Israelite nation became tantamount to observing the holy days of the religious calendar "as written" in the book of Moses.[114]

The Rise of Ethnic Religion

Outside Judah, the most significant consequence of the promulgation of the Torah was the diffusion of a common festival calendar among Jewish communities throughout the Persian Empire. This general diffusion must be inferred from the Elephantine Passover papyrus. Hananiah's letter to the Elephantine community was sent from Memphis, where the Persian satrap had his residence.[115] Other Jewish communities in Egypt must have received the same or a similar message.[116] It is unlikely that the dissemination of a common calendar and a common rite for Passover and Matzoth was limited to the Jewish diaspora in Egypt. Since Ezra came from the Babylonian diaspora, the Judean communities in Mesopotamia were probably familiar with the same festival calendar. Darius himself had authorized Hananiah's mission, which presupposes recognition by the Persian authorities of the Jews as a legitimate and distinct ethnic community in the empire. For outsiders, the most visible expression of Jewish identity was the observance of the Jewish festivals. Among themselves, Jews might have had great differences of opinion and belief; they did not all speak the same language; and their personal names were not necessarily distinctly Jewish. But one could recognize them by their rituals.

The promulgation of one festival calendar for all Jews is correlated to a phenomenon of far greater significance than a ritual innovation. It signals the emergence of the Jews as an ethnic community. For the religion of Israel, this is the greatest transformation of the Persian period. Religious identity was no longer linked to membership in a tribe (the tribal religion of premonarchic times) or citizenship of a state, as it had been in the days of the Israelite and the Judean kingdoms. During the first decades in Babylonia, when diaspora still felt like exile, the Judeans continued to think of themselves as deported Judean citizens. But when a return to Judah became an option, and exile turned into diaspora, they developed a double identity. They were Persian subjects in Babylon politically, but Judeans by descent and religion. This was true also in a way for the Babylonian Judeans who had migrated back to Judah. Even in the "holy land" (Zech 2:16) and in the "holy city" (Neh 11:1, 18), they were Persian subjects (cf. Ezra 9:8–9; Neh 9:36–37). The demographic situation in Judah was mixed. The *qāhāl*, "community," as the consecrated term in Ezra-Nehemiah has it, did not coincide with the population of the province. Not every inhabitant of Judah belonged to the *qāhāl*. The latter consisted only of "all the people of Israel who had returned from the exile" plus "all who had joined them and separated themselves from the pollutions of the nations of the land to worship the LORD, the God of Israel" (Ezra 6:21). As is clear from the last reference, the *qāhāl* was both a religious and an ethnic community.[117]

In Ezra-Nehemiah, this community is referred to as "Israel" or "the children of Israel," on the one hand, and as the "Judeans," on the other.[118] Both are terms of ethnicity, though "Israel" has strong religious connotations.[119] Non-Judeans did not use the term "Israel" but spoke of "Judeans."[120] Many of these Judeans were not inhabitants of Judah, though, and a fair number of them descended from Samarian families. But in the terminology of the Persian administration they were *Yĕhûdayyē*, which is perhaps best translated as "Jews" to mark the distinction between the Jewish ethnic community, on the one hand, and the citizens of Judah, on the other.[121] As an ethnic community, all of these Jews were "brothers." When Hananiah wrote to the leadership of the Elephantine community (the "Jewish garrison," as his letter says), he addresses them as "my brothers" (*'ḥy*) and signs off as "your brother Hananiah" (*'ḥwkm ḥnnyh*).[122] In the same vein, Nehemiah refers to fellow Judeans abroad as "our Jewish brothers" (*'aḥênû hayyĕhûdîm*) (Neh 5:8 NJPS; cf. 5:1, 7). Nearly all English translations render *yĕhûdîm* in this passage as "Jewish" rather than "Judean." Understandably so, for it is nearly impossible here to distinguish between ethnicity and religion. In former times, the Israelites used the term "brothers" for members of their kin group. Its extension to the wider Jewish community is telling of a new sensibility. During the Persian period, ties of ethnicity and religion gave Jews the feeling they were members of one family, wherever they might happen to live. Judahites and Samarians, whether at home or in the diaspora, became Jews.[123]

Ethnicity formation is a complex process. While the language of ethnicity privileges terms of kinship and consanguinity—the group is united by birth and blood—the reality of ethnicity owes as much if not more to common culture and shared tradition. These two facets of ethnicity correspond to different concepts. The one is the racial concept of ethnicity; the other, the cultural one. They existed side by side during the Persian period. The racial concept of ethnicity comes to the fore in such expressions as the "holy race" (zera' haqqōdeš, Ezra 9:2) or "the divine race" (zera' 'ĕlōhîm, Mal 2:15) and led in Judah on occasion to measures of ethnic cleansing by the collective dismissal of foreign women and their offspring by Judean husbands (Ezra 9–10; Neh 13:1–3, 23–31). The proponents of the narrow view of ethnicity were priests. They used the priestly terminology of pure (ṭāhôr) and impure (ṭāmē'), as well as the attendant notion of separation (the verb is hibdîl, "to separate," the transitive form of bādal), to conceptualize notions of ethnic purity. Though some degree of separateness is necessary for any ethnic group to survive, the priestly separatists carried the principle to an extreme.[124] Just as in the Priestly account of creation God had separated day from night (Gen 1:14–19), so the real Judeans "had separated themselves [nibdal] from the pollutions [ṭum'at] of the nations of the land" (Ezra 6:21 NRSV; cf. 9:1; Neh 9:2, 10:29, 13:3). This gave a racial twist to the old separation principle. The separatists considered themselves the pure Judeans.

Many Judeans did not subscribe to the narrow racial definition of Jewish identity. Mixed marriages, for one thing, were not generally frowned upon. According to the book of Ruth, they could be part of God's plan. While the separatists advocated the excommunication of Ammonites and Moabites (Neh 13:1–13; cf. Deut 23:4–7), the book of Ruth implies that the great King David himself would not have seen the light of day if it had not been for the marriage of his great-grandfather Boaz of Bethlehem to Ruth the Moabite (Ruth 4:13–22).[125] Outside separatist circles, most Judeans did not think of Samarians as gentiles (Ezra 6:21; Neh 5:9; 6:6, 16), "adversaries" (ṣārîm, Ezra 4:1–2; Neh 4:5, 5:9), or "enemies" ('ōyĕbîm, Neh 4:9; 5:9; 6:1, 16).

Various members of the Judean political elite (the "nobles of Judah") were allies of "Tobiah the Ammonite" and kept up a brisk correspondence with the man (Neh 6:17–18). Both Tobiah and his son Jehohanan had married into prominent Judean families (Neh 6:18).[126] Thanks to Tobiah's connections to the Jerusalem priesthood (Neh 13:4), the high priest Eliashib had given him an office in the temple (Neh 13:5).[127] The Samarian governor Sanballat had close connections to this Eliashib as well, since Eliashib's grandson had married Sanballat's daughter (Neh 13:28; Josephus, *Ant.* 11.302–303). The nuptial links between these prestigious families—the Jerusalem high priest, the Samarian governor, and the Tobiads of Ammon—attest to an open attitude toward Samarians. Also in the eyes of the priestly authors of 1–2 Chronicles, presumably writing toward the end of the fourth century BCE, the Samarian population counted a significant number of loyal and God-fearing Yahwists (e.g., 2 Chr 28:8–15, 30:1–26, 34:1–35:19).[128]

Eventually, it was the broad definition of Jewish ethnicity that carried the day. In this respect, the Elephantine papyri are quite telling. The 419 BCE letter of Hananiah to "the Jewish garrison" addresses the leadership of the community unconditionally as "brothers."[129] Intermarriage was not uncommon at Elephantine, and the community's religion left room for other gods, but to Hananiah its Jewish credentials were not at issue. Some ten years later, when the temple on the island is in ruins, the leaders of the community solicit the support of their Jewish brothers both in Jerusalem and in Samaria. In their petition to the Judean governor, they tell him they also wrote to the sons of Sanballat the Samarian governor.[130] Clearly they assume that relations are cordial between the leaders of the two provinces. In the end, they manage to obtain the joint endorsement of the governors of both Judah and Samaria.[131] Both the Passover papyrus and the correspondence with Judah and Samaria are witness to a shared sense of ethnic solidarity among the various Jewish communities in the empire. Some groups may still have subscribed to a more narrowly racial view of Jewish identity, but they did not sway the general opinion. They may have started what has been called "proto-sectarian movements," thereby tacitly admitting that the Jewish mainstream went another way.[132] For the vast majority of Jews and non-Jews, observance of the Jewish festivals was the most reliable indication of Jewish identity. Israelite religion was no longer tribal, royal, or local. It had become ethnic.

6 Scriptural Religion

The Persian domination of Samaria and Judah came to an abrupt end. In 333 BCE Alexander the Great, king of Macedonia, defeated Darius III (r. 336–330 BCE) in the battle of Issus and had the city of Persepolis burned down in retaliation of the Persian sack of Athens more than fifty years before. It spelled the end of the Persian Empire. The next year Alexander conquered Tyre and Gaza. The way to Egypt lay open, and soon the Macedonian monarch was crowned as the new pharaoh. For the cities of Samaria and Jerusalem, it meant the end of an era and a brutal transition to a new one. Shortly after the Macedonian conquest of Palestine, when Alexander was in Egypt, the Samarians rose up against their new masters. Tradition has it they killed Andromachus, the recently appointed prefect of Syria. The response was swift and ruthless. The Macedonian troops destroyed the city of Samaria and went after the suspected conspirators. Many inhabitants had already left the city. One group of refugees had set out for Jerusalem in search of shelter for themselves and their possessions. They never reached their destination. The Macedonian troops overtook them at Wadi Daliyeh, a small tributary of the Jordan River north of Jericho, where the Samarians had withdrawn into a cave. It was to be their grave. Alexander's troops set fire to the entrance, and everybody inside died of asphyxiation. When the cave was discovered in 1962, archaeologists found the skeletal remains of between two hundred and three hundred men, women, and children, all buried under layers of bat guano. The coins they had carried as well as much of their archives were still mostly intact. It turns out these families had made their money by trading slaves. The Wadi Daliyeh papyri are now a precious source of information on Samarian society in the late Persian period.[1]

The Samarian revolt rises above the level of historical anecdote insofar as it foreshadows the resistance that the rule of Alexander and his successors would elicit among Samarians and Judeans. Whereas Judeans had hailed Cyrus as a godsend—Second Isaiah had called him a messiah (Isa 45:1)—no one in Judah or Samaria saw Alexander as God's chosen servant. They had been loyal to the Persians, but the new rulers met with a mixed reception at best. Alexander's conquest was to be the beginning of the Hellenistic era for the Eastern Mediterranean. His successors divided his legacy. Palestine passed into the hands of the Ptolemaic dynasty between 320 and 198 BCE, after which the Seleucid kings managed to bring it under their control. For a while, that is, for the heavy taxation imposed by the Seleucids and the suppression of the traditional cult by Antiochus IV Epiphanes (r. 175–164 BCE) sparked the Maccabean revolt in 168 BCE, which prepared the way for the Jewish rule by the Hasmonean high priest Jonathan and his successors (152–63 BCE).[2] For Judeans and Samarians the encounter with Hellenism was the catalyst that triggered the transformation of Israelite religion into Judaism. In fact, the very term "Judaism" originated as the ideological counterpart to the notion of Hellenism. Whereas the Persians had authorized the Judeans to rebuild their temple and to live by their own religious laws, the encounter with the Hellenistic culture of the Ptolemies and Seleucids, and especially the Seleucid attempts to Hellenize the Jerusalem temple cult and to repress Jewish religious customs, gave Jewish religion traits of a counterculture.

From Israelite Religion to Judaism

Where does Israelite religion end and Judaism begin? Or better: When does the Jewish turn of Israelite religion begin? When did Judeans become Jews? Even if the encounter with Hellenism precipitated the emergence of Judaism, the transformation was the outcome of a process that had been going on for quite some time. Much in these things is a matter of definition. If we define Judaism as a typical mix of ethnicity and religion, in which religion determines ethnicity and vice versa, the development goes back to the Persian era. By that time already, Samarians could be called *yĕhûdayyēʾ* because of their religion. The custom continued during the Hellenistic era. The book of Esther calls Mordechai a "Jew" (*ʾîš yĕhûdî*), even if he is a Benjaminite (Esth 2:5). In a similar vein, the book of Tobit refers to the Samarian exiles in Nineveh as "Jews" (*Ioudaioi*, Tob 11:18). Here the fundamental shift has been from territorial to religious identity. Formerly one's religious loyalty was to the god of the place where one lived; to be driven out of YHWH's estate was to go and serve other gods (1 Sam 26:19). The diaspora experience had given a new perspective: religion created common ethnicity independent of territorial origins. It made all those who worshipped the God of heaven "Judeans" or "Jews," and therefore "brothers" of one another.[3] The Persian period had consolidated this development and turned Israelite religion into ethnic religion.

The new focus on the national religion as the major locus of group identity promoted the interest in the national past and accelerated the decline of family religion. When Nehemiah mourned the devastation of Jerusalem, he called it "the place of my ancestors' graves" (Neh 2:3 NRSV). These ancestors (literally, "fathers") may have been those of his own family, but the reference is more likely to the national ancestors. During the Hellenistic era, at any rate, Greek adjectives meaning "ancestral" gain unprecedented prominence in Jewish writings. Their anti-Hellenistic edge is unmistakable.[4] The second book of Maccabees refers to the Jewish "law" or "laws" (*nomos*, plural *nomoi*) time and again as "ancestral" (*patrios* or *patrōios*, 2 Macc 6:1; 7:2, 24, 37). The religious festivals are likewise "ancestral" (2 Macc 6:6). At moments of special solemnity, devout Jews use "the ancestral language," that is, Hebrew (*tēi patriōi phōnēi*, 2 Macc 7:8, 21, 27; 12:37; 15:29). And the prologue to the Greek translation of the Wisdom of Ben Sira refers to the literary heritage of the Jews as "the Law and the Prophets and the other ancestral books." Clearly, these ancestors are the ancestors of the nation who embody the national identity. Their veneration made Jewish parents of this period choose to name their children after such biblical heroes as Miriam, Jacob, Joseph, Judah, Levi, and Phinehas.[5] Up to a point, the nation took the place of the family as the anchor of identity. This development led to the almost complete erosion of the traditional ancestor cult by the family. In the new religious climate, it continued to be important to honor the dead (Sir 22:11–12; 38:16–23), but as a patriotic duty rather than as a family rite. Tobit went to some lengths to give a decent burial to "any of my people thrown out behind the wall of Nineveh" (Tob 1:17–18). To bury the corpse of a fellow Jew was perhaps the most important charitable act one could perform (Tob 2:3–8, 4:3–4, 6:15, 14:10–13).[6] The religious community was the new family, with God as their heavenly Father.[7] In family religion, people had venerated "the god of the father"; in the new dispensation, the nation worshipped "God the lord of our ancestors" (Jdt 7:28, 10:8).

An important innovation in the religious realities of the time was the phenomenon of converts. The Hebrew term for them is *gērîm*, which originally means "strangers." The classic phrase from the Decalogue about "the stranger in your settlements" (Deut 5:14; Exod 20:10) uses the term *gēr*. Initially it did not imply religious conversion. In the Hellenistic period, however, the *gērîm* were proselytes, meaning non-Jews who had embraced Judaism. The many references to such proselytes throw into relief just how much Judaism had become a religion. Tobit was reputedly pious with the dead and generous with proselytes. While living in northern Israel, he would often go to Jerusalem for the festivals and distribute tithes to "the orphans and widows and to the converts [*tois prosēlytois*] who had attached themselves to Israel" (Tob 1:8 NRSV).[8] An example of such a convert is the Ammonite Achior: "When Achior saw all that the God of Israel had done, he believed firmly in God. So he was circumcised, and joined the house of Israel, remaining so to this day" (Jdt 14:10 NRSV). Joining the house of Israel meant becoming a Jew. Indeed, the non-Israelite convert to Judaism was said to "become a *Ioudaios*," a Jew (2 Macc 8:21). Many Jews believed that in the final era conversion to Judaism would be universal: "Then the nations in the whole world will be converted [*epistrepsousin*] and worship God in truth. They will all abandon their idols" (Tob 14:6 NRSV).

If Judaism is characterized sociologically as a mix of ethnicity and religion, a more substantial definition would say that it is "the Jewish way of life characterized by conformity to the rules and regulations of the Torah."[9] The Torah is not an invention of the Hellenistic era, since it gained its position as law for Samarians and Judeans during the Persian period. Yet "Judaism" as such was yet unknown. This may be related, materially, to the fact that the precepts of the Torah did not put their stamp on the lifestyle of the masses in Persian Samaria and Judah and, terminologically, because "Judaism" is a neologism coined by analogy with "Hellenism." Hellenism was the Greek way of life; Judaism, the Jewish way of life. For the author of 2 Maccabees, who apparently invented the terms, it was either/or. In 174 BCE, one Jason obtained the high priesthood by bribing the Seleucid ruler Antiochus IV Epiphanes. Once in office, Jason tried to turn Jerusalem into a Greek polis. He allegedly established a gymnasium, made it fashionable for young men to wear a Greek hat, and introduced various other "customs contrary to the law" (2 Macc 4:11–12). Yet what kindled a popular revolt was Antiochus's attempt to abolish some of the Jewish ancestral laws (circumcision, Sabbath observance, avoidance of pork).[10] The anti-Hellenists, led by Judas Maccabeus and his brothers, "fought bravely for Judaism" (2 Macc 2:21 NRSV; cf. 8:1, 14:38). The Maccabean wars ended with victory for the supporters of Judaism and prepared the way for the Hasmonean rule that began with the installation of Jonathan as high priest (in 152 BCE; see 1 Macc 10:15–21) and ended with Aristobulus II (r. 67–63 BCE). From the reign of Aristobulus I (r. 104–103 BCE) onward, the Hasmonean rulers combined the high priesthood with kingship. Though following a Hellenistic lifestyle, they promoted an emphatically Jewish identity for themselves and their subjects, in which observance of the ancestral laws—the Torah—was a civic duty.[11] If Judaism is defined in terms of widespread adherence to the Torah, then its emergence must be dated to the second half of the second century BCE.[12]

The Spread of Education and the Rise of a Money Economy

The opposition between Judaism and Hellenism in 2 Maccabees is both illuminating and misleading—illuminating inasmuch as the adepts of the Jewish way of life thought of themselves as resisting the Greek way of life; misleading because the opposition misrecognizes the actual debt of Judaism to Hellenism.[13] Many scholars have observed that the author of 2 Maccabees, while projecting an image of himself as a staunch opponent of Hellenism, is in fact heavily indebted to the conventions of contemporary Greek historical writing. His praise of the Jewish martyrs follows Greek modes of expression.[14] He must have had the benefit, then, of a good literary education. Such an education—*paideia* is the Greek term—was a major Hellenistic ideal. The citizens of the polis were to be educated men and women. The spread of Hellenistic civilization went in tandem, therefore, with the spread of schools and a significant rise of literacy rates. The inhabitants of Judah participated in this development. Ben Sira had a *bêt midraš*, that is, a "house of instruction" or a school, in Jerusalem. In the Greek text of Ben Sira this is a house of *paideia* (Sir 51:23). Jews embraced the ideal of education. In the Septuagint version of such wisdom books as Proverbs and Ben Sira, traditional terms for "fool" (such as Hebrew *'ĕwîl* and *sākāl*) were rendered in Greek as "uneducated" (*apaideutos;* e.g., Prov 24:7; Sir 6:20, 8:4, 51:23).

The substantial increase of literacy rates during the Hellenistic period created an important condition for the emergence of Judaism as book religion. The reading revolution of the period led to the production of a spectacular amount of new religious literature (wisdom texts, apocalyptic literature, novellas), contributed to the creation of the synagogue (where the reading and interpretation of scripture had a central place), and stimulated the development of the new literary genre of commentary (known as *pēšer,* "interpretation"). While the spread of literacy was part of a long-term development in Palestine, it is fair to say that the advent of Hellenism provided the impetus for the transition from professional literacy (in which reading and writing were a scribal art) to popular literacy (in which the ancestral books became accessible to a general readership). The consequences were tremendous. They are not without some resemblance to the printing revolution in the early modern period and its impact on the Reformation.[15]

Another major change in the Hellenistic era was the transition to a money economy. The economy in Palestine had long been based on a mix of barter (in which one commodity was exchanged for another) and payment in weighted silver (in which the shekel—derived from the verb *šāqal,* "to weigh, to weigh out"—was the unit).[16] The standardization of weights and measures prepared the way for the coinage of silver, which in Palestine started in the Persian period. Yet the transition to a full-blown money economy, in which goods and services were paid for in minted coins, came about only in the Hellenistic period (fig. 40).[17] The societal impact is hard to overestimate. Loans, debts, credits, payments, and savings were nothing new, but the use of coins as the medium of transaction changed everything.[18] Payment in kind did not cease altogether (Tob 2:11–12), but employers normally paid in money: "I will pay you a drachma a day as wages" (Tob 5:15 NRSV; cf. 4:14, 5:7). The money economy facilitated a growing labor division, as partially reflected in the catalogue of trades that Ben Sira deploys as a foil to stress the superiority of the scribal profession (Sir 38:24–34). It also had its effects on religious practice. The "righteousness" (*ṣĕdāqâ*) that saved such legendary figures as Noah, Daniel, and Job (Ezek 14:14, 20) became in the Hellenistic era the technical term for "almsgiving" (Greek *eleēmosynē*). "Almsgiving atones for sin," says Ben Sira (*ṣdqh tkpr ḥṭ't,* which in the Greek version becomes *eleēmosynē exilasetai hamartias;* Sir 3:30). Along with monotheism, prayer, fasting, and the pilgrimage to Jerusalem, almsgiving became one of the pillars of Judaism.[19] An act of human kindness took the form of a monetary transaction. Greed was the reverse of almsgiving. The love of money came to be regarded as the mother of all evils. It was generally deplored as the chief cause of corruption of people in positions of leadership.[20]

Another effect of living in a money economy was its influence on the religious imagination. The most significant example is probably the reconceptualization of sin in terms of debt. Whereas sin previously was

Fig. 40. Coin of the Hasmonean king Alexander Jannaeus (r. 103–76 BCE).
(Wikimedia Commons, CC-BY-SA-4.0, https://creativecommons.org/licenses/
by-sa/4.0/deed.en.)

thought of as a burden or a stain, in the environment of Hellenistic Palestine it came to be likened to a monetary debt.[21] The metaphor first occurs
in texts from the Persian period (e.g., Isa 40:2, 65:6), then became common
during the Hellenistic era. In the Aramaic vernacular spoken in Palestine
at the time, "debt" (*ḥôbāʾ*) was the regular equivalent of "sin," and a "sinner"
was a "debtor" (*ḥayyābāʾ*). This metaphorical use of the notion of debt is
in evidence in many of the ancient Aramaic translations, interpretations,
and paraphrases of the Hebrew scriptures (the targumim) and echoes in
the petition "and forgive us our debts, / as we also have forgiven our debtors" (from the Lord's Prayer, Matt 6:12 NRSV).[22] The elaboration of the
metaphor in some of Jesus's parables shows that divine remission of sins
had come to be understood on the model of a cancellation of debts (Matt
18:23–35; Luke 7:36–50). A metaphor is rarely just a metaphor since it creates its own logic. It is no coincidence that the debt metaphor and the
insistence on almsgiving were more or less simultaneous developments in
early Judaism. Almsgiving atones for sin (Dan 4:24 [4:27]; Sir 3:30) because
it restores the balance: it is a way to pay off one's debt.[23]

The Reading Revolution and the Turn to Scripture

The Qurʾan calls Jews and Christians "people of the book" (*ahl al-kitāb*)
because they adhere to a scriptural religion, whether that scripture be the
Torah or the Gospel (Qurʾan 5:68–69). The Arabic phrase captures an

important aspect of early Judaism. Though Judaism is a community of practice rather than a reading club, the study of the "ancestral books," as Ben Sira's grandson calls them, determined Judaism's profile in a major way. This would not have happened without the reading revolution that occurred during the Hellenistic era.

Both the Ptolemies and the Seleucids sought to implant a Hellenistic culture in the territories over which they ruled. To them it was out of the question to adopt Aramaic as the language of empire, the way the Persians had done before them. They believed in the superiority of Greek language and culture; non-Greeks were *barbaroi*, "uncivilized."[24] Their way to achieve the Hellenization of the East included the recruitment of Greek colonists, often settled in such new cities as Alexandria and Antioch; the establishment of Greek cultural institutions, such as the gymnasium and the theater; and the patronage of centers of learning and research, such as the museum and library of Alexandria. These institutions spread *paideia*, education, with the purpose of forming a competent elite, drawn from both colonist and local families, with a shared set of cultural values. This was a Greek education, in the Greek language, and based on the classics of Greek literature.[25] Though out of reach for the general population, a formal Greek education attracted youths of the local upper classes since it opened up prospects of a public career and paved the way to positions of influence. Also, Hellenism was the culture of prestige. For many Jews, both in Palestine and in the diaspora, it seemed the most natural thing in the world. Even if they were unable to pursue a formal education, they would emulate Greek manners and fashions. In this cultural climate, literacy came to be a social skill found in many layers of the population, especially among Jews in Jerusalem and the Jewish diaspora in cities abroad.

The rising rates of literacy propelled the written word to unprecedented prominence. Records of financial transactions, marriage contracts, chronicles, and memoirs were nothing new, but they became present everywhere now that writing skills had trickled down from class to class. When Tobias asks for the hand of Sarah, her father immediately agrees. To him it is a match made in heaven and "in accordance with the decree in the book of Moses" (Tob 7:12 [7:11]). He gives his daughter in marriage: "Then he called her mother and told her to bring writing material; and he wrote out a copy of a marriage contract" (Tob 7:14 [7:13] NRSV). The patriarchal atmosphere of the story is reminiscent of the past, but the reference to the book of Moses, the domestic availability of writing material (*biblion*), and the personal preparation of a marriage contract reflect the literate culture of the new age. Popular literacy and the money economy meet in records of financial transactions. "When you make a deposit, be sure it is counted and weighed, / and when you give or receive, put it all in writing," advises Ben Sira (Sir 42:7 NRSV). People write themselves without recourse to a scribe.[26] Compare the parable about the dishonest manager who summons his master's debtors and tells them to take their bills (*grammata,* plural of *gramma*) and personally write out (*graphein*) a lower figure than what they actually owe (Luke 16:1–9). Written records were so omnipresent that in heaven, too, nearly all of the administration was imagined to be done in writing. God kept a ledger of good and evil deeds (e.g., Neh 13:14; Isa 65:6; Mal 3:16; 1 En. 81:4), which explains why, at the time of judgment, the heavenly court sat down "and the books were opened" (Dan 7:11; cf. 1 En. 90:20).[27] Human prayer also entailed paperwork in heaven. Angels had to make a transcript so they could read out the petitions before God (Tob 12:12).

Though much of the writing was for administrative purposes, the texts of prestige were literary. In the institutions of *paideia* and the great libraries those texts were mostly Greek, but the inherent claim of the superiority of Hellenistic culture also spurred a renewed interest in the native eastern scribal legacies. Local experts produced treatises in Greek on the antiquity and eminence of their own civilization. The Babylonian priest Berossus (Bel-re'ušu) wrote the *Babyloniaca* (ca. 280 BCE); about the same time, the priest Manetho from Heliopolis wrote the *Aegyptiaca;* and the priest Sanchuniathon wrote a presentation of Phoenicia that was to provide Philo of Byblos (ca. 64–141 CE) with material for his *Phoenician History.*[28] Josephus's *Jewish Antiquities* is a late representative of this genre, but the Jewish turn to ancestral tradition goes back to the early Hellenistic period. It had an outspoken literary slant for ancestral tradition was extant primarily in the "ancestral books." Ben Sira had, as his grandson says, "devoted himself especially to the reading of the Law and the Prophets and the other books of our ancestors, and had acquired considerable proficiency in them" (Prologue to Ben Sira, NRSV). A similar zeal for the study of the ancestral texts transpires in the book of Daniel, where the fictive hero "perceived in the books" (*bassĕpārim*) the word of God to the prophet Jeremiah about the seventy years of desolation of Jerusalem (Dan 9:2 NRSV). The quotation from Amos in Tob 2:6, the mention of Adam and Eve as archetype of the Jewish marriage in Tob 8:6, and the reference to Nahum in Tob 14:4 are further indications of the point to which the Jewish literary culture of the time was permeated by the veneration for the national written legacy.[29] It would be an anachronism to call these books the Jewish Bible, for there was no canon as yet. But it is clear that the "ancestral books" had a special status. Opinions may have differed about their number, but the belief in a national body of venerable texts was common. Some of them were definitely "sacred," such as the five books of Moses, excerpts of which had the power to keep evil at bay.[30]

Jews of the time, whether in Palestine or the diaspora, owed their knowledge of the ancestral books primarily to collective readings.[31] Even though books began to circulate in an increasing number of copies, they remained anchored in a culture in which the transmission and dissemination of knowledge traditionally were oral.[32] The solitary reader was an exception. Private reading did occur, but only as a derivative of public reading and hardly ever in complete silence: the performance was reduced to a murmur, yet loud enough for others to overhear (Acts 8:26–40).[33] Also, people who could fluently read and write and had the means to acquire books came from a culture that had programmed them for reading as a communal experience. Where formerly the priest had dispensed torah from oral tradition, and the bard told his tales from memory, the performer now read aloud from a scroll, stopping from time to time for explanations, interpretations, summaries, and other forms of commentary. Reading, then, was normally a group event, in which the audience actively participated in construing the meaning. Such oral performances before a group left their marks in the manuscripts in the form of comments, terminological elucidations, congregational responses, and the like.[34] In this setting originated new flexible genres such as that of textual interpretation (*pēšer*, as in the *pēšer* of Habakkuk from Qumran), midrashic expansion (often referred to as "rewritten scripture"), and Halakhic instruction.[35] The reception of the ancestral scriptures was a creative process during which various "interpretive communities" emerged.[36]

The turn to scripture during the Hellenistic era went beyond the revaluation of the old ancestral books. It also led to the production of a profusion of new books of all kinds: edifying novellas (such as Esther, Tobit, Judith, 3 Maccabees), wisdom literature (such as Qoheleth, Ben Sira, Wisdom of Solomon), apocalyptic literature (such as 1 Enoch and Daniel), historiography (such as 1 and 2 Maccabees), prayers and psalms, and various more hybrid genres (such as the Testaments of the Twelve

Patriarchs, a mix of wisdom, prophecy, and apocalyptic sections). These new books in no way took the place of the old ones. Rather the contrary: in various ways they paid homage to the ancient Hebrew scriptures by explicit mention, quotation, or the borrowing of their main personae. The latter phenomenon is known as pseudepigraphy: the authors borrowed the identity of a famous figure from the past, presumably to enhance the significance of their own work. Enoch, Daniel, and Solomon are cases in point. The practice predates the advent of Hellenism: the Deuteronomists claimed Moses was the author of their book of the law (2 Kgs 23:25). But in the Hellenistic and Roman periods the phenomenon became so common that it was more a genre convention and a hermeneutical key than a claim to authority. The real authors were not trying to get away with fraud. Compared with previous periods, the literary production of the Hellenistic era was staggering. It may have seemed there was no end to the making of many books (Eccl 12:12), but with so much on offer there must have been a real demand. Judaism had entered the reading era; there was a public for books (2 Macc 2:25).

Scripture as Source of Revelation

Though most studies of the Hellenistic era in Palestine focus on political events and the battle for the Jewish identity, the lasting significance of the period for the evolution of Israelite religion is the turn to scripture as the essential source of revelation. It inaugurated a truly new phase. Although the promulgation of "the book of the Torah" during the Persian period had used a written text to regulate religious practice, it had not brought about a reading revolution on the scale seen during the Hellenistic period. Literacy had still been the preserve of a professional elite. Also, during the Persian period scriptural authority was restricted to the Pentateuch; other traditional texts circulated in scholarly circles but did not have the status of national heritage. By the second century BCE, however, the scriptures had come to include "the Prophets and the other books of our ancestors," as Ben Sira's grandson put the matter in his prologue. Reading, moreover, was no longer an esoteric skill. This does not mean there was a formal canon of sacred literature that everybody was studying at home, but the classics of the Jewish tradition—the national library, so to speak—now consisted of "the Law and the Prophets," as the common phrase had it (see, e.g., 4 Macc 18:10–19; Matt 7:12, 22:40; Acts 13:15).[37] They were "the holy books" (*ta biblia ta hagia*, 1 Macc 12:9), and communal readings of this sacred literature became a central ritual in the religious practice of Judaism.

The reading revolution of the Hellenistic era also affected the devotional practices in the synagogue. The synagogue was a new institution, not attested before the third century BCE.[38] Though the oldest synagogue inscriptions are from Egypt (Jewish) and Delos (Samaritan), the phenomenon was not limited to the diaspora. Jerusalem, too, had synagogues. These synagogues had a variety of functions, one of which was the accommodation of visitors from abroad. But rather than mere community centers, the synagogues were places for devotional practice. The first-century CE Theodotus inscription from Jerusalem says that the synagogue there was built "for the reading of the Law" (*eis anagnōsin nomou*) and "instruction in the commandments" (*eis didachēn entolōn*), in addition to being an inn "for lodging visitors from abroad."[39] The prominence of communal readings is striking. Even though another Greek term for synagogue, from the earliest inscriptions on, is *proseuchē*, "(place of) prayer," many early literary descriptions of synagogal gatherings focus on the public reading and interpretation of scripture (see, e.g., Matt 4:23, 9:35, 13:54; Luke 4:14–30; John 18:20; Acts 13:13–43, 14:1, 18:4; for a reference to the synagogue as place of prayer, see Matt 6:5).[40] Gatherings for a collective reading of the sacred texts also occurred outside synagogues. The Rule of the Community from Qumran speaks about communal readings "in the book" (*bspr*) in conjunction with its interpretation (*drš mšpṭ*, 1QS 6:6–8). The commentaries on Habakkuk and Nahum (the pesharim) provide an illustration of what such interpretations might entail.

The Qumran commentaries reveal a new approach to the literary legacy from the ancestors.[41] It is as though the reading revolution had transformed the nature of the texts: they were not viewed merely as a record of the past, but as a revelation for the present.[42] The Prophets were full of oracles that were pertinent to events that had recently occurred or were still taking place. The pesher of Habakkuk bristles with examples. Habakkuk 1:6 speaks about God rousing "the Chaldeans, / that fierce and impetuous nation" (NRSV). The historical reference is to the Babylonians and their wars of expansion during the sixth century BCE. But the interpretation offered in the Qumran pesher says that this concerns the Romans (here designated as the Kittim), who "will take possession [of many countries] and will not believe in the precepts of [Go]d" (1QpHab 2:11–15). Many other utterances of Habakkuk are interpreted as references to conflicts with those of the

Jerusalem temple and its priests who opposed the Qumran community and its leadership in the late second century BCE.[43] The interpretation of Jeremiah's prophecy about the seventy-year desolation of Jerusalem in the book of Daniel reflects a similar hermeneutical stance. An angel tells Daniel that the seventy years are seventy weeks and that they are now nearing the end, which means that the temple desecration by "the troops of the prince" will soon be over (Dan 9:20–27). The prince in question is Antiochus IV Epiphanes, and the temple desecration apparently refers to the temple's dedication to Zeus Olympius in 168 BCE.

The new attitude toward received scriptures is especially manifest in the way people read the prophetical books. The Prophets were regarded as the repository of oracles that predicted events that were happening or about to happen in the time of the readers. This perception of prophecy was common at the time. As the book of Tobit puts it, "everything that was spoken by the prophets of Israel, whom God sent, will occur. None of all their words will fail, but all will come true at their appointed times" (Tob 14:4 NRSV). In due course, readers came to regard other books as prophecy as well. There was a common belief that King David had been a prophet too, and that the psalms contained predictions about the present time.[44] And Moses, of course, had also been a prophet: his own book said so, and also contained predictions (Deut 18:15–18). All the ancestral books could be read as prophecy then. The prophets were now buried in their graves, just as King David (Acts 2:29); maybe their bones could still work miracles, but they themselves were silent (Sir 49:10). The era of revelation had come to an end.[45] "When the latter prophets, Haggai, Zechariah, and Malachi died, the Holy Spirit departed from Israel," later Jewish tradition says.[46] Prophetic succession ceased in the time of Artaxerxes I (r. 465–424 BCE), according to Josephus (*C. Ap.* 1.40–41).[47] The prophetical books had now taken the place of the prophets: they contained "oracles of God" (*logia tou theou,* Rom 3:2). The prophets might be dead, but these oracles were alive (Acts 7:38, *logia zōnta*).

Owing to Israel's scribal legacy, the end of the era of revelation did not mean the end of divine communication. The ancestral books provided a mediated revelation—mediated on more than one account. The written text itself is a medium. It is there as material record, waiting to be opened, read, and interpreted, so that its audience may receive a revelation from God.[48] But the sacred scriptures had been mediated as well. First by those who had committed the texts to writing—Moses, the prophets, David—though their role had been purely instrumental: "The Holy One . . . dictated, Moses repeated, and Moses wrote" (b. B. Bat. 15a). In some quarters it was held that the law had been handed down by angels (Acts 7:53; Heb 2:2). The practical consequence of such theories of divine inspiration and angelic mediation was that the prophets did not know about which time they were speaking (1QpHab 7:1–2; 1 Pet 1:10–12). Even to themselves, their prophecies were "mysteries" (1QpHab 7:5, *kwl rzy dbry 'bdyw hnb'ym*). They had produced oracle books that needed the intervention of an angel (Dan 9:20–23) or a specially gifted teacher to decipher their code (1QpHab 7:4–5). Untrained eyes and ears would miss their meaning.

Since the scriptures were believed to hold many riddles and mysteries, all of them of the highest importance, the act of interpretation became key to unlocking the treasures of the text. The pesher had to provide the solution. Interpretation was the province of the scribe:

> He seeks out the wisdom of all the ancients,
>   and is concerned with prophecies;
> he preserves the sayings of the famous
>   and penetrates the subtleties of parables;
> he seeks out the hidden meanings of proverbs
>   and is at home with the obscurities of parables. (Sir 39:1–3 NRSV)

These words in praise of the scribal profession come from a man who had little use for apocalyptic dreams and esoteric speculations (Sir 34:5–8). Yet his references to the "subtleties" (*strophais*), "hidden meanings" (*apokrypha*), and "obscurities" (*ainigmasi*) of the text reflect a view of scripture that was quite close to the one found in Daniel and at Qumran.[49] For the uninitiated, scribes and teachers like Ben Sira had to determine the meaning of the scriptures. It put some of these men in a powerful position. Their students and disciples would form schools and sects. The reading revolution fostered a new approach to scripture and led to the emergence of various reading communities. These differed from one another with respect to the books they recognized as revelation as well as to their interpretation. These reading communities are more commonly known as the Jewish "sects" of the period.

Mainstream Judaism and the Rise of Jewish Sects

Writing around 75 CE, Josephus gives his readers several descriptions of what he considered the three main Jewish groups of his day: Pharisees, Sadducees, and Essenes.[50] The word Josephus uses for these groups is *hairesis,* traditionally translated as "sect."[51] If we stay with the *OED* definition of a sect as "a body of people subscribing to views divergent from those of others within the same religion," the term is quite appropriate. In any case, the words "sect" and "sectarian," when applied to religious associations in Hellenistic Judaism, do not have any of the derogatory overtones they tend to assume in colloquial use today. This is connected to the absence, at the time, of normative Judaism. There was what may be called mainstream Judaism ("common Judaism" is another possible term), but "mainstream" did not mean orthodox as approved of by a body of clerics with doctrinal authority. With the rise of Jewish ethnic religion during the Persian period, the mainstream religion of the Jewish community in the various parts of the empire materialized most visibly in the observation of a common religious calendar. It manifested in the more or less uniform celebration of the great Jewish festivals: Passover, Feast of Unleavened Bread, and Festival of Booths. In some of the Jewish communities of the Persian period, the religious practices included the observation of the Sabbath, circumcision, the avoidance of pork, and the profession of monotheism. In the Hellenistic period, and especially under the Hasmoneans, the full package became the common hallmark of all Jews—or at least those in Judah.[52]

The existence of mainstream Judaism is the necessary condition for the emergence of Jewish sects, for it belongs to the profile of sects to rally people around a set of particular views and values in full respect of the basic beliefs and customs shared by the wider religious community. When religion was tribal, royal, or local, there were no sects. Religious diversity used to be related to family origins, gender, profession, place of residence, and a variety of other factors, but none of them was conducive to the emergence of the kind of voluntary associations that saw the day in the later Hellenistic period. A necessary condition is not a sufficient condition, though, as logicians would say. The actual cause that called sects into being is closely related to another phenomenon typical of Israelite religion during the Hellenistic era, that is, the turn to scripture as source of revelation. The three sects Josephus mentions—Pharisees, Sadducees, and Essenes—were voluntary associations, with different views on how many and which books counted as sacred scripture, and how they should be interpreted.[53] What all of them agreed on was the sanctity and absolute authority of the Torah— the five books of Moses that had become the uncontested charter of the religious community during the Persian period. But the Torah was like a sacred symbol. How it translated into practical rules for conduct today required the intervention of interpreters who could expound the law with authority. And this is where the sects parted ways.

According to the information provided by Josephus, the New Testament, and early rabbinical sources, the Sadducees saw themselves as the staunchest believers in the sanctity of the Torah.[54] To them, there was no revelation but the Torah and the Torah alone—no other tradition, whether written or oral, could claim separate authority. They embraced the Law without the Prophets. The Torah they held fast to was the written Torah, for they rejected the authority of oral tradition. This was a statement of principle for the Sadducean interpretation of Pentateuchal law was based on the oral transmission of priestly lore in their own circles. They believed themselves to be the descendants and successors of the "sons of Zadok," who had been serving as legitimate priests of Jerusalem for centuries.[55] Though most of the reported discussions involving Sadducees concern rules of purity, the greater social impact of their position concerned the belief in heavenly spirits, resurrection, predestination, and reward and retribution in the afterlife. Since none of these topics was mentioned in the Torah, they held belief in them to be erroneous and misleading.[56] The Sadducees originated as a priestly faction, but their rejection of the belief in resurrection and the afterlife gave them the status of a sect. All who subscribed to their views were Sadducean.

By denying the existence of angels or the possibility of resurrection (Mark 12:18–27; Acts 23:8), the Sadducees were dissociating themselves from ideas that had gained wide currency among the general population.[57] Many people found the belief in angels comforting and the notion of resurrection a welcome prospect in a life full of injustice. They found the Pharisees at their side. The Pharisees also venerated the Torah as God's ultimate revelation but took the Prophets and some of the Writings as authoritative commentary on the Torah. In conjunction with the oral law (*tôrâ šebě'al-peh*), purportedly passed on since the days of Moses, these complements to the Torah allowed the Pharisees to offer an interpretation of the law that was within reach of the ordinary man and woman.[58] Some of the Essene writings found among the Dead Sea Scrolls refer to the Pharisees as "seekers of smooth things" (*dršy hhlqwt, dōrěšê hahălāqôt*), an expression that seems to be a pun on *dōrěšê hălākôt*, from Halakhah, "(oral) legal tradition."[59] In the eyes of the Essenes, the Pharisees were people of easy solutions, always willing to bend the law a little so as to make its observance less demanding. That is not how the Pharisees thought of themselves, however. Their search for the meaning of the law was as genuine and serious as that of anybody else, but they followed a different set of hermeneutical principles.[60]

Until the discovery of the Dead Sea Scrolls in the caves near Qumran (in 1947), the Essenes were the most elusive of the three Jewish sects Josephus mentions.[61] Careful comparison of the "sectarian" texts of Qumran— that is, texts authored by members of the sect on practices and ideas of the community—with the description of the Essenes in Josephus and other ancient sources has led a majority of scholars to identify the group that created the library at Qumran with the Essenes.[62] Close to the caves the community had a settlement at Khirbet Qumran, but Essenes could be found throughout Judah, living as close-knit communities in various cities and towns.[63] Like the Sadducees and the Pharisees, the Essenes were a scriptural community committed to elucidating the sacred texts. Though close to the Sadducees in their interpretation of purity laws, they sided with the Pharisees in their recognition of the Prophets and other Writings (including much of the pseudepigraphic Enoch literature). Their writings do not cite oral tradition as a source of revelation, though. Leaders of the sect claim they understand the mysteries of the law (literally, "the hidden things," *nistārôt*) because of a divine revelation (the verb is *gālâ*, "to reveal, to lay bare").[64] One of their texts likens the path to illumination to the digging of a well: "He disclosed it to them, and they dug a well of plentiful water. . . . The well is the law. And those who dug it are the converts of Israel, who left the land of Judah and lived in the land of Damascus. . . . And the staff [with which they dug the well] is the interpreter of the law [*dwrš htwrh, dōrēš hattôrâ*]."[65] For the Essenes, revelation springs from interpretation.[66]

The one Jewish sect was more formally organized than the other. The Sadducees and the Pharisees were essentially factions among an elite of priests and religious scholars, each with its own sympathizers among the general population. According to Josephus, the Sadducees had their supporters primarily among the affluent class, whereas the Pharisees and the Essenes enjoyed the sympathy of the middle and lower classes.[67] The Essene movement was organized more strictly as a society with members who had to pass a period of probation at the end of which they were registered by name.[68] Joining the community was an act of separation. The members "will be separated [*ybdlw*] from the dwelling of the evil ones."[69] "We have separated ourselves [*pršnw*] from the multitude of the people (*mrwb h*ʾ[*m*]) and from mixing ([*w*]*mht'rb*) with these things."[70] Entry into the community meant entry "into a covenant [*bbryt*] before God to carry out all that he commanded."[71] This was a covenant by oath, freely sworn in token of the novice's commitment to the rules and duties of the community.[72] These procedures bear a striking similarity to the voluntary covenants in the days of Ezra and Nehemiah by which repatriated Judeans pledged to perform specific religious duties (Ezra 10:3, 5; Nehemiah 10). The record of one such ceremony also uses the language of separation: "We make a firm agreement in writing . . . [we] and all who have separated themselves [*kol hannibdāl*] from the peoples of the lands to adhere to the law of God, . . . join . . . and enter into a curse [*'ālâ*] and an oath [*šĕbû'â*] to walk in God's law" (Neh 10:1, 29–30 [9:38, 10:28–29] NRSV). There is no historical connection between these voluntary associations in the early Persian period and the Essene movement. Their structural similarity reflects a social context in which religious observance is a private commitment rather than an externally imposed duty.[73] Such voluntary associations of private citizens flourished elsewhere in the Hellenistic world as well.[74]

Josephus does not include Samaritans or Christians among his "sects." In his eyes, they apparently did not qualify as Jewish. Yet before the development of a properly Samaritan or Christian literature, Samaritans and Christians were also Jewish reading communities, the first adhering to the Samaritan Pentateuch and the second to the Alexandrian canon extant in the Septuagint.[75] Among the five groups mentioned here there were significant doctrinal differences, but they were at one in their focus on a body of sacred scripture. Every community always had people "trained in the holy books from the days of their youth" (Josephus, *J. W.* 2.159). They had disciples whom they gave instruction in foretelling the future on the basis of the scriptures (Josephus, *Ant.* 13.311; *J. W.* 1.78). These references from Josephus pertain to the Essenes, but much the same could be said of the other groups. In all of them, an elite of "learned ones" (*maśkîlîm*) was to instruct "the masses" (*hārabbîm*), that is, the rank and file of the community (Dan 11:33; cf. 1 QS 3:13, 6:8).[76] Scribal teachers and preachers had taken the place of the prophets.

Deciphering the Future: Apocalyptic Writings

Since God's revelation was believed to be encoded in a written text, reading had become the principal mode of access to meaning. It brought about a paradigm change. The concept of a text to be deciphered proved a useful angle of approach to nontextual realities as well. Wasn't everything, in a way, like a text? Jewish scribes and scholars of the Hellenistic era started to use the act of reading as metaphor in order to make sense of both the cosmos and the course of human history. Babylonian and Persian scholars had preceded them. Babylonian astronomy was based on the concept of the stars as a "heavenly writing" (*šiṭir šamê*), the patient reading of which would disclose the immutable laws that determined their movements.[77] The Astronomical Book of Enoch (1 Enoch 72–82) uses a different language but moves in the same sphere of ideas. Enoch learns the itinerary of the heavenly luminaries because an angel has shown their books—the tablets of heaven (1 En. 72:1, 81:1–2). The movement of human history could be read in a similar manner. By the instruction of another angel, Daniel understood that history was not a cycle but a succession of world eras leading up to a final apotheosis. The author offers an exegesis of world history as though it were a book written by God—a sealed book, impossible to read for the noninitiate, unless an angel would open it and reveal its meaning (cf. Isa 29:11). In the logic of the apocalypse, the end is ineluctable and history unfolds according to a predetermined plan—much as the stars follow their predetermined paths.

Both the first book of Enoch and the book of Daniel belong to the literary genre of the apocalypse.[78] This type of literature enjoyed a special vogue among Jewish authors of the Hellenistic era. Just as the synagogue was the institutional counterpart of the reading revolution, so the apocalypse was its literary companion. The reading revolution had taught Jews to read their scriptures not as mere record but as revelation. As a type of literature, the apocalypse catered to the need to read the universe and world history as the unfolding revelation of God's plan and designs. The authors who wrote works in this genre invoked extraordinary experiences to explain how the heroes of their books—men like Enoch and Daniel—had obtained their insights. Mantic dreams and visions, otherworldly journeys, explanations by angels, and access to heavenly books—they belonged to the standard repertoire of the genre. But however extraordinary the alleged experience, in the end it was all literature. The apocalypse is typically a written genre for a public of readers. As such, it differs from prophecy. The prophets were preachers. They spoke their messages, and the books that carry their names are secondary records in writing of their deeds and oracles. But Enoch and Daniel are cast as scribes and scholars rather than as prophets of the old mold. Enoch was "the scribe of righteousness" (1 En.

12:3–4, 15:1–3) and "the first who learned writing and knowledge and wisdom . . . who wrote in a book the signs of heaven" (Jub. 4:17).[79] He did not speak about his secret knowledge, but wrote it down in a book (1 En. 81:6, 82:1). Daniel, for his part, was "versed in every branch of wisdom, endowed with knowledge and insight," and trained in "the literature and language of the Chaldeans" (Dan 1:4 NRSV). The choice of Baruch as the pseudonymous author of an apocalypse rather than Jeremiah is equally telling: the scribe rather than the prophet is the hero of the genre.[80]

The conspicuous role of scribes and books in Jewish apocalyptic literature suggests that the genre originated in a scribal milieu. The many borrowings of motifs, phrases, and characters from Mesopotamian, Canaanite, Persian, and Egyptian literature provide further evidence of a scholarly setting.[81] In view of the prominence of Babylonian and Persian lore in the earliest extant works of Jewish apocalyptic writing, that is, the Book of the Watchers (1 Enoch 1–36) and the Astronomical Book (1 Enoch 72–82), the first apocalyptic authors were from the eastern diaspora.[82] But scribes were known to travel far and wide (Sir 39:4), and the milieu in which they moved was one of intercultural contacts and influences. A typical scribal genre like the apocalypse soon spread around the Eastern Mediterranean and flourished in Egypt and Palestine as much as in Syria and Mesopotamia. Striking features of the genre are the mediating role of angels (as guides, interpreters, and intercessors); the afterlife as place of reward and retribution for actions performed in this life; the division of world history into periods following a predetermined sequence; and the expectation of a final judgment, often in combination with the belief in resurrection. All of these elements occur separately in the various sources from which the scribes took their material. It is their conjunction in the context of a revelation that gives the apocalyptic genre its distinctive character.

Though there are non-Jewish works that have been qualified as apocalyptic, the texts most commonly associated with the genre are all either Jewish or rooted in the Jewish tradition. There may have been preludes to the genre, such as the Mesopotamian dream reports, Neo-Babylonian prophecies, and Persian apocalyptic literature, but the full-fledged apocalypse was apparently a Jewish invention.[83] It was a creation, more specifically, of the Jewish diaspora. Through their exposure to the scribal heritage of Mesopotamian and Persian scholars, the Jewish scribes of the eastern diaspora took a new interest in some of the less conspicuous elements of their own tradition. Enoch is a biblical figure, but almost marginal by comparison to Moses; angels play a role in many Hebrew stories, but mostly as stand-ins for God and seldom as mediators of revelation; the world below had a place in the collective imagination of the Israelites, but usually as the abode where the dead were leading a dim afterlife; and although the Day of the Lord had been a prophetic theme, the prophets had not thought of it as the end of history. The Jewish apocalyptic authors took these various elements and gave them new roles in a cosmic drama of mythological dimensions. Much of the apocalyptic imagination reads like a mythicizing of history and the cosmos. Rather than demythologizing the world, the Jewish apocalypses invoke mythological themes and scenarios to make sense of events and phenomena that would otherwise remain puzzling.[84] It has been said that the pseudepigraphic authorship of the apocalypses taxes the credulity of the readers, but the belief in angelic hierarchies, miraculous journeys into the unknown, resurrection, and a final judgment may have required a greater leap of faith.[85]

The apocalyptic literature saw the day in a time when many Jews were apparently ready to put their faith in these pseudepigraphic revelations. The genre was a scribal phenomenon, but its proliferation during Hellenistic and Roman times proves its broad popular appeal.[86] There was a real demand for this kind of literature. The world people lived in had lost the simplicity it once had. Many Jews felt out of their depth when confronted with social and cultural changes that seemed to sap the foundations of much of what they had been taught to believe in. The apocalypse was a means to get a grip. It did not stop the avalanche of disturbing events but offered a perspective that allowed readers to rise above their own sense of helplessness. Everything that happened was part of a plot masterminded by God. Right now things were bad, but the present was a transition to an imminent day of judgment when God would put all records straight. It is perhaps just as much a sign of the times that this apocalyptic message was packaged as science ("wisdom"). Scribes were the scholars of the time. Their astronomical speculations, calendrical calculations, and historical periodizations were a superior kind of knowledge acquired through revelation. It gave members of the apocalyptic reading communities a sense of tapping into a secret source that sprang from the very heart of heaven.

While it is clear that the floruit of apocalyptic literature owes much to the mood of the times, it would be a mistake to assume all sections of Jewish society embraced its worldview. Those who belonged to the relatively well-to-do conservative classes, such as the Sadducees and wisdom teachers like Qoheleth and Ben Sira, dismissed the idea of resurrection.[87] If they did not deny the existence of angels, they were reluctant to regard them as channels of revelation, just as they were suspicious of visionary dreams and alleged extraterrestrial journeys (Eccl 5:3; Sir 34:5–8). Most Jews, however, were in sympathy with the apocalyptic message. Especially the ideas of resurrection, miraculous angelic interventions, and retribution in the afterlife gained wide currency, often without regard for their original literary contexts. The apocalyptic worldview did not dictate one particular lifestyle. To the Essenes, as we know them from the Dead Sea Scrolls, the Enoch literature had almost as much significance as the law of Moses. It led them to live a life of withdrawal in conventicles where they waited for the imminent end of the world. The Maccabees, on the other hand, had a very different response. They, too, were convinced they were living in the time of tribulation and believed in resurrection and retribution in the afterlife. But instead of waiting for judgment day to come, they took up arms to fight for the Jewish way of life. Between the quietism of the Essenes, on the one side, and the activism of the Maccabees, on the other, the majority population was glad to navigate a middle course.

Living in the Shadow of the End

In the eschatological scenario of many a Jewish apocalypse, the readers are living in the final days. It is one minute before midnight, as people would say in the world of watches and chronometers; it is the last of the seventy weeks, as the angel told Daniel in his apocalyptic visions (Dan 9:24–27). The religious intelligentsia had caught the popular mood in a formula. They lived in the age of wrath—the era of God's ire during which he had turned against his own people. The choice of words shows some variation, but the underlying idea is the same. The book of Daniel calls it "the period of wrath" (*za'am*, Dan 8:19, 11:36; *orgē* in the Greek), a phrase that echoes in the words of Mattathias, the father of Judas Maccabeus, on his deathbed ("this is a time of ruin and furious anger," *kairos katastrophēs kai orgē thymou*, 1 Macc 2:49; cf. Rom 2:8). The Qumran treatises speak of "the era of anger," *qṣ ḥrwn*, pronounced as *qēṣ ḥārôn*, to make it rhyme with *qēṣ hā'aḥārôn*, "the final era" (*qṣ h'ḥrwn*).[88] Another expression in the Dead Sea Scrolls for the same world period is "the era of iniquity" (*qṣ hrš'h*, 1 QpHab 2:7–8), human iniquity being the cause of the divine anger (see also Matt 24:12, where *anomia* is "iniquity" or "lawlessness"). During this era, both divine wrath and human iniquity will build up to a paroxysm.

Toward the end there will be "a time of anguish [ṣārâ, Greek *thlipsis*], the like of which has never been since nations came into being" (Dan 12:1). This "time of anguish as never before" became a standard item in the apocalyptic eschatology, from the Maccabean period until early Christianity (1 Macc 9:27; Matt 24:21). According to the Essene eschatology, it would lead up to the "day of the great battle," predetermined by God since ancient times (1QM 13:14), which eventually would usher in "the era of salvation" (*'t yšw'h*, 1QM 1:5).

Though the apocalyptic literature offered detailed and elaborate descriptions of the various events of the final era, the general public could paraphrase it in a simple and easily remembered paradigm: times are bad and are getting worse; there will be great anguish like never before; all this will lead up to an imminent day of judgment that will bring salvation for the righteous and damnation for sinners. When were these things to happen? Jeremiah had said God's wrath would last seventy years (Jer 25:11, 29:10), and Zechariah had echoed his prediction (Zech 1:12, 7:5). When the seventy years were over, God would "show his mercy" (Zech 1:12; *raḥēm*, same verb in Sir 36:17). But seventy years had passed and the age of wrath was not over. This led to all sorts of speculations and ingenious text exegesis. The book of Daniel interpreted Jeremiah's seventy years as seventy weeks, each day of the week lasting one year, which amounted to a total of 490 years.[89] With some arithmetic gymnastics, this would put the end of the seventy years in the reign of Antiochus IV—the very time of the composition of the Daniel apocalypse.[90] The Qumran commentary to Habakkuk, written some fifty years later, refrains from giving a figure. It simply states that "the final age [*hqṣ h'ḥrwn*] will be long and go beyond all that the prophets say, because God's mysteries are baffling" (1QpHab 7:7–8). The formulation suggests that the end has been delayed. An earlier Essene text implies that the end would come "about forty years" after the death of the Teacher of Righteousness (CD 20:13–15). Predictions like these were precarious, yet popular belief in an imminent end proved resilient. Many people continued to believe they were "the last generation" (*hdwr h'ḥrwn*, 1QpHab 7:2; cf. Matt 24:34), even though successive generations before them had thought so too. Though no society can sustain a constant eschatological fever, the belief in the imminent "consummation of the era" (1QpHab 7:2) was smoldering throughout much of the late Hellenistic and Roman periods, ready to set minds afire the moment something happened.

Opinion differed when it came to the best attitude to adopt in the face of the present anguish and the imminent day of judgment. The first two books of the Maccabees are an apology of the Hasmonean rulers (152–63 BCE) and present the Maccabees as their vanguard. They embody the activist attitude. The authors deploy the eschatological paradigm to cast the military resistance of the Maccabees in an apocalyptic light. On his deathbed, the founder of the Maccabean movement, Mattathias, had prophetically characterized the times they lived in as the era of wrath (1 Macc 2:49). Jerusalem was being turned into a Greek polis (2 Macc 4:7–17); the temple had been rededicated to Zeus (2 Macc 6:2); circumcision and Sabbath observance were proscribed (2 Macc 6:6, 10–11; Dan 7:25); and pigs were offered in sacrifice (2 Macc 6:5, 18–20; 7:1). Under such circumstances, nonviolence was not an option: "If we . . . refuse to fight with the Gentiles for our lives and for our ordinances, they will quickly destroy us from the earth" (1 Macc 2:40 NRSV). The Maccabees took their example from Phinehas and Elijah, who had killed out of zeal for the law (1 Macc 2:54, 58; Num 25:1–16; 1 Kgs 18:40). For them, war was not an apocalyptic scenario for the future but a sacred duty today. According to the description of 2 Maccabees, angels participated in the combat (e.g., 2 Macc 3:25–30, 5:1–4, 10:29, 11:6–8). Riding on horses and armed with weapons of gold (2 Macc 3:25, 5:2), these heavenly warriors embodied the cosmic dimension of the battle and secured its successful outcome. The descriptions are propaganda. By presenting the Hasmonean priests and kings as the inheritors of the Maccabees, the authors imply that the Hasmonean kingdom realized, at least for the time being, the rule by "the people of the holy ones of the Most High" that Daniel had announced in his vision (Dan 7:26–27).

It is questionable whether the Hasmoneans actually believed they were establishing the eschatological reign promised by the prophets. Yet the regime they founded had more traits of a theocracy than any previous kingdom in Judah. Since Aristobulus I (r. 104–103 BCE), high priesthood and kingship were united in one person (Josephus, *Ant.* 13.301). Though the coins of John Hyrcanus I (r. 135–104 BCE) present him only as "Johanan the high priest," the existence of a military alliance with the Seleucid ruler Antiochus VII (Josephus, *Ant.* 13.249, *philia kai symmachia*) shows that he was in fact ruling as autonomous king.[91] His successors used both the titles "high priest" and "king" (*melek, basileus*).[92] The priestly rulers of the Judean dynasty extended the border of the kingdom all the way to Galilee in the north and Idumea in the south. They razed the Gerizim temple near Shechem and implemented a Judaizing policy with mandatory circumcision for all their male subjects (Josephus, *Ant.* 13.254–258).[93] The pro-Hasmonean literature of the period (esp. 1–2 Maccabees and the book of Judith) presents these priest-kings as reincarnations of David and Solomon, reigning over "Israel" rather than Judah, with Jerusalem as the holy city for all "Israelites" or "Hebrews." Much of this was propaganda, but the Hasmoneans did succeed in imposing a Jewish lifestyle on many of their subjects. Critical analysis of the inscriptional and archaeological records suggests that the beginnings of Judaism, in which adherence to the Torah was a way of life, go back to the Hasmonean period.[94] It seemed a golden age.

At the same time, though, the Hasmonean period was also the heyday of sectarian dissent. Though initially supporters of the Hasmonean rule, the Pharisees were increasingly ill at ease about the combination of high priesthood and kingship (Josephus, *Ant.* 13.288–296, 372). The Essenes were more radical in their rejection of the Hasmoneans. Texts authored by the Qumran leadership depict their opponents as "the priests of Jerusalem who lead [the people] astray" (1Q14 = 1QpMic frag. 11:1). In the eyes of the Essenes, the Hasmoneans had defiled the temple by their lax interpretation of the purity laws and their observance of the wrong religious calendar. The priests who had founded the Essene community were priests in exile who had left Jerusalem because they believed the temple cult was corrupt beyond salvaging.[95] Under Hasmonean rule, the Essenes lived in "the days of Belial's dominion" (*ywmy mmšlt bly'l*, 1QS 2:19), Belial being the name of God's supernatural opponent.[96] It is a classic doctrine in the apocalyptic repertoire, gladly espoused by groups that feel their deepest convictions have become marginal in the society they live in. The Qumran commentaries to Habakkuk and Nahum present the antagonism between the community and the Jerusalem priesthood in terms of a dualistic conflict.[97] To the followers of the Teacher of Righteousness (the founder of the community), the Hasmonean rule marked the "era of wickedness" (*qṣ hrš'h*, 1 QpHab 2:7–8) that would lead up to the "day of the great battle" (1QM 13:14) when the "sons of light," aided by a heavenly host of angels, would put a definite end to the "sons of darkness" and "the angels of destruction" (1QS 3:20–21; 1QM 13:10–12).

The apocalyptic mood of the times gave particular acuity to disputes that focused on the temple cult. Still, the fierceness of the quarrels cannot be fully accounted for by the belief in an imminent end or personal enmity between religious leaders (such as the Teacher of Righteousness versus the Wicked Priest). It is linked to the very special place the Jerusalem temple had acquired in the religious imagination of many Jews. This was a relatively recent development. In the time of the First Temple, the Jerusalem sanctuary had been an important religious center because it was the principal royal temple of Judah. However, there had been many other temples in Judah, some quite close to Jerusalem, each of which drew its regular worshippers. But during the Hellenistic era, the Jerusalem temple came to be the sacred center of Judaism. Since Jerusalem was the very dwelling place of God, those in the diaspora said their daily prayers with their face turned toward Jerusalem (Dan 6:11 [6:10]; 1 Esdr 4:58; Tob 4:11; cf. Jdt 9:1; m. Ber. 4.5).[98] For the same reason, the pilgrimage to Jerusalem became a duty for all Jews, even if many diaspora Jews were unable to make the journey more than once in a lifetime.[99] Because of the holiness of God, the purity of the temple cult was a highly sensitive issue. Just as the sacrificial animal had to be perfect and without a blemish (cf. Num 19:2, *tĕmîmâ . . . 'ēn-bâ mûm*), so the cult rendered unto God could not tolerate imperfection. Hence the vehemence of the debates about the festival calendar (364 or 354 days) and the rules of ritual purity, as reflected in the Qumran treatise known as "Some of the Works of the Law" (*Miqṣat Ma'aśê ha-Tôrāh*, 4QMMT = 4Q394–399).[100] When Judaism became a religion without a temple (after 70 CE), disputes about purity rules lost much of their edge, and disagreements no longer bred sectarianism.[101]

Prophets, Messiahs, and the End of the Second Temple

To some people, the kingdom of the Hasmoneans may for a time have seemed like the everlasting kingdom anticipated in Daniel's visions (Dan 7:27). By the mid-first century BCE, however, it was a thing of the past. In 64 BCE the Roman forces defeated the Seleucids, and Palestine became part of their empire a year later. However Jew-friendly local Roman rule might endeavor to be, those who wielded power over Palestine, whether as king (Herod the Great, r. 37–4 BCE), governor (Quirinius, r. ca. 6–12 CE), or proconsul (Pontius Pilate, r. ca. 27–37 CE), owed their first loyalty to Rome. Even Herod, a Jewish convert from Idumea who as king rebuilt, extended, and embellished the Jerusalem temple, was a controversial figure; the Pharisees and the Essenes refused to take the loyalty oath he demanded (Josephus, *Ant.* 15.368–371).[102] Taxation put a heavy burden on the population; the further spread of Hellenistic customs and practices put many a

Jew ill at ease; and the introduction of the imperial cult in the Jerusalem temple by the mid-first century CE met with strong resistance.

For most people in Palestine, however, the transition to Roman rule did not greatly change their outlook on life. Whoever was reigning, they would always impose taxes; making a living would never be easy; and life's many hardships and few joys were much the same now as they had been in previous generations. The real glory days of Israel lay in the distant past, when David and his descendants had ruled from Jerusalem, and the prophets were still among the living. But King David was in his grave (Acts 2:29), and the prophets had long since ceased to appear (1 Macc 9:27). They, too, had their tombs and decorated graves, but those merely put the seal to their silence (Matt 23:29–30). Yet though the time of the prophets was over, many people lived in the expectation of one more prophet to come. He would be the final prophet, no less important than Moses. The scriptural basis for these speculations was a passage from the book of Deuteronomy: "I will raise up for them a prophet like you from among their own people; I will put my words in the mouth of the prophet, who shall speak to them everything that I command" (Deut 18:18 NRSV). Various texts from the period refer to this coming prophet. Judas Maccabeus stored away the stones of the Jerusalem altar, "until the prophet would come to tell what to do with them" (1 Macc 4:46); Simon was appointed as high priest and governor of the Jews, "until the reliable prophet shall arise" (1 Macc 14:41); and the Community Rule from Qumran was to be followed, "until the coming of the prophet" (1QS 9:11).[103] The Samaritan woman from the Gospel of John refers to this prophet like Moses as the "Messiah, that is the anointed one" (*Messias . . . ho legomenos christos*), who, when he comes, "will proclaim all things to us" (John 4:25).[104]

The use of the title messiah for the prophet to come is both somewhat unusual and not entirely surprising considering the messianic expectations of the time. The term "messiah" is a loan from Hebrew *māšîaḥ*, which means "the anointed one." It is rendered in Greek as *christos*, with the same meaning. The title originally refers to the anointment ceremony by which the king and the high priest were consecrated at the inauguration of their office, in token of their divine appointment (see discussion in Chapter 2). Most Israelites associated the term first of all with the king. Because King Saul was "the LORD's anointed" (*mešîaḥ yhwh*), David would never dare to raise a hand against him (1 Sam 24:7, 11 [24:6, 10]; 26:9, 11, 16, 23). After the Babylonians put an end to the Kingdom of Judah and the heirs of the

Davidic dynasty had lost the throne, there had been occasional flurries of hope for a new king from the house of David. After all, God had promised that the throne of David would be established forever (2 Sam 7:11–16). For a time, the messianic hope had fastened on Zerubbabel (Zech 6:9–15; cf. Hag 2:20–23; Zech 4:6–10) who, alongside the high priest Joshua, would be God's anointed one (Zech 4:14). Because of the political reality of Persian rule, the messianic mood had been short-lived. Under the rule of the Hasmoneans, however, the messianic hopes revived, especially when the Hasmoneans claimed the royal title without being of Davidic descent. After the Roman conquest of Judah, the hope for a Jewish messiah grew only stronger (Pss. Sol. 17:4–6, 21–44).

The sectarian texts among the Dead Sea Scrolls link "the coming of the prophet" with the coming of "the messiahs of Aaron and Israel" (1QS 9:11).[105] The Essenes were expecting two messiahs, then, the one a high priest (the messiah of Aaron) and the other the messianic king (the messiah of Israel).[106] Add to this duo the coming prophet, and there are three eschatological figures: prophet, priest, and king. The scriptural basis for this doctrine came from a combination of three classic passages: Deut 18:18–19 (the prophet like Moses), Num 24:15–17 (the Balaam oracle promising a star from Jacob and a scepter from Israel), and Deut 33:8–11 (blessing of Levi).[107] Other passages in the scrolls fill out the profile of the messianic figures.[108] How far these eschatological speculations were alive outside Essene circles is a moot question. For most people, the future prophet and the royal messiah were part of the collective repertoire of eschatological figures; whether this was true for the priestly messiah is uncertain. Also, there was no clear distinction in everyone's mind between prophet and messiah. Though some believed the prophet would come first to prepare the way for the messiah (Mal 3:23–24 [4:5–6]; cf. Sir 48:10, Luke 1:17), many found it hard to keep the two apart. Hence the occasional reference to the prophet as messiah (John 4:25), and the expectation that the prophet would restore the kingdom to Israel (Acts 1:6). Some self-styled prophets had obvious messianic pretentions, while a revolutionary figure like Simon bar Kosiba could be hailed as messiah (hence his nickname Bar Kokhba, "Son of the Star," given him by Rabbi Akiba in reference to the Balaam oracle).[109]

The diffuse popular sentiment that the present conditions were provisional, "until the prophet shall come," fueled the anticipation of his imminent appearance. The general expectation created room for a wave of would-be prophets. One of them might be the real one. "Are you the one who is to come, or are we to wait for another?" (Matt 11:3) was a useless question, for the answer would always be affirmative. Toward the mid-first century CE, a man named Theudas, claiming to be a prophet, persuaded a great many people to take up their possessions and follow him to the Jordan River. At his command, the waters would part, affording all of them a dry passage. It would have been a replica of the miracle performed by Joshua (Josh 3:1–17). Before Theudas could create a path through the waters, however, Roman troops captured and killed him (Josephus, *Ant.* 20.97–99; Acts 5:36).[110] Since Joshua was "the successor of Moses in the prophetic office" (Sir 46:1 NRSV), the miracle Theudas had promised was meant to prove that he was the "prophet like Moses" the people had all had been waiting for. A few years later, an Egyptian Jew came to Judah. He too had gained for himself the reputation of a prophet and had a serious following (Josephus estimates their number at thirty thousand). He invited his followers to come to the Mount of Olives overlooking Jerusalem. From there he would only have to say the word, and the city walls would come falling down. They would then enter the holy city and take control. It would be Jericho all over, this time with a Jewish prophet from Egypt in the role of Moses's successor Joshua. Here too, however, the miracle did not materialize. The march upon Jerusalem ended in an armed confrontation with the Romans in which many people lost their lives or were captured. The Egyptian himself had a narrow escape (Josephus, *J. W.* 2.261–263, *Ant.* 20.169–172; Acts 21:38).

Some twenty years earlier, when Pontius Pilate held the office of proconsul (ca. 27–37 CE), a Samaritan prophet had caused a stir. He too presented himself as the new Moses. Under the spell of his charisma, a great crowd undertook the journey to Mount Gerizim where the prophet would show them the sacred vessels that Moses himself had buried.[111] Many believed him. Before the prophet and his followers had actually begun their ascent, however, Pontius Pilate sent Roman soldiers to block their way. The ranks of the prophet's followers had been steadily growing, and many of the men were armed. It did not look like a harmless outburst of popular devotion—more like the preparation of a popular revolt. A battle ensued and the crowd dispersed. There were casualties, captives, and fugitives, and the prophet was not heard of again (Josephus, *Ant.* 18.85–87).[112] Others, however, were sure to take his place. Some were quite successful. The Dositheans, a Samaritan sect that existed for centuries, traced their beginnings to Dositheus, another Samaritan prophet who identified as the "prophet like Moses" in the first century CE.[113]

In view of the Roman response to many of these self-styled prophets, it was often not easy to establish the difference between a charismatic preacher and a revolutionary ringleader. Even if the prophet did not preach insurrection, his followers were often eager to believe he would lead the way to independence. Perhaps Paul was mistaken when he said the Jewish prophet from Egypt had been heading a group of four thousand assassins (*andras tōn sikariōn,* from Latin *sica,* "curved dagger"; Acts 21:38), but there could be little doubt about the man's intent to rule from Jerusalem over a free Jewish state (Josephus, *J.W.* 2.261–263). The Samaritan prophet, too, had followers who came "in arms" (*en hoplois;* Josephus, *Ant.* 18.86). Around the turn of the century, shortly after the death of Herod the Great (4 CE), Judas the Galilean stirred up a revolt in Judah in response to the Roman census of the province in preparation for tax assessment. That imperial taxation should cause a popular grudge is not surprising. But Judas resisted taxation on the religious principle that Jews could recognize only God as their Lord; to pay taxes was to bow before human masters (Josephus, *Ant.* 18.4–10). On account of the ostensibly religious motives of this resistance movement, Josephus qualifies the followers of Judas as another Jewish "sect" (*hairesis; J.W.* 2.118, 7.253–257; *Ant.* 18.9–10, 23–25).[114]

The Roman suspicion of Jewish prophets could be fatal also to those who were nonviolent. To the authorities, every prophet with a serious following represented a potential threat to the status quo. Better to nip things in the bud than to let them run out of hand. John the Baptist had been a prophet and a "good man" (Josephus's words) whose only crime had been to exhort his fellow Jews to mend their lives, practice justice, and be undivided in their devotion to God. Yet when Herod saw the effect of John's sermons on the masses, he became alarmed. He had the prophet killed before there was even the slightest sign of insurrection (Josephus, *Ant.* 18.116–119). Likewise Jesus, the Galilean prophet from Nazareth. Though explicit in his condemnation of violence—"all who take the sword will perish by the sword" (Matt 26:52)—and laconic about paying taxes—"render unto Caesar the things that are Caesar's, and unto God the things that are God's" (Matt 22:21 and parr.)—the Roman authorities had him executed for fear his message would give people the wrong ideas. Rumor had it he pretended to be the king of the Jews (Matt 27:11, 37).

In his description of the dramatic events of 70 CE, when troops of Titus burned and sacked the temple during an expedition against the Jewish revolt, Josephus mentions the unsavory role played in the event by "false prophets" (*pseudoprophētai*). One of them had deluded six thousand refugees into thinking they would be safe in the temple; all of them died in the fire (Josephus, *J.W.* 6.284–285). In those days, the "pseudo-prophets" were numerous, and many people listened to them, for "in adversity, man is quickly persuaded," as Josephus wryly observes (*J.W.* 6.286–287). In the eyes of Josephus, all of the self-styled prophets of his time were "frauds, charlatans," and "pseudo-prophets."[115] Such qualifications are inappropriate in an historical survey. Here we must be content to note that the Roman period proved particularly propitious for the emergence of Samaritan and Jewish prophets of various cloth and kind. Most of them died forgotten; some left a memory among later generations; but only two or three had a real afterlife owing to the zeal of their disciples and later apostles. The Samaritan sect of the Dositheans survived for centuries, and "the sect of the Nazoreans" (Acts 24:5) became a world religion. It should be cause for caution not to disqualify this eruption of prophecy as a passing vogue of little importance. Among the many prophets of the time, some came with a message that had a very long echo.

The destruction of the Second Temple in 70 CE inaugurated a new phase for what had once begun as the tribal religion of the Israelites. Judaism became a religion without a temple. Prophets would still arise from time to time, but rabbis (the "sages") took the place of priests as spiritual leaders of the religious community. In the decades following the temple destruction, many of these rabbis would meet at Jamnia (Jabneh), a town situated on the Mediterranean some ten miles south of Jaffa. Their discussions launched the process that yielded the Mishnah some one hundred years later. Differences of opinion were openly tolerated as part of the scholarly debate. In the absence of a temple, these differences lost much of their acuity and no longer produced sects.[116] Since most of the rabbis at Jamnia were Pharisees, it was their collection of "sacred books" (*ta biblia ta hagia,* 1 Macc 12:9, the Greek equivalent of the Hebrew *kitbê haqqōdeš;* cf. Rom 1:2, *graphai hagiai*) that became the Jewish Bible. Though there never was a formal canonization at Jamnia, the text of the Hebrew Bible from the Pharisaic tradition did effectively become the canon of Judaism.[117] Prophets and priests had had their day in earlier phases of Israelite religion. In the wake of the Jamnia meetings, the rabbis became the central figures of Jewish religion, in keeping with the turn to scripture. Judaism became a religion of the book, and scholars held the key to Israelite religion's scribal legacy—the Torah, the Prophets, and the other ancestral books.

Epilogue

This book has told the story of Israelite religion from its tribal beginnings, around 1200 BCE, to the informal canonization of its scribal legacy in the aftermath of the destruction of the Second Temple (70 CE). There are, admittedly, other ways to tell this story. Every historical narrative has its own angle and its own take on the evidence—which does not mean that one narrative is as good or bad as another, for there are documented facts to be respected and methodological rules to be observed (see the Introduction). Even though the perspective may be personal, the story need not, for that reason, be arbitrary. But what inevitably involves a degree of arbitrariness is the decision where to begin and where to end. While it is hardly possible for a scholar to speak about Israelite religion before the Early Iron Age for lack of reliable sources, that argument does not hold for late antiquity. Rather the contrary. For the time after 70 CE, the sources run freely and data are abundant. So the decision to bring the narrative to a close toward the end of the first century CE hinges on the definition of "Israelite religion." Religion continued, but it was apparently no longer exactly Israelite.

The End of Israelite Religion

Many scholars would say that Israelite religion had reached its end well before the Common Era. In fact, there is a striking tendency, especially among authors with a Protestant background, to focus on the preexilic era as the heyday of Israelite religion and to treat the postexilic era as its aftermath.[1] This tendency continues an old tradition. The earliest histories of Israelite religion—then still called "history of the religion of the Old Testament"—discuss the preexilic period under the rubric "Israelite religion" and qualify the postexilic period as "the religion of early Judaism."[2] Those designations were anything but neutral. Israelite religion was good, whereas Judaism was bad—or, at least, inferior. Informing the opposition of the two was the history model developed by Hegel: thesis—antithesis—synthesis.

Israelite religion led to its antithesis Judaism, and out of the clash emerged Christianity as the synthesis.[3] All's well that ends well. Now that the days of Hegel are over, histories of Israelite religion often run up to the Maccabean period.[4] Around 150 BCE Israelite religion would have morphed into Judaism.[5] Only very few authors follow a timeline that takes Israelite religion up to the first century of the Common Era, the way this book does.[6]

There is, however, something deeply problematic with the separation between Israelite religion and Judaism.[7] What we call Judaism is a later phase of Israelite religion. There never was a moment when Judaism branched off from Israelite religion the way the sect of the Christians (the "Nazoreans," or "the Way") would branch off from Judaism. To posit a break or a rupture is to disown Judaism of its past. While it is entirely legitimate and even useful to distinguish between Israelite religion and Judaism, the two should not be divorced as though they were separate religions. Essentializing religion is always a bad strategy, and especially so when the Jews of the time were convinced they were carrying on their Israelite past. The division between Israelite religion and Christianity is a slightly different matter. Slightly—because here too, the demarcation lines are fuzzy. If Judaism is a later phase of Israelite religion, and if Jesus and his followers were Jews, where should we draw the line between Israelite religion and Christianity? Certainly not at the hypothetical year zero that separates the Common Era from everything that went on before. As the discussion in the last chapter ("Scriptural Religion") shows, it is not really possible, from an historical point of view, to ignore events of the first century CE when discussing trends and developments of early Judaism.

Nevertheless, every parent knows that a good story must have an ending, even if tomorrow evening you will be telling the next episode. Since there must be an ending, the end of the Second Temple and the subsequent Jamnia meetings provide a convenient closure of sorts. Around that time Judaism and Christianity parted ways. Though the curse against the heretics (the Birkat Ha-Minim, literally, "the 'blessing' of the heretics," one of the eighteen blessings of the Jewish daily prayer, the Amidah) has been the subject of intense discussion, its earliest formulations point to a Jewish condemnation of Christians as non-Jews by the early second century CE.[8] This tallies with the fact that Josephus does not include the Christians in his discussion of the Jewish sects (*haireseis*), and with Justin Martyr's references, around 160 CE, to Jews cursing Christians in the synagogal service (*Dialogue with Trypho*, 16:4, 93:4, 95:4, 96:2, 108:3, 123:6, 133:6, 137:2). The sect of the Nazoreans may at one time have been regarded as a deviant form of Judaism, but by the mid-second century it had definitely put itself outside the Jewish fold.

A Story Without a Moral and with Multiple Endings

One of the principles of divination by signs, practiced in many parts of the ancient world, is summed up in the Latin phrase *post hoc ergo propter hoc,* "after this, therefore because of this." In Mesopotamia, too, many people believed that events in the past were portents of the future. This is a form of magical thinking that is difficult to get rid of. While most people today would agree that neither the past nor the present can be read as a prediction of the future, a fair number would argue there is a causal relation between the past and the present. Acts have consequences, don't they? It is true that the present is a seamless continuation of the past, so much so that any periodization always feels a bit artificial. But that does not mean that the present is the inevitable outcome of the past. History does not move in one direction, but in many directions simultaneously, along ways and byways that wind and bend, in search of destinations no one knows. Past and present entertain a very close connection, but one that is neither fully predictable nor monocausal. Historical sequences often exhibit a high degree of unpredictability because they depend on so many factors that supernatural gifts would be required to foresee exactly what will happen.

These philosophical musings have implications for the way in which we think of the relationship between Israelite religion (including early Judaism), on the one hand, and Christianity and its origins, on the other. Christianity began as one of several Jewish sects and would grow into a world religion. Especially in those parts of the world conventionally known as the West, the impact of Christianity has been immense, pervading the culture to such a degree that no Westerner can escape its influence completely. For those who believe Christianity is superior to other religions, it has often proved tempting to think of it as the natural end of the religious history of humankind. Looking at religion in the ancient Near East, this point of view would mean there is an evolution from the ritualistic polytheism of Israel's neighbors, to the prophetic religion of Israel—morality and monotheism—and from there to the lofty spirituality of the religion of Christ the savior. This reads like the unfolding of a divine plan. But though the interpretation of Israelite religion as exodus from paganism and prelude to Christianity may put some people in their comfort zone, it is ultimately based on belief. As such, it is an article of faith and not a statement of fact. The historical reality is far more complex. It involved countless contingencies and could just as well have taken a different turn and then have followed another course. It did not. But that does not mean Christianity is logically the one obvious sequel of the religious history of Israel. To take Israelite religion as a *praeparatio evangelica* turns it into a support act in a show where Christianity is the real ticket.[9]

History has much to tell us, but it is essentially a story without a moral. And even if there were a moral, it would be largely lost on us for we go on making the same mistakes. The one moral I sometimes see is that we might have been them and they might have been us—though that is perhaps a moral which, like beauty, is mostly in the eyes of the beholder. When I was young, my parents taught me it would be silly to think of my situation as an entitlement. There was no reason to feel superior. Had I been born in a different part of the world, my life would have looked very different. It's a lottery. The same holds good with respect to one's place in time. I could have been born in a different era. Many of us think, simply because we find ourselves at the end of millennia of recorded history, that we are where history has always been heading to. We are the destiny, history's culmination. Predestination. But that belief is just as silly as the idea that one deserved to be born to the prosperity of the place where one was born. In a different life we could have been living in Palestine, sometime between 1200 BCE and 100 CE—the time span this book covers. We would have partaken of the same food as those around us, dressed in a similar manner, cared about the same things they cared about, and most likely thought the same thoughts. Why shouldn't we take them as seriously as we take ourselves? After all, in the bigger picture we're family.

Looked at from this perspective, the story of Israelite religion has the charm of a family album. The faces in these photographs look familiar, but the world they lived in seems very different. Leafing through the album we leap from one generation to the next. Each time we turn the page, the pictures look somewhat different. The faces still have the same family resemblance, but the people dress differently, and with each new generation the scenery changes—almost imperceptibly, but nonetheless. From a distance—the advantage of our perspective—it is possible to discern slow yet unmistakable shifts in the contours and orientation of Israelite religion. From the tribal religion in which blood ties, by birth or by covenant, determined the community to which one belonged, the god one would call upon, and the ancestors one kept in touch with; to the royal religion in which God was king and the king his son and deputy, chief of the army and chief judge; where religion at a local level was about honor and shame, and the continuity of the family was a major concern. From the end of the monarchy, first in Israel and then in Judah, and the ensuing diaspora, to the use of religion as hallmark of ethnicity during the Persian period. And at last, during the Hellenistic and early Roman periods, the turn to scripture as locus of revelation, while the religious focus shifted from the present to the future (day of judgment, afterlife), and from the world "down here" to a higher one "up there," situated in the realm of stars and constellations, of angels and God's heavenly presence.

But it's time to close the album. We have come to a crossroads where it is up to you, the reader, to decide where to go. If you want to continue the journey, you have to choose which path to take—or, to put it less metaphorically, whose history you would like to study: the history of rabbinical Judaism and Jewish communities in Palestine and the diaspora; or that of Samaritanism, with a growing body of Samaritan literature and Samaritan communities around the Eastern Mediterranean; or that of Christianity and the early church, with its own sacred writings, on its way to becoming the official religion of an empire. All of those communities have their own stories, and for the unbiased historian there is no reason to declare one a more legitimate successor of Israelite religion than another. In a way, the history of Israelite religion has not really come to close, but the next episodes are parallel chapters that lead in different directions. It is like a book or a film where the author or screenwriter challenges the expectations of the audience by presenting the choice between different endings. But this is not fiction. History itself has offered multiple sequels to the story of Israelite religion. The choice is yours.

Notes

Introduction

1. See Mark S. Smith, *God in Translation: Deities in Cross-Cultural Discourse in the Biblical World* (Grand Rapids: Eerdmans, 2010).
2. The phrase "against its environment" is borrowed from G. Ernest Wright, *The Old Testament Against Its Environment*, SBT 2 (Chicago: Henry Regnery, 1950).
3. See A. Leo Oppenheim, *Ancient Mesopotamia: Portrait of a Dead Civilization*, rev. ed. completed by Erica Reiner (Chicago: University of Chicago Press, 1977), 172.
4. See Julius Wellhausen, *Prolegomena zur Geschichte Israels*, 6th ed. (Berlin: de Gruyter, 1927), translated by J. Sutherland Black and Allan Menzies as *Prolegomena to the History of Israel* (Edinburgh: Adam & Charles Black, 1885; repr. Cambridge: Cambridge University Press, 2013).
5. See, e.g., Niels Peter Lemche, *Early Israel: Anthropological and Historical Studies on the Israelite Society Before the Monarchy*, VTSup 37 (Leiden: Brill, 1985), 415.
6. See, e.g., Yehezkel Kaufman, *The Religion of Israel*, trans. and abridged by Moshe Greenberg (Chicago: University of Chicago Press, 1960); Theodoor C. Vriezen, *De godsdienst van Israël* (Zeist: W. de Haan; Arnhem: Van Loghum Slaterus, 1963), translated by Hubert Hoskins as *The Religion of Ancient Israel* (Philadelphia: Westminster, 1967); Helmer Ringgren, *Israelitische Religion*, Die Religionen der Menschheit 26 (Stuttgart: Kohlhammer, 1963), translated by David E. Green as *Israelite Religion* (London: SPCK, 1966); Georg Fohrer, *Geschichte der israelitischen Religion* (Berlin: de Gruyter, 1969), translated by David E. Green as *History of Israelite Religion* (Nashville: Abingdon, 1972); Frank Moore Cross, *Canaanite Myth and Hebrew Epic: Essays in the History of the Religion of Israel* (Cambridge, MA: Harvard University Press, 1973); Rainer Albertz, *Religionsgeschichte Israels in alttestamentlicher Zeit*, 2 vols., ATD Ergänzungsreihe 8/1–2 (Göttingen: Vandenhoeck & Ruprecht, 1992), translated by John Bowden as *A History of Israelite Religion in the Old Testament Period*, 2 vols., OTL (Louisville: Westminster John Knox, 1994); Susan Niditch, *Ancient Israelite Religion*

(New York: Oxford University Press, 1997); Patrick D. Miller, *The Religion of Ancient Israel*, LAI (Louisville: Westminster John Knox, 2000); J. Alberto Soggin, *Israele in epoca biblica: istituzioni, feste, ceremonie, rituali* (Torino: Claudiana, 2000), translated by John Bowden as *Israel in the Biblical Period: Institutions, Festivals, Ceremonies, Rituals* (Edinburgh: T&T Clark, 2001); George Mendenhall, *Ancient Israel's Faith and History: An Introduction to the Bible in Context*, ed. Gary A. Herion (Louisville: Westminster John Knox, 2001); Richard S. Hess, *Israelite Religions: An Archaeological and Biblical Survey* (Grand Rapids: Baker Academic, 2007).

7. For a historical survey of the various approaches to the history of Israelite religion in the late-nineteenth and twentieth centuries, with particular attention to the history vs. theology debate, see Joachim Schaper, "Problems and Prospects of a 'History of the Religion of Israel,'" in *Hebrew Bible/Old Testament: The History of Its Interpretation*, ed. Magne Saebø (Göttingen: Vandenhoeck & Ruprecht, 2015), 3.2:622–641.

8. See "The Deir 'Alla Plaster Inscription," trans. Baruch A. Levine, *COS* 2.27:140–145; Jacob Hoftijzer and Gerrit van der Kooij, eds., *The Balaam Text from Deir 'Alla Re-evaluated: Proceedings of the International Symposium Held at Leiden 21–24 August 1989* (Leiden: Brill, 1991).

9. See "Kuntillet 'Ajrud," trans. P. Kyle McCarter, *COS* 2.47:171–173; Shmuel Aḥituv, Esther Eshel, and Ze'ev Meshel, "The Inscriptions," in *Kuntillet 'Ajrud (Ḥorvat Teman): An Iron Age II Religious Site on the Judah-Sinai Border*, ed. Ze'ev Meshel (Jerusalem: Israel Exploration Society, 2012), 73–142; Brian Schmidt, ed., *Kuntillet 'Ajrud: Iron Age Inscriptions and Iconography*, Maarav 20.1 (Rolling Hills Estate, CA: Western Academic Press, 2013).

10. See *TAD* A4.7–10, C3.15.

11. See, e.g., William G. Dever, "Material Remains and the Cult in Ancient Israel: An Essay in Archaeological Systematics," in *The Word of the Lord Shall Go Forth: Essays in Honor of David Noel Freedman in Celebration of His Sixtieth Birthday*, ed. Carol L. Meyers and Michael O'Connor (Winona Lake, IN: Eisenbrauns, 1983), 571–587; William G. Dever, "The Contribution of Archaeology to the Study of Canaanite and Early Israelite Religion," in *Ancient Israelite Religion*, ed. Patrick D. Miller, Jr., Paul D. Hanson, and S. Dean McBride (Philadelphia: Fortress, 1987), 209–247; Gösta W. Ahlström, "An Archaeological Picture of Iron Age Religions in Ancient Palestine," in *Studia Orientalia memoriae Jussi Aro dedicatae*, ed. Heikki Palva, StOr 55 (Helsinki: Finnish Oriental Society, 1984), 117–145; John S. Holladay, Jr., "Religion in Israel and Judah Under the Monarchy: An Explicitly Archaeological Approach," in *Ancient Israelite Religion*, ed. Miller, Hanson, and McBride, 249–299.

12. See Ziony Zevit, *The Religions of Ancient Israel: A Synthesis of Parallactic Approaches* (London: Continuum, 2001); Rüdiger Schmitt, *Die Religionen Israels/Palästinas in der Eisenzeit: 12.–6. Jahrhundert v. Chr.*, ÄAT 94 (Münster: Zaphon, 2020), 2–3, 23–138.

13. See Othmar Keel and Christoph Uehlinger, *Göttinnen, Götter und Gottessymbole: Neue Erkenntnisse zur Religionsgeschichte Kanaans und Israels aufgrund bislang unerschlossener ikonographischer Quellen*, Quaestiones Disputatae 134 (Freiburg im Breisgau: Herder, 1992), translated by Thomas H. Trapp as *Gods, Goddesses, and Images of God in Ancient Israel* (Philadelphia: Fortress, 1998).

14. See Ernst Axel Knauf, review of *Göttinnen, Götter, und Gottessymbole*, by Othmar Keel and Christoph Uehlinger, *Biblica* 75 (1994): 298–302, quotation at 299. In keeping with Knauf's verdict, the focus in his own discussion of Israelite religion during preexilic times is overwhelmingly on the iconographical record; see Ernst Axel Knauf and Hermann Michael Neumann, *Geschichte Israels und Judas im Altertum* (Berlin: de Gruyter, 2021), 101–111, esp. 102.

15. For an introduction to the comparative study of Israelite culture and religion in the context of the ancient Near East, see John H. Walton, *Ancient Near Eastern Thought and the Old Testament: Introducing the Conceptual World of the Hebrew Bible*, 2nd ed. (Grand Rapids: Baker Academic, 2018). For a collection of contributions on the subject by a variety of authors, see Carl D. Evans, William W. Hallo, and John B. White, eds., *Scripture in Context: Essays on the Comparative Method*, PTMS 34 (Pittsburgh: Pickwick Press, 1980); William W. Hallo, James C. Moyer, and Leo G. Perdue, eds., *Scripture in Context II: More Essays on the Comparative Method* (Winona Lake, IN: Eisenbrauns, 1983); William W. Hallo, Bruce William Jones, and Gerald L. Mattingly, eds., *The Bible in the Light of Cuneiform Literature: Scripture in Context III*, Ancient Near Eastern Texts and Studies 8 (Lewiston, NY: Edwin Mellen Press, 1990).

16. The phrase "common theology of the ancient Near East" is from Morton Smith, "The Common Theology of the Ancient Near East," *JBL* 71 (1952): 135–147, reedited in *Studies in the Cult of Yahweh, 1: Historical Method, Ancient Israel, Ancient Judaism*, ed. Shaye J. D. Cohen, RGRW 130/1 (Leiden: Brill, 1996), 15–27 [contains additional notes].

17. See Jonathan Z. Smith, *Map Is Not Territory: Studies in the History of Religions* (Leiden: Brill, 1978; repr. Chicago: University of Chicago Press, 1993).

18. See Jonathan Z. Smith, *Drudgery Divine: On the Comparison of Early Christianities and the Religions of Late Antiquity* (Chicago: University of Chicago Press, 1990), 36–53.

19. See Oppenheim, *Ancient Mesopotamia*, 171–227.

20. See Brent Nongbri, *Before Religion: The History of a Modern Concept* (New Haven: Yale University Press, 2013).

21. See Charles Taylor, *A Secular Age* (Cambridge, MA: Harvard University Press, 2007).

22. See Jacob Klein, "The God Martu in Sumerian Literature," in *Sumerian Gods and Their Representations,* ed. Irving L. Finkel and Mark J. Geller, CM 7 (Groningen: Styx, 1997), 99–116, esp. 116.

23. See Gary A. Anderson, *Sin: A History* (New Haven: Yale University Press, 2009); Joseph Lam, *Patterns of Sin in the Hebrew Bible: Metaphor, Culture, and the Making of a Religious Concept* (New York: Oxford University Press, 2016).

24. One of the first scholars to systematically explore the internal diversity in ancient Israelite religion was Rainer Albertz, *Persönliche Frömmigkeit und offizielle Religion: Religionsinterner Pluralismus in Israel und Babylon* (Stuttgart: Calwer, 1978). The subtitle of the book is programmatic. Religious diversity within Israelite religion is now commonly acknowledged and studied. See, e.g., Francesca Stavrakopoulou and John Barton, eds., *Religious Diversity in Ancient Israel and Judah* (London: T&T Clark, 2010).

25. See Karel van der Toorn, *Family Religion in Babylonia, Syria, and Israel: Continuity and Change in the Forms of Religious Life,* SHCANE 7 (Leiden: Brill, 1996).

26. See Gösta W. Ahlström, *Royal Administration and National Religion in Ancient Palestine,* SHCANE 1 (Leiden: Brill, 1982); Nicholas Wyatt, "Royal Religion in Ancient Judah," in Stavrakopoulou and Barton, *Religious Diversity,* 61–81; Philip Davies, "Urban Religion and Rural Religion," in Stavrakopoulou and Barton, *Religious Diversity,* 104–117.

27. See Carol Meyers, "Household Religion," in Stavrakopoulou and Barton, *Religious Diversity,* 118–134; Rainer Albertz and Rüdiger Schmitt, *Family and Household Religion in Ancient Israel and the Levant* (Winona Lake, IN: Eisenbrauns, 2012).

28. See Manfred Weippert, "Synkretismus und Monotheismus: Religionsinterne Konfliktbewältigung im alten Israel," in *Kultur und Konflikt,* ed. Jan Assmann and Dietrich Harth (Frankfurt: Suhrkamp, 1990), 143–179; Albertz, *History of Israelite Religion,* 1.17–21 ("official—local—family").

29. See Aage Westenholz, "The Earliest Akkadian Religion," *Orientalia* (NS) 45 (1976): 215–216.

30. See Phyllis Bird, "Women's Religion in Ancient Israel," in *Women's Earliest Records from Ancient Egypt and Western Asia,* ed. Barbara S. Lesko, BJS 166 (Atlanta: Scholars Press, 1989), 283–298; Susan Ackerman, *Women and the Religion of Ancient Israel,* AYBRL (New Haven: Yale University Press, 2022).

31. See "The Inscription of King Mesha," trans. Klaas A. D. Smelik, *COS* 2.23:137–138, lines 4–5 ("Omri was the king of Israel"; line 31, "And in Horonaim lived the House of [Da]vid (i.e., Judah)." For the correct reading, see Manfred Weippert, *Historisches Textbuch zum Alten Testament*, GAT 10 (Göttingen: Vandenhoeck & Ruprecht, 2010), 248 note 49; "Kurba'il Statue," trans. K. Lawson Younger, Jr., *COS* 2.113E:268–269, lines 25–27, "At that time, I received the tribute of the Tyrians, the Sidonians, and Jehu (*Iá-u-a*), (the man) of Bīt-Ḫumri (Omri)"; the Tel Dan Stela, see Weippert, *Historisches Textbuch*, 267–269, no. 116, lines 7–9, "[I killed Jeho]ram the son [of Ahab] the king of Israel, and [I killed Ahaz]iahu the son of [Jehoram the ki]ng of the House-of-David."

32. See Cornelis H. J. de Geus, *The Tribes of Israel*, SSN 18 (Assen: Van Gorcum, 1976).

33. The use of the terms "Israel" and "Israelites" is in particular evident in the pro-Hasmonean literature of the times, such as the books of Judith and 1 and 2 Maccabees.

34. See, e.g., Zevit, *Religions of Ancient Israel*; Hess, *Israelite Religions*.

35. The historical approach has long been the dominant one in textbooks of Israelite religion. Over the past twenty to thirty years authors have tended to prefer a more thematic approach, see, e.g., Niditch, *Ancient Israelite Religion* (1997); Miller, Jr., *Religion of Ancient Israel* (2000); Soggin, *Israel in the Biblical Period* (2001); Zevit, *Religions of Ancient Israel* (2001); Schmitt, *Die Religionen Israels/Palästinas*, 23–138 (2020); and Ackerman, *Women and the Religion of Ancient Israel* (2022). The reasons for the disenchantment with a historical approach are related to (1) the conviction that there is strong ideological bias in the biblical account of Israelite history, and (2) the wish to avoid the impression that Israelite religion leads up to Christianity and is, as it were, its prologue. Those are absolutely legitimate concerns, but they do not annul the need for a historical approach. Over the long millennium of its existence, Israelite religion went through all sorts of developments that only an historical presentation can throw into the appropriate relief. What distinguishes my historical approach from the one that was dominant in the late nineteenth and most of the twentieth centuries is the absence of a teleological bias: this book does not treat Israelite religion as a prelude to Christianity or Judaism, even though it fully recognizes their historical connections.

36. See "Kuntillet 'Ajrud: Inscribed Pithos 2," trans. P. Kyle McCarter, *COS* 2.47B:171–172; "Kuntillet 'Ajrud: The Two-Line Inscription," trans. P. Kyle McCarter, *COS* 2.47C:172.

37. See "Kuntillet 'Ajrud: Inscribed Pithos 1," trans. P. Kyle McCarter, *COS* 2.47A:171.

38. See P. Kyle McCarter, "Aspects of the Religion of the Israelite Monarchy: Biblical and Epigraphic Data," in *Ancient Israelite Religion,* ed. Miller, Hanson, and McBride, 137–155, esp. 140–142.

39. On the situation at Elephantine, see Karel van der Toorn, *Becoming Diaspora Jews: Behind the Story of Elephantine,* AYBRL (New Haven: Yale University Press, 2019); on the Leontopolis temple, see Meron M. Piotrkowski, *Priests in Exile: The History of the Temple of Onias and Its Community in the Hellenistic Period,* SJ 106 (Berlin: de Gruyter, 2019).

Prologue

1. Melford E. Spiro, "Religion: Problems of Definition and Explanation," in *Anthropological Approaches to the Study of Religion,* ed. Michael Banton (London: Tavistock, 1966), 85–126, esp. 96.

2. See, e.g., Thomas Römer, *The Invention of God,* trans. Raymond Geuss (Cambridge, MA: Harvard University Press, 2015); Theodore J. Lewis, *The Origin and Character of God: Ancient Israelite Religion Through the Lens of Divinity* (New York: Oxford University Press, 2020); Daniel E. Fleming, *Yahweh Before Israel: Glimpses of History in a Divine Name* (New York: Cambridge University Press, 2020); Francesca Stavrakopoulou, *God: An Anatomy* (New York: Knopf, 2022).

3. See Pascal, *Oeuvres complètes,* ed. Jacques Chevalier, Bibliothèque de la Pléiade (Paris: Gallimard, 1954), 1113, no. 91. The French phrase reads, "Le silence éternel de ces espaces infinis m'effraie."

4. The literary topos of the inaccessibility of heaven and the underworld as metaphor for the inscrutability of the mind of the gods also occurs in Babylonian literature; see, e.g., the Dialogue of Pessimism, lines 83–84. For an introduction to this text, edition, and translation, see Peter Machinist, "The Dialogue of Pessimism Revisited," in *Historical Settings, Intertextuality, and Biblical Theology: Essays in Honor of Marvin A. Sweeney,* ed. Hyun Chul Paul Kim, Tyler D. Mayfield, and Hye Kyung Park, FAT 160 (Tübingen: Mohr Siebeck, 2022), 105–128. For the pertinent lines, see p. 111, lines 83–84, *ayyu arku ša ana šamê elû / ayyu rapšu ša erṣetim ugammeru,* which translates as "Who is the tall one who has gone up to heaven? Who is the broad one who encompasses the underworld?" See also Wilfred G. Lambert, *Babylonian Wisdom Literature* (Oxford: Oxford University Press, 1960), 40:33–38, 76:82–83, 86:256–257.

5. See Wilfred G. Lambert, "Himmel," *RlA* 4:411–412; Lambert, *Ancient Mesopotamian Religion and Mythology,* ed. A. R. George and T. M. Oshima, Orientalische Religionen in der Antike 15 (Tübingen: Mohr Siebeck, 2016), 108–121; Wayne Horowitz, *Mesopotamian Cosmic Geography,* MC 8 (Winona Lake, IN: Eisenbrauns, 1998), 3–19.

6. See Horowitz, *Mesopotamian Cosmic Geography,* 9.

7. See Horowitz, *Mesopotamian Cosmic Geography*, 208–220.

8. See "The Descent of Ishtar to the Underworld," trans. Stephanie Dalley, *COS* 1.108:381–384.

9. "Descent of Ishtar," lines 16–20; cf. "Nergal and Ereshkigal," *COS* 1.109:388, lines 26–27.

10. For *ukultu* in the sense of "epidemic," see *CAD* 20, 64, s.v. *ukultu*. For an interesting instance of a prophet eating (*akālu*) a lamb that was still alive and then announcing that there will be an epidemic (*ukultu*), see Jean-Marie Durand, *Archives épistolaires de Mari I/1*, ARM 26 (Paris: Éditions Recherche sur les Civilisations, 1988), 434, no. 206. For an English translation, see Wolfgang Heimpel, *Letters to the King of Mari: A New Translation, with Historical Introduction, Notes, and Commentary*, MC 12 (Winona Lake, IN: Eisenbrauns, 2003), 256.

11. For a Neo-Assyrian instance, see Simo Parpola, *Assyrian Royal Rituals and Cultic Texts*, SAA 20 (Helsinki: Neo-Assyrian Text Corpus Project, 2017), 93–94, no. 34, "Burial of a Queen."

12. On purity rules more generally, see Sarah Iles Johnston, ed., *Religions of the Ancient World: A Guide* (Cambridge, MA: Harvard University Press, 2004), 496–505, by various authors.

13. For the royal harem, see Guillaume Cardascia, "Gesetze B. Assyrien," *RlA* 3:279–287, esp. 286–287; Marten Stol, *Women in the Ancient Near East*, trans. Helen and Mervyn Richardson (Berlin: de Gruyter, 2016), 459–554. For women's quarters in private houses, see Stol, *Women in the Ancient Near East*, 46; Gustaf Dalman, *Arbeit und Sitte in Palästina*, 7 vols. (Gütersloh: C. Bertelsmann, 1928–1942), 6:12–59.

14. See Dalman, *Arbeit und Sitte*, 6:140.

15. See Karel van der Toorn, *From Her Cradle to Her Grave: The Role of Religion in the Life of the Israelite and the Babylonian Woman*, trans. Sara J. Denning-Bolle (Sheffield: JSOT Press, 1994), 20–21.

16. The practice of ablutions after sexual intercourse to nullify its defiling effects was widespread in the ancient world. It is attested in Hittite texts, see Billie Jean Collins, "Sin, Pollution, and Purity: Anatolia," in Johnston, *Religions of the Ancient World*, 504–505, esp. 504; for ancient Greece, see Eugen Fehrle, *Die kultische Keuschheit im Altertum* (Giessen: A. Töpelmann, 1910), 25–38; Robert Parker, *Miasma: Pollution and Purification in Early Greek Religion* (Oxford: Clarendon, 1983), 74–75; Martin L. West, *Hesiod Works and Days: Edited with Prolegomena and Commentary* (Oxford: Oxford University Press, 1978), 336–337; Andreas Bendlin, "Purity and Pollution," in *A Companion to Greek Religion*, ed. Daniel Ogden (Oxford: Blackwell, 2007), 178–189; for Babylonia, see Herodotus, *Hist.* 1.198; for pre-Islamic South Arabia, see Jacques Ryckmans, "Les confessions publiques sabéennes: le code sud-arabe de pureté rituelle," *AION* 32 (1972): 1–15, esp. 7–9.

17. See Mary Douglas, *Purity and Danger: An Analysis of the Concepts of Pollution and Taboo* (London: Routledge & Kegan Paul, 1966), 41–57.

18. On the name Jericho, see Wilhelm Borée, *Die alten Ortsnamen Palästinas,* 2nd ed. (Leipzig: Eduard Pfeiffer, 1930), 65–67. For the veneration of the moon, see Brian B. Schmidt, "Moon," *DDD,* 585–593; see also Andrew George and Manfred Krebernik, "Two Remarkable Vocabularies: Amorite-Akkadian Bilinguals," *RA* 116 (2022): 113–166, esp. 115, line 4: Yaraḫum = Sîn. On sun worship, see Edouard Lipiński, "Shemesh," *DDD,* 764–768; Morton Smith, *Studies in the Cult of Yahweh, 1: Historical Method, Ancient Israel, Ancient Judaism,* ed. Shaye J. D. Cohen, RGRW 130/1 (Leiden: Brill, 1996), 248–253.

19. See Jeremy Black and Anthony Green, *Gods, Demons and Symbols of Ancient Mesopotamia: An Illustrated Dictionary* (London: British Museum Press, 1992), 182–184.

20. See the Babylonian "Prayer to the Gods of the Night," trans. Benjamin R. Foster, *COS* 1.115:417, "The true judge, father of the orphaned, Shamash has gone off to his bedchamber."

21. See Ivan Starr, *The Rituals of the Diviner,* Bibliotheca Mesopotamica 12 (Malibu, CA: Undena, 1983), 37, 50–51.

22. See Marie-Joseph Seux, *Hymnes et prières aux dieux de Babylonie et d'Assyrie,* LAPO 8 (Paris: Cerf, 1976), 165.

23. See Th. Hartmann, "*šemeš* Sonne," *THAT* 2:987–999, esp. 992–994.

24. See Roland de Vaux, *Les institutions de l'Ancien Testament,* 3rd rev. ed., 2 vols. (Paris: Cerf, 1976), 1:278, translated by John McHugh as *Ancient Israel: Its Life and Institutions* (New York: McGraw-Hill, 1961), 178–194, esp. 183; *CAD* 3, 134, s.v. *dibdibbu,* "clepsydra."

25. See Benno Landsberger, *Der kultische Kalender der Babylonier und Assyrer,* LSS 6/1–2 (Leipzig: J. C. Hinrichs, 1915); Benno Landsberger, "Jahreszeiten in Sumerisch-Akkadischen," *JNES* 8 (1949): 260–297; René Labat, *Un calendrier babylonien des travaux des signes et des mois* (Paris: Honoré Champion, 1965); Mark E. Cohen, *Festivals and Calendars of the Ancient Near East* (Bethesda, MD: CDL Press, 2015). For the Gezer calendar, see "The Gezer Calendar," trans. W. F. Albright, *ANET,* 320.

26. See Josephus, *Ant.* 14.65; m. Pesaḥ. 5:1.

27. See Hermann Hunger, "Kalender," *RlA* 5:297–303, esp. 297.

28. See the text of 2 Sam 4:5–7 as preserved in the Septuagint: "The sons of Rimmon the Beerothite, Rechab and Baanah, set out and, when the day was growing hot, came to the house of Ishbaal as he was taking his midday rest. The portress of the house had been gathering wheat; she had nodded and fallen asleep. So Rechab and Baanah, his brother, slipped by and went into the house, where [Ishbaal] was lying upon a couch in his bedchamber"; P. Kyle McCarter, *II Samuel: A New*

Translation with Introduction, Notes and Commentary, AYB 9 (New York: Doubleday, 1984; repr. New Haven: Yale University Press), 123, 125–126.

29. See *CAD* 10/2, 243–245, s.v. *muṣlalu,* "midday, afternoon, siesta time."

30. See Ludwig Köhler, *Der hebräische Mensch* (Tübingen: Mohr Siebeck, 1953), 88–89, translated by Peter R. Ackroyd as *Hebrew Man* (London: SCM, 1956), 101–102.

31. See Jean Bottéro, "Küche," *RlA* 6:277–298, esp. 295–297; Jean Jacques Glassner, "Mahlzeit A," *RlA* 7:259–267, esp. 260; Lambert, *Ancient Mesopotamian Religion and Mythology,* 173.

32. See Karel van der Toorn, *Family Religion in Babylonia, Syria, and Israel: Continuity and Change in the Forms of Religious Life,* SHCANE 7 (Leiden: Brill, 1996), 49–50.

33. See de Vaux, *Ancient Israel,* 183–186, esp. 183.

34. See the discussion by P. Kyle McCarter, *I Samuel: A New Translation with Introduction, Notes and Commentary,* AYB 8 (New York: Doubleday, 1980; repr. New Haven: Yale University Press), 337–338.

35. See Fritz R. Kraus, *Briefe aus dem British Museum (CT 43 und 44),* AbB 1 (Leiden: Brill, 1964), no. 106:4–19, esp. lines 17–19: "What else should I give all year for the funerary offering [*kispu*] of the new moon [*bibbulu*] of your family?" See also Jean Bottéro, "La mythologie de la mort en Mésopotamie ancienne," in *Death in Mesopotamia,* ed. Bendt Alster, RAI 26 (Copenhagen: Akademisk Forlag, 1980), 25–52, esp. 38–39. According to Atrahasis III ii 39–43, Atrahasis invited his family for a banquet (*qerētu*) at the time of the moon's disappearance and used the occasion to have them board his boat. See Wilfred G. Lambert and Alan R. Millard, *Atra-Ḥasīs: The Babylonian Story of the Flood* (Oxford: Clarendon, 1969), 93: "[. . .] the moon disappeared [. . .] he invited his people [. . .] to a banquet [. . .] he sent his family on board, they ate and they drank."

36. See Claus Wilcke, "Nachlese zu A. Poebels Babylonian Legal and Business Documents from the Time of the First Dynasty of Babylon Chiefly from Nippur (BE 6/2), Teil 1," *ZA* 73 (1983): 48–66, esp. 49–54.

37. See *CAD* 17/1, 449–450, s.v. *šapattu* (*šabattu*), "fifteenth day of the month"; Landsberger, *Kultische Kalender,* 131–136.

38. See also *KTU* 1.123:6, for the pair *yrḫ w ksa',* "Moon and Full Moon"; see Dennis Pardee, *Ritual and Cult at Ugarit,* WAW 10 (Atlanta: SBL, 2002), 150–153, no. 47; *KAI* 43:12, inscription on votive statue of Yatonbaal, referring to funerary offerings "on the new moons [*ḥdšm*] and the full moons [*ksʼm*], month after month, forever."

39. For the Gezer calendar, see *ANET,* 320; Johannes Renz, *Die althebräischen Inschriften: Text und Kommentar,* Handbuch der althebräischen Epigraphik 1 (Darmstadt: Wissenschaftliche Buchgesellschaft, 2016), 30–37.

40. See Hunger, "Kalender," esp. 298–299; Beate Pongratz-Leisten, "Neujahr(sfest). B. Nach akkadischen Quellen," *RlA* 9:294–298.
41. The evidence for a Ugaritic New Year festival in spring is circumstantial and based mainly on the Baal myth. See discussion in Johannes C. de Moor, *The Seasonal Pattern in the Ugaritic Myth of Ba'lu*, AOAT 16 (Kevelaer: Butzon & Bercker; Neukirchen-Vluyn: Neukirchener Verlag, 1971), 61–62. The spring festival to inaugurate the seafaring season was celebrated widely around the Mediterranean; see, e.g., the Greek festival of *ploiaphesia*, the "Launching of the Ships," and see J. Gwyn Griffiths, *Apuleius of Madauros: The Isis-Book (Metamorphoses, Book XI)*, EPRO 39 (Leiden: Brill, 1975), 31–47, who also discusses Egyptian parallels. On the importance of shipping for the port city of Ugarit, see Elisha Linder, "Ugarit: A Canaanite Thalassocracy," in *Ugarit in Retrospect: Fifty Years of Ugarit and Ugaritic*, ed. Gordon D. Young (Winona Lake, IN: Eisenbrauns, 1981), 31–42.
42. See Robert R. Wilson, *Genealogy and History in the Biblical World*, YNER 7 (New Haven: Yale University Press, 1977).
43. See Bertil Albrektson, *History and the Gods: An Essay on the Idea of Historical Events as Divine Manifestation in the Ancient Near East and in Israel*, ConBOT 1 (Lund: Gleerup, 1967).
44. See Wilfred G. Lambert, "A Catalogue of Texts and Authors," *JCS* 16 (1962): 59–77, esp. 64–65, lines 1–4, referring to Ea as the god who dictated some of the Mesopotamian classics believed to originate in antediluvian times.
45. See Karel van der Toorn, *God in Context: Selected Essays on Society and Religion in the Early Middle East*, FAT 123 (Tübingen: Mohr Siebeck, 2018), 126–130.
46. There is a vast introductory literature on the gods worshipped in the ancient Near East, most of it dedicated to a specific area (Mesopotamia, Syria, Egypt, etc.). Among the more recent and illuminating monographs, see Brigitte Groneberg, *Die Götter des Zweistromlandes: Kulte, Mythen, Epen* (Düsseldorf: Artemis & Winckler, 2004); Jean Bottéro, *La plus vieille religion: En Mésopotamie* (Paris: Gallimard, 1998), translated by Teresa Lavender Fagan as *Religion in Ancient Mesopotamia* (Chicago: University of Chicago Press, 2001); Corinne Bonnet and Herbert Niehr, *Religionen in der Umwelt des Alten Testaments, II: Phönizier, Punier, Aramäer*, Studienbücher Theologie 4/2 (Stuttgart: Kohlhammer, 2010); Herbert Niehr, ed., *The Aramaeans in Ancient Syria*, HdO 1/106 (Leiden: Brill, 2014), 127–203 [on religion, by Herbert Niehr]; Jan Assmann, *Ägypten: Theologie und Frömmigkeit einer frühen Hochkultur* (Stuttgart: Kohlhammer, 1984), translated by David Lorton as *The Search for God in Ancient Egypt* (Ithaca, NY: Cornell University Press, 2001); George Hart, *The Routledge Dictionary of Egyptian Gods*

and Goddesses (London: Routledge, 2005); Emily Teeter, *Religion and Ritual in Ancient Egypt* (New York: Cambridge University Press, 2011).

47. See Frans A. M. Wiggermann, "Mythological Foundations of Nature," in *Natural Phenomena: Their Meaning, Depiction, and Description in the Ancient Near East*, ed. Diederik J. W. Meijer (Amsterdam: Royal Netherlands Academy of Arts and Sciences, 1992), 279–306.

48. See Gebhard J. Selz, "'The Holy Drum, the Spear, and the Harp': Towards an Understanding of the Problems of Deification in Third Millennium Mesopotamia," in *Sumerian Gods and Their Representations*, ed. Irving L. Finkel and Mark J. Geller, CM 7 (Groningen: Styx, 1997), 167–213. For the Mesopotamian conception of divinity, see also the observations of Michael B. Hundley, "Here a God, There a God: An Examination of the Divine in Ancient Mesopotamia," *AoF* 40 (2013): 68–107 (reference courtesy of John H. Walton).

49. See Wilfred G. Lambert, "Götterlisten," *RlA* 3:473–479; Wilfred G. Lambert and Ryan D. Winters, *An = Anum and Related Lists: God Lists of Ancient Mesopotamia, Volume I*, ed. Andrew George and Manfred Krebernik, Orientalische Religionen in der Antike 54 (Tübingen: Mohr Siebeck, 2023).

50. See *CAD* 16, 67, s.v. *ṣalālu*, "to lie asleep, to fall asleep," lexical section.

51. Among the more influential such authors are Edward B. Tylor, *Primitive Culture: Researches into the Development of Mythology, Philosophy, Religion, Art, and Custom* (London: John Murray, 1871); and F. Max Müller, *Natural Religion*, Gifford Lectures delivered before the University of Glasgow in 1888 (London: Longmans, Green, 1889).

52. See Dominique Collon, "The Near Eastern Moon God," in *Natural Phenomena: Their Meaning, Depiction, and Description in the Ancient Near East*, ed. Diederik J. W. Meijer (Amsterdam: Royal Netherlands Academy of Arts and Sciences, 1992), 19–37.

53. See Thorkild Jacobsen, "The Graven Image," in *Ancient Israelite Religion*, ed. Patrick D. Miller, Jr., Paul D. Hanson, and S. Dean McBride (Philadelphia: Fortress, 1987), 15–32, esp. 18.

54. See Werner Mayer, *Untersuchungen zur Formensprache der babylonischen "Gebetsbeschwörungen,"* StPohl 5 (Rome: Biblical Institute Press, 1976), 505, line 110, "You can read the enveloped tablet that has not been opened" (*ṭuppa arma la petâ tašassi*); see also the translation in Seux, *Hymnes et prières*, 283–286.

55. See Wilfred G. Lambert, *Babylonian Oracle Questions*, MC 13 (Winona Lake, IN: Eisenbrauns, 2007), 1–5.

56. See Paul-Alain Beaulieu, *The Reign of Nabonidus King of Babylon 556–539 B.C.*, YNER 10 (New Haven: Yale University Press, 1989), 43–65.

57. See Erik Hornung, *Der Eine und die Vielen: Ägyptische Gottesvorstellungen* (Darmstadt: Wissenschaftliche Buchgesellschaft, 1973), 240–246,

translated by John Baines as *Conceptions of God in Ancient Egypt: The One and the Many* (Ithaca, NY: Cornell University Press, 1996).

58. For an edition of the text, see Wilfred G. Lambert, *Babylonian Creation Myths*, MC 16 (Winona Lake, IN: Eisenbrauns, 2013), 3–144. For an English translation, see also "Epic of Creation," trans. Benjamin R. Foster, *COS* 1.111:390–402.

59. See Theodore E. Mullen, Jr., *The Assembly of the Gods: The Divine Council in Canaanite and Early Hebrew Literature*, HSM 24 (Chico, CA: Scholars Press, 1980); Oswald Loretz, *Ugarit und die Bibel: Kanaanäische Götter und Religion im Alten Testament* (Darmstadt: Wissenschaftliche Buchgesellschaft, 1990), 56–65.

60. See Samuel Noah Kramer, *Le mariage sacré*, trans. and supplemented by Jean Bottéro (Paris: Berg International, 1983); Martti Nissinen and Risto Uro, eds., *Sacred Marriages: The Divine-Human Sexual Metaphor from Sumer to Early Christianity* (Winona Lake, IN: Eisenbrauns, 2008); Martti Nissinen, "Love Lyrics of Nabû and Tašmetu: An Assyrian Song of Songs?" in *Und Mose schrieb dieses Lied auf: Festschrift Oswald Loretz*, ed. Manfried Dietrich and Ingo Kottsieper, AOAT 250 (Münster: Ugarit-Verlag, 1998), 585–634; Tawny L. Holm, "Nanay and Her Lover: An Aramaic Sacred Marriage Text from Egypt," *JNES* 76 (2017): 1–37.

61. For "the seventy sons of Asherah," see *KTU* 1.4.vi:46 (*šb'm bn aṯrt*). For Asherah in her role as intercessor, see *KTU* 1.4.iv (for Baal and Anat).

62. See, e.g., "Tashmetu [. . .] I have turned to you [. . .]. Please intercede for me with Nabu, your husband, the Lord [. . .] at the command of your mouth may he accept my petition" ("Tašmētu 1"); and from a prayer to Shamash, "May Aya the great bride, who dwells in the bedchamber, keep your features ever aglow and speak favorably of me every day," Benjamin R. Foster, *Before the Muses: An Anthology of Akkadian Literature*, 2 vols. (Bethesda, MD: CDL Press, 1993), 2:753. See in general Mayer, *Untersuchungen zur Formensprache der babylonischen "Gebetsbeschwörungen,"* 234–235.

63. See Francesco Pomponio, "Nabû. A Philologisch," *RlA* 9:16–24; Lambert, *Babylonian Creation Myths*, 346–349 ("The Exaltation of Nabû").

64. See Peggy Day, "Anat," *DDD*, 36–43; Tzvi Abusch, "Ishtar," *DDD*, 452–456; Jan Assmann, "Isis," *DDD*, 456–458.

65. See Walter Sommerfeld, *Die Aufstieg Marduks: Die Stellung Marduks in der babylonischen Religion des zweiten Jahrtausend v. Chr.*, AOAT 213 (Kevelaer: Butzon & Bercker; Neukirchen-Vluyn: Neukirchener Verlag, 1982).

66. For the text, see "Memphite Theology," trans. James P. Allen, *COS* 1.15:21–23. For a discussion, see James P. Allen, *Genesis in Egypt: The Philosophy of Ancient Egyptian Creation Accounts*, Yale Egyptological Studies 2 (New Haven: Yale Egyptological Seminar, 1988), 42–47.

67. See Lambert, *Babylonian Creation Myths*, 294–295, iv 7–17.

68. See Jacob Klein, "The God Martu in Sumerian Literature," in *Sumerian Gods and Their Representations*, ed. Irving L. Finkel and Mark J. Geller, CM 7 (Groningen: Styx, 1997), 99–116.

69. See Walter Sommerfeld, "Marduk. A. Philologisch. I. In Mesopotamien," *RlA* 7:360–370, esp. 360–362.

70. See Karel van der Toorn, "Amurru," *DDD*, 32–34.

71. See Marten Stol, "Old Babylonian Personal Names," *SEL* 8 (1991): 191–212, esp. 203; Elizabeth C. Stone and David I. Owen, *Adoption in Old Babylonian Nippur and the Archive of Mannum-mešu-liṣṣur*, MC 3 (Winona Lake, IN: Eisenbrauns, 1991), 55, no. 23:11.

72. Euhemerism is named after the Sicilian writer Euhemerus (ca. 300 BCE), who maintained that the gods and goddesses of Greek mythology were deified men and women. See Nickolas Roubekas, *An Ancient Theory of Religion: Euhemerism from Antiquity to the Present*, Routledge Monographs in Classical Studies (London: Routledge, 2017).

73. See Andrew George, *The Epic of Gilgamesh: A New Translation* (London: Allen Lane Penguin, 1999), 114, Yale tablet, lines 268–271.

74. See Van der Toorn, *God in Context*, 293–296.

75. See "The 'Aqhatu Legend," trans. Dennis Pardee, *COS* 1.103:344, i 26–34. For a discussion, see Theodore J. Lewis, *Cults of the Dead in Ancient Israel and Ugarit*, HSM 39 (Atlanta: Scholars Press, 1989), 53–71.

76. See "The Descent of Ishtar to the Underworld," trans. Stephanie Dalley, *COS* 1.108:381–384, esp. 381, lines 7–10; cf. *COS* 1.109, iii 1–5.

77. For the practice of necromancy, see Josef Tropper, *Nekromantie: Totenbefragung im Alten Orient und im Alten Testament*, AOAT 223 (Kevelaer: Butzon & Bercker; Neukirchen-Vluyn: Neukirchener Verlag, 1989).

78. See Van der Toorn, *God in Context*, 325, 329.

79. See Hedwige Rouillard, "Rephaim," *DDD*, 692–700.

80. See *CAD* 8, 425–427, s.v. *kispu*, "funerary offering." Akio Tsukimoto, *Untersuchungen zur Totenpflege (*kispum*) im alten Mesopotamien*, AOAT 216 (Kevelaer: Butzon & Bercker; Neukirchen-Vluyn: Neukirchener Verlag, 1985).

81. See Van der Toorn, *Family Religion*, 52–55.

82. See Jacob Joel Finkelstein, "The Genealogy of the Hammurapi Dynasty," *JCS* 20 (1966): 95–118; Pardee, *Ritual and Cult at Ugarit*, 195–210, no. 56.

83. See Theodore J. Lewis, "Teraphim," *DDD*, 844–850.

84. See Wilfred H. van Soldt, *Letters in the British Museum, Part 2*, AbB 13 (Leiden: Brill, 1994), 22–23, no. 21:5–9, "My son Sukkukum disappeared from me eight years ago and I did not know whether he was still alive and I kept making funerary offerings for him [*kispam aktasipšum*] as if he were dead."

85. See Walter Farber, *Lamaštu: An Edition of the Canonical Series of Lamaštu Incantations and Rituals and Related Texts from the Second and First Millennia* B.C., MC 17 (Winona Lake, IN: Eisenbrauns, 2014), 280–281.

86. See Thorkild Jacobsen, *The Treasures of Darkness: A History of Mesopotamian Religion* (New Haven: Yale University Press, 1976), 13.

87. See *CAD* 20, 339–342, s.v. *utukku*, "demon, ghost," citation p. 341.

88. See Irving L. Finkel, "A Study in Scarlet: Incantations Against Samana," in *Eine Festschrift für Rykle Borger zu seinem 65. Geburtstag: Tikip santakki mala bašmu*, ed. Stefan Maul, CM 10 (Groningen: Styx, 1998), 71–106, esp. 73–74.

89. See Farber, *Lamaštu*, 283.

90. See Walter Farber, "Lamaštu," *RlA* 6:439–446.

91. See Frans A. M. Wiggermann, "Lamaštu, Daughter of Anu: A Profile," in *Birth in Babylonia and the Bible: Its Mediterranean Setting*, by Marten Stol, CM 14 (Groningen: Styx, 2000), 217–252, esp. 234.

92. See Manfred Hutter, "Lilith," *DDD*, 520–521.

93. See Jacobsen, *Treasures of Darkness*, 12–13.

94. See Tzvi Abusch and Karel van der Toorn, eds., *Mesopotamian Magic: Textual, Historical, and Interpretative Perspectives*, Ancient Magic and Divination 1 (Groningen: Styx, 1999); David P. Wright, *The Disposal of Impurity: Elimination Rites in the Bible and in Hittite and Mesopotamian Literature*, SBLDS 101 (Atlanta: Scholars Press, 1987). On the false opposition of religion and magic, see Jan Bremmer, "Magic *and* Religion?," in *Greek Religion and Culture, the Bible and the Ancient Near East*, Jerusalem Studies in Religion and Culture 8 (Leiden: Brill, 2008), 347–352.

95. See George, *Epic of Gilgamesh*, 94, XI 161; cf. Lambert and Millard, *Atra-Ḫasīs*, 98–99, lines 34–35.

96. See George, *Epic of Gilgamesh*, 114, Yale tablet, lines 268–271: "When you camp for the night, dig a well; in your bottle shall be fresh water always! You must offer chilled water to Shamash, and remember your [god,] Lugalbanda."

97. See Finkelstein, "Genealogy of the Hammurapi Dynasty," 96–97, lines 39–43: "Come ye, eat this, drink this, and bless Ammiṣaduqa the son of Ammiditana, the king of Babylon!" See also 2 Sam 18:18.

98. See Ziony Zevit, *The Religions of Ancient Israel: A Synthesis of Parallactic Approaches* (London: Continuum, 2001), 178–180.

99. See Lambert, *Babylonian Creation Myths*, 112–113, line 62; *COS* 1.III:401, Tablet VI, line 62.

100. See *CAD* 10/2, 50–51, s.v. *miḫirtu*, "copy, equivalent, counterpart."

101. See Elena Cassin, *La splendeur divine: Introduction à l'étude de la mentalité mésopotamienne*, Civilisations et Sociétés 8 (Paris: Mouton, 1968).

102. See Angelika Berlejung, *Die Theologie der Bilder: Herstellung und Ein-weihung von Kultbildern in Mesopotamien und die alttestamentliche Bilderpolemik*, OBO 162 (Freiburg: Universitätsverlag; Göttingen: Vandenhoeck & Ruprecht, 1998); Michael B. Dick, ed., *Born in Heaven, Made on Earth: The Making of the Cult Image in the Ancient Near East* (Winona Lake, IN: Eisenbrauns, 1999).

103. See Tryggve N. D. Mettinger, *No Graven Image? Israelite Aniconism in Its Ancient Near Eastern Context*, ConBOT 42 (Stockholm: Almqvist & Wiksell, 1995).

104. See *DULAT* 747–748, s.v. *skn* II, "stela"; see also Herbert Donner, "Zu Gen 28, 22," *ZAW* 74 (1962): 68–70.

105. See, e.g., Jacobsen, "Graven Image."

106. See Erle Leichty, *The Royal Inscriptions of Esarhaddon, King of Assyria (680–669 BC)*, RINAP 4 (Winona Lake, IN: Eisenbrauns, 2011), 196, "Esarhaddon 104" i 44–46, "The gods dwelling in it flew up to the heavens like birds"; 203–204, "Esarhaddon 105" ii 8–11; for a variant see p. 212, "Esarhaddon 106" i 12–31, "Its [Babylon's] gods and goddesses became frightened, abandoned their cellas, and went up to the heavens."

107. See, e.g., "Erra and Ishum," trans. Stephanie Dalley, *COS* 1.113:404–416, esp. tablet II; see also Jacobsen, "Graven Image," 16–17.

108. See Pardee, *Ritual and Cult at Ugarit*, 31, no. 6:16.

109. See A. Leo Oppenheim, *Ancient Mesopotamia: Portrait of a Dead Civilization*, rev. ed. (Chicago: University of Chicago Press, 1977), 183–198.

110. See "Atra-ḫasis," trans. Benjamin R. Foster, *COS* 1.130:450–453.

111. See Mordechai Cogan, *Imperialism and Religion: Assyria, Judah and Israel in the Eighth and Seventh Centuries B.C.E.* (Missoula, MT: SBL and Scholars Press, 1974), 77–83; Alberto R. W. Green, *The Role of Human Sacrifice in the Ancient Near East*, ASOR Dissertation Series 1 (Missoula, MT: Scholars Press, 1975); V. Daphna Arbel, Paul C. Burns, J. R. C. Cousland, Richard Menkis, and Dietmar Neufeld, eds., *Not Sparing the Child: Human Sacrifice in the Ancient World and Beyond. Studies in Honor of Paul G. Mosca* (London: T&T Clark, 2015).

112. See Heath D. Dewrell, *Child Sacrifice in Ancient Israel*, EANEC 5 (Winona Lake, IN: Eisenbrauns, 2017).

113. See Wright, *Disposal of Impurity*, 31–74.

114. See, e.g., Wilhelm Vatke, *Die Religion des Alten Testaments* (Berlin: Bethge, 1935); Rudolf Smend, *Lehrbuch der alttestamentlichen Religionsgeschichte*, 2nd ed. (Freiburg: J. C. B. Mohr, 1899), esp. 173–264; Samuel Hirsch, *Die Religionsphilosophie der Juden oder das Prinzip der jüdischen Religionsanschauung und sein Verhältniss zum Heidenthum, Christenthum und zur absoluten Philosophie* (Leipzig: Hunger, 1842); Hermann Cohen, *Religion der Vernunft aus den Quellen des Judentums* (Leipzig: Gustav Fock, 1919).

115. Wilfred G. Lambert, "A Further Attempt at the Babylonian 'Man and His God,'" in *Language, Literature, and History: Philological and Historical Studies Presented to Erica Reiner*, ed. Franscesca Rochberg-Halton, AOS 67 (New Haven: American Oriental Society, 1987), 187–202, quotation at 193, lines 62–63. For another translation in English, see "Dialogue Between a Man and His God," trans. Benjamin R. Foster, *COS* 1.151:485.

116. See, e.g., Lambert, *Babylonian Wisdom Literature*, 102:61–65: "Give food to eat, beer to drink, grant what is asked, provide for and honour. In this a man's god takes pleasure, it is pleasing to Šamaš, who will repay him with favour. Do charitable deeds, render service all your days."

117. See Erica Reiner, *Šurpu: A Collection of Sumerian and Akkadian Incantations*, AfOB 11 (Graz: E. Weidner, 1958), 13–16, tablet II, lines 1–128.

118. The text is accessible in English translation in Miriam Lichtheim, *Ancient Egyptian Literature*, 3 vols. (Berkeley: University of California Press, 1975–1980), 2:124–132; *ANET*, 34–36 (trans. John A. Wilson).

119. See the Laws of Hammurabi, xlviii 95–xlix 5, as translated by Martha T. Roth, *Law Collections from Mesopotamia and Asia Minor*, WAW 6 (Atlanta: Scholars Press, 1995), 135–136: "I am Hammurabi, king of justice, to whom the god Shamash has granted (insight into) the truth. My pronouncements are choice . . . ; they are meaningless only to the fool, but to the wise they are praiseworthy."

120. See for this, and for the entire section, Giorgio Buccellati, "Ethics and Piety in the Ancient Near East," *CANE* 3:1685–1696.

Chapter 1. Tribal Religion

1. For translations of the text, see "The (Israel) Stela of Merneptah," trans. James K. Hoffmeier, *COS* 2.6:40–41; Manfred Weippert, *Historisches Textbuch zum Alten Testament*, GAT 10 (Göttingen: Vandenhoeck & Ruprecht, 2010), 168–171, no. 066 (trans. Manfred Weippert).

2. Based on the Balaam inscription from Deir Alla, see "The Deir 'Alla Plaster Inscriptions," trans. Baruch A. Levine, *COS* 2.27:140–145, esp. 142.

3. For the Baal toponyms, see Nadav Na'aman, "Baal Toponyms," *DDD*, 140–141.

4. The much-acclaimed study by Eric Cline, *1177 B.C.: The Year Civilization Collapsed* (Princeton, NJ: Princeton University Press, 2014), pays due attention to the impact of climate change but ultimately underestimates its significance in relation to other factors of upheaval, many of which were actually a consequence of the climate change of the period.

5. See Werner Nützel, "The Climate Changes of Mesopotamia and Bordering Areas," *Sumer* 32 (1976): 11–24; Jehuda Neumann and Simo

Parpola, "Climatic Change and the Eleventh-Tenth-Century Eclipse of Assyria and Babylonia," *JNES* 46 (1987): 161–182; Brandon L. Drake, "The Influence of Climatic Change on the Late Bronze Age Collapse and the Greek Dark Ages," *Journal of Archaeological Science* 39 (2012): 1862–1870.

6. See Israel Finkelstein, *The Archaeology of the Israelite Settlement* (Jerusalem: Israel Exploration Society, 1988). For a discussion of some of the newer approaches to the emergence of Israel in Canaan (including a useful bibliography), see Omer Sergi, "Israelite Identity and the Formation of the Israelite Polities in the Iron I–IIA Central Canaanite Highlands," *WO* 49 (2019): 206–235; Sergi, *The Two Houses of Israel: State-Formation and the Origins of Pan-Israelite Identity*, ABS 33 (Atlanta: SBL, 2023), 25–99. See also the useful discussion by Ernst Axel Knauf and Hermann Michael Neumann, *Geschichte Israels und Judas im Altertum* (Berlin: de Gruyter, 2021), 75–92.

7. The word "transhumance" is a contraction of "trans" and "humus" and refers to the movement "across ground." For a brief description, see Robert G. Hoyland, *Arabia and the Arabs: From the Bronze Age to the Coming of Islam* (London: Routledge, 2002), 89. For an anthropological description, see Bibhash Dhar, "Anthropology and Transhumance," *Human Ecology Special Issue* 10 (2001): 151–156. For a study of the differences between pastoralists and peasants from the perspective of the *longue durée*, see Ian Scoones, "Pastoralists and Peasants: Perspectives on Agrarian Change," *Journal of Peasant Studies* 48 (2021): 1–47. For an application of the concept of transhumance as a key to the historical geography of Palestine, see Jeremy M. Hutton, "Mahanaim, Penuel, and Transhumance Routes: Observations on Genesis 32–33 and Judges 8," *JNES* 65 (2006): 161–178.

8. On the Destroyer (*mašḥit*), see Samuel A. Meier, "Destroyer," *DDD*, 240–244. For an interpretation of these rites as transhumance rituals, see Leonhard Rost, "Weidewechsel und altisraelitischer Festkalender," *ZDPV* 66 (1943): 205–251, reprinted in an updated version in Rost, *Das kleine Credo und andere Studien zum Alten Testament* (Heidelberg: Quelle & Meyer, 1965), 101–112.

9. The dominance of agriculture as the primary mode of existence of the Israelites commands the perspective of the narratives devoted to the primeval and patriarchal history, as thoughtfully demonstrated by Theodore Hiebert, *The Yahwist's Landscape: Nature and Religion in Early Israel* (Minneapolis: Fortress, 2008 [first published 1996]), esp. 141.

10. See Oswald Loretz, *Habiru-Hebräer: Ein sozio-linguistische Studie über die Herkunft des Gentiliziums* 'ibrî *vom Apellativum* Habiru, BZAW 160 (Berlin: de Gruyter, 1984); Nadav Na'aman, "Ḥabiru and Hebrews: The Transfer of a Social Term to the Literary Sphere," *JNES* 45 (1986): 271–288; Niels Peter Lemche, "Ḥabiru, Ḥapiru," *AYBD* 3:6–10.

11. See Gesenius[18], 918, s.v. *'ibrî.*

12. See *CAD* 1/1, 45–47, s.v. *abātu* B, "to run away, to flee."

13. See Na'aman, "Habiru and Hebrews," 280–281.

14. For the phrase "emergence in Canaan," see Baruch Halpern, *The Emergence of Israel in Canaan,* SBLMS 29 (Chico, CA: Scholars Press, 1983).

15. For a sober approach from an Egyptological perspective, see Donald B. Redford, *Egypt, Canaan, and Israel in Ancient Times* (Princeton, NJ: Princeton University Press, 1992); Bernd U. Schipper, *Geschichte Israels in der Antike* (Munich: C. H. Beck, 2018), 21–23.

16. For the somewhat loose use of the toponym "Egypt," cf. Gen 21:21 where "the wilderness of Paran" is located in close proximity to "the land of Egypt."

17. See John Wijngaards, "*ḥwṣy'* and *h'lh:* A Twofold Approach to the Exodus," *VT* 15 (1965): 91–102; Gerhard Wehmeier, "*'lh* hinaufgehen," *THAT* 2:272–290, esp. 287–290 = *TLOT* 2:883–896, esp. 894–895; Ernst Jenni, "*jṣ'* hinausgehen," *THAT* 1:755–761, esp. 760–761 = *TLOT* 2:561–566, esp. 565; Hans Ferdinand Fuhs, "*ālāh*," *ThWAT* 6:84–105, esp. 93–97 = *TDOT* 11:76–95, esp. 85–89.

18. See Gösta W. Ahlström, *Who Were the Israelites?* (Winona Lake, IN: Eisenbrauns, 1986).

19. Baal and Anat are prominent deities in the mythological texts from Ugarit, in which they represent the generation of the ruling gods. On Baal, see the various essays in *Mighty Baal: Essays in Honor of Mark S. Smith,* ed. Stephen C. Russell and Esther J. Hamori, HSS 60 (Brill: Leiden, 2020). On Anat, see Neal H. Walls, *The Goddess Anat in Ugaritic Myth,* SBLDS 135 (Atlanta: Scholars Press, 1992). On the legacy of Baal and Anat in Israelite religion and the Hebrew Bible, see Mark S. Smith, *The Early History of God: Yahweh and the Other Deities in Ancient Israel,* 2nd ed. (Grand Rapids: Eerdmans; Dearborn, MI: Dove, 2002), 65–107. For the occurrence of Anat and Addu (Baal) in Middle Bronze Age Canaanite names in Palestine, see, e.g., Wayne Horowitz, Takayoshi Oshima, and Seth L. Sanders, *Cuneiform in Canaan: The Next Generation,* 2nd ed. (University Park, PA: Eisenbrauns, 2018), 69.

20. See Na'aman, "Baal Toponyms."

21. See Amihai Mazar, "Notes and News on Khirbet Marjama ('Ain Sâmiya)," *IEJ* 26 (1976): 138–139, esp. 138. For the Mesha stela, see "The Inscription of King Mesha," trans. Klaas A. D. Smelik, *COS* 2.23:137–138.

22. See also J. Andrew Dearman, "Baal in Israel: The Contribution of Some Place Names and Personal Names to an Understanding of Early Israelite Religion," in *History and Interpretation: Essays in Honour of John H. Hayes,* ed. M. Patrick Graham, William P. Brown, and Jeffrey K. Kuan, JSOTSup 173 (Sheffield: Sheffield Academic Press, 1993), 173–191.

23. See Martin Noth, *Die israelitischen Personennamen im Rahmen der gemeinsemitischen Namengebung,* BWANT 3/10 (Stuttgart: Kohlhammer, 1928), 45 and note 1.

24. See Herbert B. Huffmon, *Amorite Personal Names in the Mari Texts: A Structural and Lexical Study* (Baltimore: Johns Hopkins University Press, 1965), 203–204.

25. See Daniel Bodi, "Is There a Connection Between the Amorites and the Arameans?" *ARAM* 26 (2014): 383–409.

26. See Smith, *Early History of God,* 35–43.

27. See *KTU* 1.108:10; for translation and discussion, see Dennis Pardee, *Ritual and Cult at Ugarit,* WAW 10 (Atlanta: Society of Biblical Literature, 2002), 192–195, 205–206 note 13.

28. For an edition of the Balaam text, see Jacob Hoftijzer and Gerrit van der Kooij, eds., *The Balaam Text from Deir 'Alla Re-evaluated: Proceedings of the International Symposium Held at Leiden 21–24 August 1989* (Leiden: Brill, 1991), esp. 151–184, "The Balaam Text from Deir 'Allā and the Study of the Old Testament," by Manfred Weippert. See also Erhard Blum, "Die Kombination I der Wandinschrift vom Tell Deir 'Alla: Vorschläge zur Rekonstruktion mit historisch-kritischen Anmerkungen," in *Berührungspunkte: Studien zur Sozial- und Religionsgeschichte Israels und seiner Umwelt. Festschrift für Rainer Albertz zu seinem 65. Geburtstag,* ed. Ingo Kottsieper, Rüdiger Schmitt, and Jacob Wöhrle, AOAT 350 (Münster: Ugarit-Verlag, 2008), 573–601. For an English translation, see "The Deir 'Alla Plaster Inscriptions," trans. Baruch A. Levine, *COS* 2.27:142–145. For El, see Combination I:2; Combination II:6; the Shaddayin are mentioned in Combination I:5, 6.

29. See Ernst Axel Knauf, "Shadday," *DDD,* 749–753, esp. 750–751.

30. See Manfred Weippert, "Šaddaj (Gottesname)," *THAT* 2:873–881, esp. 876 = *TLOT* 3:1304–1310, esp. 1306.

31. See *CAD* 17/1, 49–59, s.v. *šadû* A; 43, s.v. *šaddû'a.*

32. For the profile of the deity, see also the literary text traditionally known as the Marriage of Martu (= Amurru); see Jacob Klein, "The God Martu in Sumerian Literature," in *Sumerian Gods and Their Representations,* ed. Irving L. Finkel and Mark J. Geller, CM 7 (Groningen: Styx, 1997), 99–116.

33. See Karel van der Toorn, *Family Religion in Babylonia, Syria and Israel: Continuity and Change in the Forms of Religious Life,* SHCANE 7 (Leiden: Brill, 1996), 90.

34. See Steve Wiggins, *A Reassessment of Asherah: With Further Considerations of the Goddess,* Gorgias Ugaritic Studies 2 (Piscataway, NJ: Gorgias Press, 2007), 153–172.

35. See Douglas Frayne, *Royal Inscriptions of Mesopotamia: Old Babylonian Period (2003–1595),* RIME 4 (Toronto: University of Toronto Press,

1990), 359–360. See also "Elkunirša and Ašertu," trans. Gary Beckman, *COS* 1.55:149.

36. See Roland de Vaux, *Histoire ancienne d'Israël: Des origines à l'installation en Canaan* (Paris: Gabalda, 1971), 263–265, translated by David Smith as *The Early History of Israel*, 2 vols. (London: Darton, Longman & Todd, 1978), 1:274–282; Frank Moore Cross, *Canaanite Myth and Hebrew Epic: Essays in the History of the Religion of Israel* (Cambridge, MA: Harvard University Press, 1973), 57–58.

37. See Klein, "The God Martu," 100.

38. See "Kuntillet 'Ajrud: Plaster Wall Inscription," trans. P. Kyle McCarter, *COS* 2.47D:173.

39. See "Kuntillet 'Ajrud: Inscribed Pithos," trans. P. Kyle McCarter, *COS* 2.47A:171.

40. See Wilhelm Borée, *Die alten Ortsnamen Palästinas*, 2nd ed. (Leipzig: Eduard Pfeiffer, 1930), 105–106, §32.

41. For the southern origins of the worship of Yhwh, which is the prevailing view among contemporary biblical scholars, see, e.g., Lars Eric Axelsson, *The Lord Rose Up from Seir: Studies in the History and Traditions of the Negev and Southern Judah*, ConBOT 25 (Stockholm: Almqvist & Wiksell, 1987); Frank Moore Cross, *From Epic to Canon: History and Literature in Ancient Israel* (Baltimore: Johns Hopkins University Press, 1998), 53–70, esp. 66–68; Thomas Römer, *The Invention of God*, trans. Raymond Geuss (Cambridge, MA: Harvard University Press, 2015), 35–50; Juan Manuel Tebes and Christian Frevel, eds., *The Desert Origins of God: Yahweh's Emergence and Early History in the Southern Levant and Northern Arabia*, Entangled Religions 12/2 (Bochum: Center for Religious Studies, 2021); Robert D. Miller II, *Yahweh: Origin of a Desert God*, FRLANT 284 (Göttingen: Vandenhoeck & Ruprecht, 2021). For a thorough discussion and a reasoned rebuttal of the thesis of Yhwh's northern origins, see Martin Leuenberger, "Yhwh's Provenance from the South: A New Evaluation of the Arguments Pro and Contra," in *The Origins of Yahwism*, ed. Jürgen van Oorschot and Markus Witte, BZAW 484 (Berlin: de Gruyter, 2017), 157–179.

42. See Weippert, *Historisches Textbuch*, 183–184, no. 075, trans. Manfred Weippert.

43. See Ernst Axel Knauf, *Midian* (Wiesbaden: Harrassowitz, 1988), 46–48.

44. See P. Kyle McCarter, Jr., "The Origins of Israelite Religion," in Hershel Shanks, William G. Dever, Baruch Halpern, and P. Kyle McCarter, Jr., *The Rise of Ancient Israel* (Washington, DC: Biblical Archaeology Society, 1992), 119–136, esp. 124.

45. See John R. Bartlett, *Edom and the Edomites*, JSOTSup 77 (Sheffield: Sheffield Academic Press, 1989), 37–44; Diana V. Edelman, "Edom: A Historical Geography," in *You Shall Not Abhor an Edomite for He Is Your*

Brother: Edom and Seir in History and Tradition, ed. Diana V. Edelman, ABS 3 (Atlanta: Scholars Press, 1995), 1–11.

46. For another discussion of the three "southern" theophany texts, see Henrik Pfeiffer, *Jahwes Kommen von Süden: Jdc 5; Hab 3; Dtn 33 und Ps 68 in ihrem literatur- und theologiegeschichtlichen Umfeld,* FRLANT 211 (Göttingen: Vandenhoeck & Ruprecht, 2005). Pfeiffer's analysis leads him to dismiss these texts as proof of a southern origin of YHWH. He argues that YHWH's profile as storm god points to a northern origin. Daniel E. Fleming, *Yahweh Before Israel: Glimpses of History in a Divine Name* (New York: Cambridge University Press, 2020), also argues in favor of a northern origin of the cult of YHWH.

47. See Ze'ev Meshel, *Kuntillet 'Ajrud (Ḥorvat Teman): An Iron Age II Religious Site on the Judah-Sinai Border* (Jerusalem: Israel Exploration Society, 2012), 73–142.

48. See Cross, *From Epic to Canon,* 66.

49. On YHWH as divine warrior, see Theodore J. Lewis, *The Origin and Character of God: Ancient Israelite Religion Through the Lens of Divinity* (New York: Oxford University Press, 2020), 428–473.

50. See Smith, *Early History of God,* 148–159; Daniel Sarlo, *The Solar Nature of Yahweh: Reconsidering the Identity of the Ancient Israelite Deity* (Lanham, MD: Lexington Books/Fortress Academic, 2022).

51. For a study of Habakkuk 3, see Theodore Hiebert, *God of My Victory: The Ancient Hymn in Habakkuk 3,* HSM 38 (Atlanta: Scholars Press, 1986), with a discussion of Deber and Resheph on pp. 92–94. See also Gregorio del Olmo Lete, "Deber," *DDD,* 231–232; Paolo Xella, "Resheph," *DDD,* 700–703. For the references to Asherah as consort of YHWH, see the inscriptions from Kuntillet Ajrud (ca. 800 BCE) and Hirbet el-Qom, for which see the English translations in *COS* 2.47A and B and *COS* 2.52, all by P. Kyle McCarter.

52. See also Meshel, *Kuntillet 'Ajrud,* 76 no. 1.2, *yhw.*

53. See David E. Aune, "Iao," *RAC* 17:1–12; Frank Shaw, *The Earliest Non-Mystical Jewish Use of Iaô,* CBET 70 (Leuven: Peeters, 2014).

54. Cuneiform documents from the Neo-Babylonian and Persian periods conventionally render the theophoric element *-yāh* at the end of Hebrew names as *-yāma.* Some scholars have argued that the pertinent cuneiform signs are to be read as *ia-wa₆,* and thus retain a faint echo of the pronunciation of the divine name as *Yahweh; see Martin Noth, *Die israelitischen Personennamen im Rahmen der gemeinsemitischen Namengebung* (Stuttgart: Kohlhammer, 1928), 105 note 2; Manfred Weippert, *Jahwe und die anderen Götter: Studien zur Religionsgeschichte des antiken Israel in ihrem syrisch-palästinischen Kontext,* FAT 18 (Tübingen: Mohr Siebeck, 1997), 35–44, esp. 38; Cornelia Wunsch, *Judaeans by the Waters of Babylon,* Babylonische Archive 6 (Dresden: ISLET, 2022), 11. In the

rare cases where we can match the cuneiform spelling of the name with the Hebrew or Aramaic, it is clear that -yāma stands for Hebrew -yāh. See Matthew W. Stolper, *Entrepreneurs and Empire: The Murašû Archive, the Murašû Firm, and Persian Rule in Babylonia*, PIHANS 54 (Leiden: NINO, 1985), no. 94, ᵐ*pi-li-ia-a-ma // plyh*, cf. Pelaiah in 1 Chr 3:24, see Gesenius[18], 1055; Laurie E. Pearce and Cornelia Wunsch, *Documents of Judean Exiles and West Semites in Babylonia in the Collection of David Sofer*, CUSAS 28 (Bethesda, MD: CDL Press, 2014), no. 10, ᵐ*šá-lam-mi-iá-a-ma // šlmyh*, cf. biblical Shelemiah, see Edward R. Dalglish, "Shelemiah," *AYBD* 5:1191–1192.

55. See Martin Rose, *Jahwe: Zum Streit um den alttestamentlichen Gottesnamen* (Zürich: Theologischer Verlag, 1978); Römer, *Invention of God*, 30–31. Note also the indirect biblical evidence for the pronunciation "Yāhû" in Ezek 48:35 (the new name for Jerusalem will be *yhwh šmh* = *Yāhû-šámah, a theological pun on *Yerûšālayim, not unlike the understanding of the name Babylon as "Bāb-ilī," "Gate of the gods") and Jer 5:12 (*lōʾ hûʾ*, "not Him," as a pun on *Yāhû); see B. D. Eerdmans, "The Name Jahu," *Oudtestamentische Studiën* 5, ed. P. A. H. de Boer (Leiden: Brill, 1948), 1–29.

56. Many authors have adduced the Greek transcriptions Iaoue/Iaouai, Iabe, and Iabai as proof for the pronunciation *yahweh, see, e.g., de Vaux, *Histoire ancienne d'Israël*, 321–337, esp. 322, *Early History of Israel*, 1:338–348, esp. 340–341; Weippert, *Jahwe und die anderen Götter*, 39. These Greek transcriptions are all from the Common Era; the earliest is from the third century (Clement of Alexandria) and the latest from the fifth (Theodoret of Cyrrhus). They are based on the theological etymology of the divine name offered in Exod 3:13–15 and have no independent historical value.

57. As suggested by Römer, *Invention of God*, 31.

58. See Borée, *Die alten Ortsnamen Palästinas*, 65–67. Note also the name Megiddo, consistently written as *mgdw*, but in cuneiform texts with a long final vowel *ma-gi-du-ú, ma-ga-du-u*; see Mordechai Cogan, "Megiddo. A. Philologisch," *RlA* 8:12–14, esp. 12 §1.

59. See Raymond Westbrook, *Property and the Family in Biblical Law*, JSOTSup 113 (Sheffield: Sheffield Academic Press, 1991), 58–68 ("Redemption of Land"), 90–117 ("The Price Factor in the Redemption of Land").

60. See H. Wheeler Robinson, *Corporate Personality in Ancient Israel*, rev. ed. (Philadelphia: Fortress, 1980).

61. On the grave of Rachel, see Joachim Jeremias, *Heiligengräber in Jesu Umwelt* (Göttingen: Vandenhoeck & Ruprecht, 1958), 75–76; Lamotte M. Luker, "Rachel's Tomb," *AYBD* 5:608–609.

62. See *CAD* 2, 15–16, s.v. *dāmu;* Marten Stol, review of *Supplement to the Akkadian Dictionaries, Vol. 2: D, Ţ, Ṭ,* by Michael P. Streck, *BiOr* 78 (2021): 431–458, esp. 437.

63. See Piotr Steinkeller, *Sale Documents of the Ur-III Period,* FAOS 17 (Stuttgart: Franz Steiner Verlag Wiesbaden, 1989), 143–144.

64. See Karel van der Toorn, *God in Context: Selected Essays on Society and Religion in the Early Middle East,* FAT 123 (Tübingen: Mohr Siebeck, 2018), 99–111.

65. See Meir Malul, *Studies in Mesopotamian Legal Symbolism,* AOAT 221 (Kevelaer: Butzon & Bercker; Neukirchen-Vluyn: Neukirchener Verlag, 1988), 122–138.

66. See Eugen J. Pentiuc, *West Semitic Vocabulary in the Akkadian Texts from Emar,* HSS 49 (Winona Lake, IN: Eisenbrauns, 2001), 133–134.

67. See Khaled Nashef, "Zur Frage des Schutzgottes der Frau," *WZKM* 67 (1975): 29–30; Dominique Charpin, "Les divinités familiales des Babyloniens d'après les légendes de leurs sceaux-cylindres," in *De la Babylonie à la Syrie, en passant par Mari: Mélanges offerts à Monsieur J.-R. Kupper à l'occasion de son 70e anniversaire,* ed. Önhan Tunca (Liège: Université de Liège, 1990), 59–78.

68. The classic study on "the god of the father" in early Israelite religion is Albrecht Alt, *Der Gott der Väter,* BWANT 3/12 (Stuttgart: Kohlhammer, 1929), reissued in *Kleine Schriften zur Geschichte des Volkes Israels,* 3 vols. (Munich: C. H. Beck, 1953–1959), 1:1–78, translated by R. A. Wilson as "The God of the Fathers," in *Essays on Old Testament History and Religion* (Oxford: Basil Blackwell, 1966), 1–77. Alt's hypothesis on the identity of family gods as more or less anonymous divine agents, based in part on the comparison with data from Nabatean texts (pp. 32–48), is to be abandoned in light of the cuneiform evidence. On the Nabatean evidence, see John F. Healey, "The Nabataean 'God of the Fathers,'" in *Genesis, Isaiah, and Psalms: A Festschrift to Honour Professor John Emerton for His Eightieth Birthday,* ed. Katherine J. Dell, Graham Davies, and Yee Von Koh, VTSup 135 (Leiden: Brill, 2010), 45–57.

69. See Samuel J. Greengus, "The Old Babylonian Marriage Contract," *JAOS* 89 (1969): 505–532, esp. 515–520; Malul, *Studies in Mesopotamian Legal Symbolism,* 161–179; Marten Stol, *Women in the Ancient Near East,* trans. Helen and Mervyn Richardson (Berlin: de Gruyter, 2016), 79–82.

70. See Karel van der Toorn and Theodore J. Lewis, *ThWAT* 8:765–778, s.v. *tĕrāpîm* = *TDOT* 15:777–789.

71. See Malul, *Mesopotamian Legal Symbolism,* 123–138, 197–208.

72. See Malul, *Mesopotamian Legal Symbolism,* 153; Van der Toorn, *God in Context,* 107–109.

73. For the interpretation of circumcision as an ancient rite of passage, see Bob Becking, "Then Zipporah Took a Flint . . . : Circumcision as a Rite

of Passage in Exod 4, 24–26," *SJOT* 37 (2023): 3–16. The circumcision of the Shechemites, imposed by the sons of Jacob as a condition for giving their sister in marriage to Shechem, implies entry into a covenant of nonaggression and connubium (Genesis 34, esp. vv. 9–10). For the reinterpretation of circumcision as a covenant rite for all Israelite newborn males, apparently a development in the Judean diaspora in Babylonia, see Daniel L. Smith-Christopher, *The Religion of the Landless: The Social Context of the Babylonian Exile* (Eugene, OR: Wipf & Stock, 2015), 139–152.

74. On the History of David's Rise, see Leonhard Rost, *Die Überlieferung von der Thronnachfolge Davids*, BWANT 3/6 (Stuttgart: Kohlhammer, 1926), reprinted in Rost, *Das kleine Credo und andere Studien zum Alten Testament* (Heidelberg: Quelle & Meyer, 1965), 119–253, translated by Michael D. Rutter and David M. Gunn as *The Succession to the Throne of David* (Sheffield: Almond Press, 1982); P. Kyle McCarter, Jr., *I Samuel: A New Translation with Introduction and Commentary*, AYB 8 (New York: Doubleday, 1980; repr. New Haven: Yale University Press), 27–30.

75. See Menahem Haran, *Temples and Temple-Service in Ancient Israel: An Inquiry into Biblical Cult Phenomena and the Historical Setting of the Priestly School* (Winona Lake, IN: Eisenbrauns, 1985), 293, 301–303.

76. On the term *šālôm*, "peace," as referring to a covenant, see Franz Josef Stendebach, "šālôm," *TDOT* 15:13–49, esp. 31–32, cf. Akkadian *salīmātu*, see *CAD* 15, 99–100, s.v. *salīmātu*, "ally, alliance, friendship."

77. See Jacob L. Wright, *War, Memory, and National Identity in the Hebrew Bible* (Cambridge: Cambridge University Press, 2020).

78. See Mark S. Smith, *Poetic Heroes: Literary Commemorations of Warriors and Warrior Culture in the Early Biblical World* (Grand Rapids: Eerdmans, 2014), 211–266; Mark S. Smith and Elizabeth Bloch-Smith, *Judges 1: A Commentary on Judges 1:1–10:5*, Hermeneia (Minneapolis: Fortress, 2021), 367–376.

79. On the connection between tribe and territory, see Cornelis H. J. de Geus, *The Tribes of Israel*, SSN 18 (Assen: Van Gorcum, 1976), 110–111.

80. See Hans Ulrich Steymans, *Deuteronomium 28 und die adê zur Thronfolgeregelung Asarhaddons: Segen und Fluch im Alten Israel*, OBO 145 (Fribourg: Academic Press; Göttingen: Vandenhoeck & Ruprecht, 1995); Karen Radner, "Assyrische *ṭuppi adê* als Vorbild für Deuteronomium 28,20–44?" in *Die deuteronomistische Geschichtswerke: Redaktions- und religionsgeschichtlichen Perspektiven zur "Deuteronomismus"-Diskussion in Tora und Vorderen Propheten,* ed. Jan Christian Gertz, Konrad Schmid, and Markus Witte, BZAW 365 (Berlin: de Gruyter, 2006), 351–378; Bernard M. Levinson and Jeffrey Stackert, "Between the Covenant Code and Esarhaddon's Succession Treaty: Deuteronomy 13 and the Composition of Deuteronomy," *JAJ* 3 (2012): 123–140. For a critical reassessment of the

connection between the Assyrian treaties and Deuteronomy, see Carly L. Crouch, *Israel and the Assyrians: Deuteronomy, the Succession Treaty of Esarhaddon, and the Nature of Subversion,* ANEM 8 (Atlanta: SBL, 2014).

81. For the text, see Dominique Charpin and others, *Archives Épistolaires de Mari I/2,* ARM 26/2 (Paris: Éditions Recherche sur les Civilisations, 1988), 33, text A.2730; Wolfgang Heimpel, *Letters to the King of Mari: A New Translation, with Historical Introduction, Notes, and Commentary,* MC 12 (Winona Lake, IN: Eisenbrauns, 2003), 509; Dominique Charpin, *"Tu es de mon sang": Les alliances dans le Proche-Orient ancien* (Paris: Collège de France, Les belles lettres, 2019), 74–78, 288–290.

82. See Jesper Eidem, *The Royal Archives from Tell Leilan: Old Babylonian Letters and Treaties from the Lower Town Palace East,* PIHANS 117 (Leiden: Nederlands Instituut voor het Nabije Oosten, 2011), 160 no. 89:34.

83. See "The Inscriptions of Bar-Ga'yah and Mati'el from Sefire," trans. Joseph A. Fitzmyer, *COS* 2.82:213–217, esp. 214.

84. See André Lemaire and Jean-Marie Durand, *Les inscriptions araméennes de Sfiré et l'Assyrie de Shamshi-ilu* (Geneva: Droz, 1984), 114, lines 39–40.

85. See Jean-Marie Durand, "Sumérien et Akkadien en pays Amorite," *MARI* 1 (1982): 79–89, esp. 86–87.

86. See Klaas R. Veenhof, review of *Salbung als Rechtsakt,* by Ernst Kutsch, *BiOr* 23 (1966): 308–313, esp. 310.

87. See *CAD* 15, 322, s.v. *sissiktu,* "fringe, edge, hem (of a garment)"; Charpin, *"Tu es de mon sang,"* 86.

88. See Malul, *Mesopotamian Legal Symbolism,* 197–208.

89. See Durand, *Archives Épistolaires de Mari I/1,* 152–154, no. 24:10–12; for an English translation, see Heimpel, *Letters to the King of Mari,* 189.

90. See Charpin, *"Tu es de mon sang,"* 81–82.

91. See Charpin, *"Tu es de mon sang,"* 93–126.

92. See Charpin, *"Tu es de mon sang,"* 84–85.

93. See Adam Falkenstein, "Zu den Inschriften der Grabung in Uruk-Warka 1960–1961," *BaghM* 2 (1963): 1–82, esp. 59, iv 16–19.

94. See Friedrich Schwally, *Der heilige Krieg in Israel,* Semitische Kriegsaltertümer 1 (Leipzig: Dieterich'sche Verlagsbuchhandlung Theodor Weicher, 1901); Gerhard von Rad, *Der Heilige Krieg im alten Israel,* ATANT 20 (Zürich: Zwingli-Verlag, 1951), translated by Marva J. Dawn as *Holy War in Ancient Israel* (Grand Rapids: Eerdmans, 1991).

95. See Weippert, *Jahwe und die anderen Götter,* 71–97.

96. See also "The Inscription of King Mesha," trans. Klaas A. D. Smelik, *COS* 2.23:137–138, lines 11–13, 16–17 ("and from there [i.e., the city of Nebo] I took t[he ves]sels of YHWH, and I hauled them before the face of Kemosh"). Ezra 1:7 commemorates how Nebuchadnezzar put the vessels from the Jerusalem temple in the temple of his own god.

97. See *CAD* 8, 55–56, s.v. *kakku* 3, "standard with divine symbol."

98. See Patrick D. Miller, Jr., and J. J. M. Roberts, *The Hand of the Lord: A Reassessment of the "Ark Narrative" of 1 Samuel,* JHNES (Baltimore: Johns Hopkins University Press, 1977).

99. The Hebrew Bible has various references to the tabernacle being kept in the temple. First Samuel 2:22 speaks of the tent of meeting at Shiloh, presumably set up either in or next to the Shiloh temple (the "house of the Lord" in Shiloh, 1 Sam 1:7, 9, 24). According to 1 Kgs 8:4, at the solemn inauguration of Solomon's Temple, "the Levites brought the Tent of Meeting and all the holy vessels" (NJPS). Several passages of 1–2 Chronicles suggest the tabernacle was indeed somewhere in the temple; see, e.g., 1 Chr 16:33, 23:32; 2 Chr 24:6, 29:5–7. There is no logical inconsistency here, for in times of peace the tent sanctuary was likely to be stored in a holy place.

100. See "Inscription of King Mesha," trans. Smelik, esp. 138, lines 14, 32.

101. See Robert Bach, *Die Aufforderungen zur Flucht und zum Kampf im alttestamentlichen Prophetenspruch,* WMANT 9 (Neukirchen: Neukirchener Verlag 1962), 51–91.

102. For the quotations from the Mesha stela, see "Inscription of King Mesha," trans. Smelik, 137–138, lines 11–12, 16–17.

103. For studies, see Diana Vikander Edelman, *King Saul in the Historiography of Judah,* JSOTSup 121 (Sheffield: Sheffield Academic Press, 1991); Joachim J. Krause, Omer Sergi, and Kristin Weingart, eds., *Saul, Benjamin, and the Emergence of Monarchy in Israel: Biblical and Archaeological Perspectives,* AIL 40 (Atlanta: SBL, 2020); Omer Sergi, *The Two Houses of Israel: State-Formation and the Origins of Pan-Israelite Identity,* ABS 33 (Atlanta: SBL, 2023).

104. For the Tel Dan stela, see Weippert, *Historisches Textbuch,* 267–269, no. 116, lines 7–9: "[I killed Jeho]ram the son [of Ahab] the king of Israel, and [I killed Ahaz]iahu the son of [Jehoram the ki]ng of the House-of-David."

105. See Israel Finkelstein, "Saul and Highlands of Benjamin Update: The Role of Jerusalem," in Krause, Sergi, and Weingart, *Saul, Benjamin, and the Emergence of Monarchy,* 33–56.

106. On settlement patterns of extended families and clans, see Lawrence E. Stager, "The Archaeology of the Family in Ancient Israel," *BASOR* 260 (1985): 1–35. On the link between tribe and territory, see de Geus, *Tribes of Israel,* 110–111.

107. On Aramaic elements in Northern Hebrew, see C. F. Burney, *Notes on the Hebrew Text of the Books of Kings* (Oxford: Clarendon, 1903), 208–209; Mordechai Cogan and Hayim Tadmor, *II Kings: A New Translation with Introduction and Commentary,* AYB 11 (New York: Doubleday, 1988; repr. New Haven: Yale University Press), 58. On the Aramaic elements of the Balaam inscription, see P. Kyle McCarter, "The Dialect

of the Deir 'Alla Texts," in *Balaam Text from Deir 'Alla Re-evaluated*, ed. Hoftijzer and Van der Kooij, 87–99; for a more cautious approach, see Jonas C. Greenfield, "Philological Observations on the Deir 'Alla Inscription," in the same volume, pp. 109–120.

108. See Meshel, *Kuntillet 'Ajrud*, 105–119, nos. 4.1–4.5.

109. See Aline Tenu, "Assyrians and Aramaeans in the Euphrates Valley viewed from the Cemetery of Tell Shiukh Fawqâni (Syria)," *Syria* 86 (2009): 83–96. For a survey of the archaeological evidence, see Silvia Ferreri, "Cremation Burials in North Mesopotamia in the First Millennium BC: Evidence of Social Differentiation in the Assyrian Empire?" (Ph.D. diss., St. Edmund's College, University of Cambridge, 2015). The suggestion that the burning of the bodies of Saul and his sons was "a sign of vengeance" (so W. L. Reed, "Burial," *IDB* 1:474–476, esp. 475) misses the point altogether, for the inhabitants of Jabesh-gilead were honoring the man who had saved them from the Ammonites (1 Sam 11:1–13).

110. Saul had another son named Ishbaal or Eshbaal, for whom see the discussion by P. Kyle McCarter, Jr., *II Samuel: A New Translation with Introduction, Notes and Commentary*, AYB 9 (New York: Doubleday, 1984; repr. New Haven: Yale University Press), 86–87. He makes the point that *ba'al*, "lord," "was considered an acceptable epithet of Yahweh in the early days of the monarchy" (87).

111. See Joseph Blenkinsopp, *Gibeon and Israel* (Cambridge: Cambridge University Press, 1972), 14–27, 59–62.

112. See P. Kyle McCarter, Jr., "Aspects of the Religion of the Israelite Monarchy: Biblical and Epigraphic Data," in *Ancient Israelite Religion*, ed. Patrick D. Miller, Jr., Paul D. Hanson, and S. Dean McBride (Philadelphia: Fortress, 1987), 137–155, esp. 140–141.

113. See also 1 Sam 10:1 LXX; cf. McCarter, *I Samuel*, 171.

114. The relatively high incidence of personal names referring to the god Baal in the Samaria ostraca may be taken as further evidence that, even though the Northern Kingdom had YHWH as its patron deity, worship of Baal continued in some sections of the population. See Jeremy M. Hutton, "Southern, Northern and Transjordanian Perspectives," in *Religious Diversity in Ancient Israel and Judah*, ed. Francesca Stavrakopoulou and John Barton (London: T&T Clark, 2010), 149–174, esp. 153–156.

115. See Smith, *Early History of God*, 32–35.

116. See Meshel, *Kuntillet 'Ajrud*, 87, no. 3.1, YHWH of Samaria; 95 no. 3.6; 98 no. 3.9; 105 no. 4.1.1, YHWH of Teman.

117. See Karel van der Toorn, *Papyrus Amherst 63*, AOAT 448 (Münster: Ugarit-Verlag, 2018), 127, comments to 8:7.

118. On the cult of Asherah in Israel and Judah, see Judith Hadley, *The Cult of Asherah in Israel and Judah: Evidence for a Hebrew Goddess*, UCOP 57 (Cambridge: University of Cambridge Press, 2000).

119. See *DULAT,* 916, s.v. *ṯr* I, 2.a, "Bull, divine title."
120. For the bronze bull of the Hazor temple, see Yigael Yadin, *Hazor: The Head of All Those Kingdoms,* Schweich Lectures of the British Academy 1970 (London: Oxford University Press, 1972), 94. For the Bull Site, see Amihai Mazar, "The 'Bull Site': An Iron Age I Open Cult Place," *BASOR* 247 (1982): 27–42; Amihai Mazar, "On Cult Places and Early Israelites: A Response to Michael Coogan," *BAR* 15/4 (1988): 45; Ziony Zevit, *The Religions of Ancient Israel: A Synthesis of Parallactic Approaches* (London: Continuum, 2001), 176–180.
121. The identification of El and Yhwh is strikingly emphatic in the Balaam oracles in Numbers 22–24, including the use of *rĕ'ēm,* "wild ox," with reference to El: "Yhwh their god is with them, acclaimed as king among them. El, who brings them out of Egypt, is like the horns of a wild ox for them" (Num 23:21b–22; cf. 24:8; translation adapted from the NRSV). The prominence of El in the Balaam oracles may point to their Transjordanian background.
122. See Norbert Lohfink, "Beobachtungen zur Geschichte des Ausdrucks *'m Jhwh,"* in *Probleme biblischer Theologie: Gerhard von Rad zum 70. Geburtstag,* ed. Hans Walter Wolff (Munich: Chr. Kaiser, 1971), 275–305, esp. 282.

Chapter 2. Royal Religion

1. For an English translation of the Sumerian King List, see Jean-Jacques Glassner, *Mesopotamian Chronicles,* WAW 19 (Atlanta, GA: Society of Biblical Literature, 2004), 117–126, quotation at 118–119.
2. Among the rich literature on the subject, see esp. Marc Zvi Brettler, *God Is King: Understanding an Israelite Metaphor,* JSOTSup 7 (Sheffield: Sheffield Academic Press, 1989).
3. Compare the Old Babylonian prophecies warning the king of Mari against a pact of peace (*salīmu* or *salimātu*) offered by the king of Eshnunna; see Jean-Marie Durand, *Archives Épistolaires de Mari I/1,* ARM 26 (Paris: Éditions Recherche sur les Civilisations, 1988), 424, no. 197:11–12, "the alliance [*salimātu*] which the man of Eshnunna offers is deceit"; 426, no. 199:24–25, "I am afraid you will trust the alliance [*salīmu*] of the man of Eshnunna." The covenant context is clear from no. 199:30–32, "I am afraid that the king will make a treaty [lit., 'touch his throat'] without first consulting the god."
4. See Enuma Elish, V, 77–116; for an English translation, see "Epic of Creation," trans. Benjamin R. Foster, *COS* 1.111:390–402, esp. 399–400. Though the story of the Baal Cycle bears distinct similarities to the plot of the Enuma Elish, the conflicts of Baal with Yamm and Mot read more like a struggle between pretenders to the dynastic throne, with Asherah in the role of queen mother.

5. See Klaus Dieter Seybold, "māšaḥ," *ThWAT* 5:46–59, esp. 49–50 = *TDOT* 9:43–54, esp. 45–48; Tryggve N. D. Mettinger, *King and Messiah: The Civil and Sacral Legitimation of the Israelite Kings*, ConBOT 8 (Lund: C. W. K. Gleerup, 1976), 185–232.

6. See Georges Boyer, *Textes juridiques et administratifs*, ARM 8 (Paris: Imprimerie nationale, 1957), no. 13:11′–14′.

7. See Meir Malul, *Studies in Mesopotamian Legal Symbolism*, AOAT 221 (Kevelaer: Butzon & Bercker; Neukirchen-Vluyn: Neukirchener Verlag, 1988), 161–179; Marten Stol, *Women in the Ancient Near East*, trans. Helen and Mervyn Richardson (Berlin: de Gruyter, 2016), 77–82.

8. See, e.g., "The Inscription of Zakkur, King of Hamath," trans. Alan Millard, *COS* 2.35:155, A, lines 2–3, "Ba'lshamayn [raised] me and stood beside me, and Ba'lshamayn made me king [*hmlkny*] over Hazrach"; and "The Tell Dan Stela," trans. Alan Millard, *COS* 2.39:161, lines 4–5, "[but] Hadad [ma]de [me] king [*yhmlk*]"; Manfred Weippert, *Historisches Textbuch zum Alten Testament*, GAT 10 (Göttingen: Vandenhoeck & Ruprecht, 2010), 267–269, no. 116.

9. See Charles August Briggs, *The Book of Psalms*, ICC, 2 vols. (Edinburgh: T&T Clark, 1906–1907), 1:384; Hermann Gunkel, *Die Psalmen*, HKAT II/2 (Göttingen: Vandenhoeck & Ruprecht, 1929), 193. On the possible northern background of Psalm 45, see also Gary A. Rendsburg, *Linguistic Evidence for the Northern Origin of Selected Psalms*, SBLMS 43 (Atlanta: Scholars Press, 1990), 45–50.

10. For another example, see Psalm 110. Though damaged in the process of transmission, and in places hard to understand, the text suggests that "the ordination rites are linked imaginatively with a god-like birth; the king, freshly anointed with holy unguent, is greeted as new-born," quotation from John H. Eaton, *Kingship and the Psalms*, SBT Second Series 32 (London: SCM, 1976), 147. Another possible reference to the Judean king as "mighty god" (*'ēl gibbôr*) is found in Isa 9:5; see J. J. M. Roberts, "Whose Child Is This? Reflections on the Speaking Voice in Isaiah 9:5," *HTR* 90 (1997): 115–129, who argues, following Gerhard von Rad's earlier proposal ("Das judäische Königsritual," *TLZ* 72 [1947]: 211–216), that the passage has its ideological setting in the Judean coronation ritual, which he believes was modeled after the Egyptian royal ritual.

11. For a survey, see John A. Emerton, "The Syntactical Problem of Psalm XLV, 7," *JSS* 13 (1968): 58–63, who himself opts for the translation "your throne is like the throne of God for ever and ever." See also Johannes S. M. Mulder, "Studies on Psalm 45" (Ph.D. diss. University of Nijmegen, 1972), 33–80, who after an extensive discussion of all previous interpretations settles on the translation "your throne is God's forever and ever." Cf. NJPS, "your divine throne is everlasting."

12. See the short but balanced and insightful comments on this psalm by Erhard S. Gerstenberger, *Psalms: Part 1 with an Introduction to Cultic Poetry*, FOTL 14 (Grand Rapids: Eerdmans, 1988), 186–190, esp. 189 on v. 7. In the words of Theodore J. Lewis (*The Origin and Character of God: Ancient Israelite Religion Through the Lens of Divinity* [New York: Oxford University Press, 2020]), the kings of Israel and Judah were believed to be "'infused' with divinity" (507); see his discussion of divine kingship at pp. 503–507.

13. On the name Ben-Hadad, see Mordechai Cogan and Hayim Tadmor, *II Kings: A New Translation with Introduction and Commentary*, AYB 11 (New York: Doubleday, 1988; repr. New Haven: Yale University Press), 78–79. On Assurbanipal's claim of divine descent, see Alasdair Livingstone, *Court Poetry and Literary Miscellanea*, SAA 3 (Helsinki: Helsinki University Press, 1989), 10–13, no. 3:13–15 ("I knew no father or mother, I grew up in the lap of my goddesses"), r. 14–16 ("The Lady of Nineveh, the mother who bore me . . . the Lady of Arbela, my creator").

14. For Egypt, see the survey in Adela Yarbro Collins and John J. Collins, *King and Messiah as Son of God: Divine, Human, and Angelic Messianic Figures in Biblical and Related Literature* (Grand Rapids: Eerdmans, 2008), 1–24; Miroslav Bárta, "Egyptian Kingship During the Old Kingdom," in *Experiencing Power, Generating Authority: Cosmos, Politics, and the Ideology of Kingship in Ancient Egypt and Mesopotamia*, ed. Jane A. Hill, Philip Jones, and Antonio J. Morales (Philadelphia: University of Pennsylvania Museum of Archaeology and Anthropology, 2013), 257–283. For Syria, see, e.g., the reference to royal infants drinking the milk of Astarte and suckling at the breast of Anat; see *KTU* 1.15.ii:26–28, for translation see "The Kirta Epic," trans. Dennis Pardee, *COS* 1.102:333–343, esp. 337; for discussion, see Neal H. Walls, *The Goddess Anat in Ugaritic Myth*, SBLDS 135 (Atlanta: Scholars Press, 1992), 152–154.

15. The funerary rites for Judean kings included a ritual burning (*miśrāpôt*, Jer 34:5 [King Zedekiah]; *śĕrēpâ gĕdôlâ*, 2 Chr 16:14 [King Asa]; "his people did not make a fire [*śĕrēpâ*] for him like the fire for his fathers," 2 Chr 21:19 [King Jehoram]), comparable to the *šuruptu*, "burning as a funerary rite," performed for Neo-Assyrian kings at their death, see *CAD* 17/III, 373, s.v. *šuruptu* 2; Simo Parpola, *Letters from Assyrian Scholars to the Kings Esarhaddon and Assurbanipal, Part II: Commentary and Appendices*, AOAT 5/2 (Kevelaer: Butzon & Bercker; Neukirchen-Vluyn: Neukirchener Verlag, 1983), 190–191. Several scholars have interpreted the cultic platforms excavated from underneath about twenty tumuli west of Jerusalem as installations designed for the performance of such royal funerary burnings; see discussion by Ziony Zevit, *The Religions of Ancient Israel: A Synthesis of Parallactic Approaches* (London:

Continuum, 2001), 210–213, 303–306, esp. 213. Funerary fires were not customary as burial rites for ordinary people. For an Ugaritic funerary rite in connection with the interment of a king, see Dennis Pardee, *Ritual and Cult at Ugarit*, WAW 10 (Atlanta: SBL, 2002), 85–88, no. 24 (*KTU* 1.161), also translated and discussed in Klaas Spronk, *Beatific Afterlife in Ancient Israel and in the Ancient Near East*, AOAT 219 (Kevelaer: Butzon & Bercker; Neukirchen-Vluyn: Neukirchener Verlag, 1986), 189–193.

16. The Hadad Inscription of King Panamuwa of Ya'udi states that "Hadad and El and Rakib-El and Šamaš and Rašap gave the scepter of dominion into my [Panamuwa's] hands"; see "The Hadad Inscription," trans. K. Lawson Younger, Jr., *COS* 2.36:156.

17. For the liturgy of the Babylonian New Year festival in spring, in the month of Nisan, see "Temple Program for the New Year's Festivals at Babylon," trans. Abraham Sachs, *ANET,* 331–334; Marc J. H. Linssen, *The Cults of Uruk and Babylon: The Temple Ritual Texts as Evidence for Hellenistic Cult Practice*, CM 25 (Leiden: Brill Styx, 2004), 215–237. Though the parallel with Babylonia would lead one to expect that in Israel the investiture of the king would take place in spring, there is no evidence, biblical or otherwise, for a New Year festival in spring on the scale of the autumn New Year festival. Also, it seems very unlikely that the celebration of YHWH's kingship should be entirely separate from the reinvestiture of his representative on earth.

18. See Jean-Marie Durand, "Le mythologème du combat entre le dieu de l'orage et la mer en Mésopotamie," *MARI* 7 (1993): 41–61, esp. 45.

19. See Choon Leong Seow, *Myth, Drama, and the Politics of David's Dance*, HSM 44 (cover: 46) (Atlanta: Scholars Press, 1989).

20. On the possibility that the innovations at Bethel, while attributed to Jeroboam I (r. 922–901 BCE), actually occurred under Jeroboam II (r. 786–746 BCE), see the discussion in note 52 to this chapter.

21. See "The Gezer Calendar," trans. P. Kyle McCarter, *COS* 2.85:222.

22. See Gustaf Dalman, *Arbeit und Sitte in Palästina*, 8 vols. (Gütersloh: Bertelsmann, 1928–1942), 4:343.

23. See Erhard S. Gerstenberger, *Psalms: Part I with an Introduction to Cultic Poetry*, FOTL 14 (Grand Rapids: Eerdmans, 1988), 19.

24. See Sigmund Mowinckel, *The Psalms in Israel's Worship*, trans. D. R. Ap-Thomas, 2 vols. (Oxford: Blackwell, 1962), 1:107.

25. See Gerstenberger, *Psalms*, 197.

26. For a case where the editorial interventions in a psalm can be reconstructed on the basis of extrabiblical evidence, see Karel van der Toorn, *God in Context: Selected Essays on Society and Religion in the Early Middle East*, FAT 123 (Tübingen: Mohr Siebeck, 2018), 209–219 (on the history of Psalm 20).

27. See Karel van der Toorn, "Celebrating the New Year with the Israel-ites," *JBL* 136 (2017): 657–673.

28. The passage reads, in a simplified transcription, *'dny nqm l'ryk,* "Lord, take vengeance on your adversaries." For a similar phrase, see Deut 32:4; Nah 1:2; Ps 94:1–2. Karel van der Toorn, *Papyrus Amherst 63,* AOAT 448 (Münster: Ugarit-Verlag, 2018), 172 is to be corrected accordingly.

29. All the above references to papyrus Amherst 63 are to the edition by Van der Toorn, *Papyrus Amherst 63,* 165–175. See there for commentary and further literature.

30. See Mowinckel, *Psalms in Israel's Worship,* 1:106–192.

31. See Rykle Borger, "Amos 5,26, Apostelgeschichte 7,43 und Šurpu II, 180," *ZAW* 100 (1988): 70–81.

32. See Mowinckel, *Psalms in Israel's Worship,* 1:121–122.

33. See P. Kyle McCarter, Jr., *I Samuel: A New Translation with Introduction, Notes and Commentary,* AYB 8 (New York: Doubleday, 1980; repr. New Haven: Yale University Press), 408.

34. See Gösta W. Ahlström, *Royal Administration and National Religion in Ancient Palestine,* SHCANE 1 (Leiden: Brill, 1982), 1–9.

35. For an edition of the text, see *KAI* 181. For a translation, see "The Inscription of King Mesha," trans. Klaas A. D. Smelik, *COS* 2.23:137–138.

36. See Ahlström, *Royal Administration and National Religion,* 13–17.

37. See Klaus D. Schunck, "Zentralheiligtum, Grenzheiligtum und 'Hohenheiligtum' in Israel," *Numen: International Review for the History of Religions* 18 (1971): 132–140, esp. 136–137; Ephraim Stern, "Religion in Palestine in the Assyrian and Persian Periods" in *The Crisis of Israelite Religion,* ed. Bob Becking and Marjo C. A. Korpel, OTS 42 (Leiden: Brill, 1999), 245–255, esp. 247; Susan Ackerman, *Women and the Religion of Ancient Israel,* AYBRL (New Haven: Yale University Press, 2022), 155–164.

38. See Patrick M. Arnold, "Mizpah," *AYBD* 4:879–881, esp. 879–880.

39. On Vered-Jericho, see Amihai Mazar, *Archaeology of the Land of the Bible 10,000–586 B.C.E.,* AYBRL (New York: Doubleday, 1990; repr. New Haven: Yale University Press), 452; Ephraim Stern, "The Eastern Border of the Kingdom of Judah in Its Last Days," in *Scripture and Other Artifacts: Essays on the Bible and Archaeology in Honor of Philip J. King,* ed. Michael Coogan, J. Cheryl Exum, and Lawrence E. Stager (Louisville: Westminster John Knox, 1994), 399–409. Though Avraham Eitan, the excavator, claims the site had a cultic function, there is no unambiguous evidence of a shrine of sorts; see Hershel Shanks, "Antiquities Director Confronts Problems and Controversies: BAR Interviews Avraham Eitan," *BAR* 12 (1986): 30–38; Ephraim Stern, *Archaeology of the Land of the Bible 2: The Assyrian, Babylonian, and Persian Periods, 732–332* BCE, AYBRL (New York: Doubleday, 2002; repr. New Haven: Yale University Press), 134.

40. On Michmash, see Stern, *Archaeology of the Land of the Bible 2,* 138, 202. On Lachish, see David Ussishkin, "Lachish," *AYBD* 4:114–126, esp. 120–121, 5.b. "Level IV"; David Ussishkin, "Lachish," *OEANE* 3:317–323; David Ussishkin, "Lachish," *NEAEHL* 3:897–911, esp. 905–910. For Horvat Uza and Horvat Radum, see Itzhaq Beit-Arieh, ed., *Ḥorvat 'Uza and Ḥorvat Radum: Two Fortresses in the Biblical Negev* (Tel Aviv: Emery and Claire Yass Publications in Archaeology, 2007), esp. 31 on the Bamah complex in Horvat Uza. For Horvat Qitmit, see Itzhaq Beit-Arieh, "Qitmit, Ḥorvat," *NEAEHL* 4:1230–1233; Itzhaq Beit-Arieh, "Qitmit, Horvat," *OEANE* 4:390; P. M. Michèle Daviau, "Diversity in the Cultic Setting: Temples and Shrines in Central Jordan and the Negev," in *Temple Building and Temple Cult: Architecture and Cultic Paraphernalia of Temples in the Levant (2.–1. Mill. B.C.E.),* ed. Jens Kamlah, ADPV 41 (Wiesbaden: Harrassowitz, 2012), 435–458, esp. 446–449. On Arad, see Dale W. Manor and Gary A. Herion, "Arad," *AYBD* 1:331–336; Yohanan Aharoni et al., "Arad," *NEAEHL* 1:75–87, esp. 82–85; Ze'ev Herzog, "Arad, Iron Age Period," *OEANE* 1:174–176; Diana V. Edelman, "Cult Sites and Complexes Beyond the Jerusalem Temple," in *Religious Diversity in Ancient Israel and Judah,* ed. Francesca Stavrakopoulou and John Barton (London: T&T Clark, 2010), 82–103, esp. 94–96. On Beersheba, see Ze'ev Herzog, "Beersheba," *OEANE* 1:287–291; Ze'ev Herzog, "Tel Beersheba," *NEAEHL* 1:167–173; Ze'ev Herzog and Lily Singer-Avitz, *Beer-Sheba III: The Early Iron IIA Enclosed Settlement and the Late Iron IIA–Iron IIB Cities* (Tel Aviv: Emery and Claire Yass Publications in Archaeology; Winona Lake, IN: Eisenbrauns, 2016), 1452–1485.

41. On Megiddo, see David Ussishkin, "Megiddo," *AYBD* 4:666–679; David Ussishkin, "Megiddo," *OEANE* 3:460–469, esp. 464–468; Yohanan Aharoni and Yigal Shiloh, "Megiddo," *NEAEHL* 3:1003–1024, esp. 1012–1023; Israel Finkelstein, David Ussishkin, and Baruch Halpern, "Megiddo," *NEAEHL* 5:1944–1950; Eric Cline, "Megiddo," *EBR* 18:465–471. On Mount Carmel as a border sanctuary, see Albrecht Alt, "Das Gottesurteil auf dem Karmel," in *Kleine Schriften zur Geschichte des Volkes Israels,* 3 vols. (Munich: Beck, 1953–1959), 2:135–149; Michael C. Astour, "Carmel, Mount," *IDBSup* 141; Henry O. Thompson, "Carmel, Mount," *AYBD* 1:874–875. For Dan, see Avraham Biran, *Biblical Dan* (Jerusalem: Israel Exploration Society and Hebrew Union College–Jewish Institute of Religion, 1994); "Dan," *AYBD* 2:12–17; Avraham Biran, "Dan," *NEAEHL* 1:323–332, esp. 326–331; David Ilan, "Dan," *OEANE* 2:107–112; Merja Alanne, "Tel Dan—Biblical Dan: An Archaeological and Biblical Study of Dan from the Iron Age II to the Hellenistic Period" (Ph.D. diss., University of Helsinki, 2017). On Bethsaida, see Rami Arav and Richard A. Freund, eds., *Bethsaida, a City on the North Shore of the Sea*

of Galilee, 4 vols. (Kirksville, MO: Thomas Jefferson University Press, 1995–2009); Rami Arav, "Bethsaida," *OEANE* 1:302–305. On Ramah, see Patrick M. Arnold, "Ramah," *AYBD* 5:613–614. On Mizpah, see Ackerman, *Women and the Religion of Ancient Israel*, 157. The evidence for sanctuaries at Mount Carmel, Bethel, Ramah, Mizpah, and Gilgal is only biblical, not archaeological.

42. On Ataroth and Nebo, see also Num 32:1–5, Deut 34:6, and Frank Moore Cross, "Reuben, the Firstborn of Jacob," in *From Epic to Canon: History and Literature in Ancient Israel* (Baltimore: Johns Hopkins University Press, 1998), 53–70, esp. 57–58. In Khirbet Ataruz (biblical Ataroth) a Moabite inscribed cylindrical (portable) stone altar was found in a small cult building, presumably from the time of Mesha; see Chang-Ho Ji, "A Moabite Sanctuary at Khirbat-Ataruz, Jordan," *Levant* 50 (2018): 173–210; see also Chang-Ho Ji, "The Early Iron Age II Temple at Ḥirbet 'Aṭārūs and Its Architecture and Selected Cultic Objects," in *Temple Building and Temple Cult*, ed. Kamlah, 203–221. See also P. M. Michèle Daviau, "Diversity in the Cultic Setting: Temples and Shrines in Central Jordan and the Negev," in *Temple Building and Temple Cult*, ed. Kamlah, 435–458, esp. 439–440.

43. See also the reference to a future Yahwistic *maṣṣēbâ* as border marker with Egypt in Isa 19:19.

44. For Bethel as a southern border sanctuary of the Northern Kingdom, see its pairing with Dan as northern border sanctuary in 1 Kgs 12:28–30. The Jerusalem temple was at the border between Judah and Benjamin, the latter at the time a more or less independent polity (2 Sam 3:17–19); see Klaus-Dietrich Schunck, *Benjamin: Untersuchungen zur Entstehung und Geschichte eines isarelitischen Stammes*, BZAW 86 (Berlin: Töpelmann, 1963), esp. 139–169 ("Benjamin zwischen dem Reich Israel und dem Reich Juda").

45. See Martha T. Roth, *Law Collections from Mesopotamia and Asia Minor*, WAW 6 (Atlanta: Scholars Press, 1995), 76–81.

46. On the expression "navel of the earth," see Walther Zimmerli, *Ezechiel*, 2 vols., BKAT 13/1–2 (Neukirchen-Vluyn: Neukirchener Verlag, 1969), 2:955–957.

47. The evidence for mass pilgrimage to the national temple is from later times; see Joachim Jeremias, *Jerusalem in the Time of Jesus: An Investigation into Economic and Social Conditions During the New Testament Period*, trans. F. H. and C. H. Cave (London: SCM, 1969), 58–60. The number of pilgrims must have been significantly lower during the monarchic period.

48. See Zimmerli, *Ezechiel*, 1:211; David Ussishkin, "Jerusalem as a Royal and Cultic Center in the 10th–8th Centuries B.C.E.," in *Symbiosis, Symbolism, and the Power of the Past: Canaan, Ancient Israel, and Their Neighbors from*

the Late Bronze Age Through Roman Palestine, ed. William G. Dever and Seymour Gitin (Winona Lake, IN: Eisenbrauns, 2003), 529–538.

49. The biblical passages on the royal temple at Samaria define it as a Baal sanctuary (1 Kgs 16:32; 2 Kgs 10:18–29); however, the Omride kings worshiped Yhwh as the patron god of their state, as is clear from the Mesha inscription. It is very unlikely that the main temple at Samaria would not be devoted primarily to "Yhwh of Samaria," as the Kuntillet Ajrud inscriptions call the deity. Note also the reference to "the calf of Samaria" (*'ēgel šōmrôn*) in Hos 8:5–6. It is not clear whether the name "Samaria" refers here (and at Kuntillet Ajrud) to the city or to the Northern Kingdom as a whole.

50. See Andrew R. Davis, *Reconstructing the Temple: The Royal Rhetoric of Temple Renovation in the Ancient Near East and Israel* (New York: Oxford University Press, 2019).

51. See, in the Ugaritic texts, the expressions "the Bull, his [Kirta's] father El," *KTU* 1.14.iv:6; "El . . . the father of humankind," *KTU* 1.14.i:36–37.

52. Although the biblical record ascribes to Jeroboam I (r. 922–901 BCE) the inauguration of the Bethel temple as a Yahwistic sanctuary, a growing group of archaeologists and biblical scholars argue it is more likely that the inauguration happened under Jeroboam II (r. 786–746 BCE). For a lucid presentation of this hypothesis, plus references to pertinent archaeological publications, see Thomas Römer, "Jeroboam II and the Invention of Northern Sanctuaries and Foundation Stories," in *Stones, Tablets, and Scrolls: Periods of the Formation of the Bible*, ed. Peter Dubovský and Federico Giuntoli, Archaeology and Bible 3 (Tübingen: Mohr Siebeck, 2020), 127–140. The argument is compelling when it comes to Dan, which did not become part of Israel until the eighth century BCE; with respect to Bethel, an eighth-century dating of the sanctuary, the identification of the bull with Yhwh, and the reference to the ascent from Egypt are less persuasive.

53. See Herbert B. Huffmon, "Shalem," *DDD*, 755–757.

54. The Ugaritic expression is found in *KTU* 1.5.i:1–2. For a discussion, see John Day, *God's Conflict with the Dragon and the Sea: Echoes of a Canaanite Myth in the Old Testament* (Cambridge: Cambridge University Press, 1985), 142–145. Ugaritic *bṯn* has a Mesopotamian counterpart in Akkadian *bašmu*, "sea dragon."

55. For a study on the defeated monsters and deities displayed in temples, see Frans A. M. Wiggermann, *Mesopotamian Protective Spirits: The Ritual Texts* (Groningen: Styx & PP Publications, 1992), 143–188; Frans A. M. Wiggermann and Anthony Green, "Mischwesen," *RlA* 8:222–264, esp. 226–229, §§2.2 and 2.3.

56. See Arad ostracon no. 18:9, for which see Johannes Renz, *Die althebräischen Inschriften: Text und Kommentar*, Handbuch der althebräischen

Epigraphik 1 (Darmstadt: Wissenschaftliche Buchgesellschaft, 2016), 384; Pierre Bordreuil, Felice Israel, and Dennis Pardee, "Deux ostraca paléo-hébreux de la collection Sh. Mousaïeff," *Semitica* 46 (1996): 49–76, and Planches 7–8, no. 1. For some sobering observations concerning the authenticity of this ostracon, see Israel Eph'al and Joseph Naveh, "Remarks on the Recently Published Mousaïeff Ostraca," *IEJ* 48 (1998): 269–273. The pomegranate inscription referring to the "Temple of Yhwh" is probably a forgery; see Yuval Goren, Shmuel Ahituv, Avner Ayalon, Miryam Bar-Matthews, Uzi Dahari, Michal Dayagi-Mendels, Aaron Demsky, and Nadav Levin, "A Re-examination of the Inscribed Pomegranate from the Israel Museum," *IEJ* 55 (2005): 3–20. Note also the reference to a *byt yhw*, "temple of Yaho," in an Idumean ostracon, referring to a sanctuary in Hirbet el-Qom (ancient Makkedah); see André Lemaire, *Nouvelles inscriptions araméennes d'Idumée II: Collections Moussaïeff, Jeselsohn, Welch et divers* (Leuven: Peeters, 2002), no. 283:2; see discussion by André Lemaire, "New Aramaic Ostraca from Idumea," in *Judah and the Judeans in the Persian Period*, ed. Oded Lipschits and Manfred Oeming (Winona Lake, IN: Eisenbrauns, 2006), 413–456, esp. 416–417.

57. For the expression *byt yhw/byt yhh* in the texts from Elephantine, see *TAD* A3.3:1, D4.9:1, D7.18:2–3.

58. See *TAD* C3.15:123–128 and the discussion in Karel van der Toorn, *Becoming Diaspora Jews: Behind the Story of Elephantine*, AYBRL (New Haven: Yale University Press, 2019), 100–114.

59. See Saul Olyan, *Asherah and the Cult of Yahweh in Israel*, SBLMS 34 (Atlanta: Scholars Press, 1988), 1–22, esp. 9.

60. For this insight, see Susan Ackerman, *Gods, Goddesses, and the Women Who Serve Them* (Grand Rapids: Eerdmans, 2022), 151–169, revised version of "The Queen Mother and the Cult in Ancient Israel," *JBL* 112 (1993): 385–401.

61. For the meaning of the expression *'al pānay*, cf. Gen 25:9, "the cave of Machpelah, in the field of Ephron . . . , facing Mamre [*'al pĕnê mamrē'*]." Note also 1 Kgs 11:7, "At that time, Solomon built a shrine for Chemosh the abomination of Moab on the hill facing [*'al-pĕnê*] Jerusalem." Note that the rather general term *kēlim*, "vessels," used in 2 Kgs 23:4 in connection with Baal and Asherah, can refer to sculpted images, as is clear from a comparison of 1 Sam 6:8 and 1 Sam 6:11: the "golden vessels" (*kĕlê hazzāhāb*) are in fact "golden mice" (*'akbĕrê hazzāhāb*) and "images of hemorrhoids" (*ṣalmê ṭĕḥôrêhem*).

62. See Dominique Charpin, *"Tu es de mon sang": Les alliances dans le Proche-Orient ancien* (Paris: Collège de France, Les belles lettres, 2019), 154–165.

63. See Charpin, *"Tu es de mon sang,"* 117–118.

64. The fact—or fiction—that Solomon had Moabite and Ammonite women in his harem (1 Kgs 11:1) and built a "high place" (*bāmâ*) for Chemosh, the god of Moab, plus one for Molech, the god of the Ammonites (1 Kgs 11:7, 33), must imply treaty relations with Moab and Ammon.

65. For the expression *bêt yhwh*, see Harry A. Hoffner, "bayit," *ThWAT* 1:629–638, esp. 633–635 = *TDOT* 1:107–116, esp. 111–113; Ernst Jenni, "*bayit* Haus," *THAT* 1:308–313, esp. 310, 312–313 = *TLOT* 1:232–236, esp. 234–236. For the expression *hêkal yhwh*, see Magnus Ottoson, "hêḵāl," *ThWAT* 2:408–415, esp. 410 = *TDOT* 3:382–388, esp. 383.

66. For the Ain Dara temple, see Mirko Novák, "The Temple of *'Ain Dāra* in the Context of Imperial and Neo-Hittite Architecture and Art," in *Temple Building and Temple Cult*, ed. Kamlah, 41–54; for the Tell Tayinat temple, see Timothy P. Harrison, "West Syrian *megaron* or Neo-Assyrian *Langraum?* The Shifting Form and Function of the *Tell Ta'yīnāt* (*Kunulua*) Temples," in *Temple Building and Temple Cult*, ed. Kamlah, 3–21.

67. See Roland de Vaux, *Les institutions de l'Ancien Testament*, 3rd rev. ed., 2 vols. (Paris: Cerf, 1976), 2:148–155, translated by John McHugh as *Ancient Israel: Its Life and Institutions* (New York: McGraw-Hill, 1961), 312–330; Carol Meyers, "Temple, Jerusalem," *AYBD* 6:350–369.

68. The usual term for the side chambers is *liškâ*, for which see Gesenius[18], 617–618, s.v. *liškâ*, and Diether Kellerman, "liškāh," *ThWAT* 4:606–611 = *TDOT* 8:33–38. The reference to the temple's *ṣĕlā'ôt*, the plural of *ṣēlā'*, in 1 Kgs 6:5, may refer to side chambers (so Mordechai Cogan, *I Kings: A New Translation with Introduction and Commentary*, AYB 10 [New Haven: Yale University Press, 2008], 238–239), but this technical term more likely designates "floor, story"; see Gesenius[18], 1120–1121, s.v. *ṣēlā'*, 3.

69. See de Vaux, *Institutions*, 2:242; English translation: *Ancient Israel*, 379.

70. See Elias Bickerman, *Studies in Jewish and Christian History*, 2 vols. (Leiden: Brill, 1980), 2:210–224; Peretz Segal, "The Penalty of the Warning Inscription from the Temple of Jerusalem," *IEJ* 39 (1989): 79–84.

71. See Paul Volz, *Der Prophet Jeremia*, 2nd ed., KAT 10 (Leipzig: A. Deichertsche Verlagsbuchhandlung D. Werner Scholl, 1928), 94.

72. See Jeremias, *Jerusalem in the Time of Jesus*, 48–49.

73. See J. M. Myers "Sandals and Shoes," *IDB* 4:213–214, esp. 213

74. For the holiness of Mesopotamian temples, see *CAD* 4, 105, s.v. *ellu* 2, "holy, sacred."

75. See Wilfred G. Lambert, *Babylonian Oracle Questions*, MC 13 (Winona Lake, IN: Eisenbrauns, 2007), 88–89, no. 12 i 12–13; 92 no. 13, Obverse 2–3.

76. See A. Leo Oppenheim, *Ancient Mesopotamia: Portrait of a Dead Civilization*, rev. ed. (Chicago: University of Chicago Press, 1977), 95–109.

77. See George F. Moore, *Judges,* ICC (Edinburgh: T&T Clark, 1908), 242; Jeremias, *Jerusalem in the Time of Jesus,* 24.

78. For the temple "merchant" (*makkār*), see also Ugaritic *mkr,* "merchant, commercial agent, runner," also a temple employee. Merchants (*mkrm*) occur in *KTU* 4.36, 4:38, 4.68:72–75, 4.126:6–9 alongside *khnm* ("priests") and *qdšm* ("consecrated ones," sometimes interpreted as male temple prostitutes). On the economic role of the temple in Israel, see also Marty E. Stevens, *Temples, Tithes, and Taxes: The Temple and the Economic Life of Ancient Israel* (Peabody, MA: Hendrickson, 2006).

79. See Van der Toorn, *God in Context,* 69–84.

80. See Lawrence E. Stager and Samuel R. Wolff, "Production and Commerce in Temple Courtyards: An Olive Press in the Sacred Precinct at Dan," *BASOR* 243 (1981): 95–102; Ackerman, *Gods, Goddesses,* 19–56, which contains the updated version of "Asherah, the West Semitic Goddess of Spinning and Weaving?," *JNES* 67 (2008): 1–30. Note the presence of loom weights in the Philistine temples at Ekron and Ashkelon; see Zevit, *Religions,* 135, which points to weaving.

81. On 2 Kgs 11:10 note the observation by Mordechai Cogan and Hayim Tadmor, *II Kings: A New Translation with Introduction and Commentary,* AYB 11 (New York: Doubleday, 1988; repr. New Haven: Yale University Press), 128: "The quivers issued by Jehoiada to the guards were probably the ones taken by David from the servants of Hadadezer and brought to Jerusalem (2 Sam 8:7)."

82. See A. Leo Oppenheim, "A Fiscal Practice of the Ancient Near East," *JNES* 6 (1947): 116–120.

83. See Van der Toorn, *God in Context,* 21–43.

84. The quotation is from a song to the god Bethel preserved in papyrus Amherst 63, 9:3–4; see Van der Toorn, *Papyrus Amherst 63,* 135.

85. See *CAD* 8, 559, s.v. *kurību,* "representation of a protective genius with specific non-human features"; Philippe Abrahami and Stéphanie Anthonioz, eds., *Les Chérubins/Keruvim dans l'Antiquité: Approche historique et comparée,* Kasion 6 (Münster: Zaphon, 2021).

86. For a discussion of the Taanach cult stand, see Zevit, *Religions,* 318–324; Lewis, *Origin and Character of God,* 411–415.

87. See the passage in the Baal Cycle where the god Athtar proves too small to fill Baal's throne: "his feet do not reach the footstool, his head does not reach the top (of the seat)," *KTU* 1.6.i:54–64; for an English translation, see "The Ba'lu Myth," trans. Dennis Pardee, *COS* 1.86:241–274, esp. 269.

88. See Tryggve N. D. Mettinger, *No Graven Image? Israelite Aniconism in Its Ancient Near Eastern Context,* ConBOT 42 (Stockholm: Almqvist & Wiksell, 1995), 100–106.

89. See Delbert R. Hillers and Eleonora Cussini, *Palmyrene Aramaic Texts* (Baltimore: Johns Hopkins University Press, 1996), 273, no. 1931.

90. See *DNWSI,* 697–698, s.v. "mšb₁," esp. 698. Less common than the empty throne was the suggestion of divine presence by the representation of huge artificial footprints as found in the Iron Age temple at Ain Dara in Syria; see Lewis, *Origin and Character of God,* 340–343. The underlying logic is similar: both the empty thrones and these footprints evoke the invisible presence of a deity.

91. Herbert Niehr is one of the scholars who have argued there was in fact a YHWH image in the Jerusalem temple; see his "In Search of Yhwh's Cult Statue in the First Temple," in *The Image and the Book: Iconic Cults, Aniconism, and the Rise of Book Religion in Israel and the Ancient Near East,* ed. Karel van der Toorn, CBET 21 (Leuven: Peeters, 1997), 73–95. For tentative identifications of YHWH statuary, see Christoph Uehlinger, "Anthropomorphic Cult Statuary in Iron Age Palestine and the Search for Yahweh's Cult Images," in Van der Toorn, *Image and the Book,* 97–155; Tallay Ornan, "The Throne and the Enthroned: On the Conceived Human Image of Yahweh in Iron II Jerusalem," *TA* 46 (2019): 198–210.

92. The references to "seeing God's face" in the psalms do not imply the presence of a divine image. The expression is metaphorical, as shown by Ps 30:8. To see God's face, then, means to experience his favor. When God is displeased, on the other hand, he "hides his face." See also Friedrich Nötscher, *"Das Angesicht Gottes schauen" nach biblischer und babylonischer Auffassung* (Würzburg: Becker, 1924); Friedhelm Hartenstein, *Das Angesicht JHWHs: Studien zu seinem höfischen und kultischen Bedeutungshintergrund in den Psalmen und in Exodus 32–34,* FAT 55 (Tübingen: Mohr Siebeck, 2008); Simeon Chavel, "The Face of God and the Etiquette of Eye-Contact: Visitation, Pilgrimage, and Prophetic Vision in Ancient Israelite and Early Jewish Imagination," *JSQ* 19 (2012): 1–55, esp. 23–24 note 78.

93. See Mark S. Smith and Elizabeth Bloch-Smith, *Judges 1,* Hermeneia (Minneapolis: Fortress, 2021), 569.

94. For the bronze bull of the Hazor temple, see Yigael Yadin, *Hazor: The Head of All Those Kingdoms,* Schweich Lectures of the British Academy, 1970 (London: Oxford University Press, 1972), 94. For the Bull Site, see Amihai Mazar, "The 'Bull Site': An Iron Age I Open Cult Place," *BASOR* 247 (1982): 27–42; Amihai Mazar, "On Cult Places and Early Israelites: A Response to Michael Coogan," *BAR* 15/4 (1988): 45; Zevit, *Religions of Ancient Israel,* 176–180.

95. See, e.g., Manfred Weippert, *Jahwe und die anderen Götter,* FAT 18 (Tübingen: Mohr Siebeck, 1997), 53.

96. For the use of Hebrew *'ăbîr* in the meaning "bull," cf. Ugaritic *ibr*, "bull," used in parallel with *ṯr*, see *DULAT*, 11–12, s.v. ibr, "bull." For the reference to Yaho as "our Bull" (*trn*), see papyrus Amherst 63, 12:17. Note also the personal name *'glyw*, "Yнwн is a bull" (Samaria ostracon no. 41, see Johannes Renz and Wolfgang Röllig, *Handbuch der althebräischen Epigraphik*, 3 vols. [Darmstadt: Wissenschaftliche Buchgesellschaft, 1995–2003], 1:100), to be compared with the name *'glhdd*, "Hadad is a bull" (Nahman Avigad and Benjamin Sass, *Corpus of West Semitic Stamp Seals* [Jerusalem: Israel Academy of Sciences and Humanities; Israel Exploration Society; and Institute of Archaeology, Hebrew University of Jerusalem, 1997], 312 no. 835). The divine name Aglibol, belonging to the moon god worshipped at Palmyra, is best rendered as "Bull of Bol" or "Bull Bol," Bol being a variant name of Baal; see Jean Starcky and Michel Gawlikowski, *Palmyre*, Édition revue et augmentée des nouvelles découvertes (Paris: Librairie d'Amérique et d'Orient, 1985), 94.

97. See Julius Wellhausen, *Die kleinen Propheten*, 3rd ed. (Berlin: G. Reimer, 1898), 120; Alexander Rofé, *The Prophetical Stories: The Narratives About the Prophets in the Hebrew Bible, Their Literary Types and History* (Jerusalem: Magnes, 1988), 97–98.

98. For the providing of regular offerings and prayer, and the repair of cult statues and temples as royal duty in Mesopotamia, see the omen series Šumma ālu, XI, 22'–40', see Sally M. Freedman, *If a City Is Set on a Height: Volume 1*, Occasional Publications of the Samuel Noah Kramer Fund 17 (Philadelphia: University of Pennsylvania Museum, 1998), 182–185. Like the Advice to a Prince (Wilfred G. Lambert, *Babylonian Wisdom Literature* [Oxford: Oxford University Press, 1960], 110–115), the royal duties were phrased as behavioral omens but functioned in fact as admonitions.

99. See *CAD* 17/1, 377–382, s.v. *šangû*, "chief administrator of a temple."

100. See Marie-Joseph Seux, "Königtum. B. II. und I. Jahrtausend," *RlA* 6:140–173, esp. 169–170, §§96–100.

101. See "The Sarcophagus Inscription of Tabnit, King of Sidon," trans. P. Kyle McCarter, *COS* 2.56:181–182, lines 1–2.

102. In the border sanctuary of Arad, archaeologists found two bowls inscribed with the ancient Hebrew characters *Q* and *K*, an abbreviation for *qōdeš kōhănîm*, "sacred item of the priests"; see Ze'ev Herzog, Miriam Aharoni, Anson F. Rainey, and Shmuel Moshkovitz, "The Israelite Fortress at Arad," *BASOR* 254 (1984): 1–34, esp. 12, 32. For the use of such abbreviations, cf. Jer 7:4, *hmh* = *hammāqôm hazzeh*, referring to the Jerusalem temple. For cultic vessels inscribed with *qdš*, "sacred item," see Gabriel Barkay, "A Bowl with the Hebrew Inscription *qdš*," *IEJ* 40 (1990): 124–129, esp. 126.

103. See Walter Sallaberger and F. Huber Vulliet, "Priester. A. I. Mesopotamien," *RlA* 10:617–640, esp. 624 §4.2.

104. See Alt, *Kleine Schriften*, 3:359–360, 373.

105. On the Deuteronomistic History, see Jan Christian Gertz, Doris Prechel, Konrad Schmid, and Markus Witte, eds., *Die deuteronomistischen Geschichtswerke: Redaktions- und religionsgeschichtliche Perspektiven zur "Deuteronomismus"-diskussion in Tora and Vorderen Propheten*, BZAW 365 (Berlin: de Gruyter, 2006).

106. See Jeremy M. Hutton, "Levitical Aspirations and Saintly Foundation Stories in Judges 17–18," in *ErIsr 33: Lawrence E. Stager Volume* (Jerusalem: Israel Exploration Society, 2018), 98*–108*.

107. For the role of migrant priests in the implantation and spread of religious worship of specific gods, cf. the Babylonian evidence collected and discussed by Paul-Alain Beaulieu, "Temple Towns and Nation Building: Migrations of Babylonian Priestly Families in the Late Periods," *JANER* 19 (2019): 3–17.

108. See Jeremy M. Hutton, "The Levitical Diaspora (I): A Sociological Comparison With Morocco's Ahansal," in *Exploring the Longue Durée: Essays in Honor of Lawrence E. Stager*, ed. J. David Schloen (Winona Lake, IN: Eisenbrauns, 2009), 223–234; Hutton, "The Levitical Diaspora (II): Modern Perspectives on the Levitical Cities Lists (A Review of Opinions)," in *Levites and Priests in History and Tradition*, ed. Mark A. Leuchter and Jeremy M. Hutton, AIL 9 (Atlanta: Society of Biblical Literature, 2011), 45–81.

109. For a study of the Levites and their Egyptian connection, see Leuchter and Hutton, eds., *Levites and Priests;* Mark A. Leuchter, *The Levites and the Boundary of Israelite Identity* (New York: Oxford University Press, 2017).

110. See Benjamin Mazar, "The Sanctuary of Arad and the Family of Hobab the Kenite," *JNES* 24 (1965): 297–303; Frank Moore Cross, *Canaanite Myth and Hebrew Epic: Essays in the History of the Religion of Israel* (Cambridge, MA: Harvard University Press, 1973), 195–215.

111. See Caroline Waerzeggers, *The Ezida Temple of Borsippa: Priesthood, Cult, Archives*, Achaemenid History 15 (Leiden: NINO, 2010), 36.

112. On the connection of prophets with temples, see the survey by Martti Nissinen, *Ancient Prophecy: Near Eastern, Biblical, and Greek Perspectives* (Oxford: Oxford University Press, 2017), 201–256. For Israelite prophets making the rounds of temples, see the Elisha narratives (found mostly in 2 Kgs 2–14), which mention Carmel, Gilgal, Jericho, and Samaria, all places with a sanctuary, as places where Elisha was active, and see the reference to Bethel, Gilgal, Mizpah, and Ramah as the places where Samuel made the rounds (1 Sam 7:15–17).

113. The allusion here is a reversal of the classic epigram *vox populi vox Dei*, "the voice of the people is the voice of God," which has its origins in medieval Europe rather than in Roman antiquity. On prophecy as the voice of popular opposition, see the contributions by André Finet, Jean Bottéro, and Jean-Robert Kupper in *La voix de l'opposition en Mésopotamie: Colloque organisé par l'Institut des Hautes Études de Belgique, 19 et 20 mars 1973,* ed. André Finet (Brussels: Institut des Hautes Études de Belgique, 1973).

114. See, e.g., the Hadad inscription of King Panamuwa of Ya'udi, which states, "Hadad and El and Rakib-El and Šamaš and Rašap gave the scepter of dominion into my [Panamuwa's] hands"; see "The Hadad Inscription," trans. K. Lawson Younger, Jr., *COS* 2.36:156. King Zakkur of Hamath simply says that the god Baal-shamayin "made me king"; see "The Inscription of Zakkur, King of Hamath," trans. Alan Millard, *COS* 2.35:155.

115. For the Zakkur inscription, see "Inscription of Zakkur," trans. Millard; for the Assyrian prophecies, see Simo Parpola, *Assyrian Prophecies,* SAA 9 (Helsinki: Helsinki University Press, 1997); for references to prophecies in Neo-Assyrian royal inscriptions, see Martti Nissinen, *References to Prophecy in Neo-Assyrian Sources,* SAAS 7 (Helsinki: Neo-Assyrian Text Corpus Project, 1998), 13–65. For a general survey, see Karel van der Toorn, "L'oracle de victoire comme expression prophétique au Proche-Orient ancien," *RB* 94 (1987): 63–97.

116. See Lambert, *Babylonian Oracle Questions,* 52–53, no. 3a; *CAD* 5, 14–17, s.v. *gallābu,* "barber," esp. 17; Waerzeggers, *Ezida Temple,* 54–55; for Israel, see Jeremias, *Jerusalem in the Time of Jesus,* 26.

117. For a comparable arrangement in Babylonia, see Waerzeggers, *Ezida Temple,* 55; *CAD* 16, 225–226, s.v. *ṣubātu* in *ša (ina) muḫḫi ṣubāti,* "keeper of the temple wardrobe."

118. See Oppenheim, *Ancient Mesopotamia,* 183–198.

119. See Jacob Milgrom, "Sin-offering or Purification-offering?," *VT* 21 (1971): 237–239.

120. See David P. Wright, "Day of Atonement," *AYBD* 2:72–76.

121. See Mowinckel, *Psalms in Israel's Worship,* 1:177–180.

122. For a discussion, see Karel van der Toorn, "Before the Decalogue: In Search of the Oldest Written Torah," *CBQ* 85 (2023): 385–401.

123. See Sigmund Mowinckel, "L'origine du Décalogue," *RHPR* 6 (1926): 409–433, 501–525; Mowinckel, *Le Décalogue* (Paris: Félix Alcan, 1927), 141–156.

124. See Erhard S. Gerstenberger, *Wesen und Herkunft des "apodiktischen Rechts,"* WMANT 20 (Neukirchen-Vluyn: Neukirchener Verlag, 1965).

125. For a discussion of the Urim and Thummim, see Jacob Milgrom, *Leviticus 1–16: A New Translation with Introduction and Commentary,* AYB 3 (New York: Doubleday, 1991; repr. New Haven: Yale University Press),

507–511. For the linen ephod, cf. the Akkadian term *epattu,* plural *ep-adātu,* "a costly garment," see *CAD* 4, 183, s.v. *epattu.*

126. See Werner Dommershausen, *"gôrāl,"* *ThWAT* 1:991–998 = *TDOT* 2:450–456.

127. See Samuel R. Driver, *Notes on the Hebrew Text and the Topography of the Books of Samuel,* 2nd ed. rev. and enlarged (Oxford: Clarendon, 1913), 117–118; McCarter, *I Samuel,* 247–248.

128. See Anne Marie Kitz, "The Plural Form of *'ûrîm* and *tummîm," JBL* 116 (1997): 401–410.

129. Compare the expression "breastpiece of judgment" (*ḥošen mišpāṭ*) in Exod 28:15, 29, 30; Sir 45:10.

130. For the finds of dice and astragali in a cultic context, see Philip J. King and Lawrence E. Stager, *Life in Biblical Israel,* LAI (Louisville: Westminster John Knox, 2001), 329–330 (faïence die at Dan), 340–341 (astragali); Zevit, *Religions of Ancient Israel,* 237.

131. On Mesopotamian divination, see Jean Bottéro, "Symptômes, signes, écriture en Mésopotamie ancienne" in *Divination et rationalité,* ed. J. P. Vernant, L. Vandermeersch, J. Gernet, J. Bottéro, R. Crahay, L. Brisson, J. Carlier, D. Grodzynski, and A. Retel-Laurentin, (Paris: Seuil, 1974), 70–197; Bottéro, *Mesopotamia: Writing, Reasoning, and the Gods,* trans. Zainab Bahrani and Marc Van De Mieroop (Chicago: University of Chicago Press, 1992), 125–137.

132. For a Neo-Assyrian oracle that parallels this theme, see Simo Parpola, *Assyrian Royal Rituals and Cultic Texts,* SAA 20 (Helsinki: Neo-Assyrian Text Corpus Project, 2017), 14–18, no. 7.ii:34–35, "Expand your country with your just scepter!" (from a coronation ritual).

133. See King and Stager, *Life in Biblical Israel,* 239–242.

134. See the Hittite soldiers' oath, documented in "The First Soldiers' Oath," trans. Billie Jean Collins, *COS* 1.66:165–167, and "The Second Soldiers' Oath," trans. Billie Jean Collins, *COS* 1.67:167–168. For an allusion to a loyalty oath by other royal servants in Israel, see Eccl 8:2, "Keep the king's command because of your sacred oath" (NRSV).

135. See *COS* 1.66:166 §9; cf. 1.65:164 §8.

136. For the pleasures of the palace, see 2 Sam 19:35–36, which implies the existence of a royal harem and mentions fine food and drink and "the sound of male and female singers." See also Amos 8:3 ("the female singers of the palace").

137. Cf. "Erra and Ishum," tablet I, line 58, see "Erra and Ishum," trans. Stephanie Dalley, *COS* 1.113:404–416, esp. 406, "Best beer, however sweet, cannot compare with water from a water-skin," said in the context of a celebration of warfare.

138. For the *'eṣ'ādâ,* often translated as "bracelet" or "armlet," see Helga Weippert, "Schmuck," *BRL2,* 282–289, esp. 284–285. On royal insignia, see also Angelika Berlejung, "Insignia," *EBW,* 530–539.

139. See Herbert Niehr, *Rechtsprechung in Israel: Untersuchungen zur Geschichte der Gerichtsorganisation im Alten Testament,* SBS 130 (Stuttgart: Katholisches Bibelwerk, 1987), 66–87.

140. See "The Kirta Epic," trans. Dennis Pardee, *COS* 1.102:333–343, esp. 342, "You let your hands fall slack: you do not judge the widow's case, you do not make a decision regarding the oppressed." (*KTU* 1.16.vi:33–34 // 45–47). See also "The 'Aqhatu Legend," trans. Dennis Pardee, *COS* 1.103:343–356, esp. 346, 351, "He judged the widow's case, made decisions regarding the orphan" (*KTU* 1.17.v:7–9; 1.19.i:23–25).

141. See "'Aqhatu Legend," trans. Pardee, esp. 346, 351, *KTU* 1.17.v:6–7; 1.19.i:21–23.

142. For the audience hall in the palace, see 1 Kgs 7:7 and the discussion by King and Stager, *Life in Biblical Israel,* 203–204.

143. Note also the actual instance of a judiciary petition sent to "the official [*śar*], my lord," preserved in "The Meṣad Ḥashavyahu (Yavneh Yam) Ostracon," trans. Dennis Pardee, *COS* 3.41:77, lines 1–2.

144. See Fritz R. Kraus, "Ein zentrales Problem des altmesopotamischen Rechtes: Was ist der Kodex Hammu-rabi?," *Genava* 8 (1960): 283–296; Raymond Westbrook, "Biblical and Cuneiform Law Codes," *RB* 92 (1985): 247–267.

145. See Sara J. Milstein, *Making a Case: The Practical Roots of Biblical Law* (New York: Oxford University Press, 2021).

Chapter 3. Local Religion

1. See Cornelis H. J. de Geus, *Towns in Ancient Israel and in the Southern Levant,* Palaestina Antiqua 10 (Leuven: Peeters, 2003), for an introduction to the study of ancient Israelite towns. According to de Geus, many towns "were no larger than one or two hectares" (p. 1). He stresses the difficulties involved in any estimates of population numbers. If we reckon fifty people per dunam, we obtain an average population figure of about five hundred (pp. 185–186). Paula McNutt, *Reconstructing the Society of Ancient Israel,* LAI (Louisville: Westminster John Knox, 1999), 151–154, esp. 152 ("populations of between two hundred and three hundred people").

2. See also Ps 35:26; 44:16; 69:8, 20; 71:13; 109:29 for similar complaints.

3. On agriculture in ancient Israel, see Oded Borowski, "Agriculture and Agricultural Tools," *EBW,* 1–18.

4. The rules for the Jubilee Year distinguish houses in a "walled town" (*'îr ḥômâ*) from houses in unwalled "farmsteads" (*ḥăṣērîm*); the latter count as "open country" (*śĕdê hā'āreṣ*) (Lev 25:29–34). Town houses have a redemption period of one year, after which their sale becomes final; on the other hand, there is no limit to the redemption period of houses in

the open country, and they shall be released through the Jubilee (Lev 25:31). The different treatment suggests that town houses were for permanent habitation, whereas houses in open country were designed for temporary habitation (e.g., by shepherds).

5. See the discussion in De Geus, *Towns in Ancient Israel*, 170–174, on the differences between the Israelite city, town, and village. See also Avraham Faust, "Cities, Villages, and Towns, Bronze and Iron Age," *Oxford Encyclopedia of the Bible and Archaeology*, ed. Daniel Master (New York: Oxford University Press, 2013), 203–211, esp. 203–204 (on the distinction between city and village).

6. The name Ramathaim is the dual of Ramah and literally means "Twin Heights." It suggests that the town of Ramah had expanded over time and had come to consist of two neighborhoods.

7. See De Geus, *Towns in Ancient Israel*, 27–39; Philip J. King and Lawrence E. Stager, *Life in Biblical Israel*, LAI (Louisville: Westminster John Knox, 2001), 234–236.

8. The market was usually near or "in" the gate (2 Kgs 7:1) and could give the gate its name, as in the case of the Fish Gate of Jerusalem (Neh 3:3, 12:39; 2 Chr 33:14). A market "in the gate" may have been situated between the outer and the inner gates, as, for example, in Lachish; see David Ussishkin, "Lachish," *NEAEHL* 3:897–911, esp. 906. As a rule, though, commercial activity would be conducted mainly right next to the gate, inside the walls, for reasons of room and safety. See also Kyle Keimer and Lahpai Fanang Lum, "Gate, Gates," *EBR* 9:1005–1009, esp. 1008–1009; Joachim Jeremias, *Jerusalem in the Time of Jesus: An Investigation into Economic and Social Conditions During the New Testament Period*, trans. F. H. Cave and C. H. Cave (London: SCM, 1969), 20.

9. See Ludwig Köhler, *Der hebräische Mensch* (Tübingen: Mohr Siebeck, 1953), 143–171 ("Die Hebräische Rechtsgemeinde"), translated by Peter R. Ackroyd as *Hebrew Man* (London: SCM, 1956), 149–175 ("Justice in the Gate").

10. See Tina Haettner Blomquist, *Gates and Gods: Cults in the City Gates of Iron Age Palestine. An Investigation of the Archaeological and Biblical Sources*, ConBOT 46 (Stockholm: Almqvist & Wiksell, 1999), 179. For a similar situation in Mesopotamia, see the Epic of Gilgamesh, VII 115–119: "[The junction] of highways shall be where you sit! [A field of ruins shall be] where you sleep! The shadow of the rampart shall be where you stand! [Thorn and] briar shall skin your feet!" (from the curse directed at Shamhat the prostitute, trans. Andrew George, *The Epic of Gilgamesh: A New Translation* [London: Allen Lane Penguin, 1999], 58).

11. The dung heap is the "impure place" outside the city mentioned in Lev 14:40; cf. the Babylonian *tubkinnu*, "refuse heap," for which see *CAD* 18, 446, s.v. *tubkinnu*.

12. On these "goat-demons," see Bernd Janowski, "Satyrs," *DDD*, 732–733.

13. See Monika Bernett and Othmar Keel, *Mond, Stier und Kult am Stadttor: Die Stele von Bethsaida (et-Tell)*, OBO 161 (Freiburg: Universitätsverlag; Göttingen: Vandenhoeck & Ruprecht, 1998); Avraham Biran, "Sacred Spaces: Of Standing Stones, High Places and Cult Objects at Tel Dan," *BAR* 24 (1998): 38–45, 70; Haettner Blomquist, *Gates and Gods*.

14. For the Babylonian use of Humbaba masks for apotropaic purposes, see Claus Wilcke, "Ḫuwawa/Ḫumbaba," *RlA* 4:530–535; Frans A. M. Wiggermann, *Mesopotamian Protective Spirits: The Ritual Texts* (Groningen: Styx & PP Publications, 1992), 146.

15. The expression is *bmt zʾt lkmš*, "this sanctuary for Chemosh," see *KAI* 181:3; "The Inscription of King Mesha," trans. Klaas A. D. Smelik, *COS* 2.23:137–138.

16. Aside from the (royal) border sanctuaries, there is no archaeological evidence for cultic complexes inside Israelite cities. There is some literary evidence. The description of Gideon's destruction of the Baal altar in Ophrah and the erection of a Yнwн altar "on the top of the stronghold here" (*ʿal rōʾš hammāʿōz hazzeh*, Judg 6:26) suggests a location inside town, on the acropolis (Judg 6:25–32, 8:22–27). The Jerusalem temple, too, was located on the city's acropolis. The sanctuary of Micah in the hill country of Ephraim (Judg 17:5, lit., a *bêt ʾĕlōhîm*, "house of god," the normal designation of a temple) was presumably inside the town as well in view of the question, "Do you know that in these buildings there are an ephod, teraphim, and an idol of cast metal?" (Judg 18:14 NRSV). For Philistine city temples, see Tel Qasile, for which see Amihai Mazar, *Excavations at Tell Qasile, Part One: The Philistine Sanctuary: Architecture and Cult Objects* (Jerusalem: Israel Exploration Society, 1980); and Tel Miqneh (Ekron), see Seymour Gitin, Steven M. Ortiz, and Trude Dothan, *Field IV Upper and Field V: The Elite Zone, Part 1: Iron Age IIC Temple Complex 650*, Tel Miqne-Ekron Excavations 1994–1996 (University Park, PA: Eisenbrauns, 2022).

17. See the observations in A. Leo Oppenheim, *Ancient Mesopotamia: Portrait of a Dead Civilization*, rev. ed. (Chicago: University of Chicago Press, 1977), 113–114.

18. The quotation is from Diana V. Edelman, "Cultic Sites and Complexes Beyond the Jerusalem Temple," in *Religious Diversity in Ancient Israel and Judah*, ed. Francesca Stavrakopoulou and John Barton (London: T&T Clark 2010), 82–103, quotation at 90.

19. See Shua Kisilevitz, "The Iron IIA Judahite Temple at Tel Moẓa," *TA* 42 (2015): 147–164; Shua Kisilevitz and Oded Lipschits, "Another Temple in Judah! The Tale of Tel Moza," *BAR* 46 (2020): 40–49. Compare also the biblical references to the temple at Nob (1 Sam 21:2–10), about

a mile north of Jerusalem (Isa 10:32). Second Samuel 15:32 mentions a place of worship on top of the Mount of Olives, which McCarter tentatively identifies with Nob (*II Samuel: A New Translation with Introduction, Notes and Commentary*, AYB 9 [New York: Doubleday, 1984; repr. New Haven: Yale University Press], 371). For a different—and, in my eyes, untenable—view, see Avraham Faust, "Where Was Israelite Cult Not Practiced, and Why," *Religions* 10(2) (2019), 106, https://doi.org/10.3390/rel10020106 ("Israelite cultic buildings were extremely rare").

20. On the inhabitants of villages and towns as kinship groups (extended families and lineages), see Avraham Faust, "The Rural Community in Ancient Israel During Iron Age II," *BASOR* 317 (2000): 17–39.

21. See Jeffries M. Hamilton, "Ophrah," *AYBD* 5:27–28.

22. See King and Stager, *Life in Biblical Israel*, 10–12; Susan Ackerman, *Women and the Religion of Ancient Israel*, AYBRL (New Haven: Yale University Press, 2022), 43.

23. See *TAD* A4.10. For a translation, see "Offer of Payment for Reconstruction of Temple (Draft)," trans. Bezalel Porten, *COS* 3.53:131–132.

24. The literature on the archaeology of Palestinian sanctuaries is overwhelming. Among the surveys, see Wolfgang Zwickel, *Der Tempelkult in Kanaan und Israel: Studien zur Kultgeschichte Palästinas von der Mittelbronzezeit bis zum Untergang Judas*, FAT 10 (Tübingen: Mohr Siebeck, 1994); Ziony Zevit, *The Religions of Ancient Israel: A Synthesis of Parallactic Approaches* (London: Continuum, 2001), 122–266; Edelman, "Cultic Sites"; Jens Kamlah, ed., *Temple Building and Temple Cult: Architecture and Cultic Paraphernalia of Temples in the Levant (2.–1. Mill. B.C.E.)*, ADPV 41 (Wiesbaden: Harrassowitz, 2012); William E. Mierse, *Temples and Sanctuaries from the Early Iron Age Levant: Recovery After Collapse*, HACL 4 (Winona Lake, IN: Eisenbrauns, 2012); Beth Alpert Nakhai, "Where to Worship? Religion in Iron II Israel and Judah," in Nicola Laneri, ed., *Defining the Sacred: Approaches to the Archaeology of Religion in the Near East* (Oxford: Oxbow, 2015), 90–101.

25. On Horvat Qitmit and the so-called Bull Site, see Itzhaq Beit-Arieh, *Horvat Qitmit: An Edomite Shrine in the Biblical Negev* (Tel Aviv: Tel Aviv University, Institute of Archaeology, 1995); Amihai Mazar, "The 'Bull Site': An Iron Age I Open Cult Place," *BASOR* 247 (1982): 27–42; Zevit, *Religions of Ancient Israel*, 142–149, 176–180.

26. See Patrick H. Vaughan, *The Meaning of 'bāmâ' in the Old Testament: A Study of the Etymological, Textual and Archaeological Evidence*, SOTSMS 3 (Cambridge: Cambridge University Press, 1974), esp. 31–35, who takes *bāmâ* essentially as a synonym for *mizbēaḥ*, "altar." Note the occurrences of the expression *bêt (hab)bāmôt*, var. *bāttê habbāmôt* (1 Kgs 12:31, 13:32; 2 Kgs 17:29, 23:19), *bāmâh* houses, i.e., temples.

27. On the forms and functions of Israelite altars, see Joachim Brettschneider, "Altar," *EBW,* 18–29.

28. See McCarter, *I Samuel,* 55.

29. See Elizabeth LaRocca-Pitts, *"Of Wood and Stone": The Significance of Israelite Cultic Items in the Bible and Its Early Interpreters,* HSM 61 (Winona Lake, IN: Eisenbrauns, 2001).

30. See Jean-Marie Durand, "Le culte des bétyles en Syrie," in *Miscellanea Babylonica: Mélanges offerts à Maurice Birot,* ed. Jean-Marie Durand and Jean-Robert Kupper (Paris: Éditions Recherche sur les Civilisations, 1985), 79–84, for a discussion of some Old Babylonian Mari letters that mention the need for new stone stelae (the word is *sikkanu,* plural *sikkanātu*) in connection with a sacrificial ceremony to be performed. The stone stelae had to be cut (*nakāsu*) so as to be of the appropriate dimensions. The heights mentioned vary between four cubits (*ammatu;* about six feet) and twelve cubits (about eighteen feet). By comparison, the tale about Jacob's dream suggests a rather moderate size for the Israelite bethel (Gen 28:16–22).

31. For a survey of the archaeological evidence for cultic stone stelae (*maṣṣēbôt*), see Elizabeth Bloch-Smith, "Will the Real *Massebot* Please Stand Up: Cases of Real and Mistakenly Identified Standing Stones in Ancient Israel," in *Text, Artifact, and Images: Revealing Ancient Israelite Religion,* ed. Gary Beckman and Theodore J. Lewis, BJS 346 (Providence: Brown Judaic Studies, 2006), 64–79; Elizabeth Bloch-Smith, "Masseboth Standing for Yhwh: The Fall of a Yhwistic Cult Symbol," in *Worship, Women, and War: Essays in Honor of Susan Niditch,* ed. John J. Collins, Tracy M. Lemos, and Saul M. Olyan, BJS 357 (Providence: Brown Judaic Studies, 2015), 99–115; P. M. Michèle Daviau, "Standing Stone/s," *EBW,* 898–905.

32. See Édouard Lipiński, "Bétyle," in *Dictionnaire de la Civilisation Phénicienne et Punique,* ed. E. Lipiński (Turnhout: Brepols, 1992), 70–71; Eberhard Merkel, "Baitylos," in *Götter und Mythen im Vorderen Orient,* Wörterbuch der Mythologie 1/1, ed. Hans Wilhelm Haussig, 2nd ed. (Stuttgart: Klett-Cotta, 1983), 430; Christoph Auffahrt and Hans Georg Niemeyer, "Baitylia," *Brill's New Pauly: Encyclopaedia of the Ancient World,* Antiquity Volume 2 (Leiden: Brill, 2003), 466–467.

33. See Durand, "Culte des bétyles," for a letter about new stone stelae needed to perform sacrifices (*niqû,* siskur$_2$-re) on the occasion of an Ishtar festival.

34. See Karel van der Toorn, *God in Context: Selected Essays on Society and Religion in the Early Middle East,* FAT 123 (Tübingen: Mohr Siebeck, 2018), 335–345.

35. See Kurt Galling, "Aschera," *BRL2,* 12–13.

36. For "the seventy sons of Asherah" (*šb'm bn aṯrt*), see *KTU* 1.4.vi:46, "The Ba'lu Myth," trans. Dennis Pardee, *COS* 1.86:241–274, esp. 262. In an Amorite-Akkadian bilingual, Bēlet-ilī ("mistress of the gods") occurs as the Akkadian counterpart of Asherah (*a-še-ra-tum*); see Andrew George and Manfred Krebernik, "Two Remarkable Vocabularies: Amorite-Akkadian Bilinguals," *RA* 116 (2022): 113–166, esp. 115, line 3. On Asherah in general, see Judith M. Hadley, *The Cult of Asherah in Israel and Judah: Evidence for a Hebrew Goddess*, UCOP 57 (Cambridge: Cambridge University Press, 2000); Steve Wiggins, *A Reassessment of Asherah: With Further Considerations of the Goddess*, Gorgias Ugaritic Studies 2 (Piscataway, NJ: Gorgias Press, 2007); Nicholas Wyatt, "Asherah," *DDD*, 99–105.

37. See Susan Ackerman, *Under Every Green Tree: Popular Religion in Sixth-Century Judah*, HSM 46 (Atlanta: Scholars Press, 1992), 185–194; Ackerman, *Gods, Goddesses, and the Women Who Serve Them* (Grand Rapids: Eerdmans, 2022), 192–198. For a critical assessment of the evidence and discussion of various positions in the secondary literature, see Mark S. Smith, *The Early History of God: Yahweh and the Other Deities in Ancient Israel*, 2nd ed. (Grand Rapids: Eerdmans; Dearborn, MI: Dove, 2002), xxx–xxxvi ("Asherah/asherah Revisited").

38. Philo of Byblos says that the Phoenicians "built temples [*naous*] and also consecrated stelae [*stēlas*] and wooden poles [*rabdous*]" for the ancestors they venerated as deities; see Harold W. Attridge and Robert A. Oden, Jr., *Philo of Byblos: The Phoenician History*, CBQMS 9 (Washington, DC: Catholic Biblical Association of America, 1981), 32–33. For images of tree worship, see Othmar Keel and Christoph Uehlinger, *Göttinnnen, Götter und Gottessymbole: Neue Erkenntnisse zur Religionsgeschichte Kanaans und Israels aufgrund bislang unerschlossener ikonographiser Quellen*, Quaestiones Disputatae 134 (Freiburg im Breisgau: Herder, 1992) 171–174, §95, with illustration nos. 179a–181, translated by Thomas H. Trapp as *Gods, Goddesses, and Images of God in Ancient Israel* (Minneapolis: Fortress, 1998), 152–154, §95, with illustration nos. 179a–181. Possibly the Akkadian *ēqu* refers to an asherah-like object, if the etymological connection with Aramaic *'q*, "wood" (Hebrew *'ēṣ*), holds good; see *CAD* 4, 253–254, s.v. *ēqu*, "a cultic object." Note also the report on the cutting down of an *ēqu* ("sacred tree") in the acropolis temple of Sidon by a local king in view of its transportation to Tyre, in a letter of an Assyrian official to King Tiglath-Pileser III (r. 745–727 BCE); see Mikko Luukko, *The Correspondence of Tiglath-Pileser III and Sargon II from Calah/Nimrud*, SAA 19 (Helsinki: Neo-Assyrian Text Corpus Project, 2012), 30 no. 23:8–16: "[H]i[r]am cut down [the verb is *nakāsu*] the sacred tree (*ēqu*) of his temple on the acropolis of Sidon

planning to transport it to Tyre, but I had him deported. The sacred tree (*ēqu*) that he felled is at the foot of the mountain." The Hiram in question is Hiram II (r. 736–729 BCE), king of Tyre, who also had the title "king of the Sidonians."

39. See also Judg 9:6, where the tree is referred to as the "pillar terebinth," the word *muṣṣāb* referring to the erected stone underneath the tree.

40. See also the name "teacher terebinth" (*ēlôn môreh*) given to the tree at Shechem in Gen 12:6, which also preserves the memory of dendromancy; see Hermann Gunkel, *Genesis*, GAT 1/1 (Göttingen: Vandenhoeck & Ruprecht, 1917), 166–167 ("Orakelterebinthe").

41. See *KTU* 1.3.iii:22–23 and parallels, translated by Mark S. Smith in "The Baal Cycle," *Ugaritic Narrative Poetry*, ed. Simon B. Parker, WAW 9 (Atlanta: Scholars Press, 1997), 81–176, esp. 110. For an interpretation of these lines as an allusion to divination, see Nicholas Wyatt, "Word of Tree and Whisper of Stone: El's Oracle to King Keret (Kirta), and the Problem of the Mechanics of Its Utterance," *VT* 57 (2007): 483–510.

42. See *KTU* 1.17.i:26–27; see Parker, ed., *Ugaritic Narrative Poetry*, 53: "(a son . . .) [t]o set up his Ancestor's stela, the sign of his Sib in the sanctuary" (trans. Simon B. Parker); cf. *COS* 1.103:344: "Someone to raise up the stela of his father's god, in the sanctuary the votive emblem of his clan" (trans. Dennis Pardee).

43. On the Katumuwa stela from Zincirli, see Virginia Rimmer Herrmann and J. David Schloen, eds., *In Remembrance of Me: Feasting with the Dead in the Ancient Middle East*, OIMP 37 (Chicago: Oriental Institute of the University of Chicago, 2014), 27–60.

44. See Klaas Spronk, *Beatific Afterlife, in Ancient Israel and in the Ancient Near East*, AOAT 219 (Kevelaer: Butzon & Bercker; Neukirchen-Vluyn: Neukirchener Verlag, 1986), 206–213; Herbert Niehr, "The Katumuwa Stele in the Context of Royal Mortuary Cult at Sam'al," in Hermann and Schloen, *In Remembrance of Me*, 57–60.

45. The funerary statue of Panamuwa I (ca. 750 BCE) was located in the necropolis of Gercin, located about four miles northeast of Zincirli; see "The Hadad Inscription," trans. K. Lawson Younger, Jr., *COS* 2.36:156–158. The memorial monument for Absalom (*yad 'abšālôm*) consisted of a pillar (*maṣṣebet*) erected in the Valley of the King (2 Sam 18:18), which may well have been a necropolis of sorts.

46. See Mark Smith and Elizabeth Bloch-Smith, *Judges 1*, Hermeneia (Minneapolis: Fortress, 2022), 568–569; McCarter, *I Samuel*, 350.

47. See Van der Toorn, *God in Context*, 271–288.

48. See Julius Wellhausen, *Die Composition des Hexateuchs*, 3rd ed. (Berlin: G. Reimer, 1899), 227–228; George F. Moore, *Judges*, ICC, 2nd ed. (Edinburgh: T&T Clark, 1908), 366.

49. See Benjamin R. Foster, *Before the Muses: An Anthology of Akkadian Literature*, 2 vols. (Bethesda, MD: CDL Press, 1993), 1:409. The Akkadian line reads *mītūti lilûnimma qutrin liṣṣinu* (Ishtar's Descent, line 138).

50. Though the burning of cannabis is not mentioned in the Hebrew Bible, archaeologists have established its use at the Judean shrine in Arad; see Eran Arie, Baruch Rosen, and Dvory Namdat, "Cannabis and Frankincense at the Judahite Shrine of Arad," *TA* 47 (2020): 5–28.

51. See Seymour Gitin, "The Four-Horned Altar and Sacred Space: An Archaeological Perspective," in *Sacred Time, Sacred Place: Archaeology and the Religion of Israel*, ed. Barry M. Gittlen (Winona Lake, IN: Eisenbrauns, 2002), 95–123, esp. 96–99; Jeremy M. Hutton, "Upon the Roof of the Temple: Reconstructing Cognitive Aspects of Ancient Levantine Small-Scale Altar Usage," *JANER* 22 (2022): 161–223, esp. 174–176.

52. See the Taanach cult stand discovered by Ernst Sellin in 1902; see Sellin, *Tell Taʿannek* (Vienna: Carl Gerold's Sohn, 1904), 76, and the discussion in Zevit, *Religions of Ancient Israel*, 318–320. See also the incense burners and/or cult stands from Tel Rehov that depict towers; see Amihai Mazar and Nava Panitz-Cohen, "To What God? Altars and a House Shrine from Tel Rehov Puzzle Archaeologists," *BAR* 34 (2008): 40–47.

53. On the social demography of Israelite towns and villages in Iron Age Palestine, see Faust, "Rural Community."

54. The Samaria ostraca (early eighth century BCE) attest to private land ownership. The ostraca register receipt of wine and oil from territories that bear the names of clans. See Manfred Weippert, *Historisches Textbuch zum Alten Testament*, GAT 10 (Göttingen: Vandenhoeck & Ruprecht, 2010), 278–284; Johannes Renz and Wolfgang Röllig, *Handbuch der Althebräischen Epigraphik*, 3 vols. (Darmstadt: Wissenschaftliche Buchgesellschaft, 1995–2003), 1:79–109, esp. 86–87.

55. For the sanctuary as location for ceremonies of communal fasting, see Judg 20:26 (in Bethel, "weeping before the Lord"), 1 Sam 7:6 (Mizpah), Jer 36:9 (Jerusalem), Neh 9:1 (Jerusalem), and Jdt 4:11–12 (Jerusalem).

56. It has long been assumed that the central courtyard was unroofed to let out smoke of the house, but there is no solid evidence in support of this idea. As De Geus (*Towns in Ancient Israel*, 82) writes, "Modern archaeologists nowadays think that the open central space did exist, but on the second floor."

57. For the Israelite house, see King and Stager, *Life in Biblical Israel*, 28–35; De Geus, *Towns in Ancient Israel*, 75–85; Avraham Faust, "House/s," *EBW*, 395–408.

58. As observed by Kurt Galling and Hartmut Rösel, "Ordinary houses [in Israel] are to be imagined as having open entrances that could on

occasion be closed by a curtain." See Galling and Rösel, "Tür," *BRL2* 348–349, quotation at 348. See also Mirko Novák, "Door/s," *EBW,* 245–247.

59. The Mesopotamian domestic sanctuary was called the *aširtu,* Sumerian zag-gar-ra. See *CAD* I/II, 439, s.v. *aširtu* A, 2, "a special room in a private house for cultic purposes." Šumma ālu VI 97 says that such a cult room is not to be built either on the roof of the house or in its courtyard; see Sally M. Freedman, *If a City Is Set on a Height: Volume 1,* Occasional Publications of the Samuel Noah Kramer Fund, 17 (Philadelphia: University of Pennsylvania Museum, 1998), 118–119. Apparently, it had to be a secluded place.

60. The reference is Gilgamesh Epic, VI, 165–166, which says that Gilgamesh put the golden horns for anointing the statue of his father Lugalbanda "on the bed where he slept as head of the family [*ina urši ḫammūtišu*]"; see commentary by Stephanie Dalley, *Myths from Mesopotamia: Creation, the Flood, Gilgamesh and Others* (Oxford: Oxford University Press, 1989), 129 note 68.

61. The praise of Yʜᴡʜ in Ps 22:10–11 [22:9–10)] as the god who protects from the moment of birth ("Yet it was you who took me from the womb; / you kept me safe on my mother's breast. / On you I was cast from my birth, and since my mother bore me you have been my God," NRSV) may allude to the transformation of the ancient practice of presenting newborn children to the house gods, that is, the ancestors.

62. Though references to this practice are more in the nature of allusions, the wedding banquet at the "ceremonial table" (*paššūr sakkê*) in possession of the paterfamilias implies a rite of passage in the presence of the ancestors. See E. Prang, "Das Archiv des Imgûa," *ZA* 66 (1976): 1–44, esp. 16, 28; Prang, "Das Archiv des Bitûa," *ZA* 67 (1977): 217–234, esp. 224; Andrew George, *The Epic of Gilgamesh: A New Translation* (London: Allen Lane, the Penguin Press, 1999), 105, Pennsylvania tablet 149–152 (iv 14–18).

63. See Thorkild Jacobsen, *The Harps That Once . . . : Sumerian Poetry in Translation* (New Haven: Yale University Press, 1976), 22: "O my bride, [. . .] / To the chapel of my (personal) god I have brought you. / You will sleep before my (personal) god, / and on the seat of honor of my (personal) god, my bride, you will sit!" For a commentary, see Claus Wilcke, "Familiengründung im alten Babylonien," in *Geschlechtsreife und Legitimation zur Zeugung,* ed. E. W. Müller (Freiburg: Karl Alber 1985), 213–317, esp. 279–281.

64. As noted by McCarter, *I Samuel,* 325, the story of David's escape and Michal's ruse with the teraphim is a direct continuation of 1 Sam 18:27 ("Saul then gave him his daughter Michal in marriage"). Incidentally, the passage suggests that the teraphim statuette was roughly anthropomorphic.

65. So much may be extrapolated from the texts from Nuzi and Emar. For Nuzi, see, e.g., Karlheinz Deller, "Die Hausgötter der Familie Šukrija S. Ḫuja," in *Studies on the Civilization and Culture of Nuzi and the Hurrians: In Honor of Ernest R. Lacheman,* ed. Martha M. Morrison and David I. Owen (Winona Lake, IN: Eisenbrauns, 1981), 47–76, esp. 73–74: "After my death my sons shall not make [the verb is *epēšu*] additional gods. I herewith give my gods to my firstborn son. Whoever from my sons wants to bring sacrifice should go to him. Should they [the brothers] wish to bring the gods into their houses to bring sacrifice, then the gods may go there, but they shall not make other gods [dingir.meš *šanûti*]." For Emar, see, e.g., the characteristic sentences from inheritance texts: "The gods belong to the main house. The main house is the share of PN, my eldest son"; see Daniel Arnaud, *Textes syriens de l'âge du Bronze récent,* AuOrSup 1 (Barcelona: Editorial AUSA, 1991), 80–81, no. 42:12–18, discussion in Van der Toorn, *God in Context,* 291.

66. Compare such names as Abiasaph, "My ancestor has added (a child)"; Jeroboam, "May the paternal uncle enlarge (the family)"; Rehoboam, "May the paternal uncle extend (the family)"; and Jokneam, "May the paternal uncle create (offspring)"; see Karel van der Toorn, *Family Religion in Babylonia, Syria and Israel: Continuity and Change in the Forms of Religious Life,* SHCANE 7 (Leiden: Brill, 1996), 230.

67. For a survey and some informed speculation on their background and function, see Zevit, *Religions of Ancient Israel,* 336–343. See also Joachim Brettschneider, "Götter in Schreinen: Eine Untersuchung zu den syrischen und levantinischen Tempelmodellen, ihre Bauplastik und ihren Götterbildern," *Ugarit-Forschungen* 23 (1991): 13–32; Mazar and Panitz-Cohen, "To What God?"

68. See George, *Epic of Gilgamesh,* 24–26, Standard Version, tablet III, 35–119, quotation at 24, lines 44–45. For other Akkadian references to rituals performed on the rooftop, see *CAD* 20, 262–263, s.v. *ūru* A, "roof," (e) as place of ritual.

69. For a discussion of the textual evidence for rooftop sacrifices, see Hutton, "Upon the Roof of the Temple," esp. 189–202.

70. See Tryggve N. D. Mettinger, "Yahweh Zebaoth," *DDD,* 920–924.

71. See Martha T. Roth, *Law Collections from Mesopotamia and Asia Minor,* WAW 6 (Atlanta: Scholars Press, 1995), 167–168, MAL A§40: "Wives of a man, or [widows], or any [Assyrian] women who go out into the main thoroughfare [shall not have] their heads [bare]. [. . .] [they] shall be veiled."

72. For a comprehensive study of women's life-cycle rituals, see Susan Ackerman, *Maturity, Marriage, Motherhood, and Mortality: Women's Life-Cycle Rituals in Ancient Israel* (New York: Oxford University Press, forthcoming).

73. See *HAL*, 1620, s.v. *tnh*, "to sing antiphonically, in choir," and cf. Judg 5:11 ("chant").

74. For a discussion with slightly different conclusions, see Peggy L. Day, "From the Child Is Born the Woman: The Story of Jephthah's Daughter," in *Gender and Difference in Ancient Israel*, ed. Peggy L. Day (Minneapolis: Fortress, 1989), 109–124; Ackerman, *Women and the Religion of Ancient Israel*, 246–249.

75. According to an incantation against Ardat-lilî (cf. the biblical Lilith), the demon is one "who did not rejoice with the other girls, who was not seen at the city festival"; see Egbert von Weiher, *Spätbabylonische Texte aus Uruk, II*, Ausgrabungen der Deutschen Forschungsgemeinschaft in Uruk-Warka 10 (Berlin: Mann, 1983), no. 7:5–6. The Instructions of Šūpê-amēli, known from a copy from Ugarit, advise a man "not to marry a young girl during festival time." A Hittite parallel explains: "An unworthy *karšanza* girl will dress up for a festival. She will dress up in a loaned garment and she will anoint herself with oil that has been borrowed." See Yoram Cohen, *Wisdom from the Late Bronze Age*, WAW 34 (Atlanta: Society of Biblical Literature, 2013), 94–95. Roth, *Law Collections*, 175, MAL A§55, mentions the city festival as one of the typical occasions on which extramarital sex might occur.

76. See Raz Kletter and Katri Saarelainen, "Judean Drummers," *ZDPV* 127 (2011): 11–28. Several authors interpret the drummer figurines as representations of the goddess Asherah; see, e.g., Delbert R. Hillers, "The Goddess with the Tambourine: Reflections on an Object from Taanach," *Concordia Theological Monthly* 41/9 (1970): 606–619. According to Lucian, *Dea Syria*, XV, the image of the Syrian Goddess (Atargatis) was holding a drum in her hand.

77. Hebrew *ṣārâ*, 1 Sam 1:6, cf. Akkadian *ṣerretu*, *CAD* 16, 137–138, s.v. *ṣerru* B, "enemy, second wife, rival."

78. A Babylonian diagnostic list of childhood diseases says that "vows have seized the baby," which implies that failure to fulfill the vows might cause infant disease and death; see René Labat, *Traité akkadien de diagnostics et pronostics médicaux* (Paris: Académie internationale d'histoire des sciences; Leiden: Brill, 1951), 228:103, 104, 105, 109; 230:113, etc.

79. See Van der Toorn, *God in Context*, 85–97.

80. Note also "the mother whose son was taken captive prays to you constantly and without cease," Wilfred G. Lambert, *Babylonian Wisdom Literature* (Oxford: Clarendon, 1960), 134–135:134 (Shamash hymn); Luke 2:36–37. See also the prayer by the mother of Gilgamesh, mentioned earlier in this chapter.

81. On personal names as a reflection of the position of Yhwh in Israelite religion, see Jeffrey H. Tigay, *You Shall Have No Other Gods: Israelite Religion in the Light of Hebrew Inscriptions*, HSS 31 (Atlanta: Scholars Press), 1986.

82. On local forms of Yʜwʜ (and other gods), see P. Kyle McCarter, Jr., "Aspects of the Religion of the Israelite Monarchy: Biblical and Epigraphic Data," in *Ancient Israelite Religion*, ed. Patrick D. Miller, Jr., Paul D. Hanson, and S. Dean McBride (Philadelphia: Fortress, 1987), 137–155, esp. 140–142.

83. On the role of Asherah as intercessor with El, see *KTU* 1.4.iv, "The Ba'lu Myth," trans. Dennis Pardee, *COS* 1.86:241–274, esp. 258–259.

84. First published by William G. Dever, "Iron Age Epigraphic Material from Khirbet el-Qom," *HUCA* 40–41 (1970–1971): 139–204, esp. 158–169, 200–201. For translation and interpretation, see P. Kyle McCarter, "Khirbet el-Qom," *COS* 2.52:179; Renz and Röllig, *Die althebräischen Inschriften*, 1:202–211.

85. See, e.g., "Tashmetu [. . .] I have turned to you [. . .]. Please intercede for me with Nabu, your husband, the Lord [. . .] at the command of your mouth may he accept my petition" ("Tašmētu 1," Marie-Joseph Seux, *Hymnes et prières aux dieux de Babylonie et d'Assyrie*, LAPO 8 [Paris: Cerf, 1976], 331–334); and from a prayer to Shamash, "May Aya the great bride, who dwells in the bedchamber, keep your features ever aglow and speak favorably of me every day" (Benjamin R. Foster, *Before the Muses: An Anthology of Akkadian Literature*, 2 vols. [Bethesda, MD: CDL Press, 1993], 2:753). See in general Werner Mayer, *Untersuchungen zur Formensprache der babylonischen "Gebetsbeschwörungen,"* StPohl 5 (Rome: Biblical Institute Press, 1976), 234–235.

86. See Erhard S. Gerstenberger, *Der bittende Mensch: Bittritual und Klagelied des Einzelnen im Alten Testament*, WMANT 51 (Neukirchen-Vluyn: Neukirchener Verlag, 1980), 137–139; cf. Mayer, *Untersuchungen*, 59–66.

87. See Zevit, *Religions of Ancient Israel*, 314–328; Andreas Reichert, "Kultgeräte," *BRL2*, 189–194; King and Stager, *Life in Biblical Israel*, 340–348.

88. The Akkadian *tamītu* texts show that people consulted the diviner at specific times of the year, especially at the New Year festival and during the new moon. This is clear from the fact that the oracle is valid for a year ("from the month Nisan, the beginning of the year, up to the month Addar, the end of the year") or a month ("within this month, up to the 30th day, and the following month, up to the second day." See Wilfred G. Lambert, *Babylonian Oracle Questions*, MC 13 (Winona Lake, IN: Eisenbrauns, 2007), 112–113:5–6; 34–35:235–239; 68–69:3; 86–87:20; 116–117:14–15; 24–25:27–28; 28–29:97–99; 32–33:166–167; 56–57:5–6; 96–97:1–2. Compare, in the biblical record, Hannah's visit to the Shiloh temple at the annual sacrifice to obtain a priestly oracle (1 Sam 1:17), and the reference to the visit of a prophet at the Carmel sanctuary on the day of the new moon in 2 Kgs 4:27.

89. See also Albrecht Alt, "Die Wallfahrt von Sichem nach Bethel," in *Kleine Schriften zur Geschichte des Volkes Israels*, 3 vols. (Munich: C. H.

Beck, 1953–1959), 1:79–88; Martin Noth, "Der Wallfahrtsweg zum Sinai (4. Mose 33)," *Palästina-Jahrbuch* 36 (1940): 5–28.

90. The pioneering study of the terracotta figurines is James B. Pritchard, *Palestinian Figurines in Relation to Certain Goddesses Known from Literature*, AOS 24 (New Haven: American Oriental Society, 1943). For a catalogue of the Judean pillar figurines discovered up until 1995, see Raz Kletter, *The Judean Pillar-Figurines and the Archaeology of Asherah*, BARIS 636 (Oxford: Tempus Reparatum, 1996). See also Thomas A. Holland, "A Study of Palestinian Iron Age Baked Clay Figurines with Special Reference to Jerusalem: Cave 1," *Levant* 9 (1977): 121–155. For a study of the modes of production, see David Ben-Shlomo and Eric D. Darby, "A Study of the Production of Iron Age Clay Figurines from Jerusalem," *TA* 41 (2014): 180–204. See also Kurt Galling, "Götterbild, weibliches," *BRL2*, 111–119. For the possibility that some of the pillar figurines represent mourning women, see Candida Felli, "Mourning and Funerary Practices in the Ancient Near East: An Essay to Bridge the Gap Between the Textual and the Archaeological Record," in *How to Cope with Death: Mourning and Funerary Practices in the Ancient Near East: Proceedings of the International Workshop Firenze, 5th–6th December 2013*, ed. Candida Felli, Ricerche di Archeologia del Vicino Oriente 5 (Pisa: ETS, 2016), 83–132.

91. For the plaque figurines, see Miriam Tadmor, "Female Cult Figurines in Late Canaan and Early Israel: Archaeological Evidence," in *Studies in the Period of David and Solomon and Other Essays: Papers Read at the International Symposium for Biblical Studies, Tokyo 5–7 December, 1979*, ed. Tomoo Ishida (Tokyo: Yamakawa, 1982), 139–173; Amihai Mazar, "Pottery Plaques Depicting Goddesses Standing in Temple Facades," *Michmanim* 2 (1985): 5–17; Izak Cornelius, "A Preliminary Typology for the Female Plaque Figurines and Their Value for the Religion of Ancient Palestine and Jordan," *JNSL* 30 (2004): 21–39. On pillar figurines and plaque figurines, see Izak Cornelius, "Iconography of Human Beings," *EBW*, 459–475. For a discussion of the horse-with-rider figurines, see Othmar Keel and Christoph Uehlinger, *Göttinnen, Götter und Gottessymbole: Neue Erkentnisse zur Religionsgeschichte Kanaans und Israels aufgrund bislang unerschlossener ikonographischer Quellen*, Quaestiones Disputatae 134 (Freiburg im Breisgau: Herder, 1992), 390–399, §§198–200, translated by Thomas H. Trapp as *God, Goddesses, and Images of God in Ancient Israel* (Philadelphia: Fortress, 1998), 341–348. Note that in Akkadian, Nergal (god of the netherworld) bears the title *rākib sīsû*, "horseman"; see *CAD* 15, 328–334, s.v. *sīsû*, "horse," esp. 330 (c); see also G. Kenneth Jenkins, "Two New Tarsos Coins," *Revue Numismatique* 15 (1973): 30–34, coins with inscription, with a horseman on one side and a standing figure and *nrgl trz*, "Nergal of Tarsus," on the other.

In the Israelite context, the god of the underworld (and pestilence) would be Resheph (cf. Hab 3:5).

92. On the midwife as a "wise woman," see Hennie J. Marsman, *Women in Ugarit and Israel: Their Social and Religious Position in the Context of the Ancient Near East*, OTS 49 (Leiden: Brill, 2003), 412. The designation is common in the Mishnah.

93. On the Mesopotamian rites for Tammuz, see Walter Farber, *Beschwörungsrituale an Ištar und Dumuzi* (Wiesbaden: Franz Steiner, 1977), 188–206; Simo Parpola, *Letters from Assyrian and Babylonian Scholars*, SAA 10 (Helsinki: Helsinki University Press, 1993), 15–16, nos. 18–19; Parpola, *Letters from Assyrian Scholars to the Kings Esarhaddon and Assurbanipal: Part II: Commentary and Appendices*, AOAT 5/2 (Kevelaer: Butzon & Bercker; Neukirchen-Vluyn: Neukirchener Verlag, 1983), 8–10; Alasdair Livingstone, *Mystical and Mythological Explanatory Works of Assyrian and Babylonian Scholars* (Oxford: Oxford University Press, 1986), 137–141.

94. For a study of mourning performances in the ancient Near East, including a discussion of the iconographic evidence, see Felli, "Mourning and Funerary Practices." The author makes a plausible case for interpreting some of the Palestinian pillar figurines of women holding their breasts as mourners.

95. See Saul M. Olyan, *Biblical Mourning: Ritual and Social Dimensions* (Oxford: Oxford University Press, 2004), 28–61.

96. For Arabic *kâhin* as "prophet," see Julius Wellhausen, *Reste arabischen Heidentums*, 2nd ed. (Berlin: Georg Reimer, 1897), 134–140; Toufic Fahd, *La divination arabe: Études religieuses, sociologiques et folkloriques sur le milieu natif de l'Islam* (Leiden: Brill, 1966), 92–97.

97. See Alexander Rofé, *The Prophetical Stories* (Jerusalem: Magnes, 1988), 13–22.

98. For the interpretation of *nāyôt* (plural of *nāweh*) as pasturage, shepherd camp, see McCarter, *I Samuel*, 328.

99. See André Lemaire, *Les écoles et la formation de la Bible dans l'ancien Israël*, OBO 39 (Fribourg: Presses Universitaires; Göttingen: Vandenhoeck & Ruprecht, 1981), 50–52; Bernhard Lang, *Wie wird man Prophet in Israel? Aufsätze zum Alten Testament* (Düsseldorf: Patmos, 1980), 31–58, esp. 33–35.

100. See, e.g., Jean Bottéro, "Symptômes, signes, écritures," in *Divination et Rationalité*, J. P. Vernant, L. Vandermeersch, J. Gernet, J. Bottéro, R. Crahay, L. Brisson, J. Carlier, D. Grodzynski, and A. Retel-Laurentin (Paris: Seuil, 1974), 70–197, esp. 162–165.

101. See Jean-Georges Heintz, ed., *Oracles et prophéties dans l'Antiquité: Actes du Colloque de Strasbourg, 15–17 juin 1995* (Paris: De Boccard, 1997); Jonathan Stökl, *Prophecy in the Ancient Near East: A Philological*

and Sociological Comparison, CHANE 56 (Leiden: Brill, 2012); Manfred Weippert, *Götterwort in Menschenmund: Studien zur Prophetie in Assyrien, Israel und Juda,* FRLANT 252 (Göttingen: Vandenhoeck & Ruprecht, 2014); Martti Nissinen, *Ancient Prophecy: Near Eastern, Biblical, and Greek Perspectives* (New York: Oxford University Press, 2017).

102. See Jean-Marie Durand, *Archives Épistolaires de Mari I/1,* ARM 26 (Paris: Éditions Recherche sur les Civilisations, 1988), 377–452, Deuxième partie: Les textes prophétiques, nos. 191–223.

103. See Simo Parpola, *Assyrian Prophecies,* SAA 9 (Helsinki: Helsinki University Press, 1997); Martti Nissinen, *References to Prophecy in Neo-Assyrian Sources,* SAAS 7 (Helsinki: Neo-Assyrian Text Corpus Project, 1998).

104. See, e.g., "The Inscription of Zakkur, King of Hamath," trans. Alan Millard, *COS* 3.35:155, A lines 11–15: "Now I raised my hands to Ba'lshamayn and Ba'lshamayn answered me. Ba'lshamayn spoke to me through seers (*ḥzyn*) and diviners ('*ddn*). Ba'lshamayn said to me, 'Do not be afraid! Since I have made [you king, I will stand] beside you. I will save you from all [these kings who] have besieged you.'" See also James F. Roth, "Prophecy in Hamath, Israel, and Mari," *HTR* 63 (1970): 1–28.

105. See Jean Bottéro, "Le pouvoir royal et ses limitations d'après les textes divinatoires," in *La voix de l'opposition en Mésopotamie: Colloque organisé par l'Institut des Hautes Études en Belgique, 19 et 20 mars 1973,* ed. André Finet (Brussels: Institut des Hautes Études de Belgique, 1973), 119–165.

106. See Esther J. Hamori, *Women's Divination in Biblical Literature: Prophecy, Necromancy, and Other Arts of Knowledge,* AYBRL (New Haven: Yale University Press, 2015).

107. For Mesopotamian necromancy, see *CAD* 17, 109–112, s.v. *šā'iltu,* "woman diviner," and *šā'ilu,* "diviner (interpreting dreams, practicing necromancy)." According to the lexical section of *šā'ilu* (pp. 110–111), he is a *mušēlû eṭemmē,* "who raises the spirits," and a *mupaššēr šunāti,* "interpreter of dreams." For the use of incense by the necromancer, see the sentences "the haruspex does not enlighten him by means of divination, the necromancer does not reveal (the fate) to him by means of incense (*še-e-ta, ina mušakka*)," at 110–111; "the necromancer has used up the incense (*maššakka*)" (viz. without reaching a verdict); see Jean Nougayrol, Emmanuel Laroche, Charles Virolleaud, and Claude F. A. Schaeffer, *Ugaritica V,* MRS 16 (Paris: Imprimerie nationale and Geuthner, 1968), 162:6; "the necromancer could not proclaim the verdict for me with the incense (*ina maššakka*)," with comment *maššakku = surqinnu ša šā'ilu,* "Maššakku is the incense offering of the necromancer," Wilfred G. Lambert, *Babylonian Wisdom Literature* (Oxford: Clarendon, 1960), 38:7 (Ludlul). See also Irving L. Finkel, "Necromancy in Ancient Mesopotamia," *AfO* 29–30 (1983–1984): 1–17, for the use of a skull.

108. The Babylonian Talmud says the *baʿal ʾōb* denotes both he "who con-
jures up the dead by calling names, and one who consults a skull"
(b. Sanh. 65b). Eitan Klein and Boaz Zissu, "Oil Lamps, Spearheads
and Skulls: Possible Evidence of Necromancy During Late Antiquity
in the Teʿomim Cave, Judean Hills," *HTR* 116 (2023): 399–421, suggest
that the skulls found in a cave in the Jerusalem Hills were used for
purposes of necromancy during the Roman period.

109. The Sarcophagus Inscription of Tabnit, king of Sidon, warns not to
open the sarcophagus and disturb (*ʾl trgzn*) him; see "The Sarcophagus
Inscription of Tabnit King of Sidon," trans. P. Kyle McCarter, *COS*
2.56:181–182. For other examples of *rgz* in this sense, see *DNWSI* 2:1059,
s.v. rgz₁. For a similar use of the Hebrew verb *rāgaz*, see Isa 14:9.

110. Compare, e.g., the Old Babylonian myth of Atrahasis, in which the
gods decide to decimate humankind because humans make too much
noise and deprive the gods of sleep; see Wilfred G. Lambert and Alan
R. Millard, *Atra-Ḥasīs: The Babylonian Story of the Flood* (Oxford: Clarendon, 1969), 72–73 (Tablet II I 1–10). The theme of noise keeping the
dead awake also occurs in Old Babylonian baby incantations; see Walter Farber, *Schlaf, Kindchen, Schlaf! Mesopotamische Baby-Beschwörun-
gen und -Rituale*, MC 2 (Winona Lake, IN: Eisenbrauns, 1989), 34–35,
where the baby's crying has woken "the god of the house" (*ì-lí bi-tim*),
presumably a reference to the ancestor(s). See also Alasdair Livingstone, *Court Poetry and Literary Miscellanea*, SAA 3 (Helsinki: Helsinki
University Press, 1989), 74, no. 32:21, with a reference to "din" (*ḫubūru*)
keeping the dead from falling asleep.

Chapter 4. Diaspora Religion

1. See A. Kirk Grayson, "Shalmaneser," *AYBD* 5:1155. For the twofold conquest of Samaria, see Bob Becking, *The Fall of Samaria: A Historical and
Archaeological Study*, SHCANE 2 (Leiden: Brill, 1992), 21–45.

2. For the little we do know about the Israelite exiles in Assyria, see Becking, *Fall of Samaria*, 61–93; Bob Becking, *Israel's Past Seen from the Present: Studies on History and Religion in Ancient Israel and Judah*, BZAW
535 (Berlin: de Gruyter, 2021), 66–80 (four Israelites who were most
likely descendants of those taken to the River Habur in Gozan). On
the impact of the Assyrian conquest on the demographic situation in
what used to be the kingdom of Israel, see also Avraham Faust, *The
Neo-Assyrian Empire in the Southwest: Imperial Domination and Its Consequences* (Oxford: Oxford University Press, 2021), 73–115.

3. On the office of royal secretary (*sōpēr*), see Tryggve N. D. Mettinger,
*Solomonic State Officials: A Study of the Civil Government Officials of the
Israelite Monarchy*, ConBOT 5 (Lund: Gleerup, 1971), 31–42. Mettinger

emphasizes the role of the royal *sōpēr* as secretary and writer of royal annals. Compare the critical stance taken by Paul Mandel, "Between *sōpēr* and *sāpar:* The Evolution of the Second Temple Period Scribe," in *The Scribe in the Biblical World: A Bridge Between Scripts, Languages, and Cultures,* ed. Esther Eshel and Michael Langlois, BZAW 547 (Berlin: de Gruyter, 2023), 295–320, who casts the scribe mostly in the role of clerk, registrar, accountant.

4. For a description of this demographic movement, see Israel Finkelstein, *The Forgotten Kingdom: The Archaeology and History of Northern Israel,* ANEM 5 (Atlanta: Society of Biblical Literature, 2013), 154–155. For a critical appraisal of Finkelstein's interpretation of the evidence, see Nadav Na'aman, "Dismissing the Myth of a Flood of Israelite Refugees in the Late Eighth Century BCE," *ZAW* 126 (2014): 1–14. For a reply, see Finkelstein, "Migration of Israelites into Judah after 720 BCE: An Answer and an Update," *ZAW* 127 (2015): 188–206. See also Ernst Axel Knauf, "Was There a Refugee Crisis in the 8th/7th Centuries BCE?," in *Rethinking Israel: Studies in the History and Archaeology of Ancient Israel in Honor of Israel Finkelstein,* ed. Oded Lipschits, Yuval Gadot, and Matthew J. Adams (Winona Lake, IN: Eisenbrauns, 2017), 159–172. For the archaeological evidence, see also the literature mentioned in the following notes to this chapter.

5. Magen Broshi, "Expansion of Jerusalem in the Reigns of Hezekiah and Manasseh," *IEJ* 24 (1974): 21–26; Nahman Avigad, *Discovering Jerusalem: Recent Archaeological Excavations in the Upper City* (Oxford: Blackwell, 1984), 23–60; Eliat Mazar and Benjamin Mazar, *Excavations in the South of the Temple Mount* (Jerusalem: Institute of Archaeology, Hebrew University, 1989); Ronny Reich and Eli Shukron, "The Urban Development of Jerusalem in the Late Eighth Century B.C.E.," in *Jerusalem in Bible and Archaeology: The First Temple Period,* ed. Andrew G. Vaughn and Ann E. Killebrew, SBLSS 18 (Atlanta: Society of Biblical Literature, 2003), 209–218.

6. Moshe Kochavi, ed., *Judaea, Samaria and the Golan: Archaeological Survey 1967–1968* (Jerusalem: Carta, 1972), 20–21 [Hebrew]; Aaron Burke, "An Anthropological Model for the Investigation of the Archaeology of Refugees in Iron Age Judah and Its Environs," in *Interpreting Exile: Interdisciplinary Studies of Displacement and Deportation in Biblical and Modern Contexts,* ed. Brad E. Kelle, Frank Ritchel Ames, and Jacob L. Wright, AIL 10 (Atlanta: Society of Biblical Literature, 2011), 41–56.

7. Note that Huldah speaks an oracle in the name of the "the god of Israel" to "the king of Judah" (2 Kgs 22:15–18).

8. The priests from Anathoth are the descendants of Abiathar (2 Kgs 1:26–27), who survived the massacre of the priests at Nob (1 Sam 22:18–23). The priests of Nob had their roots in Shiloh and settled in Nob

after the destruction of Shiloh, as is evident from the genealogy of Abiathar son of Ahimelech (also known as Ahijah) son of Ahitub son of Phinehas son of Eli, "the priest of Yʜwʜ at Shiloh" (1 Sam 14:3, 22:20). According to the genealogies preserved in 1 Chr 5:37–40, 9:10–11; Ezra 7:1; and Neh 11:11, the priest Hilkiah was son of Shallum (var. Meshullam) son of Zadok (son of Meraioth) son of Ahitub.

9. See Robert R. Wilson, *Prophecy and Society in Ancient Israel* (Philadelphia: Fortress, 1980), 219–223.

10. For Maaseiah son of Shallum, see Shemuel Yeivin, "Families and Parties in the Kingdom of Judah," *Tarbiz* 12 (1941): 241–267, esp. 261 [Hebrew].

11. For a discussion of the event, see William L. Holladay, *Jeremiah 2,* Hermeneia (Minneapolis: Fortress, 1989), 433–434.

12. Note his genealogical connection ("Shaphan son of Azaliah son of Meshullam," 2 Kgs 22:3), as well as the names of his sons and grandson ("Ahikam son of Shaphan," Jer 26:24; "Elasah son of Shaphan," Jer 29:3; "Jaazaniah son of Shaphan," Ezek 8:11; "Gedaliah son of Ahikam son of Shaphan," Jer 39:14).

13. For a discussion of a northern scribal family integrated in the Judean administration, see William M. Schniedewind, "Northern Refugees in Jerusalem: The Case of Menaḥem, Son of Yawbana," in *Linguistic and Philological Studies of the Hebrew Bible and Its Manuscripts in Honor of Gary A. Rendsburg,* ed. Vincent D. Beiler and Aaron D. Rubin, SSN (Leiden: Brill, 2023), 262–269. Schniedewind bases his case on the seal impressions listed in Nahman Avigad, *Corpus of West Semitic Stamp Seals,* rev. and completed by Benjamin Sass (Jerusalem: Israel Academy of Sciences and Humanities, 1997), 248–249, nos. 676–678.

14. For the expression "new elite," see Mordechai Cogan and Hayim Tadmor, *II Kings: A New Translation with Introduction and Commentary,* AYB 11 (New York: Doubleday, 1988; repr. New Haven: Yale University Press), 295.

15. Note the correspondences between several of Jeremiah's oracles and the books of Amos and Hosea, e.g., the time of the desert wanderings as the honeymoon between Yʜwʜ and Israel (Hos 2:17, 9:10, 11:1–4, 13:3; Jer 2:2–6, 31:2–3), and the nonsacrificial character of the early worship of Yʜwʜ (Amos 5:25, "Did you bring me sacrifices and offerings during the forty years in the wilderness, O house of Israel?" [NRSV]; Jer 7:22–23, "For in the day that I brought your ancestors out of the land of Egypt, I did not speak to them or command them concerning burnt offerings and sacrifices" [NRSV]). Another "northern" aspect of Jeremiah is the veneration for Moses and Samuel (Jer 15:1). For Amos as a northern prophet, in terms of ideology and language, see, e.g., Gary A. Rendsburg, "Israelian Hebrew in the Book of Amos," in *New*

Perspectives in Biblical and Rabbinic Hebrew, ed. Aaron D. Hornkohl and Geoffrey Khan (Cambridge: Cambridge University Press, 2021), 717–739. The prophet's refusal to identify neither as "a prophet" (*nābî*') nor as "a prophet's son" (*ben-nābî*', Amos 7:14) reflects familiarity with the northern traditions about Elijah and Elisha and "the sons of the prophets," for which see Karel van der Toorn, "The Sons of the Prophets: Movement, Guild, Order, or Sect?," in *A Sage in New Haven: Essays on the Prophets, the Writings, and the Ancient World in Honor of Robert R. Wilson,* ed. Alison Acker Gruseke and Carolyn R. Sharp, ÄAT 117 (Münster: Zaphon, 2023), 33–42.

16. See C. F. Burney, *The Book of Judges* (London: Rivingtons, 1918), xlvi; Adam C. Welch, *The Code of Deuteronomy: A New Theory of Its Origin* (London: James Clarke, 1924); Albrecht Alt, "Die Heimat des Deuteronomiums," in *Kleine Schriften zur Geschichte des Volkes Israels,* 3 vols. (Munich: C. H. Beck, 1953–1959), 2:250–275; Ernest Wilson Nichelson, *Deuteronomy and Tradition* (Oxford: Basil Blackwell, 1967), 58–82; Johannes Lindblom, *Erwägungen zur Herkunft der josianischen Tempelurkunde* (Lund: C. W. K. Gleerup, 1971), 50–54; Harold Louis Ginsberg, *The Israelian Heritage of Judaism* (New York: Jewish Theological Seminary, 1982), 19–24; Moshe Weinfeld, "The Emergence of the Deuteronomic Movement: The Historical Antecedents," in *Das Deuteronomium: Entstehung, Gestalt, und Botschaft,* ed. Norbert Lohfink, BETL 68 (Leuven: Peeters, 1985), 76–98.

17. See the discussions in Rainer Albertz, *Religionsgeschichte Israels in alttestamentlicher Zeit,* 2 vols., ATD Ergänzungsreihe 8/1–2 (Göttingen: Vandenhoeck & Ruprecht, 1992), 1:307–321, translated by John Bowden as *A History of Israelite Religion in the Old Testament Period,* 2 vols., OTL (Louisville: Westminster John Knox, 1994), 1:195–216; Gösta W. Ahlström, *The History of Ancient Palestine from the Palaeolithic Period to Alexander's Conquest,* JSOTSup 146 (Sheffield: JSOT Press, 1993), 777–780; Christoph Uehlinger, "Was There a Cult Reform Under King Josiah? The Case for a Well-Grounded Minimum," in *Good Kings and Bad Kings,* ed. Lester Grabbe (London: T&T Clark, 2005), 279–316; Michael Pietsch, *Die Kultreform Josias: Studien zur Religionsgeschichte Israels in der späten Königszeit,* FAT 86 (Tübingen: Mohr Siebeck, 2013), is optimistic about the historical reality of the reform although he admits there is little support for this in the archaeological evidence.

18. See *TAD* A2.1:1; Karel van der Toorn, *Becoming Diaspora Jews: Behind the Story of Elephantine,* AYBRL (New Haven: Yale University Press, 2019), 112–114.

19. Jean-Jacques Glassner, *Mesopotamian Chronicles,* WAW 19 (Atlanta: Society of Biblical Literature, 2004), 230–231, no. 24, Reverse 11–13.

20. See Jer 52:30; Josephus, *Ant.* 10.180–182. On the campaign against Egypt in 582–581 BCE (the twenty-third year of Nebuchadnezzar), see Dan'el Kahn, "Nebuchadnezzar and Egypt: An Update on the Egyptian Monuments," *HBAI* 7 (2018): 65–78, esp. 72–74.

21. For a discussion of the number of exiled Judeans, see Sigmund Mowinckel, *Studien zu dem Buche Ezra-Nehemia, I: Die nachchronische Redaktion des Buches. Die Listen* (Oslo: Oslo University Press, 1964), 94–97. Mowinckel argues that the figures given in Jer 52:28–30 are broadly reliable (forty-six hundred deportees), but that the reference has omitted to count deportees from the city of Jerusalem. He surmises a total of seven thousand to eight thousand exiles.

22. For an archaeological study of Judah in the period 609–539 BCE, see Oded Lipschits, *The Fall and Rise of Jerusalem: Judah Under Babylonian Rule* (Winona Lake, IN: Eisenbrauns, 2005), who observes that the majority of the population lived in the territory of Benjamin, north of Judah.

23. For an insightful discussion of the ideological issues involved in the study of the Judean diaspora in Babylonia, as well as the history of Judah in the sixth century BCE, see Hans M. Barstad, *The Myth of the Empty Land*, SO 28 (Oslo: Scandinavian University Press, 1996).

24. For an example of a prosperous Judean family that had adapted well to the Babylonian culture, see the case of the royal merchant Hosea from Sippar, who named his sons Bel-iddin, Bel-uballiṭ, Nabu-ittannu, and Šamaš-iddin, and whose daughter, Kaššaya, married into an elite Babylonian family; see Martha Roth, *Babylonian Marriage Agreements 7th–3rd Centuries B.C.*, AOAT 222 (Kevelaer: Butzon & Bercker; Neukirchen-Vluyn: Neukirchener Verlag, 1989), 92–95, no. 26. For a discussion of this mixed marriage, the Amušê/Hosea family and their connections, with references to earlier literature, see Cornelia Wunsch, *Judaeans by the Waters of Babylon: New Historical Evidence in Cuneiform Sources from Rural Babylonia in the Schøyen Collection*, Babylonische Archive 6 (Dresden: ISLET-Verlag, 2022), 57–60. For a discussion of the revival of Yahwistic personal names in the Babylonian diaspora after the establishment of Achaemenid rule, see Yigal Bloch, "Judeans in Sippar and Susa in the First Century of the Babylonian Exile: Assimilation and Perseverance Under Neo-Babylonian and Achaemenid Rule," *JANEH* 1 (2014): 119–172; Elias Bickerman, "The Babylonian Captivity," *CHJ* 1:342–358, esp. 355–357. Name-giving patterns at Al-Yaḫudu, where Judeans with Babylonian names are relatively rare, indicate than one has to distinguish between Judeans in an urban context and Judeans in the countryside.

25. For the texts, see Francis Joannès and André Lemaire, "Contrats babyloniens d'époque achéménide du Bît-abi Râm avec une épigraphe

araméenne," *RA* 90 (1996): 41–60; Francis Joannès and André Lemaire, "Trois tablettes cunéiformes à l'onomastique ouest-sémitique," *Transeuphratène* 17 (1999): 17–34; Kathleen Abraham, "West Semitic and Judean Brides in Cuneiform Sources from the Sixth Century BCE: New Evidence from a Marriage Contract from Āl-Yaḫudu," *AfO* 51 (2005–2006): 198–219; Wilfred G. Lambert, "A Document from a Community of Exiles in Babylonia," in *New Seals and Inscriptions: Hebrew, Idumean, Cuneiform,* ed. Meir Lubetski, HBM 8 (Sheffield: Sheffield Phoenix Press, 2007), 201–205; Laurie E. Pearce and Cornelia Wunsch, *Documents of Judean Exiles and West Semites in Babylonia in the Collection of David Sofer,* CUSAS 28 (Bethesda, MD: CDL Press, 2014); Wunsch, *Judaeans by the Waters of Babylon.* In addition to some hundred "new" texts, the last book also contains a reedition of all the texts previously published (pp. 383–459) plus a study of the Aramaic and Hebrew epigraphs on the tablets by James D. Moore (pp. 371–382). Another source of—mostly indirect—information is the Murashu archive consisting of legal documents from Nippur during the last half of the fifth century BCE. These texts contain a variety of Judean names and attest to the presence and economic activities of members of the Judean diaspora in Persian-period Babylonia; see Matthew W. Stolper, "Murashû, Archive of," *AYBD* 4:927–928.

26. For a survey, see Muhammad A. Dandamaev, "Twin Towns and Ethnic Minorities in First-Millennium Babylonia," in *Commerce and Monetary Systems in the Ancient World: Means of Transmission and Cultural Interaction,* ed. Robert Rollinger and Christoph Ulf, Melammu Symposia 5 (Stuttgart: Franz Steiner, 2004), 137–149.

27. See Israel Eph'al, "The Western Minorities in Babylonia in the 6th–5th Centuries B.C.: Maintenance and Cohesion," *Orientalia* (NS) 47 (1978): 76–90, esp. 80–83. See also Pearce and Wunsch, *Documents of Judean Exiles,* 81 s.v. Ṣurāia; Wunsch, *Judaeans by the Waters of Babylon,* 2–3.

28. See Pearce and Wunsch, *Documents of Judean Exiles,* no. 1:16 ("town of the Judeans," 572 BCE); Wunsch, *Judaeans by the Waters of Babylon,* no. 1:13 ("town of the Judeans," 567 BCE); Pearce and Wunsch, *Documents of Judean Exiles,* no. 20:2 ("the *šušānû* fields of the Judeans," 511 BCE).

29. See, e.g., in Pearce and Wunsch, *Documents of Judean Exiles,* Bethel-ab-uṣur son of Bethel-šar-uṣur (nos. 17:14–15, 18:15, 19:16, 20:14, 21:10–11, 22:7, 24:7–8; cf. Wunsch, *Judaeans by the Waters of Babylon,* no. 6:17); Bethel-šar-uṣur son of Šalammu (nos. 17:12–13, 18:16, 24:6–7); Bethel-šar-uṣur son of Ile'i-Nabu (no. 101:8–9); Bethel-šūru son of Arad-Banītu (no. 26:20–21); Bethel-aḫ-iddin son of Il-du-nūr (no. 17:15–16; cf. Wunsch, *Judaeans by the Waters of Babylon,* no. 6:18); Bethel-dīni-īpuš son of Mamanna (no. 72:2–3); Bethel-idra son of Nabu-šum-iddin (no. 45:17–18);

Adad-idri son of Zabūdu (no. 47:6–7); Urkittu-šarrat daughter of Bethel-šūru (no. 51:1–2); Bethel-ḫisni son of Bethel-šar-uṣur (no. 53:4–5); Arad-Banītu son of Ḫanana (Joannès and Lemaire, "Contrats babyloniens," no. 2:13–14); Itti-Nabu-balāṭu son of Zu-Batil (Pearce and Wunsch, *Documents of Judean Exiles*, 93 s.v. Zū-Bāt-il; cf. Wunsch, *Judaeans by the Waters of Babylon*, no. 18:5–6, Zu-Batil son of Nabu-aḫḫē-bulliṭ).

30. For the devotion of the Aramean diaspora in Egypt to Bethel, Nabu, and Banitu, see Van der Toorn, *Becoming Diaspora Jews*, 45–53.

31. See Pearce and Wunsch, *Documents of Judean Exiles*, 172, note to no. 45:5. Note also the family of Bethel-ab-uṣur son of Bethel-šar-uṣur son of Šalammu son of Baḫi-Esu, the latter name being Egyptian, "Desired-by-Isis," see nos. 17:12–13, 14–15; 27:4, 11; 46:4 (Šalammu son of Baḫi-Esu rented out his house in Al-Yaḫudu to Neriah son of Ahikam). See also Wunsch, *Judaeans by the Waters of Babylon*, no. 73:6, Bethel-šar-uṣur son of Ḫanapsi, the latter being an Egyptian name meaning "Shining One of Karnak."

32. See the ration lists from 595–570 BCE published by Ernst F. Weidner, "Jojachin, König von Juda, in babylonischen Keilschrifttexten," in *Mélanges syriens offerts à Monsieur René Dussaud* (Paris: Geuthner, 1939), 2:923–935; "Historical Documents, Nebuchadnezzar II (605–562), Varia," trans. A. Leo Oppenheim, *ANET*, 308; Manfred Weippert, *Historisches Textbuch zum Alten Testament*, GAT 10 (Göttingen: Vandenhoeck & Ruprecht, 2010), 425–430, nos. 265–267; discussion by Ran Zadok, *The Jews in Babylonia During the Chaldean and Achaemenian Periods According to the Babylonian Sources* (Haifa: University of Haifa, 1979), 39–40.

33. See Tero Alstola, *Judeans in Babylonia: A Study of Deportees in the Sixth and Fifth Centuries BCE*, CHANE 109 (Leiden: Brill, 2020), 87–91.

34. For a description of the agricultural activities of the diaspora Judeans, see Wunsch, *Judaeans by the Waters of Babylon*, 81–113.

35. See Pearce and Wunsch, *Documents of Judean Exiles*, nos. 14, 15, 19, 20, 21, etc. The *imittu* tax on fields was paid in kind to the local tax collector (in Al-Yaḫudu this was the Judean Ahikam), who might convert the crops into silver for payment to the royal administration, see no. 17.

36. See Pearce and Wunsch, *Documents of Judean Exiles*, nos. 12, 41, 86; Wunsch, *Judaeans by the Waters of Babylon*, nos. 4, 94.

37. See Pearce and Wunsch, *Documents of Judean Exiles*, nos. 5, 26, 32, 41, 44, 45, 61, 77, 98, 100.

38. According to Pearce and Wunsch, *Documents of Judean Exiles*, 114, comments to no. 12, the corvée period in Elam lasted two months.

39. See Wunsch, *Judaeans by the Waters of Babylon*, 115–119.

40. See Pearce and Wunsch, *Documents of Judean Exiles*, no. 96.

41. Pearce and Wunsch, *Documents of Judean Exiles,* no. 45, lists Abdi-Yaḫû as slave in the household of Ahikam (504 BCE). This is likely the same Abdi-Yaḫû who contracted a debt to Ahikam in 517 BCE, see no. 41.

42. See Abraham, "West Semitic and Judean Brides," esp. 206–208.

43. See Abraham, "West Semitic and Judean Brides." In view of the name of the bride, Nanaya-kānat, she may in fact have been an adopted Aramean rather than a native Judean. For this marriage, see also the discussion by Wunsch, *Judaeans by the Waters of Babylon,* 28. It should be noted that in both upper-class and lower-class mixed marriages, the women were sworn to loyalty by the gods of their Babylonian husbands; see Abraham, "West Semitic and Judean Brides," 198:23–28; Roth, *Babylonian Marriage Agreements,* no. 26:23–26.

44. The book of Ezekiel normally refers to the Judean elders as "the elders of Israel" (Ezek 14:1, 20:1). See also Jer 29:1, "the elders of the Golah."

45. For the text, see Johann N. Strassmaier, *Inschriften von Cambyses, König von Babylon (529–521 v. Chr.),* Babylonische Texte 8–9 (Leipzig: Eduard Pfeiffer, 1890), no. 85. For a discussion, see Johannes Hackl and Michael Jursa, "Egyptians in Babylonia in the Neo-Babylonian and Achaemenid Periods," in *Exile and Return: The Babylonian Context,* ed. Jonathan Stökl and Caroline Waerzeggers, BZAW 478 (Berlin: de Gruyter, 2015), 157–172, esp. 166. Wunsch, *Judaeans by the Waters of Babylon,* no. 27, refers to a lawsuit about which the Persian official consults with the citizens (*mār bānê*) and the city elders (*šībūt āli,* ˡúAB.BA.MEŠ URU); no. 82 deals with a legal case decided by the bailiff (*paqudu*) and the assembly of the citizens (*puḫur mār bānê*) of Bit-Abiram.

46. See Pearce and Wunsch, *Documents of Judean Exiles,* no. 10.

47. Note especially the Aramaic summary on the edge of an Akkadian contract, Pearce and Wunsch, *Documents of Judean Exiles,* no. 53:23–24: *byt'l ḥsny tmrn krn 6,* "Bethel-ḥisni [will deliver] six kor of dates." See also the Aramaic epigraphs in Joannès and Lemaire, "Contrats babyloniens," nos. 1, 5, 7, and the Aramaic epigraphs in nos. 40, 41, 42, 71B. For a study of the three Hebrew and sixteen Aramaic epigraphs on the tablets presently known, see James D. Moore, "Traces of Administrative Reform in the Hebrew and Aramaic Epigraphs of the Al-Yahudu and Related Tablets," *NABU* 2023/1, 66–69, no. 28. Moore argues that the shift from Hebrew to Aramaic was related to the imperial transfer after the rise of Cyrus: the three Hebrew epigraphs are all from the Neo-Babylonian period; the sixteen in Aramaic, from the Persian period.

48. Cf. Jer 10:11 (Aramaic phrase in a polemic against the Babylonian cult of idols) and Isa 44:15 (also against Babylonian idols, using the Aramaic verbs *slq, sgd,* and *p'l*). Note that the names Shabbetai, "born on the Sabbath," and Haggai, "born during the festival," are both linguistically Aramaic (cf. the Hebrew form *ḥaggî*) and come into use from the early

Persian period onward; see Gesenius[18], 323 s.v. *ḥaggay;* 1322 s.v. *šabbĕtay.*
Both names are found among Judeans in Babylonia, Egypt, and Judah.

49. See Roth, *Babylonian Marriage Agreements,* 92–95, no. 26.

50. See Pearce and Wunsch, *Documents of Judean Exiles,* no. 77. For the
    name Aqabi-Yāma, cf. the Hebrew name *'qbyh,* for which see Ran
    Zadok, *The Pre-Hellenistic Israelite Anthroponymy and Prosopography,*
    OLA 28 (Leuven: Peeters, 1988), 289–290. See also Nabu-uṣur son of
    Dalā-Yāma (Delaiah), no. 101:4–5 (533 BCE).

51. The author of the book of Esther, a novella about events at the Persian
    court, chose to provide his Judean heroes with the typically Babylonian
    names Esther (Hadassah) and Mordechai, both of them referring to
    Babylonian deities (Ishtar and Marduk).

52. See Pearce and Wunsch, *Documents of Judean Exiles,* nos. 2:1, 3:2, 4:2–3,
    and see discussion on p. 101. Cornelia Wunsch (*Judaeans by the Wa-
    ters of Babylon,* 38, 58 note 105) compellingly argues that Bel-šarru-uṣur
    changed his name to Yaḫu-šarru-uṣur after the accession of Naboni-
    dus so as not to be named after the crown prince Belshazzar (Bel-
    šarru-uṣur). Similarly, the Babylonian scribe Nabû-na'id (Nabonidus)
    changed his name to Nabû-nāṣir at the same time.

53. See Zadok, *Pre-Hellenistic Israelite Anthroponymy,* 12–13. See also the
    double name of Esther-Hadassah (Esth 2:7); see Frederick W. Bush,
    "Hadassah (person)," *AYBD* 3:13–14.

54. See Hanspeter Schaudig, "'Bel bows, Nabû stoops!' The Prophecy of
    Isaiah xlvi 1–2 as a Reflection of Babylonian 'Processional Omens,'" *VT*
    58 (2008): 557–572.

55. Pearce and Wunsch, *Documents of Judean Exiles,* no. 45, documents the
    division of the paternal estate by the sons of Ahikam in the city of Bab-
    ylon, in the presence of various Judean witnesses, on day 7 of Tashritu,
    in 504 BCE.

56. See the ration lists from 595–570 BCE published by Weidner, "Jojachin,
    König von Juda," and the other references mentioned in note 32 (above)
    in this chapter.

57. Note the occurrence of "the town of the Kabara river" (uru i₇ *Ka-ba-ra*)
    in Joannès and Lemaire, "Contrats babyloniens," no. 7:8, as the name of
    a settlement of West Semitic exiles.

58. See H. Jacob Katzenstein, *History of Tyre: From the Beginning of the
    Second Millennium B.C.E. Until the Fall of the Neo-Babylonian Empire
    in 538 B.C.E.* (Jerusalem: Schocken Institute for Jewish Research of the
    Jewish Theological Seminary of America, 1973), 328; Stefan Zawadski,
    "Nebuchadnezzar's Campaign in the 30th Year (575 B.C.): A Conflict
    with Tyre?," in *Treasures on Camels' Humps: Historical and Literary Stud-
    ies from the Ancient Near East Presented to Israel Eph'al,* ed. Mordechai
    Cohen and Dan'el Kahn (Jerusalem: Magnes, 2008), 331–336; Stefan

Zawadski, "The Chronology of Tyrian History in the Neo-Babylonian Period," *AoF* 42 (2015): 276–287.

59. For the intercessory prayer for foreign authorities, see also Ezra 6:10; *TAD* A4.7:26 // A4.8:25; note also the Cyrus Cylinder reference to intercessory prayer to the Babylonian gods for Cyrus and his son, see *COS* 2.124.

60. See, e.g., Oracle collection 3, "The Covenant of Aššur," in Simo Parpola, *Assyrian Prophecies*, SAA 9 (Helsinki: Helsinki University Press, 1997), 22–27, esp. 23; Marc J. H. Linssen, *The Cults of Uruk and Babylon: The Temple Ritual Texts as Evidence for Hellenistic Cult Practices*, CM 25 (Leiden: Brill-Styx, 2004), 223, lines 445–446 (Akkadian), 232 (translation), "Bel will bless you . . . [f]orev[er], he will ruin your enemy and overthrow your adversary."

61. See Ezek 32:1–16, pronounced in year 12, XII/1 = 586 BCE, March 22; Ezek 29:17–20, pronounced year 27, month I/1 = 571 BCE, April 22. For XII/1 as a religious high holy day in the city of Uruk, see Mark E. Cohen, *Festival and Calendars of the Ancient Near East* (Bethesda, MD: CDL Press, 2015), 447; Shana Zaia and Rosaura Cauchi, "Destination Eanna: Cultic Assemblies Visiting Uruk During the Neo-Babylonian Period," *Akkadica* 140 (2019): 161–178, esp. 167 and note 28 (references courtesy Paul-Alain Beaulieu).

62. On Ezekiel's familiarity with Babylonian culture, see Isaac Gluska, "Akkadian Influences on the Book of Ezekiel," in *An Experienced Scribe Who Neglects Nothing*, ed. Y. Sefati, Festschrift Jacob Klein (Bethesda, MD: CDL Press, 2005), 718–737; Martti Nissinen, "(How) Does the Book of Ezekiel Reveal Its Babylonian Context?," *WO* 45 (2015): 85–98.

63. For discussion of the text (é ᵈXXX uru *ša* ᶫⁱ*Arbāyyā*, dated on 9 Nabonidus = 547 BCE), see Israel Eph'al, *The Ancient Arabs: Nomads on the Borders of the Fertile Crescent 9th–5th Centuries B.C.* (Jerusalem: Magnes, 1984), 189–190; Muhammad A. Dandamaev, "Twin Towns and Ethnic Minorities in First-Millennium Babylonia," in *Commerce and Monetary Systems in the Ancient World: Means of Transmission and Cultural Interaction*, ed. Robert Rollinger and Christoph Ulf, Melammu Symposia 5 (Stuttgart: Franz Steiner, 2004), 137–149, esp. 145.

64. So Mowinckel, *Studien zu dem Buche Ezra-Nehemia*, 76. See the discussion by Joseph Blenkinsopp, *Ezra-Nehemiah*, OTL (London: SCM, 1989), 165–166; Hugh Williamson, *Ezra-Nehemiah*, WBC 16 (Grand Rapids: Zondervan, 1985), 116–117; Tamara Cohn Eskenazi, *Ezra: A New Translation with Introduction and Commentary*, AYB 14A (New Haven: Yale University Press, 2023), 329. For a critical appraisal of the suggestion, see Bob Becking, *Ezra and Nehemiah*, HCOT (Leuven: Peeters, 2018), 125.

65. Both Babylonian and biblical texts emphasize the importance of praying "with washed hands"; see Marten Stol, *Letters from Collections in Philadelphia, Chicago and Berkeley,* AbB 11 (Leiden: Brill, 1986), no. 60:25–28, "I pray for you constantly before my Lord and my Mistress with both my hands washed." See also Wilfred G. Lambert, *Babylonian Wisdom Literature* (Oxford: Clarendon, 1960), 146:54–55; Erica Reiner, *Šurpu: A Collection of Sumerian and Akkadian Incantations,* AfOB 11 (Graz: E. Weidner, 1958) 20:44 (Šurpu III 44); Ps 26:6–7, Jdt 12:8. Cf. Acts 16:13, "On the sabbath day we went outside the gate [of Philippi in Macedonia] by the river [*para potamon*], where we supposed there was a place of prayer [*proseuchē*]; and we sat down and spoke to the women who had gathered there" (NRSV).

66. On the possibility of communal readings from the prophets in the Babylonian diaspora, see Albertz, trans. Bowden, *History of Israelite Religion,* 2:380–381.

67. See Bryan E. Beyer, "Zerubbabel," *AYBD* 6:1084–1086. "Offspring of Babylon" is the proud designation of a man born as a citizen of Babylon; see Johann Jakob Stamm, *Die akkadische Namengebung* (Leipzig: Hinrichs, 1939), 269–270. See also the occurrence of one Zēr-Bābili son of Ḫanapsi/Panapsi (Egyptian name meaning "shining one of Karnak") and brother of Bitil-šar-uṣur (cf. Bethel-sharezer, Zech 7:2), in a contract from Bīt-Abiram; see Wunsch, *Judaeans by the Waters of Babylon,* no. 73:13. See also Pearce and Wunsch, *Documents of Judean Exiles,* 53 s.v. "Ḫanapsi."

68. See Yair Hoffman, "The Fasts in the Book of Zechariah and the Fashioning of National Remembrance," in *Judah and the Judeans in the Neo-Babylonian Period,* ed. Oded Lipschits and Joseph Blenkinsopp (Winona Lake, IN: Eisenbrauns, 2003), 169–218.

69. The only one of those fasts preserved in contemporary Judaism is Tisha B'Av (V/9), in commemoration of the destruction of Jerusalem. The fast for the murder of Gedaliah was celebrated on the second day of Tashritu in order to avoid coincidence with New Year's day.

70. On Gedaliah, the stamp seals attributed to him, and the political role of the Shaphanides, see Peter van der Veen, "Gedaliah ben Aḥiqam in the Light of Epigraphic Evidence (a Response to Bob Becking)," in *New Seals and Inscriptions, Hebrew, Idumean and Cuneiform,* ed. Meir Lubetski, HBM 8 (Sheffield: Sheffield Phoenix Press, 2007), 55–70.

71. See Hoffman, "Fasts in the Book of Zechariah," 196–197.

72. For Ezekiel, see Ernst Kutsch, *Die chronologischen Daten des Ezechielbuches,* OBO 62 (Freiburg: Universitätsverlag; Göttingen: Vandenhoeck & Ruprecht, 1985), 35 note 74: "Diese Art, bei Daten nicht nur Jahr und Monat . . . sondern auch den Tag eines Ereignisses anzugeben, findet

sich in Israel erst vom Exil an." For Haggai and Zechariah, see Hag 1:1, 15; 2:1, 10, 20; Zech 1:1, 7; 7:1.

73. For the Beersheba ostraca, see Joseph Naveh, "The Aramaic Inscriptions," in *Beer-Sheba I: Excavations at Tel-Beer-Sheba 1969–1971 Seasons*, ed. Yohanan Aharoni (Tel Aviv: Tel Aviv University, Institute of Archaeology, 1973), 79–82, Pls. 35–38; Joseph Naveh, "The Aramaic Ostraca from Tel Beer-sheba (Seasons 1971–1976)," *TA* 6 (1979): 182–198, Pls. 24–31.

74. For the ritual significance of the seventh day in Babylonia, see already the Old Babylonian Atrahasis Epic, tablet I, lines 221–222: "On the first, seventh, and fifteenth days of the month, let me [the god Enki] establish a purification, a bath," *COS* 1.130:451, trans. Benjamin R. Foster. See also the Epic of Creation, V, 15–18, *COS* 1.111:399, trans. Benjamin R. Foster. In Babylonian hemerologies, days 7, 14, 21, and 28 count as "unpropitious" (*ūmu lemnu*, "evil day"), for which reason the execution of plans should be postponed to another day. The underlying logic is based on numerology, in which 7 is an evil number, as demonstrated by the fact that day 19 is the ultimate unfavorable day, since day 19 is in fact day 49 reckoned from the previous month, and 49 is 7 multiplied by 7; see Benno Landsberger, *Der kultische Kalender Babylonier und Assyrer*, LSS 6/1–2 (Leipzig: J. C. Hinrichs, 1915), 119–120.

75. It should be noted that the personal name Shabbethai, "born on the Sabbath," is linguistically Aramaic and occurs first in the Persian period, among the Judeans in Babylonia (Šabbataya), in the diaspora in Egypt (Šbty, fem. Šbtyt), and in Judah; see Gesenius[18], 1322 s.v. *šabbětay*.

76. For studies of the intellectual interaction between Babylonians and Judeans in the sixth century BCE, see, e.g., Isaac Gluska, "Akkadian Influences on the Book of Ezekiel," in *An Experienced Scribe Who Neglects Nothing: Ancient Near Eastern Studies in Honor of Jacob Klein*, ed. Yitschak Sefati, Pinhas Artzi, Chaim Cohen, Barry L. Eichler, and Victor Avigdor Hurowitz (Bethesda, MD: CDL Press, 2005), 718–737; Abraham Winitzer, "Assyriology and Jewish Studies in Tel Aviv: Ezekiel Among the Babylonian Literati," in *Encounters by the Rivers of Babylon: Scholarly Conversations Between Jews, Iranians, and Babylonians in Antiquity*, ed. Uri Gabbay and S. Secunda, TSAJ 160 (Tübingen: Mohr Siebeck, 2014), 163–216; Dalit Rom-Shiloni and Corrine Carvalho, eds., "Ezekiel in Its Babylonian Context," *WO* 45 (2015): 3–110.

77. Pearce and Wunsch, *Documents of Judean Exiles*, 170–173, no. 45. The document is dated 7/VII, 504 BCE. Possibly the sons of Ahikam were in the city on account of the autumn Akitu festival and used the occasion to settle part of the business of their father, who had been selling his beer in Babylon for a while; see no. 44. For Judeans in the city of Babylon, see also Wunsch, *Judaeans by the Waters of Babylon*, 127–128.

78. See Alstola, *Judeans in Babylonia,* 100–101.
79. Lachish Letter 3, lines 19–21, trans. Dennis Pardee, *COS* 3.42:79–80:
    "(Herewith) I am also sending to my lord the letter of Ṭobyahu, servant
    of the king, which came to Shallum son of Yada from the prophet and
    which says 'Beware.'" For the Hebrew text and discussion, see Johannes
    Renz and Wolfgang Röllig, *Handbuch der althebräischen Epigraphik,*
    3 vols. (Darmstadt: Wissenschaftliche Buchgesellschaft, 1995–2003),
    1:412–419. The exact meaning of the Lachish letter is hard to establish,
    but the practice of prophets communicating their messages by writing
    (not as a means of preservation) is well-attested in the Mari archives;
    see, e.g., Jean-Marie Durand, *Archives Épistolaires de Mari I/1,* ARM 26
    (Paris: Éditions Recherche sur les Civilisations, 1988), no. 194: "Speak
    to Zimrilim: Thus says the prophet (*āpilum*) of Shamash, 'Thus says
    Shamash. . . .'" The tradition about the letter of Elijah to King Jehoram
    of Judah (2 Chr 21:12–15) belongs to the realm of legend.
80. For the earliest mention, see Pearce and Wunsch, *Documents of Judean
    Exiles,* no. 18:7–8 (512 BCE).
81. See Matthew W. Stolper, *Entrepreneurs and Empire: The Murašû Ar-
    chive, the Murašû Firm, and Persian Rule in Babylonia,* PIHANS 54
    (Leiden: NINO, 1985).
82. For an English translation of the Cyrus Cylinder, see "Cyrus Cylinder,"
    trans. Mordechai Cogan, *COS* 2.124:314–316.
83. See Gauthier Tolini, "From Syria to Babylon and Back: The Neirab
    Archive," in *Exile and Return: The Babylonian Context,* ed. Jonathan
    Stökl and Caroline Waerzeggers, BZAW 478 (Berlin: de Gruyter, 2015),
    58–93; Alstola, *Judeans in Babylonia,* 237–250.
84. See Hag 1:1, VI/1, 2 Darius (cf. 1:15, VI/24, 2 Darius); 2:1, VII/21, [2
    Darius]; 2:10, IX/24, 2 Darius; 2:20, IX/24, [2 Darius]; Zech 1:1, VIII, 2
    Darius; 1:7, XII/24, 2 Darius; 7:1, IX/4, 4 Darius.
85. A cuneiform contract of sale of oxen and sheep, drawn up at Haran
    in 521 ("accession year of Darius," presumably Darius I) but found at
    Tawilan in Edom, more than six hundred miles south of Haran, has
    been taken as evidence of an Edomite return from exile around 520
    BCE; see Ernst Axel Knauf, "Bethel: The Israelite Impact on Judean
    Language and Literature," in *Judah and the Judeans in the Persian Pe-
    riod,* ed. Oded Lipschits and Manfred Oeming (Winona Lake, IN:
    Eisenbrauns, 2006), 291–349, esp. 303 and note 57. For the tablet, see
    Stephanie Dalley, "The Cuneiform Tablet from Tell Tawilan," *Levant*
    16 (1984): 19–22; John R. Bartlett, *Edom and the Edomites,* JSOTSup 77
    (Sheffield: JSOT Press, 1989), 225–227.
86. The name Bethel-sharezer (Zech 7:2) occurs several times in the ar-
    chives of Al-Yaḫudu and vicinity; see Pearce and Wunsch, *Documents of
    Judean Exiles,* 47, under Bīt-il-šar-uṣur.

87. On the significance of the reign of Darius for the position of Judah in the Persian Empire, see Kenneth G. Hoglund, *Achaemenid Imperial Administration in Syria-Palestine and the Missions of Ezra and Nehemiah*, SBLDS 125 (Atlanta: Scholars Press, 1992), esp. 23–29.

88. For linguistic indications of the Babylonian background, see Hugh G. M. Williamson, "The Setting of Deutero-Isaiah: Some Linguistic Considerations," in *Exile and Return: The Babylonian Context*, ed. Jonathan Stökl and Caroline Waerzeggers, BZAW 478 (Berlin: de Gruyter, 2015), 253–267, esp. 259–267, with discussion of Akkadian loans in Isa 45:2, *dūru*, "city wall"; Isa 40:20, *musukkannu*, "Indian hardwood"; Isa 44:4, *bīnu*, "tamarisk." One could add the expressions *kesep ṣōrep* = *kaspu ṣarpu*, "refined silver" (Isa 40:19); *bdym* = *brym* = *bārû*, "(the signs of) the diviners" (Isa 44:25; cf. 47:13; Jer 50:36). See also Shalom M. Paul, "Deutero-Isaiah and Cuneiform Royal Inscriptions," *JAOS* 88/1 = AOS 53, *Essays in Memory of A. E. Speiser* (New Haven: American Oriental Society, 1968), 180–186.

89. The translation follows the NRSV but has "city walls" instead of the NRSV's "mountains" on the assumption that *wahădûrîm* uses the Babylonian loanword *dūru*, "city wall"; see previous note.

90. In the words of the Cyrus Cylinder, "He [Marduk] made him enter his city Babylon without fighting or battle; (. . .). All the people of Babylon (. . .) bowed to him and kissed his feet," *COS* 2.124:315, trans. Mordechai Cogan. Cf. "The Babylonian Chronicle," trans. Allan Millard, *COS* 1.137:467–468, which also says, in more sober prose, that Cyrus entered Babylon "without battle."

91. See Cyrus Cylinder, line 12 (*ittamaḫ qātuššu*); see Hanspeter Schaudig, *Die Inschriften Nabonids von Babylon und Kyros' des Grossen samt den in ihrem Umfeld entstandenen Tendenzinschriften: Textausgabe und Grammatik*, AOAT 256 (Münster: Ugarit-Verlag, 2001), 550–556.

92. The text is known as the Verse Account of Nabonidus; see Schaudig, *Inschriften Nabonids*, 563–578.

93. See Peter Machinist, "Mesopotamian Imperialism and Israelite Religion: A Case Study from the Second Isaiah," in *Symbiosis, Symbolism, and the Power of the Past: Proceedings of the Centennial Symposium of the Albright Institute 2000*, ed. William G. Dever and Seymour Gitin (Winona Lake, IN: Eisenbrauns, 2003), 237–264.

94. See also the summons in Zech 2:10–11 [2:6–7], the urgency of which betrays the disillusion of the returnees with their small number: "Up, up! Flee from the land of the north, says the Lord; . . . Up! Escape to Zion, you that live with daughter Babylon" (NRSV).

95. For traditions about the death of Jeremiah and the location of his grave, see Joachim Jeremias, *Heiligengräber in Jesu Umwelt* (Göttingen: Vandenhoeck & Ruprecht, 1958), 108–111.

96. For a discussion of the various allusions to Jeremiah in Second Isaiah, see Benjamin D. Sommer, "New Light on the Composition of Jeremiah," *CBQ* 61 (1999): 646–666, esp. 647–664.

97. For Jeremiah as God's suffering servant, see the so-called Confessions of Jeremiah, esp. Jer 11:18–12:6, 15:10–21, 18:18–23, 20:7–18. Note the parallels between Jer 1:5 ("Before I formed you in the womb I knew you, / and before you were born I consecrated you; / I appointed you a prophet to the nations," NRSV) and Isa 49:1 ("The LORD called me before I was born, / while I was in my mother's womb he named me," NRSV); Jer 11:19 ("But I was like a gentle lamb / led to the slaughter," NRSV) and Isa 53:7 ("like a lamb that is led to the slaughter / . . . / so he did not open his mouth," NRSV). For a discussion, see Katherine J. Dell, "The Suffering Servant of Deutero-Isaiah: Jeremiah Revisited," in *Genesis, Isaiah and Psalms: A Festschrift to Honour Professor John Emerton for His Eightieth Birthday,* ed. Katherine J. Dell, Graham Davies, and Yee Von Koh (Leiden: Brill, 2010), 119–134.

98. From a wealth of literature on the subject, see, e.g., Daniel Boyarin, *Dying for God: Martyrdom and the Making of Christianity and Judaism* (Stanford, CA: Stanford University Press, 1999).

99. The description echoes the title of a landmark publication on Elephantine by Bezalel Porten, *Archives from Elephantine: The Life of an Ancient Jewish Military Colony* (Berkeley: University of California Press, 1968). Porten's study was the main source for the first chapter of Simon Schama's *The Story of the Jews* (London: Bodley Head, 2013).

100. See Yonatan Adler, *The Origins of Judaism: An Archaeological-Historical Reappraisal,* AYBRL (New Haven: Yale University Press, 2022).

101. The evidence has been surveyed on more than one occasion in the context of an investigation of ethnicity at Elephantine. See, e.g., Bob Becking, *Identity in Persian Egypt: The Fate of the Yehudite Community of Elephantine* (University Park, PA: Eisenbrauns, 2020), 18–20, with references to earlier literature.

102. For an introduction and description, see the contributions by Tawny Holm and Karel van der Toorn in *Elephantine in Context: Studies on the History, Religion and Literature of the Judeans in Persian Period Egypt,* ed. Reinhard G. Kratz and Bernd U. Schipper, FAT 155 (Tübingen: Mohr Siebeck, 2022), 323–351 ("Papyrus Amherst 63 and the Arameans of Egypt"), 353–365 ("The Background of the Elephantine Jews in Light of Papyrus Amherst 63").

103. The Aramean diaspora communities at Syene are best known through the Hermopolis letters, for which see *TAD* A2.1–7.

104. There are three translations in English of the full text; see Richard C. Steiner, "The Aramaic Text in Demotic Script," *COS* 1.99:309–327; Karel van der Toorn, *Papyrus Amherst 63,* AOAT 448 (Münster:

Ugarit-Verlag, 2018), the English translation being also available, with some corrections, in Van der Toorn, *Becoming Diaspora Jews*, 149–197; and Tawny Holm, *Aramaic Literary Texts*, WAW (Atlanta: SBL, forthcoming).

105. Amherst 63, 17:1–6.

106. Amherst 63, 12:11–19 and 13:1–17. The title "our Bull" (*trn*) is found in 12:17 and the reference to Bethel in 12:18.

107. Cf. *TAD* B7.3:3 with *TAD* C3.15:128. For the identification of Bethel and Yaho, compare also the name Bethel-nathan son of Yeho-nathan, *TAD* B6.4:10.

108. See József Zsengellér, "The Samaritan Diaspora in Antiquity," *ActAnt* 56 (2016): 157–175, esp. 164–165. For a study of the village, see Clemens Kuhs, *Das Dorf Samareia im griechisch-römischen Ägypten: Eine papyrologische Untersuchung* (MA Thesis, University of Heidelberg, 1996), accessible through http://www.ub.uni-heidelberg.de/archiv/497 (references courtesy Tawny Holm).

109. See *TAD* B7.3:3; B7.2:7–8.

110. See *TAD* C3.15:1, 123–128.

111. For Eshem-Bethel and Herem-Bethel in papyrus Amherst 63, see 16:1, 14, 15 (Eshem-Bethel) and 17:14 (Herem-Bethel).

112. See Van der Toorn, *Becoming Diaspora Jews*, 45–49.

113. One possible case of Judean-Aramean intermarriage may be reflected in the names Malkiah son of Yathom son of Hadad-Nuri (*TAD* C3.15:23; cf. B2.2:19). Another case involves Ahutab, a prominent woman in the ostraca, whose name echoes her Babylonian-Aramean background; see Hélène Lozachmeur, *La collection Clermont-Ganneau: Ostraca, épigraphes sur jarre, étiquettes de bois*, Mémoires de l'Académie des Inscriptions et des Belles-Lettres 35 (Paris: De Boccard, 2006), 489–490.

114. See *TAD* B3.3 (marriage of Judean temple servant with Tapamet, Egyptian woman servant in the household of Meshullam son of Zakkur); B2.6 (marriage of Lady Mibtahiah with Eshor, Egyptian architect in the service of the Persian government). See also C4.6:5; C4.4:2; C3.15:4; B2.2:17; Cl.-G. 177; A4.4:5; D3.17:10 for various other cases. The list is not exhaustive.

115. See *TAD* D7.21:3 (greeting "by Yaho and Khnum"), B2.8:5 (Mibtahiah's oath by the Egyptian goddess Satet).

116. Biblical "Pathros" (Isa 11:1; Jer 44:1, 15) renders Egyptian *p3-t3-rsj*, the Paturisi of Assyrian sources, "southern country," to which both Elephantine and Syene belonged.

117. See *TAD* A4.7, A4.8 (drafts of petition to Bagohi in Jerusalem, with mention of a previous message to the authorities in Samaria), A4.9 (memorandum registering the support of Bagohi and Delaiah for the

reconstruction of the temple). The memorandum makes mention of vegetal offerings (*minḥâ*) and incense (*lĕbônâ*) to be brought in the new temple, but omits any reference to animal sacrifice—probably on purpose; see also the written offer of a bribe by leading members of the Elephantine community extant in *TAD* A4.10, which also avoids the mention of animal sacrifice (lines 10–11).

118. See *TAD* C3.28:85, 113, 114. For a discussion, see Sylvie Honigman, "Jewish Communities in Hellenistic Egypt: Different Responses to Different Environments," in *Jewish Identities in Antiquity: Studies in Memory of Menahem Stern*, ed. Lee I. Levine and Daniel R. Schwartz, TSAJ 130 (Tübingen: Mohr Siebeck, 2009), 117–135, esp. 121–123.

119. See Erle Leichty, *The Royal Inscriptions of Esarhaddon, King of Assyria (680–669 BC)*, RINAP 4 (Winona Lake, IN: Eisenbrauns, 2011), 196, "Esarhaddon 104" ii 2–9: "The merciful god Marduk wrote that the calculated time of its abandonment (should last) 70 years, (but) his heart was quickly soothed, and he reversed the numbers and (thus) ordered its (re)occupation to be (after) 11 years." In cuneiform, 70 is written with one vertical stroke (60) followed by a wedge (10); 11, with a wedge (10) followed by one vertical stroke (1).

120. The purpose of Hananiah's mission to Egypt in 419 BCE was to bring the various Judean diaspora communities in line with the official calendar for the Feast of Unleavened Bread (and presumably Passover); see *TAD* A4.1 and the discussion by Ingo Kottsieper, "Die Religionspolitik der Achämeniden und die Juden von Elephantine," in *Religion und Religionskontakte im Zeitalter der Achämeniden*, ed. Reinhard G. Kratz (Gütersloh: Kaiser, 2002), 150–178, esp. 150–158. For a fuller discussion, see Chapter 5, "Ethnic Religion," in the present book.

121. For an outspoken and rather radical position in this debate, see Steve Mason, "Jews, Judaeans, Judaizing, Judaism: Problems of Categorization in Ancient History," *JSJ* 38 (2007): 457–512.

Chapter 5. Ethnic Religion

1. See "The Cyrus Cylinder," trans. Mordechai Cogan, *COS* 2.124:314–316, esp. lines 24–25. For a critical edition of the text, see Hanspeter Schaudig, *Die Inschriften Nabonids von Babylon und Kyros' des Grossen*, AOAT 256 (Münster: Ugarit-Verlag, 2001), 550–556.

2. See, e.g., Eric M. Meyers, "The Persian Period and the Judean Restoration: From Zerubbabel to Nehemiah," in *Ancient Israelite Religion*, ed. Patrick D. Miller, Jr., Paul D. Hanson, and S. Dean McBride (Philadelphia: Fortress, 1987), 509–521; Frank Moore Cross, *From Epic to Canon: History and Literature in Ancient Israel* (Baltimore: Johns Hopkins University Press, 1998), 151–202, chapters entitled "A Reconstruction of

the Judaean Restoration" and "Samaria and Jerusalem in the Era of Restoration."

3. On the Persian royal mail system and the royal couriers, see Pierre Briant, *From Cyrus to Alexander: A History of the Persian Empire*, trans. Peter T. Daniels (Winona Lake, IN: Eisenbrauns, 2002), 369–371. An echo of the marvel at, and fantasies about, Persian court life can be found in the book of Esther, e.g., Esth 1:5–9.

4. For the influence of Persian religion on Israelite religion during the Persian and Hellenistic periods, see Mary Boyce, "Persian Religion in the Achaemenid Age," *CHJ* 1:279–307; Shaul Shaked, "Iranian Influence on Judaism: First Century B.C.E. to Second Century C.E.," *CHJ* 1:308–325. Most cases of Persian influence surface in texts only from the Hellenistic period, such as the dualism found in the sectarian texts from Qumran (see Chapter 6, "Scriptural Religion," in the present book). One indubitable instance of religious borrowing is the demon Asmodeus in the book of Tobit, whose name is plausibly explained only through reference to Aešma-daeva, "wrath demon"; see Shaked, "Iranian Influence," 318. Ab de Jong, "Iranian Connections in the Dead Sea Scrolls," in *The Oxford Handbook of the Dead Sea Scrolls*, ed. Timothy H. Lim and John J. Collins (New York: Oxford University Press, 2010), 479–500, shows that the Persian influence reflected in the post-Persian-period Dead Sea Scrolls is mostly evident in loanwords and imagery, a major element of the latter being the representation of God as emperor surrounded by courtiers.

5. On Persian loanwords in Hebrew, see Aren Wilson-Wright, "From Persepolis to Jerusalem: A Reevaluation of Old Persian-Hebrew Contact in the Achaemenid Period," *VT* 65 (2015): 152–167. Note that the Persian term *dāta*, "law," which entered Hebrew as *dāt*, is used in modern Hebrew as the word for "religion."

6. On the book of Tobit, see Carey A. Moore, "Tobit, book of," *AYBD* 6:585–594, esp. 591 for a brief discussion of the date. The Dead Sea Scrolls have yielded five fragments of Tobit, four in Aramaic and one in Hebrew (4Q196–200).

7. George W. E. Nickelsburg, "Enoch, First Book of," *AYBD* 2:508–516, esp. 509, with reference to Matthew Black, *The Books of Enoch or 1 Enoch: A New English Edition with Commentary and Textual Notes*, SVTP 7 (Leiden: Brill, 1985), 387.

8. The term also occurs in Job 5:1, "To which of the holy ones will you turn?," here too in reference to mediating angels.

9. For a study of heaven modeled after a palace with a king (God) surrounded by courtiers (angels) in the Book of the Watchers (1 Enoch 1–36), a work of roughly the same period as the Astronomical Book; see Philip F. Esler, *God's Court and Courtiers in the Book of the Watchers:*

Re-Interpreting Heaven in 1 Enoch 1–36 (Eugene, OR: Cascade Books, 2017).

10. The parallel passage of 1 Esdr 8:11 speaks about "the seven Friends [*philoi*] the counselors."

11. For a discussion of the college of seven counselors, see Briant, *From Cyrus to Alexander*, 128–130.

12. See Briant, *From Cyrus to Alexander*, 369–371.

13. See E. Theodore Mullen, *The Assembly of the Gods: The Divine Council in Canaanite and Early Hebrew Literature*, HSM 24 (Chico, CA: Scholars Press, 1980), 113–280; Simon B. Parker, "Saints," *DDD*, 718–720; John J. Collins, "Saints of the Most High," *DDD*, 720–722.

14. Hecataeus of Abdera, writing around 300 BCE, praises the Jews for the sacrifices they are willing to make to hold on to the monotheism of their law; see Josephus, *C. Ap.* 1.190–193.

15. See Karel van der Toorn, *Papyrus Amherst 63*, AOAT 448 (Münster: Ugarit-Verlag, 2018), 174, commentary on papyrus Amherst 63, 13:14–15.

16. The quotation of words put in the mouth of Cyrus is from the Cyrus Cylinder, trans. Cogan, 315.

17. See Gard Granerød, "YHW the God of Heaven: An *interpretatio persica et aegyptiaca* of YHW in Elephantine," *JSJ* 52 (2021): 1–26. See also the reference to "the sun of righteousness . . . , with healing in its wings" (Mal 3:20 [4:2] NRSV).

18. Nearly all we know about Sheshbazzar is his name, which is an adaptation into Hebrew of the Babylonian name Sin-ab-uṣur, "Sin-protect-the-father"; see Cross, "Samaria and Jerusalem in the Era of the Restoration," in *From Epic to Canon*, 173–202, esp. 179–180 note 21. The name Sin-ab-uṣur occurs among the witnesses in tablets from Al-Yaḫudu and Našar; see Laurie E. Pearce and Cornelia Wunsch, *Documents of Judean Exiles and West Semites in Babylonia in the Collection of David Sofer*, CUSAS 28 (Bethesda, MD: CDL Press, 2014), no. 27:19–20 ("Barik-Il son of Sin-ab-uṣur"), no. 71:13–14 ("Iddinâ son of Sin-ab-uṣur"). The occurrences have no connection with Sheshbazzar but demonstrate that the name was current at the time and familiar to Babylonian Judeans. Note that the Samarian governor Sanballat also carries a theophoric name referring to the moon god (Sin-uballiṭ).

19. Note the references to the reign of Darius in Hag 1:1, VI/1, 2 Darius (cf. 1:15, VI/24, 2 Darius); 2:1, VII/21, [2 Darius]; 2:10, IX/24, 2 Darius; 2:20, IX/24, [2 Darius]; Zech 1:1, VIII, 2 Darius; 1:7, XII/24, 2 Darius; 7:1, IX/4, 4 Darius. For the Neirabians returning, see Gauthier Tolini, "From Syria to Babylon and Back: The Neirab Archive," in *Exile and Return: The Babylonian Context*, ed. Jonathan Stökl and Caroline Waerzeggers, BZAW 478 (Berlin: de Gruyter, 2015), 58–93; Tero Alstola, *Judeans in Babylonia: A Study of Deportees in the Sixth and Fifth Centuries BCE*, CHANE 109

(Leiden: Brill, 2020), 237–250. A cuneiform contract of sale of oxen and sheep, drawn up at Haran in 521 ("accession year of Darius," presumably Darius I) but found at Tawilan in Edom, some more than six hundred miles south of Haran, has been taken as evidence of an Edomite return from exile around 520 BCE; see Ernst Axel Knauf, "Bethel: The Israelite Impact on Judean Language and Literature," in *Judah and the Judeans in the Persian Period,* ed. Oded Lipschits and Manfred Oeming (Winona Lake, IN: Eisenbrauns, 2006), 291–349, esp. 303 and note 57. For the tablet, see Stephanie Dalley, "The Cuneiform Tablet from Tell Tawilan," *Levant* 16 (1984): 19–22; John R. Bartlett, *Edom and the Edomites,* JSOTSup 77 (Sheffield: JSOT Press, 1989), 225–227.

20. See also Briant, *From Cyrus to Alexander,* 47, who observes, "it is possible that many of the events dated by the chronicler [i.e., the author of Ezra-Nehemiah] to the beginning of the reign of Cyrus actually took place during the reign of Cambyses or even later." In the same vein, he suggests, "It is possible that the province of Judah was not created until the time of Cambyses" (49).

21. On the particular ideological slant of Ezra-Nehemiah, see Tamara Cohn Eskenazi, *In an Age of Prose: A Literary Approach to Ezra-Nehemiah,* SBLMS 36 (Atlanta: Scholars Press, 1988); Eskenazi, *Ezra: A New Translation with Introduction and Commentary,* AYB 14A (New Haven: Yale University Press, 2023), 33–35. On the meaning of *qāhāl* in Ezra-Nehemiah and 1–2 Chronicles, see Sigmund Mowinckel, *Studien zu dem Buche Ezra-Nehemia, I: Die nachchronische Redaktion des Buches. Die Listen* (Oslo: Oslo University Press, 1964), 87–89.

22. For the dating of the sacred precinct and the adjacent building on Mount Gerizim, see Yitzhaq Magen, "The Dating of the First Phase of the Samaritan Temple at Mount Gerizim in Light of the Archaeological Evidence," in *Judah and the Judeans in the Fourth Century B.C.E.,* ed. Oded Lipschits, Gary N. Knoppers, and Rainer Albertz (Winona Lake, IN: Eisenbrauns, 2007), 157–211.

23. Inscriptions from the Hellenistic period found in the vicinity of Gerizim refer to it as the "sacrifice house" (*byt dbḥ*'); see Yitzhak Magen, Haggai Misgav, and Levana Tsfania, *Mount Gerizim Excavations, Volume 1: The Aramaic, Hebrew and Samaritan Inscriptions,* Judea and Samaria Publications 2 (Jerusalem: Israel Antiquities Authority, 2004), no. 199. The terminology is in keeping with the designation of the Jerusalem temple as *byt zbḥ* ("house of sacrifice") in 2 Chr 7:12 and the reference to the Elephantine temple as *byt mdbḥ*' ("altar house") in *TAD* A4.9:3.

24. It is entirely possible that John Hyrcanus meant to force the Samaritans to conform to Jewish practices and to accept Jerusalem as sole religious center, as argued by Jonathan Bourgel, "The Destruction of

the Samaritan Temple by John Hyrcanus: A Reconsideration," *JBL* 135 (2016): 505–523. The practical consequence of his action was a widening of the rift between the two communities.

25. See Josephus, *Ant.* 11.310–324. For a discussion of the Aaronide pedigree of both priesthoods, see Gary N. Knoppers, *Jews and Samaritans: The Origins and History of Their Early Relations* (New York: Oxford University Press, 2013), 190–191.

26. The Hebrew text of the passage shifts from third-person singular to third-person plural. Though most Bible translations opt to read this as a reference to one priest, the historical likelihood lies with the plural. See the observations by James A. Montgomery and Henry Snyder Gehman, *The Books of Kings*, ICC (Edinburgh: T&T Clark, 1951), 473. For the phenomenon of priests instructed to relocate to a different geographical area to implant or reinforce the cult of a particular deity, see Paul-Alain Beaulieu, "Temple Towns and Nation Building: Migrations of Babylonian Priestly Families in the Late Periods," *JANER* 19 (2019): 3–17. Beaulieu observes that the migrations of priests attested in the Neo-Babylonian period "were motivated primarily by political reasons such as imposing the cult of official deities in local sanctuaries, or the need to maintain a memory landscape of venerable cult centers" (from the Abstract on p. 3). See also the discussion of the mission of Ezra in the present chapter.

27. On the date of Josiah's expansion to the north and his actions against Bethel, see Mordechai Cogan and Hayim Tadmor, *II Kings: A New Translation with Introduction and Commentary*, AYB 11 (New York: Doubleday, 1988; repr. New Haven: Yale University Press), 298–299.

28. Aramaic inscriptions from the Hellenistic period, found in the close vicinity of Gerizim, refer to the Samarian temple as [*byt*] *yhwh*; see Magen, Misgav, and Tsfania, *Mount Gerizim Excavations*, no. 383. See also nos. 149–155, which contain the phrase "before God/the Lord [*'lh'*, *'dny*] in this place."

29. See Jan Dušek, *Les manuscrits araméens du Wadi Daliyeh et la Samarie vers 450–332 av. J.-C.*, CHANE 30 (Leiden: Brill, 2007), 486–494; Knoppers, *Jews and Samaritans*, 109–120, esp. 117.

30. See the discussion by Cogan and Tadmor, *II Kings*, 176–180; Wilhelm Rudolph, *Jeremia*, 3rd ed., HAT 1/12 (Tübingen: Mohr Siebeck, 1968), 289.

31. On the history of the Tobiads of Ammon, see Benjamin Mazar, "The Tobiads," *IEJ* 7 (1957): 137–145, 229–238.

32. See Ulrich Hübner, "Idumea," *AYBD* 3:382–383.

33. During the Neo-Babylonian period, the area of Judah had shrunk considerably; see Oded Lipschits, *The Fall and Rise of Jerusalem: Judah Under Babylonian Rule* (Winona Lake, IN: Eisenbrauns, 2005), esp. ch. 3:

"Changes in the Borders of Judah Between the End of the Iron Age and the Persian Period" (134–183).

34. See Diana Vikander Edelman, "Edom: A Historical Geography," in *You Shall Not Abhor an Edomite for He Is Your Brother: Edom and Seir in History and Tradition*, ed. D. V. Edelman, ABS 3 (Atlanta: Scholars Press, 1995), 1–11.

35. See Yigal Levin, "The Religion of Idumea and Its Relationship to Early Judaism," *Religions* 11, no. 10 (2020): 487, see esp. p. 5 of 27, https://doi.org/10.3390/rel11100487.

36. See Jacob M. Myers, "Edom and Judah in the Sixth–Fifth Centuries B.C.," in *Near Eastern Studies in Honor of William Foxwell Albright*, ed. Hans Goedicke (Baltimore: Johns Hopkins University Press, 1971), 377–392; John R. Bartlett, *Edom and the Edomites*, JSOTSup 77 (Sheffield: Sheffield Academic Press, 1989), 168–172. Note also the fifth-century BCE Aramaic inscription on a silver vessel, found in Lower Egypt (Tell el-Maskhuta), mentioning "Qaynu, son of Gashmu, king of Qedar"; see William J. Dumbrell, "The Tell el-Maskhuṭa Bowls and the 'Kingdom' of Qedar in the Persian Period," *BASOR* 203 (1971): 33–44.

37. André Lemaire, "New Aramaic Ostraca from Idumea," in *Judah and the Judeans in the Persian Period*, ed. Lipschits and Oeming, 413–456, esp. 416–417. For a general introduction to the Idumean ostraca, see Bezalel Porten and Ada Yardeni, *Textbook of Aramaic Ostraca from Idumea*, 5 vols. (University Park, PA: Eisenbrauns, 2014–2023), 1:xv–xxii. See also Porten and Yardeni, "Social, Economic, and Onomastic Issues in the Aramean Ostraca of the Fourth Century B.C.E.," in *Judah and Judeans*, ed. Lipschits and Oeming, 457–488.

38. See André Lemaire, *Nouvelles inscriptions araméennes d'Idumée II: Collections Moussaïeff, Jeselsohn, Welch et divers* (Leuven: Peeters, 2002), no. 283:2; see discussion in André Lemaire, "New Aramaic Ostraca from Idumea," in *Judah and the Judeans in the Persian Period*, ed. Lipschits and Oeming, 413–456, esp. 416–417. On the location of Khirbet el-Qom, see John S. Holladay, Jr., "Kom, Khirbet el-," *AYBD* 4:97–99.

39. See Oded Lipschits, Yuval Gadot, Benjamin Arubas, and Manfred Oeming, eds., *What Are the Stones Whispering? Ramat Raḥel: 3,000 Years of Forgotten History* (Winona Lake, IN: Eisenbrauns, 2017), 95–112; 108–111 for the Persian garden at Ramat Rahel; and Dafna Langgut, Yuval Gadot, Naomi Porat, and Oded Lipschits, "Fossil Pollen Reveals the Secrets of the Royal Persian Garden at Ramat Rahel, Jerusalem," *Palynology* 37 (2015): 115–129. Many studies of Judah in the Persian period posit a scenario in which the Persian administration was located first at Mizpah, the place where the Babylonians had their administrative center in Judah after the destruction of Jerusalem (see, e.g., 2 Kgs 25:23, Jer 40:5–6). There is no inscriptional evidence to support this claim.

40. See Briant, *From Cyrus to Alexander,* 442–444. For the Samarian palace garden, see John W. Crowfoot, "Introduction," in John W. Crowfoot, Grace M. Crowfoot, and Kathleen M. Kenyon, *Samaria–Sebaste III: The Objects from Samaria* (London: Palestine Exploration Fund, 1957), 1–8, esp. 3.

41. The presence of mercenaries may be indirectly reflected by references to "bow land" (*qšt*), in WDSP iiv. 3, 4 (Plate XII), and Israel Eph'al and Joseph Naveh, *Aramaic Ostraca of the Fourth Century BC from Idumaea* (Jerusalem: Magnes, Israel Exploration Society, 1996), nos. 39:1, 40:1. Bow fiefs were given by the king on the basis of the land-for-service system; see *CAD* 13, 153–155, s.v. *qaštu* 4 ("bow fief"), *qaštu* in *bēl qašti* ("holder of a bow fief"), and *qaštu* in *bīt qašti* ("bow fief").

42. The Persian taxes are referred to with the standard enumeration of *mindâ-bēlô wāhălāk* in Ezra 4:13, 20; 7:24. The Aramaic terms correspond to Akkadian *maddattu, biltu,* and *ilku.* The *mindâ* is a collective rent on landed domains, and the *hālak* is here also a land tax, not the mandatory service required of the landholder as was the *ilku* in the Al-Yaḫudu documents. See the discussion in Joseph Naveh and Shaul Shaked, *Aramaic Documents from Ancient Bactria from the Khalili Collections* (London: Khalili Family Trust, 2012), 30; and see also *CAD* 7, 77–79, s.v. *ilku* A, 3, "delivery of part of the yield of land held from a higher authority." Nehemiah 5:4 speaks about "the king's tax" (*middat hammelek*), the Aramaic equivalent of which is found in Naveh and Shaked, *Aramaic Documents from Ancient Bactria,* 120, A8:2 (*mndt mlk'*). Its payment forced some Judeans to borrow money on their fields and vineyards (Neh 5:4). See also the reference to the *mindat haylā',* the "tribute of the troop," in Judah B. Segal, *Aramaic Texts from North Saqqâra* (London: Egyptian Exploration Society, 1983), no. 24:11; *TAD* C3.5:7. Aramaic *kargā'* is a variant of *hālak* (*ilku*); see *TAD* D7.27:8. The nature of *bēlô* is unclear. If the connection with *biltu* holds good, it must have been a "tribute" to be paid to the king; see *CAD* 2, 234–236, s.v. *biltu* 5, "tribute paid by subject rulers."

43. The references to hired laborers (Hebrew *śākîr*) multiply in texts from the Persian period; see Hag 1:6, Mal 3:5, and the so-called worker texts among the Aramaic ostraca from Idumea.

44. See Briant, *From Cyrus to Alexander,* 343–344. Cf. also A. Leo Oppenheim, "The Eyes of the Lord," *JAOS* 88 (1968): 173–180, for the possibility that the postexilic prophets picked up the metaphor and applied it to Yhwh.

45. See the observations by Knoppers, *Jews and Samaritans,* 71–73, who contrasts the "very open and conciliatory attitude toward residents of the north" of Chronicles with the "much more hostile perspective toward the northern community" of Ezra-Nehemiah (72). This is one of

the differences Knoppers adduces to substantiate his claim, also made by Sara Japhet and Hugh Williamson, that 1–2 Chronicles, on the one hand, and Ezra-Nehemiah, on the other, have different authors.

46. For an eloquent exposition of the historical problems that beset both the text of Ezra-Nehemiah and the allegedly Persian documents it contains, see Lester L. Grabbe, *A History of the Jews and Judaism in the Second Temple Period*, 3 vols. (London: Continuum, 2004, 2008, 2021), 1:324–331; and Grabbe, "The 'Persian Documents' in the Book of Ezra: Are They Authentic?," in *Judah and the Judeans in the Persian Period*, ed. Lipschits and Oeming, 531–570.

47. For the sources of Ezra-Nehemiah, see the groundbreaking studies of Sigmund Mowinckel, *Studien zu dem Buche Ezra-Nehemia*, 3 vols. (Oslo: Oslo University Press, 1964–65). See also Hugh Williamson, *Ezra-Nehemiah*, WBC 16 (Grand Rapids: Zondervan, 1985), xxiii–xxxiii; Joseph Blenkinsopp, *Ezra-Nehemiah*, OTL (London: SCM, 1989), 41–47.

48. At first glance, the Masoretic vocalization of "Joshua" as "Jeshua" might be taken as a reference to the Succoth celebration mentioned in Ezra 3:4, but the patronymic "son of Nun" dispels possible confusion; see Williamson, *Ezra-Nehemiah*, 296.

49. For references to the province Yehud, see Oded Lipschits and David Vanderhooft, *Yehud Stamp Impressions: A Corpus of Inscribed Stamp Impressions from the Persian and Hellenistic Periods in Judah* (Winona Lake, IN: Eisenbrauns, 2011). The traditional view according to which Judah was part of the Persian province of Samaria until Nehemiah (so Albrecht Alt) has to be modified in light of the references to Yehud and its governor in late sixth- and early fifth-century BCE documents; see the discussion by Reinhard Gregor Kratz, *Das Judentum im Zeitalter des Zweiten Tempels*, FAT 42 (Tübingen: Mohr Siebeck, 2004), 93–119 ("Statthalter, Hohepriester und Schreiber im perserzeitlichen Juda"), esp. 97–100. In the interpretation here advanced, the reconstruction of the temple—or the erection of the Second Temple—symbolically marked the status of Judah as a separate Persian province (since Darius I). For references to "the province of Samaria," see the Wadi Daliyeh papyri studied by Dušek, *Manuscrits araméens de Wadi Daliyeh*. Most of the papyri are contracts made out "in the fortress of Samaria which is in the province of Samaria" (*bšmryn byrt' zy bšmryn mdynt'*), see, e.g., WDSP 1:1, 4:1, 5:1.

50. Note that the letter sent to Artaxerxes cited in Ezra 4:8–16 has been misplaced on the assumption it was dealing with the temple project. But v. 12 makes it clear that the subject concerns the rebuilding of the walls.

51. For a brief but balanced assessment of Ezra's mission and its historical circumstances, see John J. Collins, *The Invention of Judaism: Torah and*

Jewish Identity from Deuteronomy to Paul, Taubman Lectures in Jewish Studies 7 (Oakland: University of California Press, 2017), 52–61.

52. Nehemiah was "cupbearer of the king" (*mašqeh lammelek,* Neh 1:11; LXX, *oinochoos tōi basilei,* which in later tradition was corrupted as *eunouchos,* "eunuch"). The office of cupbearer normally entailed much more than that of royal sommelier. The Neo-Assyrian title Rabshakeh (Hebrew *rab-šāqēh,* 2 Kings 18–19) means "chief cupbearer," but the man who had this function occurs in 2 Kings 18–19 // Isaiah 36–37 as army officer; see A. Kirk Grayson, "Rabshakeh," *AYBD* 5:605. See also Tob 1:22: "Now Ahikar was cupbearer [*oinochoos,* var. *archioinochoos,* "chief cupbearer"], keeper of the signet [*epi tou daktyliou*], and in charge of administration of the accounts under King Sennacherib of Assyria." The Aramaic Ahiqar says he was scribe (*spr*), counselor of all of Assyria (*yʿṭ ʾtwr klh*), and seal-bearer (*šbyt ʿzqh*) of the king; see *TAD* C1.1, A 1–3, B 18–19. For the title "seal-bearer" (*šbyt ʿzqh*), see Jonas C. Greenfield, "Studies in Aramaic Lexicography I," in *ʾAl Kanfei Yonah: Collected Studies of Jonas C. Greenfield on Semitic Philology,* ed. Shalom M. Paul, Michael E. Stone, and Avital Pinnick, 2 vols. (Leiden: Brill; Jerusalem: Magnes, 2001), 1:6–21, esp. 18–21.

53. See Wilhelm Rudolph, *Esra und Nehemia, samt 3. Esra,* HAT 20 (Tübingen: Mohr, 1949), 74, who stresses that Ezra's activity as teacher of Torah was to embrace all Jews in Beyond the River, not only those in Judah. Ezra's promulgation of the law was to consist of public instruction plus the appointment of "magistrates [*šāpěṭîn*] and judges [*dayyānîn*]" (Ezra 7:25). In the description of Ezra's activity, there is no reference to any such appointment. During the Persian period, the "judges" (*dayyānîn*) were Persian appointees and often of Persian extraction. Perhaps the term "magistrates" refers to priests or Levites with judicial duties, cf. Deut 16:18.

54. The chronological order of the missions of Ezra and Nehemiah is a much-debated issue among biblical scholars and historians of Israel. For a brief presentation of the arguments, see Mowinckel, *Studien zu dem Buche Ezra-Nehemia,* 3:99–106; Williamson, *Ezra-Nehemiah,* xxxix–xliv; Blenkinsopp, *Ezra-Nehemiah,* 139–144; Eskenazi, *Ezra,* 30–31. Taking their cue from Ezra 7:7–8, most scholars date Ezra's mission occurring either in 458 BCE (seventh year of Artaxerxes I) or in 398 BCE (seventh year of Artaxerxes II). Considering the purpose and the effects of Ezra's mission, neither of these dates is entirely satisfactory. In view of its purpose—the introduction of a common constitution for Yhwh worshippers in Beyond the River—one would suspect Ezra to have been active after Nehemiah's career as governor (445–433 BCE). In view of its effects, on the other hand, one would suspect Ezra to have been active before 419 BCE, the date of the Elephantine Passover

papyrus (see discussion later in this chapter). Ezra reportedly worked together with the high priest Jehohanan son of Eliashib (1 Esd 9:2, Ezra 10:6, Neh 12:22–23). If this was the high priest Eliashib who built the Sheep Gate (Neh 3:1), his son (or grandson) Jehohanan must have succeeded him in the high priesthood around 430 BCE. It is not impossible that this is the same high priest Jehohanan (*yhwḥnn khn' rb'*) to which the leadership of the Elephantine community sent a petition for support around 410 BCE (*TAD* A4.7:18 // A4.8:17). This would put Ezra's mission sometime between 430 and 420 BCE and implies that the "seventh year of Artaxerxes" is to be corrected into a later year (twenty-seventh? thirty-seventh?), as various scholars have proposed. See also H. H. Rowley, "The Chronological Order of Ezra and Nehemiah," in *The Servant of the Lord and Other Essays on the Old Testament*, 2nd ed. (Oxford: Blackwell, 1965), 135–168. For a different reconstruction, see Cross, "A Reconstruction of the Judaean Restoration," in *From Epic to Canon*, 151–172, esp. 161–164.

55. For the classic exposition of the theory, see Peter Frei, "Zentralgewalt und Lokalautonomie im Achämenidenreich," in *Reichsidee und Reichsorganisation im Perserreich*, ed. Peter Frei and Klaus Koch, 2nd rev. and exp. ed., OBO 55 (Göttingen: Vandenhoeck & Ruprecht; Fribourg: Universitätsverlag, 1996), 8–131. Frei's thesis has met with almost as much criticism as support. For a discussion by various authors, some in favor and some against, see James W. Watts, ed., *Persia and Torah: The Theory of Imperial Authorization of the Pentateuch*, SBLSS 17 (Atlanta: Society of Biblical Literature, 2001). In a volume published in 2007, Konrad Schmid revisited Frei's thesis and proposed some refinements, partly based on discussions with Frei; see Schmid "The Persian Imperial Authorization as a Historical Problem and as a Biblical Construct: A Plea for Distinctions in the Current Debate," in *The Pentateuch as Torah: New Models for Understanding Its Promulgation and Acceptance*, ed. Gary N. Knoppers and Bernard M. Levinson (Winona Lake, IN: Eisenbrauns, 2007), 23–38. For a survey and discussion of all the pertinent evidence, with conclusions broadly sympathetic to the idea of imperial authorization, see Kyong-Jin Lee, *The Authority and Authorization of the Torah in the Persian Period*, CBET 64 (Leuven: Peeters, 2011). For a more critical evaluation from the perspective of an Iranist, see Josef Wiesehöfer, "Gerechtigkeit und Recht im achämenidischen Iran," in *Recht und Religion: Menschliche und göttliche Gerechtigkeitsvorstellungen in den Antiken Welten*, ed. Heinz Barta, Robert Rollinger, and Martin Lang (Wiesbaden: Harrassowitz, 2008), 191–204, translated into English as "Law and Religion in Achaemenid Iran," in *Law and Religion in the Eastern Mediterranean: From Antiquity to Early Islam*, ed. Anselm C. Hagedorn and Reinhard G. Kratz (Oxford: Oxford University Press, 2013), 40–57, esp. 50–53.

56. For a presentation and translation of the text, see Amélie Kuhrt, *The Persian Empire: A Corpus of Sources from the Achaemenid Period* (London: Routledge, 2007), 141–158.

57. The Behistun inscription refers to its translation and dissemination at the end of column IV: "Both on clay tablets and on parchment it has been placed. . . . Afterwards, I sent off this form of writing everywhere into the countries"; trans. Kuhrt, *Persian Empire*, 149, §70.

58. The text is *TAD* C2.1. For a discussion, see Reinhard G. Kratz, "Aḥiqar and Bisitun: The Literature of the Judeans at Elephantine," in *Elephantine in Context*, ed. Reinhard G. Kratz and Bernd U. Schipper, FAT 155 (Tübingen: Mohr Siebeck, 2022), 301–322, esp. 312–314.

59. For the text, see Schaudig, *Die Inschriften Nabonids*, 550–556; for an English translation, see "Cyrus Cylinder," trans. Cogan, *COS* 2.124:314–316.

60. Cyrus Cylinder, lines 27–27 (*ana yâti Kuraš šarru pāliḫšu u Kambuziya mar ṣīt lib[biya u an]a napḫ[ar] ummânīya damqiš ikrubma*); see also lines 35–36.

61. See Kuhrt, *Persian Empire*, 148, §62.

62. For an English translation and commentary, see Kuhrt, *Persian Empire*, 117–122. For a study, see Alan B. Lloyd, "The Inscription of Udjahorresnet: A Collaborator's Testament," *JEA* 68 (1982): 166–180.

63. See Kuhrt, *Persian Empire*, 118–119, sections (d)–(h).

64. See Kuhrt, *Persian Empire*, 122–124, no. 12, epitaph of Apis bull; 124, no. 13, inscription on Apis sarcophagus; and 125–127, no. 14, reverse of the Demotic Chronicle, section (c), Cambyses's decree concerning the incomes of Egyptian temples.

65. See Alan H. Gardiner, "The House of Life," *JEA* 24 (1938): 157–179; Aksel Volten, *Demotische Traumdeutung*, AAeg 3 (Copenhagen: Munsksgaard, 1942), 17–44; Manfred Weber, "Lebenshaus I," *LÄ* 3:954–957.

66. See Kuhrt, *Persian Empire*, 119, section (j). For a study of the mission of Udjahorresnet as a possible parallel for the missions of Ezra and Nehemiah, see Joseph Blenkinsopp, "The Mission of Udjahorresnet and Those of Ezra and Nehemiah," *JBL* 106 (1987): 409–421. See also the discussion in Briant, *From Cyrus to Alexander*, 57–59.

67. The Egyptian word used here for "law" is *ḥp*, for which term see Charles Nims, "The Term *HP*, 'Law, Right,' in Demotic," *JNES* 7 (1948): 243–260; Donald B. Redford, "The So-Called 'Codification' of Egyptian Law Under Darius I," in *Persia and Torah: The Theory of Imperial Authorization of the Pentateuch*, ed. James W. Watts, SBLSS 17 (Atlanta: Society of Biblical Literature, 2001), 135–159, esp. 138–150. For a discussion of Darius's initiative to produce a compilation of Egyptian law, see Christoph J. Tuplin, "The Justice of Darius: Reflections on the Achaemenid Empire as a rule-based environment," in *Assessing Biblical and Classical Sources for the Reconstruction of Persian Influence,*

History and Culture, ed. Anne Fitzpatrick-McKinley, Classica et Orientalia 10 (Wiesbaden: Harrassowitz, 2015), 73–126, esp. 102–105. For a more critical assessment, see Redford, "So-Called 'Codification' of Egyptian Law," who argues there was no "codification" of Egyptian law, only translation into Aramaic.

68. The text is found on the reverse of the Demotic Chronicle, middle section. For an English translation and commentary, see Kuhrt, *Persian Empire,* 124–127, esp. 125 section (b).

69. John MacGinnis, "A Judgment of Darius the King," *JCS* 60 (2008): 87–99, argues, on the basis of several legal cuneiform documents from the reign of Darius I, that it is highly likely that Darius also "commanded a recension of Babylonian law" that judges in the Babylonian satrapy might use (quotation at 96).

70. Several scholars have argued that the "Legal Code of Hermopolis West," a document from the Ptolemaic period, was modeled on the codification of Egyptian law ordered by Darius. See, e.g., Shafik Allam, "Réflexions sur le 'Code légal' d'Hermopolis dans l'Égypte ancienne," *CdE* 61 (1986): 50–75; Allam, "Traces de 'codification' en Égypte ancienne (à la basse époque)," *RIDA* 40 (1993): 11–26; Janet H. Johnson, "The Persians and the Continuity of Egyptian Culture," in *Continuity and Change: Proceedings of the Last Achaemenid History Workshop, April 6–8, 1990, Ann Arbor,* ed. Heleen Sancisi-Weerdenburg, Amélie Kuhrt, and M. C. Rood, Achaemenid History 8 (Leiden: NINO, 1994): 149–159.

71. See also Jan Quaegebeur, "Sur la 'loi sacrée' dans l'Égypte gréco-romaine," *Ancient Society* 11–12 (1980–1981): 227–240.

72. For the transition from papyrus (preexilic) to skin (postexilic), mainly under the influence of Aramean practice in Babylonia, see Menahem Haran, "Book-Scrolls at the Beginning of the Second Temple Period: The Transition from Papyrus to Skins," *HUCA* 54 (1983): 111–122.

73. The Greek term *hē pentateuchos* (*biblos*) first occurs in texts from second-century CE Alexandria (see Epiphanius, *Pan.* 33.4), presumably as a translation of Hebrew *ḥămiššâ ḥûmšê hattôrâ,* "the five fifths of the Torah." Greek *pentateuchos* combines *pente/penta,* "five," with *teuchos,* "vessel, jar," the jar being used as container of a scroll. The Greek term entered Latin as *pentateuchus* (scil. *liber*), first attested in Tertullian, *Marc.* 1.10. See Otto Eissfeldt, *Einleitung in das Alte Testament,* 4th ed. (Tübingen: Mohr Siebeck, 1976), 206.

74. For a defense of the view that Ezra's law was the Pentateuch, see Sigmund Mowinckel, *Studien zu dem Buche Ezra-Nehemia,* 3 vols. (Oslo: Oslo University Press, 1964–1965), 3:124–141; Williamson, *Ezra-Nehemiah,* xxxvii–xxxix; Cross, *From Epic to Canon,* 171. For different views, see Ulrich Kellermann, "Erwägungen zum Esragesetz," *ZAW* 80 (1968):

373–385 (Ezra's Torah is Deuteronomy); Cornelis Houtman, "Ezra and the Law," in *Remembering All the Way,* ed. Bertil Albrektson, OtSt 21 (Leiden: Brill, 1981), 91–115 (Ezra's Torah is a Hebrew law collection unknown to us); Blenkinsopp, *Ezra-Nehemiah,* 152–157 (it is forerunner of the Pentateuch, consisting of Deuteronomy 12–26, supplemented with cultic legislation). For a discussion of the issue, see Juha Pakkala, *Ezra the Scribe: The Development of Ezra 7–10 and Nehemiah 8,* BZAW 347 (Berlin: de Gruyter, 2004), 284–290.

75. The clearly composite nature of the biblical flood narrative has made it a showcase in studies of source criticism; see, e.g., John A. Emerton, "An Examination of Some Attempts to Defend the Unity of the Flood Narrative in Genesis," *VT* 37 (1987): 401–420, and *VT* 38 (1988): 1–21. For Deuteronomy 12, see the parallels between vv. 4–7 // 8–12 and 13–19 // 20–27.

76. See the pertinent observations of Seth Sanders, "What If There Aren't Any Empirical Models for Pentateuchal Criticism?," in *Contextualizing Israel's Sacred Writings: Ancient Literacy, Orality, and Literary Production,* ed. Brian B. Schmidt, AIL 22 (Atlanta: Society of Biblical Literature, 2015), 281–304. See also Mark Leuchter, "The Aramaic Transition and the Redaction of the Pentateuch," *JBL* 136 (2017): 249–268, who argues that the incorporation of dissonant sources in the Pentateuch is to be attributed to the scribal culture of the Persian Empire, where much of the classical literature had to be retextualized in Aramaic script.

77. According to the tale of the rediscovery of the Cyrus edict relating to the temple of Jerusalem, the archive (*bêt siprayyāʾ*) was located in the place where the treasures (*ginzayyāʾ*) were stored in Babylon, Ezra 6:1.

78. This insight, developed by Theodor Nöldeke, *Untersuchungen zur Kritik des Alten Testaments* (Kiel: Schwers'sche Buchhandlung, 1869), 1–144 ("Die s.g. Grundschrift des Pentateuchs"), remains one of the cornerstones in the critical study of the Pentateuch.

79. See Martin Noth, *Das zweite Buch Mose: Exodus,* ATD 5 (Göttingen: Vandenhoeck & Ruprecht, 1961), 42; Hugo Gressmann, *Mose und seine Zeit: Ein Kommentar zu den Mose-Sagen* (Göttingen: Vandenhoeck & Ruprecht, 1913), 50–56.

80. Freely paraphrased after Baruch J. Schwartz, "Bible," in *The Oxford Dictionary of the Jewish Religion,* ed. R. J. Zwi Werblowsky and Geoffrey Wigoder (New York: Oxford University Press, 1997), 121–125, esp. 121–122.

81. For references to the Pentateuch in Chronicles, see Zipora Talshir, "Several Canon-Related Concepts Originating in Chronicles," *ZAW* 113 (2001): 386–403, esp. 388–390. A majority of scholars puts the composition of Chronicles around 350 BCE. For a dissenting view (early Maccabean period), see Georg Steins, "Zur Datierung der Chronik: Ein neuer methodischer Ansatz," *ZAW* 109 (1997): 84–92.

82. See Knoppers, *Jews and Samaritans*, 178–194, esp. 189: "the conflation-ary expansions in the pre-Samaritan manuscripts were made over the course of centuries and did not occur as the result of a systematic recension at one particular time."

83. See, e.g., Samuel Sandmel, *The Genius of Paul* (New York: Farrar, Straus and Cudahy, 1958), 46–47.

84. See the observations by Yishai Kiel, "Reinventing Mosaic Torah in Ezra-Nehemiah in the Light of the Law (*dāta*) of Ahura Mazda and Zarathustra," *JBL* 136 (2017): 323–345, esp. 333–337, with many references to other pertinent literature. For a study of *tôrâ* from a variety of angles, including critical reflections on the Torah of Ezra, see David Lambert, "What Is *Tôrâ*?," in *The Pentateuch and Its Readers*, ed. Joel S. Baden and Jeffrey Stackert, FAT 170 (Tübingen: Mohr Siebeck, 2023), 307–335.

85. For the text, see Michael Jursa, J. Paszkowiak, and Caroline Waerzeggers, "Three Court Records," *AfO* 50 (2003–2004): 255–268, esp. 255–259.

86. Jursa, Paszkowiak, and Waerzeggers "Three Court Records," 259 (comment by Michael Jursa).

87. Kristin Kleber, "*Dātu ša šarri:* Gesetzgebung in Babylonien unter den Achämeniden," *ZABR* 16 (2010): 49–75, esp. 53.

88. The expression occurs both with a reference to the torah (as in Ezra 3:2; Neh 10:35, 37; 2 Chr 23:18; 25:4; 31:3; 35:12, 26; cf. Dan 9:13) and in an absolute sense (see Ezra 3:4; Neh 8:15; 2 Chr 30:5, 18).

89. The possibility that the *kakkātûb* references are mostly rhetorical counsels caution in the use of Ezra-Nehemiah passages about the performance of festivals and reform measures as a lead to identify Ezra's law. Discrepancies between Ezra-Nehemiah and the Pentateuch do not necessarily imply Ezra's law could not have been the Pentateuch. For a discussion of some of the discrepancies, see Collins, *Invention of Judaism*, 55–57.

90. So freely after the *OED* s.v. "promulgate."

91. For the Levites as teachers of Torah with a scribal training, see Deut 33:10; 2 Chr 17:7–9, 35:3; Gerhard von Rad, *Gesammelte Studien zum Alten Testament* (Munich: Kaiser, 1958), 248–261 ("Die levitische Predigt in den Büchern der Chronik"); Karel van der Toorn, *Scribal Culture and the Making of the Hebrew Bible* (Cambridge, MA: Harvard University Press, 2007), 89–96.

92. Both Passover and Mazzoth (the Feast of Unleavened Bread) were originally seasonal festivals connected with the practice of transhumance; see Leonhard Rost, "Weidewechsel und altisraelischer Fest-kalender," in *Das kleine Credo und andere Studien zum Alten Testament* (Heidelberg: Quelle & Meyer, 1965), 101–112. Their reinterpretation as commemorative rites of events on the eve of the liberation from Egypt (Exod 12:1–28) came to a conclusion in the early Persian period. See

also the discussion by Baruch M. Bokser, "Unleavened Bread and Pass-over, Feasts of," *AYBD* 6:755–765, esp. 759–760.

93. The reform measures involve the cancellation of debts, the return of fields and other property taken as security, and the manumission of people made slaves for reasons of insolvability (Neh 5:10–12). The perti-nent passages in the Torah would be Exod 21:2–11, 22:24–26 [22:25–27]; Leviticus 25; Deut 15:1–18, 23:20–21 [23:19–20], 24:10–13.

94. The terms are Aramaic *phh,* Hebrew *peḥâ,* "governor," both loans from Akkadian *bēl pīḥati,* "governor, lord of the province"; the "prefect" is Hebrew *sāgān, sĕgānîm;* Aramaic *sĕgan, signîn,* from Akkadian *šak-nu,* "governor, commander"; the "royal judges" are the *dyny mlk'* and the "provincial judges" are the *dyny' zy bmdynt* (followed by name of province). For a discussion of these functionaries, see Christopher Tu-plin, "The Administration of the Achaemenid Empire," in *Coinage and Administration in the Athenian and Persian Empires: The Ninth Oxford Symposium on Coinage and Monetary History,* ed. Ian Carradice, BARIS 343 (Oxford: Oxford University Press, 1987), 109–166, esp. 119, 122–126. On the provincial governor, see Reinhard G. Kratz, *Das Judentum im Zeitalter des Zweiten Tempels,* FAT 42 (Tübingen: Mohr Siebeck, 2004), 93–125 ("Statthalter, Hohepriester und Schreiber im perserzeitlichen Juda"), esp. 93–106. For *dyny mlk',* see *TAD* B5.1:3; for the "provincial judges," see *TAD* A4.5:9. Herodotus (*Hist.* 3.31) mentions the Persian "royal judges" (*hoi basilēioi dikastai*) and says they administer justice and interpret the old laws, all disputes being referred to their decision. For *sgn,* see WDSP no. 14; Neh 5:17. In the Elephantine papyri, the provincial governor is normally referred to with the Persian term *fra-taraka (prtrk);* see Tuplin, "Administration of the Achaemenid Empire," 125–126.

95. The evidence from Achaemenid Babylonia, the Samarian papyri (Wadi Daliyeh), and the Elephantine papyri indicates that most of the "roy-al judges," also known as "provincial judges," had Persian names and were likely Persians. See, e.g., WDSP 2:11, 3:10 ("Vahudata the judge"); *TAD* A5.2:6 ("Bagapharna, Naphaina, and Mannuki the judges"); *TAD* B2.2:6 ("Damidata and his colleagues the judges"; and *TAD* B2.9:4 ("Ramnadaina the phrataraka [member of tribunal]"). See discussion in Dušek, *Manuscrits araméens de Wadi Daliyeh,* 92, 512–513.

96. Sanballat the governor of Samaria has a Babylonian name (Sin-uballiṭ, "Sin keeps alive"; cf. the spelling *snblṭ* in *TAD* A4.7:29), but his sons carry Hebrew names with a reference to Yʜwʜ (Delaiah and Shele-miah, *TAD* A4.7:29 // 8:28); he may have been an Israelite or a Judean from the eastern diaspora. See also "Jeshua son of Sanballat" (WDSP no. 14). The question of whether Bagohi the governor of Judah was Persian or Judean is still unresolved.

97. The draft of the petition the Elephantine leadership sent to Judean governor Bagohi mentions a previous message sent to "Jehohanan the high priest and his colleagues the priests who are in Jerusalem, and Ostana (*'wstn*) brother of Anani and the nobles of the Judeans, var. Judah (*ḥwry yhwdy'*, var. *yhwd*)"; see *TAD* A4.7:18–19 // 4.8:17–18. The identity and function of Ostana are unresolved for lack of data. As a Judean with a Persian name, he is likely to have been a high official in the provincial administration. The Elephantine leadership also consists of "Jedaniah the priest and his colleagues the priests who are in Elephantine the fortress, and the Judeans" (*TAD* A4.8:1; cf. 4.8:3, 21–22; 4.7:1, 4, 22). In Ezra-Nehemiah the leadership of Judah consists of the governor, the high priest, and the "chiefs of the clans" (*rāšê hā'ābôt*, Ezra 2:68; 3:12; 4:2, 3; 8:1; 10:16; cf. Neh 7:69, 70; 11:13). The distinct terms *śābayyā'* (Aramaic, "the elders," Ezra 5:9), *śābê yĕhûdayyē'* ("elders of the Judeans," mentioned alongside the "governor of the Judeans," *paḥat yĕhûdayyē'*, Ezra 6:7), *hazzĕqēnîm* ("the elders," mentioned alongside the *śārîm*, "officials," Ezra 10:8), *ziqnê-'îr* ("town elders," Ezra 10:14), *ḥōrîm* ("nobles," in the enumeration of the priests, the nobles, the prefects, and the rest of the officials, Neh 2:16; cf. 4:8, 13; 5:7), *ḥōrê yĕhûdâ* ("the nobles of Judah," Neh 6:17; 13:17, 30; cf. *TAD* A4.7:18–19 // 4.8:17–18), and *hayyĕhûdîm* ("the Judeans," as designation of Judean leaders, Neh 5:17; cf. *TAD* A3.8:12, A4.3:12, A4.7:22, A4.8:22) presumably refer to one and the same category of people. Where the book of Ezra speaks of the Judean "elders," Nehemiah calls them the Judean "nobles."

98. See Dušek, *Manuscrits araméens de Wadi Daliyeh,* who notes that the contracts of slave sales and house sales follow local customs, with influence of Neo-Babylonian contracts (pp. 65–80) and some similarities with Persian tradition (p. 82 note 53). See also Knoppers, *Jews and Samaritans,* 110.

99. For the dating of the sacred precinct and the adjacent building on Mount Gerizim, see Yitzhaq Magen, "The Dating of the First Phase of the Samaritan Temple at Mount Gerizim in Light of the Archaeological Evidence," in *Judah and the Judeans in the Fourth Century B.C.E.,* ed. Lipschits, Knoppers, and Albertz, 157–211.

100. See Lemaire, "New Aramaic Ostraca from Idumea."

101. For the messages to Jerusalem, see *TAD* A4.7–8. *TAD* A4.9 is the memorandum that contains the Judean governor's endorsement. For evidence of the existence of a reconstructed temple at Elephantine, see *TAD* B3.12:18–19, a contract from 402 BCE that mentions "the temple of Yaho" as topographical reference. See also *TAD* 3.15, the temple collection text, most likely dated in 400 BCE. For a reconstruction of the events, see Van der Toorn, *Becoming Diaspora Jews,* 136–142.

102. See van der Toorn, *Becoming Diaspora Jews,* 54–55; Bob Becking, *Identity in Persian Egypt: The Fate of the Yehudite Community of Elephantine* (University Park, PA: Eisenbrauns, 2020), 78–86. For evidence on intermarriage among the Judeans of Babylonia, see Martha Roth, *Babylonian Marriage Agreements 7th–3rd Centuries B.C.,* AOAT 222 (Kevelaer: Butzon & Bercker; Neukirchen-Vluyn: Neukirchener Verlag, 1989), 92–95, no. 26; Kathleen Abraham, "West Semitic and Judean Brides in Cuneiform Sources from the Sixth Century BCE: New Evidence from a Marriage Contract from Āl-Yaḫudu," *AfO* 51 (2005–2006): 198–219; Cornelia Wunsch, *Judaeans by the Waters of Babylon: New Historical Evidence in Cuneiform Sources from Rural Babylonia in the Schøyen Collection,* Babylonische Archive 6 (Dresden: ISLET-Verlag, 2022), 57–60.

103. See Alejandro F. Botta, *The Aramaic and Egyptian Legal Traditions at Elephantine: An Egyptological Approach,* LSTS 64 (London: T&T Clark, 2009). The legal documents of the Judean communities in Babylonia have been written by Babylonian scribes in accordance with Babylonian legal traditions; see Wunsch, *Judaeans by the Waters of Babylon,* 123–139.

104. The wording of these lines (*mn mlk' šlyḥ 'l 'rš[m . . .*]) may be compared with Ezra 7:14, *mn-qdm mlk' (. . .) šlyḥ. . . .*

105. See *TAD* A4.1:3–8; Manfred Weippert, *Historisches Textbuch zum Alten Testament,* GAT 10 (Göttingen: Vandenhoeck & Ruprecht, 2010), 479–480, no. 283.

106. See Bernd U. Schipper, "The Judeans/Arameans of Elephantine and Their Religion: An Egyptological Perspective," in *Elephantine in Context,* ed. Kratz and Schipper, 209–233, esp. 217–221.

107. See Weippert, *Historisches Textbuch,* 480 note 167.

108. For the significance of the Passover papyrus with respect to the religious policy of the Persians and their recognition of the Judean community, see Ingo Kottsieper, "Die Religionspolitik der Achämeniden und die Juden von Elephantine," in *Religion und Religionskontakte im Zeitalter der Achämeniden,* ed. Reinhard G. Kratz, Veröffentlichungen der Wissenschaftlichen Gesellschaft für Theologie 22 (Gütersloh: Kaiser, 2002), 150–178, esp. 150–158.

109. The patronym of this man (Meshezabel) is a Hebraicized version of either Mušēzib-El or, more plausibly, Mušēzib-Bēl, since the name is Babylonian; see Martin Noth, *Die israelitischen Personennamen im Rahmen der gemeinsemitischen Namengebung* (Stuttgart: Kohlhammer, 1928), 156. For the occurrence of the name Mušēzib-Bēl ("Bel saves") in documents from Bīt-Abirām, see Pearce and Wunsch, *Documents of Judean Exiles,* 67. This suggests that Pethahiah was from the Judean diaspora in Babylonia. On his possible function as an advisor or

ambassador of Judean affairs at the Persian court, see Jacob M. Myers, *Ezra-Nehemiah: A New Translation with Introduction and Commentary*, AYB 14 (Garden City, NY: Doubleday, 1965; repr. New Haven: Yale University Press), 189. See also the cautious discussion by Terry L. Brensinger, "Pethahiah," *AYBD* 5:287–288, esp. 288.

110. Elsewhere in the Elephantine papyri and ostraca there is no mention of Matzoth. Passover, on the other hand, is mentioned in the ostraca (all from before 419 BCE). See *TAD* D7.6:8–10 ("Send me word when you observe the Passover [*psḥ*]") and D7.24:5 ("on the Passover"). The reference to *psḥ* in Cl.-G. 62, rev. 4, for which see Lozachmeur, *La collection Clermont-Ganneau*, 229–230, is to be read as *pshḥnty*, "the temple scribe," a calque on Egyptian *pз sḥ ḥt-nṯr;* see Günter Vittmann, "Arameans in Egypt," in *Wandering Arameans: Arameans Outside Syria, Textual and Archaeological Perspectives*, ed. Angelika Berlejung, Aren M. Maeir, and Andreas Schüle, Leipziger Altorientalische Studien 5 (Wiesbaden: Harrassowitz, 2017), 229–279, esp. 259.

111. Scholars have correctly noted the phraseological parallels between the Passover papyrus and Lev 23:5–8 (prohibition to work during the Feast of Unleavened Bread) and Exod 12:15–20 (command to remove leaven from houses). Neither of these two passages, however, refers to the need for purification the way both Ezra 6:20 and the Passover papyrus, line 5 (*dkyn hww*), do.

112. See *TAD* A4.3:7.

113. In this respect, the discussion by Yonatan Adler, *The Origins of Judaism: An Archaeological-Historical Reappraisal*, AYBRL (New Haven: Yale University Press, 2022), 145–155, esp. 153–155, minimizes the significance of the Elephantine evidence in an unacceptable way.

114. See Ezra 3:3–5 (Passover, Matzoth, Succoth); see also Ezra 6:19–22 (Passover and Matzoth), Neh 8:9–12 (New Year, VII/1), Neh 8:13–18 (Succoth), Zech 14:16–19 (Succoth). In view of the emphasis on the communal celebration of Passover "as prescribed," the story of Josiah's celebration of Passover "as prescribed" in 722 BCE, reported in 2 Kgs 23:21, is most plausibly a retrojection of ritual practices that took shape during the Persian period. See, e.g., Laura Feldt, "Total Devotion: Dismantling Religious Practices and Training Devotion in 2 Kings 22–23," *JSJ* 51 (2020): 309–338.

115. The Passover papyrus begins by referring to an order of King Darius to Arsames, the Persian satrap in Egypt (*TAD* A4.1:2). Hananiah was in Egypt when he sent his letter (*TAD* A4.3:7). The most likely assumption puts him at the court of Arsames in Memphis.

116. The biblical reference to sixth-century BCE Jewish communities in Migdol, Tahpanhes (both Nile delta), Noph (Memphis), and "the

land of Pathros" (southern Egypt) (Jer 44:1) finds confirmation in the references to Jewish communities in these places in Aramaic papyri from the Persian period.

117. On *qāhāl*, see Mowinckel, *Studien zu dem Buche Ezra-Nehemia*, 1:87–89.

118. Although the History of Ezra favors the use of the term "Israel" (Ezra 7:6, 7, 10, 28; 8:35; 9:1, 4, 15; 10:1, 2, 5, 25; Neh 8:1, 14, 17), the Nehemiah Memoir nearly always speaks of "Judah" and "Judeans" (Neh 1:2, 3:33, 4:6, 5:14, 13:24). The difference reflects the more elevated religious language of the priestly milieu of Ezra versus the more administrative language of Nehemiah as governor.

119. For "Israel" as a term of ethnicity, see Ezra 2:59: "they were unable to tell whether their families and their offspring were from Israelite stock." On the religious connotations of "Israel," see the observations by Mowinckel, *Studien zu dem Buche Ezra-Nehemia*, 1:85–87.

120. In this respect, the occurrence of the expression "people of Israel" (*'ammâ yiśrā'ēl*) in the transcript of the Artaxerxes letter to Ezra (Ezra 7:13) betrays a Judean hand. The Persian chancellery would have spoken of *'ammâ yĕhûdayyē'*, as pointed out by Mowinckel, *Studien zu dem Buche Ezra-Nehemia*, 3:21 note 1. See also the pertinent observations by Grabbe, "'Persian Documents' in the Book of Ezra," 543 note 53 and p. 551.

121. The debate about the most appropriate translation of *Yĕhûdîm* (Hebrew), *Yĕhûdayyē* (Aramaic), and *Ioudaioi* (Greek) is unlikely to reach a consensus conclusion anytime soon. For a discussion, see Van der Toorn, *Becoming Diaspora Jews*, 15–18, 124–128. While it may be claimed with some confidence that Judaism did not come into being until the mid-second century BCE (see Adler, *Origins of Judaism*), Jewish ethnicity did see the light of day in the Persian period.

122. See *TAD* A4.1:1, 10, 419 BCE.

123. In an essay on the missions of Ezra and Nehemiah, Tamara Cohn Eskenazi writes that "under Ezra's guidance, Judahites and exiles become Jews"; see Eskenazi, "The Missions of Ezra and Nehemiah," in *Judah and the Judeans in the Persian Period*, ed. Lipschits and Oeming, 509–529, esp. 511. This puts a little too much weight on the shoulders of one man. The process of Jewish ethnicity formation had been going on since the beginning of the Persian era, first in the diaspora and later in Palestine too.

124. Like any ethnic group in the diaspora, Jews abroad would always have to navigate between assimilation and separation. For group survival, some form of separation was unavoidable. Cf. Esth 3:8: "There is a certain people scattered and separated [*mĕpuzzār ûmĕpôrād*] among the peoples in all the provinces of your kingdom; their laws [*dātêhem*] are different from those of every other people" (NRSV).

125. For another voice against the particularism of Deut 23:2–7, see Isa 56:1–8 (both "foreigners," *běnê hannēkār,* and "eunuchs," *sārîsîm,* will be welcome to the altar of Yhwh).

126. For a discussion of the Judean connections of Tobiah, see Knoppers, *Jews and Samaritans,* 158–159.

127. This Eliashib is the very priest who rebuilt the Sheep Gate in the walls of Jerusalem, and a close collaborator of Nehemiah (Neh 3:1). His decision to grant Tobiah the use of a room in the temple soured his relations with Nehemiah (Neh 13:7–9).

128. See the discussion by Knoppers, *Jews and Samaritans,* 73–97.

129. *TAD* A4.1:1, *h*[*yl'*] *yhwdy'.* For the use of the term "brother(s)," see lines 1, 2, and 10.

130. See *TAD* A4.7:29 // A4.8:27–28: "Also, we sent all these words in a letter, in our name, to Delaiah and Shelemiah sons of Sanballat governor of Samaria."

131. *TAD* A4.9:1–2: "Memorandum (*zkrn*) of what Bagohi [governor of Judah] and Delaiah [from the province of Samaria] said to me."

132. See Richard J. Bautch, "A Response and Further Thoughts," *JHebS* 18 (2018): 43–48, esp. 47–48, where he speaks about "proto-sectarian groups" that used covenant practices to form group identity at the beginning of the Second Temple period. He refers to Ezra 9–10 and Nehemiah 10 as examples.

Chapter 6. Scriptural Religion

1. On the Samarian revolt and the Wadi Daliyeh discovery, see Frank Moore Cross, "Papyri of the Fourth Century B.C. from Dâliyeh," in *New Directions in Biblical Archaeology,* ed. David Noel Freedman and Jonas C. Greenfield (Garden City, NY: Doubleday, 1969), 45–69, esp. 57–58; Paul W. Lapp and Nancy L. Lapp, eds., *Discoveries in the Wadi ed-Dâliyeh,* AASOR 41 (Cambridge, MA: American Schools of Oriental Research, 1974); Frank Moore Cross, "Daliyeh, Wadi ed-," *AYBD* 2:3–4; Jan Dušek, *Les manuscrits araméens du Wadi Daliyeh et la Samarie vers 450–332 av. J.-C.,* CHANE 30 (Leiden: Brill, 2007), 439–485. The historical reference to the killing of Andromachus by Samarian conspirators comes from Q. Curtius Rufus, *Hist. Alex.* 4.8.9–10.

2. On the causes of the Maccabean revolt, see John J. Collins, "Temple or Taxes? What Sparked the Maccabean Revolt?," in *Revolt and Resistance in the Ancient Classical World and the Near East in the Crucible of Empire,* ed. John J. Collins and J. G. Manning, CHANE 85 (Leiden: Brill, 2016), 189–201. See also, in the same volume, Robert Doran, "Resistance and Revolt: The Case of the Maccabees," 173–188.

3. Judas Maccabeus refers to the inhabitants of Gilead as "brothers" of the Jews; see 1 Macc 5:32; see also 1 Macc 9:10.

4. The anti-Hellenistic and anticolonial slant of the adjective also comes to the fore in the use of the noun *patēr*, "ancestor," in 1 Macc 2:19–20: "But Mattathias answered and said in a loud voice: 'Even if all the nations that live under the rule of the king [Antiochus IV Epiphanes] obey him, and have chosen to obey his commandments, every one of them abandoning the religion of their ancestors [*latreia paterōn autou*], I and my sons and my brothers will continue to live by the covenant of our ancestors [*diathēkē paterōn hēmōn*]'" (NRSV).

5. The evidence for such names comes from early Hellenistic inscriptions found in the close vicinity of Mount Gerizim; see Yitzhak Magen, Haggai Misgav, and Levana Tsfania, *Mount Gerizim Excavations, Volume 1: The Aramaic, Hebrew and Samaritan Inscriptions*, Judea and Samaria Publications 2 (Jerusalem: Israel Antiquities Authority, 2004); Jan Dušek, *Aramaic and Hebrew Inscriptions from Mt. Gerizim and Samaria Between Antiochus III and Antiochus IV Epiphanes*, CHANE 54 (Leiden: Brill, 2012). For a brief but illuminating discussion, see Gary N. Knoppers, *Jews and Samaritans: The Origins and History of Their Early Relations* (New York: Oxford University Press, 2013), 125–128.

6. Compare the talmudic saying that burying the dead takes precedence over studying Torah; see b. Meg. 3b.

7. The address of God as "our Father in heaven" (Matt 6:9 and parr.) has antecedents in several biblical passages from the Persian and Hellenistic periods; see Isa 63:16; Mal 2:10; Sir 23:1, 4; 51:10. On the invocation of God as Father, see also Joachim Jeremias, *Abba: Studien zur neutestamentlichen Theologie und Zeitgeschichte* (Göttingen: Vandenhoeck & Ruprecht, 1966), 15–67.

8. This is the text as given in the Codex Sinaiticus; neither the Aramaic nor the Hebrew version of the passage is extant in the Tobit fragments from Qumran.

9. This is the definition given by Yonatan Adler, *The Origins of Judaism: An Archaeological-Historical Appraisal*, AYBRL (New Haven: Yale University Press, 2022), 5. Adler loosely models his definition upon the entry "Judaism" in *Webster's Third New International Dictionary:* "conformity to Jewish rites, ceremonies and practices . . . the total complex of cultural, social and religious beliefs and practices of the Jews" (quoted on p. 3). Adler's variant puts the stress on Judaism as a way of life rather than as a complex of beliefs.

10. For the religious policy of Antiochus IV Epiphanes, see Robert Doran, "The Persecution of Judeans by Antiochus IV Epiphanes: The Significance of 'Ancestral Laws,'" in *The "Other" in Second Temple Judaism: Essays in Honor of John J. Collins*, ed. Daniel C. Harlow, Karina Martin Hogan, Matthew Goff, and Joel S. Kaminsky (Grand Rapids: Eerdmans, 2011), 423–433.

11. The coins from the reign of John Hyrcanus I carry inscriptions in an archaizing paleo-Hebrew script, which, as Tessa Rajak ("Hasmonean Dynasty," *AYBD* 3:67–76), writes, "visibly evoked the days of the First Temple" (70).

12. For a more elaborate demonstration of this point, see Adler, *Origins of Judaism*, 228–236.

13. On the impact of Hellenism on Judaism, see the pioneering studies of Saul Lieberman, *Hellenism in Jewish Palestine: Studies in the Literary Transmission, Beliefs and Manners of Palestine in the I Century B.C.E.— IV Century C.E.* (New York: Jewish Theological Seminary, 1950); and Martin Hengel, *Judentum und Hellenismus: Studien zur ihrer Begegnung unter besonderer Berücksichtigung Palästinas bis zur Mitte des 2. Jh.s v. Chr.* (Tübingen: Mohr Siebeck, 1969), translated by John Bowden as *Judaism and Hellenism: Studies on Their Encounter in Palestine During the Early Hellenistic Period*, 2 vols. (London: SCM; Philadelphia: Fortress, 1974). For a more recent treatment, see the various contributions in John J. Collins and Gregory E. Sterling, eds., *Hellenism in the Land of Israel* (Notre Dame, IN: University of Notre Dame Press, 2001).

14. See the discussion by Martha Himmelfarb, "Judaism and Hellenism in 2 Maccabees," *Poetics Today* 19 (1998): 19–40, with references to earlier treatments of the topic.

15. For a voice of caution in the debate on Jewish popular literacy during the late Hellenistic and early Roman periods, see Catherine Hezser, *Jewish Literacy in Roman Palestine*, TSAJ 81 (Tübingen: Mohr Siebeck, 2001); and Hezser, "Jewish Literacy and Languages in First-Century Roman Palestine," *Orientalia* (NS) 89 (2020): 58–77. In the absence of statistics, it is possible that the literacy rate among the general population was actually lower than my treatment of the matter suggests. Nevertheless, the occurrence of such related phenomena as the private possession of (sacred) books, synagogal readings, paratext genres like the pesharim, and the profusion of new literary texts warrants the use of the phrase "reading revolution." On this "revolution," see the section that follows.

16. See, e.g., Gen 38:16–17 (a kid from the flock as the wages of a harlot, instead of the silver mentioned in Prov 7:14–20 and Deut 23:19 [23:18]), Deut 14:22–26 (tithes can be paid in kind or converted into silver), 1 Sam 9:7–8 (Saul pays the prophet a quarter shekel as a gift), 1 Kgs 21:2 (a vineyard for another property or a price in silver), Jer 32:9–11 (a piece of land for seventeen shekels), Hos 3:1–2 (the prophet "buys" a woman for fifteen shekels of silver and a homer of barley and a measure of wine), and Amos 2:6 (a bribe in silver or in kind). The prevalence of barter in the earliest periods explains why the Hebrew verb *mākar*, like its Aramaic equivalent *zĕban*, is used for both "selling" and "buying," the root meaning being

"to barter, to bargain." On the practice of barter and the use of weighted silver, see Philip J. King and Lawrence E. Stager, *Life in Biblical Israel,* LAI (Louisville: Westminster John Knox, 2001), 194–198.

17. See King and Stager, *Life in Biblical Israel,* 198–200; Helga Weippert, "Geld," *BRL2,* 88–90; Kurt Galling, "Münze," *BRL2,* 233–234; Ulrich Hübner, "Finance," *EBW,* 260–269. Note that in the Wadi Daliyeh papyri, economic transactions use weighted silver as means of payment; see Dušek, *Manuscrits araméens du Wadi Daliyeh,* 496.

18. The impact of the money economy is reflected in the book of Qohelet (Ecclesiastes), as demonstrated by James L. Kugel, "Qohelet and Money," *CBQ* 51 (1989): 32–49. The book reflects the economic conditions of the Hellenistic age; see Robert Gordis, *Koheleth—The Man and His World: A Study of Ecclesiastes,* 3rd augm. ed. (New York: Schocken, 1968), 63–68, esp. 67; George A. Barton, *The Book of Ecclesiastes,* ICC (Edinburgh: T&T Clark, 1908), 58–65, esp. 59. See also Sir 29:1–13 on the effects of the money economy on human interaction.

19. On the importance of almsgiving, see Dan 4:24 [4:27] ("Atone for your sins by almsgiving [ṣidqâ], and your iniquities by generosity to the poor"); Tob 4:10–11, 12:8–9, 14:11; Sir 7:10, 32; 12:3; 17:22; 29:8–13; 35:4; 40:24. On fasting as a means to atone for sins and obtain divine mercy, see Sir 34:31; Jdt 4:8–15, 8:6. On the annual pilgrimage to Jerusalem, especially for the celebration of Passover, see Joachim Jeremias, *Jerusalem in the Time of Jesus,* trans. F. H. Cave and C. H. Cave (London: SCM, 1969), 58–84. On prayer as religious duty, see Sir 7:10, 14; 28:2; 35:20–21; Tob 3:1–6, 11–15; 8:4–8, 15–17; 13:1–17; Jdt 8:31, 12:7–9, 13:3–5.

20. See, e.g., 2 Macc 4:7–9. The Dead Sea Scrolls say that the "wicked priest" (the principal opponent of the Teacher of Righteousness) "deserted God and betrayed the laws for the sake of riches. And he robbed and hoarded wealth from the violent men who had rebelled against God. And he seized public money, incurring additional serious sin" (1QpHab 8:10–12, Florentino García Martínez and Eibert J. C. Tigchelaar, eds., *The Dead Sea Scrolls: Study Edition,* 2 vols. [Leiden: Brill; Grand Rapids: Eerdmans, 2000]), 1:16–17. See also Sir 26:29: "A merchant [*emporos*] can hardly keep from wrongdoing, nor is a tradesman [*kapēlos*] innocent of sin . . . a sin is wedged in between selling and buying."

21. See Gary A. Anderson, *Sin: A History* (New Haven: Yale University Press, 2009).

22. See Bruce Chilton, "Debts," *AYBD* 2:114–116, esp. 115. Chilton elaborates the point by a discussion of the Targum Jonathan of Isaiah, in which Isa 50:1 is rendered as, "Thus says the LORD, where is the bill of divorce that I gave to your congregation, that it is rejected? Or who had a debt against me, to whom I have sold you? Behold, for your debts you were sold, and for your apostasies your congregation was rejected."

23. The counterpart of debt is credit, and almsgiving is a way of building up credit with God; see Matt 6:19–21, 19:21 ("sell your possessions, and give the money to the poor, and you will have a treasure in heaven"); Luke 12:33–34 ("Sell your possessions, and give alms. . . . an unfailing treasure in heaven").

24. Compare the complaint of a Syrian employed in Ptolemaic Egypt that he has not received his pay, was slighted, and had been forced to go home to Syria because he was *barbaros* and did not want to act as a Hellene (*ouk epistamai hellēnizein*); see William Linn Westermann, Clinton Walker Keyes, and Herbert Liebesny, *Zenon Papyri, Vol. II: Business Papers of the Third Century B.C. Dealing with Palestine and Egypt* (New York: Columbia University Press, 1940), no. 66.

25. See F. W. Walbank, *The Hellenistic World*, 2nd ed. (Glasgow: Fontana, 1986), 182–184.

26. See, e.g., 1 Macc 13:42: "and people began to write in their documents and contracts, 'In the first year of Simon the great high priest . . . '" (NRSV).

27. For the interpretation, see John J. Collins, *Daniel*, Hermeneia (Minneapolis: Fortress, 1993), 303.

28. See Felix Jacoby, *Die Fragmente der Griechischen Historiker, C: Autoren über einzelne Länder* (Leiden: Brill, 1958), 5–112, no. 609 (Manetho); 364–395, no. 680 (Berossus); 802–824, no. 790 (Philo of Byblos). For translations, see W. G. Waddell, *Manetho: History of Egypt and Other Works*, LCL 350 (Cambridge, MA: Harvard University Press, 1940); Stanley Mayer Burstein, *The Babyloniaca of Berossus*, SANE 1/5 (Malibu, CA: Undena Publications, 1978); Harold W. Attridge and Robert A. Oden, Jr., *Philo of Byblos: The Phoenician History*, CBQMS 10 (Washington, DC: Catholic Biblical Association of America, 1981).

29. See also 1 Macc 7:12–18, where the citation of Ps 79:2–3 is applied to the massacre of sixty Jerusalem scribes by Alcimus.

30. The silver rolls found at Ketef Hinnom (close vicinity of Jerusalem), inscribed with biblical blessings (based on Num 6:24–26), were used as amulets. Though the rock tomb in which they were found dates back to the late seventh or early sixth century BCE, it continued to be used until the first century CE. On the basis of paleographic and stylistic considerations, the inscriptions on the silver rolls are most likely from the second century BCE; see the discussion in Johannes Renz and Wolfgang Röllig, *Handbuch der Althebräischen Epigraphik*, 3 vols. (Darmstadt: Wissenschaftliche Buchgesellschaft, 1995–2003), 1:447–456, esp. 448–449. Note also the reference to "twenty silver amulets" in a third-century BCE Aramaic inventory from Egypt (otherwise unprovenanced); see *TAD* C3.28:106 (*tplḥ zy zhb* 20). See also Angelika Berlejung, "Amulet/s," *EBW*, 29–37, esp. 34–35.

31. See for the following, Mladen Popović, "Reading, Writing, and Memorizing Together: Reading Culture in Ancient Judaism and the Dead Sea Scrolls in a Mediterranean Context," *DSD* 24 (2017): 447–470.

32. On the private possession of books among Jews, see, e.g., 1 Macc 1:56–57: "The books of the law that they [the inspectors appointed by Antiochus IV] found they tore to pieces and burned with fire. Anyone found possessing the book of the covenant . . . was condemned to death by decree of the king" (NRSV).

33. See also the revealing instance of a solitary reader inadvertently pronouncing the holy name "by reading a book" (*qwr' bspr*), 1QS 7:1. According to 2 Macc 15:39, "the style of the story delights the ears of those who read the work" (NRSV).

34. Most glosses to the text were originally written in the margin and later entered the main text in the process of copying; see Ernst Würthwein, *Der Text des Alten Testaments,* 4th ed. (Stuttgart: Württembergische Bibelanstalt, 1973), 108–109, translated by Erroll F. Rhodes as *The Text of the Old Testament: An Introduction to the Biblia Hebraica,* 2nd ed. rev. and enlarged (Grand Rapids: Eerdmans, 1994). For an example of a congregational response, see Jer 10:6–7.

35. See Molly M. Zahn, "Rewritten Scripture," in *The Oxford Handbook of the Dead Sea Scrolls,* ed. John J. Collins and Timothy H. Lim (Oxford: Oxford University Press, 2011), 323–336; Zahn, "Genre and Rewritten Scripture: A Reassessment," *JBL* 131 (2012): 271–288; Adiel Schremer, "'[T]he[y] Did Not Read in the Sealed Book': Qumran Halakhic Revolution and the Emergence of Torah Study in Second Temple Judaism," in *Historical Perspectives: From the Hasmoneans to Bar Kokhba in Light of the Dead Sea Scrolls,* ed. David Goodblatt, Avital Pinnick, and Daniel R. Schwartz, STDJ 37 (Leiden: Brill, 2001), 105–126.

36. For the term "interpretive community," see Stanley Fish, *Is There a Text in This Class? The Authority of Interpretive Communities* (Cambridge, MA: Harvard University Press, 1980).

37. See also John Barton, *Oracles of God: Perceptions of Ancient Prophecy in Israel After the Exile* (London: Darton, Longman & Todd, 1986), 91–93.

38. There is a vast amount of literature on the historical development of synagogues; see, e.g., Rachel Hachlili, "The Origin of the Synagogue: A Re-Assessment," *JSJ* 28 (1997): 34–47; Lee I. Levine, *The Ancient Synagogue: The First Thousand Years,* 2nd ed. (New Haven: Yale University Press, 2005); Anders Runesson, Donald D. Binder, and Birger Olsson, *The Ancient Synagogue from Its Origins to 200 C.E.: A Source Book,* Ancient Judaism and Early Christianity 72 (Leiden: Brill, 2008); Lee I. Levine, "Synagogues," in *The Eerdmans Dictionary of Early Judaism,* ed. John J. Collins and Daniel C. Harlow (Grand Rapids: Eerdmans, 2010), 1260–1271; Eric M. Meyers, "Synagogue/s," *EBW,* 947–957; Jodi

Magness, *Ancient Synagogues in Palestine: A Re-evaluation Nearly a Century After Sukenik's Schweich Lectures,* Schweich Lectures of the British Academy 2022 (Oxford: Oxford University Press, 2024).

39. For the dedicatory text, see Walter Ameling et al., *Corpus Inscriptionum Iudaeae/Palaestinae,* 5 vols. (Berlin: de Gruyter, 2010–2023), vol. 1, no. 9. See also Jeremias, *Jerusalem in the Time of Jesus,* 66.

40. See also Charles Perrot, "The Reading of the Bible in the Ancient Synagogue," in *Mikra: Text, Translation, Reading and Interpretation of the Hebrew Bible in Ancient Judaism and Early Christianity,* ed. Martin J. Mulder and Harry Sysling, CRINT 2/1 (Assen: Van Gorcum, 1988), 137–159.

41. On the Qumran commentaries, see Maurya P. Horgan, *Pesharim: Qumran Interpretations of Biblical Books,* CBQMS 8 (Washington, DC: Catholic Biblical Association of America, 1979).

42. For a study of this phenomenon from a variety of angles, see Hanna Tervanotko and Jonathan Stökl, eds., *Text as Revelation,* LHBOTS (London: Bloomsbury, 2023). The contributions to this volume focus on the Hellenistic period, though some show that the phenomenon occurs before that period as well.

43. On the Pesher Habakkuk from Qumran, see Timothy H. Lim, *The Earliest Commentary on the Prophecy of Habakkuk,* Oxford Commentary on the Dead Sea Scrolls (Oxford: Oxford University Press, 2020).

44. For David as "prophet," see, e.g., 11Q5 = 11QPs^a 27:11 (David spoke his songs "by prophecy," *bnbw'h*), Acts 2:30 (David "being a prophet," *prophētēs oun hyparchōn*).

45. Rudolph Meyer, "Prophetentum und Propheten im Judentum der hellenistischen-römischen Zeit," *TWNT* 6:813–828, esp. 817–820; Ragnar Leivestad, "Das Dogma von der prophetenlosen Zeit," *NTS* 19 (1972–1973): 288–299. See also the reference to the era without prophets in 1 Macc 9:27: "So there was great distress in Israel, such as had not been since the time that prophets ceased to appear among them" (NRSV).

46. Tosephta on m. Soṭah; cf. b. Yoma 9b; b. Sanh. 11a; y. Soṭah 9, 13.

47. Josephus's reference to Artaxerxes is apparently to Artaxerxes I, under whose reign Ezra and Nehemiah were active in Judah, according to Ezra 7:1; Neh 2:1, 13:6.

48. The perception of the scriptures as oracle book led at times to the practice of bibliomancy, where a chance passage might be interpreted as divine oracle for the hour. See, e.g. 1 Macc 3:48: "And they opened the book of the law to inquire into those matters about which the Gentiles consulted the likenesses of their gods" (NRSV). On bibliomancy in late antiquity, see Pieter W. van der Horst, "Sortes Biblicae Judaicae," in *My Lots Are in Thy Hand: Sortilege and Its Practitioners in Late Antiquity,* ed. AnneMarie Luijendijk and William Klingshirn, RGRW 188 (Leiden: Brill, 2018), 154–172.

49. See Helge Stadelmann, *Ben Sira als Schriftgelehrter: Eine Untersuchung zum Berufsbild des vor-makkabäischen Sofer unter Berücksichtigung seines Verhältnisses zu Priester-, Propheten- und Weisheitslehrertum*, WUNT 2/6 (Tübingen: Mohr, 1980).

50. For Josephus on the various Jewish "sects," see *Ant.* 13.171–173 (Pharisees, Sadducees, and Essenes) and 13.295–298 (Pharisees and Sadducees); *J.W.* 2.119–161 (Essenes) and 2.162–166 (Pharisees and Sadducees).

51. So, e.g., the NRSV translations of Acts 5:17, "the sect [*hairesis*] of the Sadducees"; 15:5, "the sect [*hairesis*] of the Pharisees"; 26:5, "I [Paul] have belonged to the strictest sect of our religion [*kata tēn akribestatēn hairesin tēs hēmeteras thrēskeias*] and lived as a Pharisee."

52. From a study of the archaeological evidence, Adler (*Origins of Judaism*, 25–49) concludes that abstention from pork and scaleless fish did not become the prevalent dietary practice among Jews until the late second century BCE. His observation agrees with the fact that references to self-imposed dietary restrictions out of respect for the Jewish way of life occur in texts only from the Hellenistic period and later. See, e.g., Dan 1:8–16; OG Esth 14:17; Tob 1:10–11; Jdt 11:12 ("all that God by his laws has forbidden them to eat," NRSV), 12:1–4; 1 Macc 1:61–62; 2 Macc 6:18–20, 7:1.

53. The term "voluntary association" is used here in a sociological sense for a group one adheres to by personal choice, even though family tradition and class consciousness play their part in the determination of that choice. The Qumran writings emphasize the voluntary character of the association by the frequent use of the verb *hitnaddēb*, "to volunteer"; see, e.g., 1QS 5:1, "This is the rule for the men of the Community who freely volunteer to convert from all evil"; 1Q14 (1QpMic), frags. 8–10:7–8, "a[l]l those volunteering to join the chosen of [God . . .]." On the merits and pitfalls of the analogy of private associations in the Hellenistic world, see Benedikt Eckhardt, "Temple Ideology and Hellenistic Private Associations," *DSD* 24 (2017): 407–423.

54. On the Sadducees, see Gary G. Porton, "Sadducees," *AYBD* 5:892–895.

55. For the interpretation of the name Sadducees, see Porton, "Sadducees," 892.

56. For these views of the Sadducees, see Acts 23:8 (no resurrection, angels, or spirits); Josephus, *J.W.* 2.164–165 (belief in free will as opposed to predestination, no immortality of the soul, no punishments and rewards in the afterlife); Mark 12:18–27; Josephus, *Ant.* 18.16–17 (no afterlife, no resurrection, no oral tradition besides the law)

57. For the popular belief in angels, see Carol Newsom, "Angels (Old Testament)," *AYBD* 1:248–253, esp. 252–253. Note also the popular conception of personal guardian angels (e.g., Matt 18:10, Acts 12:15), an adaptation of the earlier notion of a personal god to the logic of

a monotheistic universe; see Hermann Vorländer, *Mein Gott: Die Vorstellungen vom persönlichen Gott im Alten Orient und im Alten Testament,* AOAT 23 (Kevelaer: Butzon & Bercker; Neukirchen-Vluyn: Neukirchener Verlag, 1975). On resurrection, see, e.g., the tale of the martyrdom of the Seven Sons and Their Mother, 2 Maccabees 7, esp. vv. 9, 11, 14, 23, 29, 36. See also 2 Macc 12:38–45. For general studies, see George W. E. Nickelsburg, Jr., *Resurrection, Immortality, and Eternal Life in Intertestamental Judaism and Early Christianity,* 2nd expanded ed., HTS 26 (Cambridge, MA: Harvard University Press, 2006); James H. Charlesworth, "Where Does the Concept of Resurrection Appear and How Do We Know That?," in *Resurrection: The Origins and Future of a Biblical Doctrine,* ed. James H. Charlesworth, Faith and Scholarship Colloquies (London: T&T Clark, 2006), 1–21; C. D. Elledge, *Resurrection of the Dead in Early Judaism, 200 BCE–CE 200* (New York: Oxford University Press, 2017).

58. The oral Torah (lit., the Torah by word-of-mouth) is reminiscent of the Mesopotamian notion of *šut pi ummāni,* "oral lore of the masters." The doctrine of the oral law could be traced back to Deut 24:8, which implies that the Levitical priests possessed knowledge that Moses had imparted to them (cf. Deut 17:8–13). See also Ephraim E. Urbach, *The Sages: Their Concepts and Beliefs,* trans. Israel Abrahams (Jerusalem: Magnes, 1979), 290–292.

59. See James C. VanderKam, "Those Who Look for Smooth Things, Pharisees, and Oral Law," in *Emanuel: Studies in Hebrew Bible, Septuagint and Dead Sea Scrolls in Honor of Emanuel Tov,* ed. Shalom M. Paul, Robert A. Kraft, Lawrence H. Schiffman, and Weston W. Fields, VTSup 94 (Leiden: Brill, 2003), 465–477.

60. See discussion in John J. Collins, *The Invention of Judaism: Torah and Jewish Identity from Deuteronomy to Paul,* Taubman Lectures in Jewish Studies 7 (Oakland: University of California Press, 2017), 110–111.

61. For a survey of the Dead Sea Scrolls and their discovery, see James C. VanderKam, *The Dead Sea Scrolls Today,* 2nd ed. (Grand Rapids: Eerdmans, 2010); John J. Collins, *The Dead Sea Scrolls: A Biography* (Princeton, NJ: Princeton University Press, 2012). An accessible presentation of nearly all of the texts in transcription with English translation is available in García Martínez and Tigchelaar, eds., *Dead Sea Scrolls.*

62. For a lucid presentation of the evidence and a cogently argued conclusion, see Sidnie White Crawford, *Scribes and Scrolls at Qumran* (Grand Rapids: Eerdmans, 2019), 269–308.

63. Josephus, *J.W.* 2.124–127. The Rule of the Community speaks about the members "in all their places of residence" (1QS 6:2 // 4QSd 2:6); see Sarianna Metso, *The Community Rule: A Critical Edition with Translation,* EJL 51 (Atlanta: Society of Biblical Literature, 2019), 32–33. See John J.

Collins, *Beyond the Qumran Community: The Sectarian Movement of the Dead Sea Scrolls* (Grand Rapids: Eerdmans, 2010). Sidnie White Crawford, "The Identification and History of the Qumran Community in American Scholarship," in *The Dead Sea Scrolls in Scholarly Perspective: A History of Research,* ed. Devorah Dimant, STDJ 99 (Leiden: Brill, 2012), 1–18, esp. 15, observes that the different editions of the Community Rule reflect the existence of multiple settlements of "Qumranites."

64. See CD 3:13–14. See also 1QpHab 7:4–5, "the Teacher of Righteousness, to whom God has made known all the mysteries (*rzy*) of the words of his servants, the prophets"; 1QS 8:11–12, "And every matter hidden (*nstr*) from Israel but which has been found out by the Interpreter."

65. Quotations from CD 3:16; 6:4–5, 7.

66. The description here given draws its inspiration from Collins, *Invention of Judaism,* 110–111.

67. See Josephus, *Ant.* 13.298, who writes that the Sadducees had the confidence of the wealthy alone but no following among the general population, whereas the Pharisees had the support of the masses. See also *Ant.* 13.288, where it is said that the Pharisees have a great "influence with the masses" (*ischun para tōi plēthei*). For the Essenes, note the reference to "the simple ones of Judah who observe the Law" (*pt'y yhwdh 'wśh htwrh*), in 1QpHab 12:4–5; cf. 1Q14 (1QpMic), frags. 8–10:5.

68. See 1QS 5:23, 6:13–23, 8:19; CD 13:11–12, 14:3–6. For a critical edition of the Community Rule (1QS and parr.), see Metso, *Community Rule.*

69. See 1QS 8:12–13.

70. See 4QMMT C 7–8.

71. See 1QS 1:16–17. On the use of the notion of covenant in the Essene community, see John J. Collins, "Jewish Communities in the Dead Sea Scrolls," in *Torah, Temple, Land,* ed. Markus Witte, Jens Schröter, and Verena M. Lepper, TSAJ 184 (Tübingen: Mohr Siebeck, 2021), 105–116, esp. 108–110.

72. See 1QS 5:8–10, CD 15:5–9.

73. See the somewhat sweeping but judicious observations by Moshe Weinfeld, "The Crystallization of the 'Congregation of the Exile' (*qhl hgwlh*) and the Sectarian Nature of Post-Exilic Judaism," in *Normative and Sectarian Judaism in the Second Temple Period,* LSTS 54 (London: T&T Clark, 2005), 232–238.

74. See Moshe Weinfeld, *The Organizational Pattern and the Penal Code of the Qumran Sect: A Comparison with Guilds and Religious Associations of the Hellenistic-Roman Period,* NTOA 2 (Fribourg: Éditions Universitaires; Göttingen: Vandenhoeck & Ruprecht, 1986); John S. Kloppenborg and Stephen G. Wilson, eds., *Voluntary Associations in the Graeco-Roman World* (London: Routledge, 1996); Yonder M. Gillihan, *Civic Ideology, Organization, and Law in the Rule Scrolls: A Comparative*

Study of the Covenanters' Sect and Contemporary Voluntary Associations in Political Context, STDJ 97 (Leiden: Brill, 2011).

75. The early Christians are also referred to as a *hairesis*, "sect," in Acts 24:5, "[Paul,] a ringleader of the sect of the Nazarenes [*tēs tōn Nazōraiōn haireseōs*]"; 24:14, "the Way, which they call a sect [*hairesis*]"; 28:22, "this sect" (*hairesis*, for Christians).

76. For a discussion of the background, see Collins, *Daniel*, 385.

77. See *CAD* 17/3, 144–147, s.v. *šiṭru*, esp. 146, *šiṭir šamê*. On the notion of the stars as "heavenly writing" and astrology/astronomy in Mesopotamian culture, see Francesca Rochberg, *The Heavenly Writing: Divination, Horoscopy, and Astronomy in Mesopotamian Culture* (Cambridge: Cambridge University Press, 2004).

78. For an excellent introduction to the apocalypse as literary genre plus a survey of the various Jewish apocalyptic texts, see John J. Collins, *The Apocalyptic Imagination: An Introduction to Jewish Apocalyptic Literature*, 3rd ed. (Grand Rapids: Eerdmans, 2016).

79. For Enoch as "scribe," see also 4Q203 (EnGiants[a]) 8:1–4; 4Q530 (EnGiants[b]) 2:14.

80. For a discussion of the apocalyptic literature ascribed to Baruch, see Collins, *Apocalyptic Imagination*, 264–280, 311–315. For the figure of Baruch, see J. Edward Wright, *Baruch Ben Neriah: From Biblical Scribe to Apocalyptic Seer* (Columbia: University of South Carolina Press, 2003).

81. See the discussion by John J. Collins, "Where Should We Look for the Roots of Jewish Apocalypticism?," in *Dreams, Visions, Imaginations: Jewish, Christian and Gnostic Views of the World to Come*, ed. Jens Schröter, Tobias Nicklas, and Armand Puig i Tàrrech, BZNW 247 (Berlin: de Gruyter, 2021), 5–26. On Babylonian lore in Jewish apocalyptic traditions, see Wilfred G. Lambert, *The Background of Jewish Apocalyptic*, Ethel M. Wood Lecture delivered before the University of London on 22 February 1977 (London: Athlone, 1978); Helle S. Kvanvig, *Roots of Apocalyptic: The Mesopotamian Background of the Enoch Figure and of the Son of Man*, WMANT 61 (Neukirchen-Vluyn: Neukirchener Verlag, 1988); Gebhard J. Selz, "Of Heroes and Sages: Considerations on the Early Mesopotamian Background of Some Enochic Traditions," in *The Dead Sea Scrolls in Context: Integrating the Dead Sea Scrolls in the Study of Ancient Texts, Languages, and Cultures*, ed. Armin Lange, Emanuel Tov, and Matthias Weigold, 2 vols., VTSup 140 (Leiden: Brill, 2011), 2:779–800. For the presence of motifs from the Canaanite mythology as known from the Ugaritic texts, see John Day, *God's Conflict with the Dragon and the Sea: Echoes of a Canaanite Myth in the Old Testament* (Cambridge: Cambridge University Press, 1985), 141–178 ("The eschatologization of the divine conflict with the dragon and the sea"). For a discussion of possible Persian influence, see Collins, *Apocalyptic*

Imagination, 36–41. For Egyptian influence, especially Egyptian conceptions about the judgment of the dead, see Jiří Janák and Michael Sommer, "Ancient Egyptian Judgment of the Dead in Visual Memory of Jewish Apocalyptic Literature," in *Social Memory Theory and Conceptions of Afterlife in Jewish and Christian Antiquity,* ed. Thomas R. Hatina and Jiří Lukeš, Studies in Cultural Contexts of the Bible 8 (Paderborn: Brill Schöning, 2023), 77–97.

82. See Mark J. Geller, "The Fiction of a Jewish Hellenistic Magical-Medical *Paideia," JAOS* 142 (2022): 443–454, esp. 445–446; Henryk Drawnel, "Some Notes on the Aramaic Manuscripts from Qumran and Late Mesopotamian Culture," *RevQ* 26 (2013): 145–168. The biblical book of Ezekiel offers an early (pre-Hellenistic) example of the impact of Babylonian scribalism on Judean authors from the eastern diaspora; see Isaac Gluska, "Akkadian Influences on the Book of Ezekiel," in *An Experienced Scribe Who Neglects Nothing: Ancient Near Eastern Studies in Honor of Jacob Klein,* ed. Yitschak Sefati, Pinhas Artzi, Chaim Cohen, Barry L. Eichler, and Victor Avigdor Hurowitz (Bethesda, MD: CDL, 2005), 718–737; Abraham Winitzer, "Assyriology and Jewish Studies in Tel Aviv: Ezekiel Among the Babylonian Literati," in *Encounters by the Rivers of Babylon: Scholarly Conversations Between Jews, Iranians, and Babylonians in Antiquity,* ed. Uri Gabbay and S. Secunda, TSAJ 160 (Tübingen: Mohr Siebeck, 2014), 163–216.

83. For a discussion of non-Jewish apocalypses, see Anders Hultgård, "Persian Apocalypticism," in *The Encyclopedia of Apocalypticism,* ed. John J. Collins, Bernard McGinn, and Stephen J. Stein, 2 vols. (New York: Continuum, 1998), 1:39–83; Lambert, *Background of Jewish Apocalyptic;* Françoise Dunand, "L'Oracle du Potier et la formation de l'apocalyptique en Égypte," in *L'Apocalyptique,* ed. Freddy Raphael et al. (Paris: Geuthner, 1977), 39–67; Giovanni Battista Bazzana, "The 'Oracle of the Potter' and the 'Apocalyptic Worldview' in Egypt," *ETL* 94 (2018): 207–222.

84. See Collins, *Apocalyptic Imagination,* 65: "The perplexing problems of the present . . . are overcome by the superimposition of the myth."

85. In the words of John J. Collins, *Apocalyptic Imagination,* 49, "the effectiveness of the device [of pseudepigraphy] presupposes the credulity of the masses."

86. The term "scribal phenomenon" is borrowed from Jonathan Z. Smith, "Wisdom and Apocalyptic," in *Map Is Not Territory: Studies in the History of Religion* (Chicago: University of Chicago Press, 1993), 67–87, esp. 74.

87. See Matt 22:23–33; Josephus, *J.W.* 2.165; Eccl 9:5–6, 11:8; Sir 41:1–4. Though Ben Sira also saw world history as a succession of empires similar to the sequence of kingdoms in Daniel 2 and 7 (a model frequently referred to with the Latin phrase *translatio imperii),* he believed their

rise and decline were of human making (Sir 10:8; cf. 15:14–15; contrast Jdt 9:5–6).

88. For references to the *qṣ ḥrwn*, see CD 1.5.

89. For the equation one day = one year, see Ezek 4:5, Num 14:34. See also Walther Zimmerli, *Ezechiel 1–24*, BKAT 13/1 (Neukirchen-Vluyn: Neukirchener Verlag, 1969), 118–119, who identifies it as a Priestly way of reckoning.

90. See discussion in Collins, *Daniel,* 352–360.

91. For the coins of John Hyrcanus I, see Oliver D. Hoover, "The Seleucid Coinage of John Hyrcanus I: The Transformation of a Dynastic Symbol in Hellenistic Judaea," *American Journal of Numismatics* 15 (2003): 29–39. On Seleucid military alliances with autonomous political entities, see John Ma, *Antiochos III and the Cities of Western Asia Minor* (New York: Oxford University Press, 1999), 164–165.

92. See Tessa Rajak, "Hasmonean Dynasty," *AYBD* 3:67–76, esp. 70.

93. For the dates of the Hasmonean expansion, see Dan Barag, "New Evidence on the Foreign Policy of John Hyrcanus I," *INJ* 12 (1992–1993): 1–12; Gerald Finkielsztejn, "More Evidence on John Hyrcanus I's Conquests: Lead Weights and Rhodian Amphora Stamps," *BAIAS* 16 (1998): 33–63; Israel Shatzman, "The Expansionist Policy of John Hyrcanus and His Relations with Rome," *Iudea socia—Iudea capta*, ed. Gianpaolo Urso (Rome: ETS, 2020), 29–77, esp. 37–45.

94. See Adler, *Origins of Judaism,* esp. 231–233, where he argues that the practice of Judaism as a religion emerged as a result of the religious politics of the Hasmonean kings.

95. For the notion of "exile" (*glwt*) in Qumran texts, see, e.g., the self-designation *glwt hmdbr,* "the exiled of the desert," in 1Q33 (1QM) 1:2; and "the house of his exile" as designation of the dwelling of the Teacher of Righteousness, 1QpHab 11:6.

96. See S. David Sperling, "Belial," *DDD,* 169–171.

97. In the dualistic worldview of the Qumran sectarian scrolls, the community was involved in a conflict between "the sons of light" and "the sons of darkness" (1QS 1:9–10); the former are "the men of God's lot," and the latter are "the men of the lot of Belial" (1QS 2:1–5). Up to a point, this dualism echoes the traditional antithesis between the "righteous" (*ṣaddîqîm*) and the "wicked" (*rěšā'îm*) in the Psalms, or the wise versus the fools in Proverbs. But whereas the older texts use the opposition as a rhetorical device (for pedagogical purposes, or to make the argument more compelling), the Qumran writings take it literally. The conflict between two opposing camps has cosmic dimensions. It is a battle between God and Belial, each assisted by a host of heavenly beings. The Prince of Light (*śr 'wrym, śr m'wr*) is the commander of God's "angels of justice," whereas the Angel of Darkness (*ml'k ḥwšk*)

leads "the angels of destruction" (1QS 3:20–21, 1QM 13:10–12). While the discussion about the possible Persian background of this dualism is far from closed, it seems difficult to deny all Iranian influence. See the discussion by Florentino García Martínez, "Iranian Influences in Qumran?," in *Qumranica Minora I: Qumran Origins and Apocalypticism,* ed. E. J. C. Tigchelaar and F. García Martínez, STDJ 63 (Leiden: Brill, 2007), 227–242; Paul Heger, "Another Look at Dualism in the Qumran Writings," in *Dualism in Qumran,* ed. Géza G. Xeravits (London: T&T Clark, 2010), 39–101; Albert de Jong, "Iranian Connections in the Dead Sea Scrolls," in *The Oxford Handbook of the Dead Sea Scrolls,* ed. Timothy H. Lim and John J. Collins (Oxford: Oxford University Press, 2010), 479–500, esp. 490–495.

98. Initially, Muhammad and his early followers took over the Jewish practice of saying their prayers facing Jerusalem. They changed the *qibla* (prayer orientation) toward Mecca as the relationship with the Jews deteriorated; see Qur'an 2:142–145 and Fred M. Donner, *Muhammad and the Believers: At the Origins of Islam* (Cambridge, MA: Harvard University Press, 2010), 44–45, 214–215.

99. On the importance of the pilgrimage to Jerusalem, from either Palestine or the diaspora, see Tob 1:5–8; Jdt 16:18–20; Mark 11:11; Luke 2:41–51; Acts 2:5–13, 8:27–28; Jeremias, *Jerusalem in the Time of Jesus,* 58–84. The parallel with the Muslim pilgrimage to Mecca known as the hajj (etymologically related to Hebrew *ḥag,* "festival") is not fortuitous.

100. See Lawrence H. Schiffman, "The New Halakhic Letter (4QMMT) and the Origins of the Dead Sea Sect," *BA* 53 (1990): 64–73; Collins, *Invention of Judaism,* 109–112; Crawford, *Scribes and Scrolls at Qumram,* 280–284.

101. See Shaye J. D. Cohen, "The Significance of Yavneh: Pharisees, Rabbis, and the End of Jewish Sectarianism," *HUCA* 55 (1984): 27–53, esp. 31, "With the disappearance of the temple, the focal point of sectarianism also disappeared."

102. On the reign of Herod the Great, see Lee I. Levine, "Herod the Great," *AYBD* 3:161–169.

103. All of these passages refer to the coming not just of any prophet but of the prophet like Moses promised in Deut 18:18, which explains the emphasis on the oral instruction he shall give. The qualification of the prophet as "reliable" (*pistos,* 1 Macc 14:41) echoes the use of the same adjective for Moses in Num 12:6–8 LXX, cf. Heb 3:5. The Community Rule from Qumran actually speaks of the coming of the prophet "and the messiahs of Aaron and Israel" (*'d bw' nby' wmšyḥy 'hrwn wyśr'l*), to be discussed below.

104. For the Samaritan doctrine of the Messiah (the Taheb), see Ferdinand Dexinger, *Der Taheb: Ein "messianischer" Heilsbringer der Samaritaner*

(Salzburg: Müller, 1986); Dexinger, "Samaritan Eschatology," in *The Samaritans*, ed. Alan D. Crown (Tübingen: Mohr Siebeck, 1989), 266–292, esp. 267–276.

105. See also CD 12:3, 14:19, 19:10–11, which speak about "the messiah of Aaron and Israel" (*mšyḥ 'hrwn wyšr'l*); cf. 20:1, *mšyḥ m'hrwn wmyšr'l*.

106. On the expectation of a dual leadership in the eschatological time, see John J. Collins, *The Scepter and the Star: The Messiahs of the Dead Sea Scrolls and Other Ancient Literature*, 2nd ed. (Grand Rapids: Eerdmans, 2010), 81–83.

107. See 4Q175 (4QTestimonia) 1–20. The quotation of Deut 18:18–19 is preceded by Deut 5:28b–29, which resembles the catena consisting of Exod 20:19–22 + Deut 5:29 + Deut 18:18–20, 22, found in 4Q158 frag. 6 (4QReworked Pentateuch^a, frag. 6). The Qumran catena has a parallel in the catena in Exodus 20 of the Samaritan Pentateuch (Deut 5:24–27 + 5:28b–29 + 18:18–22 + 5:30–31).

108. For a full discussion, see Collins, *Scepter and the Star*.

109. See Stefan Beyerle, "'A Star Shall Come Out of Jacob': A Critical Evaluation of the Balaam Oracle in the Context of Jewish Revolts in Roman Times," in *The Prestige of the Pagan Prophet Balaam in Judaism, Early Christianity and Islam*, ed. George H. van Kooten and Jacques van Ruiten, Themes in Biblical Narrative 11 (Leiden: Brill, 2008), 163–188.

110. See Clayton N. Jefford, "Theudas," *AYBD* 6:527–528; David E. Aune, *Prophecy in Early Christianity and the Ancient Mediterranean World* (Grand Rapids: Eerdmans, 1983), 126–162.

111. For the tradition about the disappearance of the "sacred vessels," see the preface of 2 Maccabees, which says that the prophet Jeremiah, so instructed by an oracle, had taken the tabernacle (the tent sanctuary from the time of Moses), the ark, and the incense altar to a cave dwelling in the mountain and sealed it. Nobody knew their location. As Jeremiah had said, "the place shall remain unknown until God gathers his people together again and shows his mercy" (2 Macc 2:1–8). The absence of these holy items—the so-called sacred vessels—symbolized the discontinuity between the cult in the days of Moses and the monarchy, on the one hand, and the postexilic period, on the other. A variant Samaritan tradition says that Moses had hidden the sacred vessels; see also the next note.

112. For this episode, see Marilyn F. Collins, "The Hidden Vessels in Samaritan Traditions," *JSJ* 3 (1972): 97–116.

113. See Stanley J. Isser, *The Dositheans: A Samaritan Sect in Late Antiquity*, SJLA 17 (Leiden: Brill, 1976).

114. For a discussion of Judas the Galilean and his movement, see David Rhoads, "Zealots," *AYBD* 6:1043–1054.

115. The Greek terms are *goēs* (Josephus, *Ant.* 20.97, about Theudas; *J.W.* 2.261, the Jewish prophet from Egypt) and *pseudoprophētēs* (*J.W.* 2.261, the Jewish prophet from Egypt; cf. *Ant.* 18.85, where *pseudos* qualifies the Samaritan prophet in the days of Pontius Pilate).

116. See Cohen, "Significance of Yavneh.

117. See Timothy H. Lim, *The Formation of the Jewish Canon*, AYBRL (New Haven: Yale University Press, 2013); see also Lim, "How Was the Canon Formed," *ExpTim* 133 (2022): 1–13.

Epilogue

1. See, e.g., Richard S. Hess, *Israelite Religions: An Archaeological and Biblical Survey* (Grand Rapids: Baker Academic, 2007), who devotes no more than ten of four hundred pages to a discussion of "Exilic and Postexilic Religion" (pp. 337–346). Patrick D. Miller, *The Religion of Ancient Israel,* LAI (London: SPCK; Louisville: Westminster John Knox, 2000), has chosen a thematic approach and explains, "The decision not to present the religion of Israel in this volume in a primarily historical mode has at least some justification in the very fuzzy lines that mark the beginning and end of Israelite religion" (208). In practice, his focus is overwhelmingly on the preexilic period. The same focus on the preexilic period is in Susan Niditch, *Ancient Israelite Religion* (New York: Oxford University Press, 1997); Susan Ackerman, *Women and the Religion of Ancient Israel,* AYBRL (New Haven: Yale University Press, 2022), esp. 2–4; and Rüdiger Schmitt, *Die Religionen Israels/Palästinas in der Eisenzeit, 12.–6. Jahrhundert v. Chr.,* ÄAT 94 (Münster: Zaphon, 2020).

2. See, e.g., Rudolf Smend, *Lehrbuch der alttestamentlichen Religionsgeschichte,* 2nd rev. ed. (Freiburg: J. C. B. Mohr, 1899), esp. 265–268. The earliest history of Israelite religion is Wilhelm Vatke, *Die Religion des Alten Testaments nach den kanonischen Büchern* (Berlin: Bethge, 1835). The title as here given is actually the subtitle, the main title being *Die biblische Theologie wissenschaftlich dargestellt,* which is telling of the intellectual climate of the times. See also Archibald Duff, *Old Testament Theology or: The History of Hebrew Religion,* 2 vols. (London: Adam and Charles Black, 1891–1900).

3. The developmental scheme devised by Vatke and followed by Smend also informs William Foxwell Albright, *From the Stone Age to Christianity: Monotheism and the Historical Process* (Baltimore: Johns Hopkins University Press, 1940), and still echoes in George Mendenhall, *Ancient Israel's Faith and History: An Introduction to the Bible in Context,* ed. Gary A. Herion (Louisville: Westminster John Knox, 2001).

4. See, e.g., Theodoor C. Vriezen, *De godsdienst van Israël* (Zeist: W. de Haan; Arnhem: Van Loghum Slaterus, 1963), translated by Hubert

Hoskins as *The Religion of Ancient Israel* (Philadelphia: Westminster, 1967). Frank Moore Cross, *Canaanite Myth and Hebrew Epic: Essays in the History of the Religion of Israel* (Cambridge, MA: Harvard University Press, 1973), starts with the chapter "The Religion of Canaan and the God of Israel" and ends with "Exile and Apocalyptic." Rainer Albertz, *Religionsgeschichte Israels in alttestamentlicher Zeit*, 2 vols. ATD Ergänzungsreihe 8/1–2 (Göttingen: Vandenhoeck & Ruprecht, 1992), Teil 1: Von den Anfängen bis zum Ende der Königszeit; Teil 2: Vom Exil bis zu den Makkabäern; translated by John Bowden as *A History of Israelite Religion in the Old Testament Period*, 2 vols. (London: SCM, 1994).

5. See Yonatan Adler, *The Origins of Judaism: An Archaeological-Historical Reappraisal*, AYBRL (New Haven: Yale University Press, 2022).

6. One notable example is B. D. Eerdmans, *The Religion of Israel* (Leiden: Leiden University Press, 1947), whose ch. 35 has the title "From the Maccabees to 70 A.D." (pp. 250–260).

7. On this issue, see Marc Zvi Brettler, "Judaism in the Hebrew Bible? The Transition from Ancient Israelite Religion to Judaism," *CBQ* 61 (1999): 429–447. Brettler observes that "there is not a neat transition between ancient Israel and Judaism" (443) and that "Judaism incorporates what others call biblical Israel" (446). His discussion emphasizes continuity, without ignoring the religious and social developments that make Judaism a transformative sequel of Israelite religion.

8. Among a wealth of studies of the Birkat Ha-Minim, see esp. Pieter W. van der Horst, "The birkat ha-minim in Recent Research," *ExpTim* 105 (1994): 363–368; Uri Ehrlich and Ruth Langer, "The Earliest Text of the *Birkat Haminim*," *HUCA* 76 (2005): 63–112; Joel Marcus, "*Birkat Ha-Minim* Revisited," *NTS* 55 (2009): 523–551.

9. The term *preparatio evangelica* is taken from the title of a treatise by the church father Eusebius of Caesarea (ca. 260–340 CE). Most scholars of Israelite religion would not make the phrase their own, but in nineteenth-century books on Israelite religion, it is not uncommon to find Israelite religion qualified as "Vorgeschichte des Christenthums"; see Smend, *Lehrbuch des alttestamentlichen Religionsgeschichte*, v.

Acknowledgments

I owe a huge debt of gratitude to a great many people who were involved, one way or another, in the writing of this book. Most of them inspired me with ideas and insights without even knowing that they did. Colleagues and students with whom I have interacted, in Amsterdam, Leiden, Utrecht, and elsewhere; participants in conferences and workshops I have attended over the years; family and friends with whom I have discussed about a thousand things rarely related to Israelite religion directly—all of them have helped me in identifying some of the real issues by asking the inconvenient questions, by venturing their own views, and by providing a congenial context in which ideas came to me unannounced, as if I were the one who had thought of them first.

A few people deserve to be singled out for their special help. They are, in alphabetical order, Susan Ackerman (Dartmouth College), whose observations, especially on the first part of the book, have caused me to rethink and rephrase several passages; Bob Becking (Utrecht University), whose insightful comments have helped me shape the discussion of diaspora religion in Chapter 4; Elizabeth Bloch-Smith (Princeton Theological Seminary), who read through Chapters 2 and 3 and generously shared her intimate knowledge of the archaeology of the Levant in the Iron Age; Pieter van der Horst (Utrecht University), who kindly offered to submit Chapter 6 to a critical and very helpful review; and Konrad Schmid (University of Zurich), who read through the entire manuscript, suggested improvements, and provided me with additional references to important literature.

Despite the help of these and other colleagues, this book is not without flaws and imperfections. No one is to blame but the author, as the ethics of scholarly accountability tell me to say at this point. Absolutely. All the same, a book like this is not the work of just one author. It also reflects the prejudice of its time, and the particular concerns and interests of a given generation. A hundred years ago, the history of Israelite religion looked very different from the way it does today. Another hundred years from now—most likely much sooner—new generations will have developed views that are again quite different. Not only because of new discoveries, archaeological and otherwise, but also because none of us can look at the past from outer space. We are locked within the perspective of our own time. In that respect, this book, caught in the tides and turns of the present, will pass the way its predecessors have passed. The sands are constantly shifting, and so do the contours of the past. It doesn't matter. After all, the fun is in trying to tell the story as it emerges from the data as we see them right now, even though we know that tomorrow people will be smiling at what we have come up with today.

Index of Subjects

accusations, false, and slander, 46, 113, 119

acropolis: of Jerusalem, 93, 292n16; of Ophrah, 292n16; site of city temple, 125; temple of Sidon, 295–296n38

adoption, 61, 65

adultery, 46, 88, 112, 113

afterlife, 226, 230, 232, 347n56

agricultural year, 24–25

Ahikam: beer trader in Babylon, 316n77; member of Judean community in Al-Yaḫudu, 160, 168, 312n41; tax collector, 161, 311n35

Ahuramazda (god), 193, 194, 195

Akhenaten (pharaoh), 29

Akitu festival, 25, 84, 163–164, 277n17, 301n88, 316n77; Ezekiel at, 164–165

alcohol: avoided by Rechabite community, 157; not permitted for priests on duty, 110

Alexander the Great, 178, 211–212

almsgiving, 216, 217, 343n19, 344n23

altars: of Bethel, 53, 106, 187; dedication of new, 112; of earth, 39; fourhorned, 99–100; incense altar, 97, 126; of King Ahaz, 106; large, for animal sacrifice, 97; at Ophrah, 292n16; place at Mount Gerizim, 185; of Shechem, 53; temple as "altar house," 324n23

Al-Yaḫudu: archives from, 309–310n25; Judean settlement, 160

Amherst papyrus, 76, 86–87, 173, 174

Amorites, 32–33, 53, 55, 60, 66, 76

Amos (prophet), 108, 151, 307–308n15

Amurru (god), 32, 33, 55, 76

Anat (goddess), 3, 30, 31, 47, 258nn61,64, 264n19, 276n14

Anat-Bethel (goddess), 3, 94, 157, 174, 175

Anathoth (priestly city), 14, 47, 147, 155, 157, 306n8

Anat-Yaho (goddess), 3, 94, 174

ancestor cult, 24, 33–36, 130–132, 136–139, 305n110; erosion of, 213; for royal ancestors, 36

angels, 93, 182–183, 229, 232, 234, 347–348n57; angel of darkness, 352–353n97; archangels, 181; of destruction, 352–353n97; gods demoted to, 182–183; as intermediaries, 224, 230; of justice, 352–353n97; personal guardian, 347–348n57; Sadducees reject belief in, 226, 347n56; seven "angels of the presence," 181

anguish, eschatological "time of," 233

ankle bones (astragali), used for divinatory purposes, 114, 289n130

anointment: as covenant rite, 79–80; priestly, 237; royal, 79–83, 237

anthropomorphism, 28, 30, 42, 46, 111

Antiochus IV Epiphanes, 212, 214, 233, 341n10; as "the prince" in Daniel, 223

Anu (god), 37

apocalypse and apocalyptic literature, 228–232

Arad (fortress), 57, 90, 129, 188, 279n40, 286n102, 297n50

Arad ostraca, 281–282n56

Aramaic: adopted by Judean diaspora in Babylonia, 163; as dominant vernacular in Palestine, 217; elements of, in Northern Hebrew, 272–273n107; as spoken language of the Elephantine community, 173

Ardat-lilî (demon), 300n75

ark (portable shrine), 68, 84, 85, 101, 354n111

armory, temple serving as, 101

army, 116

Artaxerxes I (Persian king), 185, 192; confusion of, with Artaxerxes II, 329–330n54, 346n47; edict of, 181, 339n120

asherah (cult symbol), 128, 130, 295n38

Asherah (goddess), 3, 12, 30–31, 33, 55, 57, 76, 94, 95, 109, 128, 130, 143, 144, 145, 258n61, 265n34, 267n51, 273n118, 274n4, 282nn59,61, 284n80, 295nn36–37, 300n76, 301n83

Ashratu (goddess), 33, 55, 76

Asmodeus (demon), 322n4

astronomy: Astronomical Book of 1 Enoch, 181, 229, 230, 322–323n9; Babylonian, 229, 350n77

asylum, temple as, 99, 101

Atargatis (goddess), 300n76

Atrahasis, epic of, 44, 255n35, 305n110, 316n74

Aya (goddess), 22, 30

Azazel (demon), 49

Baal (god), 12, 25, 27, 30, 43, 47, 52, 57–58, 75, 94, 264n19, 273n114, 274n4, 281n49, 286n96

Baal-berith (god), 63

Baal Cycle, 94, 129, 274n4, 284n87

Baal-shamayin, Baal-shamin (god), 41, 87, 288n114

Baal toponyms, 52

Baal-zaphon (god), 87

Babylon (city), 31, 32, 40, 81, 156, 158, 160, 161, 164, 166, 168, 170, 176, 268n55

Babylonian story of creation (Enuma Elish), 29–30, 31, 40, 79, 84, 274n4

Balaam inscription from Deir Alla, 3, 54–55, 73, 262n2, 272–273n107

Balaam oracle, 238, 354n109

Banit (title of goddess Nanay), 160, 173

Bar Kokhba (Simon bar Kosiba), 238

barter, 6, 134, 216, 342–343n16

Baruch (secretary of Jeremiah), 146; as alleged author of apocalyptic literature, 230, 350n80

bedrooms, 136; sites of domestic cult, 137–138; of sun god, 22; in temple, 98

Beersheba (Judean fortress town), 90, 100, 145, 188

Beersheba ostraca, 167, 316n73

Behistun rock inscription, 193, 195, 331n57

Bel (god), 31, 163, 164, 165, 170, 178, 314n60. See also Marduk

Belial (leader of the forces of darkness), 235, 352–353n97

Benjamin (tribe, territory), 72, 90, 280n44, 309n22

Ben Sira, 215, 219, 224, 232, 347n49, 351–352n87

Berossus, 219, 344n28

Bethel (god), 127, 157, 160, 174–175, 187, 320nn105–106

Bethel (place): altar at, 53; Amos active in, 151; bull statue of, 76; prophets at, 149. See also temples

bethel (sacred stone), 42, 127. See also stela, stone

Bethel-sharezer, 160, 315n67, 317n86

Bethsaida, 90, 292n13

Birkat Ha-Minim, 243, 356n8

birth: ancestors witnessing, of offspring, 138; cause of impurity, 112; kings' divine, 275n10; Yhwh present at, 298n61

blessing, 35–36, 39, 44, 148

blood, 59, 60, 66, 112; taboo on spilling, 70
Book of the Dead, 46
books: "book of Moses," 198; "book of the law," 154–155, 203; consultation of royal rule book, 202; "people of the book," 217; as private possessions, 345n32; scrolls, 198, 200, 332n72
Booths, Festival of. *See* Succoth
border fortresses, 90–92, 278–280n37–44, 286n102
bride price, 134
Bull Site, 40, 76–77, 126, 128
bull statues, 76–77, 86, 94, 105, 174, 274n120, 286n96
burial, 213, 253n11, 276–277n15

calendars, 22; adoption of Babylonian, 167; festival, 15, 207–208, 236; use of calendar dates by Judeans, 167
Cambyses II (king), 195, 324n20
cannabis, used as incense, 132, 297n50
Carmel, Mount, 58, 90, 279–280n41, 287n112, 301n88
catalogues: of gods, 1; of texts and authors, 256n44; of trades, 216
cella (inner sanctum), 93, 97–98, 101, 103, 261n106
Chemosh (god), 11, 32, 69, 70, 77, 89–90, 282n61, 283n64
cherubs, cherubim: flanking the ark, 101–102; throne of, 102
Christians, 217, 228, 243–244, 350n75
circumcision, 14, 62, 214, 225, 234, 235, 269–270n73
cities: and towns, 120; walls of, 120, 125
code of conduct, 44
coinage, 216, 234, 342n11, 352n91
commentary texts (*pesharim*), 216, 217, 222–223, 233
community: interpretive or reading, 220, 224; religious (*qāhāl*), 185, 189, 208, 213, 324n21

conquest of Canaan, 51
conversion, converts, 214, 236
cosmology, 18
council, divine, 29–30, 182
Covenant Code, 139
covenants, 62–67, 73–74, 79–80, 82–83, 87–89, 228, 269–270n73, 270n76, 274n3
cremation, 73, 273n109
critiques: of Babylonian religion, 171; of divine images, 131; of the sacrificial cult, 111
cult centralization, 14, 199
cult stands, clay and limestone, 134, 144, 297n52. *See also* Taanach cult stands
curses, 46, 67, 114, 116, 148, 228
Cyrus (king): conquers Babylon, 168, 178; hailed as YHWH's servant and messiah, 170, 212
Cyrus cylinder, 169, 170–171, 194, 314n59, 318n90

Dan (city in northern Israel), 42, 43, 64, 76, 90, 105, 131
Daniel (book), 223, 229, 233
Daniel (prophet), 163, 219, 229–230
Darius I (king), 169, 185, 193, 195, 202, 317n85, 318n87, 328n49; orders codification of Egyptian law, 196, 332n69
Darius II (king), 205, 207
David (king), 51, 62, 71–76, 80, 138, 223, 235
Day of Atonement (Yom Kippur), 49, 98, 112
Day of the LORD, 231
deber ("Pestilence," divine being), 57, 93
Deborah (prophetess), 69; Song of, 64
Deborah (wet nurse of Rebekah), 93
demons, 17, 37–39, 44, 45, 49, 123, 300n75, 322n4
dendromancy, 128
Destroyer (*mašḥit;* demon), 49

Deutero-Isaiah (Second Isaiah), 158, 164, 169–170, 171, 172, 318n88

Deuteronomy, northern background of, 155, 156

diaspora: Israelite, in Judah, 154–158; Judean, in Babylonia, 158–172; Judean and Samarian, in Egypt, 172–177; Samarian, in Assyria, 154, 212; Samaritan, 222, 246, 320n108

divine kingship, 80–81

divorce, 62, 67

domestic cult, 13, 35, 36, 105, 136–139, 144, 298n59

Dositheans (Samaritan sect), 239, 241

dreams: deceitful, 224, 232; dream interpretation and necromancy, 304n107; prophetic, 149, 229

dualism, 180, 322n4, 352–353n97

dung heap, 122

economy: as mitigated form of capitalism, 134–135; money, 6, 134, 216–217, 343n18

Edomites (ethnic group), 57, 74, 188, 317n85

education, in Hellenistic Palestine, 215, 218

El (god), 12, 30, 33, 61, 75–76, 93–94, 127, 128, 274n121; "sons of El," 182

El-berith (god), 63

elders: in Babylonia, 161, 163, 168; city, 135; of Judah, 312n45; justice by, 117; local governance by priests and, 205; tribal, 79–80

Elephantine, 157; intermarriage at, 210; Jewish community of, 15, 154, 172–177, 193; papyri, 58, 94, 182, 184, 193, 210; priests, 205; Yaho temple at, 3, 14, 94, 126, 165, 177, 189, 205, 324n24. See also "Passover papyrus" from Elephantine

Eli (priest at Shiloh), 147, 306–307n8

Elijah (prophet), 14, 96, 151, 234, 307–308n15, 317n79

El-shaddai (god), 53–55, 76

Emar (Syrian city), 34, 42, 60, 299n65

Enlil (god), 27, 32

Enoch (book), 181, 220, 227, 229–230, 322–323n9

Enoch (prophet), 229, 230–231; qualified as "scribe," 229–230, 350n79

enthronement: of the king, 80, 82–83, 106, 116; of Yhwh, 83–89

ephod (priestly garment), 114, 147, 288–289n125

ephod (statue), 105, 114, 131–132

eschatology, eschatological, 233, 234, 238, 354n106; eschatological prophet, 237–238; eschatological "time of anguish," 233

Eshem-Bethel (god), 3, 94, 174, 320n111

Essenes, 226–227, 228, 232, 235, 236, 238

ethnicity: cultural concept of, 209; Jewish, 177, 178–179, 194, 208–210, 339nn119,121,123; racial concept of, 209–210

etiquette, 44, 110

euhemerism, 33

eunuchs, 329n52, 340n125

exodus (from Egypt), 14, 51, 156, 203

Ezekiel (priest, prophet), 147; oracles of victory at Babylonian Akitu, 164–165

Ezra, 15, 185; law of, 198–202; mission of, 189–198, 202–207; as scribe, 192

Ezra-Nehemiah (books), 185, 190–191, 324nn20–21, 327–328n45, 328nn46–47

families: by covenant, 65; gods and ancestors of, 136–138; incorporation into by anointment, 79–80; Israelites as one family, 77, 209, 213; and kinship, 59–62; patrilineal, patrilocal, 59–60, 136, 140; periodical celebrations, 35–36, 62; religion, 7, 60–61, 120, 125, 213 fast days, fasting, 92, 135, 166–167, 169, 216, 297n55, 315nn68–69, 343n19

festivals: autumn, 25; calendar of, 15, 207–208; city, 141; harvest, 25, 203; wine, 86. *See also* Akitu festival; Matzoth; New Year festival; Passover; Succoth

figurines: horse with rider, 145, 302–303n91; pillar, 145–146, 302nn90–91; plaque, 145, 302–303n91

flood story, 19, 199, 333n75; Babylonian, 39, 44–45

funerary customs, 276–277n15; for royalty, 253n11, 276–277n15

gates: of city or town, 122–123; cult at, 123

Gedaliah (grandson of Shaphan), 158, 166

genealogies, 26

Gerizim, Mount, 156; sanctuary at, 185–187, 199, 201, 205, 234–235, 239, 324nn22–23, 325n28, 336n99

Geshem, Gashmu (Idumean ruler), 185, 188

Gezer calendar, 25, 85

ghosts, 17, 37–39; consultation of, 151–152

Gibeon (town), 74

Gideon, 79, 105, 125, 292n16

Gilead (region), 55, 64, 71, 72–73, 79, 273n109, 340n3. *See also* Jabesh-gilead

Gilgal (Israelite town), 90, 149, 287n112

Gilgamesh, 34, 138, 291n10; mother of, 139

goat-demons *(śĕʿîrîm)*, 37, 123

"God of heaven" (title of Yhwh), 184, 202, 323n17

gods: hierarchy among, 29; lists of, 26; of nature, 26–29; tribal and city, 31–33; tribal and territorial deities, 89

Golden Age, 26

golden calf. *See* bull statues

greed, 216

guardian of the threshold (high priestly function), 98, 110, 156

Habiru (Hebrews), 50–51

Hadad, Haddu, Adad, Addu (god), 29, 32, 45, 52, 81, 82, 131, 275n8, 277n16

Hammurabi, laws of, 46, 92, 118

Hananiah (commissioner for Jewish affairs in Memphis), 205–207, 208, 210, 338n115

Haran (city), 53, 67, 317n85

Hasmoneans, Hasmonean dynasty, 8, 186, 212, 215, 234–235, 238, 251n33, 352n94

Hazor (city), 52, 76, 105

headscarf, worn by married women, 61, 140–141

healers: ancestors called, 35; prophets acting as, 148

heaven: modeled after a palace, 322–323n9; three-tiered and seven-tiered, 18–19; used as code for "God," 184

Hebron (city), 74–75, 80, 144

hereditary priesthood, 108

Herem-Bethel (god), 174

Herod (king), 150, 236; convert from Idumea, 236, 240

high place *(bāmâ;* sanctuary), 74, 90, 123–125, 283n64

Hilkiah (high priest under King Josiah), 154–156, 306–307n8

holiness, of temple, 98, 283n74

Holofernes (character in book of Judith), 117

holy: books, 16, 221–222, 228; city, 14, 208; days, 21, 204, 207; "holy ones" as designation of angels, 181–182; land, 208; race, 192, 209; spirit, 223

host of heaven, 86, 139, 235, 352–353n97

house, Israelite, 136

Huldah (prophetess, wife of Shallum), 155–156
Humbaba (mythological creature), masks of, 123–124, 292n14
Hyrcanus, John, 234, 342n11; destroys Gerizim temple, 186, 201, 324–325n24

Idumea, Idumeans, 185, 188; Herod, 236; "temple of Yaho," 205, 281–282n56
Idumea ostraca, 281–282n56, 326n37, 327n41, 327n43
image, divine, 42–43, 131–132
incense: burned for gods, 39, 98, 111, 132; burned on rooftops, 133–134, 139; burners, 90, 132–133, 297n52; used in necromantic rituals, 304n107
intercession, by goddess with her divine spouse, 144
investiture, 60; royal, 81, 82, 83, 277n17
Isaiah (prophet), priestly connections of, 147
Ishtar (goddess), 30, 31; descent of to the underworld, 19, 132
Isis (goddess), 31

Jabesh-gilead (town), 73, 273n109
Jacob tradition, 50, 52–53, 72, 93, 158
Jamnia (Jabneh), 241, 243
Jehoiachin, Jeconiah (Judean king): deported to Babylon, 158, 159; food allowance, 164; grandfather of Zerubbabel, 166, 192; imprisoned, 164
Jephthah, 79; daughter of, 141
Jericho (city), 22, 58, 149, 287n112
Jerusalem: extension of after fall of Samaria, 155; "holy city," 14, 171; pilgrimage to, 135–136; temple of, as sacred center of Judaism, 236

Jesus, 65, 240, 243
Jewish ethnicity: formation of, 208–209, 339n123; Jews or Judeans? 173, 177; and religion, 207–210
Jezebel (Phoenician princess), 109
John the Baptist, 240, 250
Josiah (Judean king), 14, 123, 154–156, 187, 308n17
Judaism, 16, 23, 167, 173, 177, 200, 212–215, 217; Israelite religion and, 242–244; mainstream, and Jewish sects, 224–228
Judas Maccabeus, 214–215, 232, 237. See also Maccabeans
Judas the Galilean (leader of popular revolt), 240
judgment: of the dead in Egyptian literature, 350–351n81; final, 219, 230, 231, 233–234; royal throne as "seat of," 118
Judith, 117, 143

Kenites (ethnic group), 57
Ketef Hinnom amulets, 344n30
Khnum (Egyptian god), 175
kings: ambivalent attitude of toward prophets, 108–109; as commander of the army, 115–117; divine mandate of, 79–83, 87, 109; enthronement oracles as royal propaganda, 109; as highest judge, 115, 117–118; as priests, 106
Kuntillet Ajrud inscriptions, 3, 12, 55, 56, 58, 73, 76, 248n9, 251nn36,37, 266nn38,39, 267nn47,51,52, 273nn108,116, 281n49

labor, division of, 216
Lachish (Judean town), 90, 279n40, 291n8
Lachish letters, 317n79
Lamashtu (demon), 37–38
land-for-service system, in Judean diaspora in Al-Yaḥudu, 161, 327n41

laws: absence of a code, 118; codification of Egyptian under Darius I, 196; family, 15, 99, 204–205; "of the God of heaven," 184, 202; "of the king" (*dātā᾽ dî malkā᾽, dātu ša šarri*), 193, 202; royal verdicts based on common, 118
Leontopolis (Egyptian city), 14, 252n39
letters, sent by prophets, 168
Leviathan (adversary of Baal), 94
Levites (guild of priests), 107–108, 203
libations, cultic, 87, 127, 139
Lilith (demon), 37, 300n75
literacy: as professional skill, 221; rising rates of in Hellenistic period, 215–216, 218–219, 324n15
lots, casting of, 114

Maccabeans: movement, 234; revolt of, 212, 215, 340n2
magic, 39, 260n94
Manetho, 219, 344n28
Marduk (god), 30, 31, 32, 40, 79, 84, 176, 313n51
marriage: as covenant, 65; intermarriage, 73, 96, 161, 175, 204, 209, 320nn113,114, 337n102; levirate, 59; religious transition at, 60–61; sacred rites, 30. *See also* weddings
martyrs, martyrdom, 172, 215, 347–348n57
maṣṣēbâ. See stela, stone
Matzoth (Feast of Unleavened Bread), 204, 206–207, 225, 321n120, 334–335n92, 338nn110,111, 114
meal, daily, 23–24
Megiddo (city in northern Israel), 52, 54, 90, 123, 268n58
Memphis (Egyptian city), 31; Judean diaspora in, 154, 174–175; residence of Persian satrap, 207, 338n115, 338–339n116
Merenptah stela, 47, 48, 52, 72
Mesha (Moabite king), 45

Mesha stela, 52, 89–90, 125, 251n31
Messiahs, 170, 212, 237–238, 353–354n104
Micah: divine statue of, 105, 131–132; sanctuary of, 105, 125–126, 131–132, 292n16; son acting as priest, 107
Midianite hypothesis, 57
Midianites (ethnic group), 57
midwives, 145, 303n92
Milcom (god), 32. *See also* Molech
miracles, prophets as miracle workers, 148, 223, 239
model shrines, 139–140
Molech (god), 283n64
monotheism, 29, 45, 135, 347–348n57; central tenet of Judaism, 216, 225, 244, 323n14; turn to, 182–183
monsters, 37, 281n55
month names, 25
moon: full, 24, 88; god, 24, 165; new, 24, 62, 86–88, 255n35, 301n88
morals, and religion, 44–46
Mordechai, 212, 313n51
morning and evening offerings, 22, 98, 111
morning star, 33, 132, 144
Moses tradition, 72, 147, 198, 200, 223, 239
Mot (god), 25, 274n4
motherhood, 143, 300n80; Asherah as mother, 30–31, 128; mother of Gilgamesh, 139; Samuel's mother, 147
mourners and mourning: mourning as rite of passage, 145–146; mourning women, 302n90; professional mourners, 145
mysophobia, 112
mysteries: of God, 233; of the law, 227; meaning of revealed to Teacher of Righteousness, 349n64; of the prophetic texts, 224
mythology, solar, 22

Nabonidus (king), 29, 170, 313n52
Nabu (god), 31, 160, 164, 173, 188, 258n62, 311n30

Nanay (goddess), 30; consort of Nabu, 173; worshipped by Arameans in Egypt, 160

Nazoreans, 241, 243–244

Nebo, Mount, 58, 69, 90

necromancy, 35, 132, 146, 151–152, 304n107, 305n108

Nehemiah, 185, 189, 191–192, 213, 328n49; cupbearer of the king, 329n52, 339n118

Nehushtan (bronze serpent), 94

neighbors: disputes between, 88, 119; reputation among, 120

Neirab (Syrian city), 169, 185

Nergal (god), 31, 302–303n91

New Year festival, 81, 83–89; at Bethel, 106; and celebration of the harvest, 25; at Ugarit, 25, 256n41; *See also* Akitu festival; Succoth

Nippur (Babylonian city), 169: Arab migrants in region, 165; Judean settlements in the vicinity of, 160–161, 164

Nob (town), 155, 292–293n19, 306–307n8

nomads, 6, 48–50, 52, 62–63, 66, 119, 157

oaks: of Bethel, 93–94; of Shechem, 128; "of weeping," 93

oaths, 63, 66–67, 73–74, 75, 79, 99–100, 116, 174, 175, 228, 289n134; of innocence, 139; loyalty, 116, 289n134; Pharisees and Essenes refusal to take loyalty oath, 236; and trial by ordeal, 101

omnipresence, 40

oracles, 28–29; enthronement, 106; prophetic, from Mesopotamia, 82, 150, 289n132, 314n60; Scripture as oracle book, 346n48

oral tradition, 220, 226, 227, 347n56, 348nn58–59

ordeals, 67, 101

palaces, royal, 92–93, 98, 100; audience halls, 115, 290n142; gardens, 189, 327n40; harems, 20; impact on cultural development, 118; Persian, 180; pleasures of, 289n136; revolutions, 156; soldiers living close to, 116

Palmyra (caravan city), 41, 103, 286n96

pantheon, 29, 30, 31, 32, 33, 57

Passover, 25, 49, 204, 207, 210, 225, 334–335n92, 338nn110,111, 114, 343n19

"Passover papyrus" from Elephantine, 205–207

pastoralism, pastoralists, 49, 51–52

paterfamilias, 35–36, 59–60, 62, 135, 138, 298n62; king as, 72, 75

patternism, 4–5

Pentateuch: comprehensive compilation, 199; lawbook of Ezra identified with, 198–202; Samaritan, 201

Pharisees, 226–227, 235, 236, 241, 348n59, 349n67

Philistines, 49, 68, 160, 284n80, 292n16

Philo of Byblos, 219, 295n38, 344n28

pilgrimages, 144–145; to graves of holy women, 59; to Jerusalem, 216, 236, 280n47, 353n99

pluralism, religious, 7

polytheism, 29; at Elephantine, 95

Pomegranate inscription, 282n56

Pontius Pilate, 236, 239

pork, avoidance of, 214, 225, 347n52

prayers, 143–144; facing Jerusalem, 236, 353n98; intercessory, by prophets, 148; intercessory, for the authorities, 165, 194, 314n59; the Lord's Prayer, 217; practices by Judeans in Babylonia, 166; as religious duty for Jews, 343n19; silent, 144; transmitted by angels, 182

predestination, 226, 347n56

Priestly Source (P), 167, 200, 209

priests, 13, 14, 45, 98, 101, 106–108, 110, 167–168, 226, 227, 325n26; deputy

high, 156; high, 13, 80, 83, 98, 110,
186–187, 205, 215, 234–235; priestly instruction, 112–113; priestly
oracles, 114–115; and prophecy, 147;
remuneration of, 106–107. *See also*
guardian of the threshold; Levites;
Sadducees; *tôrâ, tôrôt;* Urim and
Thummim; Zadokites
prisons: King Jehoiachin in Babylonian,
164, 166; temples serving as, 101
processions, religious, 42, 85, 87, 89, 101,
164
prophets: of Baal and Asherah, 109;
court, 147; David as, 223, 346n44;
the eschatological prophet,
237–238; Jewish, in the Roman era,
239–240; Judean, in Babylonia,
164; and kings, 108–109; Moses as
the ancestor of, 147; and prophecy,
146–151, 253n10; prophetic frenzy,
148–149; prophetic schools, 149;
"prophet like Moses" to come,
353n103; prophet of Adad, 82;
prophet of Shamash, 317n97;
reference to, in Lachish letter,
317n97; "sons of," 149, 307–308n15;
wages of, 148, 342–343n16
prostitutes, 110, 121, 122, 284n78, 291n10;
prostitution in payment of vows, 143
Proto-Israelites, 49, 51
pseudepigraphy: Deuteronomy as
pseudepigraph, 155; in Hellenistic
and Roman periods, 221
Ptah (god), 31
pure/impure binary, 21, 111–112, 209
purity: laws, 98, 227, 235, 236; ritual,
70, 98, 108, 110, 112, 206, 226, 236,
253n16; rules as court etiquette, 110

Qos, Qaush (god), 188
queen mother, 95; Asherah as, 274n4
Queen of Heaven (goddess), 132, 143–
144, 173, 175; title of Anat-Bethel,
157

Queen of the Underworld (goddess),
37
Qumran, 227

Raphael (angel), 181, 182
reading: collective, 220; communities,
224; as metaphor, 229; revolution,
215, 217–221, 222, 224, 229, 342n15;
silent, 220
Rebekah (wife of Isaac), 93
Rechabites (clan group), 57, 75, 157
religion: concept of, 5–6; definition, 17;
freedom of, 194; Judaism as religion of the book, 215; nature, 28
Resheph ("Plague," divine being), 57,
302–303n91
resurrection, 226, 230, 231–232, 347n56,
347–348n57
retribution, 38, 44, 46, 67, 226, 230, 232
return to Judah, 169
rites of passage, 19, 21, 62, 112, 136–138,
141, 146, 149, 269–270n73, 298n62
roofs, as place for ritual activity, 139

Sabbath, 23, 24, 167–168, 203, 204, 214,
225, 234, 312–313n48
sacrifices and sacrificial cult, 23–24,
39, 44–45, 111–112, 126–127, 324n23;
annual sacrifice, 62, 65, 301n88; human sacrifice, 45, 70, 261n111; purifying sacrifice, 111–112; sacrificial
meal (*šĕlāmîm*), 79, 87; substitute
sacrifice, 45
Sadducees, 224, 226, 227
Sakkun (god, deified stela), 127
salt, as offering material for the deity,
111
Samana (demon), 37
Samaria (city), 93, 287n112; pool of, 121;
fall of, 153, 305n1
Samaria (province), 175, 186, 187; and
Ezra's mission, 192; Persian,
328n49; Yahwistic population, 187,
210

Samarians: as adversaries of the Judeans, 185, 190, 209; among the Jewish diaspora in Egypt, 173–174; at Elephantine, 177; referred to as Jews, 212–213; and Samaritans, 186

Samaria ostraca, 273n114, 286n96, 297n54

Samaritans, 186, 200, 237, 354n111; Samaritan Pentateuch, 201; Samaritan prophets, 239, 240, 241; Samaritan synagogue, 222

Samuel, 108, 121–123, 135, 147–148, 287n112, 307–308n115

Sanballat (governor of Persian Samaria), 186–187, 190, 210, 323n18, 335n96

Sanchuniathon, 219

sanctuaries, 39–43, 287n112; border, 90–92, 286n102; with dining hall for communal meals, 127; domestic, 298n59; at Hirbet al-Qom (Makkedah), 282n56; local (*bāmâ*), 123–134; of Mount Gerizim, 185, 187, 325n28; sanctuary enclosure (*temenos*), 96, 126; tent (tabernacles), 68, 354n111. *See also* tabernacles; temples

Satet (Egyptian goddess), 175

Saul (king), 62, 71–74, 151, 273nn109,110

schools: in Hellenistic Palestine, 215; prophetic, 149

scribes, 224, 230, 305–306n3; Ahiqar, 329n52; Babylonian, 337n103; place of, in Jewish apocalyptic literature, 230; scribal training, 118, 203

Sea, bronze (in Jerusalem temple), 94

Sea Peoples, 48, 49, 50

sects: Jewish, 224–228; in Rechabite community, 157

secular slaughter, 127

seers, 146–147, 304n104

separation principle, 19–21, 37, 98, 112, 125, 146; racial interpretation of, 209

Shadday (god), 47, 265n28. *See also* El-shaddai

Shalem (god), 94

Shamash (god), 21, 22, 28–29, 30, 31, 34, 39, 139, 188, 254n20, 258n62, 262n119, 300n80, 317n79

shame and honor, 64, 116, 119, 143

Shaphan (royal secretary), 154, 156, 166, 307n12, 315n70

Shapshu (goddess), 21

Shechem (city), 53, 63, 85, 128, 185, 187, 235, 269–270n73, 296n40

Sheol (underworld), 18, 34. *See also* underworld

Sheshbazzar, 185, 323n18

Shiloh (town), 58, 127, 135, 136, 147, 155, 156, 187, 272n99, 301n88, 306–307n8

siestas, 23

sin, 6, 112, 216–217, 343n20

Sin (god), 32, 67, 165, 188, 254n18

Sinai, Mount, 56; Sinai covenant, 88–89

Sippar (Babylonian city), 32, 160, 163; Judean merchants in, 161

skulls, used in necromancy, 151, 304n107, 305n108

slavery, slaves, 160, 202; debt slavery, 164, 312n41; manumission, 134–135; manumitted slave adopted into family, 61, 136–138; slave trade, 211, 336n98

soldier's oath of loyalty, 116

spirit possession, 149

stela, stone (*maṣṣēbâ, sikkanu*), 40, 42, 93, 127, 131; funerary, 131

Succoth (Festival of Booths), 25, 85, 88, 191, 203–204, 225

Succoth (place in Gilead), 55

sun: winged disk of, 184; worship of in Palestine, 21–22

Syene (city in southern Egypt), 320n16; Aramean diaspora community of, 157, 173, 174, 175

synagogues, 166; in Hellenistic period, 222, 345–346n38

Taanach cult stands, 102–103, 297n52

tabernacles, 68, 272n99, 354n111

taboos: on plotting against anointed king, 80; on the spilling of blood, 70; social, 88

Tammuz (god), 145, 303n93

taxes: collected by temple, 101, 106; imposed by the palace, 118; imposed by Seleucid kings, 212; paid by Judeans in Babylonia, 161; paid to Persian authorities, 189; resistance against Roman, 240

Tayinat (Syrian city), 96–97

Teacher of Righteousness, 233, 235, 236, 343n20, 349n64, 352n95

Tel Dan Stela, 71, 251n31, 275n8

temples, 39–43; barbers, 110; Bethel temple, 84, 92–96, 281n52; Gibeon temple, 74; Hazor temple, 76, 274n120, 285n94; Hebron temple, 75; Jerusalem temple, 40, 92–101, 236, 328n49; Moza temple, 125; Samaria temple, 93; Shechem temple, 85; social functions of, 99–101; temple of Ain Dara, 96; temple of Tell Tayinat, 96–97; traders, 98; Yaho temple at Elephantine, 3, 14, 94, 126, 165, 177, 189, 205, 324n24. *See also* sanctuaries

temple wardrobe, 110; 288n117; keeper of, 98, 155–156

Ten Commandments (Decalogue), 88–89, 101, 112–113

teraphim, 36, 61, 131–132, 136–138

theft, 88, 112, 113, 139

theocracy, 204, 234

Theodotus inscription, 222

theophany, 12, 47, 55, 56–57, 87

Theudas (prophet), 239

threshing floors, 85; outside the city walls, 117; as site of Jerusalem temple, 93

thrones: empty to suggest presence of deity, 103–105; "Lord of the throne" in Palmyra, 103

Tiamat (deified primeval ocean), 79, 82, 84

time, 22; days, 23–24; months, 24; years, 24–25

tithes. *See* taxes

Tobiah, 185, 190, 340nn126–127; Judean connection through marriage, 210; ruler of Ammon, 187; worshipper of Yhwh, 187–188

Tobit, book of, 154, 181, 182, 212, 220, 223, 322nn4,6

tôrâ, tôrôt (priestly instruction), 110, 112–113; Hebrew *tôrâ* and Greek *nomos*, 201; "torah of Moses," 198; written and oral, 113, 348n58

totem, 28

towns, Israelite, 120–121

transhumance, 49, 263nn7,8, 334n92

treasuries: Jerusalem temple treasury, 42, 100, 154; written archive located in, 333n77

treaties, 65–66; of Northern Kingdom, 96

trees: grave markers, 131; symbol of divine presence, 128

tribal ethics, 113

Tyre (city), 103, 295–296n38; Babylonian campaign against, 164–165; Israelite treaty with, 96; "mirror town" in Mesopotamia, 160; princess from, 81

Udjahorresnet (Egyptian priest): adviser in religious matters, 195; autobiography on funeral statue, 195, 197; reorganization of Egyptian temples, 196

underworld, 18–19, 25, 34, 37, 145, 252n4, 302–303n91

universalism, 183, 199–200, 214

Urim and Thummim, 100, 113–115, 139, 288–289n125

violence, divine, 45, 70
voluntary associations, 225, 228, 347n53, 349–350n74
vows, 141, 143–144, 147, 149, 300n78; Nazirite vow, 112
vox populi vox dei, 288n113

Wadi Daliyeh Samarian papyri, 187, 205, 211, 327n41, 328n49, 335nn94–96, 343n17
warfare, 64, 68–71, 115–117; ideology of, 116; prophetic oracles and, 109; in spring, 115
water, 121
weddings: banquet, 298n62; canopy, 22; night, 20, 138; rites, 61, 67, 78, 138; songs, 81
wells (water point, springs): girls drawing water at, 121; location of, 121
wilderness tradition, 51, 68–69, 203; Levites possible channel of, 107; no sacrifices in the wilderness, 307–308n15
wine: new, at New Year festival in autumn, 85–86; as ritual offering, 87, 111; royal drinking, 117
women and local religion, 140–146
wrath, 176, 194; age of, 232–233

Yamm (god), 25, 27, 84, 94, 274n4
Yarikh (god), 21
Yhwh (god): and Asherah, 3, 12, 76, 95, 144, 267n51; Baal mythology transferred to, 94; enthronement festival of, 84–89; of Hebron, 144; identification El and, 12, 75–76, 274n121; images of, 101–105, 285n91; inheritance of, 89; name of, 58–59; origins of cult of, 12, 47, 55–56, 266n41, 267n46; "people of," 76–77, 84; profile of, 57–58; of Samaria, 55, 281n49; of Teman, 12; Zebaoth (*yhwh ṣĕbā'ôt*), 139

Zadokites (guild of priests), 108, 226
Zakkur (king of Hamath), inscription of, 203, 275n8, 288nn114–115, 304n104
Zarpanitu (goddess), 30
Zerubbabel, 315n67; grandson of King Jehoiachin, 166, 185, 191; kingship oracles addressed to, 191, 238
Zimrilim (king of Mari), 82, 317n79
Zion, Mount: abode of Yhwh, 33; identified with Mount Zaphon, 94
Zionist movement, among Judeans in Babylonia, 170–172
Zoroastrianism, 180, 193

Index of Modern Authors

Abraham, Kathleen, 310n25, 312nn42,43, 337n102
Abrahami, Philippe, 284n85
Abusch, Tzvi, 258n64, 260n94
Ackerman, Susan, 250n30, 251n35, 278n37, 280n41, 282n60, 284n80, 293n22, 295n37, 299n72, 300n74, 355n1
Adams, Matthew J., 306n4
Adler, Yonatan, 319n100, 338n113, 339n121, 341n9, 342n12, 347n52, 352n94, 356n5
Aharoni, Miriam, 286n102
Aharoni, Yohanan, 279nn40,41, 316n73
Ahituv, Shmuel, 248n9, 282n56
Ahlström, Gösta W., 248n11, 250n26, 264n18, 278nn34,36, 308n17
Alanne, Merja, 279n41
Albertz, Rainer, 247n6, 250n24, 250nn27,28, 308n17, 315n66, 324n22, 336n99, 356n4
Albrektson, Bertil, 256n43, 332–333n74
Albright, William Foxwell, 254n25, 355n3
Allam, Shafik, 332n70
Allen, James P., 258n66
Alster, Bendt, 255n35
Alstola, Tero, 311n33, 317nn78,83, 323–324n19
Alt, Albrecht, 269n68, 279n41, 287n104, 301–302n89, 308n16, 328n49
Ameling, Walter, 346n39
Ames, Frank Ritchel, 306n6
Anderson, Gary A., 250n23, 343n21

Anthonioz, Stéphanie, 284n85
Arav, Rami, 279–280n41
Arbel, V. Daphna, 261n111
Arie, Eran, 297n50
Arnaud, Daniel, 299n65
Arnold, Patrick M., 278n38, 280n41
Artzi, Pinhas, 316n76, 351n82
Arubas, Benjamin, 326n39
Assmann, Jan, 250n28, 256n46, 258n64
Astour, Michael C., 279n41
Attridge, Harold W., 295n38, 344n28
Auffahrt, Christoph, 294n32
Aune, David E., 267n53, 354n110
Avigad, Nahman, 286n96, 306n5, 307n13
Axelsson, Lars Eric, 266n41
Ayalon, Avner, 282n56

Bach, Robert, 272n101
Baden, Joel S., 334n84
Bahrani, Zainab, 289n131
Banton, Michael, 252n1
Barag, Dan, 352n93
Barkay, Gabriel, 286n102
Bar-Matthews, Miriam, 282n56
Barstad, Hans, 309n23
Barta, Heinz, 330n55
Bárta, Miroslav, 276n14
Bartlett, John R., 266n45, 317n85, 324n19, 326n36
Barton, George A., 343n18
Barton, John, 250nn24,26,27, 273n114, 279n40, 292n18, 345n37
Bautch, Richard J., 340n132

Bazzana, Giovanni Battista, 351n83
Beaulieu, Paul-Alain, 257n56, 287n107, 314n61, 325n26
Becking, Bob, 269–270n73, 278n37, 305nn1,2, 314n64, 319n101, 337n102
Beckman, Gary, 265–266n35, 294n31
Beiler, Vincent D., 307n13
Beit-Arieh, Itzhaq, 279n40, 293n25
Bendlin, Andreas, 253n16
Ben-Schlomo, David, 302n90
Berlejung, Angelika, 261n102, 289n138, 338n110, 344n30
Bernett, Monika, 292n13
Beyer, Brian, 315n67
Beyerle, Stefan, 354n109
Bickerman, Elias, 283n70, 309n24
Binder, Donald D., 345–346n38
Biran, Avraham, 279n41, 292n13
Bird, Phyllis, 250n30
Black, Jeremy, 254n19
Black, Matthew, 322n7
Blenkinsopp, Joseph, 273n111, 314n64, 315n68, 328n47, 329n54, 331n66, 333n74
Bloch, Yigal, 309n24
Bloch-Smith, Elizabeth, 270n78, 285n93, 294n31, 296n46
Blum, Erhard, 265n28
Bodi, Daniel, 265n25
Boer, P. A. H. de, 268n55
Bokser, Baruch M., 334–335n92
Bonnet, Corinne, 256n46
Bordreuil, Pierre, 281–282n56
Borée, Wilhelm, 254n18, 266n40, 268n58
Borger, Rykle, 278n31
Borowski, Oded, 290n3
Botta, Alejandro F., 337n103
Bottéro, Jean, 255nn31,35, 256n46, 258n60, 288n113, 289n131, 303n100, 304n105
Bourgel, Jonathan, 324–325n24
Boyarin, Daniel, 319n98
Boyce, Mary, 322n4

Boyer, Georges, 275n6
Bremmer, Jan, 260n94
Brettler, Marc Zvi, 274n2, 356n7
Brettschneider, Joachim, 294n27, 299n67
Briant, Pierre, 322n2, 323nn11,12, 324n20, 327nn40,44, 331n66
Briggs, Charles August, 275n9
Brisson, L., 289n131, 303n100
Broshi, Magen, 306n5
Brown, William P., 264n22
Buccellati, Giorgio, 262n120
Burke, Aaron, 306n6
Burney, C. F., 272n107, 308n16
Burns, Paul C., 261n111
Burnstein, Stanley Mayer, 344n28
Bush, Frederick W., 313n53

Cardascia, Guillaume, 253n13
Carlier, J., 289n131, 303n100
Carradice, Ian, 335n94
Carvalho, Corrine, 316n76
Cassin, Elena, 260n101
Cauchi, Rosaura, 314n61
Charlesworth, James H., 347–348n57
Charpin, Dominique, 269n67, 271nn81,87,90–92, 282nn62–63
Chavel, Simeon, 285n92
Chilton, Bruce, 343n22
Cline, Eric, 262n4, 279n41
Cogan, Mordechai, 261n111, 268n58, 272n107, 276n13, 283n68, 284n81, 307n14, 317n82, 318n90, 321n1, 323n16, 325nn27,30, 331n59
Cohen, Chaim, 316n76, 351n82
Cohen, Hermann, 261n114
Cohen, Mark E., 254n15, 314n61
Cohen, Mordechai, 313–314n58
Cohen, Shaye J. D., 249n16, 254n18, 353n101, 355n116
Cohen, Yoram, 300n75
Collins, Billie Jean, 253n16, 289n134
Collins, John J., 276n14, 294n31, 322n4, 323n13, 328–329n51, 334n89,

340n2, 342n13, 344n7, 345nn35,38, 348nn60,61, 348–349n63, 349nn66,71, 350nn76,78,80, 350–351n81, 351nn83–85, 352n90, 353nn97,100, 354nn106,108
Collins, Marilyn F., 354n112
Collon, Dominique, 257n52
Coogan, Michael, 278n39
Cornelius, Izak, 302n91
Cousland, J. R. C., 261n111
Crahay, R., 289n131, 303n100
Crawford, Sidnie White, 348n62, 348–349n64, 353n100
Cross, Frank Moore, 247n6, 266nn36,41, 267n48, 280n42, 287n110, 321n2, 323n18, 330n54, 332n74, 340n1, 356n4
Crouch, Carly L., 270–271n80
Crowfoot, Grace M., 327n40
Crowfoot, John W., 327n40
Crown, Alan D., 353–354n104
Cussini, Eleonora, 285n89

Dahari, Uzi, 282n56
Dalglish, Edward R., 268n54
Dalley, Stephanie, 253n8, 259n76, 261n107, 289n137, 298n60, 317n85, 324n19
Dalman, Gustaf, 253nn13,14, 277n22
Dandamaev, Muhammad A., 310n26, 314n63
Darby, Eric D., 302n90
Daviau, P. M. Michèle, 279n40, 280n42, 294n31
Davies, Graham, 269n68, 319n97
Davies, Philip, 250n26
Davis, Andrew R., 281n50
Day, John, 281n54, 350n81
Day, Peggy L., 258n64, 300n74
Dayagi-Mendels, Michal, 282n56
Dearman, J. Andrew, 264n22
Dell, Katherine J., 269n68, 319n97
Deller, Karlheinz, 299n65
Demsky, Aaron, 282n56

Dever, William G., 248n11, 266n44, 281n48, 301n84, 318n93
Dewrell, Heath D., 261n112
Dexinger, Ferdinand, 353–354n104
Dhar, Bibhash, 263n7
Dick, Michael B., 261n102
Dietrich, Manfried, 258n60
Dimant, Devorah, 348–349n63
Dommershausen, Werner, 289n126
Donner, Fred M., 353n98
Donner, Herbert, 261n104
Doran, Robert, 340n2, 341n10
Dothan, Trude, 292n16
Douglas, Mary, 254n17
Drake, Brandon L., 262–263n5
Drawnel, Henryk, 351n82
Driver, Samuel R., 289n127
Dubovsky, Peter, 281n52
Duff, Archibald, 355n2
Dumbrell, William J., 326n36
Dunand, Françoise, 351n83
Durand, Jean-Marie, 253n10, 271nn84,85,89, 274n3, 277n18, 294nn30,33, 304n102, 317n79
Dušek, Jan, 325n29, 328n49, 335n95, 336n98, 340n1, 341n5, 343n17

Eaton, John H., 275n10
Eckhardt, Benedikt, 347n53
Edelman, Diana V., 266–267n45, 272n103, 279n40, 292n18, 293n24, 326n34
Eerdmans, B. D., 268n55, 356n6
Ehrlich, Uri, 356n8
Eichler, Barry L., 316n76, 351n82
Eidem, Jesper, 271n82
Eissfeldt, Otto, 332n73
Elledge, C. D., 347–348n57
Emerton, John A., 275n11, 333n75
Eph'al, Israel, 282n56, 310n27, 314n63, 327n41
Eshel, Esther, 248n9, 306n3
Eskenazi, Tamara Cohn, 314n64, 324n21, 329n54, 339n123

Esler, Philip F., 322–323n9
Evans, Carl D., 249n15
Exum, J. Cheryl, 278n39

Fahd, Toufic, 303n96
Falkenstein, Adam, 271n93
Farber, Walter, 260nn85,89,90, 303n93, 305n110
Faust, Avraham, 291n5, 293nn19,20, 297nn53,57, 305n2
Fehrle, Eugen, 353n16
Feldt, Laura, 338n114
Felli, Candida, 302n90, 303n94
Ferreri, Silvia, 273n109
Fields, Weston W., 348n59
Finet, André, 288n113, 304n105
Finkel, Irving L., 250n22, 257n48, 259n68, 260n88, 265n32, 304n107
Finkelstein, Israel, 263n6, 272n105, 279n42, 306n4
Finkelstein, Jacob Joel, 259n82, 260n97
Finkielsztejn, Gerald, 352n93
Fish, Stanley, 345n36
Fitzmeyer, Joseph A., 271n83
Fitzpatrick-McKinley, Anne, 331–332n67
Fleming, Daniel E., 252n2, 267n46
Fohrer, Georg, 247n6
Foster, Benjamin R., 254n20, 258nn58,62, 261n110, 262n115, 274n4, 297n49, 301n85, 316n74
Frayne, Douglas, 265n35
Freedman, David Noel, 340n1
Freedman, Sally M., 286n98, 298n59
Frei, Peter, 330n55
Freund, Richard A., 279–280n41
Frevel, Christian, 266n41
Fuhs, Hans Ferdinand, 264n17

Gabbay, Uri, 316n76, 351n82
Gadot, Yuval, 306n4, 326n39
Galling, Kurt, 294n35, 297–298n58, 302n90, 343n17
García Martínez, Florentino, 343n20, 348n61, 352–353n97

Gardiner, Alan H., 331n65
Gawlikowski, Michel, 286n96
Gehman, Henry Snyder, 325n26
Geller, Mark J., 250n22, 257n48, 259n68, 265n32, 351n82
George, Andrew R., 252n5, 254n18, 257n49, 259n73, 260nn95–96, 291n110, 295n36, 298n62, 299n68
Gernet, J., 289n131, 303n100
Gerstenberger, Erhard S., 276n12, 277nn23,25, 288n124, 301n86
Gertz, Jan Christian, 270n80, 287n105
Geus, Cornelis H. J. de, 251n32, 270n79, 272n106, 290n1, 291nn5,7, 297nn56–57
Gillihan, Yonder M., 349–350n74
Ginsberg, Harold Louis, 308n16
Gitin, Seymour, 280–281n48, 292n6, 297n51, 318n93
Gittlen, Barry M., 297n51
Giuntoli, Federico, 281n52
Glassner, Jean Jacques, 255n31, 274n1, 308n19
Gluska, Isaac, 314n62, 316n76, 351n82
Goedicke, Hans, 326n36
Goff, Matthew, 341n10
Goodblatt, David, 345n35
Gordis, Robert, 343n18
Goren, Yuval, 282n56
Grabbe, Lester L., 308n17, 328n46, 339n120
Graham, M. Patrick, 264n22
Granerød, Gard, 323n17
Grayson, A. Kirk, 305n1, 329n52
Green, Alberto R. W., 261n111
Green, Anthony, 254n19, 281n55
Greenberg, Moshe, 247n6
Greenfield, Jonas C., 272–273n107, 329n52, 340n1
Greengus, Samuel J., 269n69
Gressmann, Hugo, 333n79
Griffiths, J. Gwyn, 256n41
Grodzynski, D., 289n131, 303n100
Groneberg, Brigitte, 256n46

Gruseke, Alison Acker, 307–308n15
Gunkel, Hermann, 275n9, 296n40

Hachlili, Rachel, 345–346n38
Hackl, Johannes, 312n45
Hadley, Judith, 273n118, 295n36
Haettner Blomquist, Tina, 291n10,
    292n13
Hagedorn, Anselm C., 330n55
Hallo, William W., 249n15
Halpern, Baruch, 264n14, 266n44,
    279n41
Hamilton, Jeffries M., 293n21
Hamori, Esther J., 264n19, 304n106
Hanson, Paul D., 248n11, 252n38, 257n53,
    273n112, 301n82, 321n2
Haran, Menahem, 270n75, 332n72
Harlow, Daniel C., 341n10,
    345–346n38
Harrison, Timothy P., 283n66
Hart, George, 256–257n46
Hartenstein, Friedhelm, 285n92
Harth, Dietrich, 250n28
Hartmann, Th., 254n23
Hatina, Thomas R., 351n81
Haussig, Hans Wilhelm, 294n32
Healey, John F., 269n68
Heger, Paul, 353n97
Heimpel, Wolfgang, 253n10,
    271nn81,89
Heintz, Jean-Georges, 303–304n101
Hengel, Martin, 342n13
Herion, Gary A., 248n6, 279n40, 355n3
Hermann, Virginia Rimmer,
    296nn43,44
Herzog, Zeʾev, 279n40, 286n102
Hess, Richard S., 248n6, 251n34, 355n1
Hezser, Catherine, 342n15
Hiebert, Theodore, 263n9, 267n51
Hill, Jane A., 276n14
Hillers, Delbert R., 285n89, 300n76
Himmelfarb, Martha, 342n14
Hirsch, Samuel, 261n114
Hoffman, Yair, 315nn68,71

Hoffmeier, James K., 262n1
Hoffner, Harry A., 283n65
Hoftijzer, Jacob, 248n8, 265n28, 273n107
Hogan, Karina Martin, 341n10
Hoglund, Kenneth G., 318n87
Holladay, John S., Jr., 248n11, 326n38
Holladay, William L., 307n11
Holland, Thomas A., 302n90
Holm, Tawny L., 258n60, 319n102,
    320nn104,108
Honigman, Sylvie, 321n118
Hoover, Oliver D., 352n91
Horgan, Maurya P., 346n41
Hornkohl, Aaron D., 307–308n15
Hornung, Erik, 257–258n57
Horowitz, Wayne, 252nn5–6, 253n7,
    264n19
Horst, Pieter W. van der, 346n48, 356n8
Houtman, Cornelis, 332–333n74
Hoyland, Robert G., 263n7
Huber Vulliet, F., 287n103
Hübner, Ulrich, 325n32, 343n17
Huffmon, Herbert B., 265n24,
    281n53
Hultgård, Anders, 351n83
Hundley, Michael B., 257n48
Hunger, Hermann, 254n27, 256n40
Hurowitz, Victor Avigdor, 316n76,
    351n82
Hutter, Manfred, 260n92
Hutton, Jeremy M., 263n7, 273n114,
    287nn106,108,109, 297n51, 299n69

Ilan, David, 279n41
Ishida, Tomoo, 302n91
Israel, Felice, 281–282n56
Isser, Stanley J., 354n113

Jacobsen, Thorkild, 257n53, 260nn86,93,
    261nn105,107, 298n63
Jacoby, Felix, 344n28
Janák, Jiří, 351n81
Janowski, Bernd, 292n12
Japhet, Sara, 327–328n45

Jefford, Clayton N., 354n110

Jenkins, G. Kenneth, 302–303n91

Jenni, Ernst, 264n17, 283n65

Jeremias, Joachim, 268n61, 280n47, 283n72, 284n77, 288n116, 291n8, 318n95, 341n7, 343n19, 346n39, 353n99

Ji, Chang-Ho, 280n42

Joannès, Francis, 309–310n25, 310–311n29, 312n47, 313n57

Johnson, Janet H., 332n70

Johnston, Sarah Iles, 253nn12,16

Jones, Bruce William, 249n15

Jones, Philip, 276n14

Jong, Ab de, 322n4, 353n97

Jursa, Michael, 312n45, 334nn85,86

Kahn, Dan'el, 309n20, 313–314n58

Kaminsky, Joel S., 341n10

Kamlah, Jens, 279n40, 280n42, 283n66, 293n24

Katzenstein, H. Jacob, 313n58

Kaufman, Yehezkel, 247n6

Keel, Othmar, 249nn13,14, 292n13, 295n38, 302n91

Keimer, Kyle, 291n8

Kelle, Brad E., 306n6

Kellerman, Diether, 283n68

Kellermann, Ulrich, 332–333n74

Kenyon, Kathleen M., 327n40

Keyes, Clinton Walker, 344n24

Khan, Geoffrey, 307–308n15

Kiel, Yishai, 334n84

Killebrew, Ann E., 306n5

Kim, Hyun Chul Paul, 252n4

Kisilevitz, Shua, 292–293n19

Kitz, Anne Marie, 289n128

Kleber, Kristin, 334n87

Klein, Eitan, 305n108

Klein, Jacob, 250n22, 259n68, 265n32, 266n37

Kletter, Raz, 300n76, 302n90

Klingshirn, William, 346n48

Kloppenborg, John S., 349–350n74

Knauf, Ernst Axel, 249n14, 263n6, 265n29, 266n43, 306n4, 317n85, 324n19

Knoppers, Gary N., 324n22, 325nn25,29, 327–328n45, 330n55, 334n82, 336nn98,99, 340nn126,128, 341n5

Koch, Klaus, 330n55

Kochavi, Moshe, 306n6

Koh, Yee Von, 269n68, 319n97

Köhler, Ludwig, 255n30, 291n9

Kooij, Gerrit van der, 248n8, 265n28, 273n107

Kooten, George H., 354n109

Korpel, Marjo C. A., 278n37

Kottsieper, Ingo, 258n60, 265n28, 321n120, 337n108

Kraft, Robert A., 348n59

Kramer, Samuel Noah, 258n60

Kratz, Reinhard G., 319n102, 321n120, 328n49, 330n55, 331n58, 335n94, 337nn106,108

Kraus, Fritz R., 255n35, 290n144

Krause, Joachim J., 272nn103,105

Krebernik, Manfred, 254n18, 257n49, 295n36

Kuan, Jeffrey K., 264n22

Kugel, James L., 343n18

Kuhrt, Amélie, 331nn56,57,61–64,66, 332nn68,70

Kuhs, Clemens, 320n108

Kupper, Jean-Robert, 288n113, 294n30

Kutsch, Ernst, 315–316n72

Kvanvig, Helle S., 350n81

Labat, René, 254n25, 300n78

Lam, Joseph, 250n23

Lambert, David, 334n84

Lambert, Wilfred G., 252nn4,5, 255nn31,35, 256n44, 257nn49,55, 258nn58,63, 259n67, 260nn95,99, 262nn115,116, 283n75, 286n98, 288n116, 300n80, 301n88, 304n107, 305n110, 310n25, 315n65, 350n81, 351n83

Landsberger, Benno, 254n25, 255n37, 316n74
Laneri, Nicola, 293n24
Lang, Bernard, 303n99
Lang, Martin, 330n55
Lange, Armin, 350n81
Langer, Ruth, 356n8
Langgut, Dafna, 326n39
Langlois, Michael, 306n3
Lapp, Nancy L., 340n1
Lapp, Paul W., 340n1
LaRocca-Pitts, Elizabeth, 294n29
Laroche, Emmanuel, 304n107
Lee, Kyong-Jin, 330n55
Leichty, Erle, 261n106, 321n119
Leivestad, Ragnar, 346n45
Lemaire, André, 271n84, 282n56, 303n99, 309–310n25, 311n29, 312n47, 313n57, 326nn37,38, 336n100
Lemche, Niels Peter, 247n5, 263n10
Lemos, Tracy M., 294n31
Lepper, Verena, 349n71
Lesko, Barbara S., 250n30
Leuchter, Mark A., 287nn108,109, 333n76
Leuenberger, Martin, 266n41
Levin, Nadav, 282n56
Levin, Yigal, 326n35
Levine, Baruch A., 248n8, 262n2, 265n28
Levine, Lee I., 321n118, 345–346n38, 353n102
Levinson, Bernard M., 270n80, 330n55
Lewis, Theodore J., 252n2, 259nn75,83, 267n49, 269n70, 276n12, 284n86, 285n90, 294n31
Lichtheim, Miriam, 262n118
Lieberman, Saul, 342n13
Liebesny, Herbert, 344n24
Lim, Timothy H., 322n4, 345n35, 346n43, 355n117
Lindblom, Johannes, 308n16
Linder, Elisha, 256n41
Linssen, Marc J. H., 277n17, 314n60
Lipiński, Edouard, 254n18, 294n32

Lipschits, Oded, 282n56, 292–293n19, 306n4, 309n22, 315n68, 317n85, 324nn19,22, 325–326n33, 326nn37–39, 328nn46,49, 336n99, 339n123
Livingstone, Alasdair, 276n13, 303n93, 305n110
Lloyd, Alan B., 331n62
Lohfink, Norbert, 274n122, 308n16
Loretz, Oswald, 258n59, 263n10
Lozachmeur, Hélène, 320n113, 338n110
Lubetski, Meir, 310n25, 315n70
Luijendijk, AnneMarie, 346n48
Luker, Lamotte M., 268n61
Lukeš, Jiří, 351n81
Lum, Lahpai Fanang, 291n8
Luukko, Mikko, 295–296n38

Ma, John, 351n83
MacGinnis, John, 332n69
Machinist, Peter, 252n4, 318n93
Maeir, Aren M., 338n110
Magen, Yitzhaq, 324nn22,23, 325n28, 336n99, 341n5
Magness, Jodi, 345–346n38
Malul, Meir, 269nn65,69,71,72, 271n88, 275n7
Mandel, Paul, 305–306n3
Manning, J. G., 340n2
Manor, Dale W., 279n40
Marcus, Joel, 356n8
Marsman, Hennie, 303n92
Mason, Steve, 321n121
Mattingly, Gerald L., 249n15
Maul, Stefan, 260n88
Mayer, Werner, 257n54, 258n62, 301nn85,86
Mayfield, Tyler D., 252n4
Mazar, Amihai, 264n21, 274n120, 278n39, 285n94, 292n16, 293n25, 297n52, 299n67, 302n91
Mazar, Benjamin, 287n110, 306n5, 325n31
Mazar, Eliat, 306n5
McBride, S. Dean, 248n11, 252n38, 257n53, 273n112, 301n82, 321n2

McCarter, P. Kyle, 56, 248n9, 251n36, 251n37, 252n38, 254n28, 255n34, 266n38, 266n39, 266n44, 267n51, 270n74, 272n107, 273n110, 273n112, 273n113, 277n21, 278n33, 286n101, 289n127, 293n19, 294n28, 296n46, 298n64, 301n82, 301n84, 303n98, 305n109
McGinn, Bernard, 351n83
McNutt, Paula, 290n1
Meier, Samuel A., 263n8
Meijer, Diederik J. W., 257nn47,52
Mendenhall, George, 248n6, 355n3
Menkis, Richard, 261n111
Merkel, Eberhard, 294n32
Meshel, Ze'ev, 248n9, 267nn47,52, 273n108, 273n116
Metso, Sarianna, 348–349n63, 349n68
Mettinger, Tryggve N. D., 261n103, 275n5, 284n88, 299n70, 305–306n3
Meyer, Rudolph, 346n45
Meyers, Carol L., 248n11, 250n27, 283n67
Meyers, Eric M., 321n2, 345–346n38
Mierse, William E., 293n24
Milgrom, Jacob, 288n119, 288–289n125
Millard, Alan R., 255n35, 260n95, 275n8, 288nn114,115, 304n104, 305n110, 318n90
Miller, Patrick D., Jr., 248n6, 248n11, 251n35, 252n38, 257n53, 272n98, 273n112, 301n82, 321n2, 355n1
Miller, Robert D. II, 266n41
Milstein, Sara J., 290n145
Misgav, Haggai, 324n23, 325n28, 341n5
Montgomery, James A., 325n26
Moor, Johannes C. de, 256n41
Moore, Carey A., 322n6
Moore, George F., 284n77, 296n48
Moore, James D., 310n25, 312n47
Morales, Antonio J., 276n14
Morrison, Martha M., 299n65
Moshkovitz, Shmuel, 286n102

Mowinckel, Sigmund, 88, 277n24, 278nn30,32, 288nn121,123, 309n121, 314n64, 324n21, 328n47, 329n54, 332n74, 339nn117,119,120
Moyer, James C., 249n15
Mulder, Johannes S. M., 275n11
Mulder, Martin J., 346n40
Mullen, Theodore E., Jr., 258n59, 323n13
Müller, E. W., 298n63
Myers, Jacob M., 283n73, 326n36, 337–338n109

Na'aman, Nadav, 262n3, 263n10, 264nn13,20, 306n4
Nakhai, Beth Alpert, 293n24
Namdat, Dvory, 297n50
Nashef, Khaled, 269n67
Naveh, Joseph, 282n56, 316n73, 327nn41,42
Neufeld, Dietmar, 261n111
Neumann, Hermann Michael, 263n6, 249n14
Neumann, Jehuda, 262–263n5
Newsom, Carol, 347–348n57
Nichelson, Ernest Wilson, 308n16
Nickelsburg, George W. E., 322n7, 348n57
Nicklas, Tobias, 350n81
Niditch, Susan, 247n6, 251n35, 355n1
Niehr, Herbert, 256n46, 285n91, 290n139, 296n44
Niemeyer, Georg, 294n32
Nims, Charles, 331n67
Nissinen, Martti, 258n60, 287n112, 288n115, 304nn101,103, 314n62
Nöldeke, Theodor, 333n78
Nongbri, Brent, 250n20
Nötscher, Friedrich, 285n92
Noth, Martin, 265n23, 267n54, 301–302n89, 333n79, 337n109
Nougayrol, Jean, 304n107
Novák, Mirko, 283n66, 298n58
Nützel, Werner, 262n5

O'Connor, Michael, 248n11
Oden, Robert A., Jr., 295n38, 344n28
Oeming, Manfred, 282n56, 317n85,
    323–324n19, 326nn37–39, 328n46,
    339n123
Ogden, Daniel, 253n16
Olmo Lete, Gregorio del, 267n51
Olsson, Birger, 345–346n38
Olyan, Saul, 282n59, 294n31, 303n95
Oorschot, Jürgen van, 266n41
Oppenheim, A. Leo, 2, 5, 44, 247n3,
    249n19, 261n109, 283n76, 284n82,
    288n118, 292n17, 311n32, 327n44
Ornan, Tallay, 285n91
Ortiz, Steven M., 292n16
Oshima, Takayoshi M., 252n5, 264n19
Ottoson, Magnus, 283n65
Owen, David I., 259n71, 299n65

Pakkala, Juha, 332–333n74
Palva, Heikki, 248n11
Panitz-Cohen, Nava, 297n52, 299n67
Pardee, Dennis, 255n38, 259nn75,82,
    261n108, 265n27, 276n14, 277n15,
    282n56, 284n87, 290nn140,141,143,
    295n36, 296n42, 301n83, 317n79
Park, Hye Kyung, 252n4
Parker, Robert, 353n16
Parker, Simon B., 296nn41,42, 323n13
Parpola, Simo, 253n11, 262–263n5,
    276n15, 288n115, 289n132, 303n93,
    304n103, 314n60
Pascal, Blaise, 18, 252n3
Paszkowiak, J., 334nn85,86
Paul, Shalom M., 318n88, 329n52,
    348n59,
Pearce, Laurie E., 267–268n54, 309–
    310n25, 310nn27–28, 310–311n29,
    311nn31,35–38,40, 312nn41,46,47,
    313nn50,52,55, 315n67, 316n77,
    317nn80,86, 323n18, 337–338n109
Pentiuc, Eugen J., 269n66
Perdue, Leo G., 249n15
Perrot, Charles, 346n40

Pfeiffer, Henrik, 267n46
Pietsch, Michael, 308n17
Pinnick, Avital, 329n52, 345n35
Piotrkowski, Meron M., 252n39
Pomponio, Francesco, 258n63
Pongratz-Leisten, Beate, 256n40
Popović, Mladen, 345n31
Porat, Naomi, 326n39
Porten, Bezalel, 293n23, 319n99, 326n37
Porton, Gary G., 347nn54–55
Prang, E., 298n62
Prechel, Doris, 287n105
Pritchard, James B., 302n90
Puig i Tarrech, Armand, 350n81

Quaegebeur, Jan, 332n71

Rad, Gerhard von, 271n94, 275n10,
    334n91
Radner, Karen, 270n80
Rainey, Anson F., 286n102
Rajak, Tessa, 342n11, 352n92
Raphael, Freddy, 351n83
Redford, Donald B., 264n15, 331–332n67
Reed, W. L., 273n109
Reich, Ronnie, 306n5
Reichert, Andreas, 301n87
Reiner, Erica, 247n3, 262n117, 315n65
Rendsburg, Gary A., 275n9, 307–308n15
Renz, Johannes, 255n39, 281–282n56,
    286n96, 297n54, 301n84, 317n79,
    344n30
Retel-Laurentin, A., 289n131, 303n100
Rhoads, David, 354n114
Ringgren, Helmer, 247n6
Roberts, J. J. M., 272n98, 275n10
Robinson, H. Wheeler, 268n60
Rochberg-Halton, Franscesca, 262n115,
    350n77
Rofé, Alexander, 286n97, 303n97
Röllig, Wolfgang, 286n96, 297n54,
    301n84, 317n79, 344n30
Rollinger, Robert, 310n26, 314n63,
    330n55

Römer, Thomas, 252n2, 266n41, 268nn55,57, 281n52
Rom-Shiloni, Dalit, 316n76
Rood, M. C., 332n70
Rose, Martin, 268n55
Rösel, Hartmut, 297–298n58
Rosen, Baruch, 297n50
Rost, Leonhard, 263n8, 270n74, 334n92,
Roth, James F., 304n104
Roth, Martha, 262n119, 280n45, 299n71, 300n75, 309n24, 312n43, 313n49, 337n102, 262n119
Roubekas, Nickolas, 259n72
Rouillard, Hedwige, 259n79
Rowley, H. H., 330n54
Rubin, Aaron, 307n13
Rudolph, Wilhelm, 325n30, 329n53
Ruiten, Jacques van, 354n109
Runesson, Anders, 345–346n38
Russell, Stephen C., 264n19
Ryckmans, Jacques, 253n16

Saarelainen, Katri, 300n76
Sachs, Abraham, 277n17
Saebø, Magne, 248n7
Sallaberger, Walter, 287n103
Sancisi-Weerdenburg, Heleen, 332n70
Sanders, Seth L., 264n19, 333n76
Sandmel, Samuel, 334n83
Sarlo, Daniel, 267n50
Sass, Benjamin, 286n96, 307n13
Schaeffer, Claude F. A., 304n107
Schama, Simon, 319n99
Schaper, Joachim, 248n7
Schaudig, Hanspeter, 313n54, 318nn91,92, 321n1, 331n59
Schiffman, Lawrence H., 348n59, 353n100
Schipper, Bernd U., 264n15, 319n102, 331n58, 337n106
Schloen, J. David, 287n108, 296nn43,44
Schmid, Konrad, 270n80, 287n105, 330n55

Schmidt, Brian B., 248n9, 254n18, 333n76
Schmitt, Rüdiger, 249n12, 250n27, 251n35, 265n28, 355n1
Schniedewind, William M., 307n13
Schremer, Adiel, 345n35
Schröter, Jens, 349n71, 350n81
Schüle, Andreas, 338n110
Schunck, Klaus Dietrich, 278n37, 280n44
Schwally, Friedrich, 271n94
Schwartz, Baruch J., 333n80
Schwartz, Daniel R., 321n118, 345n35
Scoones, Ian, 263n7
Secunda, S. 316n76, 351n82
Sefati, Yitschak, 314n62, 316n76, 351n82
Segal, Judah B., 327n42
Segal, Peretz, 283n70
Sellin, Ernst, 297n52
Selz, Gebhard J., 257n48, 350n81
Seow, Choon Leong, 277n19
Sergi, Omer, 263n6, 272nn103,105
Seux, Marie-Joseph, 254n22, 257n54, 286n100, 301n85
Seybold, Klaus Dieter, 275n5
Shaked, Shaul, 322n4, 327n42
Shanks, Hershel, 266n44, 278n39
Sharp, Carolyn R., 307–308n15
Shatzman, Israel, 352n93
Shaw, Frank, 267n53
Shiloh, Yigal, 279n41
Shukron, Eli, 306n5
Singer-Avitz, Lily, 279n40
Smelik, Klaas A. D., 251n31, 264n21, 271n96, 272nn100,102, 278n35, 292n15
Smend, Rudolf, 261n114, 355n2, 356n9
Smith, Jonathan Z., 249nn17,18, 351n86,
Smith, Mark S., 247n1, 264n19, 265n26, 266n36, 267n50, 270n78, 273n115, 285n93, 295n37, 296n41, 296n46
Smith, Morton, 249n16, 254n18
Smith-Christopher, Daniel L., 270n73
Soggin, J. Alberto, 248n6, 251n35

Soldt, Wilfred H. van, 259n84
Sommer, Benjamin D., 319n96
Sommer, Michael, 350–351n81
Sommerfeld, Walter, 258n65, 259n69
Sperling, S. David, 352n96
Spiro, Melford E., 252n1
Spronk, Klaas, 277n15, 296n44
Stackert, Jeffrey, 270n80, 334n84
Stadelmann, Helge, 347n49
Stager, Lawrence E., 272n106, 278n39,
    284n80, 289nn130,133, 290n142,
    291n7, 293n22, 297n57, 301n87,
    342–343n16, 343n17
Stamm, Johann Jakob, 315n67
Starcky, Jean, 286n96
Starr, Ivan, 254n21
Stavrakopoulou, Francesca,
    250nn24,26,27, 252n2, 273n114,
    279n40, 292n18
Stein, Stephen J., 351n83
Steiner, Richard C., 319–320n104
Steinkeller, Piotr, 269n63
Steins, Georg, 333n81
Stendebach, Franz Josef, 270n76
Sterling, Gregory E., 342n13
Stern, Ephraim, 278nn37,39, 279n40
Stevens, Marty E., 284n78
Steymans, Hans Ulrich, 270n80
Stökl, Jonathan, 303–304n101, 312n45,
    317n83, 318n88, 323–324n119, 346n42
Stol, Marten, 253n13, 259n71, 260n91,
    269nn62,69, 275n7, 315n65
Stolper, Matthew W., 267–268n54,
    310n25, 317n81
Stone, Elizabeth C., 259n71
Stone, Michael E., 329n52
Strassmaier, Johann N., 312n45
Sysling, Harry, 346n40

Tadmor, Hayim, 272n107, 276n13,
    284n81, 307n14, 325nn27,30
Tadmor, Miriam, 302n91
Talshir, Zipora, 333n81
Taylor, Charles, 250n21

Tebes, Juan Manuel, 266n41
Teeter, Emily, 257n46
Tenu, Aline, 273n109
Tervanotko, Hanna, 346n42
Thompson, Henry O., 279n41
Tigay, Jeffrey H., 300–301n81
Tigchelaar, Eibert J. C., 343n20, 348n61,
    352–353n97
Tolini, Gauthier, 317n83, 323–324n19
Toorn, Karel van der, 250n25,
    252n39, 253n15, 255n32, 256n45,
    259nn70,74,78,81, 260n94, 265n33,
    269nn64,70,72, 273n117, 277n26,
    278nn27–29, 282n58, 284nn79,83,84,
    285n91; 288nn115,122, 294n34,
    296n47, 299nn65,66, 300n79,
    308nn15,18, 311n30, 319n102, 319–
    320n104, 320n112, 323n15, 334n91,
    336n101, 337n102, 339n121
Tov, Emanuel, 350n81
Tropper, Josef, 259n77
Tsfania, Levana, 324n23, 325n28, 341n5
Tsukimoto, Akio, 259n80
Tunca, Önhan, 269n67
Tuplin, Christoph J., 331–332n67,
    335n94
Tylor, Edward B., 257n51

Uehlinger, Christoph, 249nn13,14,
    285n91, 295n38, 302n91, 308n17
Ulf, Christoph, 310n26, 314n63
Urbach, Ephraim E., 348n58
Uro, Risti, 258n60
Urso, Gianpaolo, 352n93
Ussishkin, David, 279n40, 279–280n41,
    280n48, 291n8

Van De Mieroop, Marc, 289n131
Vanderhooft, David, 328n49
VanderKam, James C., 348nn59,61
Vandermeersch, L., 289n131, 303n100
Vatke, Wilhelm, 261n114, 355nn2,3
Vaughan, Patrick H., 293n26
Vaughn, Andrew G., 306n5

Vaux, Roland de, 254n24, 255n33, 266n36, 268n56, 283nn67,69
Veen, Peter van der, 315n70
Veenhof, Klaas R., 271n86
Vernant, J. P., 289n131, 303n100
Virolleaud, Charles, 304n107
Vittmann, Günter, 338n110
Volten, Aksel, 331n65
Volz, Paul, 283n71
Vorländer, Hermann, 347–348n57
Vriezen, Theodoor C., 247n6, 355n4

Waddell, W. G., 344n28
Waerzeggers, Caroline, 287n111, 288nn116,117, 312n45, 317n83, 318n88, 323n19, 334nn85,86
Walbank, F. W., 344n25
Walls, Neal H., 264n19, 276n14
Walton, John H., 249n15, 257n48
Watts, James W., 330n55, 331n67
Weber, Manfred, 331n65
Wehmeier, Gerhard, 264n17
Weidner, Ernst F., 311n32, 313n56
Weigold, Matthias, 350n81
Weiher, Egbert von, 300n75
Weinfeld, Moshe, 308n16, 349nn73,74
Weingart, Kristin, 272nn103, 105
Weippert, Helga, 289n138, 343n17
Weippert, Manfred, 250n28, 251n31, 262n1, 265nn28,30, 266n42, 267n54, 268n56, 271n95, 272n104, 275n8, 285n95, 289n138, 297n54, 303–304n101, 311n32, 337nn105,107
Welch, Adam C., 308n16
Wellhausen, Julius, 2, 247n4, 286n97, 296n48, 303n96
Werblowsky, R. J. Zwi, 333n80
West, Martin L., 253n16
Westbrook, Raymond, 268n59, 290n144
Westenholz, Aage, 250n29
Westermann, William Linn, 344n24
White, John B., 249n15
Wiesehöfer, Josef, 330n55

Wiggermann, Frans A. M., 257n47, 260n91, 281n55, 292n14
Wiggins, Steve, 265n34, 295n36
Wigoder, Geoffrey, 333n80
Wijngaards, John, 264n17
Wilcke, Claus, 255n36, 292n14, 298n63
Williamson, Hugh G. M., 314n64, 318n88, 327–328n45, 328nn47,48, 329n54, 332–333n74
Wilson, John A., 262n118
Wilson, Robert R., 256n42, 307n9
Wilson, Stephen G., 349–350n74
Wilson-Wright, Aren, 322n5
Winitzer, Abraham, 316n76, 351n82
Winters, Ryan D., 257n49
Witte, Markus, 266n41, 270n80, 287n105, 349n71
Wöhrle, Jacob, 265n28
Wolff, Hans Walter, 274n122
Wolff, Samuel R., 284n80
Wright, David P., 260n94, 261n113, 288n120
Wright, G. Ernest, 247n2
Wright, J. Edward, 350n80
Wright, Jacob L., 270n77, 306n6
Wunsch, Cornelia, 267–268n54, 309n24, 309–310n25, 310nn27,28, 310–311n29, 311nn31,34–40, 312nn41, 43, 45–47, 313nn50,52,55, 315n67, 316n77, 317nn80,86, 323n18, 337nn102,103, 337–338n109
Würthwein, Ernst, 345n34
Wyatt, Nicholas, 250n26, 295n36, 296n41

Xella, Paolo, 267n51
Xeravits, Géza G., 353n97

Yadin, Yigael, 274n120, 285n94
Yarbro Collins, Adela, 276n14
Yardeni, Ada, 326n37
Yeivin, Shemuel, 307n10
Young, Gordon D., 256n41
Younger, K. Lawson, 251n31, 277n16, 288n114, 296n45

Zadok, Ran, 311n32, 313nn50,53
Zahn, Molly M., 345n35
Zaia, Shana, 314n61
Zawadski, Stefan, 313–314n58
Zevit, Ziony, 249n12, 251nn34,35,
    260n98, 274n120, 276–277n15,

284nn80,86, 285n94, 289n130,
    293nn24,25, 297n52, 299n67, 301n87
Zimmerli, Walther, 280nn46,48, 352n89
Zissu, Boaz, 305n108
Zsengeller, József, 320n108
Zwickel, Wolfgang, 293n24

Index of Ancient Sources

Hebrew Bible

Genesis

1	200	26:28–30	63
1:1–2:4	199	27:1–45	35
1:14–19	21, 209	27:43	53
2:4–3:24	199	28:10–22	93
2:23	59, 65	28:16–22	294n30
4:21–22	6	29:1–14	121
4:26	6	29:14	59
5:1–32	26	30:1	143
6:1–8	19	31:5	61
6:9–9:19	199	31:10–18	61
9:5	70	31:13	93
12:6	296n40	31:16	61
12:8	93	31:19	36
12:14–20	199	31:29–30	61
13:3–4	93	31:30	132
15:9	66	31:30–35	138
19:30–38	143	31:43–54	63, 90
20:1–18	199	31:51–53	61, 90
20:7	148	32:10–11	61
20:17	35	33:20	53
21:21	264n16	34	270n73
21:22–32	63	34:9–10	270n73
21:33–22:19	145	34:16	64
22:1–14	45	35:1	53
22:1–19	93	35:2–3	20
23:17–20	131	35:3	53
24:10–20	121	35:4	128
24:10–27	121	35:7	53, 93
24:11	23, 121	35:8	59, 93, 131
25:9	282n61	35:14	127
26:6–11	199	35:16–20	59

384

35:20	131	21:7–11	134
38:8–11	59	21:13–14	100, 101
38:12–26	143	21:18–22:16	118
38:14	141	22:6–8	139
38:16–17	342n16	22:9–12	139
43:23	61	22:19	135
43:30	136	22:24–26	335n93
47:22	107	23:4	119
49:1	35	23:13	39, 135
49:1–28	35	23:16	85
49:24–25	105	24:10	18
49:25	54, 94	24:20	45
50:16–17	61	25–31	68
		25:9	40
Exodus		25:40	40
2:15–22	121	26:31–34	98
2:16–22	57	28	110
3:1	57	28:15	289n129
3:5	20, 98	28:29	289n129
3:13–15	58, 268n56	28:30	289n129
4:24–26	20	29:35–37	111
6:2–7:7	200	29:36–37	112
6:3	76	30:27–28	126, 132
8:8–9	148	31:18	113
11–12	45	32	108
12:1–13	49	32:1–6	105
12:1–28	334n92	32:15–16	113
12:15–20	338n111	33:7–11	125
15:3	12, 57	34:22	25, 85
18:1	57		
18:10–12	57	Leviticus	
19–20	88	3:11	45
19:10	20	8:15	112
20	354n107	10:8–11	110
20:3	95	12	112
20:10	214	13:45–46	20
20:13	88	14:1–9	20
20:13–16	112	14:19	112
20:14	136	14:40	291n11
20:19–22	354n107	15:18	20
20:21	39	16	112
21:2–6	61, 135	16:11–17	98
21:2–11	335n93	16:12	98
21:6	136	17:4	96

Leviticus (*continued*)

19:31	151
20:27	151
21	111
21:7	110
21:16–23	110
22:25	111
23:5–8	338n111
23:27–28	112
23:34	88
23:39	25
23:39–43	203
25	335n93
25:13–18	135
25:23–24	135
25:23–55	59
25:29–34	290n4
25:31	291n4

Numbers

5:1–4	19
5:2	116
5:11–31	114, 143
6:13–20	112
6:24–26	344n30
10:35	68
11:29	76
12	108
12:1–9	147
12:6–8	353n103
14:34	352n89
19:2	236
19:14–22	19
21:14	75, 76, 116
21:29	77
22–24	3, 35, 148, 274n121
22:7	109, 148
23:21–22	274n121
23:22	76
24:15–17	238
25:1–16	234
27:21	114
28:1–6	111
28:3–8	111

30:4–17	143
32:1–5	280n42
32:34	52
35:9–28	59

Deuteronomy

1:30	115
4:13	113
4:19	21
5	88
5:7	95
5:12–15	203
5:14	214
5:17	88
5:17–20	112
5:19	113
5:24–27	354n107
5:28–29	354n107
5:29	354n107
5:30–31	354n107
9:10	113
10:2	113
10:4	113
12	199
12:4–7	333n75
12:8–12	333n75
12:13–19	333n75
12:15–16	127
12:20–25	127
12:20–27	333n75
13:17	70
14:22–26	342n16
15:1–18	335n93
15:17	61, 136
16:13	85
16:18	329n53
17:3	21
17:8–13	101, 348n58
17:14–20	156
17:18–19	198
18:11	132, 151
18:15–18	223
18:18	237, 353n103
18:18–19	238, 354n107

18:18–20	354n107
18:18–22	354n107
18:22	354n107
19:12	59
20:14	64
21:5	101
21:10–14	64
21:15–17	35
22:5	20
23:2–7	340n125
23:4–7	209
23:10–15	70
23:19	342n16
23:20–21	335n93
24:8	348n58
24:10–13	335n93
25:5–10	59
26:5	50, 53
26:12	106
26:14	138
27:4	156
27:12	156
30:1–10	199
30:11–14	18
31:9	198
31:10–13	198
31:24–26	198
32:4	278n28
32:8–9	32
32:17	123
33:1–29	35
33:2	47, 56
33:2–3	12
33:5	89
33:8	107
33:8–11	238
33:10	334n91
33:29	199
34:6	280n42

Joshua

2:1	122
2:1–5	93
2:15	122

3:1–17	239
5:15	20, 98
6:19	100
6:24	100
7	101
13:14	106
13:17	52
24:26	128

Judges

1:4–7	116
1:16	57
4:4–5	93
4:4–10	69
4:5	59
4:11	57
5:2	70
5:3	76
5:4	12
5:4–5	47, 56
5:5	76
5:8	123
5:11	76, 300n73
5:13	76
5:14–18	64
5:14–22	64
5:15–17	64
5:20	64
5:23	68, 76
5:24–27	116
5:24–30	64
5:30	64
6:25–32	292n16
6:26	292n16
8:22	79
8:22–27	105, 292n16
8:23	105
8:25–32	125
8:27	105, 131
8:33	63
9:2	59
9:4	63
9:6	296n39
9:8	80

Judges (*continued*)

9:8–15	78
9:27	85
9:37	92, 128
9:46	63
9:53–54	116
11:1–11	79
11:11	79, 90
11:23–24	11
11:34	141
11:37	141
11:39–40	141
12:5–6	72
15:1	24
17:1–6	105, 125
17:2–4	131
17:3	105
17:4	131
17:5	131, 292n16
17:5–13	107
17:6	118
17:13	105
18:14	126, 292n16
18:14–20	107
18:18	131
18:22	126
18:29–31	105
19:15–21	122
20:1	90
20:26	297n55
21:8–14	73
21:19	85
21:19–21	85
21:21	141
21:25	118

1 Samuel

1:1–8	135, 143
1:6	300n77
1:7	272n99
1:9	101, 136, 272n99
1:9–14	85
1:10	143
1:13	144
1:17	301n88
1:18	127
1:20	25
1:24	272n99
1:24–28	143
2:1–10	144
2:11	147
2:12–14	106
2:18	147
2:27–36	108
3:1–14	147
3:3	147
4–6	68
4:4	102
5:1–2	68
6:8	282n61
6:11	282n61
6:13	24
7:5–6	90
7:6	297n55
7:15–17	287n112
7:16–17	90
8:11–18	78, 118
8:20	115
9:1–10:16	121
9:6	146, 148
9:7–8	342n16
9:7–10	148
9:8	146
9:9	146
9:11	23, 121
9:11–14	62
9:12	62, 123, 125, 134, 135
9:13	126
9:14	122
9:18	122
9:22	101, 125, 126, 127, 135
9:22–25	62, 126
9:23	126
9:24	126
9:25	136
9:25–26	133
10:1	76, 89, 273n113

10:2	59	21:10	105, 131
10:5	148	22:2	51
10:5–6	149	22:18–23	308n8
10:6	149	22:20	307n8
10:7	148	23:9–12	114
10:9–13	149	23:18	74
10:10–13	149	24:7	80, 237
10:12	149	24:11	80, 237
10:14–16	62	25:2–42	74
10:17–19	78	25:4–8	51
10:17–25	90	25:10	51
10:25	87	25:28	75, 76, 116
11:1	73	25:39–43	74
11:1–13	273n109	25:43	74
11:7	66, 73	26:9	237
11:15	79	26:9–11	80
12:16–17	24	26:11	237
12:23	148	26:16	237
14:3	307n8	26:19	75, 89, 111, 213
14:41–42	114	26:23	237
14:49	138	27:8–9	51
14:49–50	74	28:3	151
14:50	116	28:3–25	146
14:50–51	62	28:6	108, 114
15:23	132, 151	28:9	151
16:1–5	135	28:13	34
16:1–13	135	28:13–15	151
16:11	62	28:20–25	151
16:11–13	138	28:24	136
18	51	29:3	51
18:3–4	74	30:7–8	114
18:17	68, 75, 76	31:11–13	73
18:27	298n64	31:13	131
19:11–17	132		
19:11–18	36	**2 Samuel**	
19:13–16	138	1:10	117
19:18–24	149	1:12	76
19:19–20	149	1:14–16	80
20:5–29	24	2:4	79, 80
20:6	36, 62	3:17–19	280n44
20:8	74	3:21	74
20:28–29	62	3:27	122
21:2–8	70	3:29	20, 116
21:2–10	292n19	4:5–7	254n28

2 Samuel (*continued*)

5:1	59, 74
5:3	74, 79, 80
5:5	74
5:13–14	74
5:21	68
5:24	115
6:1–19	84
6:2	102
6:6–11	20
6:12–18	106
7:11–16	238
7:14	13, 80
8:7	284n81
8:9–12	100
8:16	116
10:4–5	116
10:12	89
11:1	25, 115, 116
11:1–13	116
12:1–14	109
12:3	136
12:26–31	117
14:1–11	117
14:11	59
14:16	89
15:2	64, 72
15:3	118
15:4	118
15:7–8	75
15:7–9	144
15:11	126
18:18	131, 260n97, 296n45
19:13	59
19:14	59
19:35–36	289n136
20:19	89
21:6	74
21:7	74
21:9	24, 74
24:9	116
24:15–25	93

1 Kings

1:19	116
1:32–40	106
1:33	121
1:39	80
1:41	126
1:49	126
1:50–53	99, 101
2:7	109
2:26–27	106, 107
3:4	74
4:4	106
5:15	80
6:5	283n68
6:23–30	101
6:31–32	98
6:33–35	98
7:7	290n142
7:12	93
7:23–26	94
7:44	94
7:48–49	97
7:51	100
8:1–9	101
8:4	272n99
8:6–8	101
8:9	101
8:31–32	100
8:63	106
11:1	283n64
11:7	282n61, 283n64
11:33	283n64
12:16	119
12:25–31	131
12:25–33	92
12:26–30	76
12:28	76, 89, 94
12:28–29	12, 105
12:28–30	280n44
12:29	90
12:29–30	105
12:30	90
12:31	107, 293n26

12:31–32	106
12:32	25, 84, 88
12:32–33	24, 92
12:32–13:6	106
13:6	148
13:7	109, 148
13:11	148
13:14	93
13:32	293n26
13:33	107
14:1–3	148
14:1–18	144
14:3	109, 148
14:23	125
14:28	101
15:13	95
15:17	90
15:18	100
15:22	90
16:23–24	93
16:29–33	96
16:32	93, 281n49
16:32–33	96
16:33	95
17:7–10	96
17:17–24	148
18	58
18:6–14	151
18:19	109
18:20–46	147
18:28–29	149
18:29	22
18:36	22
18:40	234
19:3–14	145
19:10	147
19:18	105
20:12	117
20:22	25, 115
20:26	25, 115
21:2	342n16
21:8–14	101
21:8–16	135
21:9	135

21:10–13	148
21:12	135
21:13	135
22:5–12	70
22:6–28	109
22:10	117
22:38	121
22:44	132

2 Kings

1:1–2:12	35
1:2	96, 148
1:2–4	144
1:9–14	151
1:26–27	306n8
2–14	287n112
2:3	149
2:4–15	149
2:12	109, 149
2:19–22	35
2:23–24	148
3:2	127
3:9–20	148
3:11–20	109
3:15–20	149
3:20	22
3:27	45
4:8–11	136
4:13	60, 109, 116, 134
4:17–30	144
4:17–37	148
4:23	24
4:24–37	148
4:27	301n88
4:38	149
5:1–19	148
5:3	148
5:15	109, 148
5:17	89
6:1	149
6:1–7	149
6:12	136
6:21	149

2 Kings (*continued*)

6:26–30	117
6:32	149
7:1	122, 291n8
7:3–4	122
7:3–5	20
8:1–6	96, 117
8:7–8	148
8:8	109, 148
9:1–14	109
9:11	109
10:12–17	157
10:15–17	57
10:18–29	93, 281n49
10:22	20, 98, 110
10:25	106
10:26–27	127
11:1–3	101
11:1–8	106
11:1–20	101
11:10	101, 284n81
11:12	80, 83, 117
11:17	83
12:6	100
12:8	100
12:10	98
12:11	100
12:19	100
13:14	109, 149
13:20	25, 115
15:19–22	187
15:29	187
16:10–16	106, 147
16:10–18	106
17:26	89
17:27–28	187, 198
17:29	293n26
17:33	165
18–19	329n52
18:4	94, 95
18:32–25	11
19:10–12	11
21:5	95
21:23–26	156
22–23	154
22:3	307n12
22:4	98
22:14	98, 110, 155
22:15–18	306n7
23:4	95, 98, 282n61
23:5	21, 132
23:6–7	95
23:7	95
23:8	90, 123
23:12	139
23:15	158, 187
23:19	293n26
23:21	338n114
23:24	132
23:25	221
23:30	80
24:8–17	158
24:16	158
25:1	166
25:3–4	166
25:8–12	166
25:11–12	158
25:18	98, 110
25:22–26	166
25:23	326n39
25:27–30	164, 166

Isaiah

1:10–17	24
3:18–23	140
6:1	99, 102
6:1–7	112
6:1–8	147
6:5	21, 98
6:6–8	21
8:1–2	147
8:16	149, 152
8:19	152
8:19–20	34, 130
9:5	275n10
10:30	293n19
11:1	320n116
13:3	70

14:2	89	48:5	171
14:9	305n109	48:20	171
16:10	85	49:1	319n97
16:12	125	49:14–26	172
19:3	151	49:26	105
19:19	280n43	50:1	343n22
25:10	122	51:1–2	171
27:1	94	51:9–10	94
29:4	151	52:1	14, 171
29:11	229	52:11	171
32:11–12	145	53:4–6	172
33:14–16	113	53:7	319n97
33:18	100	56:1–8	340n125
34:6	45, 70	60:16	105
34:13–14	37	63:16	34n7
36–37	329n52	65:6	217, 219
36:18–20	11		
37:4	148	Jeremiah	
37:10–13	11	1:1	14, 147, 155
37:16	102	1:5	319n97
38:21	148	1:11–14	150
40–48	158, 170	2:2–6	307n15
40–55	170, 172	2:27	94
40:2	217	3:16–18	101
40:8	172	5:12	268n55
40:19	318n88	7	92
40:20	318n88	7:2	98
41:8–9	171	7:4	136, 286n102
43:3	172	7:9	113
44:4	318n88	7:12–15	127, 136, 156
44:9–20	171	7:16–20	157
44:15	312n48	7:21	98
44:25	318n88	7:22–23	307n15
44:28	170	8:2	21
45:1	170, 212	9:16	145
45:1–7	170	10:6–7	345n34
45:2	170, 318n88	10:11	312n48
45:13	170	11:12	132
46:1–2	171	11:13	125
46:1–3	164	11:18–12:6	319n97
46:6	100	11:19	319n97
46:6–8	171	11:21–23	155
47:13	171, 318n88	15:1	307n15
48:2	14, 171	15:7	153

Jeremiah (*continued*)

15:10–21	319n97
16:6–8	138
18:18–23	319n97
19:13	139
19:14	98
20:1–3	101
20:7–18	319n97
21:12	115
24:1	158
24:1–10	150
25:11	233
25:11–12	172, 176
26	92
26:2	98
26:6	156
26:9	156
26:10	98
26:24	156, 307n12
28:1–4	159
29:1	168, 312n44
29:1–2	158
29:1–3	168
29:3	156, 307n12
29:7	165
29:8–9	159
29:10	172, 176, 233
29:15	156, 159
29:20–23	159
29:24–28	101
29:25	168
29:26	101, 109
29:28	176
29:31–32	159
31:2–3	307n15
31:15	59
32:6–15	107, 155, 156
32:9–11	342n16
32:12	156
32:29	139
34:5	276n15
34:18	66
35	57

35:2	101, 127
35:4	98, 156
35:6–10	157
35:11	157
36:4	156
36:9	92, 297n55
36:10	92, 98, 100, 156
36:25	156
36:32	156
37:12	107
37:15–16	101
38:7	117
39:1	166
39:2–3	166
39:10	158
39:14	307n12
40:5–6	326n39
41:1–3	166
41:1–7	90
41:5	158, 187
41:10	187
41:15	187
41:16–43:7	158
42:1–12	148
43:4–7	175
44	175
44:1	154, 320n116, 339n116
44:15–19	95, 143
44:15–25	157
44:15	154, 175, 320n116
44:17	132
48:13	157, 174
48:35	132
48:46	77
49:1–2	187
49:3	145
50:36	318n88
51:39	34
51:57	34
51:59–64	156, 168
52:4	166
52:6–7	166

52:12–14	166	46:1	167
52:24	98, 110, 156	48:35	268n55
52:28	158		
52:28–30	158, 309n20	**Hosea**	
52:29	158	2:13	24
52:30	309n20	2:17	307n15
52:31–34	164	2:18	72
		3:1–2	342n16
Ezekiel		3:4	131
1:1–2	164	4:2	113
1:3	147	4:8	106
1:26–28	18	4:12	128
2:8–3:3	168	4:13	125
3:15	164	8:1	89
4:5	352n89	8:4	78
8:1	149, 161, 164, 168	8:5–6	281n49
8:11	307n12	8:12	113
8:14	145	9:3	89
10:1	18	9:4–5	87
13:17–23	146	9:5	85
14:1	149, 164, 168,	9:8	89
	312n44	9:10	307n15
14:14	216	9:15	78
14:20	216	11:1–4	307n15
16:8	99	12:3–15	55, 72
20:1	149, 164, 168,	12:12	78
	312n44	12:14	147
21:26	132, 151	13:2	105
25:12	188	13:3	307n15
26:1	164	13:9–11	78
26:7–14	164		
29:17	164	**Joel**	
29:17–20	314n61	1:6	89
29:20	165	1:13	45
29:28	164	4:19	188
32:1–16	314n61	4:21	33
36:5	188		
38:12	92	**Amos**	
41:3	98	2:6	342n16
42:13	101	2:11	149
43:8	93	3:1	63
44:12	110	5:5	90, 144
44:18	110	5:15	122
44:21	110	5:21–25	111
		5:25	307n15

Amos (*continued*)

5:26	87
7:1	25
7:9	125
7:10	106
7:10–17	92, 151
7:13	84, 92
7:14	308n15
7:17	107
8:1–2	150
8:3	289n136
8:5	24
8:14	90, 105, 131, 144
9:7	44

Obadiah

1:12–15	188

Micah

6:7	45

Nahum

1:2	86, 278n28

Habakkuk

1:6	222
3	267n51
3:3	12, 47, 56
3:5	57, 303n91
3:7	47, 56

Zephaniah

1:7	126
1:5	139

Haggai

1:1	185, 316n72, 317n84, 323n19
1:6	327n43
1:15	316n72, 317n84, 323n19
2:1	316n72, 317n84, 323n19
2:1–2	185
2:3	185
2:10	316n72, 317n84, 323n19

2:11–13	112, 198
2:20	316n72, 317n84, 323n19
2:20–23	191, 238

Zechariah

1:1	316n72, 317n84, 323n19
1:7	167, 316n72, 317n84, 323n19
1:12	176, 233
2:10–11	318n94
2:14–15	96
2:16	89, 208
4:6–10	191, 238
4:14	238
6:9–15	191, 238
7:1	167, 316n72, 317n84, 323n19
7:1–3	169
7:1–7	166
7:2	160, 315n67, 317n86
7:5	166, 176, 233
7:12	194
8:3	96
8:18–19	166
10:2	132, 151
14:16–19	338n114
14:21	98

Malachi

1:2–5	188
1:6	105
1:6–14	111
1:7	106
1:11	166, 183
2:6	198
2:7	113, 198
2:10	34n7
2:11	62
2:14	65
2:15	209
3:5	327n43

3:10	101	50:16	88
3:16	219	50:18–19	112
3:20	323n17	50:18–20	88
3:23–24	238	57:2	99
		60:12	69
Psalms		61:5	99
2:2	81	63:8	99
2:7	13	65:5	98
2:7–8	81	68:2	68
2:7–9	109	68:15	54
2:8	116	68:22	70
2:9	109	68:22–24	45
4:3	119	68:24	85
5:8	98	68:25	86
13:4	34	69:8	290n2
15	112	69:13	122
16:3–4	138	69:20	290n2
17	101	71:13	290n2
17:8	99	72:1	117
19:6	22	72:2	115
20	173, 277n26	72:12–14	117
22:10–11	298n61	74:12–17	84, 94
24:3–6	112	79:2–3	344n29
24:8	12, 57	81:4	24, 88
26:6–7	315n65	81:9–11	88, 112
30:8	285n92	81:10	88, 113
35:26	290n2	82:1	30
36:8	99	86:9	183
44:10	69	89:4	83
44:16	290n2	89:6–9	86
45	275n9	89:10–12	94
45:4–8	82	89:10–15	84
45:7	81	89:15	86
45:7–8	13, 80	89:19–20	80
45:13	81	89:20–26	109
47:6	86	89:20–38	109
47:7	86	90:10	176
47:9	86	93:5	98
48:3	94	94:1–2	278n28
50	87	94:23	86
50:4	115	95:3	86, 88
50:5	87	96:4	86
50:7	87, 88	97:2	86
50:8–13	111	97:7	86, 88

Psalms (*continued*)

99:5	101
99:6	147
101	82
101:2	82
101:8	82, 115, 117
108:12	69
109:18	67
109:29	290n2
110	275n10
110:1	109
110:2	116
110:4	106
110:7	117
119:144	202
121:8	120
132	84
132:2	105
132:5	105
132:7	101
132:11–18	109
135:14	115
138:2	98
141:2	24, 111, 132
148:1–6	18

Proverbs

2:17	65
7:12	122
7:14–20	342n16
7:19–20	24
9:18	126
16:10	115, 118
16:33	114
20:8	118
24:7	122, 215
25:1	118
27:9	111, 132
28:9	198
30:3–4	18
31:2	143
31:23	122

Job

5:1	322n8

11:7–8	18
17:13–16	34
26:9	24
29:7	122
31:26–28	21

Song of Songs

3:4	136
4:1	141
6:7	141

Ruth

1:16	61
1:20–21	55
1:22	24
2:20	59
2:23	24
3:9	59, 99
3:12	59
4:1–2	122
4:1–14	59
4:13–22	209

Lamentations

2:1	171
2:15	171

Ecclesiastes

3:1	19
5:3	232
5:4–6	143
8:2	289n134
9:5–6	351n87
10:20	136
11:8	351n87
12:12	221

Esther

1:5–9	322n3
1:14	181
2:5	212
2:7	313n53
2:16	167
2:21	98
3:8	339n124
6:2	98

Daniel

1:4	230
1:7	163
1:8–16	347n52
2	351n87
4:24	217, 343n19
6:11	236
7	351n87
7:11	219
7:25	234
7:26–27	234
7:27	236
8:19	232
9:2	176, 219
9:13	334n88
9:20–23	224
9:20–27	223
9:21	24
9:24–27	232
11:33	228
11:36	232
12:1	233

Ezra

1–2	185
1:1	176
1:1–4	168
1:2	184
1:2–4	190
1:7	271n96
1:8–11	185, 190
2:1	184
2:1–70	190
2:2	185
2:59	339n119
2:64–67	169
2:68	336n97
3:1–3	190
3:2	334n88
3:2–3	204
3:3–5	338n114
3:4	191, 334n88
3:4–5	203
3:4–6	190

3:4–7	204
3:7	190
3:8	184
3:8–13	190
3:12	185, 336n97
4:1	185
4:1–2	209
4:1–3	185
4:1–5	190, 191
4:2	185, 336n97
4:3	336n97
4:6	190
4:7–24	190
4:8–16	328n50
4:11	192
4:11–16	191
4:13	327n42
4:16	192
4:17	192
4:20	327n42
5:1–2	190
5:3–5	190
5:6–17	190, 191
5:9	336n97
5:14	185
6:1	333n77
6:1–12	190
6:7	336n97
6:10	194, 314n59
6:18	204
6:19–22	190, 204, 206, 338n114
6:20	338n111
6:21	208, 209
7:1	307n8, 346n47
7:1–6	192
7:6	190, 193, 198, 339n118
7:7	339n118
7:7–8	329n54
7:10	198, 339n118
7:11–26	190
7:12	184, 202

Ezra (*continued*)

7:14	181, 192, 193, 202, 203, 337n104
7:15–24	193
7:23	194
7:24	327n42
7:25	185, 192, 193, 329n53
7:26	193, 202
7:28	339n118
8:1	336n97
8:1–20	185
8:1–36	190
8:15–20	165
8:22	192
8:31	192
8:32	185
8:35	184, 339n118
9–10	209, 340n132
9:1	209, 339n118
9:2	192, 209
9:4	339n118
9:8–9	208
9:9	189
9:15	339n118
10:1	339n118
10:1–44	204
10:2	339n118
10:3	204, 228
10:5	228, 339n118
10:6	330n54
10:8	336n97
10:14	336n97
10:16	336n97
10:25	339n118

Nehemiah

1:1	167
1:1–3	158
1:2	184, 339n118
1:3	184
1:11	192, 329n52
2:1	167, 346n47
2:1–9	185

2:3	213
2:4–5	190
2:7–9	190
2:10	190
2:11–18	190
2:16	336n97
2:19	185, 190, 191
3:1	330n54, 340n127
3:1–32	190
3:3	291n8
3:33	339n118
3:33–35	190
4:1–8	190
4:5	209
4:6	339n118
4:8	336n97
4:9	209
4:13	336n97
5:1	208
5:1–5	189
5:1–13	204
5:4	189, 327n42
5:7	208, 336n97
5:8	208
5:9	204, 209
5:10–12	335n93
5:4	327n42
5:14	185, 339n118
5:15	189
5:17	335n94, 336n97
6:1	185, 209
6:1–14	190
6:5–7	191
6:6	188, 209
6:10–14	190
6:15	167
6:16	209
6:17	336n97
6:17–18	210
6:17–19	190
6:18	187, 190, 210
7:5–72	190
7:69	336n97
7:70	336n97

8:1	198, 339n118
8:1–3	203
8:1–12	190
8:3	198
8:4–8	199
8:5	202
8:7	203
8:8	203
8:9–12	338n114
8:13–17	204
8:13–18	190, 191, 202, 203, 338n114
8:14	339n118
8:15	334n88
8:15–16	203
8:17	191, 203, 339n118
8:18	198
9:1	297n55
9:1–3	204
9:2	190, 209
9:3	204
9:6–37	199
9:36–37	189, 208
10	228, 340n132
10:1	228
10:29	209
10:29–30	228
10:31	204
10:32	167, 204
10:33–40	204
10:35	204, 334n88
10:36–37	204
10:37	334n88
10:39–40	101
11:1	208
11:11	307n8
11:13	336n97
11:18	208
11:24	206
12:1–25	190
12:22–23	330n54
12:39	291n8
13:1	198
13:1–3	204, 209

13:1–13	209
13:3	192, 209
13:4	190, 210
13:4–9	185, 190
13:5	210
13:6	346n47
13:7–9	340n127
13:14	219
13:15–21	167
13:15–22	204
13:17	336n97
13:19	23
13:23	190
13:23–31	209
13:24	339n118
13:28	190, 210
13:30	336n97

1 Chronicles

2:55	57
3:24	268n54
5:8	52
5:37–40	307n8
9:10–11	307n8
10:2	131
10:13	151
16:33	272n99
23:32	272n99
28:2	101

2 Chronicles

3:1	93
4:2–10	94
7:12	324n23
16:14	276n15
17:7–9	334n91
17:9	203
21:12–15	317n79
21:19	276n15
23:18	334n88
24:6	272n99
25:4	334n88
28:8–15	210
29:5–7	272n99
29:25	147

2 Chronicles (*continued*)

30:1–26	210
30:5	334n88
30:18	334n88
30:25	155
31:3	334n88
32:6	122
33:14	291n8
34:1–35:19	210
34:14	154
35:3	334n91
35:12	334n88
35:26	334n88
36:22	176

Deuterocanonical Works and Septuagint

Tobit

1:5–8	353n99
1:8	214
1:10–11	347n52
1:17–18	213
1:22	329n52
2:3–8	213
2:6	219
2:11–12	216
3:1–6	343n19
3:7–9	20
3:11–15	343n19
3:16	182
4:3–4	213
4:10–11	343n19
4:11	236
4:14	216
4:17	138
5:7	216
5:15	216
6:14–15	20
6:15	213
6:17	111
7:12	218
7:14	218
8:4–8	343n19

8:6	219
8:15–17	343n19
11:18	182
12:8–9	343n19
12:12	182, 219
12:15	181
13:1–17	343n19
14:4	219, 223
14:6	214
14:10–13	213
14:11	343n19

Judith

4:8–15	343n19
4:11–12	297n55
7:28	213
8:6	343n19
8:31	343n19
9:1	24, 143, 236
9:5–6	352n87
10:8	213
10:20–23	117
11:12	347n52
12:1	117
12:1–4	347n52
12:7–9	343n19
12:8	315n65
13:3	143
13:3–5	343n19
13:4–5	144
13:15	116
14:10	214
16:18–20	353n99

Additions to Esther

14:17	347n52

Wisdom of Solomon

13:2	21

Sirach

3:30	216, 217
6:20	215

7:10	343n19	3:48	346n48
7:14	343n19	3:50	184
7:32	343n19	4:10	184
8:4	215	4:46	237
10:8	352n87	5:32	340n3
12:3	343n19	7:12–18	344n29
15:14–15	352n87	7:43	167
17:22	343n19	9:10	340n3
22:11–12	213	9:27	233, 237, 346n45
23:1	341n7	9:46	184
23:4	341n7	10:15–21	215
26:29	343n20	12:9	222, 241
28:2	343n19	13:42	344n26
29:1–13	343n18	14:41	237, 353n103
29:8–13	343n19		
30:18	138	**2 Maccabees**	
34:5–8	224, 232	2:21	215
34:31	343n19	2:25	221
35:4	343n19	3:10–15	100
35:20–21	343n19	3:25	234
36:17	233	3:25–30	234
38:16–23	213	4:7–9	343n20
38:24–34	216	4:7–17	234
39:1–3	224	4:11–12	214
39:4	230	5:1–4	234
40:24	343n19	5:2	234
41:1–4	351n87	6:1	213
42:7	219	6:2	234
42:9–14	141	6:5	234
45:10	289n129	6:6	213, 234
46:1	239	6:10–11	234
48:10	238	6:18–20	234, 347n57
49:10	223	7	348n57
51:10	341n7	7:1	234, 347n52
51:23	215	7:2	213
		7:8	213
1 Maccabees		7:21	213
1:56–57	345n32	7:24	213
1:61–62	347n52	7:27	213
2:19–20	341n4	7:37	213
2:40	234	8:21	214
2:49	232, 234	10:29	234
2:54	234	11:6–8	234
2:58	234	12:37	213

2 Maccabees (*continued*)

12:38–45	348n57
15:29	213
15:36	167
15:39	345n33
21:8	354n111

1 Esdras

2:10–15	185
4:13–63	185
4:50	188
4:58	236
7:10–15	206
8:9	192
8:11	323n10
9:2	330n54

4 Maccabees

4:3	100
18:10–19	221

New Testament

Matthew

2:16–18	59
4:23	222
5:14	121
6:5	222
6:9	341n7
6:12	217
6:19–21	344n23
7:12	221
9:35	222
11:3	239
13:54	222
14:5	150
18:10	347n57
18:23–35	217
19:21	344n23
21:12–13	98
22:21	240
22:23–33	351n87
22:40	221
23:29–30	237
24:12	232

24:21	233
24:34	233
26:52	240
27:11	240
27:37	240
27:59	19

Mark

11:11	353n99
12:18–27	226, 347n56

Luke

1:8	108
1:9–10	24
1:10	98
1:17	238
2:36–37	300n80
2:41–42	136
2:41–51	353n99
4:14–30	222
7:36–50	217
12:33–34	344n23
15:18	184
16:1–9	219

John

4:1–15	121
4:25	237, 238
11:51	147
18:20	222

Acts

1:6	238
2:5–13	353n99
2:29	223, 237
2:30	346n44
5:17	347n51
5:36	239
7:38	223
7:53	224
8:26–40	220
8:27–28	353n99
12:15	347n57
13:13–43	222
13:15	221
14:1	222

15:5	347n51
16:11–15	143
16:13	315n65
18:4	222
21:28–31	98
21:38	239, 240
22:3	149
23:8	226, 347n56
24:5	241, 350n75
24:14	350n75
26:5	347n51
27:12	25
28:11	25
28:22	350n75

Romans

1:2	241
2:8	232
3:2	223

2 Corinthians

12:2	18

Hebrews

2:2	224
3:5	353n103

1 Peter

1:10–12	224

Revelation

8:1–2	181
8:4–5	111

Pseudepigrapha

1 Enoch

12:3–3	229–230
15:1–3	229–230
72:1	229
81:1–2	229
81:4	219
81:5	181
81:6	230
82:1	230
90:20	219
90:21	181

2 Enoch

20:1	18

Jubilees

1:27	181
1:29	181
2:1	181
2:18	181
4:17	230
15:27	181

Psalms of Solomon

17:4–6	238
17:21–44	238

Testament of Levi

8:2	181

Dead Sea Scrolls and Related Texts

Book of Giants

4Q203 Frag. 8:1–4	350n79
4Q530 Frag. 2:14	350n79

Damascus Document (Cairo Genizah) (CD)

1:5	352n88
3:13–14	349n64
3:16	349n65
6:4–5	349n65
6:7	349n65
12:3	354n105
14:19	354n105
15:5–9	349n72
19:10–11	354n105
20:13–15	233

Miqṣat Maʿaśê ha-Torah (4QMMT)

C 7–8	349n70

Pesher Habakkuk (1QpHab)

2:7–8	232, 235

Pesher Habakkuk
(1QpHab) (*continued*)

2:11–15	222
7:1–2	224
7:2	233
7:4–5	224, 349n64
7:5	224
7:7–8	233
8:10–12	343n20
11:6	352n95
12:4–5	349n67

Pesher Micah
(1QpMic)

Frags. 8–10:5	349n67
Frags. 8–10:7–8	347n53
Frag. 11:1	235

Psalms Scroll[a]
(11Q5)

27:11	346n44

Reworked
Pentateuch[a] (4Q158)

Frag. 6	354n107

Rule of the
Community (1QS)

1:9–10	352n97
1:16–17	349n71
2:1–5	352n97
2:19	235
3:20–21	235, 353n97
5:1	347n53
5:8–10	349n72
5:23	349n68
6:2	348n63
6:6–8	222
6:13–23	349n68
7:1	345n33
8:11–12	349n64
8:12–13	349n69
8:19	349n68
9:11	237, 238

Testimonia
(4Q175)

1–20	354n107

War Scroll (1QM)

1:2	352n95
1:5	233
13:10–12	235, 353n97
13:11–12	349n68
13:14	233, 235
14:3–6	349n68

Josephus

Against Apion

1.40–41	223
1.190–193	323n14

Jewish Antiquities

10.180–182	309n20
11.302–303	210
11.306–312	190
11.310–324	325n25
12.160–236	187
13.171–173	347n50
13.249	234
13.254–258	235
13.282–283	147
13.288–296	235
13.295–298	347n50
13.298	349n67
13.301	234
13.311	228
13.372	235
15.368–371	236
14.65	254n26
18.4–10	240
18.9–10	240
18.16–17	347n56
18.23–25	240
18.85	355n115
18.85–87	239
18.86	240

18.116–119 240

20.97 355n115

20.97–99 239

20.169–172 239

Jewish War

1.78 228

2.118 240

2.119–161 347n50

2.124–127 348n63

2.159 228

2.162–166 347n50

2.164–165 347n56

2.165 351n87

2.261 355n115

2.261–263 239, 240

5.193–194 98

5.207 98

5.216–218 97

5.219 98, 101

5.220–221 98

6.282 100

6.284–285 241

6.286–287 241

7.253–257 240

Cuneiform Texts from Mesopotamia

For miscellaneous other cuneiform texts from Mesopotamia, see the Index of Subjects

AbB

1.106:4–19 255n35

1.106:17–19 255n35

11.60:25–28 315n65

13.21:5–9 259n84

ARM

8.13:11'–14' 275n6

26.194 317n79

26.197:11–12 274n3

26.199:24–25 274n3

26.262 253n10

26/2, p. 33, A. 2730 271n81

Pearce and Wunsch, *Documents of Judean Exiles*

1:16 310n28

2:1 313n52

3:2 313n52

4:2–3 313n52

10 267–268n54

17:12–13 311n31

17:14–15 310–311n29, 311n31

18:7–8 317n80

18:15 310–311n29

19:16 310–311n29

20:2 310n28

20:14 310–311n29

21:10–11 310–311n29

22:7 310–311n29

24:6–7 310–311n29

24:7–8 310–311n29

27:4 311n31

27:11 311n31

27:19–20 323n18

45 313n55, 316n77

45:5 311n31

46:4 311n31

71:13–14 323n18

Wunsch, *Judaeans by the Waters of Babylon*

1:13 310n28

6:18 310–311n29

17:12–13 310–311n29

17:15–16 310–311n29

18:5–6 310–311n29

18:16 310–311n29

24:6–7 310–311n29

26:2–21 310–311n29

Wunsch, *Judaeans by the Waters of Babylon* (*continued*)

45:17–18	310–311n29
46:6–7	310–311n29
51:1–2	310–311n29
53:4–5	310–311n29
53:23–24	312n47
72:2–3	310–311n29
73:6	311n31
73:13	315n67
101:8–9	310–311n29

Lambert, *Babylonian Wisdom Literature*

38:7	304n107 (Ludlul)
40:33–38	252n4 (Ludlul)
76:82–83	252n4 (Babylonian Theodicy)
86:256–257	252n4 (Babylonian Theodicy)
102:61–65	262–116 (Counsels of Wisdom)
110–115	286n98 (Advice to a Prince)
134–135:134	300n80 (Shamash Hymn)
146:54–55	315n65 (Dialogue of Pessimism)

SAA

3, 10–13, no. 3:13–15	276n13
3, 10–13, no. 3 r. 14–16	276n13
3, 74, no. 32:21	305n110
9	288n115, 314n60
9, 22–27, no. 23	305n110
10, 15–16, nos. 18–19	303n93
19, 30, no. 75, 23:8–16	295–296n38
20, 14–18, no. 7 ii 34–35	289n132
20, 93–93, no. 34	253n11

Šurpu

II 1–128	262n117

II 180	278n31
III 44	315n65

West Semitic Texts

For miscellaneous other West Semitic texts, see the Index of Subjects

KTU

1.3.iii:22–23	296n41
1.4.iv	258n61, 301n83
1.4.vi:46	258n61, 295n36
1.5.i:1–2	281n54
1.6.i:54–64	284n87
1.14.i:36–37	281n51
1.14.iv:6	281n51
1.15.ii:26–28	276n14
1.16.vi:33–34	290n140
1.16.vi:45–47	290n140
1.17.i:26–27	296n42
1.17.v:6–7	290n141
1.17.v:7–9	290n140
1.19.i:21–23	290n141
1.19.i:23–25	290n140
1.108:10	265n27
1.123:6	255n38
1.161	277n15
4.36	284n78
4.38	284n78
4.68:72–75	284n78
4.126:6–9	284n78

KAI

43:12	255n38
181	278n35
181:3	292n15

Aramaic Texts from Egypt

TAD

A2.1–7	319n103
A2.1:1	308n18
A3.3:31	282n75

A3.8:12	336n97	B6.4:10	320n107
A4.1	321n120, 339n122	B7.2:7–8	320n109
A4.1:1	340n129	B7.3:3	320nn107, 109
A4.1:2	338n115, 340n129	C1.1, A 1–3	329n52
A4.1:3–8	337n105	C1.1, B 18–19	329n52
A4.1:10	339n122, 340n129	C2.1	331n58
A4.3:7	338n112, 115	C3.5:7	327n42
A4.3:12	336n97	C3.15	248n10
A4.4:5	320n114	C3.15:1	320n110
A4.5:9	335n94	C3.15:4	320n114
A4.7	320–321n117	C3.15:23	320n113
A4.7–10	248n10	C3.15:123–125	282n58
A4.7:1	336n97	C3.15:123–128	320n110
A4.7:4	336n97	C3.15:128	320n107
A4.7:18	330n54	C3.28:85	321n118
A4.7:18–19	336n97	C3.28:106	344n30
A4.7:22	336n97	C3.28:113	321n118
A4.7:26	314n59	C3.28:114	321n118
A4.7:29	335n96, 340n130	C4.4:2	320n114
A4.8	320–321n117	C4.6:5	320n114
A4.8:1	336n97	D3.17:10	320n114
A4.8:3	336n97	D4.9:1	282n57
A4.8:17	330n54	D7.6:8–10	338n110
A4.8:17–18	336n97	D7.18:2–3	282n57
A4.8:21–22	336n97	D7.21.3	320n115
A4.8:25	314n59	D7.24:5	338n110
A4.8:27–28	340n130	D7.27:8	327n42
A4.8:28	335n96		
A4.9	320–321n117	**Papyrus Amherst 63**	
A4.9:1–2	340n131	8:7	273n117
A4.9:3	324n23	9:3–4	284n84
A4.10	293n23	12:11–19	320n106
A4.10:10–11	320–321n117	12:12–13	87
A5.2:6	335n95	12:16–17	86
B2.2:6	335n95	12:17	286n96, 320n106
B2.2:17	320n114		
B2.2:19	320n113	12:18	320n106
B2.6	320n114	12:18–19	87
B2.8:5	320n115	13:1	86
B2.9:4	335n95	13:1–17	320n106
B3.3	320n114	13:5	86
B3.12:18–19	336n101	13:5–6	86
B5.1:3	335n94	13:6–7	86

Papyrus Amherst 63
(*continued*)

13:8–10	86	13:15–16	87
13:11–12	86	13:16	86
13:12	86	16:1	320n111
13:13–15	87	16:14	320n111
13:14–15	86, 323n15	16:15	320n111
		17:1–3	320n105
		17:14	320n111